Della Beth Kallina

Beware about Progressive

Call Chuck Snyder

j. I was stopped + rear ended

16-2610394

Ev 309-407-3245

If Orenthal James Simpson did not brutally murder Nicole Brown Simpson and Ronald Goldman, they will walk through these courtroom doors.

Guilty as sin

Smart style Morton -

TRIUMPH
OF
JUSTICE

TRIUMPH
OF
JUSTICE

The Final Judgment on
the Simpson Saga

DANIEL PETROCELLI

with PETER KNOBLER

CROWN PUBLISHERS, INC., NEW YORK

Copyright © 1998 by Daniel Petrocelli

All rights reserved. No part of this book may be reproduced or transmitted in any form or by any means, electronic or mechanical, including photocopying, recording, or by any information storage and retrieval system, without permission in writing from the publisher.

Published by Crown Publishers, Inc., 201 East 50th Street, New York, New York 10022. Member of the Crown Publishing Group.

Random House, Inc. New York, Toronto, London, Sydney, Auckland www.randomhouse.com

CROWN and colophon are trademarks of Crown Publishers, Inc.

Printed in the United States of America

Design by June Bennett-Tantillo

Library of Congress Cataloging-in-Publication Data
Petrocelli, Daniel.
Triumph of justice : the final judgment on the Simpson saga /
Daniel Petrocelli with Peter Knobler
Includes index.
1. Simpson, O.J., 1947–   —Trials, litigation, etc.   2. Trials
(Murder)—California—Los Angeles.   I. Knobler, Peter.   II. Title.
KF224.S485P482   1998
345.73'02523'0979494—dc21   98-6251
                                                                CIP

ISBN 0-609-60170-9

10 9 8 7 6 5 4 3 2 1

First Edition

To Ronald Goldman and Nicole Brown Simpson.
May you rest in peace.

—DANIEL PETROCELLI

To Jane and David.

—PETER KNOBLER

CONTENTS

TRIUMPH

OF

JUSTICE

ONE

One-on-One

Fred Goldman never said the man's name; he always referred to O.J. Simpson as "the killer." Fred's son Ron Goldman and Simpson's former wife, Nicole Brown Simpson, had been brutally murdered by this man. He was a killer. That was never in doubt.

The physical evidence was conclusive: Simpson's blood was dripped at the murder scene; a cap with hairs matching his was found next to Ron's and Nicole's dead bodies; one of Simpson's large leather gloves was lying between them; and the matching glove, still holding strands of the victims' hair and stained with their blood and Simpson's, was found outside his house. Size-twelve shoe prints, slightly pigeon-toed, were clearly stamped in the victims' blood, at the murder scene. Simpson is among the 9 percent of the population who wears size-twelve shoes, and he is pigeon-toed. Those shoe prints made an impression that was matched to one sole in the world—a Silga sole, manufactured at the Silga factory in Civitinova Marche, Italy, for the upscale shoemaker Bruno Magli. We had photographs of Simpson wearing Bruno Magli shoes with the identical sole. Simpson's white Ford Bronco, parked outside his house, contained not only Simpson's blood but Ron's and Nicole's, and a shoe impression consistent with the Bruno Magli stained the carpet on the driver's side. A trail of Simpson's blood was dripped up his driveway, into his house, and up to his bedroom and bathroom. Planting of that blood was out of the question—because, just like the blood at the murder scene, it was found long before police investigators had taken any blood from his arm. Simpson had cuts all over his hands the day after the murders but had no explanation for how he got them. His socks were lying on his bedroom floor, spattered with his blood and Nicole's. Blue black cotton fibers consistent with a dark sweatsuit were found at both the crime scene and in Simpson's home, linking him to both locations. Rare carpet fibers of the type used in his Bronco were found at the murder scene. His blood, his cuts, his clothing, his gloves, his shoes, his car, his house, his ex-wife's blood, Ron Goldman's blood . . . all pointed to O.J. Simpson—and to no one else.

We spent the first eighteen days of the trial laying out this overwhelming evidence. Still, I was in no way certain we would win. Much of this same evidence had fallen on deaf ears in the criminal trial.

Our jury research showed we had a paradox on our hands: The more we emphasized the brutality of the murders, the more people thought it unlikely Simpson had committed them. The killings were chilling, vengeful, full of rage; Simpson was warm, celebrated, seductive. He wore thousand-dollar suits and flashed a million dollar smile. *How could this man have committed this crime?* I strongly believed our jury—any jury—would struggle to accept the physical evidence, no matter how incriminating, unless they were convinced that O.J. Simpson was a man *capable* of committing these murders. Far from the all-American hero who had smiled and charmed his way into our hearts, O.J. Simpson was a man who betrayed his image, a man of no conscience, no remorse, no character. He was a man who beat his wife and lied about it to everyone. He was a man who never accepted responsibility for anything. Yes, he was a man who would kill. This is what we needed to show to the jury, and that is why we had to call O.J. Simpson to the witness stand.

I made a decision not to call him "O.J." "O.J." was a celebrity. He ran through airports, winked at grandmas, and played a lovable dunce in the *Naked Gun* movies. He was handsome, mischievous, wholesome; he was "the Juice." If I permitted Simpson to endear himself to the jury on that witness stand, we would lose. If the jury believed Simpson when he looked them in the eyes and swore on his children that he did not commit these murders, the case would be over. No amount of blood, DNA, or physical evidence would overcome that one defining moment of this trial. I could not allow that to happen. This was my client's last chance for justice. I could not let him down, let his family down, let our team down, let down millions of people across the country who'd been horrified by the verdict at the criminal trial. And I could not let down Ron Goldman, or Nicole Brown Simpson, two people I never met but grew to know like my closest friends.

I resolved there would be no "O.J." on the witness stand today. I would not even refer to that sweet nickname. I would begin by calling him by his given name, Orenthal Simpson.

"Pursuant to California Evidence Code Section 776," I told the court, "we call to the stand the defendant, Orenthal James Simpson." The "James" just slipped out. I guess I was more nervous than I'd thought.

I had read everything, learned everything, spoken to everyone who would speak to me, immersed myself in Simpson's life and was ready to take him on. I had worked obsessively for more than a year to prepare for this moment. The outline our team developed was comprehensive and meticulously planned. But success would require more than knowledge and preparation. I had to take control of the examination from the beginning. I had to control a man who never once in his life let anyone control him.

Primacy is important in a trial. An attorney's first approach to a witness leaves a powerful impact with the jury. I wanted to show the jury right off the bat that Simpson would lie to them. About everything. That was the linchpin. If he lied, he was guilty. An innocent man would not lie.

Simpson was clever and calculating and when backed against a wall was not a man to be underestimated. He had managed his criminal trial from a jail cell, and he had won twelve–zip in under three hours. He was the supreme competitor. We did not expect him to break down on the witness stand and confess to the murders or lead us to the murder weapon. I was not going to make him explode in anger and turn into a raging killer right before the jury's eyes. I knew Simpson was determined, more than anything else, not to flash the slightest hint of a temper, much less anger or rage. His demeanor throughout eleven days of pretrial deposition, at which he appeared virtually sedated, assured me Simpson would do everything in his power to convince the jury he was incapable of losing emotional control—as he had on the night of June 12, 1994, at 875 South Bundy Drive. But that was fine with me. In his zeal to deceive the jury, Simpson failed to realize that a truthful, innocent man falsely accused of murdering the mother of his children and a young man, would not be able to contain his anger even for one minute.

The most important question, in terms of Simpson's credibility, was whether he had ever hit his wife. If the jury believed he had never struck Nicole, they would believe anything Simpson told them. Right from the outset, I had to disabuse them of that notion.

I began my examination with a few very safe questions that I knew he couldn't argue with concerning his first meeting with Nicole. Then, when I got to my first important question, about the nature of their relationship, Simpson immediately started to lie.

"It was a problem relationship for you throughout much of that time, true?"

I addressed him sharply. He was a killer, and I intended to treat him like one. How could I expect the jury to convict this celebrity if I treated him with deference?

"Not true," he said firmly.

I immediately impeached him with a statement he made to Los Angeles Police Department detectives Tom Lange and Phil Vannatter when they interviewed him after he came back from Chicago the day after the murders. "Did you not tell the Los Angeles police detectives who interviewed you on June 13, 1994, hours after Nicole's death, that you had always had problems with your relationship with Nicole, it was 'a problem relationship'?"

"Yes." Then he started to argue with me. "We had problems in our relationship, but I don't think it was mostly a problem."

"Did you not say that to the police detectives on June 13, 1994? Yes or no?"

"Yes."

"You said that, right?"

"Yes."

"And when you said, 'I have always had problems with her, that's— our relationship has been a problem relationship,' that was true, correct?"

"Yes."

This started the process of disciplining Simpson to answer my questions. Simpson was very skilled at putting self-serving argument and spin on his answers, rarely giving a straightforward response and hoping to deflect the aim of the question. It was critical that I not let him get away with this; whoever was in control was going to carry the day.

O.J. Simpson had been treated with deference by the authorities since he was a schoolboy. He was idolized as a football hero. In his relationships with friends, with women, with the sycophants and hangers-on in his celebrity world, he dominated his environment. The Los Angeles police had treated him with awe and respect before the murders and very gingerly after them. Even in jail during his criminal trial he was a dominant force: receiving special privileges, quarterbacking his defense, ruling his lawyers. That would end today. He was a witness in a civil trial in front of the judge, the plaintiffs, the press, and the world, and for one of the few times in his life he was not in charge, not in control.

As a result of the television coverage of the criminal trial, some of Simpson and Nicole's battles were well known to the public by this time, so I zeroed in on them. "There was more than one physical altercation," I said, "true?"

"I think you'd have to define that," he answered confidently. "There was one very physical altercation, and there were other times when they were not so physical."

"What do you mean by 'not so physical,' Mr. Simpson?"

"Well, Nicole hit me a few times, and I didn't consider that too physical." Here was the pride and ego of a professional athlete and a very narcissistic man. No mere woman could hurt him. I let him run with that ball.

"And how many times did Nicole hit you, as *you* say?" I got in his face immediately. Again, I treated him with no respect. Challenged by my tone, he took the bait. His wife's throat had been slashed to the voice box, and he was telling the jury that Nicole had hit *him*.

"Numerous times." He loved that word, "numerous."

"Okay. And how many times, Mr. Simpson, in the course of these physical altercations, did you hit Nicole?"

"Never."

There it was. The lie was simple and adamant, an explosion as he exhaled. Both of us knew where this was going. We had been through this dance in deposition; he was going to deny everything, and as far as he was concerned there was no way I could touch him. This was his story, and he was sticking to it. He wasn't going to look anybody in the eye, he was just going to put his head down and bull his way through his whole chain of lies.

"How many times did you strike Nicole?"

"Never."

"How many times did you slap Nicole?"

"Never."

"How many times did you kick her?"

"Never."

"How many times did you beat her, sir?" My mentor, Arthur Groman, thought I paid Simpson too much respect by calling him "sir," but I felt the word was ironic, and I used it condescendingly.

"Never."

"And if Nicole said you hit her, she would be lying, is that true?" I wanted to pit Simpson against Nicole in front of the jury. Now it was no longer me against him, it was him against Nicole.

Bob Baker, Simpson's lead defense attorney, objected, and Judge Hiroshi Fujisaki sustained the objection.

"If Nicole told people and wrote down in her diary that you hit her—"

Immediately Baker objected again. He wouldn't even let me finish; whether the jury was permitted to consider the information or not, he didn't want them hearing it from me. Sustained. The court was not about to let me get away with that.

I had taken two passes at informing the jury that Nicole had talked or written about her beatings at Simpson's hands and I had failed. I changed the question slightly, to focus on Simpson's knowledge and state of mind. "You are aware that Nicole has told others that you hit her?" I asked. Again Baker objected, but this time he was overruled.

Answer: "Yes."

I'd won the point, and I went for the next one. "And you are aware that Nicole has written down in writings that you hit her, true?"

"Yes."

"And you are aware that her writings describe *numerous* incidents"— his favorite word, so I gave it right back to him—"when you hit her, true?"

Bob Baker saw where this was going and tried to stop it. "I object to this, again." The judge overruled, and Baker said, "I think we need to approach." He was looking for a chance to argue at length at the judge's bench and interrupt my examination.

"No," said Fujisaki. The judge was serious and intent. Lawyers can make their objections, that's their right, but unlike in the criminal case, this judge did not intend to allow a parade up to the sidebar. He would not let the most important examination of the trial get chopped up and sidetracked. This was not the first time Judge Fujisaki had denied sidebars; he was simply refusing to make an exception for O.J. Simpson. He was quite properly treating him like any other witness, for which I was extremely grateful.

I returned to Simpson. "Please answer the question."

"Yes."

"And your view is, all that is false, true?"

He was caught. Nicole had told many people that Simpson beat her, she had written it down, and as far as he was concerned it was all false. I'd put him in the untenable position of calling the murdered, slaughtered mother of his children a liar.

Simpson had gone too far to turn back. He didn't hesitate. "Yes," he said.

"Let's talk about 1989, okay?" There was an edge to my voice. I was curt with him. People didn't treat O.J. like that, and I knew he wouldn't like it. I was now ready to take him through his blow-by-blow beating of Nicole and let him lie—in detail—to the jury. Simpson would deny everything. The jury would decide in the next few minutes if Simpson was a liar and, in all likelihood, if he was a killer. The case could easily rest on this.

After midnight on New Year's Eve 1989, Nicole Brown Simpson had called 911 and reported that her husband had beaten her. The tape recording of that call had been played all over the media for two years. When the police arrived they took Nicole's statement and photographed her. A spousal abuse complaint was later filed by the authorities against Simpson. This was the last publicly acknowledged instance of domestic violence involving Simpson and Nicole.

"That was an angry, intense, physical confrontation, true?"

Simpson began breathing heavily, his answers coming in short, explosive bursts.

"Correct."

"You're what, at the time," I asked him, "six two, two hundred fifteen pounds?" I had my facts straight and the numbers exact; I didn't want any quibbling.

"Yes."

The courtroom was swollen with lawyers; we'd had to build and install double sets of tables for both ourselves and the defense. As a result I was standing no more than four feet from Simpson. I was right in front of him. Fred Goldman sat directly behind me, glaring. He had been waiting more than two years for this day.

"Nicole, five eight, one hundred thirty-five pounds?"

"Yes."

"And you *hit* her that day, didn't you, sir?" I said it fast.

"No." He didn't look at me.

This was an obvious lie. The police photos showed her face battered and bruised.

"Did your hand make contact with her face at all to cause injuries to her face? Yes or no?" I demanded.

"I don't know." He seemed to be hearing me from a distance, his eyes focusing on a point in midair somewhere to my left, far from the jury, between the witness box and me.

He didn't know. "Didn't you testify—you remember testifying in this deposition, sir?" I held up the four-inch-thick transcript of Simpson's eleven days of pretrial testimony.

Simpson snapped out of it. He looked at the book. "Yes."

"Remember I took your deposition over a number of days? . . ."

"Yes."

"Let me read from that deposition." There was no fumbling through pages to arrive at the right spot; I had my materials ready. Our team was thoroughly prepared. "By the way . . ." (You've always got to be wary when a lawyer begins a question with "By the way"; he's anything but off the point.) "You understand and you understood then, you were under oath and subject to the same penalty of perjury, just as you are today?"

"Yes."

I began reading to him. "Question: 'You were in such a rage that you don't remember what you did; is that right?' Answer: 'I remember exactly what I did.'" Simpson had just told me he didn't know whether his hand had made contact with Nicole's face, but in the deposition he'd said he

remembered exactly what he did. I intended to impeach him every chance
he gave me. This would be an all-out assault on his credibility.

"Now, tell this jury"—I pointed with my right hand to the jury—
"exactly how you caused all those injuries on Nicole's face."

Simpson is very clever; he's a shrewd guy, and he had a prepared
response. He assumed this was a day like all days and that he'd get away
with it. "Well, as I told you throughout the deposition, I don't know how
exactly it happened, but I felt totally responsible for everything that happened at one point."

That was a mantra, not an answer. It was also an old refrain. He had
said it in deposition, he had said it on television, every time I saw Simpson
he was saying the same thing. It got to be a joke in the office; I would pace
our conference room, mocking Simpson's deep baritone, saying, "I feel
totally responsible!" As if Simpson thought "feeling responsible" would be
enough: *That will get me off, I'll say I "feel responsible" and I'm home free.*
It was almost comical; I thought he'd be smarter than to try to get away
with that at trial.

"Mr. Simpson—"

Baker cut me off. "Let him answer the question."

Baker was out of line; opposing counsel are not permitted to speak
to each other in open court, we are allowed to converse only with the witnesses and the judge. I ignored him. I wasn't about to deal with Bob Baker.
He would try hard to interrupt as much as possible; he wanted to upset
my concentration and break the flow of the examination. My battle was
not with Bob Baker. This was between me and O.J. Simpson.

"I'm not asking about your responsibility; I'm asking about your
physical movements and actions." I was harsh, angry, confrontational.
This was no mere inquiry, this was an attack. The message was: I'm in control, you're not. And you're going to answer my questions to this jury.
Simpson had a magnetic public persona, and I risked offending the jurors,
but I was willing to take that chance. This was no time to tiptoe around
him. Simpson was a killer, and I had to treat him like a killer.

Baker jumped in again, pleading. "I move to let this witness answer
the question."

Five minutes into the examination and we had hit the critical junc-
ture. Judge Fujisaki had a decision to make concerning the way in which
this examination and the course of this trial would run. My tone, while

argumentative, was completely appropriate for this witness. If the judge began sustaining the defense's objections and allowed Simpson to avoid and evade my questions, if he did not let me confront Simpson aggressively, the examination would be diluted severely. My game plan would have to be scrambled. If the judge said, "You've got your answer, Mr. Petrocelli, move on," I was in big trouble.

In the criminal trial, Judge Lance Ito had given the defense lawyers an astonishing amount of leeway. It is my opinion that Ito did so because he believed, beyond any doubt, that O.J. Simpson had murdered two people. I am sure Ito expected—at least until the end, when even he had to see the case unraveling—that Simpson would be found guilty. What rational jury, properly presented with all the evidence, wouldn't find Simpson guilty? Ito gave the defense every break and benefit so that when the inevitable appeal was filed, the verdict would be bulletproof.

This is not uncommon. Having a decision reversed on appeal usually results from a determination by an appeals court that the judge committed errors in the proceedings. A judge presiding over a high-profile criminal trial knows the case will be flyspecked by many high-powered lawyers, professors, and pundits around the country looking for just such errors on which to base a reversal. Reversal is not good for one's judicial career; it is to be avoided. Some judges will bend over backward to do so. Judge Ito did that to such an extreme in the O.J. Simpson criminal trial that he successfully solved his own problem; he did not have to worry about a successful appeal because there was none—Simpson got off.

I didn't fault Bob Baker for his objections. He was just doing his job as a defense lawyer, and he was good at it. He was trying to get whatever edge he could. If you can win something from the judge, go for it. If you don't ask, you've got no chance. Judge Fujisaki had previously been consistently neutral and given Baker a wide berth in conducting very hostile questioning of our witnesses. I still didn't know whether Simpson would get favored treatment.

"The answer was not responsive," declared the judge. "Go ahead."

He made his decision quickly. I was relieved. My way was now paved to force Simpson to answer the questions he did not want to answer and had chosen not to answer in the criminal trial with his life hanging in the balance. I turned back to Simpson. "Please tell the jury exactly what you did to cause the injuries on Nicole's face."

"Well, as I explained to you, I don't know exactly how the injuries took place, so I can't really answer that question. If you want me to say what happened, I can tell you what happened." That was another clever, elusive response and I would not let Simpson get away with it.

"You said in the deposition you remember *exactly* what you did, true?"

"And I also told you I don't know how the injuries got there."

"You said you remembered exactly what you did, true?"

"Correct." He paused. "Not to cause the injuries; I didn't say that." In his deposition Simpson had said he remembered exactly what he did, but he had not literally said that he remembered exactly how the injuries were caused. He was no fool. I thought: You got that one. But you sure won't get many more. I stopped arguing with him about what he remembered and went on to the next question.

"You caused all those injuries, did you not?" I used the word "caused" because I wanted him to say "I did not." I knew Simpson would never admit to hitting Nicole—he had refused to do so in the $29.95 video he had produced and sold to the public ten months earlier, he had refused to do so over eleven days of depositions and throughout his pre-trial public appearances—but I wanted to draw out his lies in front of the jury, to put him in a position in which he would deny causing the injuries when anyone with half a brain would know he had caused them directly.

"I feel totally responsible for every injury she had then," Simpson said, "yes." Again the familiar mantra, with an answer to his own question instead of mine.

"Sir"—I was right in his face, scolding him, "I'm not asking you about your feelings of responsibility. Do you understand?"

"Yes."

"I'm asking you about what you did. You *caused* the injuries to her face, did you not?"

"I feel responsible for every injury she had." This was the third time he had refused to answer my question.

"Move to strike as nonresponsive."

"Stricken," said the judge. "Jury is to disregard that answer."

"Please answer the question."

Simpson had clearly assumed he could get away with his evasions, but now he was trapped. As long as I asked my questions properly, the judge would make him answer them. He couldn't dodge or shortcut.

Simpson didn't have an innocent answer, an answer that didn't incriminate him. He knew he'd hit her, and he knew I knew. Now the jury would know, too. I had the upper hand. The courtroom was riveted, and Baker was trying his best to break it up, but the judge was not going to let the defendant off the hook. No favors this time. Finally, in this courtroom he was no longer "O.J.," he was "Mr. Simpson." You're a witness, answer the question.

"I don't know."

I looked derisively. "You don't know *what*?" I wanted him to repeat it.

"That I caused every injury."

I had not used the word "every." I'd said, "You caused the injuries to her face." Simpson was desperately looking for room to wriggle free.

I was so focused on Simpson, I hadn't yet looked at the jury; I couldn't be sure what they were thinking. But clearly the defendant was evading the truth, and I expected that they were getting the message. Now it was time to drive the point home.

"Let's put some photos up."

Our paralegal, Steve Foster, had the exhibit cued and ready to roll on a projector called the ELMO. He pressed a button and a picture of Nicole appeared on the thirty-five-inch TV monitor that stood like a monolith in the corner to Simpson's left between him and the jury. The jurors had to look past the screen to see him. I apologized to the jurors for having to show photographs of a severely beaten woman, and the apology was sincere—but I wanted them to watch Simpson lying while Nicole's pulpy face hung over his shoulder. I wanted them to see Simpson impeached by his dead wife, from her grave.

This was not a pretty sight. Wearing a black zippered sweatshirt, Nicole was a beautiful woman, but with her head tilted to the right she had reached up and pulled back her long blond hair as one would reveal an ugly secret. Red welts and scratches began on her forehead above the right eye and extended down to her neck. This was a beaten woman. There was no anger in her face, no rebellion, only sadness. The photograph had a bruised dignity. Look what she'd put up with. Her eyes were closed.

"You've seen those photos before, Mr. Simpson?" I wanted to make him look.

A quick glance, a sharp, "Yes." Simpson had begun to breathe heavily again.

I paused as I paced in front of the jury. I waited for the image to sink in. "By the way"—operating the ELMO, Steve began to zoom in on the most unsettling bruises—"you say that some of the marks on this photograph were caused by Nicole *picking* her face that night, true?" He had told me this in deposition and I was incredulous even recalling his testimony.

"No." He was abrupt. "I told you, *when* she cleans her face."

"That night?" I couldn't believe he was arguing with me about this.

"A lot of this redness would normally be there most nights once she picked and cleaned her face."

Simpson had been very clear in his deposition in claiming that Nicole had picked her face the night of the beating, but now even he was embarrassed by such a preposterous and offensive lie. I wouldn't let him wriggle off. I wanted the jury to know just how far he would go to lie about not hitting her. "You said in your deposition, sir, did you not, that that night she was picking at her blemishes and *that* caused marks on her chin and on her cheek, true?"

"No. I said normally, when she does pick her face, that those were marks that I'd normally see, yes."

"Did you not say in your deposition that she did so that night, and that's why those marks appear on her face? Yes or no?"

I encouraged these arguments, and not just because I wanted Simpson to try to deny what he'd said in his deposition. There was also the sheer implausibility of his answers; it was asking a lot of a jury to have them look at the photograph of a severely beaten woman, now dead, and believe that she'd caused the wounds herself as a beauty treatment.

"Tell the jury right now"—I brought the jury into this confrontation on my side—"did Nicole cause any of those marks to herself that night by *picking*"—I leaned on the word—"at her face."

"I don't know," he told me.

"You don't know! . . . Okay, let's talk about the injury to the lip, the split lip. How did she get that injury, sir?"

"That looks like more than what would normally be there. So at some point during the night, I assume that that happened, once our altercation began."

He "assumed." Simpson did a lot of assuming on the stand. *Assuming* is what Simpson did when confronted with facts he could not deny but refused to admit.

"Well, what did you do to cause that injury?"

"I wrestled her out of the room. And what happened when she was outside, I didn't see when she fell, but I feel responsible for all of that."

I was two feet from Simpson, and now I got in his face. "You've said you 'feel responsible for' a number of times. It's not necessary to keep saying it because it's not responsive to my questions."

From across the courtroom Baker yelled out, "I object to this. He can't give my client a speech!" The court sustained him, which it should have. I moved on.

"Let's talk about what you did physically with your hand, your foot, whatever. Tell us"—*us,* me and the jury, united as one—"how she got the cut on her lip, the split on her lip, that caused it to bleed that night."

"I don't know."

When Simpson gave a ridiculous answer I repeated it with disdain, giving the jury a second opportunity to be offended by it. "You don't know?"

"No."

"Okay. Tell us how she got the welt over the right eye." Steve zoomed in, and the TV screen was filled with the nasty red bruise.

"I don't know specifically how."

"You did hit her there?"

"No." They'd had an intense, angry, physical confrontation, she was beaten bloody, and he was saying he didn't hit her. Okay.

"And it's your testimony before this jury that you *never* touched her face with your hand, true?"

"I don't know. As I told you in the deposition"—now he was trying to make it appear that he was being consistent—"in wrestling her, maybe my hand hit"—he seemed for a moment to be conceding that perhaps his hand had struck her, but he immediately recognized he had gone too far and tried to retreat—"or was on her face. I certainly didn't punch or slap her." Simpson was trying to present answers that might satisfy the jury but not sound too bad. *My hand was on her face . . . My hand was on her face and then there was a mark . . . My hand was on her lip, then there was a split, and then there was blood . . . But I did not hit her.* That's what he was trying to say. "My hand was on her face." It almost sounds affectionate.

"You say your hand was 'on her face.' Did you strike her at any time?"

"As I told you, I had her in a headlock at one point, in trying to get her out of the door, so I would assume that my hand was somewhere around her face."

You don't get cuts and bruises like that from a headlock. The jury had to know this. "Are you saying that that's when that injury to her eye occurred?"

"I don't know when it occurred. But I'm assuming it occurred during the altercation or when she fell outside and—"

I cut him off. "I would ask that you not assume anything. Either tell us what happened or—"

Baker cut me off. "I would ask Mr. Petrocelli not to give my client legal advice."

"Overruled," said the judge.

Simpson wanted it both ways. He wanted to admit the obvious, which was that he caused the injuries, so the jury wouldn't think he was lying. But at the same time he was hell-bent on denying he had hit Nicole; he didn't want to admit ever lashing out in anger. He knew that if the jury believed he could do that with his fists, they would believe he could do it with a knife. He would not make it that easy for them. He would go to his grave denying he hit her.

"Are you saying now that it's possible that you might have struck her with your hand, delivered a blow to her right eye to cause that mark? Yes or no?"

"No."

"It's not possible?"

"I did not punch or slap her. That didn't happen."

"Did you strike her with your hand?"

"No."

The battered face of Nicole Simpson still stared down from the TV screen.

"Now, this thing about wrestling." I could not have been more dismissive. "Your view is that Nicole started an argument that night about something that she was absolutely wrong about, true?"

"Exactly, yes." He was putting all the blame on his dead wife. Good. The jury had to be thinking exactly what I was thinking: How could anyone do that?

"And she came into the bedroom and started hitting you, right?" He didn't say anything. "Correct?" I prodded.

"Essentially, yes."

I began to take Simpson through his version of the fight in detail: He locked her out of the bedroom, she got a key and came back in and started hitting him. "And you said Nicole is one of the most physically conditioned women you've ever known, right?"

"Yes." He had told this to police investigators on the day after she was murdered. I found that so offensive. This was O.J. Simpson; he had put his helmet down and dragged behemoth defensive linemen across goal lines, he had run through linebackers and over strong safeties and powered for 2,003 yards in a National Football League season. I guess only his dead wife could stop him one-on-one.

"You said, at least that night, she was quite a match for you, right?" What he was really saying was that she was so well conditioned, it would be a fair fight.

"It was tough to get her out of the room," said Simpson, "yes."

"At some point, you think, in the process of trying to get her out the fifteen feet or so to the door so you could close your door, you got her in a headlock; is that right?"

"I don't think that's necessarily true."

"Is that a fair description?"

"No."

"Well, tell us, then."

"She jumped on me, on the bed, and with her knees and arms . . . and then I kind of grabbed her"—he balled his right hand—"and we kind of fell over on the floor. And then I was trying to get her—to get her out of the door, and she was grabbing things and hitting. And eventually, I got her out of the door."

"And when you said you grabbed her, you put your right hand into a fist—" He had put up his fist! Even in retelling the story he had gotten so carried away that he'd reflexively raised his fist! The jury could now catch a glimpse of what Simpson did inside that room, in the heat of passion, while Nicole was supposedly attacking him. Simpson had gained around forty pounds since the criminal trial and appeared even thicker in his suit. He had large hands. The picture of a beaten Nicole was up on the monitor, Simpson was sitting on the witness stand and could see it, and he had raised his fist. He knew immediately he'd made a mistake. He cut me off.

"Yes."

I hadn't finished my question. "Just now. Is that what you did that night when you grabbed her?"

"Quite possibly when I grabbed her arm, quite possibly I did."

Despite his intense desire to keep denying it, he was actually beginning to admit that he'd hit her that night. He raised his arms to demonstrate and, I'm sure without thinking, closed both hands. The effect was extraordinary. The jury looked across a picture of a bruised and beaten Nicole to see O.J. Simpson with both fists clenched at shoulder height in a fighter's stance, denying he'd hit her.

"When you did—now, you just put *both* hands in a fist! When you did it that night did you punch her in the face with your hands?"

"No, no."

"Did you put your fingers and hands on her throat and leave marks on her throat, sir?" We had witnesses who would testify that she'd had marks on her throat that night, marks that clearly came from the beating.

"I don't recall doing that at all, no."

"You are aware that she had marks on her throat, are you not?"

"I'm aware that someone said she did, yes."

"You believe that's false?"

"I never saw them. And the next day she showed me all her bruises."

Imagine that scene. I tried to draw it out as long as possible. "She showed you everything the next day?"

Simpson pointed to the screen. His lawyers must have been cringing as their client cavalierly cataloged his murdered wife's bruises, but Simpson didn't seem to mind. "She showed me something here"—he pointed—"and this"—indicating her arm and head—"this was obvious to me."

"You didn't see any marks on her throat?"

"No."

"No handprint or anything like that?"

"No."

I forced Simpson to talk in front of the jury about Nicole's throat, because that's where he killed her. Every time they heard the word "throat" they were reminded of another slash.

"It's your testimony that you never touched her throat, right?"

"I don't know. When you say 'touched her throat,' I was wrestling her." He pronounced it "rassling." "I could have touched her throat, yes."

"And how could you have touched her throat?"

"I don't know. Maybe—I don't know." He was fumbling, trying to get off the subject. "If you want to wrestle, you know—I don't know. You know, it happens in a wrestling match."

Simpson was using gentle words—"rassling," "touched her throat," hands "on her face"—to soften the impact of the blows he had delivered. I wanted to demonstrate the complete absurdity of his attempt. I went right up to him and said, "Would you like to demonstrate to me, sir, how you had her head in a headlock?" I beckoned Simpson to come down off the witness stand, kind of like a schoolyard dare, then turned to Judge Fujisaki. "With the court's permission."

Of course, I knew the court wouldn't stand for it, and there was no way Bob Baker was going to allow his client to reenact a beating Simpson had delivered to the woman he'd killed a few years later. Still, I was prepared to have Simpson go through it and hammer me. I wanted the jury to see that his explanation was totally implausible. He was slipping and sliding all over the place, trying desperately to avoid admitting what everyone in the courtroom knew—that he had hit her, punched her, that he had choked her. But if you put someone in a headlock, they don't get finger marks on their throat or welts and bruises on their face. Put me in a headlock and show me how it happened. Go ahead, O.J.

Simpson is a very big man. I'm not. I liked the image of Simpson overpowering me in front of the jury, just as he had overpowered Ron and Nicole. And I wanted the jurors to see that I was not afraid of this man, that I would stand up to him. I would let a killer put his arm around my throat to show how much I cared and believed in my client's case. I wanted to embolden this jury. I wanted to stand up to Simpson so *they* would stand up to him.

Most of all, I had to make it clear: You cannot kill two people and get away with it, no matter how much money you have, no matter how many lies you tell.

TWO

What Have I Gotten Myself Into?

I'd had no involvement with the criminal case against O.J. Simpson other than being mesmerized by the Bronco chase. It's one of those rare events in one's life when you know exactly where you were when it happened. I was having an early dinner in a California Pizza Kitchen restaurant with my wife, Marian, my daughter, Rachel, and my son, Adam. When I looked up, everyone was watching Simpson and his friend Al Cowlings in the white Bronco, on television, take off down the freeway. I could not believe what I was seeing. All week, despite news of the mounting evidence against him, I had dismissed—I should say, wanted to dismiss—the notion that Simpson was guilty of these two brutal murders. But seeing him running from the police on national television forced me to face it: He must be guilty.

It was a textbook case of what is taught in law school as "consciousness of guilt." Fleeing was tantamount to a confession; nobody of his stature would run from the police unless he was guilty. I couldn't focus on my meal or even talk to my family, I couldn't take my eyes off the screen. I got the check quickly, drove home, and watched the rest. The specter of O.J. Simpson blowing his brains out on television with all of us watching was absolutely horrifying, yet at the same time completely transfixing.

One of my law partners, Tom Lambert, had first told me about the killings. I happened to stroll into his office one Monday morning just to shoot the breeze, and he'd said, "Did you hear what happened? O.J. Simpson's ex-wife was found murdered and they think Simpson might have done it." I was shocked. I am a big sports fan, and I had been a very big Simpson fan. I had closely followed his football career, then later his broadcasting and acting careers. I did not believe there was any possibility that the former University of Southern California all-American could be involved in such a thing.

I paid little attention to the criminal trial. As a busy litigation attorney and partner in the Los Angeles law firm of Mitchell, Silberberg & Knupp, I had little time or desire to tune in to the Simpson case. I didn't watch any of the live coverage, just scanned the newspapers, caught highlights on the evening news, and observed the trial as any casual observer might. I did make a point to watch some of the closing arguments on television before going to work. I was curious to see how the attorneys, who were receiving international acclaim, summed up their cases to the jury. The prosecutors had been hand-picked as Los Angeles's finest. The defense was being called the "Dream Team." To the general public, these lawyers were being billed as the highest-caliber lawyers in the country, and I wanted to see how they did.

I was not impressed with the prosecution's closing arguments. Marcia Clark seemed exhausted, haggard, and unfocused. Christopher Darden's opening remarks struck me as defensive and apologetic. He told the jury this was the hardest task they would ever face. "Nobody wants to do anything to the man. We don't." I thought this was absolutely the wrong thing to say; he should have told them exactly the opposite, that this was the *easiest* job a juror ever faced because the evidence showed the man they were charged with judging was entirely, 100 percent guilty.

In contrast, Johnnie Cochran was a stronger, more powerful advocate. Barry Scheck was effective in his presentation. Aided greatly by Lance Ito's rulings throughout the trial, they pounded home their twin themes of police corruption and police incompetence. From what little I knew at the time, there wasn't any concrete proof that the incriminating evidence against Simpson had actually been planted by police officers, or that all the blood evidence had accidentally become contaminated with Simpson's blood. Nor were these reasonable or plausible ideas. Yet there was Johnnie Cochran viciously excoriating veteran police detectives for framing an innocent man, and there was Barry Scheck ranting and raving that the LAPD was a cesspool of contamination and that none of the evidence could be trusted. As I sat and watched the spectacle of these clever lawyers skillfully pulling the wool over the eyes of a misguided jury, I felt no great pride in my noble profession. We were all sure to be judged and labeled for years to come by what these lawyers were doing.

But the truth is I also felt envious. This case riveted our nation and would be counted as one of the most important trials in our history. I wished I were standing in front of that jury, telling them exactly how the defense was trying to deceive, inflame, and prejudice them. The envy just added to my frustration, however, and I could not stand to watch anymore. I turned off the TV and went to work.

Despite my belief that Simpson was guilty, I was ambivalent five days later as I watched with my wife and son in our family room and waited for the verdict to be read. One part of me was still rooting for Simpson, not wanting to see the sports hero taken down, but another part could not put aside the DNA evidence or fail to see how absurd the defense arguments were.

The moment I heard the verdict, I felt a profoundly empty feeling in the pit of my stomach. I saw Fred Goldman in a state of shock. His daughter, Ron's sister Kim, buried her face in her hands. Nicole's parents, Juditha and Lou Brown, seemed stoic in their pain and anguish. I was suddenly ashamed of my own ambivalence. A terrible mistake had been made, an inhumane injustice delivered, and these people would have to suffer their loss forever. When I saw O.J. Simpson, I thought, Here's a guy who just got away with murder in plain view of the whole world. He beat the system, he would walk and be a free man for the rest of his life, while two young, innocent people were lying in their graves. I saw Marcia Clark and Chris Darden staring in disgust and disbelief, and immediately felt sorry for them. I watched as the defense lawyers' immediate reactions of relief turned to grinning satisfaction and felt even more empty. Although they had succeeded in using their skills and talents to subvert justice, they would forever be known as America's legal Dream Team.

Immediately after the verdict, I watched a reporter ask Johnnie Cochran about the civil suits filed against his client by the families of the victims. This was the first I had heard about the civil suits. Cochran confidently predicted the suits would be dismissed now that Simpson had been acquitted. Johnnie Cochran had just won the Trial of the Century, and he looked invincible. He and his defense team had just crushed one of the most massive and expensive prosecutions of all time. The victims' families, with extremely limited funds and resources, would be no match. The families, already bereft, would be victimized again. Simpson would overpower them in much the way he overpowered their children. The more I thought about it, the angrier I got.

I was not the only one in Los Angeles upset by the verdict. There was pervasive outrage and resentment about the handling of the trial, the verdict, the manipulation of the system, and Simpson himself. A few days after the trial ended, Phyllis Harvey, the wife of one of my longtime clients, Brian Harvey, was having lunch with several of her wealthy women friends. During the meal, talk developed of encouraging Fred Goldman to prosecute his civil suit against O.J. Simpson and of helping to raise money for it.

Goldman had been very outspoken during the criminal trial. It was understandable. Simpson killed his son, and Goldman hated him for it. Now Simpson and his lawyers were making a mockery of his son's murder trial. The father was relentless in his attacks, unwilling to contain his anger or his grief, and he was taking his fury out on Simpson in the media. Goldman was the face of outrage. People like Phyllis Harvey wanted to do something about it. They set about thinking, Whom do we know who could represent this man? My name came up, and they asked my friend and fellow lawyer Bob Briskin to approach me.

I was driving down the San Diego Freeway the next morning, on my way to work, when my cell phone rang. It was Briskin, recounting the ladies' lunch. "Phyllis Harvey wants to know if you'd be interested in representing the Goldmans." I laughed out loud. "Is she crazy? Fred Goldman hasn't called me, and he isn't going to." For his part, Briskin didn't know whether the Goldman family already had lawyers or had any inclination to hire new ones, much less hire me. I had never met Fred Goldman, and I would never call a person I don't know and ask if I could be his lawyer. Moreover, Briskin did not know how Phyllis or her friends intended to gain access to Goldman. "Bob," I told him, "this is bizarre. I can't imagine anything ever coming of it, so I'm not really sure. I suppose if he called I would talk to him."

I clicked off the phone and turned my attention to the traffic. There was no possibility of my ever getting involved in the Simpson case. Even if

Goldman were to contact me, how could I take a case like this? I'd been a business litigator all my professional life, I didn't practice criminal law, I didn't practice personal injury law, and I'd never handled a wrongful death case, which is what the Goldmans were bringing. I was sure the Goldmans would look for a specialist in this area. Furthermore, this case would not be a paying venture. The Goldmans, I assumed, would not have the personal wherewithal to finance what would be an extremely costly case. Whatever firm took it would have to invest substantial money of their own and take the case on a contingency basis, hopefully getting a judgment against Simpson and then recovering from him. My law firm rarely accepted contingent-fee cases; our clients paid us by the hour, and in a case like this, the fees would be in the millions. Simpson, while wealthy, had probably depleted a considerable portion of his net worth to pay his lawyers, and I wondered about his ability to make much more money.

Still, I couldn't help feeling pleased and, admittedly, a bit of a thrill to have my name injected even slightly into such a high-visibility case. By the time I got to the office, however, the daydreaming had returned to reality and I vowed to give the idea no more thought. Nevertheless, later that morning I couldn't resist mentioning the call to my partner and good friend Tom Lambert. We had a laugh about it and then went about our work.

After lunch Tom called from his office. "Dan, you know what? I think you ought to pursue what Briskin told you. It would be great to get the Simpson case. It would be great for you, it would be great for the firm. It's going to be a huge case with a lot of interest in it. And it would be a fun case to handle. . . ." Tom was no longer kidding, and though I was pleasantly surprised at what he was saying, I knew there was no point in getting too serious about this. It was too farfetched.

The next day I was in the downtown Los Angeles office of my most important client, Paul Marciano, president of Guess?, Inc. I had a very close relationship with him as both a lawyer and a friend. In the course of discussing strategy in one of a number of cases I was handling for Guess?, my mind wandered and I mentioned the overture about Goldman. Given how busy and deeply immersed I was on important legal business for Guess?, I expected Paul to dismiss and discourage the idea. The last thing he needed was to have me consumed indefinitely by the Simpson case. But his reaction caught me offguard.

"Dan," he said immediately, "you ought to do this. I am outraged that Simpson got away with these murders! Everyone else is, too. Goldman needs a good law firm and a good lawyer, otherwise he's going to get crushed. You *must* do this!"

Since Briskin's call, I had given the idea more and more thought and could feel myself becoming genuinely interested. "Well," I said, "if he calls, I'll talk to him."

Ten minutes later I was upstairs in the office of Guess? then–general counsel Stan Levy when I was told, "Paul wants to speak with you. Please come downstairs. He's got Fred Goldman on the phone."

I looked at Stan in disbelief, and we both started to laugh. Paul Marciano grew up in France, didn't go very far in school, but is one of the smartest men I've ever known. He and his brothers Maurice, Armand, and Georges founded Guess? in the early 1980s and developed it overnight into one of the premier design apparel companies in the world. Paul is a doer, very challenging, very fast. It was just like him to begin from a standing start and in ten minutes have Fred Goldman on the line.

I was still laughing as I hustled downstairs, but all of a sudden this was not just a cute story anymore. This was getting serious. As I walked into Paul's office I heard him winding up a pitch. Then he handed me the phone. "Wow," was the first word Fred Goldman said to me, "you've got some pretty happy clients there."

I introduced myself and immediately expressed my condolences for the loss of his son and the experiences of the criminal trial. Then I said, "Mr. Goldman, let me tell you right off the bat, I am flattered that my client thought so highly of me to give you a call, but I'm embarrassed that he did so. I have no interest in talking to you at all if you have a lawyer. I just want to make that clear."

"Well, I had a lawyer," Goldman told me. "Bob Tourtelot. But I'm in the process of looking for a new lawyer to replace him."

"Why is that?"

"For a number of reasons. Primarily because Bob used to represent Mark Fuhrman, and I've decided it's not a good idea to have the same attorney as Fuhrman." Mark Fuhrman, of course, was the cop who found the killer's bloody glove and was accused of planting it on Simpson's property. In the criminal trial he denied having used the word "nigger" in the previous ten years and was found to be lying, impeached by tape recordings he had made with a screenwriter years before. He was widely perceived as a racist and the symbol of everything wrong with the LAPD.

Fred said he was in the process of interviewing a number of lawyers and asked if I would meet with him. I told him I wasn't sure I was the kind of lawyer he was looking for, but I would be willing to sit down with him to discuss the situation. By the end of the conversation we had set up a time.

I got off the phone and looked at Marciano. "How did you do that?" He shrugged. I said, "Paul, I can't take this case. First of all, I'm busy with you—"

"Dan," he interrupted, "you *must* take this case. It's more important than you. It is important to this country that there is justice. All the cases are coming out the wrong way: the Rodney King trial, the Simpson trial, the Menendez brothers trial. This case needs a big law firm like yours, and it needs a lawyer like you."

I knew better than to argue with Paul when he became passionate and enthusiastic about an idea. For the next several days I walked around thinking, What have I gotten myself into? At a time when many Los Angeles law firms were downsizing or even going out of business, it was important to bring in paying clients—if, that is, you wanted to make a good living. I had a busy practice and had been quite successful in working to expand our client list and improving our bottom line. To represent the Goldmans would, at best, put all of that on hold and might actually move me and the firm in the opposite direction. I was reaching a stage of my career where I was fast developing a reputation for winning hard cases for important clients. I'd worked hard to reach that stage. I was at a point in my life where I was not willing to go careening around a blind turn. If I took this case and lost, my ego, my psyche, or even worse, my career might be hurt badly. One other thing was clear: Whoever took this case should expect it to take his life in a whole new direction—and I wasn't going to get on that train unless I really wanted to go where it took me.

On the other hand, I thought about the extraordinary opportunity. I was staring into the very heart of justice. Here was a chance to share in a part of legal history! For a year and a half, Los Angeles, the United States, and a large part of the world had been consumed with the Trial of the Century. The obsession would likely culminate in the civil trial. How would I feel if I passed up this case? How *could* I pass it up? This was a chance to make my mark.

As odd as that might sound, I had never thought in those terms before. I was not a person who sat down and set concrete goals to achieve. I never even aspired to be a lawyer. I had wanted to be a musician.

I was born August 15, 1953, in East Orange, New Jersey, the third of four sons of Ralph and Anna Petrocelli. As a boy, my father was forced to quit school to help his father support the family. He worked in coal mines, trapped furs, farmed, and wound up as a mechanic on the Pennsylvania Rail Road, rising to the position of foreman before he retired. He met and married my mother in Italy, where he was stationed as a soldier during the Second World War. My oldest brother, Gabriel, was born in Naples. The war ended and my father came back to New Jersey, with my mother and brother following about a year later. My brother John was born, then I came, then my younger brother, Dennis. When I was about ten we moved to West Orange, all of one mile away.

When my father reached the age of sixty-five he was forced to retire, but he never stopped working. He did contracting jobs, painting, and construction. He owned three acres of land thirteen miles from our house, and he farmed them religiously every summer. When we were growing up, my father insisted that his boys help him on "the farm." My brothers and I never wanted to go with him, but we dutifully did. My parents still have a basement overflowing with forty years' worth of canned tomatoes. My dad loves to work and works to live.

My mother was just as tireless. She cooked and cleaned for four boys and a husband while working full-time in a small factory, cutting diamonds. My parents were like so many other immigrants who came to this country to make a better life for their families. They worked hard, they educated their children, and they devoted themselves to providing their family with opportunities they themselves never had. In the process, they passed on the simple but priceless values of love, decency, and honesty.

I was a pretty good student, but I never really killed myself studying. My father was a trumpet player, and he taught my brothers and me to play the horn. Gabriel and I took to music more seriously than John and Dennis. I played my horn as often as I could. In high school, my friends and I formed a rock band called the Hamburgers. In spite of the name, we were pretty good. Some of the members went on to become professional musicians. I loved playing in that band.

While I was still in high school, Gabriel moved to Southern California. He got a job teaching music in a junior high school and started talking to me about coming to Los Angeles for college. He was lonely for family. In 1971 I graduated from West Orange High School and was all set to go to Rutgers University in New Brunswick, New Jersey. My friend Dan Kolkowitz and I had already agreed to be roommates, when I decided, What the hell, and put in a last-minute application to UCLA. A month later, I was accepted. My mom said to me, "You're not going to come back." "Oh, yes I am," I told her. But she was 100 percent right.

I met my wife, Marian, the first day of school. She was a singer, a superb and natural musician. I was a workmanlike trumpet player who loved big band jazz and who had to practice hard to accomplish anything; she had the gift. I had been a hotshot player in high school, but when I arrived at UCLA and showed up for my first rehearsal for the UCLA marching band (a dreaded requirement in order to play in all the other bands), I found myself surrounded by sixty trumpet players, all better than I was. I was embarrassed, but I took my horn to the bowels of the dorm and practiced four hours every day. By the end of the year I was one of the better players in the band, but still a long way from the best.

After nearly three years of studying and playing music at UCLA, I did some soul-searching. I saw the hard time my extremely talented brother was having trying to make it in the industry and realized I didn't want to be a struggling musician my whole life. I knew Marian and I were going to be together, and I figured two starving musicians in one family was not a good idea, so I decided to be sensible and try something else. I looked through the UCLA course catalog and saw that the degree with the fewest required courses was economics. I crammed down nine econ courses during four academic quarters in little over a year and graduated in 1976. Though I had done well in my classes, I knew nothing about economics and had no interest in pursuing a career in it. Marian and I had just gotten married. She was working as a singer and songwriter and was doing extremely well. I, on the other hand, had no idea what I was going to do with myself.

Gabriel had been suggesting law school to me for several years, but I had never thought about it seriously. In my last year at UCLA, I got a part-time job as a bookkeeper for a Beverly Hills civil trial attorney, Sandy Sapin. This was my introduction to the law. I observed the fast pace, diversity, and complexity of the work. I saw the lawyers interact with their clients. Sandy's expensive clothes, Beverly Hills mansion, and Rolls-Royce didn't escape my attention, either. I thought maybe I should give law school a try and see if I liked it.

But I also needed to make some money. After graduation, my friend Ken Jaffe got me a job working with him as an auditor at City National Bank. We went from one branch to another, showing up by surprise and hoping to catch and report all the mistakes of the bank's employees. It was not the most gratifying job, so I decided to enroll in Southwestern University School of Law, located near downtown Los Angeles, at night. After two months of missing more classes than I attended, I found myself unwilling and unable to keep up with the grueling workload. I dropped out. I had my first taste of learning the law, however, and I loved it. I resolved to try again when I was more serious and committed to doing the work.

By the next year, I was ready. I enrolled in night school again, but this time buckled down, rarely missed class, and studied whenever I was not working.

Halfway through law school, I quit my bank job and went to work full-time as a law clerk in a firm whose clients were insurance companies defending civil lawsuits by plaintiffs who suffered personal injuries in accidents. I found I didn't like defense work; I would read the files about how the plaintiffs got injured or hurt, and more often than not I felt sorry for them. The firm's hard-core defense lawyers chastised me: "The plaintiffs are frauds, they're making these claims up," but I didn't agree. I also didn't appreciate the anti-Semitic jokes and disparaging remarks about minorities. It was an early lesson about the culture and personality of law firms. I knew I would have to be careful to find one in which I could be comfortable.

As the work piled up in school, I went to the firm's partners and asked if I could work part-time, so I could devote more time to school. They said, "We'll make it easier on you. You can have all the time in the world. You're fired." I was devastated. Marian and I had just had our first child, and now I had no job. I went to collect unemployment, and the firm fought me. They said I had quit. The unemployment office ruled in my favor. I'd won my first case.

Nevertheless, getting fired from my first law job shook me for quite a time. It was not a good way to start a legal career. After a few months of collecting unemployment, I got up enough confidence to look for another job as a law clerk while I finished my last year of law school. A friend in school helped me get a job with a Beverly Hills law firm, then known as Freshman, Marantz, Comsky & Deutsch, that specialized in commercial and business law. The firm's practice was interesting and challenging, but more important, the people who worked there were warm and support-ive. It was here that I began to cut my teeth in the world of business liti-gation, and I enjoyed every minute of it.

I graduated law school in December 1980 and decided to go work for Mitchell, Silberberg & Knupp, a large law firm located on the west side of Los Angeles. Tom Lambert was the head of the firm's hiring com-mittee that recruited me, and over the years we got to be good friends. He was a brilliant guy, a terrific lawyer, and he helped guide my career.

Mitchell, Silberberg & Knupp is one of the oldest and most respected law firms in Los Angeles. It was founded in 1908 by Shepard Mitchell, a white Anglo-Saxon Protestant, and Mendel Silberberg, a Jew, one of the first such partnerships in California. This, no doubt, helped shape the firm's personality and culture as tolerant, egalitarian, and open-minded. MSK had a long history of developing excellent lawyers, and I was thrilled to get the chance to work there. The firm represented clients of all types in a wide variety of areas and fields of practice. It was one of the first to represent clients in the entertainment industry. MSK repre-sented, for example, Jack Warner and his brothers when they formed Warner Bros., and was the first law firm to have lawyers maintain an office right on the lots of the motion picture studios.

MSK employs more than one hundred lawyers, with about sixty in the litigation group, which is where I was assigned when I joined. As my practice developed over the years, I worked on many different types of cases, all growing out of disputes in business or industry. I especially enjoyed cases involving the entertainment industry (if I couldn't be a musician, this was the next closest thing). Typically, my cases were hard-fought battles between smart, driven businessmen. I grew used to work-ing on complex cases, handling ream after ream of documents requiring extensive pretrial work and preparation, writing intricate legal motions and briefs to the judges, and doing high-level legal wrangling.

In most cases, litigation attorneys jockey for position with the express purpose of coming to the most advantageous settlement for their client. Lawyers and clients settle because juries are notoriously unpredictable and businesses rarely want to put their fate and considerable finances in a jury's hands. Unlike in a criminal trial, in which the state takes on the defendant winner take all, a civil case usually boils down to people vying to make the best economic deal at the right time. They hire lawyers to put them in the best position to achieve that result. In the end, we litigators are usually moving money from one rich man's pocket to another rich man's pocket.

All I knew about Fred Goldman I had learned from the media. On television Goldman was the humorless man with the handlebar mustache who never let up. He was angry at the legal system, at Simpson's circle of friends, at the defense attorneys, and most of all at Simpson himself. He didn't care who was watching; he was an articulate man standing at a podium in a riot of press, saying exactly what was on his mind. And what was on his mind was avenging his son's murder. I'd never seen him smile. His was an unrelenting vision, and Goldman seemed to be an unrelenting man. He had dignity but something wild seemed to be lurking underneath. He shouted and called Johnnie Cochran a racist. "His client butchered my son!" Goldman had screamed. He was Moses on the rock, railing at Pharaoh's army.

The Goldmans' house, not far from mine and not unlike my own, sat in a nice, quiet, suburban neighborhood in Agoura Hills, next to Southern California's San Fernando Valley. As I drove up, got out of my car, and walked to the door, around seven o'clock on Saturday night, October 14, 1995, I started to get an eerie feeling: This is an ordinary man who lives with his family in an ordinary house—much like me—whose son was murdered. The idea that this was not a racial flashpoint or a media phenomenon or a celebrity mauling, but a personal tragedy and a real loss, began to sink in. In all the thinking about taking on this second Trial of the Century and the chance to make my mark, that thought had somehow been overlooked.

There was a mezuzah, a Jewish sign of faith, beside the door when I knocked. Fred Goldman answered, and the moment I saw his face I could feel the overwhelming tragedy of his loss. More than two years after his son's killing, his face was lined and etched with sorrow, his eyes were drawn and drained.

Los Angeles is stocked with celebrities. You drive down the streets or walk into restaurants and see movie stars, television personalities, people you've seen only on the screen, and you never fail to compare their image against their reality. Boy, he's short. Wow, she certainly has a glow to her. Nice hair. Fred Goldman, without wanting to, had become that kind of celebrity, but the aura he exuded was beaten and grim. Defeated. We shook hands, and he invited me into his home.

The house was dark and filled with a sad, heavy air, as if the funeral would never end. The living room was piled almost to the ceiling with letters and boxes and cards, overflowing, unopened, spilling out all over the floor. There was no urgency to pick them up, there was the sense that this home would never be tidy again. I sat on a couch in the family room while Fred, his wife, Patti, and his daughter, Kim, sat opposite me. There were pictures of Ron around the home: bar mitzvah pictures, graduation pictures. Whenever they spoke about him they began to cry; the emotions were still very, very raw. The pressure of the trial, and particularly the outcome, had kept them raw. They'd had no real time to heal. I didn't know the Goldmans, and as a stranger I didn't want to intrude on such deep feelings, so I tried to keep the conversation focused on information they would need to make an informed choice of attorneys.

Fred made it clear to me that they were going to change lawyers, and he asked about my background, which I provided. We then spoke at length about the civil suits—what they were, what they entailed, how they would be litigated, and how they differed from the criminal case. I had done my homework and was able to explain all of this in some detail. I spent a little bit of time talking about the types of damages that could be awarded for the various claims in the case, but quickly realized that Fred and his family had little interest in the subject of money. What they wanted was to hear twelve people declare that O.J. Simpson killed their Ron.

Fred made it clear he wanted to bring the case to trial as quickly as possible. I told him that, although the civil cases had been filed some time ago, they had just been sitting there, waiting for the criminal case to end. I explained that, had Simpson been found guilty in the criminal trial there would have been no need for the jury in the civil case to hear all the evidence and make a determination about his responsibility for the murders; the only question would have been how much money Simpson should pay in damages. But with the not-guilty verdict, the case had to be tried again from scratch. I told Fred it would take six months to a year to get the case to trial, and that the trial itself would be lengthy, though certainly not as long as the criminal trial.

I took for granted that the Goldmans knew the difference between a criminal and civil case but quickly found that they, like most people in this country, did not. I explained.

In the first place, no matter what the jury determined in the civil case, Simpson would never go to jail for his crimes. Once acquitted, he could never be tried again in a criminal court or face criminal consequences, even if a jury determined in the civil case that he killed Ron— even if Simpson himself *confessed* to the killings. All that could be accomplished in the civil suit was to fix responsibility on Simpson for the killing of Ron and the assault on Nicole and to make him pay monetary damages. Though he listened and acknowledged what I was saying, I could see the disgust all over Fred's face. The man who butchered his son would be a free man forever, no matter the outcome in the civil case.

In a criminal case, I explained, the defendant must be judged guilty beyond a "reasonable doubt," while in a civil case the standard is the lower "preponderance of the evidence." A criminal case demands a unanimous twelve to nothing jury vote, while in a civil case, nine to three can suffice. In criminal cases, the defendant has a constitutional right to a speedy trial. (In the Simpson case the defense hurried the prosecution into presenting their case before they were fully prepared; the prosecution was still developing it as the trial was progressing.) In the civil case, there was ample time for further factual investigation, called pretrial discovery. As part of this discovery, the parties would have the right to take pretrial depositions. This is a process by which witnesses are brought to one of the lawyers' offices and questioned under oath by the lawyers. We would have the right to take Simpson's deposition under oath; we could force him to testify against his will. Fred was astonished; that was an amazing revelation to him. Plus, I explained, if Simpson failed to appear, the judge would enter a default judgment against him and the Goldmans would win.

"How do we stop that?" Fred asked.

"No, you don't understand," I said. "That means we win the case."

Fred understood perfectly. "What if he doesn't want to testify? How do we *stop* that?"

I had never heard of a client rejecting a victory before, but Fred Goldman was looking for a lawyer to be his surrogate; he wanted to see Simpson put on the stand, confronted face-to-face, challenged on every fact, and shown to the world to be, without a doubt, the man who murdered Ron and Nicole Brown Simpson. More than anything else, this was Goldman's ultimate goal. He wanted to confront the killer, and he was very concerned that, even now, Simpson might find another way to deprive him.

I made a point of telling the Goldmans that this was no longer the *People of the State of California* v. *O.J. Simpson;* the civil trial would be *Fred Goldman* v. *O.J. Simpson.* This would be his case, and he and his family would be deeply and actively involved in it, far beyond their roles as passive spectators in the criminal case. I asked him, "Are you sure this is something you want to do? You've suffered a horrible loss and were dealt a devastating blow in the criminal trial. Do you want to take on this fight? Why do you want to put you and your family through this?"

Fred had one answer to all those questions: "Because my son lost his life fighting till the end, and it's the least that I can do for him."

The case presented some complications. Fred Goldman and Sharon Rufo had been divorced twenty-one years earlier when Ron was six years old. Goldman and Rufo were not on good terms and there had been no relationship to speak of between Ron and his mother. She had not seen him in the last fifteen years of his life, had spoken to him only a few times, and would not have recognized him if he were standing next to her. Then she showed up at his funeral with a lawyer. Both Fred's and Kim's feelings on this subject were intensely negative, but they and Rufo were on the same side of the case, so this complication had to be dealt with. The last thing in the world we needed was to have the plaintiffs fighting among themselves, while Simpson and his lawyers sat back and enjoyed the show.

Another potential trouble spot was the fact that three suits had been brought, each by a different family. There would be three teams of lawyers going in three different directions. It would be devastating if the three suits were not strictly unified in goal, purpose, and effect, as well as in the way they were handled and who was handling them. It was critical for the three families to work together.

I told Fred that I did not have experience as a criminal lawyer, had not handled a wrongful death case, and was not a personal injury lawyer, all of which would have been assets. He told me he was talking to other lawyers, and I encouraged that. He had to feel entirely comfortable with his choice. I did caution him that to go up against Simpson's army of high-powered attorneys he really needed a team effort, not a high-profile celebrity-type lawyer. He needed lawyers who were totally committed to his cause, and who would not be out-worked or out-prepared. If my firm and I agreed to take his case, and Fred decided he wanted us, these were the qualities we could promise to deliver.

I told Fred, Patti, and Kim that when I get involved in a case it is an all-consuming process. When I go into battle for a client it makes my job infinitely easier and more gratifying if the client is right there with me every step of the way. I wanted to know whether they were prepared to make that commitment. They pledged that they were.

We discussed financial issues. Obviously the Goldmans were a middle-class family; they didn't have the resources to pay our normal fees. While I couldn't be certain, I estimated this case would run well in excess of $1 million in legal fees. They told me people were sending money. Fred and Kim showed me envelopes, kids writing in barely legible letters sending dollar bills, other people sending $100, others sending $1,000. The public was reacting with extraordinary support and interest. The letters screamed to the galling injustice—not just to the Goldman and Brown families, but to everyone—of what happened in the criminal case. I told Fred that fund-raising would be necessary to raise additional money, and that some of my clients, like Brian and Phyllis Harvey and the Marcianos at Guess?, had told me they would be interested in contributing and helping to raise funds.

We spoke for several hours that night, and by the end of the evening I knew this was a special time in my life, that I was about to embark on something very important. Although I take all my cases seriously and invest tremendous amounts of time and energy and emotion in winning them, this was different. I tend to deal with corporations, and my cases are about money. Yes, I'm usually fighting for what I think is right, but never like this. This *was* personal. This was the killing of a young man, and as a lawyer and a father, I could think of nothing more natural and more profound than to represent a father fighting for his murdered son.

I wondered whether I was the right lawyer for the job. Leaving the Goldmans' house and driving home, I balanced the scales. Many other attorneys, particularly personal injury lawyers, had vast amounts more experience than I did in handling this kind of case. I had none. Many litigation attorneys had far more trial experience. My cases had made it all the way through trial about a dozen times—only once to conclusion in front of a jury. All the rest had settled. There would be no settlement here. I was not a natural for this case.

But these were fears and insecurities taking over. Deep down I had no doubt I could do the job. Fred wanted a fighter. That was me. This was a civil case. That is what I do. This case had all the same ingredients of every other case I had ever worked on: endless legal maneuvering, discovery, motion practice, the need to out-think your opponent, the struggle to uncover every last piece of information, building your case down to the last, most minute detail, and presenting your arguments and evidence to the judge and jury to persuade them that you are right and the other side is wrong.

Despite all the hype that clients hear from lawyers about their great courtroom victories and their unique specialties and fields of expertise, effective lawyering boils down to hard work and preparation. One of the beauties of the law, and one of its curses, is that there is no limit to how much you can do to prepare a case. You can always dig for more information, you can always spend more time mastering the facts and evidence, you can always learn more about the law. In the end, success is a direct function of how much desire and commitment you have. And when it came to those qualities, I could hold my own. I had the utmost confidence in the capabilities of my law firm, my partners and associates who would jump at the chance to work with me on this case. We would put together a great team.

Something else crossed my mind. I had never met O.J. Simpson, but I could remember watching the game in which he ran in the snow against the New York Jets to become the first man in NFL history to rush for over 2,000 yards in a season. I had watched in agony as, year after year, his Buffalo Bills got knocked out of the American Football Conference playoffs, usually by the Miami Dolphins, denying Simpson the opportunity to play in the Super Bowl, something I had badly wanted to see. I'd never thought he was a particularly good broadcaster—he used to wag his big head around too often and didn't have the best diction—but he was "O.J.," and he was a persona. I had seen *The Towering Inferno* and felt bad for him, a typical athlete turned actor not doing a very good job, but I'd thought he had found a perfect role for himself as a funny, lovable figure in the *Naked Gun* movies. I wondered, given my fan's adulation of him, whether I would be able to treat Simpson as what he was, a cold-blooded killer.

Could I resist the temptation to talk sports with a Hall of Famer, to revel in the locker room stories, to joke around with one of the greatest running backs of all time? It was kind of scary. There I would be, trying to prove that he slaughtered my client's young son, and yet would I be flattered if he treated me like a buddy?

What if I liked O.J. Simpson? How would I handle that?

Nevertheless, I felt a strong pull to take on Fred Goldman's fight. I felt deeply for him, for his family, for their case, and wanted the chance to give them what they so cruelly had been denied so far—a verdict in a court of law that O.J. Simpson killed their son. I was hooked, and I knew it.

On Monday I started to discuss the case with my partners at MSK, particularly the executive committee, of which Tom Lambert was a member. They asked some hard questions, specifically about how it might affect the firm economically: "How are we going to do this?" "How much time will it involve?" "How much money are we going to put into it?" "Will we have to invest our own funds?" "Who will pay the expert witnesses, the jury consultants, all the people we will need to win?" "You have a busy practice, Dan, you have good clients, how are you going to handle your practice and this case at the same time?" We very rarely took contingency-fee cases, and the committee viewed this one as unlikely to generate a significant recoverable fee and so was not willing to take it on that basis. There were many good reasons to take this case, but economics was not one of them.

One element that we hoped would bring expenses down was the fact that the case had already been tried in criminal court. We could, in effect, sift through that work, distill it, repackage and re-present it. We assumed, based on the massive work and investigation by the LAPD, the FBI, the DA's office, and many others, that we would not have to do much new or independent investigation. We could use the prosecution's consultants and experts. The idea was, the case had already been tried, it just needed to be tried better, to a more receptive jury, and to a different result.

There were good reasons for taking it. Some important clients were supporting our involvement, and even interested in raising money to support the effort. The case would certainly give the firm and me exposure and lead to more business in the future. This was a case that would make legal history, and law firms should be a part of legal history. We felt it would be good for the firm to win a case that many, many people wanted very badly to see won. Bringing O.J. Simpson to justice would bring a significant measure of goodwill and visibility to Mitchell, Silberberg & Knupp. There was also the simple fact that it was the right thing to do.

However, there was concern that the behavior of some of the attorneys in the criminal case—on both sides—had not brought honor to the legal profession. Would some of that negative publicity rub off on us? Possibly. We might be seen as another group of media-hound lawyers standing in front of the microphones, yapping away. The media would be unavoidable and we would have to learn how to handle it.

We also discussed the issue of race. MSK is a progressive firm, has always been a staunch supporter of minority rights, and would never advocate or want to be perceived as advocating a racist position. Because the Simpson criminal case had ended up being cast in racial terms, it was important that the law firm avoid a racial backlash. Would our clients think this was a white versus black issue and we were advocating for whites over blacks? That would have been unacceptable.

One of the partners astutely observed that we could use the case to turn a potential negative into a positive. "I think this is an opportunity for us to show how responsibly this racial issue can be dealt with. We've always prided ourselves on our fairness, on being color blind. Who better than us to do this?" We thought we could be good emissaries in this regard. I added, "We can make it clear to the public, to our clients, and to the lawyers here at the firm that this case is not about race and we're not going to let it devolve into a black versus white conflict. We're going to do everything we can to keep race out of the equation."

We decided that, on balance, if funds could be raised, taking this case was a good thing. MSK gave me its blessing. Assuming we could work out acceptable economic arrangements, if I got the call from the Goldmans we would take it.

On Tuesday night I was sitting in bed, reading briefs and watching television when the phone rang shortly after 10:00 P.M. It was Fred. We chatted briefly, and finally he said, "Well, I think I'd like to hire you."

"Fred," I told him, "I'd love to represent you. We need to discuss financial terms and some other issues. Let's talk about it tomorrow."

"How do you spell your name?" he asked.

Approximately an hour later I was propped up on a pillow, watching the news, when I saw my picture, with my name underneath it—spelled correctly—on the screen on Channel Four. I was being announced as Fred Goldman's new attorney.

I was stunned. I was not a guy who ever got on TV. There was no chance.

But there I was, and now there was no turning back.

Was I ready for this?

THREE

The "Big Unit"

The next morning, I had a breakfast meeting with my accountant, Mike Glynn, at Junior's, a deli in West Los Angeles where I ate often. Mike had heard the news and couldn't talk about anything else. One of my senior partners, Ed Medvene, was also having breakfast there, and he came to our booth and said, "From now on I'm going to have to call you the Big Unit!" A lot of us at MSK are passionate sports fans, and Randy Johnson, the American League's most dominating pitcher, affectionately known as "the Big Unit," was ruling the baseball playoffs at the time. I had already been bringing in lots of new clients, but this case was a major leap forward.

I got in my car to travel the half mile to my office and, as usual, picked up my voice mail from my cell phone. By nine A.M. I generally have two or three calls. The automated computer voice said, "You have twenty-five voice messages." What? I started punching them in. Some friends had called with congratulations, but mostly it was the media. Radio and TV stations from around the country, magazines, newspapers. All wanting interviews—immediately. I thought that I'd thought this all through, but I was completely unprepared. I parked in our basement garage, and when I got upstairs to my office my secretary, Maria Johnson, told me, "There are TV trucks all around the building. People are trying to get in to see

you. What do we do?" I had no idea. I had not even finalized the arrangements with Fred Goldman. Officially I was not yet on the job.

"Dan," she said, "NBC wants to do an interview with you." I think
she giggled. "Are you doing interviews?" I had never given an interview in
my life.

Tom Lambert walked into my office and said, "This place is a zoo.
What are we going to do?"

I said, "Tom, I don't have a clue." We started laughing.

Lambert suggested calling the firm's public relations consultants,
who immediately sent three representatives. They said we had to hold a
press conference.

"Press conference?" I said. "No way." Normally, our firm had a policy against talking to the media; legal matters are private and sensitive, not
things to be splashed out in newspaper headlines and TV shows. So I had
no experience dealing with the media. But obviously, this wasn't a normal
case. The PR guys were all in agreement that we should be proactive and
should act quickly.

"Dan, you don't understand. If you don't talk to the reporters, they're
going to end up writing about you anyway, it will be inaccurate because
they won't have the benefit of your thoughts. It's going to make your client
look bad. This is a very public case. Your client has been public. You can't
deal with the media one by one, you'll be here all day, you'll say different
things, it will be a disaster. We'll put together a press conference for three
this afternoon in one controlled setting."

"I really don't want to do that," I complained. "I'm not prepared, I
don't know anything about the case, I don't know what to say." I was truly
terrified. I could practice law with confidence, but meeting the press was
a whole different animal. I wasn't even dressed particularly well that day.
I had woken up that morning thinking it would be a normal day at the
office, I'd had no expectation that I was going to stand in front of the
national media that afternoon. That's how naive I was.

I called Fred Goldman, who started laughing. "Better get used to it!"

"The place is wild," I said. "You better come over here."

Within an hour Fred breezed in, cool, confident. He seemed like
such a veteran. I was a nervous wreck. We prepped before going out there.
Goldman would introduce me as his new attorney, he would make a state-

ment, I would make a very brief statement, then we would take some questions.

At the law firm we had thought, for sure, that there would be publicity. But most of us felt that the media frenzy and micro-reporting surrounding the criminal trial would subside for the civil case. The press did not understand the long, tedious, and often mundane civil litigation process, especially the pretrial process. No way the media and the public would remain transfixed. The punishment involved money. Simpson's life was no longer on the line. The idea that he might be imprisoned behind bars for the rest of his life was no longer in the air.

As it turned out, I was completely wrong. And on this day, I was totally unprepared for the onslaught. From the quiet anteroom near our elevators, waiting to meet the press, I looked down at the building's courtyard and saw it was packed with people. The plaza was jammed with reporters, camera operators, and sound technicians standing on the concrete embankment that enclosed the flower beds. They and the spectators attracted by the cameras and the news crews overflowed down the plaza steps. I was too nervous even to estimate the crowd or count the cameras and microphones. As I moved through the crush to the podium, all I could think of was walking to my execution.

Fred spoke effortlessly, eloquently. I had to follow him. I was terrified that I would say something inappropriate, or entirely wrong, and be branded for life. I didn't know my facts, I barely knew my client, I felt completely inadequate. I wasn't up to this. Cameras kept flashing in my face. My mouth went dry, I was having trouble swallowing, I was having an anxiety attack. I wanted out of there in the worst way. I said my few words and shut up. Leaving the lectern in an area I routinely strolled through at lunchtime almost every day of my working life, I turned and marched straight into a dead end. I had to face the humiliation of retracing my steps and beating a retreat.

Tom Lambert said I'd done a fine job, but he was just being his usual gracious and supportive self. Some weeks later, after I had worked with our public relations people and learned to be more at ease in front of microphones, cameras, and crowds, one of my partners told me, "Dan, I can tell you now, but . . . you didn't talk like yourself, you didn't sound like yourself, you didn't even *look* like yourself." I said, "You're right. I was terrified!"

After the press conference, Fred Goldman and I went up to my office to talk business. The door to my inner office was open, and all of a sudden a strange guy walked in. He said, "Hello, Mr. Goldman. Hello, Mr. Petrocelli." Startled, I asked, "Who the hell are you?" He identified himself as a local newspaper reporter.

"You're here from the media?"

"Well, I just was wondering whether I could sit in and take some notes—"

"Sir, are you crazy! I am meeting with my client and you're not permitted to be here. Maria, get this guy out of here!"

We immediately had my floor and office number deleted from the building's public directory. I'd been on the job one hour, I hadn't given a thought to the substance of the case, and now I had the media in the core of the law firm, *in* my office, *with* my client!

Meanwhile I had a case to prepare and a team to assemble.

Under normal circumstances, when I brought a case into the firm I worked on it with lawyers junior to me. As more important and serious cases came along, I would from time to time, not often, ask senior lawyers to get involved. One had to be aware of law firm protocol and the acute sensibilities of highly accomplished senior attorneys. The O.J. Simpson civil case would obviously be extremely high profile, and I had been hired as lead lawyer. I wanted to put together a team of excellent, experienced senior lawyers and divide responsibility in a fair and equitable manner, while still maintaining my position as quarterback. I had just turned forty-two years old. I approached my senior partners solicitously.

The first person I went to was Ed Medvene. Medvene was a senior partner in the litigation department, in his mid-sixties. He was a veteran trial lawyer, a former assistant U.S. attorney with a prominent criminal defense practice. There would be highly experienced lawyers on the other side and I wanted someone of Medvene's stature working with me. Ed was vastly experienced in both criminal and civil litigation, having been the lead lawyer for the NAACP, the ACLU, and the Mexican-American Legal Defense Fund in the landmark Los Angeles school integration case in the mid-seventies. He had defended a number of prominent people, prosecuted and defended various alleged organized crime figures. I had worked for him when I was a young, hustling lawyer on the way up, and he had been one of my significant mentors at the firm. He was a tenacious attorney, a bulldog. We had not worked together for many years and I had always wanted to try a case with him, but never had the opportunity. Well, I had my opportunity now.

I visited his office and said, "Ed, I'd love for you to work on this with me. I explained that I wanted him to play a major role in all phases of the case and the trial. At the same time, I shared my feelings that this was a rare and special opportunity for me, and I wanted to maintain my role as lead lawyer. I don't know that Ed Medvene had worked on a case in the last thirty years in which he wasn't in complete control, so this was asking a great deal of him.

"Look," he told me graciously, "I'd love to work on the team. Don't worry about it, we'll work it out." I was thrilled.

The second person I approached was Tom Lambert. During my fifteen years at MSK I had always looked up to him as a model for developing my style and practice. Tom was an impressively quick study, with the intellectual firepower to tackle areas unknown to most of us, absorb them, and bring them to bear with confidence and precision in his cases. He had been my good friend at MSK since day one, and we had worked many successful cases together. Tom was also the consummate team player. Several years earlier, the firm's senior partner Arthur Groman had turned over the reins to me in a very important case involving the estate of Armand Hammer, a complicated, hard-fought battle over a contested will worth hundreds of millions of dollars. I immediately asked Tom to work on it with me. We put together a team of lawyers, litigated all across the country for four years, and won a spectacular victory following a lengthy trial. Tom and I worked together like a machine. The Simpson case would also be trench warfare, and I knew I could spend many days and months in a foxhole with Tom Lambert.

Before I could approach him, Peter Gelblum came to me and asked to be on the case. Despite his busy practice at MSK, Peter had been drawn into the drama of the Simpson criminal case and had followed the proceedings closely. His wife had taped the television broadcasts so he could watch the coverage at home at night. It wasn't the first trial he had followed closely. Most of our own work gets settled before it goes to trial, so he enjoyed watching other lawyers try cases.

Peter and I were good friends. He had graduated number one in his class a year after I did at Southwestern Law School, also in the night program. He had bettered all my record grade-point averages and succeeded me as editor of the law review. I introduced Peter to MSK, and once out of law school he and I had followed similar career paths. Prior to law school was another matter.

Peter had been an actor. His most notable credit was as a villain on an episode of *Kojak.* He had written a screenplay for Bette Davis that was optioned but never produced. Peter tells the story that he was propelled into the law profession when his wife, Sian, an actress, got into a dispute with her agent over commissions. Peter wrote the man a legal letter and got a check in the return mail. A star lawyer was born.

Peter is a brilliant guy and an excellent legal writer. I knew I would need someone to work with me closely on brief writing and research. Peter has that type of personality and demeanor that reminds you more of a shrink than a lawyer, and I felt he would work especially well in the important areas of domestic violence and behavioral science. In a wrongful death case following a murder trial, not unlike this one, Peter had worked with Ed Medvene in defending Christian Brando at deposition after Marlon Brando's son killed a man. (Ironically, Bob Shapiro was involved in this case as well.) That was experience he could put to good use. I also needed Peter to help me direct our younger lawyers. I jumped at the opportunity to add him to the team.

I didn't know it at the time, but the MSK halls were abuzz over which junior lawyers I would ask to work on the case. One of the first I added was Yvette Molinaro, a senior associate who had worked with me before and exhibited an indefatigable ability to read, review, and digest massive volumes of documents, materials, and facts. I knew I could count on her to put in workaholic hours. Associates Jeff Goldman (no relation) and Matt Railo were brought on to take on the difficult legal research and brief writing.

With the exception of Gelblum's anecdotal knowledge, we were a collection of lawyers who knew zero about this case—and we were up against Simpson's team of attorneys, who had lived the criminal case for a year and a half and had just won it. The only significant change in their roster was that Johnnie Cochran was stepping down as lead lawyer and had handpicked Robert Baker to succeed him. I read up on Bob Baker and learned he was a very successful insurance defense lawyer, especially in defending doctors and hospitals in medical malpractice cases. Baker had considerable trial experience, was named California Trial Lawyer of the Year, and was widely considered to be one of the top trial lawyers in the western part of the United States.

The Dream Team was intact in one form or another. Cochran and his firm remained behind the scenes. F. Lee Bailey's firm was handling the case full-time. Bailey was positioned to try the case with Baker. But Bailey himself soon encountered legal problems in Florida that ultimately landed him in jail, thanks largely to the testimony of his co–Dream Teamer Robert Shapiro. Bailey's partner, Daniel Leonard, replaced Bailey on the case and in the courtroom. DNA expert Bob Blasier was working full-time and his colleagues Barry Scheck and Peter Neufeld were still in the fold. Private investigator Bill Pavelic was still on board. Law professors Gerry Uelman and Alan Dershowitz were lurking in the background. They had all the materials, they had all the evidence, they had all the transcripts and files. They had just won the Trial of the Century twelve–zip in three hours. They knew everything, we knew nothing.

Goal number one was to get the information into our office, but we immediately had a problem. The district attorney and the prosecutors didn't work for Fred Goldman, and we didn't have the right to call upon them to sit down with us, bring us up to speed, and hand everything over to us on a silver platter at the taxpayers' expense. We were private citizens, and they didn't want to be accused of playing favorites. They told me, "Look, if we were just to make copies and turn this stuff over to you, Johnnie Cochran's going to ask for an audit of the city records and it would not look good. We're going to have to play this straight."

To add to our problems, within days after we were hired, we received notification that Simpson's attorneys were racing into criminal court in front of Judge Ito to get an order requiring the return of all Simpson's property that had been seized as evidence by the police. Under California law, once a defendant is acquitted, the state has no further jurisdiction over him or his property. We, of course, wanted to resist. We suspected that if O.J. Simpson got the evidence back, it would be long gone; we'd never see it again. At best, the chain of custody would be broken. Since Fred Goldman was not a party to the criminal lawsuit, we had no sure-fire way to stop this. But we decided to file court papers and hope to be heard on it. At the same time, we sent out subpoenas for the same items Simpson was asking for. A subpoena is a court order commanding evidence and/or witnesses to be turned over. As such, it was superior to the motion the defense filed requesting the return of Simpson's property. So we subpoenaed everything. We had subpoenas served on the DA's office, the LAPD, the Los Angeles County coroner's office, even on Judge Ito's clerk for evidence that still remained in the courthouse. We then went into court to argue before Judge Ito on October 31, 1995. Halloween.

The irony was not lost on me that the first legal battle in the civil case was being fought in the criminal court. The media was out in spectacular force, again I was stunned by their numbers. You would think I would have caught on quickly to the overwhelming public fascination with everything about the O.J. Simpson case, but it took me some time to get used to being in the middle of it.

Judge Ito's courtroom, the stage for the criminal trial, was surprisingly small. So was Judge Ito. I looked around and noticed the witness box, the judge's bench, the prosecution and defense tables that had been burned as icons into so many people's minds on the live broadcasts and the evening news. It was all so unimposing in person. Only two weeks had passed since closing arguments—"If it doesn't fit, you must acquit"—yet so much had changed. O.J. Simpson was a free man, walking the streets, playing golf. Johnnie Cochran was almost as controversial a figure, yet here he was at the hearing, leaning against the back wall, a passive observer, smugly taking it all in. He had announced the hiring of Bob Baker with great bravado, and later declared, "Bob will be the best lawyer in the courtroom." There was a lot of arrogance coming out of the defense side, and like a football coach who tapes incendiary quotes to the locker room door, I used it to motivate myself and the people on my team.

Medvene and I argued against Simpson's attorney Carl Douglas that day. We argued "special circumstances." This was a unique situation, we told Judge Ito; we had a civil suit that had already been filed and all the evidence and material collected for the criminal trial was relevant. We hadn't even seen the potential evidence yet; we needed the opportunity to inspect it all, whether it had appeared in the criminal trial or not. If this material was returned to Simpson, there was every possibility that it would never show up again. Simpson wanted everything back: his luggage, his golf clubs, his clothing, his blood-spattered socks, his credit cards. We privately joked that he would ask for the bloody gloves back, thereby establishing his ownership of them. We did actually look over his list for the gloves, but no such luck. Simpson even asked for the fake goatee and mustache that had been found in his black bag inside the Ford Bronco. On Halloween, of all days, we asked Judge Ito, why does he need his fake goatee and mustache? Was he going to go trick-or-treating?

We argued that Ito should hold the evidence in abeyance and permit the civil judge, who was then Alan Haber, to decide what to do with it in view of its importance to the civil case. Ito, to the consternation of the defense lawyers, agreed. He deferred the decision by kicking it to Judge Haber. In the meantime, nothing would be returned to Simpson. Ito's ruling enabled us to go into the civil court and persuade Judge Haber to give us time to examine all these evidentiary materials, preserve anything that was biological in nature, and return anything we didn't need. We won the first big legal skirmish. Simpson didn't get his goatee back.

We set up a depot across the hall from my office to house all the material. It quickly became too small, and we moved it twice before settling down in a windowless conference room on the fifth floor that we quickly named the War Room.

The logistical task of gaining access to and duplicating all the files, documents, photographs, and massive amounts of materials that we subpoenaed was staggering. There were fifty thousand pages of trial transcript alone, and that didn't include the grand jury, preliminary hearing, and other pretrial proceedings. The court reporter wanted to charge us a dollar a page: $50,000 for one copy! We were operating on a tight budget to begin with, and that seemed an outrageous amount of money under any budget. Instead, we brought in our own photocopying machines and put paralegals on the case. The police would not let the material out of their office, and neither would the DA, so we had to do it there. It would have been easy many times to say, "Oh, no, that's all right, don't copy that." But you never knew what you would find, and I didn't want to miss a piece of evidence that might turn out to be important. We ended up copying just about everything. We duplicated audiotapes, videotapes, black and white and color photographs. We duplicated computer disks and converted them onto our firm's computer systems.

As all this material started coming in and piling up, I couldn't begin to fathom how we could possibly make a dent in it, let alone read, review, and master all of it. Once again, the doubts crept back. What had I gotten myself—my firm—into, and how were we going to deal with this?

Adding to my concerns was seeing how much of the files and materials were in a state of disarray. The LAPD's filing system was especially disorganized. We were going through some of these files one day when I came upon drawer after drawer of loose audiotapes. "What are these?" I asked. "I don't know," I was told, "various conversations, 911 calls, the Bronco chase, all kinds of stuff." Later, we distributed the tapes among the lawyers and listened on our office tape recorders whenever we had a free minute, or in our cars driving to and from work. One day Peter Gelblum popped in a cassette and heard Simpson talking to Detective Tom Lange on the cell phone during the infamous Bronco chase. Lange was trying to talk him into surrendering, and Simpson sounded completely pitiful, moaning, "You've been a good guy, man. You really have . . . I'm the only one that deserves [to be hurt]." All of it was utterly inconsistent with the notion, central to his defense, that these police officers—and in particular this individual, the lead detective in the case—were responsible for framing him.

I like to develop personal relationships with my clients; it's hard for me to work with clients I am not close to, and I find it gratifying when I know that my work means something to another person, as opposed to just putting money in the coffers of some faceless company. I stay in constant contact with my clients. I want them involved, I want them to understand all the issues and developments in the case and be part of the team every step of the way. I wanted and would need the same interaction with the Goldmans.

As the files began to arrive, I would pick up one that grabbed my attention, and read it. I would read about the Simpson case all day and at night, and bring my handheld dictating machine with me everywhere, making notes in the car on my way home, and in bed, propped up on a pillow before I went to sleep. In the evening, I called Fred, Patti, and Kim to give them reports on the day's activities. It became a ritual. They were eager to learn, and were fast learners. I was constantly amazed at how adept and astute Kim Goldman's input was on technical and complex legal points. Fred had less patience for the details but had great instincts when it came to matters of strategy and tactics. Patti was always supportive, always there, like a rock.

Sometimes at night and on weekends, I would drive to the Goldmans' house and visit with them for hours. On Sunday, Patti served coffee and bagels. These visits were important to me. I wanted to know Ron Goldman. I needed to know him. I spent my workdays looking at crime-scene pictures of his crumpled slain body and even more lifeless autopsy photographs, but that was Ron Goldman in death. I asked his sister, Kim, "Tell me about your life. Tell me about Ron's life. Tell me about your dad's life. Tell me about growing up." It wasn't easy, but Kim spent one long Sunday afternoon in my living room describing how close she and her brother had been, how they had had to band together to handle the tragedy that faced them at a young age—the separation from their mother, who abandoned them, and their parents' messy divorce.

One day, on my way to the Goldmans' house, I stopped at the cemetery and visited Ron's grave. I sat there, all by myself on a hill in Agoura, and read the inscription on his tombstone:

> *Sometimes when we're alone and lost in thought and all the*
> *world seems far away, you come to us as if in a dream, gently*
> *taking our hands and filling our hearts with the warmth of your*
> *presence, and we smile, knowing that although we cannot be*
> *together for now, you're always close in our thoughts.*

I was struck by the awesome responsibility I had undertaken. I had never met Ron Goldman, and never would. But I was now his lawyer. This case was about obtaining accountability for his life. It is an unspeakable tragedy to have a life taken before its time, but to have it taken mockingly, to have the killer walk out of the courtroom to a hero's welcome, with cheering people lining the streets and helicopters following him home to a victory party, what could be more wrong? If it were my child, how would I feel?

Unfortunately, money continued to be an issue. The legal community in Los Angeles was experiencing leaner times than in previous years, and MSK was no exception. The firm had entrusted me with directing the case, as I saw fit, and I felt obligated to protect the interests of the firm. For several weeks after we accepted the case I fretted about our ability to withstand the massive legal effort needed to litigate it properly. In taking the case, as in any case, we committed to do a first-rate job; nothing less was acceptable. The question in this case was how to pay for it. People had pledged money, I just didn't know whether they would come through and whether it would be enough.

Fred Goldman informed me that then Los Angeles radio talk show host, Bill Press on station KFI, spontaneously said on the air that he would donate $100 to the Goldman family if his listeners would contribute as well. The phones lit up. All of a sudden money began to arrive. We established the Ron Goldman Justice Fund as a bank account to accept these donations. At the suggestion of Bill Press, Kim Goldman and I appeared on the show on a Sunday afternoon. Again I was surprised when television cameras were on hand to shoot us going down the hall into the radio booth. Kim answered questions, and money started pouring in. We had had the case for all of four days.

My client, Guess?, Inc., produced and funded a newspaper advertisement asking for contributions to help support the Goldman family's fight for justice. The ads included an 800 number that people could call to make contributions and a post office box to which contributions could be sent. Guess? workers volunteered their time processing the donations, doing all the administrative work, depositing the checks, preparing and sending out thank-you notes. There were rumors that Joan Rivers had contributed $500,000, that Marvin Davis had agreed to fund the litigation, and that the Marciano brothers of Guess? were footing the entire bill. None of these rumors was true. I got calls from several anonymous wealthy donors, but in most cases they didn't come through, either. The money that came in was almost entirely from the general public and was in tens, twenties, fifties, up to a $100 per contribution. After about three weeks it totaled $100,000. KFI station representatives came to my office twice with a big box of checks, which I turned over to Guess? and the Goldmans. It all went into the Ron Goldman Justice Fund bank account and was used only for legal expenses.

The early advertisements were so successful that Guess? proposed sponsoring further newspaper ads in which Fred Goldman would make a direct pitch for donations for the case. We had a meeting at Guess? where ideas for a fund-raising campaign with Fred as the spokesman were laid out. Fred balked at the idea. He did not want to directly ask for money; he was uncomfortable with that role and feared his motives would be misunderstood. "Fred," I said firmly, "this is something we have to do." I explained my reasons. Nonetheless, he wouldn't budge, other than to say, "I'll think about it." I was disappointed because once I had made clear how important the issue was, I thought he would go along with it.

That night Fred called me at home. "Dan," he said, "I'm not comfortable with this. I don't want to be out there asking for money. It's not right. I don't feel good doing it."

I pressed him some more. "Fred, I can't overstate how important this is. I know you're uncomfortable about raising money directly, but it can be done in a tasteful way. We can get our message across with dignity."

Finally he said, "You know, we've only known each other for about a week or so and it seems like every conversation we have is about money. Maybe I didn't make the right choice."

I was going to argue with him. Money was tight; I was constantly worrying over it. But then it hit me, and I stopped in my tracks. I said, "You know what, Fred? You're absolutely right. I am so concerned about this issue that I have disregarded your feelings. And, I think you're right." I apologized to him. I had gotten carried away with my own financial insecurities regarding my firm and I had not been sensitive to him. It was an important and early reminder that this case was not like any other case of mine. From then on I tried hard to take the money issue more in stride. Fred, for his part, seemed to appreciate my change of heart. He allowed Guess? to run additional ads. He would never give speeches in which he asked for money, and there were some things he would not do, but he agreed to appear at some dignified solicitations.

I found myself asked to speak before several hundred people at a very elegant fund-raiser hosted by Phyllis and Brian Harvey. I had no speech prepared, other than wanting to introduce the lawyers on our team. All I could do was stand at the podium and tell them what visiting Ron's grave had meant to me, the feeling of responsibility I felt for this case and for Ron's life. Afterward, a friend came up with tears in her eyes. That I was able to move her and others, and communicate feelings about something so personal and important, as opposed to talking about lost profits or breach of fiduciary duty, gave me a sense of satisfaction.

Friends and supporters hosted a more formal $500-a-plate-fund-raiser at Drai's, a trendy Hollywood restaurant. A number of people in the entertainment industry attended. A large segment of the Hollywood community, I learned quickly, was especially generous and supportive of our

cause. My clear sense was that they wanted Simpson—and the public—
to know he was not welcome back. I spoke, as did the Goldmans,
Dominick Dunne, and several friends of Nicole's. The feeling was universal: Simpson had gotten away with murder and this case was the last
chance for justice.

Events like these underscored how deeply this case extended beyond
the Goldmans and Browns, beyond the victims, beyond O.J. Simpson, to
the community itself. Los Angeles had been marred by a series of controversial and unpopular court cases: the Simpson criminal case; the first
Rodney King trial, in which the white officers who beat King were acquitted by a white jury in Simi Valley; the Menendez brothers case, in which
two young men admitted killing their parents, but could not be convicted
until a second trial. The race riots triggered by the Rodney King verdict
had been extremely disturbing and unsettling, unleashing a frightening
breakdown of law, order, and civility. People in Los Angeles and throughout the country blamed the legal system. What trust and confidence in
the system survived was all but destroyed by the spectacle and result of the
Simpson criminal case. So there was a lot riding on our civil case. People
wanted to right a wrong. People wanted to know that their legal system
worked. People wanted justice.

The fund-raisers were successful, unsolicited contributions were
pouring in, and more than $500,000 was collected.

Three months later it was apparent that the flow of these contributions was coming to a close. Also apparent was that we would need significantly more money than we collected, just to pay costs and expenses.
Forget lawyers' fees, we had vendors, expert witnesses, and consultants to
pay. Audiovisual equipment, graphics, travel expenses, depositions all
added up. Without them we would be lost, and the case would be lost as
well. One of my partners, Ronald DiNicola, gave me a crash course in
professional direct-mail fund-raising and the firms who do this work.
Many worthwhile organizations, supporting many diverse and worthy
causes, used these firms to raise funds. Our appeal would require a letter
from the Goldman family to the public, prepared by direct-mail special-
ists, sent to thousands of people on professionally selected mailing lists,
asking for money to defray legal expenses.

I was very apprehensive about presenting the idea to Fred. I knew it
was likely to be an unpleasant meeting because of his feelings about the

issue. When I broached it with him, he told me flatly, no. I pushed him on it, and we built up some considerable personal tension. I let it drop again.

At the same time, the financial pressures continued to rise. I now had a clearer understanding about the level of public interest and desire that we succeed, as well as the degree of scrutiny and criticism should we fail. We would be flyspecked on everything we did, so we could make no mistakes, we had to do a first-rate job all the way, we were up against a very formidable defense team, and we would require more time and more money than I had realized. The amount of work and people needed to prepare the case properly were also far greater than expected. The entire operation was growing in all respects, and we were mounting what amounted to a small business. Fred had never signed the fee agreement with MSK that I sent him, and I was feeling pressure from the law firm to finalize our financial agreement.

Early in 1996 I met at the Goldmans' house with Fred, Patti, and Kim for a real heart-to-heart. I explained in detail the needs of the case and the financial requirements to meet those needs. I told them it was necessary to engage in direct-mail fund-raising. I said, "I admire your reasons for resisting soliciting funds personally, and I know this is difficult for you. There won't be many things I will ask of you, but this is one of them. We need these resources to bring this case to fruition in the way that you deserve. We need it to do battle with these people."

"You know I'm not comfortable with this," Fred insisted.

I had drawn up a new fee agreement to include his participation in direct-mail fund-raising and handed it to him. "Fred," I said, "you are going to have to sign this or I don't think I can go forward. We've got to get this thing taken care of. We've got to get it behind us and move on."

There was an awkward silence. Then Patti said, "Fred, just do it." He reluctantly agreed. He asked for some changes in the document, I wrote them in the margin, we signed it, put it away, and never discussed it again.

Ron DiNicola took charge of the direct-mail effort, and the mailings produced another $700,000. All told, the Ron Goldman Justice Fund received $1.2 million in contributions. These funds made a huge difference, giving us the financial wherewithal to compete with the defense on a level playing field.

Sharon Rufo filed suit first, on July 20, 1994. In all there were four plaintiffs in the civil lawsuit against Simpson: Fred Goldman, individually; the estate of Ronald Goldman; Sharon Rufo, individually; and the estate of Nicole Brown Simpson.

Under California law, when a person dies under Ron's and Nicole's circumstances, two suits are typical. One is a wrongful death suit, and the other is a survival suit. A survival suit may be brought by the estate of a person who has died; it's the decedent's suit, brought after his or her death. In this case, Ron Goldman had been assaulted, attacked, beaten, and battered by Simpson. Had Ron survived the attack, he would have been able to bring a civil suit against his assailant for assault and battery and seek damages for injury and disfigurement, plus punitive damages. Ron died, so injury and disfigurement damages were moot, but punitive damages could be significant. Because Ron was deceased, the law permitted his estate to bring suit by his personal representative. Ron had no will, so his estate was governed by the laws of intestacy succession; these are the laws by which a deceased person's estate is distributed when he or she dies without a will. Fred Goldman, as his closest family member, was appointed the personal representative of Ron's estate by the probate court. In that position it was his fiduciary duty and responsibility to bring suit, hire lawyers, and do whatever was in the best interest of the estate. Any money obtained from this suit, however, would have to be divided between Ron's heirs. In the case of an unmarried adult with no children, the heirs are both parents, if alive. Ron's estrangement from his mother made no difference in the eyes of the law; his heirs were Fred Goldman and Sharon Rufo, to share equally.

Fred Goldman also filed a wrongful death claim, which is a claim that belongs to and can be brought by the heir of a decedent for loss to the heir: loss of financial support, loss of emotional support, in this case the loss of the relationship Fred had and would have had over the years with his son. Ron was just beginning in the working world, he was not supporting Fred, and we made a decision not to ask for any damages in that area. There are cases in which the court will allow parents to seek support damages, on the theory that one day the child would have a good job and would support the parents in their old age. We decided not to take that position; we weren't trying to maximize every last dollar; this wasn't about money, this was about justice.

Although she had no relationship with her son at the time of his death, Sharon Rufo filed her own wrongful death claim. Fred and Kim Goldman were offended—indeed disgusted—by Sharon's suit, especially how she raced to file within weeks of her son's death. Indeed, she showed up at Ron's funeral with a lawyer. I said to Fred and Kim, "As right as you are, nonetheless, she is Ron's natural mother. Some people will say, 'No matter what happens, a mother feels for her son in a way no one else does.' We shouldn't impugn that. We should act with restraint. It doesn't look good to air dirty laundry in public." Rufo was represented in the civil suit by her attorney, Michael Brewer.

The fourth plaintiff in the case was the estate of Nicole Brown Simpson. Nicole died with a will that gave some gifts to her sisters and relatives and named her father, Louis Brown, not her former husband, O.J. Simpson, as executor of her estate. Her heirs and principal beneficiaries were her two children, Sydney and Justin Simpson, who were nine and six years old, respectively, when their mother was murdered. The estate's claim was a survival claim for the battery Nicole suffered that resulted in her death. Each of Nicole's children conceivably could bring a wrongful death claim against their father when they turn eighteen. Thus there exists the theoretical but unlikely specter of not one, but two more O.J. Simpson civil trials within the next decade.

Sydney's and Justin's cases against O.J. Simpson could have been brought at the same time as ours, but the decision was made by the Brown family not to pit the children directly against their father at such an early age. (He turned over temporary guardianship of his children to the Browns when he went into jail.) While I understood the sentiment, their decision didn't make much sense to me; the children's claims were virtually identical to the claim of Nicole's estate, and could have even been brought by Lou Brown without naming the children as individual plaintiffs or involving them. Nor would the children have been required to testify, unless, of course, Simpson and his lawyers elected to call them to the stand. (Can you imagine how the jury would have reacted to that?) So without the children's wrongful death claim, the only claim brought on the Brown side was by Nicole's estate, for battery.

When you total up all the suits, the jury was being asked to decide whether O.J. Simpson attacked and battered Ron Goldman, whether he killed Ron Goldman, and whether he attacked and battered Nicole Brown

Simpson. No issue was going to be submitted to this jury concerning whether O.J. Simpson killed Nicole Brown Simpson.

Nicole's estate was represented by a New York practitioner named John Q. Kelly, who had been doing some commentary for Fox TV during the criminal proceedings. Before private practice, Kelly had been a prosecutor for the Manhattan District Attorney's office. He brought in a prominent Los Angeles attorney named Michael Piuze to join him as trial counsel for Nicole's estate. Piuze was known as a lawyer who routinely got big damage awards for his clients in wrongful death cases and personal injury cases. Likewise, Michael Brewer and his firm were very successful and experienced lawyers in wrongful death cases.

Strangely, we at MSK saw this as a serious problem. It was clear to us very early on that we brought the most to the table; we would be putting in the most time, the largest number of lawyers, the most resources, the most money. Without in any way slighting the others, we thought we were the best lawyers to get the job done. I strongly believed one lawyer had to take charge and be in charge. However, the other attorneys represented major participants in this case and could not simply be ignored. It was vital to coordinate our efforts and be a unified team. Making this happen was the most daunting challenge I faced.

The surprises began early. While we were trying to get all the material assembled, a process that promised to take at least a month, Mike Brewer's firm sought to begin many of the key depositions in the case: O.J. Simpson, Kato Kaelin, Al Cowlings, Arnelle Simpson, Robert Kardashian, Allan Park, Jason Simpson. All were to be taken by him at his law firm. The move seemed extremely precipitate. In my opinion, we were in no way prepared to take these depositions; we still had much to digest and learn to get up to speed on the facts and details of the case, let alone the nuances. If we took them now, we risked losing valuable opportunities to probe subtly and intelligently for information these people possessed but might not want to deliver. Plus, I wanted to begin to take the lead in the case, and that meant I should be the principal examiner of most of these crucial witnesses. And I needed more time to get ready.

Ed Medvene and I had a couple of dinner meetings with Brewer and his partner, Nick Hornberger, at which we discussed our vision of the case. We told them that MSK expected to be the lead lawyers and explained that as well as providing the resources and manpower we also felt we had the right plaintiff. Fred Goldman, we argued, should play the lead role. He was articulate and focused and had a good relationship with the press. Fred personified the fight against Simpson. This was a case that would be played out in the media, and for obvious reasons Fred was a much more attractive plaintiff than Sharon Rufo. He held the high moral ground. Of all the plaintiffs, we felt, she ought to maintain the lowest profile.

Brewer and Hornberger were understandably concerned about taking a backseat—this was going to be a highly visible case, and they, like us, wanted their work to be noticed—but they wanted to do what was right for their client. Goldman was raising impressive sums of money, and Rufo was not. We made our commitment clear to them, and in time they recognized that this would inure directly to their client's benefit. They agreed we would assume the lead role. The depositions were rescheduled and they were team players from then on.

The road with John Kelly and Mike Piuze was bumpier. Piuze had been brought in as trial counsel and to help finance his client's share of the costs. He had a significant practice. We sat one evening with Kelly and Piuze as we had with Brewer and Hornberger, getting to know one another and finding out their thinking and approach. Time became an issue. Because of previous commitments, Piuze was unavailable to start significant work on the case, including depositions, for several months. He was in one trial and was going from there to another, then another. We had a trial date of April 2, 1996. It was now November 1995. Piuze suggested we put the trial off six months to a year. I told him I didn't think delaying the case was in our side's best interests. We wanted to capitalize on the outpouring of support and goodwill, and I was afraid that in time this support might dissipate. In fact, I was concerned it would dissipate quickly. Piuze, being a smart lawyer, said, "You're right. You guys should go ahead and take this discovery, even though I'm not available. For now, we can stay with the trial date." In his absence, Kelly would cover depositions and other discovery work.

We also expressed our views that MSK should act as the lead lawyers, but with the Brown side it was a more difficult sell. They represented Nicole Brown Simpson's estate, and she was obviously a major protagonist. We had two claims, they had only one. We let the issue ride for the time being.

Two months later Kelly asked me to come talk with him. Piuze, it turned out, was extremely busy. By that time we were moving ahead very quickly with our financing, information gathering, and building of a war room of case files, documents, and materials, and Kelly and I discussed the idea that he join our team without his having a local Los Angeles lawyer. I thought he would be a solid addition to our team and saw this as the perfect solution. While MSK retained control of the case, we would give Kelly access to our materials, promised him a share of the major witnesses to depose and examine at trial, and told him we could work together. Several weeks later he ascended as the lead counsel for the Browns when Mike Piuze stepped down. To help out, Kelly retained Los Angeles lawyers Natasha Roit and Ed Horowitz, an appellate specialist.

The Simpson defense attempted to take the initiative while we were trying to get up to speed. They raced into court and filed several motions. The first was to prevent Simpson's deposition from being videotaped. The second was to keep all depositions in the case confidential, to prevent their contents from being disclosed and disseminated to anyone outside the lawsuit. The third was to consolidate the three lawsuits brought by the various families into one.

This told me a lot about their thinking. After having gotten away with milking and manipulating the public and the media to their advantage throughout the entire criminal trial—sending surrogates on the talk shows, having his attorneys hold incendiary press conferences claiming all kinds of investigatory and police malfeasance, massaging reporters—now Simpson and his defense wanted to bury the civil case. He had played it to the hilt, but now that he would be called to testify under oath he didn't want another word of his history of domestic violence, or his other activities, breathed in public.

A deposition is a proceeding unique to civil cases. In criminal cases, the prosecutors can subpoena witnesses to testify before a grand jury, at pretrial court hearings, and at trial, and they can have search warrants executed to seize evidence. Defense lawyers also can subpoena witnesses to testify at pretrial and trial proceedings. While prosecutors and defense lawyers can interview witnesses who agree to be interviewed, they cannot compel them by legal process to appear or put them under oath. In contrast, civil lawyers can interview witnesses privately, but, in addition, each side can issue subpoenas for a pretrial deposition; such a subpoena requires a witness to appear at a designated time on a designated day, with or without counsel, and be examined under oath by lawyers for all the parties in the case. The testimony is taken by a certified court reporter, then typed up in a transcript or booklet. Depositions may also be videotaped. A good deposition will inform the lawyers what the witness knows and will say if called to testify at trial. If the witness called to testify tells a different story, the witness can be confronted with his or her earlier statement, sworn under oath.

In addition, under California law, a witness who resides out of state cannot be subpoenaed to appear and testify in court. As a result, if the attorney wants that testimony, he must find and serve the witness with a deposition subpoena, go to the witness's state, and take the deposition there. That deposition may be videotaped, and the tape or transcript may be played in court at the time of trial in lieu of the witness's appearance.

Depositions are a critical part of the investigative process in civil cases called "discovery." In recent years, discovery rules have evolved to permit broad wide-ranging inquiry and "fishing expeditions" for information, the idea being to eliminate trial by surprise. (Most veteran trial lawyers will tell you this has taken the fun out of trying cases.) If everyone has done his job beforehand, it is possible to go into the courtroom knowing *everything*.

If the Simpson defense had its way, no one could show or tell anyone outside the lawsuit—a reporter, a writer, your wife—the contents of a deposition. All the depositions would be sealed, and no one in the outside world would know what had been said. I had no interest in keeping this thing quiet. Silence wasn't helpful to our case and our cause at all. I wanted the public to be aware of what was going on and to be in a position to give us as much help as possible. This puzzle was missing quite a few pieces, and we needed help finding them. I knew there were missing witnesses out there, I knew there was missing evidence and new information to be found, and I wanted to be in a position to unearth everything the prosecution in the criminal trial had either overlooked, undervalued, or simply not turned up.

Plus, this case was not merely going to be fought in the courtroom, it was going to be number one on the docket in the court of public opinion. It was very important to Fred Goldman, in particular, to let the twelve jurors who would finally hear this case—*and* the whole world— know what happened on the day his son was murdered. Therefore we decided to resist strenuously all efforts to seal any part of this case.

More important, we wanted the discovery process to remain open in order to counter Simpson, who, while demanding secrecy in court, was orchestrating his effort to rehabilitate his image and regain his place as a rich, famous, and "innocent" celebrity. He continued to have his entourage make the rounds of the talk shows and speak fervently on his behalf, and he himself began calling television stations and radio shows and making speeches proclaiming his innocence. It didn't take much digging to find out he was preparing to produce and sell a video—$29.95 plus shipping and handling—in which he would tell his side of the story. I couldn't imagine anything more prejudicial to our case than having the defendant peddle a fully produced, two-and-a-half-hour, high-priced promotional video to the public, stating his side of the case. Not only was he skittish about adverse information seeing the light of day, he didn't want anything competing with his product. He wanted a corner on the market.

So Simpson's attorneys moved to seal all depositions, prevent Simpson's deposition from being videotaped, and to consolidate all the plaintiffs' cases into one case for a single trial. On November 15 we went into court to argue in front of Judge Haber.

Of course, the press was there. The Santa Monica courtroom was packed. The defense had a team of lawyers present, while we had Kelly and Piuze, Brewer and Hornberger, myself and four or five lawyers from MSK. This was a staking out of ground rules, and we didn't want to begin at a disadvantage.

In our legal briefs to the court, we argued Simpson couldn't have it both ways. He couldn't put out and promote a video and then claim the jury pool was being contaminated by information. That called up the old saw about a man murdering both his parents and then throwing himself upon the court's mercy because he was an orphan.

Indeed, there is a legitimate argument to be made that if you put out too much information, it could contaminate and prejudice people who might someday sit on the jury. That is a problem confronting all high-visibility cases. The solution, used in all trials that attract public interest, is to question prospective jurors at the time of trial to see to what extent they have been affected by pretrial publicity and then determine whether they are impermissibly biased. The trial judge makes a determination as to whether an individual is suitable to sit as a juror. Depositions, as the judge and the defense well knew, are typically not sealed; theirs was an unusual request. Only if there was going to be some sensitive, confidential, private information would the notion even be entertained. By now, of course, you'd have to have been living on Mars not to know something about the Simpson criminal trial. The whole case had been shouted to the world. There was nothing private Simpson could claim he needed to protect. The motion was frivolous.

Judge Haber ruled in our favor; the depositions, including Simpson's, would not be sealed.

On the second point, Bob Baker argued that Simpson's deposition should not be videotaped at all. Our position was that we had the absolute right to videotape him and to play that videotape to the jury at trial, if we wished. Simpson could fall in a hole, he could bolt, he could become mute; we needed his testimony. The judge agreed. It would be videotaped. This was good for us. We wanted Simpson videotaped when he would be questioned under oath for the first time. We didn't know how he would react or behave under fire. We also felt that Simpson, knowing his mannerisms and facial expressions were being recorded, would be more inhibited, more serious, less likely to play games, and for us, be easier to control.

Baker then made the good argument that the videotape itself should be sealed because its images could be very powerful. He argued that a videotape of Simpson's deposition would be far more prejudicial, should it get out, than a written transcript of his testimony. He told the judge, "Our concern is that each deposition, whether it be of our client or an independent witness, will be the lead story on the six o'clock P.M. news." Judge Haber decided that only Simpson's tape would be kept under seal, and imposed strict controls over the videotaping itself. At the end of each session the tapes were to be walked to a bank vault and stored in a safe-deposit box. Haber appointed a referee to sit at the deposition and take custody of the video to ensure that no one made copies of it. This referee was to be a retired judge, paid by the hour by the parties to monitor the Simpson deposition, and report back to Judge Haber.

(Although this is now a common practice in California and other jurisdictions around the country, I am not comfortable with the use of so-called rent-a-judges. I think justice should be found in courthouses open to the public and that we ought not be creating a separate system of private justice for wealthy litigants.)

Simpson's deposition was a highly anticipated event and Judge Haber became quite concerned about the issue of security. I had received several death threats, some vile voice mail at the office, saying, "I'm going to get you," "I'm going to slit your throat"; and some anti-Semitic garbage was directed at Fred Goldman. The defense claimed they were getting even more. I think they overstated their concern as part of their strategy to get the locale and time kept confidential from the press. We retired to Judge Haber's chambers, away from the media, to discuss holing up in some private place to take Simpson's depo. Given the level of madness and obsession that had already built around this case, Judge Haber gave the defense lawyers the benefit of the doubt and agreed to keep the time and place of Simpson's deposition secret. There was talk about holding it on neutral turf, in a conference room out at Los Angeles International Airport.

Ultimately, for reasons never made known to me, Baker refused to agree to the referee—and the secret location of the Simpson deposition became my law office. And since the depositions routinely were completed after banking hours, the safe-deposit box was abandoned. Although we could have walked them to the bank downstairs each morning, there were hordes of media out there, the market value of each of these tapes was in the hundreds of thousands of dollars, so we all agreed it was more secure and prudent to keep the tapes locked in the MSK vault.

There was really no basis for us to oppose the defense request to consolidate the families' claims. It made eminent sense, and Judge Haber ordered them consolidated. Obviously, the court did not intend to permit three different trials to take place; the issues and evidence would be virtually identical. So the three cases were folded into one: *Sharon Rufo, et al.* v. *Orenthal James Simpson.*

This was the first time I met Bob Baker, who was clearly the dominant force on his side of the table. He was a lean, attractive, distinguished-looking man with wavy gray hair and a great voice. Very impressive. He was self-assured and supremely confident. Arrogant and cocky, too. He struck me as the kind of lawyer who loved to be in court but didn't like to spend a lot of time worrying about the details of a case. Not a great one for paperwork but fast on his feet. His reputation preceded him: He was a tough customer, a bully, always on the attack, and extremely successful at it.

At the same time, Bob Baker was an immensely likable man. He was a big sports fan, the kind of a guy, if it weren't for the Simpson case, I'd like to go to a ball game or sit down and have a few beers with. He was witty and, when he wanted to be, friendly and charming. He had far more courtroom experience than I and would tell funny stories about his past cases. His side of the table always seemed to be having a good time. Nevertheless, he was very tough, and I always had to be mindful that he was fully capable of smiling and at the same time carving you up.

Baker was very concerned about our appealing to the public. He was very sensitive to our rhetoric. Early in the case, Mike Brewer served him with a standard request for the defense to produce documents and other pertinent information. The final request, Item 29, was to produce the knife Simpson used to kill Nicole Brown Simpson and Ronald Goldman. Baker responded, "In the future, I think it would be beneficial for us all if items such as number twenty-nine are left out of any future notice to take Mr. Simpson's deposition."

Of course, Bob Baker would not want to admit he was representing a killer. This was Los Angeles, and in many circles O.J. Simpson was a pariah, along with those who continued to associate with him. Perhaps at some level, Baker was embarrassed. He had every right to be. But he chose the case; he didn't have to take it. He *was* representing a killer, and it was in my interest to let his client be seen for what he was. I had no intention of allowing the defense to hide behind the mask of Simpson's public persona. It was not in our interests to treat Simpson like just another defendant in a lawsuit. This wasn't about sharp business practices or medical malpractice. This was about murder, and Simpson was a killer. He would get no respect from us. We were starting to get out the other side of this story—and it had nothing to do with police corruption or incompetence or racial animus. It had to do with Simpson, and the kind of man he was, and what he did on the night of June 12.

In late November I started hearing rumblings that Baker's firm might withdraw from the case because they weren't getting paid. A long article on the speculation appeared in the *Los Angeles Times.* Simpson's scheduled deposition was approaching, and I was concerned that the defense would use this as a tactic to delay it. I wrote to Baker, saying, "We will resist any attempt by Mr. Simpson to delay his deposition or any other proceedings in this case because he chooses to switch counsel again.

We cannot allow Mr. Simpson to continue to hinder the prosecution and progress of this case. We sincerely hope that the rumors of your departure are just that and nothing more."

Not long thereafter I was in Haber's courtroom on some matter concerning the case when Baker stormed in, red in the face. I politely began to greet him when he cut me off. "I don't want anything to do with you!" he shouted. "Who do you think you are?" He was livid; he couldn't contain himself. Judge Haber then summoned us into his chambers. With me was Tom Lambert. With Baker was his son, Phil, a young attorney working on the case with him. We started to address the judge on some issue and Baker came at me again. "Mr. Petrocelli—" Baker raged. "Maybe he wants to go talk to the press now. Or maybe he has a PR agent."

I tried to stay calm. "Judge," I said, "Mr. Baker is having problems controlling himself. Maybe you can put a stop to this so we can get on with our business."

Judge Haber was not amused. Like a high school principal pulling aside two students who had been fighting in the hall, he said, "Let me talk to each of you privately." This was fairly unusual. A judge does not ordinarily speak to opposing attorneys individually. First he spoke in chambers with Baker and Baker's son. I waited outside with Tom. Fifteen minutes later the Bakers stormed out, right past us. Then it was our turn.

In chambers Judge Haber said, "Dan, this is going to be a long haul, and I am trying to get this calmed down between you and Mr. Baker."

"Judge, with all due respect, there's nothing I can do about it. I don't control him. It will not affect what I have to do and what I'm going to do. It's not my problem, it's his."

"He thinks you are appealing to the media."

I was. We all were. We were vocal, we were in his face, we were in his client's face. We called his client a killer over and over again. We put it right out in the open and were not going to let him hide. I explained to the judge how Simpson was conducting his own publicity campaign, including the behavior of his entourage and the spin they were putting on the case. "His problem is, he doesn't like the fact that we're evening out the scales."

"I understand your point, and I don't disagree," Haber told me. "My concern is, I don't want to see you have a heart attack! This is only one case, and you have a long career."

I looked at the judge, and frankly, he looked more stressed out than I did. I started laughing. "Judge, I'm the last person involved in this case who's going to have a heart attack. I do this for a living, and I enjoy it."

The judge started laughing.

"Well, okay, if you do, that's fine."

The thing of it was, I was invigorated by the challenge and stimulated by the importance of the case. I *was* enjoying it. In spite of all the responsibility, the emotion, and the pressure, I was having the time of my life.

FOUR

On the Job

Our motto from day one was: "Less is more." We recognized that the nine-month criminal prosecution had been ridiculously long and that we would have to substantially streamline and simplify our case in order to win it. It was particularly important to present the science in a way that jurors could understand and accept quickly, rather than offering days and days of complex testimony and hoping that they would learn on the job.

Learning on the job was our task. Before we could begin to think about how to present the evidence, we had to master it. We had to absorb every iota of evidence, every fact, every nuance of the case. Only then could we begin the process of simplifying.

My problem was, I didn't know where to begin.

The common assumption was that having the criminal prosecution precede us gave us an enormous advantage in pursuing the civil case; we could learn from their mistakes. To some extent that was true. We certainly learned what went wrong and what not to do again. But there were equal, if not greater, disadvantages to going second. The state of the physical evidence was all but immutable—we weren't about to find new blood drops, trace evidence, or other physical evidence. All that was collected— or destroyed—following the murders and the processing of the crime scene and other locations. We had to learn this evidence cold and figure out a way to present it clearly so it convicted Simpson. But what was especially problematic in going second was that all the witnesses had already testified under oath, in great detail, not only at trial but also at the preliminary hearing; some had also testified before the grand jury. They had given police statements and interviews to numerous defense lawyers and investigators. These witnesses were locked in on and off the record, but they had not always gotten things right.

Many different people had handled these interviews, and often the witnesses had not been questioned fully and effectively. A police officer performed one interview, a separate investigator working for the district attorney's office took another, a deputy DA performed yet another, various defense people interviewed witnesses—all with varying approaches, questions, angles, and incentives, each pushing and molding the testimony to suit his or her case. Witnesses, for their part, were not always helpful or forthcoming. Many were fearful of getting involved while others rushed to get involved. Once we started reading the material, it became apparent that we had to interview the key witnesses all over again. Those who would not voluntarily speak to us would have to be subpoenaed to appear for deposition. A massive amount of work loomed ahead.

No one on our team took the responsibility, or even attempted, to read the entire trial transcript. That was fifty thousand pages, and it would have been a tremendous waste of time. We divided up the case into workable segments.

Ed Medvene, with his background as both a prosecutor and criminal defense lawyer, was assigned the FBI and police witnesses, which we called "Cops and Coroners." He, in turn, interviewed several investigative teams and then hired Bill Gailey & Associates to assist us. Gailey was a retired LAPD detective whose desk had been directly opposite Tom Lange and Phil Vannatter's, the LAPD Robbery/Homicide Division's lead investigators in the Simpson murder case. Many members of his firm were also ex-LAPD, and several had actually worked on the Simpson case before retiring from the police department and joining Gailey's firm. Gailey had been investigating homicides for twenty years; he knew the department and was able, as Medvene likes to say, "to make me smart." Gailey and his firm were particularly helpful in developing police testimony, identifying effective witnesses within the department, and pinpointing their strengths and weaknesses. It was an immense benefit for us to know how the LAPD worked, to be able to call upon officers and be accorded instant credibility rather than be met with the standard close-to-the-vest diffidence that police routinely present to outsiders.

Since leaving the Justice Department, Medvene had practiced mostly as a criminal defense attorney. It was often his job to go up against the authorities and get his clients acquitted. Cops see defense attorneys as adversaries, if not worse. Now, for the first time in many years, the police saw Ed as "the good guy." He not only had the police but also the FBI wanting and working to help him. The public got involved as well, calling and approaching each of us with words of encouragement. "It feels wonderful," Ed said.

Tom Lambert took the blood and DNA part of the case. Whereas the rest of our team (whom Lambert liked to describe as "real liberal arts types") were shy of math and science, Tom wasn't afraid of it. He had been a physics major at the beginning of his college career, admittedly a long time before, and despite the fact that he had no background in the area, Lambert went off and learned the forensics.

It was extremely clear to us that blood and DNA would be among the most important areas at trial. Barry Scheck, Peter Neufeld, and Bob Blasier had been working in the field for years, they had made careers out of it. We didn't have a clue about DNA, let alone the complete mastery of the science needed to cross-examine and challenge the smart, glib, and hostile defense expert witnesses led by expert defense lawyers. Tom took that area and became an expert, it seemed, overnight.

I spent hours listening to Tom try to explain the DNA evidence to me. I read general reference materials, and a few of the new books discussing the DNA science in the Simpson criminal trial. I accompanied Tom on a trip to Cellmark Laboratory in Maryland where our DNA expert, Dr. Robin Cotton, worked. She also tried to give me a primer on the subject. Even though I would not be handling this part of the evidence, I wanted to have some reasonable, working understanding so I could help develop our arguments and speak confidently about the subject at trial.

Peter Gelblum was concerned that he have a meaningful role in the case, above and beyond writing briefs. That was never an issue; I knew there would be plenty for him to do as the case progressed. First off, writing briefs was crucial to our success. Particularly in the state court system, where there are few research assistants or law clerks available, judges are so overburdened with stacks of legal briefs on various motions before the court that they rarely have time to read them. This is one of a lawyer's major frustrations. At law firms like MSK that deal in complex litigation, lawyers earn their spurs in the library, researching the law and writing legal memoranda and briefs. Complicated issues cannot be presented or argued with a few impassioned courtroom statements off the top of your head. Rather, reams of factual issues and intricate points of law need to be distilled and laid out persuasively and precisely in legal papers filed with the court. These papers are written and rewritten *ad nauseam* by teams of lawyers. That's the high-caliber work clients are paying for when they hire expensive law firms. The filing of legal papers is usually followed by an opportunity to present oral argument to the court. This is almost always a waste of time. In oral argument you typically have a couple of minutes to make your points, because the judge has a courtroom packed with thirty or more other cases, and an hour or two to get through all of them. So you have to make your case on paper, where 99 percent of motions are won and lost.

In the Simpson civil case, there was no chance that a brief would be overlooked. We knew the judge would be paying close attention to the legal motions, getting help on them, undoubtedly working overtime. Peter was our best brief writer, and I wanted to be certain we took full advantage of his talents. I told him, "Peter, there is no doubt in my mind this case is big enough to go around for all of us. Trust me, you'll have a major role." And he did. In addition to the motion work, he worked closely with me in the domestic violence part of the case and took responsibility for developing key portions of the forensic evidence.

On November 21, 1995, we received permission from the court for both sides to visit Parker Center, the LAPD command center in downtown Los Angeles, to inspect and analyze the physical evidence that was in the custody of the LAPD's Scientific Investigation Division (SID). This was evidence, seized from Simpson and other witnesses pursuant to search warrants, that had not been introduced in the criminal case—items found, among other places, in Simpson's home, in his Ford Bronco, in his Bentley, in Al Cowlings's Bronco after their slow-speed chase on Los Angeles's freeways. Tom Lambert, Ed Medvene, Peter Gelblum, and I all made the trip. For the defense, Bob Baker's son, Phil, arrived with one of his colleagues. Baker himself did not attend, as he was involved in another case in trial. That sent a message I was happy to hear: Bob Baker wasn't rolling up his sleeves and diving into this case, at least not yet. I could not work that way. I needed to be on top of everything right from the beginning, to be a zealot for the details. I felt I had to be better prepared than my opponent. This would be my big advantage, perhaps my biggest.

We looked at the evidence. Items recovered from Simpson's home at 360 North Rockingham and not used at trial included navy blue socks found in the master bedroom, an airline ticket receipt, an extra-large baggage tag, Reebok athletic shoes, a navy blue knit cap—just like the navy blue knit cap containing strands of hair matching Simpson's found at the Bundy crime scene the night of the murders—a navy blue knit shirt, a black shirt embroidered with the designer's name, Ellesse. Also found were two videotapes containing selected cuts from the TV pilot *Frogman* that Simpson had just finished filming at the time of the murders, and the script and call sheet from that show. Papers recovered at Rockingham included a letter from Simpson's attorney, Leroy "Skip" Taft, to Simpson, and two letters from Simpson to Nicole, dated May 31 and June 6, 1994.

Recovered from Simpson's Bronco: a plaid cap found on the driver's-side floor, a Motorola cellular phone, a note reading "Joe Stellini," a garage door opener, a pair of golf shoes inside a golf-shoe box with the words "Dan Marino Foundation" written on it, one pair of Nike green/white golf shoes (size twelve), a parking ticket, a videotape of the movie *Carlito's Way,* and two cassette tapes *(Too Funky* and *Frank Sinatra Duets).* Simpson and Nicole had had a rocky relationship and had separated a number of times, and during one of the periods when Nicole had tried to woo him back she had sent him cookies and a videotape of their daughter, Sydney, from birth to age three. That video was here, along with business cards reading "Joel Lenoff, I.Magnin," "All Systems Go. Landmark Real Estate," and "Jerry Karakjian, Artin, Fine Jewelry," a note reading "Karate/Nicole," a photograph of Simpson, the January 3, 1994, issue of *USA Today,* a piece of paper on which was written the address of O'Connor Mortuary, a wooden coat hanger, a white towel, a shovel, and a plastic sheet. (The prosecution in the criminal case made a big deal about the shovel and sheet, trying to indicate that they may have been intended for use in burying a body, but the plastic turned out to be standard issue in a Ford Bronco, and the shovel, according to the defense, was there for poop-scooping purposes. How, I wondered, could the prosecution have pursued that line of inquiry in front of a jury without knowing where it was going?)

Inside Simpson's Bentley was a map to Hollywood National Stages, a receipt for "Genesis—Streets of Rage," which sounded promising but turned out to be a video game, a pink Post-it on which was written "Jackie Cooper," and business cards from "Jeane McKenna, Douglas Property Estate" and "Gary's Pool and Spa Service."

From Cowlings's Bronco on June 17 came a black travel bag, which Simpson called his "grip," containing Simpson's passport; a plastic bag holding a fake goatee and mustache; receipts from Cinema Secrets Beauty Supply, dated May 27, 1994; one plastic pill vial (pills included), with a prescription for Xanax in the name of Naomi Fischman; a key ring holding three rings and a pocket knife, another holding two keys and a small ring with the likeness of Smokey the Bear, and yet another holding one key, with a University of Southern California pocket knife attached; coins totaling $3.93; a checkbook containing blank checks and number 1408 made out to United Jersey Bank; a yellow metal ring with blue stone, inscribed "Pro Football Hall of Fame, O.J. Simpson 1985 Running Back"; two Swiss Army wristwatches; two cuff links; eight ballpoint pens; a wooden hairbrush; a comb; one blue-and-white Nike shirt, extra-large; two pairs of socks; one pair of underwear; one Giorgio Armani eyeglass case; one brown wallet; sixty-nine business cards; credit cards (two Chevron, one Sears, one AT&T, one GTE, one New York Telephone); one Automobile Club of Southern California membership card; one Hertz card in the name of Simpson, another in the name of Nicole; a Price Club card; a United Red Carpet Club airline card and others for the American Admiral's Club, Delta's Crown Club, US AIR's club, American Advantage Gold, and Northwest's World Club; a West Hills Country Club card; two Trippo VIP guest pass cards; and one VIP Hooter's card.

Also sitting there was the Smith & Wesson .357 Magnum handgun Simpson had held to his head, with six bullets, seized from Cowlings's Bronco. It looked new. The weapon had been fully loaded when it was found, six shells in the chamber. Even unloaded in the property room, it was scary. I hate guns. One of the defense lawyers picked up the pistol and started pointing it, waving it around.

"Put that thing down!" I shouted.

I was overwhelmed by the work ahead of us. World-renowned experts had been through this evidence, FBI, LAPD, private experts, criminalists, top forensic people, investigators, and district attorneys who had tried perhaps one hundred murder cases among them, the best criminal trial attorneys and their teams of experts. Here I was, a civil litigator, looking at this stuff—clueless. I thought to myself, "What am I doing here? What can I expect to find?" I didn't know what was valuable and what was of no use at all, so not knowing what else to do I ordered copies of everything that could be duplicated. We would figure it out later. Nothing was going back to Simpson until we knew its place in the scheme of things.

After leaving SID, my partners and I met with Tom Lange and Phil Vannatter at Parker Center. It is a measure of exactly how far removed I am from the criminal justice system, and have been my whole life, that here I was, in effect trying a murder case, and this was the first time I had ever been inside Parker Center. In fact, this was the first time I'd ever been inside any police station. Vannatter and Lange walked us through the Robbery/Homicide Division's bullpen, a long open room, with its metal desks lined up all in a row, to a small dingy conference room.

The LAPD had taken a beating during the criminal trial, its honesty attacked and its competence belittled, and over the course of an hour and a half Vannatter and Lange made it very clear they didn't like the way the prosecution had handled the case. There was a lot of finger-pointing. They said the prosecutors should have used the statement Simpson gave them when he returned from Chicago on June 13, the day after the murders. I had not yet read it. They had been criticized for being soft in their questioning of Simpson and were very defensive. Lange said, "We thought the best way to handle Simpson was to go low-key with him, let him talk and open up, not put the screws to him. In this kind of interview, you just don't come out grilling the guy; you're gonna lose him. He had a roomful of lawyers next door." Skip Taft and Howard Weitzman were, in fact, sitting outside. "He could have gotten up and walked out at any time, so we eased into it, let him talk, and he made some very incriminating statements. We were not happy that it wasn't used at trial."

In the weeks and months that followed, I must have read Simpson's statement to Vannatter and Lange over one hundred times. It is, indeed, chock full of incriminating statements, some of which help destroy Simpson's alibi. While the prosecutors would never have the opportunity as I would to confront and cross-examine Simpson with his police statement, they should have introduced it into evidence anyway. Used in conjunction with other evidence, they could have hammered away at his crucial admissions—he admitted, for example, cutting his finger and dripping blood on his driveway *before* going to Chicago; he admitted he was driving in his Bronco using the cell phone—according to his cell phone records, this was a time just before the murders. There were many damning statements in these critical first words uttered sixteen hours after he killed two people. Vannatter and Lange were right; the statement should have been used.

Vannatter and Lange also expressed great dismay that the prosecutors had failed to present other important evidence they had assembled, including the fact that Simpson fled from the police, showing a consciousness of guilt; the conversation between Simpson and Lange that had been taped during the Bronco chase; and the observations of a man named Ralph Junis at Los Angeles International Airport. Junis, they told me, saw Simpson arrive at LAX in a limousine, put a travel bag on top of a trash can at the airline terminal entrance, and then reach into the trash can. The implication was that the bag may have contained the murder weapon and bloody clothes, which have never been found. (Police checked the trash several days later, but it had been emptied and they found nothing.) Vannatter and Lange had interviewed Junis and felt he'd held up well, but Marcia Clark and the district attorney's office did not use him at trial because, according to the detective, Clark didn't, as a general rule, like "one-on-one witnesses," meaning people whose testimony could not be corroborated.

Lange explained how he had identified one of the keys found in Simpson's grip as opening the gate to Nicole's condo at Bundy, giving Simpson the ability to gain entrance to the property. Unfortunately, immediately after the murders, Nicole's father, Lou Brown, had all the locks changed, and the police found themselves unable to check the key against the original lock. Six days before the murder, however, Nicole had complained to her good friend Cora Fischman that she couldn't find her extra key. Cora had been given a key to the condo and the gate, and Lange commissioned a locksmith to create a lock around Cora's key. When he took the key from Simpson's bag and tried it in the new lock, sure enough it worked. Lange's enterprising detective work had proved that Simpson had a key to the gate and, therefore, access to the murder site. As Ed Medvene later wrote in a memo to the team, "The key found on Simpson opened the lock. Why would Simpson be carrying that key when he was estranged from Nicole and not going to see her anymore? He couldn't even sit with the family that night, so why did he happen to be carrying it with him?"

These two veteran homicide detectives, with over fifty years of police experience between them, were very frustrated with how their careers had wound down. Each was about to retire with hard feelings. They felt crucial evidence they had uncovered had been dismissed, and I could see they were looking to us to bring that evidence to light and vindicate their roles in this case that would be their legacy.

They clearly had strong feelings, but I knew there was certainly a whole other side to this story as well. I wasn't interested in getting involved in the crossfire between the LAPD and the district attorney's office, I just wanted to obtain as much information as possible. At the same time, Vannatter and Lange would have to testify for us, so we needed their cooperation much more than we needed the DA's. We tried to be understanding, promised them we would give all the evidence a fresh look, and would not in any way wed ourselves to the strategies played out in the criminal case. Which was our instinct going in. The criminal case, after all, was a loser. We tried to make it clear to the detectives that we would do everything we could to restore respect for the job they and the department did. Just like Vannatter and Lange, we did not want our case to degenerate into a malpractice suit against the LAPD.

Medvene and I had a very quick meeting with Deputy District Attorney Christopher Darden, the co-lead prosecutor who had lost the criminal case. It was only a few weeks after the trial, and he was still angry about the result, still devastated. Neither his mind nor his heart was really into talking to us. But he believed Simpson was guilty and wanted to see the victims' families have some consolation. He was especially fond of Kim Goldman. We asked him to direct us to certain files and material we would be needing and asked a few questions. The meeting didn't last more than half an hour, and Darden didn't say much. He spoke in lawyer's shorthand. "Ito ruined the trial," he told us. "The judge let them ask anything they wanted." We knew what he meant.

A cardinal rule in the courtroom is that the lawyer conducting a cross-examination must limit the scope of his questions to matters raised by the first lawyer in direct examination. If, on direct, you were asked only about what movie you saw last night, it would be improper on cross for a lawyer to ask you what you did two weeks before. Judge Ito, Darden was saying, not only let the defense range far beyond permissible boundaries, he also let them ask questions on which there was no evidence to base them. "Well, Dr. Cotton, isn't it true that if blood spilled during the testing process, bindles could get contaminated?" The witness, forced to answer, might say, perhaps, if blood did spill, contamination could occur. *But there was no evidence that blood did spill,* and unless the lawyer can specifically prove that it did, such a hypothetical question is improper and the judge should not allow it, the lawyer should not be permitted to ask it, the witness should not answer it, and the jury should not hear the question or answer. It is sheer speculation, and speculation is not evidence. Our review of the transcripts confirmed Darden's complaint. Judge Ito blurred the lines in permitting open-ended questioning, and the result was that it created, in the jury, an assumption and belief that untoward things happened with the evidence when, in fact, they never did.

I tried to arrange a meeting with the criminal case's other co-lead prosecutor, Deputy District Attorney Marcia Clark, when I was preparing to take O.J. Simpson's deposition. She had been the attorney slated to examine Simpson at the criminal trial if he had testified, and in preparation for my taking Simpson's deposition, I thought it would be helpful to talk with her. We traded phone calls for several days until I finally got through and suggested we meet in my office to discuss the examination. She said she couldn't, she had to take care of her kids. I volunteered to come to her house and have the meeting there. She didn't think that would work either. Then she suggested we talk over dinner at a restaurant in Westwood. I said, "Well, okay." But after I'd thought about it I called back and canceled. I didn't want to meet in a restaurant; I didn't think we could get much accomplished there. I felt Clark was trying to return to her own life and didn't need to be dragged back in by me. That was the last time I spoke to her.

Bill Hodgman was a gem. He was one of the most senior deputy district attorneys, Darden and Clark's superior, and had begun the criminal trial as co-lead prosecutor. Stress and overwork had put him in the hospital briefly during the trial's early going and removed him from the courtroom, but not the case. He was deeply and profoundly hurt that a killer had been allowed to walk free. He knew justice had been cheated, and he felt the entire prosecution team, himself included, was responsible because none of them had done a good enough job. There was an intense sadness in his eyes as he spoke. He committed to helping us in any way he could. I admired Hodgman. He wanted to see Simpson go down.

"We made mistakes," he told me. "We didn't work together as a team. Don't you make the same mistakes. You've got a lot of lawyers on your side, in your firm and your co-plaintiffs' firms. It's important for you to be the uncontested leader. Quarterback everything. Coordinate everything. Don't let people run off in different directions, making big cases out of what should be little areas of the case. It's not that people want to build themselves up, it's that this is such an important case, there's a lot of public attention, and the urge is to do more rather than less."

No one on the prosecution had the necessary "global" view to keep the case together, Hodgman told me. Clark, he said, did not exert herself as the unquestioned leader of the team, and did not bring about enough coordination between all the attorneys. The case was divided into components, with individual lawyers assigned different segments, and each attorney then developed his or her own case. Rather than adding up to a cohesive whole, each component ballooned into a minitrial of its own.

For instance, Brian Kelberg, a brilliant lawyer, was assigned the coroner. The pressure was on—television cameras, the Trial of the Century—he wanted to do the best job he could. He went off and worked it up—and he put the medical examiner on the stand for a full week. He should have been on for no more than two to three days. Someone needed to say, "We just cannot go into this level of detail, we don't need to cover all these points." Someone had to have the bigger picture in mind. Someone had to be in charge. There had been a leadership vacuum for the prosecution. Hodgman implored me not to let that happen in our case.

By now, I was reading, talking, living, breathing, and being consumed by the case. I assimilated information almost through my pores. I was still handling cases for other clients, but I would take Goldman-Simpson material with me wherever I went.

And the material was overwhelming. It was an unprecedented experience, having more than you could possibly read at your disposal. I read some of the books on the criminal case as they came out: Vincent Bugliosi's *Outrage,* Sheila Weller's *Raging Heart,* Faye Resnick's *Nicole Brown Simpson: The Private Diary of a Life Interrupted,* Alan Dershowitz's *Reasonable Doubt,* Chris Darden's *In Contempt.* I scanned many others. I wasn't interested in the dynamics of the trial, I was interested in finding evidence, finding things people knew, finding people who might possibly have knowledge as yet undiscovered. Weller's and Resnick's books gave me a good working start in understanding the life that Simpson and Nicole lived, what kind of people they were, who their friends were. A book by M. L. Rantala called *O.J. Unmasked,* which someone sent to me in the mail, turned out to be a goldmine. It discussed the key points made by the defense in the criminal trial and, with great insight and analysis, explained why they were unsupported by the evidence and the laws of reason. The book was so helpful that I ordered copies for the whole team. It became a running joke when, instead of pouring into the trial transcript to find an answer to a question, I would pull out this book and find it in a second. But my favorite was Bugliosi's book. Apart from his acute analysis of the issues and evidence, and putting aside his unrelenting condemnation of the prosecution team, his was a book about indignation, about passion, about standing up for what you believe, and it refreshed me with new vigor and energy. Of course I read Simpson's own *I Want to Tell You,* a meaningless collection of letters and thoughts Simpson assembled while in jail for a fat $1 million. He wanted to tell us, he insisted, but even with his life hanging in the balance he didn't want to tell us enough to get on the witness stand.

Among the evidence we accumulated were the crime scene and autopsy photographs. Like any adult, I had seen newspaper photos of car wrecks and crime victims and disasters and mayhem without taking them to heart. I had seen some of the photos released to the media during the criminal trial, but I had not pored over them, and I had certainly never thought of the two bodies as people I had anything to do with.

I had never seen police crime-scene photographs. I had thought of them, if I'd thought of them at all, as stark, high-contrast, black-and-white tableaux—tabloid material, which is where, I guess, my vision of scene-of-the-crime photography comes from. This time it was different. Police photographs, taken in color like any tourist's, each in its own plastic pocket, filled several loose-leaf books and lay in the evidence room for our perusal. There were hundreds of them.

These were grim albums. They were not easy to look at. There was Nicole, a woman I was only beginning to get to know, lying in a fetal position, in a pool of her own blood at the bottom of the stairs. There was Ron, crumpled in the tiny caged area of Nicole's garden against a tree. This was brutal. But then the photographer moved in for close-ups. It was hard to turn the pages. These were real human beings, not characters in a movie, and just two minutes before they had fallen to these positions for the last time, they had been fighting desperately for their lives. They had been breathing, now they were dead. And they were dead forever. For me, death is incomprehensible because it is permanent. It is irreversible. It stops everything.

I have not had many experiences with death. Both my parents are alive and well, thank God. My family and friends are relatively young and healthy. In my life, death was unusual. One of my close friends was killed in a car accident in New Jersey five years ago, and to this day I am shaken that he is not around anymore.

It took a while before I could bear to look at the autopsy photographs. At least at the crime scene, the bodies are in the context of the life they led. They are in recognizable surroundings—a garden, a house. Autopsy photographs are clinical, and if you're not clinical with them, they can be horrifying. Even describing them is a trial. I looked because I had to learn the information they gave me, but I put them away quickly. It's not an image you want to keep with you.

After we had viewed the evidence, my partners and I thought it necessary to visit the Bundy crime scene. This was another difficult experience. As litigation attorneys, we are professionally adept at dealing with issues in cold, calculated terms. We are highly competitive individuals who get worked up over trying to win cases, but dispassion is our basic frame of mind. However, dispassion was not so easy as I walked up the path to 875 South Bundy to see how two lives were taken.

We walked through the front gate. The garden was all overgrown by now, with no one to tend it. As I stood and watched, a carload of people pulled up with cameras. One woman asked me to turn around and pose in front of the gate. I turned instinctively then stopped cold. "I'm not going to do that," I told her.

All of us on the trial team noticed that the caged area where Ron had been attacked and murdered was tiny. Although there was a path running behind it, a tree branch hung over and effectively blocked the way. Ron Goldman had been cornered, he'd had nowhere to run, there was no escape route. In fact, there was little space even to get your hands up to defend yourself. The image of Ron being overpowered by a professional athlete in this space—one of the most powerful men who ever played sports, in a state of rage, wielding a knife—was terrifying. The idea that such a one-sided knife fight could go on for twenty minutes, as Simpson's defense contended in the criminal case (and would again in the civil case), was absurd. You're dead in no time.

We looked in the alley behind the condo, where the killer had exited. A driveway ran behind this house and all the others on the block, leading south to Dorothy Street. It seemed unlikely, if he had wanted to keep his presence a secret, that Simpson had parked in this alley. But at the end of the alley, directly across the street, there was a deserted parking area where, at night, a car might not be seen.

We were scheduled to begin trial April 2, 1996, only a few months away. In the backlogged state court system, cases routinely took two and three years to arrive at trial. But this case had been assigned a relatively early trial date, and we wanted to keep it. Tactically, we wanted to take advantage of the prevailing public sentiment that Simpson had gotten away with murder. We were initially convinced the publicity would wane quickly, and we wanted to go to trial while the torrent of goodwill was still rushing to our side.

I spoke with a litigation research and consulting firm called DecisionQuest, a firm my partners and I had used in the past to provide jury research and other assistance in large, complex cases. This was the same firm, founded by a man named Dr. Donald Vinson, that was retained by the prosecution in the criminal case to assist in jury selection. As reported in the media, and later confirmed to me by Vinson himself, Marcia Clark was not especially comfortable with jury research and less comfortable with Vinson, so she chose not to work with him and his team. I decided to retain and consult him early on, long before trial. Vinson and his colleagues told me their data showed that among the public at large, Fred Goldman's approval rating was very high and Simpson's very low. In the wake of the "not guilty" verdict, DecisionQuest felt the figures were exaggerated and in time Goldman's would drop and Simpson's rise. Their advice was to anticipate that movement and act against it. We didn't want to be picking a jury months later when our client's rating was at low ebb. This reinforced our desire to get the case to trial quickly. Vinson also agreed we should maintain a very public posture. As he put it, "Dan, this case will be litigated in the public eye with or without you." So we had a choice between letting the media say and write what they wanted and living with the consequences or working with the media and keeping our client's image positive for as long as possible.

DecisionQuest helped us understand those dynamics, and we continued to hit hard on Simpson. We talked up the case in press conferences and to individuals in the media, refusing to allow the public to forget what the killer had done and bringing pressure to bear on the court system and the judges to get this case to trial.

This just frustrated Simpson and dashed his vain hopes for a quick and easy return to his old life. He and his lawyers never missed an opportunity to accuse us of being publicity hounds for talking to the media—this from the team who would each day enter and leave court to a cascade of sound bites before massive numbers of microphones and cameras.

Although his lawyers didn't want him talking to the press—because Simpson was a defendant and anything he said could be used against him in the civil trial—Simpson just couldn't help himself. He would call in to radio shows and TV talk shows devoted to the case. We created what we called our "O.J. Watch," a loose network of people who would track his TV and radio appearances and provide us with transcripts. Almost from the day he got out of jail, any time he said anything in public, we were tracking him. An interview on Black Entertainment Network, an appearance at Oxford University in England, a speech to a local college, call-in radio, we had it. Still, Simpson was very good about not making statements or admissions we could use against him. He was savvy that way.

I thought the courts would want the case moved speedily along for another reason: it was a major diversion of resources for the Santa Monica court system, where the trial would be held. They were not a huge facility and would have to gear up considerably to accommodate the crush of media and public interest in the case.

From an economic standpoint, the sooner we got the case tried, the better. Another year of pretrial discovery would add enormously to the expense. The quicker we worked, the less strapped we would be.

Also, people were starting to peel off. Witnesses were moving or, worse, writing books. Officers who had worked on the case were leaving the department. Phil Vannatter told us he was retiring and going off to a farm in Indiana. O.J. World was changing rapidly, and I was very vocal, in and out of court, trying to keep the April 2 date in place.

I wanted our first deposition to be of O.J. Simpson. I wanted to get his story committed under oath in such excruciating detail that he couldn't budge one inch without getting impeached. Simpson was the killer, he knew when he killed Ron and Nicole, he knew how. He knew how he got away, he knew how he got back on his Rockingham property, and he knew what he did with the murder weapon and bloody clothes. He wasn't going to tell me, of course. He was going to lie. But in lying, he would try to craft a story that took into account all the known evidence and concluded with Simpson being innocent. I would take that story, and then begin the laborious task of matching it against the truth. The difference would be impeachment. Impeachment equals lies. Lies equal guilt. An innocent man does not lie.

As a defendant, Simpson had the right to attend all depositions. His lawyers and investigators would presumably also be interviewing witnesses and reporting back to him. He had learned all the evidence elicited during the criminal case while sitting in jail, reading batches of witness statements as the cops and DAs performed their interviews, looking for the holes in the evidence—looking for the opportunities to lie and fabricate. Under the rules of discovery, these interviews got typed up and turned over to the defense, and Simpson was no doubt sitting there reading and laughing, realizing the prosecution didn't have it right. I had a picture in my mind of him reading the statements of those witnesses who lied to protect him and feeling smug and proud that people would lie—commit perjury if need be—to save him. He would read testimony of people lying against him, and that probably drove him crazy. But through it all he sat there, able to say, "Okay, this is what's on record. This is what they will say. Taking into account everything the prosecution knows, here's how I can reverse-engineer my story, fill in the gaps, and come out innocent."

We knew there would be new witnesses interviewed, old ones interviewed in more depth, new material developed in the course of our lengthy discovery process. I did not want to present Simpson with the opportunity to retrofit his testimony, so I wanted him to talk first.

However, I wasn't ready for Simpson in December. There was too much information to assimilate, and I didn't want to be caught unprepared. I wanted to be completely ready when I faced off against him. Still, I wanted to do something; I didn't want to wait. I knew Simpson's attorneys were not anxious to begin his deposition, and I didn't know how long they would stall me. Tom Lambert suggested, "Let's start taking some other depositions, let's get it going. Do Paula Barbieri first."

FIVE

The Hunt Begins

There were good reasons to start with Paula Barbieri. She had been Simpson's girlfriend, on and off, for several years and could be presumed to know him well. When Simpson and Nicole were divorced, Paula had been next in line. They had spent considerable time together over the past few years, up to and including the night before the murders. Even after the murders and the trial, she had stuck with him. Then, after he got out of jail, she'd dumped him. Only a few weeks earlier, she had announced to Diane Sawyer on national TV that she and Simpson had split up. She stood by his side throughout the entire time he was in jail; then he got out, went to see her at her home in Florida, and without telling her brought a photographer from *Star* magazine, who was paying him $450,000 for the pictures. Simpson had been promising Paula a quiet, idyllic life, and he showed up with a tabloid camera crew. That, she said, was when she realized she had been duped and broke off the relationship.

Now it was a month later, and I didn't know where her heart was, or her head. I thought I might be able to exploit the recent breakup and give her the opportunity to play the jilted lover. Maybe, if she was upset enough at Simpson, she would tell me the truth.

Paula had no desire to testify. None of Simpson's circle was anxious to talk about him under oath. Paula had an apartment in West Los

Angeles, but her legal address was in Florida, and she was not making her-self available. Pursuant to California law, you cannot just up and take an out-of-state deposition; you need a commission from the California court directing the foreign jurisdiction (in this case, Florida) to issue a sub-poena. So I asked MSK associate Yvette Molinaro to pursue it.

Getting a commission is a technical process of jumping through legal hoops; if you make a mistake, the whole thing backfires and you can lose the witness. If we missed and Paula got wise to us, she could fly off to Paris, London, wherever she wanted. Timing was crucial. You don't want to tip off a witness that you're about to serve her with a subpoena, especially in this case, especially this witness.

Yvette located a local Florida lawyer to help us serve Paula. There is a provision in the Florida legal code that enables you to serve an adult who lives wirh the witness you are trying to serve. Paula had listed her mother's home as her legal address, so we had our process server pretend to be an early-morning jogger in the mother's neighborhood. The mother's morn-ing newspaper was lying in a plastic bag in the driveway, and our jogger placed a copy of the subpoena inside with it. When Mom came out, he approached her, introduced himself—you don't want to jump out of the bushes and scare someone to death—and said, "You are served herewith with a subpoena . . ." Paula was not in Florida at the time, but it was good service on her.

December 14, 1995, was the first deposition of the civil case, and it brought out the traveling O.J. media circus. Again, I never ceased to be amazed at the sheer number of reporters and camera crews massed in the concrete courtyard of the Trident Center, the buildings that housed MSK's offices. Television trucks ringed the block. The press was not allowed inside, so they all huddled in the center's plaza in the chilly shadow between two towers. The plaza was a tunnel for the swirling winds that kicked up regularly. Late in the afternoon, with the wind whipping and the sun going down, it got really cold down there. You'd hardly know you were in Los Angeles. Jumbled together, fighting each other for scraps of news and battling the wind for comfort, the fourth estate was having a reunion.

I didn't know where they expected to get their information. The deposition room is off limits to the press and public. Rather than go to court over the issue, I had agreed with Paula's lawyers to treat her deposi-tion the same as Simpson's and sequester the video. I had no intention of coming downstairs at each break and briefing anyone. I had never done that during a deposition (frankly, the opportunity had never before presented itself). Reporters were scrambling up and down the streets, hanging out at every available driveway and tollgate in and out of the parking garage, looking to make contact. They were in excitement mode. O.J. II was about to begin.

Paula Barbieri was a figure of intrigue to the press. She was an aspiring actress and had appeared nude in *Playboy.* She had not spent a single day at the criminal trial, and few in the media had had access to her.

She arrived represented by three lawyers. This was a phenomenon of the Simpson case: Everybody had a team of lawyers. In a normal lawsuit, third-party witnesses will often show up without an attorney, and if they do have representation, they're paying for it. In this case, no witness ever had a problem getting a lawyer, and in all likelihood they didn't have to pay. Lawyers showed up for the publicity, for their piece of the Simpson case, for their fifteen minutes of fame, and maybe to drum up some business at the same time. Witnesses, parties, prosecutors, the FBI, the media, even jurors—everyone had a lawyer. The *lawyers* had lawyers.

Paula was shapely, tall, and slender. She had been an actress and a model, but when she walked through the door in an olive green silk suit and white shirt she was sexy without quite living up to her billing, one of those women who looks better from a distance. She was made up well, but she did not strike me as a naturally beautiful woman.

She spoke in a soft, wispy voice, very hard to hear. She gave the impression of a woman trying to please everyone and just get through this. A small smile played on her face.

The deposition took place in a tenth floor conference room at MSK's offices. Ocher leather swivel chairs surrounded the long oval wood conference table. Soft lighting, a mural that filled an entire wall, and an adjoining balcony opening to the fresh air outside made the room more pleasantly informal than a standard corporate boardroom. The videographer was positioned at the far end of the table, with the witness at the other, attorneys for the plaintiffs to her left, her own attorneys and the defendant to her right. The court reporter sat slightly to the side, between Paula and me.

Moments before her testimony began, Simpson showed up. As a party to the suit, he was allowed to attend all depositions. When told he was in the hall, I walked outside to usher him in. He stuck out his hand.

"I'm O.J."

Not, "I'm O.J. Simpson." Not, "I'm Mr. Simpson." Hand out-stretched. Smiling. "I'm O.J."

Instinctively I shook it.

Then I felt terrible. This was a double murderer. I shook the hand that held the knife that killed my client's son, the one that cut a huge, gaping hole in Nicole's throat. I didn't have the power, the fortitude, to resist. For all my wariness, for all the compassion and understanding I had for Fred Goldman's anger and passion, I had been taken in by Simpson immediately. He exuded power and confidence. He was physically imposing, with a personality that overflowed the room.

Normally I will shake someone's hand when it is offered to me. It's my natural reaction, and it's good manners. I am accustomed to hard-fought, contentious litigation between companies and people fighting over millions of dollars, when feelings turn raw and the tone has grown acrimonious. But most of the time we all try to keep things on a professional level, so grilling your adversary in a deposition and then shaking his hand to bid him good-bye is not at all unusual. But shaking Simpson's hand disturbed me because I got sucked in. I wasn't able to stand up to him. In the first moment, Simpson had a step on me. That stayed with me.

Depositions are measured affairs. No witness is there willingly, and their attorneys generally counsel them to answer only what is being asked, to volunteer nothing, and to think carefully before they speak. That's the counsel I give my clients. As a result, depositions produce few conversations and a lot of one-word answers. Lawyers, guardians of their clients' rights, set the tone.

I decided to take a formal but friendly approach with Paula, as opposed to being confrontational. I did not know where she stood with Simpson, and rather than accuse her of cooperating with him, I wanted to give her every opportunity to tell us what she knew. I began the deposition by getting some general background about who she was and her career in the entertainment business. Then I moved into her first meeting Simpson, with the intent of learning the general outline and chronology of their relationship.

"When did you first meet Mr. Simpson?" I asked.

"I couldn't recall, exactly," she said, "but it was in 1992."

"Mr. Stein," I said. Larry Stein, a well-known Los Angeles entertainment lawyer representing Barbieri, was sitting next to her. I'd had a case or two against him in previous years, and he is a formidable lawyer and a good guy. It appeared to me that he had put his hand on her arm. Lawyers will do that as a signal to the witness to slow down, or not answer, or not volunteer information. It's a lawyer's way of controlling his witness. "It would probably be better if you weren't touching the witness."

"He is not," said Paula.

"I am not," said Stein.

"It appears that way from my angle."

"I am actually touching the arm of the chair."

"Okay." I had made my point and returned my attention to Paula. "You first met Mr. Simpson in 1992?"

"Yes, sir."

"What month?"

"I can't remember."

I thought that was a little unusual. I had just found *my* meeting "O.J." for the first time quite memorable, and I suspected Paula's introduction had far more fireworks.

"Well, was it early in the year? Later in the year?"

"It seemed it was summertime."

"Summertime, okay. Now, when you met Mr. Simpson, had he split up from his wife, Nicole?"

"Yes, they were separated." Some witnesses are clearly hostile, but Paula seemed to be actively listening to my questions. Simpson's divorce from Nicole became final in October 1992. We pinned their meeting down to July.

Being a witness can be a stressful experience, and each person finds his own way of handling it. Paula was sighing with almost every answer, taking a breath and blowing out through pursed lips as if she were doing deep-breathing exercises or using relaxation techniques.

She was clearly not there to speak in paragraphs. I would have to draw her out, slowly. "So I can get a little picture of what's happened here," I said, "did there come a time when your relationship with Mr. Simpson, that you said became serious in July of '92, came to an end? Was there any interruption or end to that relationship?"

"Could you repeat the question?"

Whenever a witness asks an attorney to repeat a question, it is usually a sign that they want more time to think. "I'm trying to find out, Miss Barbieri, whether there was a time following July of 1992 when your serious relationship with him came to an end."

Phil Baker, who again was present in the absence of his father, said, "I'm going to object. What do you mean by 'came to an end'?"

It was a silly objection, and I ignored it.

A few words about lawyer objections. Lawyers have the right to object to any question they believe is improper. Many types of legal objections must be made at the deposition or else they are waived. There is no judge at a deposition—unless the court orders one (usually a retired judge paid by the parties) to attend and monitor the proceedings. In depositions where no judge has been ordered to attend—as in this and every other deposition in the Simpson case—there is no one to instantly rule on the objection. This means there is no way to know if the objection is proper, in which case the question need not be answered, or if the objection is without merit, in which case the question must be answered. The procedure, therefore, calls for the witness to answer the question in spite of the objection. (If the question calls for privileged information or has no conceivable relevance, the witness may be instructed by her lawyer not to answer at all.) At the time of the trial, the objecting lawyer can ask the judge to rule on the objections raised at the deposition: if the objection was proper, the witness's deposition answer is stricken; if the objection was improper, the answer remains—no harm, no foul. Lawyers, therefore, tend to object liberally and often. But beyond the legal niceties, lawyers object at depositions for tactical reasons: to interrupt the flow of the examination; to throw the examiner off track; to send signals and messages to the witness. To counter these ploys, it is essential for the lawyer asking the questions to keep his focus, avoid the distractions, and maintain control of the deposition. There is a considerable element of gamesmanship, and to succeed you have to play the game better than your opponent.

Without acknowledging Baker's objection, I said to the witness, "You may answer."

"Yes."

"When was that?"

"Nineteen ninety-three."

"When was that in 1993?"

"It seems approximately April." Breathe in, blow out.

"Can you describe any event with which you associate your relationship coming to an end . . . something that happened which caused it to come to an end in April of 1993?"

Phil Baker objected again, and I ignored it.

"Not in particular," she said.

"There was no special reason why the relationship ended in April of 1993?"

Stein broke in: "Asked and answered."

Now, I'd gotten an answer that didn't make sense to me, plus an objection from each attorney. Clearly I was on to something sensitive. "Is that what you're saying?"

Stein interrupted. "Dan, excuse me, it's been asked and answered. I am trying to give you latitude because I realize the seriousness of this matter to everyone concerned, but I would appreciate it if you would deal with those issues that are most pertinent to this matter."

When an opposing lawyer feels you have gone on too long or roamed too far afield, he will object and tell his client not to answer. Before doing so, an experienced lawyer like Stein often will give you a warning that he believes the questions are straying into fringe areas.

But we were nowhere near the fringes; we were getting right to the heart of the issues. I told Stein, "We're in that issue right now, and I intend to spend quite a bit of time exploring the relationship between Miss Barbieri and Mr. Simpson, and the relationship between Mr. Simpson and Ms. Brown Simpson, and it's going to take some time." Stein would have liked to confine me only to examining Paula Barbieri about her relationship with Simpson and her knowledge of the events in June 1994, when the murders occurred. But to evaluate what happened at the end, I had to go back to the beginning and get the whole picture. "I would like to disabuse you of the idea that I'm not dealing with relevant information." Then I said to Paula, "I have no prurient interest in prying into your life."

Phil Baker broke in. "Well, you sure hold a press conference about it."

Phil Baker had been practicing only a couple of years. His little smart remark was another reminder that our public comments must really be irking their side. So guess what? If it bothered them, we would step it up.

"What I am trying to find out, Miss Barbieri, is what reason was there for the breakup of your relationship with Mr. Simpson in April of 1993."

Again, the objection: "Asked and answered. . . . Does his question refresh your recollection any more than it did a minute ago? That's the question."

"That wasn't my question, Mr. Stein."

Finally Paula said, "I would say we both changed. We both wanted different things."

This was an evasive, bullshit answer. Baker knew, from his conversations with Simpson, why they had broken up. Stein knew, because he had prepped her for the depo. I was the only one who was in the dark, and they wanted to keep it that way. I was asking a simple, innocuous question, she asked me to repeat it, and there was a flurry of objections and colloquy. Obviously, I was treading into an area troubling to the witness and the defense.

"Did the relationship ever resume?" I asked.

"We were taking small steps."

"So, between April of '93 and April of '94, you and Mr. Simpson did not see each other. Correct?" I knew this was the year Simpson and Nicole had attempted a reconciliation.

"We weren't dating."

"You were not romantically involved?"

"No."

"Now, when the relationship resumed in April of 1994"—two months before the murders—"were you about to tell me before that you and he decided to take 'small steps' toward rebuilding that relationship?"

Another flurry of objections. She asked me to repeat the question. What was here that I was missing?

I asked again if they resumed their relationship, and she said yes. "And did there come a time when that process came to an end?"

"Yes."

"When was that?"

"The morning of June 11."

"Sunday morning?" June 11 was a Saturday, but I sensed she meant Sunday, the morning of the murders.

Answer: "Yes."

This was an astonishing revelation. Paula had just admitted that her relationship with Simpson ended on the same day he killed Nicole and Ron. She volunteered no details, and we didn't know the reasons for the breakup, or most important, who initiated the breakup. We would get to all of that in time. Her conflicting testimony about the date was problematic. I would have to clarify this, but now was not the time.

When I am dealing with adverse witnesses, one technique I use frequently to prevent them from rolling out a prepared story is to skip all over the place. It's easy for a person to tell a tale from beginning to end; it's considerably harder to keep the lies straight when you are being bounced around, back and forth, by months and years, from one topic to another. I changed the subject and asked whether Simpson had supported her financially when he was in jail. Her evasive answers had made me suspicious of her honesty, and I was trying to find out whether she had been and might still be financially beholden to Simpson. She answered Simpson had, in fact, given her financial support. I was getting the picture of a woman who didn't have much money and had to borrow from her friends and his. There was a sense that she was still on the payroll. After a while, I ducked back into the chronology of the relationship.

"Following your breakup with Simpson—" I corrected myself. "Mr. Simpson—the second breakup, on the morning of June 11—" I decided to use her incorrect date for now. "Did there come a time when you resumed your relationship with him again?"

Baker objected, saying, "It misstates the testimony as to 'breakup.'" What he was saying—to me and to Paula Barbieri, should she not get it— was that there never was a second breakup, that they were together all the way from April 1994 until only one month before this deposition. This only underscored to me how damning Paula's admission was.

Johnnie Cochran had emphasized Paula's relationship with Simpson in the criminal trial. Simpson, he told the jury, had no motive to kill Nicole because he was deeply involved with Paula at the time of the murders. They were back together, he said. Simpson had even called an interior decorator to design a bedroom at the Rockingham estate to Paula's tastes. They had attended a fancy party Saturday night, June 11, and witnesses saw Simpson and Paula there, happy as lovebirds. They were embarking on a life together, perhaps even looking toward marriage. So, according to Cochran, why kill Nicole? Simpson wasn't obsessed with Nicole, he had Paula.

I ignored Baker's objections and told the witness she could answer. If I was wrong, a judge would rule the testimony inadmissible. But I wasn't wrong.

She asked me to repeat it again.

"Did there come a time when your relationship began again?"

"Yes," she told me. "While he was in jail." Now she was admitting they had, indeed, broken up in June. She then proceeded to say that she broke up with him again on the day she was interviewed on television by Diane Sawyer.

Up to this point, Simpson remained relatively quiet. He confined his role to writing feverishly but in spurts on a yellow legal pad. Rarely did Paula look down the table to meet his eyes. But as we started to enter more important, sensitive terrain, Simpson began to get more animated, reacting visibly to answers he didn't like.

I decided the time was not right to press Paula on her breakup the day of the murders. She was still too guarded in her answers, and I needed more time to break down her resistance. So I broke chronology and delved into details about Simpson's advisers, his contacts. This was my first opportunity to learn about Simpson's world, to load up on background information, and Paula became a resource. I probed Paula's relationship with Simpson's family, his children Sydney, Justin, Jason, and Arnelle. Paula and Simpson, I found, did not exhibit the characteristics of two people who were in love and close to being married. They didn't do things as a family. Paula didn't spend time with the children, they didn't go shopping, they didn't go to church together, she was not part of their lives. There was family, and then there was Paula. This confirmed everything I had read and seen in preparing for the deposition. Paula was the sex object. Paula was an armpiece. She was the person Simpson would summon during interruptions in his relationship with Nicole, or even on the side. But it was clear she would never be Mrs. Simpson, because he truly loved Nicole. If he didn't love Nicole, he would not have killed her. He killed her because he was rejected by a woman he wanted badly and who did not want him anymore, and he could not live with that rejection. He killed her in anger, in retaliation, in rage. Throughout the criminal trial and now in the civil case, Simpson sought to diffuse and conceal this motive by trying to create the impression that he had a life with Paula, that they had a future, that Nicole was out of the picture, and Paula was the one for him. As I spoke with the woman, it became increasingly clear that this was not true.

I began asking Paula about her jailhouse conversations with Simpson. She admitted they talked constantly, either by phone or in person. She had told Diane Sawyer that Simpson promised in jail their life would be idyllic. At the deposition she told me, "He said that we would have just a life of simplicity. We were sharing scripture readings together."

Then I asked her a question: "Did you and he talk about Nicole's death?"

"No."

"At any time?"

"No."

I found that incomprehensible. She was spending hours and hours talking with him in jail, he's on trial for his life for the brutal murder of his ex-wife, and they never once talked about Nicole's death? Who could believe that for a second? I realized then that her testimony would not be candid. I knew then she would remain loyal to Simpson.

"Was there a particular reason for that?" I asked calmly.

"I think I was going through a healing process as well as he was. He was having a difficult time in jail. So I imagine he spoke mostly with Rosey Grier." Roosevelt Grier was a former New York Giants lineman turned minister.

"In all of the conversations that you had with Mr. Simpson while he was incarcerated, are you saying at no time did you and he talk about Nicole's death?" I asked incredulously. "Is that right?"

"Nothing that I could recall," she said softly. "We really didn't talk about Nicole."

"When you first broke up with Mr. Simpson in April of 1993—" I began.

"It was actually," she corrected me, "it wasn't that I broke up with him. It was mutual."

"Okay, when the two of you broke up . . ."

"Yes." This was a point she was intent on making.

"In April of 1993, did that breakup have anything to do with an attempted reconciliation between Mr. Simpson and Nicole?"

"It had something to do with it, yes."

"In other words, Mr. Simpson was going to attempt a reconciliation with Nicole. Is that right?"

"Yes."

A few minutes earlier, when I'd asked whether anything had caused that breakup, she had said, "Not in particular." She had just contradicted herself. (This is one of the advantages of jumping back and forth between topics and revisiting questions three and four times.)

"You were not in favor of splitting up with him at this time," I said. "You didn't want to split up with him, he wanted to go back to Nicole, right?"

Answer: "Yes."

Now we're full circle. It wasn't mutual, as she had said a moment before. She got dumped. After finally being divorced and completely free of Nicole, after finding a sexy woman who doted on and satisfied him, Simpson had dumped Paula and run back to Nicole. What pull this woman must have had on him. This was the important piece of information I needed to develop the motive aspect of the case. Simpson truly loved Nicole.

"Did Mr. Simpson ever explain to you why Nicole and he were divorced in the first place?"

"No."

"Did you ever ask him?"

"No." The subject never once came up between them.

I jumped off the subject again and explored Paula's relationship with Simpson's personal secretary, Cathy Randa, who hated Nicole, and then returned. "In April of '94, you and Mr. Simpson got back together again. . . . Is that because Mr. Simpson's attempted reconciliation failed?"

"Yes."

Simpson, five seats from her, became more obvious in his reactions, often quite childishly. He did a lot of mugging: the "Who, me?" face; the "Naw, never happened" face. In a room full of lawyers doing business, he would get quite animated, as if playing to a crowd. His head bobbed inappropriately, as it did when he failed as a broadcaster on Monday Night Football. His facial expressions were exaggerated and almost comical. This all might have played in the *Naked Gun* movies, where his character was a caricatured dunce, but at this deposition the only character revealed was his own. When Paula said, or I asked, something he didn't agree with, he would react visibly, looking around the table and making sure everybody saw his disagreement. I could hear his deep baritone as he rumbled his asides to his attorneys. Paula must have been terribly intimidated, but she didn't respond visibly.

"Was Nicole ever a topic of controversy or conflict between you and Mr. Simpson?" I asked.

"No."

This was foolishness. Paula was the other woman, Simpson had left her to return to Nicole, she had already admitted that Nicole had come between them. As a lawyer, you expect most people under oath to tell the truth. It's a combination of honesty, respect for the law, and fear of going to jail for perjury. I expected Simpson to lie, of course; otherwise he would have had to confess to a double homicide. After murder, what's a little perjury? But in a sense I found it more offensive that this woman would lie, to protect a man who killed two people. Now, I decided, it was time to zero in on what happened with the breakup the morning of the murders.

"Now, what happened to cause your relationship to Mr. Simpson to come to an end on Sunday morning?" I deliberately left out the date.

Breathe, blow. "It was just a compilation of things. It was just so difficult to pinpoint one thing. I think between the time that we first discussed getting back together to the time that I decided it wasn't working out, he was always on the road. I think I've seen him maybe a week and a half out of that period of time. . . . He was on the road. Golf. . . ."

"Are you here with us?" Stein asked her. "You seem to be spacing out somewhere. Come on back here to the deposition."

Paula denied having an argument or fight on the Saturday night before the murders when Simpson and she had attended a party. "Did you call Mr. Simpson up and tell him that you wanted to end the relationship?" I asked.

"Yes."

There it was. Paula had dumped O.J. On the day of the murders!

"Where did you reach him?"

"I didn't. I left a message."

This was virgin territory. This had never come out at the criminal trial. This directly shredded Cochran's representations to the jury.

"Where did you leave that message?"

"I think it was his car phone."

"There's an answering machine on his car phone?"

"Yes."

"When did you leave that message?"

"Approximately seven in the morning."

"On Sunday morning?"

"Yes."

"What was your message?"

"I can't remember exactly, but 'Between work, the kids, golf, my schedule . . . it was just too difficult to work things out.' Something to that effect."

Why had she left a phone message rather than telling Simpson in person? He was going to Chicago, she said, she was going to Las Vegas; it was her only way to get in touch with him.

"Did you receive any messages back from him at any time on June 12?" I asked.

Answer: "Yes."

She remembered picking up three messages from Simpson by calling her message service. "What did they say?" I asked.

"Something about we were talking the night before about filling the house with babies and what was wrong now."

"Did you understand that Mr. Simpson had already picked up your message?"

Baker objected, "Calls for speculation."

"You can answer."

"Yes," she said, "I assumed."

"In other words, from the contents of the messages he left, you understood that he had already received the message. Is that right?"

"Yes."

Paula was in Las Vegas, it turned out, with Michael Bolton. She did not return Simpson's calls.

Paula Barbieri had left O.J. Simpson a "Dear John" message at seven in the morning, the day the murders were to take place! This kind of thing didn't happen to "O.J." Women don't leave him, he leaves them in his wake. When he returned from his round of golf, Simpson was faced with an ex-wife who no longer wanted him and a girlfriend who dissed him over the phone. June 12 had not begun well for him.

We broke for lunch a few minutes later. In the middle of the afternoon I got a call from Patti Goldman, who said, "What's this about Paula breaking up with the killer?"

Mike Brewer, I was later told, had gone downstairs and reported Paula's revelation to the press. It was on television within minutes and in the papers that afternoon. We were hours into the first deposition and there was important new information! If we had any illusions about the civil trial being covered more civilly than the criminal, they went out the window with that report. From then on, the high-profile depositions were media feasts.

After the break, Paula became more tight-lipped. I did not know whether and to what extent her lawyers were talking to and cooperating with Simpson's lawyers during breaks in the deposition. I did know that her testimony after lunch became more and more incredible. Simpson's daughter, Sydney, had been scheduled to perform in an evening dance recital on Sunday, June 12. Paula claimed, although she wanted to see Sydney dance, and Simpson had never expressed any uneasiness about her attending functions at which Nicole would also appear, she never asked to attend.

Paula had already said she and Simpson had had no conversations about Nicole or the murders. Now she added domestic violence to the list. "Did you ever discuss the subject at all with Mr. Simpson?"

"Nothing that I remember. Uh-uh." She said she had never heard the 911 tapes or seen the pictures of a battered Nicole.

"To be clear on this . . ." What could I do in the face of such testimony—except document the story and pin it down completely? "[You] had many, many telephone conversations each day, and you made many, many visits once you came to Los Angeles while Mr. Simpson was incarcerated. In all those conversations, not once did the subject of abuse towards Nicole come up. Is that right?"

"Not anything I remember."

"And you never inquired. Right?"

"Not that I remember."

This was absurd. Everybody heard those tapes. You had to be on the moon to miss them. After several more hours of being deposed, she eventually admitted she had heard one 911 call, the one with him "yelling in the background." "I couldn't believe that he was hitting her," she testified. "I just heard him yelling, and then I thought, Well, gosh, who knows." She never asked about it. "I was just trying to be supportive." Did she believe, as she sat there at the deposition, that Simpson had hit Nicole? "I really don't know."

In other words, here's a guy she had been close to marrying. They were planning to fill up the house with babies. He dumps her, goes back to Nicole, comes back to her, kills Nicole. He's in jail. Now they're back together, and she finds no need to ask a single question like "Gee, O.J., I love you and all, but, you know, I did hear Nicole screaming on the tape, and I heard you screaming on the tape, and now they're talking about 911 calls, and a battering case brought against you in 1989 for spousal abuse. You know, I'd sort of like to know before I get involved with you any deeper, what's the deal here? Is any of this true?" She said she never saw fit to ask those questions.

Paula was by the pool in Las Vegas on Monday when someone told her Nicole had been murdered. She didn't hop on a plane back to Los Angeles. She didn't come until the next day, when Cathy Randa arranged for her to be with Simpson at the home of Robert Kardashian, one of Simpson's tennis partners, business associates, and confidants. Two days after Nicole's murder, Simpson was sleeping with Paula in Bob Kardashian's house. Shows how grief-stricken he was.

Paula was assigned to watch over O.J. "The doctor came and gave us some medicine for him, which was really strong." She could not recall the doctor's name.

"Did he tell you that Mr. Simpson was on suicide watch?"

"I just don't remember."

In the beginning of the criminal proceedings, Paula had been called to testify before the grand jury investigating Al Cowlings's role in Simpson's flight from the police in Cowlings's Bronco. I had to confront Paula with her grand jury testimony, given under penalty of perjury, in which she said exactly that. "If you told that to the grand jury, would that be a true statement?"

"Yes, sir."

"But you don't remember it now?"

"Yes, sir. No, sir, I don't."

"You look like you're glazing over. Would you like to take a short break?"

"Yeah, thanks."

Fifteen minutes later we were back to Paula's grand jury testimony. During the two days she stayed with Simpson at Kardashian's, she now said she was concerned that he might commit suicide. On the phone from Las Vegas before she'd arrived, Simpson told her he had picked up a gun and threatened to kill himself. The only thing that had stopped him was Simpson's sister Shirley. "He's come close many times," Paula had told the grand jury. When I asked her at the deposition whether Simpson had come close to killing himself many times, she claimed not to recall.

Again I had to impeach her with her own words. "I am reading from the witness's grand jury testimony. . . ." I read it to her. "Was that true testimony that you gave?"

"That was the testimony I gave."

Suicide was an issue forced on Simpson. The world had seen him running around the freeways with a gun to his head. He had two options: Either he was planning to kill himself, or he was fleeing the police and pulled a gun when the game was up and he was about to get caught. I did not want to get trapped into taking one position to the exclusion of the other, because I thought both were incriminating. An innocent man in Simpson's position would not be planning to kill himself, he would be planning his outraged defense. But feigning suicide was better than the other alternative, which was to admit that he was running from the police.

The truth, I suspect, was somewhere in between. Simpson considered killing himself because he believed, sitting around Kardashian's house at various times during the week, with the net tightening around him, that he was going to spend the rest of his life in jail. He loved being "O.J.," he loved being the center of his world, and when the police were finally about to come for him, he was finished, a goner. He was going to jail and not getting out. The vision must have been chilling. His survival instincts took over. He grabbed his grip (his travel bag) containing his passport, credit cards, a disguise, an armful of clothes, and his .357 Magnum, threw it in the car, and ran.

Paula claimed she had not tried to get in touch with Simpson during the Bronco chase. She had his cell phone number and Al Cowlings's;

she could have called up and spoken to him directly. She chose not to. "I didn't think he had his cellular phone with him," she said. "I remember thinking, How could I get in touch with him? but I couldn't."

I questioned Paula Barbieri in detail on everything from the location of Simpson's passport to the contents of his grip to a sapphire bracelet he had given her to whether Simpson had beaten her to whether she was aware of anything Simpson had done to find Nicole's "real killer." Her answers were all predictably supportive of the defendant.

After more than five hours I finished, and Mike Brewer began his examination. He was more confrontational. Had she ever seen gloves like the murder gloves in Simpson's possession? Had she ever seen him wear Bruno Magli shoes? Did Simpson have a knife collection? Had he had any specific training with knives? No, no, no, no. She never saw him hit a wall, break a dish, throw a lamp. According to Paula, Simpson was not aggressive, she had never seen him go into a fit of rage, and he had never hit her.

Then Bob Baker took over.

Brewer and I had asked hundreds of questions concerning Simpson's activities on June 17, the day of the Bronco chase, particularly about the suicide note and whether he was fleeing the police. It was clear from the first deposition that, unlike the criminal case, the civil case would delve into the question of Simpson's conduct after the murders and whether it was the conduct of an innocent or guilty man. Baker came right out and tried to demonstrate that actions that at first blush might seem incriminating were not incriminating at all. Before leaving in the Bronco, Simpson had given Cowlings seven or eight thousand dollars that he had on his person. "Did Mr. Simpson generally carry a lot of cash?" he asked. "And when I say 'a lot of cash,' Mr. Simpson usually had in excess of five thousand dollars in cash on him at any given time, did he not?"

Brewer said, "Objection. Leading." When questioning a friendly witness, it is improper for an attorney to ask questions in a form that suggests the answer he is seeking, as Baker did here.

She said he always had a big wad on him.

"Those bills were basically hundred-dollar bills, were they not?"

I interrupted. "Leading."

"Big bills," she agreed.

"Mr. Simpson had a grip bag that he took with him on most occasions when he traveled, did he not?"

"Leading." This was obviously his style; he wanted to barrel along with a witness without stopping for the legal niceties. Paula Barbieri was obviously going to agree with whatever Baker suggested, she was clearly in Simpson's corner, and it was making her testimony a farce. All I could do was object, and I did.

"You can have a standing objection, if you want," he told me. A standing objection is one that applies to each and every question. If, at time of trial, the judge decides I'm right, then all of her answers get stricken.

"That you're leading the witness," I wanted my objection clear for the record.

"You can have any objection you want that's standing or sitting or laying down. Doesn't matter to me. Okay." This was also Baker's style: he preferred informality, while I wanted clarity so there would be no problems.

"The Gospel According to Simpson," as revealed by Baker through Paula was that at the time of the murders, everything between him and Paula was hunky-dory. She had picked him up at the airport when he had arrived that Friday from New York. On Saturday evening, the night before the murders, they had gone to a lovely dinner party in honor of the then–First Lady of Israel, no problems, Simpson's mood was jovial. He dropped her off at her apartment on Wilshire Boulevard and went on home to Rockingham. Simpson woke up early the next morning to play golf. Sydney's dance recital, which Paula did not attend, was simply a family affair.

They needed an innocent explanation for the fake goatee and mustache found in O.J.'s bag. "Did O.J. ever indicate to you that he would wear those disguises so he wouldn't have to give autographs, and he could spend some time with his children?"

"Something about getting a tired hand," she said gamely.

"Tired hand?" Baker asked quizzically.

"A cast or something." Between them they were fumbling for an answer. She appeared a little at sea.

"And had you ever seen him in any disguise before the murders?"

"No."

Baker had been caught unprepared. Probably at the insistence of his client sitting next to him, he was asking questions and not getting the expected answers. Baker got a little frustrated and began to lead Paula through what it appeared he thought would be a set piece. "Do you have a recollection of a makeup artist giving him a disguise and having a board full of props?"

"No, I don't." Another misfire.

"Did you ever go to Disneyland with Mr. Simpson and his children?"

"No."

"Did you ever go to any amusement—Knotts Berry Farm, Magic Mountain, anything—with Mr. Simpson and his younger two children?"

"We went to Magic Mountain, but not with the children."

"And at that time he did not wear any disguise, is that correct?" He threw in the towel on this one and moved on.

Baker led Paula through a series of questions designed to show that Simpson routinely used his cellular phone as a portable phone, setting up his alibi that on the night of the murders he was calling her from his driveway and not from his Bronco driving to the scene of the murders. Even there, Paula had to be prodded to agree.

Baker's approach to the "Dear John" call tipped us off that Simpson would go to the mat to deny receiving it. "Now, you don't have, even as you sit here today, any knowledge whether he ever picked that message up, do you?"

"No, sir," she said dutifully. The moment went by very quickly. I made a note not to let that be the last word on the matter.

As much as Baker would have liked Paula to deny it, Simpson got dumped on the day of Nicole's murder. Clearly concerned that this would show a buildup of tension and anger, the sense that Simpson's life was spiraling out of control—and then his wife shows up dead that night—Baker tried to defuse the obvious significance of that evidence. He asked Paula, wasn't it true that they broke up all the time, hadn't she broken up with him two weeks before the murders in Palm Springs, and then gotten back together. Paula, in her submissive, compliant fashion, went right along with it.

I hadn't heard about this Palm Springs breakup. They had given me another lead.

By now, Simpson was very active, an imposing physical presence in the deposition room. The criminal trial appeared fresh in his mind, and he was still very focused and on top of his facts and angles. He was constantly telling Baker what to ask, sometimes in words and phrases I could hear across the table. Think of a bear rumbling. Baker would be satisfied with a topic and go on to something else, but Simpson would drag him back, forcing Baker to say, "Oh, I apologize for jumping around, but I want to get back to another subject for a minute."

Baker closed his examination by eliciting a scene from Paula in which Simpson, studying the Bible, moans to the heavens, "Why is God doing this to me? I didn't do it. I never killed anyone." This piece of piety was so saccharine, I had to get it off the table.

"Notwithstanding our stipulation, I can't help but object on leading grounds to all these questions, Mr. Baker." He just smiled.

Depositions continue until all attorneys are satisfied and no further questioning is requested. I couldn't allow Paula's flip-flop as to whether Simpson received the "Dear John" message to stand. "I think Mr. Baker asked you if you knew if Mr. Simpson had ever picked that message up. Do you remember that question?"

"Yes, sir."

"And you responded that you didn't know. Do you remember your answer?"

"Yes, sir."

"But you testified earlier today, did you not, that by Mr. Simpson's three messages to you, you could tell he had picked up your earlier message. Correct?"

Larry Stein broke in. "No, that's not accurate."

"Is that correct?" I asked her again.

"She assumed," Stein answered.

"I believe I said I assumed."

"You assumed it because Mr. Simpson said in words or in substance, 'What happened now? Last night we were talking about a house full of kids.' Is that correct?"

"Yes, sir."

"So, it's your belief that he had picked up your earlier message of seven o'clock, correct?"

"I assume." This was now her mantra. She "assumed."

"That's your belief," I followed.

"Yes, sir."

Baker and I did some more jousting over Simpson's passport and cash. Paula said quite directly that during her vigil over Simpson at Bob Kardashian's, Simpson's passport and cash were both kept on his nightstand.

Now I was covering the bases. I asked her, "Has O.J. Simpson ever told you where he was between the hours of ten and eleven on June 12, 1994?"

"I really don't recall."

"Well, would you like to give me your best recollection?"

"I really couldn't recall."

"Did Mr. Simpson ever tell you that he had an alibi?"

"No."

"Has Mr. Simpson ever told you the name of a single person who was with him between the hours of ten and eleven on June 12, 1994?"

Of course, he hadn't. This was a big problem: Simpson could not identify a single living human being who could vouch for his whereabouts during the time of the killings. It was entirely unbelievable that Paula Barbieri never once asked him, "O.J., where were you?"

"It is true," I said, "that as of the time you left Mr. Kardashian's house on the seventeenth of June . . . you believed that O.J. Simpson would take his life. Correct?"

She had been in that chair for ten hours, and it was as if she were disappearing in front of us; her voice small, her eyes not sharp. "I felt he was suicidal. I did believe the police were on their way. It was a concern."

"Did you have a private conversation with Mr. Simpson in the pool area just shortly before you left?"

"I don't recall, exactly."

Again she had to be reminded of her grand jury testimony.

"And did you reiterate to Mr. Simpson how much you loved him?"

"Yes, sir."

"And you *did* love him," I said softly.

She spoke more softly than I did. "Yes, sir."

I looked straight at her. "And you *still* love him, don't you."

She didn't look at me, she looked at Simpson, directly, for the first time all day. "Yes, sir." Simpson looked up, and flashed a silly little smile. He was happy with that answer. He liked women loving him, you could almost see him preening. The admission destroyed her credibility as an independent witness—I needed it to show her testimony was highly biased and unreliable—but Simpson appeared to prefer it that way.

Usually, depositions end at five o'clock, but Paula didn't want to come back a second day, so we pushed on through. We had begun at ten in the morning and ended at eight at night. I was not pleased with how the day had gone. Much of Paula's story was incomplete, some of it was painfully untrue, but I did not feel I had made a dent in it. I had amassed more detail to sift through and many stories to run down. It was obvious that Paula knew a lot more than she was telling, but I didn't yet have the command of the evidence that I needed to pry the truth out of her. I had a lot of work in front of me.

I did get some basic information about Paula's relationship with Simpson and how she fit into the puzzle, and we found out about the crucial Sunday morning breakup. I vowed I would be much better prepared when it came time to depose Simpson himself.

Paula's deposition also served notice that there would be a group of Simpson loyalists who would hunker down for him. Not only would Simpson be difficult to crack, there was a circle of people around him who would lie to protect him. I didn't know how wide or deep that circle would be.

But it was also apparent there was no great amount of ground preparation involved on their side. Paula was no ace. They were doing a lot of seat-of-your-pants flying, and Baker didn't seem up to speed. Good. It appeared their case would be guided largely by the same battle plan that won the criminal case, the same arguments made, more people telling the same lies. All the better.

Paula revealed her "Dear John" message for reasons that escape me. I suspect it was because she thought she would get caught if she didn't. Perhaps she thought there were phone records that showed her having made the call, or Simpson's cell phone having received it, and if she denied it, she would be charged with perjury. We didn't have any such records that we knew of. Not yet. But whatever informed her decision, it supplied a crucial piece of the puzzle that would help to reveal the motive for these murders.

SIX

Locked in to Lies

In December things began to heat up in the courtroom. Under
California law, when a defendant's guilty conduct is committed
intentionally and with malice, a plaintiff may be granted punitive
damages. Punitive damages are permitted to punish the defendant and
discourage others from committing the same or similar acts. The punitive damages must bear some relationship to the defendant's wealth. A
$1 fine might be appropriate punishment for a penniless man, while it
might take millions of dollars to have the same effect on a company with
unlimited funds. The plaintiff must prove the defendant's financial condition in order to enable the jury to decide what constitutes appropriate
punishment.

Until several years ago, a plaintiff could simply request that information and a defendant would be required to supply it. The California
State Legislature changed that law in response to what they determined
was a surfeit of unwarranted, unmeritorious, even frivolous punitive damage requests. No one, simply by filing a complaint, should have the right
to obtain such private, sensitive financial information. A new hurdle was
erected; defendants must provide such information only when a judge
decides they are likely to lose the case at trial. It is up to the plaintiff who
wants the financial information to show the judge the defendant will
likely lose.

Normally such motions are not filed by the plaintiff until the end of the discovery phase, when each side has accumulated all its evidence. From the very outset of this case, I resolved we would not be reactive or defensive; instead, we would go on the offensive at every step. We went to court in December to request discovery of Simpson's finances and could start laying the groundwork for punitive damages. We wanted to launch this discovery process right away, we wanted to set the agenda.

We presented an interesting argument. Judge Kathleen Kennedy Powell, in the preliminary hearing preceding Simpson's criminal trial, had determined that there was enough evidence to allow the case to go to trial. Thereafter, Judge Lance Ito reached the same determination and later concluded there was enough evidence to allow the case to go to the jury after the prosecution had rested its case. We argued in our discovery motion that two judges had already made a determination that the evidence was sufficient to show Simpson's guilt. In the face of these rulings, and after reviewing the evidence himself, Judge Haber agreed and ruled in our favor. We won the right to take punitive damage discovery.

Baker went ballistic. He took the decision right up on appeal under a special writ procedure and lost. We moved forward. We had served notice that we would come out firing.

Shortly thereafter, right before Christmas and with Simpson's long-awaited deposition just one week away, Baker fired back. He filed a motion to disqualify Mitchell, Silberberg & Knupp and me from representing the Goldman family in this lawsuit, claiming we had a conflict of interest.

This was a serious charge. Years earlier, MSK had represented a partnership between two corporations involved in running a Honey-Baked Ham franchise. The managing partner was a company run by a man named Ron Reynolds; the other partner was a company called Pigskins. Pigskins was a corporation 100 percent owned by O.J. Simpson. My firm did some legal work for Reynolds that did not involve our dealing or meeting with Simpson, and that did not render Simpson our "client." Nevertheless, Simpson's attorneys were charging conflict of interest. They were crowing, *Ah ha!*, you can't sue Simpson because you previously represented him.

It was a frivolous claim, but we had to deal with it and a one in a million chance the judge would rule in their favor. Eliminating MSK from the case would have been a devastating blow to the Goldmans' case, and a huge victory for Simpson and his defense.

Not coincidentally, Simpson was scheduled to begin his deposition on January 6. His $29.95 video had not come out, and he needed time to get it into stores. The disqualification motion, even if unsuccessful, would likely stall Simpson's deposition—and give Simpson time to get his video out before testifying. On January 5, the day before Simpson's scheduled deposition, I went into court before Judge Haber and argued that the deposition should proceed as scheduled. "This is ridiculous. This is frivolous. They're just trying to get out of this deposition. Make him appear tomorrow."

Judge Haber said he was not in a position, right then, to decide whether the conflict of interest was real or not, but the defense was taking a position that it had to be sorted out before Simpson was subjected to cross-examination by me and my firm, so he had no choice but to postpone it.

The judge was right, but I was very disappointed with the ruling. The defense had succeeded in putting up a roadblock. In a subsequent hearing, Judge Haber eventually concluded there was no conflict, my firm and I could not be disqualified, and Simpson's deposition would proceed without further delay. Simpson, however, had bought several weeks' time. Shortly thereafter, his video hit the stores.

Simpson made over $300,000 from sales of that video.

The deposition was finally scheduled to begin on January 22, and I spent weeks preparing for it. All of us on the team helped out, dictating memos with thoughts, ideas, and questions for the deposition. I had to review and digest a massive amount of materials, which I organized in hanging files by topic: the cuts, the blood evidence, the gloves, the shoes, the suicide note, the Bronco chase. The files of topics alone filled two banker's boxes. I had a couple of big, black, three-ring notebooks with each area I wanted to pursue broken down in extensive detail. Under "Domestic Violence," for instance, there were over thirty individual incidents involving Simpson and Nicole, most of which we had discovered in her diaries, each of which I intended to question Simpson about. The mail and phone messages offering suggestions poured in. Radio and TV talk shows were flooded with commentary, analysis, and advice. I was on overload with all this information. With the deposition a few days away, I slumped into my chair in my office. It was late into the evening, and I was alone. I took a deep breath, and tried to relax and collect my thoughts. With all the expectations, anticipation, and hype, I realized that I just had to put it all aside. I had to treat this like any other of the hundreds of depositions I'd taken. I could not be concerned with the public expectations or my own client's desires, for that matter. I had to take my time and conduct a thorough, methodical examination. No need for drama. No need for theatrics. There would be no jury in the room. Just do your job. With that, I began to focus.

When I thought about this case, which was all the time, what troubled me more than anything was that despite all the blood and forensic evidence showing that Simpson murdered Ron and Nicole, I didn't really understand why he did it. Not that we needed to *show* why he did it. The law imposed no such requirement. But I wanted—and felt the jury would want—to have some sense of why this charismatic all-American stabbed two people to death. This question had not been adequately answered at the criminal trial. The prosecution had presented some episodes of violence by Simpson toward Nicole, but it was patchwork, as if because Simpson had hit Nicole on January 1, 1989, the jury was expected to assume he had killed her on June 12, 1994. There were snippets of evidence about what happened in the intervening years, but no thread had sewn them together. The defense had mocked the prosecution for their failure of proof in this area.

So I was haunted by the perplexing question: Why? *Why* had he killed her, and *why* on June 12, 1994? If that question bothered me, it certainly would bother the jury. We had to present some explanation. Whether we could find it remained to be seen. Perhaps, if the physical evidence was so convincing, we would not need to give the jury an answer, but I had the visceral feeling that to convict Simpson, the jury would have to understand what drove him.

Motive. It was the area of the case that was most elusive and required the most work. I read the criminal trial lawyers' opening statements and closing arguments, then went back and read the pretrial hearings and briefs concerning domestic violence. I found the prosecution had presented it to the judge largely as a social issue. "Domestic violence, including battered woman syndrome, is a very serious issue in today's society, and this is a classic case of 'domestic homicide.'" All of this was true but struck me as too esoteric. I was not convinced that framing the killing in social terms was the best way to go in a murder trial.

There had been significant haggling between the lawyers about whether domestic violence evidence should be allowed in the case and whether various experts in this particular field of social science should be allowed to testify. The defense, of course, had tried to keep all references to domestic violence out. Cochran and company did not want any of Simpson's history with Nicole to enter into the case, their position being there had been no domestic violence, and if there had, it was so far in the past as not to be relevant.

The prosecution relied on California case precedents ruling that the history between a victim and an alleged perpetrator is relevant to prove whether the perpetrator had a motive to harm or kill the victim. Where a couple's behavior shows animosity, enmity, hostility, conflict, or violence between them, this evidence may be introduced to show motive. After all the arguments back and forth, Judge Ito had issued a comprehensive order permitting certain incidents in the Simpsons' relationship to be offered at the trial but prohibiting the vast majority of them as barred by hearsay law's and other rules of evidence. At one of our early meetings concerning discovery issues, Baker said to me arrogantly, "We won't see any of that evidence in this case. It's pillow talk. It's not coming in this case."

I didn't argue the issue with him at the time, but, again, he showed that his defense would attempt to mirror the defense in the criminal case. We would be better prepared for their effort to exclude Simpson's history of abuse from the civil case.

Domestic violence groups had weighed in on the side of the criminal prosecution. During and since the murder trial, Nicole's sister Denise Brown had become a symbolic activist in that movement and was devoting her time and life to the field.

But we were trying to prove a murder, trying to show what happened on one given night. My view was, Let's get back to basics. Let's talk common sense. Let's look at the two people and what they did and how they behaved toward each other. Let's explore what happened between them that led this particular man to pull a knife on his ex-wife, stab her in the head over and over again, and finally slash her throat. Why did he do it?

I dug deeper into the materials assembled by the district attorney's office and the LAPD. They had done extensive interviewing among

Nicole's friends, some of Simpson's friends, family members, baby-sitters, house-sitters, domestic workers. I found the interviews mechanical, formulaic, and not very penetrating, especially those performed by non-lawyers. Investigators, detectives, and police officers often covered the main points but rarely went deep or far enough. To pursue this case properly, we would need more in-depth interviews with even the most peripherally involved. Still, the initial interviews were a start, and I began, through bits and pieces, to pull the story together.

One afternoon, Tom, Peter, Ed, and I visited the DecisionQuest offices and viewed the exhibits they had prepared for the prosecution in the criminal case. They showed us large graphics boards, plus hundreds of photographs of Simpson's house and property, all on laser disk. They showed us two life-size mannequins, like the ones you would see in a department store window, except mutilated with Ron's and Nicole's wounds, the gaping hole in the neck, the stab in the side, the ear sliced off. The generic mannequin faces bore no resemblance to the two dead victims, but the effect was all the more horrific for being so lifeless. Medvene, slated to handle the coroner part of the case at trial, had the mannequins sent to his office, where they stood, draped so no one would stare at them. They were eerie, shrouded in a corner like ghosts, and I could feel their presence each time I walked in.

I spent a month developing the history of Simpson and Nicole. By the time his deposition arrived I was very well informed.

A deposition is testimony given under oath, written down, and recorded for later use in a court proceeding. The deponent is subject to the penalties of perjury, just as though he were testifying on a witness stand in a court of law. Everything gets transcribed: the questions, the answers, the arguments, the asides, the colloquy between the lawyers. At the end of the process, it's all typed up into a transcript and sent to the witness for review. If, at that point, there are errors, they are corrected and the document is signed. If it doesn't get corrected or signed, it is binding anyway.

Depositions serve several functions. First, they put the witness on the record. If the witness is unavailable to attend the trial, the deposition may be used instead. If the witness appears and testifies at trial and gives testimony at odds with that given in deposition, he or she has been caught in a lie. When you contradict a witness with an inconsistent statement previously made to you or someone else, orally or in writing, it's called impeachment. The best way to impeach someone is to produce evidence of his prior statement made under oath. When a witness's credibility is attacked in this way, a jury is not inclined to believe the witness.

The second function depositions serve is to elicit all information that the witness possesses. This includes information that may never come into use at trial, but may help lead to discovery of other more relevant information.

It is not uncommon for witnesses, especially those who are parties to the lawsuit with a financial or other incentive at stake, to exaggerate or shade the truth, perhaps saying they don't recall an incident when, in fact, they do. So an attorney expects to hear some lying at a deposition. Still, perjury is a serious felony; you can go to jail for it. Depositions are creatures of civil suits, which invariably involve fights over money. Though money is a powerful motive to lie, most witnesses do not want to go to jail. The perjury statute acts as a governor, a deterrent on people's inclination or desire to help themselves out by lying. Given that leverage, an attorney can usually keep a witness's feet to the fire. Generally speaking, you don't have witnesses who just commit wholesale perjury day after day.

Not this time. Not Simpson. Having beaten a double-murder rap, perjury was small change for him. With the array of legal firepower he assembled the first time, what state or federal official would risk going to battle with him over the charge of lying in court? On the issue of perjury, Simpson had a "Get Out of Jail Free" card.

I found myself in a unique position. Simpson had pulled off the biggest fraud on the American public ever seen in a court of law, and now he was trying to perpetuate that fraud to reclaim his position in society. He wanted his image restored, he wanted his stature, he wanted his money; he wanted his life back. With that at stake, he could care less about perjury, because the only other option was to tell the truth and be a confessed murderer. Not too many lawyers take a deposition in these circumstances: We knew Simpson would lie about every important fact in the case.

Okay. My goal was to get him to say as much as I could. This would be my only opportunity, before going to trial, to have this man sitting in a chair, under compulsion of law, forced to answer my questions. If he was going to lie, go right ahead. But in the midst of the lies, I would surely gain important information—about him, his friends, their standing in his life, Nicole, Nicole's friends, his life with Nicole, the places they went, the things they did together, the things they did separately, the clothes he and she wore, the course of their lives. Learn as much as possible, make Simpson tell his story, get it set in concrete, then my team and I can set about to attack that story from every angle, really take a hammer to it, and reduce him to dust.

Simpson had not testified at the criminal trial; his only running account of the case had been on his $29.95 video, hardly complete and completely one-sided. His entire story had never been told. My game plan was to question him on every last detail of his story, not only on the issue of motive and his relationship with Nicole, but also on his alibi, the murder clothing, the shoes, the gloves, the cuts on his fingers, the trip to Chicago the night of the murders, the return, the statement to the police, the Bronco chase, the suicide note. In the hopes of getting more information and drawing fewer objections and lawyer arguments, I thought a more low-key approach in dealing with Simpson and Baker would get me further. I would not be warm to Simpson—this would have been unseemly, especially since Fred Goldman would be present. But there was no need to be consistently chilly. My job, for the moment, was to get information out of him, not berate him.

As the deposition approached, commentators and pundits appeared all over the television and in the daily press, speculating whether Simpson would show up. The thinking was, he could put the case behind him simply by absenting himself, refusing to testify, and defaulting. He would eliminate the embarrassment of being grilled; after a flurry, he would short-circuit the media and get his name and face off the screen and front page; he would not have to endure month after month of extended public inquiry; he would avoid embarrassment and never be forced to answer, under oath, whether he killed two people.

Fred Goldman was very concerned about these rumors. "What can we do?" he asked. "What's going to happen?" I explained that if Simpson didn't show, the only thing we could do was get a default judgment entered against him. Fred and the Brown family and Sharon Rufo would win, and there would be a setting of damages done by the judge, not a jury. We would never get the chance to question Simpson. "Is there anything we can do to stop that?" he demanded.

"Nothing. You can't force a person to testify against his will."

Fred's anxiety was almost too much to bear. But ultimately he felt arrogance would compel the "killer" to appear. ("Arrogant" was how Fred often described Simpson. Also "piece of shit." These struck me as moderate words to describe the person who killed your son.) Fred believed Simpson was so arrogant, he would think he could pull this off. Of course, it would have been difficult for Simpson to continue maintaining his innocence after ducking a trial; to have any chance of being "O.J." in the future, he would have to swear to the world he was not guilty. So in the end he appeared.

The "secret date" chosen by the court for the Simpson deposition was January 22. The "secret place" was the MSK office. The secrecy was laughable. I got calls a week in advance from members of the media, asking if we intended to hold press conferences and where they could set up the microphones. I told them, "I can't confirm or deny." I felt like an idiot.

Downstairs on the morning of the first session, the plaza was full. Everybody in the media wanted the "Simpson enters depo" shot. Because they had almost trampled Paula Barbieri on our premises, the media were no longer allowed inside the Trident Center's first-floor parking garage and had to content themselves with crowding outside the lobby's plate-glass windows, trying to catch a glimpse of Simpson when he arrived. We had arranged for him and his lawyers to enter through a special driveway so they wouldn't have to walk through the press, unless they wanted to. The uniformed security guard station, however, housed a bank of monitors showing black-and-white images from half a dozen strategically placed security cameras, and from outside in the plaza, several enterprising cameramen trained their lenses on these screens, waiting to catch Simpson on his way up in the elevators. TV wasn't getting inside the deposition room, and they were desperate for images.

After the Barbieri deposition, in which the quarters had been a little close, all depositions taken at MSK offices were held in the larger tenth-floor conference room, nicknamed the "bowling alley" because it was extremely long and narrow. This room was less warm and more sterile with fluorescent lighting, a dropped ceiling, and little artwork on the walls.

Security had progressed from day one. I wasn't about to have any more reporters ambling into my office and sitting down with my client for a chat. This time I had special locks installed on the deposition room doors, and only those people in my firm working directly on the case had a key. We also secured the neighboring conference rooms, just to be sure. I arranged for vacant attorney offices on the floor to be reserved, one for the witnesses and their representatives, one for the plaintiffs, and another for the defense, all with telephone access, so everyone could huddle up. We had luncheon served every day and coffee brought in when requested. We were a citadel of hospitality. In fact, the defense had noticed their depositions to be held at Baker's offices, but our operation ran so smoothly that they asked permission to hold them at our place as well, which was fine with me. They said it was because they wanted to keep the media away from their door—but I suspect it was the accommodations.

We had reason to be concerned about security. Many of us thought shenanigans had gone on in the criminal case. Francine Florio-Bunten, a juror most felt was sympathetic to the prosecution and would have hung that jury, got knocked off the panel under highly suspicious circumstances. An anonymous letter was sent to Judge Ito, claiming that she was working on a book about the case. When Ito interviewed her, she denied the charge, and Ito found it to be without basis. However, the judge thought Ms. Florio-Bunten had been untruthful during his investigation and bounced her anyway. It was widely speculated that someone loyal to the defense fabricated the letter to get this juror dismissed. I got a tip that it was someone from the defense team, and passed it on to Bill Hodgman. His office investigated the issue and could not pin down sufficient hard evidence to make an affirmative accusation. But I believed Simpson and his most ardent cronies, whoever they might be, would break laws to get him off again. Security was put in place to prevent that from happening.

There was also the fact that almost everybody even vaguely related to the case was trying to make a buck. I'd never seen anything like it. Even tangential witnesses had been wooed and won by tabloid television dollars. Important witnesses like Nicole's best friend, Faye Resnick, had written books instead of first presenting their testimony to the court. People were selling everything. If some enterprising miscreant planted a videocamera or recording device in the deposition room and obtained a tape of O.J. Simpson testifying, he could make a small fortune. Or even a large one. Harvey Levin, then an investigative reporter for KCBS-TV News, told me he had been approached by someone who showed him a photograph of the deposition room and said he could also provide an audiotape, for money.

I couldn't believe someone had breached our security. We heightened our precautions and asked the Trident Center to reassign the security staff. We had new people brought on board to try and solve the problem.

Several months earlier, the defense had said they were getting death threats, and we had originally considered installing a metal-detector system to check every person before they entered the deposition room. We backed off that one, but we were very careful. I told the defense lawyers that Simpson's bodyguard would not be permitted to bring a firearm into the building and would not be allowed in the deposition room.

"There he is! There he is! He's here, he's here!"

The building's black-and-white monitors were flashed on the air as TV cameras tried to follow Simpson. Our security people brought him and his entourage of attorneys up in the elevator. Simpson was accompanied by his armed bodyguard, Tom Gleason, but security made him stash the weapon. He stood sentinel outside the deposition room door.

The atmosphere in the conference room was very tense. This was the first time Fred Goldman had been in the same room with Simpson since the criminal trial. No bailiffs were posted, and Fred didn't look at Simpson often. He just listened.

Simpson sat at the end of the bowling alley table, with three of his lawyers to his right: Bob Baker, Dan Leonard, and Bob Blasier. Leonard was a partner in F. Lee Bailey's firm. I sat directly to Simpson's left, and next to me were Peter Gelblum, Ed Medvene, MSK senior partner and my mentor Arthur Groman, Fred Goldman, and Mike Brewer. John Kelly sat across the table, opposite Brewer. The younger lawyers at the firm who were working on the case took turns sitting in to see the show. All the guns were rolled out for this one.

Simpson had spent fifteen months in jail, poring over testimony and evidence. He had just finished his video; he knew the facts of his case cold. He had recently made a speech to a local community college and told the students he could "run rings around" his lawyers. I expected a formidable adversary.

He was dressed California casual in a gray V-neck cardigan sweater over a white golf shirt, slacks, and loafers. He was carrying a large wad of cash in his sock, every time he crossed his legs, you'd see it. It was nine-forty in the morning, so maybe he had just woken up, but I was no more than two feet from him, and Simpson's face seemed unusually puffy. For a defendant about to be grilled, he seemed oddly sedate, perhaps even sedated. He stretched often, like a man who wanted to go back to bed.

I sit very close to the witnesses I depose—it's easier to establish a rapport—and I began this deposition by asking some routine warm-up questions, not unlike pregame stretches. How many times, prior to the murder of Nicole Brown Simpson and Ron Goldman, had he previously testified in depositions?

"I believe twice," he said. He wasn't looking at me.

I delivered a question designed to let him know I would be challenging his honesty and credibility right from the get-go and that I knew he would be lying about everything. "When you gave those depositions, you understood you were under oath."

"Yes."

"And did you tell the truth in those depositions?"

"Yes."

"Did you say anything untrue?" The question was completely redundant, but I asked it anyway, just to annoy him.

"I don't believe so, no."

"You told the truth, right?" Each time I asked, my voice got a slight bit more arch.

"The best I knew it."

Baker stopped me. "That's enough, that's enough." The edge to his voice told me he would try to take control early on. I had asked the same question several times concerning depositions, so now I changed the question slightly to one to which Baker could not object.

"And have you ever testified at a trial?"

"Yes."

"You were just a witness?"

"Yes."

"And you told the truth in those criminal cases?"

He had been under oath at those trials; any time you testify under oath you have to tell the truth. For me to ask him that question impugned his honesty. He must have been thinking, What am I supposed to tell you, that I lied and committed perjury? Screw you. Fine. I just wanted to tease him a bit.

"Tell me who the parties were."

"Instruct him not to answer," said Baker. "It's irrelevant and immaterial."

"What I would like to do," I quickly responded, "is get a copy of the transcript of his testimony." A legitimate request. Anything a witness has previously said under oath may be relevant to impeach his credibility in a current proceeding. For example, it may show a propensity to lie. Baker, however, was in the driver's seat. He could tell his client not to answer, which he did. I returned to my questioning.

"This is the first time you're testifying under oath since the death of Nicole and the death of Ron Goldman?"

"Yes."

"So you've never been questioned under oath about the events surrounding Ron and Nicole's death. Is that right?" I had already gotten an answer to that question, but I asked it once more, to emphasize the point. Baker again instructed him not to answer.

"When you gave an interview [to] Ross Becker recently, you were not under oath, correct?" This was the major component of his $29.95 video.

"Correct."

"Did you tell the truth?"

"Best that I knew it, yes."

"Would you have said anything differently if you were under oath?" I thought this was pretty clever; to answer, he had to either certify the video as the full truth or admit he had lied in it.

"It's argumentative," barked Baker. "Don't answer that question." Usually, lawyers do this more formally, by saying, "I instruct the witness not to answer." But Baker's style was tough, without much regard for formalities.

"Are you instructing him?" I tweaked him. Meaning, "Is that a formal instruction?"

"Yes."

"Can we have a stipulation that if you instruct him not to answer, he will abide by your instructions?"

If an attorney instructs his witness not to answer, it does not necessarily mean the witness will heed him. The witness may decide to disregard his lawyer's advice and answer anyway, in which case, technically, I would have to keep asking Simpson, "Okay, your lawyer has told you not to answer. Are you going to listen to him?" To dispense with this formality, I asked Baker if he would stipulate that every time he instructed his client, Simpson would be deemed to have obeyed him. This would inoculate me from later on being accused of having waived my right to go to court and require that answers be given. It's a routine stipulation, and even Baker agreed to it.

This sort of early jockeying between lawyers is common, especially when it's one of the first depositions in a case. The lawyers are feeling each other out to see how much they can get away with and how far they can go. It's a battle for control. I wanted Baker to know I wasn't a pushover. He came in with the big reputation, I was the unknown. I had seen his lightning-quick temper at the courthouse during the hearings. He was a hotheaded guy, prone to tantrums, who could get instantly angry and even vicious, and then five minutes later joke around with you. I had to fight back and establish the battle lines. I wanted Baker and his client to know that I wasn't going to back down.

If a lawyer starts objecting and pushing you around, and you let him, he will continue the manhandling to his benefit. Early on, I wanted both Baker and Simpson to realize that no amount of objecting, arguing, or evading would deter me from plugging away, that Simpson would have to answer all my questions, that I wasn't going to let him off the hook until I got my answers, and it was simply a matter of whether he intended to answer me in five minutes or five hours. The sooner they realized this, the faster the deposition would go.

"Now, you recall giving a statement to the Los Angeles Police Department on June 13?"

"Yes."

"Were you under oath?"

"I don't believe so."

"Did you tell the truth?"

"Best as I could remember it—"

Often, I deliver questions rapidly, and sometimes when I can predict an unsatisfactory answer, I get a little impatient. Witnesses pause, and I will have my next question in the air already. I cut him off, and Baker jumped in.

"Just a minute."

Acknowledging my error, I said, "I'm sorry."

"Let him finish his answer," he sneered.

Baker likes to provoke his adversary. When I represent a witness, I, too, try to engage opposing counsel with questions and objections, to get him off his game. On the other hand, when I'm deposing a witness I want as few distractions as possible. I don't want a dialogue with opposing counsel, I want a dialogue with the witness. It was not difficult to see what he was doing or to counter it. If I could keep Baker at bay, this deposition would go better. "I apologize, Mr. Baker," I said. Let me not fight with him here; there was a greater prize.

"Go ahead and finish your answer," Baker told Simpson.

"As best as I could *at that time*, yes."

This was a clear indication that Simpson was no *Naked Gun* dunce witness; he would answer questions very carefully, very cleverly, and not very truthfully. He did not say his police statement was true, because there were serious problems for Simpson in that statement that he needed to sidestep. Baker had prepared his client for this examination and was obviously attuned to that fact, which was why he was so insistent that Simpson present his answer fully. They knew more than I did, but I would catch up.

I inquired further into the making of his video and whether that was the only time he had been recorded discussing the facts and circumstances surrounding the murders. Again Baker jumped in. "Don't answer that question unless you exclude anything that was done vis-à-vis your attorneys. Any questions that he puts to you, I don't want you to answer and include anything that was done with your attorneys."

If you know what the law entitles you to ask, you can be pretty facile at getting information. If not, you're sure to get buried at the hands of a seasoned lawyer like Baker. I didn't accept Baker's qualification, and I was not going to move on. The contents of Simpson's conversations with his lawyers were private under the lawyer-client privilege, but I was absolutely permitted to know whether certain tape recordings and documents existed, and I was permitted to know who was present at those conversations. If, for example, strangers or persons other than Simpson's attorneys were present, those conversations might not be privileged and I may be entitled to learn about them; it would depend on who was there and what was being discussed. I had the right to bring this to the judge and ask for a ruling on the issue. Directing a litany of time-consuming follow-up questions to test the claim of privilege also tends to make the other lawyer think twice before asserting needless objections. He wants to get his witness out of the chair as quickly as possible. But that would not happen with this witness. I intended to keep him there as long as it took to get every last question answered.

"I would like to know if he is excluding anything," I said to Baker.

"He is going to exclude everything that was done with and through and by his attorneys."

"But all I am saying, Mr. Baker, so we know whether or not there is a relevant contact with an attorney where we might want to attack the assertion of the attorney-client privilege, we have to know the basic foundational facts. That's all I'm saying."

"I understand what you're saying," Baker told me abruptly, "and I'm not assenting to that, and we are not going to allow you to inquire as to what he did with his attorneys, whether he was taped, videotaped, or anything else."

"Well, I am going to inquire into that," I answered. And to counter his assertions that I was delving into privileged information, I continued, "I haven't asked so far about any communications. I have simply asked for the mere existence of such recordings, if they do exist."

"And I am going to instruct him not to answer that, and you can certify it, and we can argue that point with the court."

"Okay," I agreed. "Let me get back to my question: Other than this recent video, have you ever been recorded on videotape or audiotape discussing facts and circumstances and events surrounding the deaths of Ron and Nicole?"

Baker broke in, "And I want you to answer that, other than anything you did with your attorneys."

Simpson, getting the hint, said, "Other than anything that I did with my attorney, not that I knew of."

"And what about with respect to things you did with your attorneys?"

Baker, in a voice dripping with sarcasm said, "Could you be more vague?"

Pretty cute, and pretty funny. If I answered, "Yes," I would admit to being vague, and if I answered, "No," I would admit to the same. But as I would discover, he overused it. By the third time, it's enough.

I had learned that while Simpson was in jail during the criminal trial, the defense had brought in a woman from San Francisco to subject him to a mock cross-examination, and that Simpson had performed miserably. "Did a lawyer named Christina Arguellas subject you to a practice or mock cross-examination?" I asked.

"Don't answer that question," Baker told Simpson. "I instruct him not to answer," he told me.

"What are the grounds of these objections?"

"I think it's pretty evident."

"It's not to me," I said. "I just would like the record to be clear."

"It's attorney-client privilege and attorney work-product privilege."

"Okay." I took a fresh tack. I wanted to see if Simpson regarded her as his attorney. "Is Christina Arguellas an attorney that has ever worked for you in the past two years?"

"I don't know," said Simpson. "The name really doesn't mean anything to me."

"Have you ever been cross-examined about the facts and circumstances of the death of Ron and Nicole by a person who you did not know? . . . I am trying to find out if anybody ever subjected you to a cross-examination when the person was not acting as your attorney, other than this video that just happened? Can you answer that yes or no, please?"

Baker, realizing he was being pushed, began to think out loud. "That assumes that an attorney that was hired through another attorney of his is not—may or may not be his attorney. . . ." As I listened to him, he came to the conclusion that if Cochran or Shapiro had hired this woman, even without Simpson knowing her, their conversations would still be privileged. He made his decision: "I am not going to allow him to answer that question." It wasn't a bad argument, and I realized it.

I could have continued to argue and insist that Simpson answer, but once Baker told his client not to answer, my only recourse would have been to haul us all before a judge. That would have been counterproductive. One of the big mistakes made by lawyers taking depositions is they get so angry and frustrated at the opposing counsel that they throw a fit and get thrown off their game. Many times they say, "That's it, I'm suspending this deposition," and run off into court to have a dispute adjudicated. But between drawing up motions, filing papers, and getting a hearing date, that can take weeks. Considering all the time and work it had taken to get this far, I wasn't going to do anything that would break off these depositions. I intended to ask all my questions, then pile up the objections, and then take them all to court at the same time.

But I had served notice on the defense that we would be dogged and they would not evade our questions. I could now expect Baker to give me more room. That's what was happening here. It was grueling work, this squabbling back and forth, but if we didn't persevere, if we got lazy or tired, we would not get much out of Simpson.

I asked whether Simpson had taken notes during the criminal trial. He had. "Where are those notes?"

"I don't know."

"What did you do with them?"

"I have absolutely no idea."

He had taken them back to his jail cell each night, he said, had not given them to his attorneys, his assistant, or anyone else, yet he did not know where they were as we spoke. This was vintage Simpson; when he couldn't come up with a good lie, he would give a ridiculous answer.

I asked him about prior injuries, prior surgeries, and had him go through the various parts of his body that had been scarred during his football days. I asked him to name his friends, family, and business associates, in an effort to get a general picture of the Simpson inner circle. Kato Kaelin, Simpson made a point of telling me, was not a close friend, just an acquaintance.

Early in the deposition I asked Simpson, "As of June of 1994, is it true that you had generally favorable relations with the Los Angeles Police Department?" Baker wouldn't let him answer the question, and later, when I brought that point to Judge Haber for ruling, neither would the judge. I thought they both were wrong. If Simpson himself believed he had positive relations with the police, that belief must have been grounded in reality. And if he did, in fact, get on well with the LAPD, then it wasn't likely that they would have framed him, as he claimed in the criminal trial. I pursued the issue further.

How many times had he signed footballs for the LAPD? How many times did he let various police officers use his pool and/or tennis court? Did he attend any police functions? Christmas parties? Had his son Jason been given an LAPD hat? Toward the end of that portion of the depo, I asked Simpson, "So your dealings with the LAPD were cordial."

"Yeah," he answered. "For the most part, yes." That was a pretty good answer for me.

"Do you have any information that you were framed by the LAPD?" I asked.

"You are not going to try this case through him," Baker snapped. "You are going to try this case through evidence." We started arguing.

"Give me an objection so we can just have a clean record." He did so.

"When did you first think you were being framed by the LAPD?" I continued.

"Don't answer that question."

"Do you contend that you were framed by the LAPD?"

"I will do the contentions," Baker told me, "and he is not going to answer that question."

"As of June 17, Mr. Simpson, did you have any information that caused you to believe that you were being framed or set up by the LAPD?"

This time there was no objection because I had directly asked for "information," rather than Simpson's state of mind. A subtle distinction, but lawyers engage in this all the time. Simpson said, "No."

What I was trying to show was that there existed no rational basis to believe the LAPD framed him, and not even Simpson himself believed it as of the day he was arrested. Why didn't he? If he didn't commit the murders, and he knew the cops were saying they had found a bloody glove on his property and his blood all over the murder scene, he should have had some reason to suspect a police frame-up. His state of mind against the LAPD as of June 17 was absent any belief or opinion or information that the LAPD framed him. I thought that was helpful to show that the whole frame-up theory was concocted after the fact.

As I had done with Paula, I was moving around. Rather than give Simpson the opportunity to regurgitate a scripted story, I flowed from area to area, constantly branching off into new and different topics. For instance, in examining Simpson about the events of June 17—the Bronco chase—we knew the contents of the Bronco included his black grip. Inside the grip there were perhaps fifty items. A bottle of pills was among them. I asked about the pills, then detoured to some other item, maybe the passport, then the knife. In the context of investigating the Bronco chase, we were amassing a great deal of information about other subjects.

Who was with Simpson the morning of June 17, before he bolted? I ran down the guest list and asked about each name. Bob Shapiro, Simpson's lead attorney at the time, had put together a team of top-notch people with lightning speed. Dr. Michael Baden and Dr. Henry Lee, both expert witnesses of considerable renown, were taking pictures and examining Simpson at the Kardashian home as the cabal was trying to figure out what the cops had on him. As well as performing for the accused killer, these preeminent forensic experts were now unavailable to be hired by the prosecutors.

Simpson said he was on medication at the time of the Bronco chase. "What were you on?" I asked.

"I have no idea." The pills were prescribed by Dr. Saul Faerstein, he said, and, "When I needed them, Cathy [Randa] or Paula would get them." A vial of the prescription drug Xanax, a mild tranquilizer for short-term relief of anxiety and nervous tension, written in the name of Naomi Fischman, was found in his black grip.

"By the way," I asked, "are you on any drugs or medication now?"

"Yes. Sulfasalazine and prescription Motrin."

"For what?"

"Pain."

"What kind of pain?"

"Just arthritic, whatever, general arthritic pains."

"Do those medications in any way interfere with your ability to hear, understand, and answer truthfully my questions?" Another lawyer's safety question. You don't know whether a witness is under the influence of prescription drugs, and you don't want to be told later, "Oh, I was taking medication, that's why I gave you that wrong answer."

"Not that I know of," he said.

He said he "did some writing" that morning. I asked him about those letters, the so-called suicide note that Kardashian read to the press and that received such wide play. In it, he wrote: "I've had a good life. I'm proud of how I lived, my mamma taught me to do unto others. I treated people the way I wanted to be treated. I always tried to be up and helpful. So why is this happening? I'm sorry for the Goldman family. I know how much it hurts. . . .

"I think of my life and feel I've done most of the right things. So why do I end up like this? I can't go on. No matter what the outcome, people will look and point. I can't take that. I can't subject my children to that. This way they can move on and go on with their lives. . . .

"Don't feel sorry for me. I've had a great life, made great friends. Please think of the real O.J. and not this lost person. Thank you for making my life special. I hope I help yours. Peace & Love, O.J."

There were many misspellings. The punctuation was poor. The "O" in "O.J." was a happy face.

"You wrote that?" I asked.

"Yes."

"In your own handwriting?"

"Yes."

"And you wrote it the morning of the seventeenth?" It was dated June 15.

"Yes."

"Did anybody assist you in writing it?"

"No."

"Did anybody dictate anything to you?"

"No." If I had been making any eye contact with him before, it stopped here. He seemed to pick a spot on the conference table and stare at it, eyes not entirely focused, head tilted, listening to my questions without seeming willing to hear them. Simpson can be a glib and engaging speaker, a raconteur. Now his breath was labored, and he spoke deliberately, softly, without energy. Life seemed to ebb from him as he got more somber, more serious, more uncomfortable. It was as if he were in a robotic trance. Simpson appeared to be bringing himself back to the morning these letters were written. I had hit on a sensitive area, and I bored in. Sitting only a few seats away, Mike Brewer couldn't hear his answers and asked him to speak up.

Simpson had put the letter in an envelope, sealed it, and given it to either Bob Kardashian or Al Cowlings. "Did you tell them what to do with it?" I asked.

"Just keep it."

"Did you tell them to open it?"

"No."

"To read it?"

"No."

"Did you tell him that he'll know when it's appropriate to open and read this?"

"No."

"What was your purpose in giving it to them?"

"It was just some thoughts I wanted to share with some people."

"When did you understand that the thoughts would be shared?"

Baker interjected, "If you had an understanding." Translation: If you didn't have an understanding, tell him that. Simpson picked up on the clue.

"If I had an understanding. I don't know. I thought that if I had harmed myself in any way, that they would read it to my friends."

Subtle or indirect answers were not sufficient. I wanted to get to the marrow. "Such as if you killed yourself," I continued. I wanted him to say those words, to get it out on the table.

"Yes."

"You were suicidal that week, right?"

"Evidently, yes."

"And you were on suicide watch?"

"I don't know about that week. I don't know. You say 'suicide watch.' I wasn't aware that I was suicidal, so I don't know."

"When you wrote that letter, though, you had thoughts of suicide. Right?"

"Yeah, I had thoughts of ending what I was feeling, yes."

When testifying about the events of that day, Simpson tried to cover himself by claiming he couldn't really remember what he was thinking or feeling. These thoughts, however, he could not deny. I asked, "What were you feeling?"

Now all the jockeying back and forth, the preliminary skirmishing, the toying, the testing of different paths, was over. It was an important question. What was he going to say: Remorse, because he had just killed two people? Anger, because he'd been framed by the Los Angeles police?

What had he been feeling?

"A lot of pain." I was sitting right next to him, and his deep baritone voice was hard to hear.

"What kind of pain?"

"Pain."

"Pain over what?"

"My wife had been murdered, and I was being attacked."

"By whom?"

"Media." He was staring at the table, chin down. Clearly more was going on in his head than he was saying.

"They were attacking you?"

"Yes."

"Meaning they were blaming you?"

"No. They were attacking me during the week, saying things that weren't true."

"You felt the media were saying things, attacking you, that were not true?"

"I knew they were. I saw it on TV."

If you take his story at face value, O.J. Simpson was contemplating suicide because the media was attacking him. He was forty-six years old, wealthy, celebrated, he had four children, two very young who had just lost their mother, he had women at his fingertips and fans worldwide; he had suffered a horrible tragedy, but he was going to kill himself because he was being falsely accused by the media? The reaction revealed how extremely important his public image was to him. It also revealed that Simpson was more concerned about the media attacks than about his wife. In fact, the "suicide" note never expressed any sorrow for Nicole, not one word. I found that astonishing. It was all about him, O.J., and the media.

"Can you tell us back then what you were thinking that was being said about you that was untrue?"

A television reporter, Simpson complained, said he had been boisterous when he had arrived in Chicago the night of the murders, "as if I was trying to be noticed, which was a flat-out lie. And I'm sure you talked to the people in Chicago when I arrived, and they made that clear, that I was anything but loud and boisterous. But things of that nature." He assumed I'd been doing my homework, had spoken to everyone and knew everything. I hadn't. Not yet. I was only beginning to go down that road.

So it was the implication that Simpson might have been working on an alibi—*Hey, they all saw me in Chicago, outgoing and gregarious. I wasn't acting frantic or upset, like a man who had just committed two murders*—that drove him to consider taking his own life. The fact that his wife had just been brutally murdered didn't enter into it.

"You believed the press was pointing the finger at you as the person who killed Nicole?"

"I can't say the press in general. Just a few things that I had heard, because I stopped watching it after a while."

"But the gist of it was that these few things were pointing the finger at you, right?"

He saw where I was leading him, and he stepped back. "My pain was for Nicole more than what they were doing," he said. "That was just all a part of it."

"The loss of Nicole?"

"Yes."

"You loved her?"

"Very much."

"And you loved her on June 12?"

"I loved her. Yeah. I didn't want to live with her, but I loved her, yes."

Simpson was smart. He had thought all this out in advance: He would confess to still loving Nicole—any decent man would still have feelings for the mother of his two children, a woman he had known for nearly seventeen years—but would make it clear that he was no longer attached to her. He was trying to have it both ways. So now the media *wasn't* the primary reason for his suicide run, it was grief over Nicole.

But if the media was not a large part of it, and if he loved Nicole but didn't want to be with her any longer, then why was he killing himself?

The tone had been quiet, subdued, as Simpson contemplated the moments he said had almost ended his life. Now I challenged him.

"You loved her so much that you were prepared to kill yourself?!"

Any answer he gave was good for me. "Yes, I loved her that much" contradicted the thrust of his criminal trial assertion that he had moved on to a new life with Paula. "No, I didn't" brought on the question "Then why were you trying to kill yourself?" Simpson didn't know which way to go. Of course, the real reason for contemplating suicide was that the police were on his trail and he would be spending the rest of his life in jail for murdering two people. He'd rather kill himself than do that. But Simpson couldn't say that. He preferred to remain vague, while I wanted him to be very specific, on the record.

Baker tried to save him. "That's argumentative," he broke in. "Don't answer."

But Simpson wanted to talk. "That's not why," he answered.

"You loved her so much that you were feeling so much pain that you had thoughts of ending your life?"

"I just had pain for a lot of reasons, for everything that was going on that week, yes."

He wanted to answer yes, but he was smart, well prepared, and quick enough on his feet to insert a lot of qualifiers. Nothing came out of him that hadn't been given significant thought. He had begun by saying the loss of Nicole and the attack of the media had caused his pain. When I went after him and tried to pin him down, he started to duck away.

"Well, besides the loss of Nicole and your feeling of being attacked, was there any other source of your pain?"

"Just everything that was going on was my source of pain."

"What do you mean by that, 'everything that was going on'?"

"Everything that was going on."

"Can you be more specific?"

"No."

"Do you mean in the sense that people were blaming you?"

"No. I just mean everything that was going on, and I can't be more specific."

"You cannot be more specific than that?"

"No."

I had done my job. I had asked him all the questions designed to elicit what he knew and what he was thinking, why he had run from the police, and he could not come up with anything more than two vague comments. Simpson had been pinned down. If at trial he tried to present a new answer, something carefully crafted, something in the manner of "I knew the police had framed me and I didn't think there was any chance I would be able to convince anyone of my innocence," I would be able to roll out the deposition in front of the jury and say, "Wait a second, I asked you all these questions before, when you were under oath, and here's what you said. Let us read it." And then he would be impeached.

I established that Simpson saw his children for the first time after the death of their mother on Tuesday, two days after the killings, and that they left the next day. What kind of man waits two days before comforting his children over the death of their mother and then has them whisked away? I also got him to admit that he specifically left the Kardashian house because he knew he was about to be arrested by police officers and that he was not going to the police station. He would not be able to testify that he didn't know the police wanted him; he was definitely fleeing. He asked Al Cowlings to drive him. He took three family photographs and a loaded gun.

After we took a short break and moved away from the subject of his suicide note, Simpson's mood cleared. I asked him to recall the contents of his black bag when he arrived in his office on the evening of June 13, after returning from Chicago and being interviewed by Vannatter and Lange. He named his overnight kit, a novel, his travel folder of tickets and schedule. "What else?" I asked.

"What *you guys* now refer to as a disguise—"

Simpson's disdainful answer made clear his sensitivity toward the well-publicized reports that he fled the police with a disguise in hand. I declined to follow his lead. "When you say 'you guys,'" I asked, "what do you mean by that?"

"Well, I seen some people in this room refer to it on the news, and the press and the prosecution."

"Okay. So what do you refer to it as?"

"It was a beard and a goatee."

"So you had a beard and a goatee in that bag."

"Yeah. I never really opened the package to see what, but it was like a Vandyke thing, I believe. I never really looked at it, so I don't know."

"It was in a sealed package?"

"Yes."

"It had never been opened?"

"I had never opened it, no."

"Was it opened? You can't tell if it had been opened?"

"I don't know what Vannatter did, because he took my bag and—"

"That was later."

"I don't know. No, I'm only basing it on his testimony. . . . He perjured himself on the stand and testified that I told him he can look in my bag, which I didn't, but I would have if he would have asked, and he testified that he did look in my bag that Monday." He had fully digested the smoke and mirrors of the criminal trial and couldn't wait to accuse Vannatter of perjury, when all I had asked him was whether the bag had been opened. It was one of the few moments all day when Simpson got the least bit animated.

On the face of it, a beard and goatee would appear to be a disguise, helpful in camouflaging the identity of a man trying to elude the authorities. Simpson tried to negate the inference that he had carried the items to flee from the police. He described how he came to acquire them. "I asked a girl who had a bunch of them on the shoot that I was doing for *Playboy.* She had a bunch of mustaches and beards and while they were doing my makeup, I said, 'You know, I can use one of them,' and I explained why." When he took his kids to Knotts Berry Farm, he said, people were "after me all the time."

"Did you ever wear a disguise to conceal your identity on those occasions?" I asked.

"Sunglasses, fake casts on my hands, hats, yes."

"The fake cast on your hand wouldn't conceal your identity as O.J. Simpson. Correct?"

"It keeps me from signing autographs. It's all for the same purpose."

I made Simpson tell me the exact point in time the fake beard and goatee went into his black bag and whether it ever came out. He said he received the package a few days after asking for it, at his office in Brentwood, and put it in his black bag the same day. It had been there ever since. Now I had something I could work with. He was committed.

So when he bolted from Kardashian's house and hit the road with Cowlings in the Bronco on Friday, June 17, Simpson had among his possessions in his black bag his passport, credit cards, a gun, and a fake beard and goatee. He knew he had killed two people and that if he stuck around, he would end up in jail for life. He knew he couldn't handle that, so he had to do something. He had options, he had mobility, he had flexibility, he had a guy with him who would do anything he wanted and to whom he had given a wad of cash in the neighborhood of $8,000, and he had a huge problem he wanted desperately to leave behind. It surprised me that in the criminal case, this issue had been entirely ignored. Simpson never had to respond to or account for it. The prosecutors elected not to pursue. In my judgment, that was a mistake. They lost a golden opportunity to argue to the jury that such a convincing compilation of evidence shows guilt.

Putting the issue into play would have allowed the prosecution to stand before the jury and argue, "Mr. Simpson ran for his life. Ladies and gentlemen, in these circumstances, what kind of man runs? What kind of man puts a loaded gun to his head when his children have just lost their mother to a vicious killer? An innocent man would have even more reason to live: He must take care of his family. He could devote his entire life to finding their mother's killer. But Mr. Simpson did none of that. What did he do? He ran, and put a gun to his head, and was too much of a coward to pull the trigger. That is astonishing evidence of guilt. Nobody who is innocent acts that way. Nobody."

How would the defense have responded? They would have had to develop arguments to show Simpson always carries his passport around. But what about the gun? The disguise? Such arguments might even have pushed Simpson over the edge and forced him to take the stand to explain his behavior. At that point he would have had a lot to answer for—and no innocent answers.

"Did you put anything into the bag before you left?" I continued.

"I'm not sure. . . ."

"Wasn't your passport on the bedside table?"

"No." Funny, Paula Barbieri testified she saw it sitting on the nightstand when they slept there a few nights that week.

"You're positive of that?"

"Yeah. I read everything you read. The answer is no."

"Did you read any statements by Miss Barbieri—"

"Yes."

"—that the passport was on the table?"

"Yes."

"And she's incorrect?"

"Yes."

"Have you discussed that with her?"

"No."

"When you said you've read everything I've read, what have you read, Mr. Simpson?"

"I've read most of the discovery in this case."

"What do you mean by 'discovery'?" Simpson was throwing legal terms around; I figured I'd call him on it.

"I don't know. You tell me. Whatever discovery is."

"You've read a number of witness statements."

"Yes."

"You've read the trial transcript."

"No."

"Any part of it?"

"No."

"Have you read any of the transcripts of the grand jury proceeding—"

"Yes."

"—in your matter?"

"Yes."

"And in Mr. Cowlings's matter?"

"Only in Mr. Cowlings's matter. I don't think it was my matter."

"Where are those documents that you read?"

"I don't know."

"When you read them, where were they?"

"In jail."

"Did you read any of these documents after you got out of jail?"

"No."

"Did you read any of them in preparation for this deposition?"

"No."

"Have you reviewed any documents to prepare for this deposition in the last three weeks?"

"Yes."

"What did you review?"

"My divorce, and I believe my divorce deposition."

"Anything else?"

"Probably Nicole's divorce deposition."

This was interesting. I, too, had read those divorce depositions. They had been taken in 1992, and the major issue involved was the violence Simpson had inflicted on Nicole. They had both acknowledged the New Year's Day 1989 incident, the lone one to become public knowledge because a spousal abuse charge had been brought by the City of Los Angeles. (Even there, Simpson admitted the physical confrontation but did not admit actually hitting her.) But Simpson and Nicole both denied, under oath, the existence of any other similar such incidents. In my view, they had chosen to cover up the dark, dirty secret of all their other episodes of his violence in order not to destroy Simpson's earning ability, which would injure not only Simpson but also Nicole and her children. What national advertiser would want a known wife-beater for a spokesman? And where would Nicole be without Simpson's money?

Simpson had been familiarizing himself with their lies. He had sworn under oath in 1992 that, outside of the 1989 incident, he had never hit her. No one would know this unless they had read his divorce deposition. It was clear then and there, the first day of his deposition, that in our case, Simpson would continue to deny ever having hit Nicole. "I never hit her": That would be his story, and he would stick to it. To forgo that denial would be to admit to perjury in the divorce deposition. Plus, Simpson knew in his bones that he had to deny hitting Nicole. He had to face a jury, and he could not allow that jury—or his public—to keep in their mind his confession of striking her.

From my point of view, the fact that Simpson had read so few documents to prepare for this deposition was a sign that he was taking this trial for granted. Sitting in a jail cell on trial for his life, he was immersed in his defense. Out and about, being "O.J.," on trial for money and honor, he was more cavalier with his time and attention. Good. Had he read anything else? I asked.

"The thing with the police," he said.

"What thing?"

Bob Baker chimed in, "Your statement?"

Simpson said, "Yes."

"The recorded statement?" Baker prompted. Simpson picked up the reference.

"The recorded statement, that portion of it, yes."

"The statement to Vannatter and Lange?" I inquired.

"Yes."

"Is that what you meant by 'recorded statement'?"

"Yes."

"Now, your lawyer put the word 'recorded' there." Did he really think we would let that go by? "Is there some other statement that was made that was not recorded?"

"A lot, yes."

"What are those statements?"

"Whatever the police were asking me that day."

"You mean there's a portion of the statement that's not recorded that you gave to the police?"

"Yes. Yes, quite a bit, as a matter of fact."

Baker broke in. "What I'm talking about is the conversations that he had with the police other—"

"I know what you're talking about," I told him sharply. "He's talking about something different, though."

"No, he is not."

"Let him testify, okay?"

"I think I've really let him testify."

"I'm not complaining so far, except for a couple of parts, Mr. Baker."

"I'm euphoric."

I inquired of Simpson in great detail whether he had ever met, talked to, seen, or heard the name of Ron Goldman. Simpson's very cagey response was, "Not that I know of." A clever answer, he must have rehearsed it a hundred times. He was covered in case we had witnesses who said they saw Simpson talking to Goldman, leaving open the possibility that they had met without being introduced or without Simpson knowing his identity. I tried to close that loophole: "Did anyone ever point out a person who was not identified to you by name but who you later discovered was Ron Goldman?"

"Not that I have any knowledge of."

"Did you have any knowledge of any kind that he was in a relationship with Nicole?"

"No."

"Did you have any information or knowledge that he was a friend of Nicole's?"

"No."

"Did Nicole ever mention him to you?"

"No."

I thought at the time and still think that all these answers were false.

I returned to the Bronco chase and asked Simpson about his supposed attempts to visit Nicole's gravesite. He said he felt "at peace" in the Bronco.

"If you felt at peace in that Bronco," I asked, "why did you want to kill yourself?"

"Because that's why I felt at peace: I thought all my pain was about to end."

"You felt at peace in contemplation of dying?"

"I felt at peace that I was going to stop feeling the way I was feeling."

"Is it fair to say that virtually all of the pain you were feeling came from the loss of Nicole?" I asked. I had already questioned him about this, but I was hoping for a better answer.

He hesitated. I could see him thinking. Why didn't he say, "Absolutely, yes. Of course"? Because he was stuck; how could he be suicidal over a woman he no longer cared for?

"Obviously it was the—yeah, the genesis of it all, but I would say the—yes, I would say that had a lot to do with it, yes. Yes."

All this stammering was doubletalk. He didn't know which way to go. But my job was to close all doors and pin him down. Which we did. Simpson had no innocent basis for his pain.

At 2:24 in the afternoon, day one of Simpson's deposition concluded. There hadn't been any great revelations. This was a slow, methodical, laborious process. It would be a scorched-earth deposition.

I had spent the first day roaming, trying to get a feel for Simpson, trying to find my own bearings. In the process, I covered some key areas but had barely scratched the surface. Some of the lawyers on our side of the table thought we hadn't gotten to the meat of the case and should move ahead more quickly—What did he do on the night of the murders? But my instincts were to keep on plodding. I didn't care how long it took. In fact, the more impatient Simpson got, the more chance he might make a mistake and tell us something or reveal some insight that might prove useful. This would be our only opportunity to question Simpson under oath until trial. Why do it in two days when we could do it in five or ten?

SEVEN

Deep Cuts

You could hear Simpson coming. He always drew a lot of attention to himself. Our paralegal, Steve Foster, heard him in the elevator three floors down, laughing, telling jokes, talking loudly. Once Simpson strutted past Steve and the videographer in the MSK hallway while he was making farting noises with his mouth. As Steve said, Simpson was "just letting people know that O.J. was here." Whichever room he entered, Simpson started out in a good mood.

When Simpson arrived, he cased Kim Goldman, Ron's sister and closest friend. She mourned her brother deeply and hated Simpson with overwhelming passion for killing him. At the criminal trial she had looked at Simpson, stared at him each day, with intense hatred and contempt. Unfortunately, because she was Ron's sister and not an heir with legal standing, she was not a party to this case, and had no legal right to be in the deposition room. I asked Bob Baker if he would agree to allow Kim to be present. "No way," he said. "She's not coming in." No surprise. Kim was very disappointed, but I had warned her and Patti Goldman that they would not be able to attend. They had to remain in an adjacent office and were briefed at each break.

On day one, Kim had a confrontation with Simpson. He stood in the doorway and gave her the once-over, staring her up and down from head to foot, checking her out as if she were in a singles bar. Kim was incensed that "this asshole who killed my brother would do this," but she could only stand helplessly and demand, "Don't . . . do . . . that!" It is the only thing she has ever said to him.

Simpson and his lawyers must have thought he'd done fine in the depo. He hadn't made any dramatic mistakes in the first day, he had held his temper and not been provoked, he had stuck to his script. For my part, I was pleased with the way the first day had gone. Simpson, for all his caginess, didn't have innocent answers, and had given me some angles to play. I went back to working the excavator.

I focused on the contents of the black bag, asked about the vial of Xanax, asked whether he had taken any Xanax on the day of the Bronco chase, asked whether he had ever taken any Xanax, then arrived at marijuana.

"Did you smoke any marijuana on the twelfth of June?" I asked.

"No."

"Did you smoke any marijuana on the eleventh of June?"

"No."

"Did you smoke any marijuana one week before June 12, 1994?"

"No."

"Did you take any drugs during that week?"

"Other than Motrin, no."

"Did you take any other kind of drugs or medication on June 12?"

"No."

"Cocaine?"

"No."

"Methamphetamine?"

"No."

"Were you a cocaine user in June of 1994?" Faye Resnick had said in her book that Simpson had used cocaine in her presence as late as 1993. Many people who knew Simpson called or spoke to me and told me about Simpson's drug use. Several reported he had earned the nickname "Hoover" because he would vacuum up so much cocaine.

"No," Simpson said firmly.

"Don't answer that," Baker jumped in. "You—"

Simpson rolled over him. "No." Just ignored his lawyer.

"The answer is you were not?" I continued.

"No."

"In May of 1994?"

"No."

"That's enough," Baker told me. To Simpson he said, "Don't answer any more questions about that."

I just kept going. I knew Simpson was hell bent on lying about his drug use regardless of what his lawyer advised him. "Did you take cocaine at any time in the period January 1994 through June 12, 1994?"

"No."

Baker was yelling at him now. "I am instructing you not to—"

"Did you take—"

Baker cut me off. "Am I a potted plant?"

I wasn't paying any attention to Baker. "Did you take any kind of amphetamines during that period?"

Nor was his client. "No," Simpson answered.

"Did you take any kind of illegal narcotics at any time in the period January to June of 1994?"

"No."

"Did you use cocaine in the year 1993?"

"Don't answer that!" Baker whined.

"No," said Simpson.

Baker was beside himself. He was about to get up and leave. Simpson, I think, finally felt bad for his lawyer's inability to control him.

"I'm sorry," he said. He said "I'm sorry" to his lawyer! At that point, he began to heed Baker's advice. But this little episode revealed how headstrong Simpson could be. No matter how many bright legal minds counseled him, when it came to certain issues near and dear to Simpson's heart—that is, his image—he would follow his own instincts.

Denying drug use was a good example of this. Too bad. I intended to go year by year back into the 1980s. I had a toxicology report taken on June 13, 1994, by the LAPD that showed traces of THC, the primary intoxicant in marijuana and hashish, in Simpson's blood. I wanted to see what he was going to say about that.

"Did you use any kind of illegal narcotics in the year 1993?"

"Don't answer that!" This time Simpson listened.

"You refuse to answer?" I asked.

"Yes," Baker shot back, "he refuses to answer."

Although Simpson was very insistent on denying he had used drugs, his criminal defense had spent considerable time implying that Nicole did. He was quoted many times saying that the "real killer" could be found "in the world of Faye Resnick"—Faye had admitted using cocaine, had been the object of an intervention in which her friends confronted her with her problem, and had been in a rehabilitation clinic at the time of the murders—bringing visions of drug cartel hit men invading Brentwood.

"You said yesterday that you were concerned about possible drug and/or alcohol abuse by Nicole Simpson. Do you recall that?" I asked him. He did. "Did you and she participate in using narcotics in 1994?"

"No."

"Did you see her do so?" He said he hadn't. "At any time, did you see her do so?"

Simpson seemed troubled by this question. I could tell he wanted to communicate that there was a problem with Nicole and drugs, so that we would all believe that it had something to do with her death. But he didn't want to appear too anxious to trash his dead ex-wife. He was in the middle of denying it when Baker broke in. "Don't answer that, O.J.!" Now he was "O.J." "Don't answer, O.J.!" As if we were in a bar, or something.

"I think the answer was no," I said. "Do you have any information whatsoever that in 1994 Nicole Brown Simpson abused or took illegal narcotics?"

"Yes," Simpson "reluctantly" admitted.

"What is that information?" If he planned to trash Nicole, I wanted to hear all of it so we would be prepared to counter it at trial.

"She told me on one occasion. . . ."

"When is the first time in 1994 that she told you that she was using drugs?" I asked.

"I think it was the middle or the end of January. . . . She called me. She was crying."

"What did she say?"

"She was in trouble. . . . She thought she was going to get in some trouble. She needed my help."

"What did she say she had done?"

To my surprise, from across the table I heard John Kelly say, "I am going to object at this time."

Simpson looked at Kelly and said, "Thank you."

"I want to speak to you for a minute, Mr. Petrocelli," Kelly said.

He and I went to a nearby conference room and spoke for about ten minutes. He, of course, represented Nicole's estate and expressed concern that Simpson might be about to put on record some considerable amount of unpleasant information about his deceased client. This was understandable. He wanted to know why I needed to get into this line of questioning and where it was going to lead. I explained, "At some point we really need to find out what he intends to say about all of this, because he's now referring to some specific incident in January or February of 1994, five months before the murders. You know we'll be hit with all of this at trial when he takes the witness stand and testifies. Who knows what he's going to say? Obviously, we've got to find out."

I compromised with Kelly. "I'll tell you what," I said. "Since you find this troubling, I won't get into it now. We can come back to it more indirectly." We were right in the middle of the deposition; I didn't want to stop everything and have an hour-long discussion to convince him.

But I was concerned about being blocked from discovering the full extent of the Simpsons' relationship even if it meant eliciting unflattering details of Nicole's life. I felt it was important to understand who Nicole really was, and not cast her as some perfect angel. In the criminal case, and in a great deal of the press coverage, the tendency had been to blame Simpson for all the problems in their relationship and to absolve Nicole entirely. I wanted to bring out the warts in her life because I thought it would make her more real and understandable as a person. Many felt the jury in the criminal case did not like Nicole because she was portrayed as a perfect white woman and Simpson as a black devil. It was important to prevent these stereotypes from disfiguring our case. In no way was I suggesting that Nicole deserved to be killed—just the opposite. By eliciting and explaining her flaws, I wanted to explain how they affected Simpson and prevent him from exploiting them.

As it turned out, Simpson said Nicole and Faye Resnick were driving in Nicole's Ferrari, apparently doing drugs, when Nicole hit a car in front of her. Concerned that her notoriety as O.J. Simpson's wife would turn the incident into headline news, they switched seats and said Faye had been driving. Nicole, Simpson said, had been hysterical when she called to tell him of the incident. This, in a town where, in a certain strata of society, you are probably in the minority if you are *not* a recreational user of drugs. He combined that with later examples of what he portrayed as her erratic behavior to show how her life was spiraling out of control. Therefore, she must be on drugs; therefore, she must be dealing with people in the drug world; therefore, people in Faye Resnick's "drug world" killed her.

Despite his attempts at character assassination, it was apparent that Simpson would not admit to firsthand knowledge of drug use by his ex-wife. He insisted he had no direct evidence of Nicole doing drugs. How, from that standing start, did he plan to leap to Colombian cartel hit men running amok in upper-class Los Angeles?

I jumped to another subject entirely. I showed Simpson a copy of the daily calendar Cathy Randa maintained for him and focused on the months April, May, and June 1994. I used this as an opportunity to discuss the last time Simpson was at Nicole's condominium on Bundy. What I was really trying to do was trace Simpson's exact whereabouts that day, to see if he intended to say that he visited all the locations where blood was found and that he was bleeding that day or an earlier day from some innocent wound. I backed into it by asking him about the last time he spoke to Faye Resnick. I knew the answer from Faye's book—Sunday, June 5. He said it was Sunday or Monday, June 5 or 6. He went to Bundy to pick up his dog, Chachi, and saw Faye there. This was the last time, he said, he went to Nicole's house, or at least the last time known to anyone but the victims.

He said he stayed outside, in the front of the house. "By the way," I asked, "is there a buzzer at the front that you could ring the doorbell?"

"Yes."

"And was that operable?"

"As far as I knew, yes."

In fact, it was not operable. Detective Tom Lange, in his crime scene notes, indicated that it was not in working order. I then traced Simpson's movements very carefully. I was able to establish that he entered the property, which ran partway down the alleyway, to get the dog. Simpson was so busy dissing Resnick—"Faye was, in my judgment, totally plastered . . . She was babbling"—that he seemed to pay no attention to the real reason for my walking him through this scenario, which was to check for blood drops.

"Was that the last time you were at the Bundy property before Nicole's death?" I asked.

"I believe so, yes."

"Were you bleeding on that occasion?"

"Not that I know of."

"Did you have any cuts that you knew of?"

"Not that I was aware of." By the time I asked these questions, he knew where I was going, but there was nothing he could do about it.

"Were you wearing any Band-Aids?"

"Not that I was aware of."

This quickly eliminated any answer he might try to concoct at trial that would innocently explain why his blood was found at the Bundy crime scene. He had not visited the specific places at which his blood had been found. We had him roped off.

I took him back to previous visits to the property and made him go through the same chain of events. All his answers were good, except at one point when he said he thought he had cut his finger closing his car door and Sydney had had to get a bandage for him. But that was in the driveway and would not have explained his blood being in other locations.

I could have gone the direct route and asked him, "Mr. Simpson, you were at the trial, you know where the blood was found at the murder scene, you saw all the markers. Had you ever bled there before?" But that would have been an open invitation, to which Simpson would have answered, "Might have. I've got cuts on me. I bleed. I might have bled there." As always, I tried to make it a little more difficult for him to lie, and this time I nailed him down before he wised up. Now, the only way his blood was at Bundy was if he dripped it on the night of the murders.

I had heard Alan Dershowitz say on television that there was evidence that Simpson's blood found at Bundy was dried over and "looked like taco sauce," the implication being, the blood could have been there for a long time. This was not true, there was never any such testimony from police personnel, and it was important to dispel that notion.

In passing, Simpson told me he saw Nicole on her balcony, but had not talked to her when he had come for the dog. No "Hey, how're you doing?" No casual conversation or friendly banter. "I mean, we acknowledged each other, but, you know . . ." So despite the fact that he tried to dismiss it, one week before her murder, Nicole and Simpson were not even talking to each other.

Nicole always kept a key to her property in one specific place in her house. Shortly before her death, she told her mother it was missing. The key was found in his bag, but Simpson denied he took it. The key worked the gate at Bundy, the gate through which the murderer walked, dressed in dark clothing. He blamed his best friend. "I know A.C. got a key," he told me.

"How do you know that?"

To try and explain Nicole's key in his bag, Simpson claimed Lou Brown might have given it to Cowlings the week after Nicole's death, so Al could get some things from the condo for Nicole's children. A clever attempt by Simpson to give an innocent explanation for an incriminating fact.

"Are you telling me that . . . This is a . . . This is access—" I almost started sputtering. "Withdrawn." I started over. "Are you saying that A.C. got a key to Nicole's condo—"

"Got access," Simpson corrected me. "I think a better word would be 'access.' "

"What does 'access' mean?" I asked him sarcastically.

"The ability to get in."

"How do you know that?"

"Because there was some conversation about it."

"Were you present?"

"I just heard it being spoken about."

"You don't know that A.C. actually received a key to the condo. Correct?"

"That's correct."

"And you have never seen A. C. Cowlings possess a key to Nicole's condo. Correct?"

"That's correct."

Satisfied I had debunked his explanation, I moved on. I handed Simpson Exhibits 10 through 21, all pictures of the clothes found in the back of the Bronco after the chase, in hopes that he might just admit it was all his. "You recognize that clothing?" I asked him.

"Not necessarily, no."

"Do you recognize any of it?"

"Not necessarily, no."

"When you say 'not necessarily'—"

"I mean, I recognize Calvin Klein underwear—"

Okay, be that way. Now I had to go one by one.

"Exhibit 10 is a picture of a jacket. Do you see that?"

"Yeah."

"Is that yours?"

"I don't know."

"Do you know whose jacket that is?"

"No."

"No idea if it's your jacket?"

"No."

"Could it be?"

"Don't answer that," Baker advised him. "That is irrelevant and has no probative value, and it's immaterial whether it could be when he has no recollection. There is no foundation, and I instruct him not to answer the question."

I couldn't resist replying, "If that standard were applied to the criminal trial, it would have lasted half the time." I showed Simpson Exhibit 11 and asked, "Is that your shirt?"

"I really couldn't say."

"Are those your pairs of underwear?"

"I have no way of knowing."

He wouldn't even admit to owning his underwear.

Simpson went on and on with these evasive answers as I went through every piece of clothing. I was trying to find out if Simpson had truly planned to visit Nicole's grave before killing himself as he contended, why he had packed the car for a trip. Simpson kept evading me, his memory distinctly indistinct. I cast about for a way to pin him down. Finally I said, "So, if these items were recovered from your bag, you would have no way of saying that these are *not* your items, is that correct?" If I could not get him to admit that he owned these clothes, I was trying to at least get him to admit that he could not *disclaim* ownership.

"That's kind of a double negative," Baker brooded.

"I don't get it," said Simpson.

"In other words, if these items were found in or near your bag in the Bronco, you can't say that they're not your items. Correct?"

"Wait a minute," Baker jumped in. "If they were found in or near his bag in the Bronco, you can't say that they're your items—" I could almost hear his mind working—"and I am going to instruct him not to answer, based on pictures, because you can't tell from the pictures whether they're his, whether they're A.C.'s, or someone else's."

Baker had pulled another lawyer's maneuver: When attorneys want to suggest an answer, they insert it in the context of their objection. It's called a "speaking objection," and I got upset with Baker for trying it. "Who's talking about A.C.? He never mentioned A.C." I challenged him directly. "Why did you mention A.C., Mr. Baker?"

"My depo isn't being taken," he shot back.

"Exactly. That's my point."

"I don't care what your point is." Baker didn't like getting taken to task and didn't want to be made a fool of in the transcript. "And I'm trying to respond to your question."

"My point is, stop trying to suggest answers. The witness can speak for himself. Just make an objection."

"Well, thank you very much for your speech, and I really am not taking legal advice from you, so I will put anything on the record that I feel like I am going to, so you—"

"You know better than that, Mr. Baker." Now we were getting angry.

"Don't tell me what I know and what I don't know—"

"Then don't testify—"

"—in court, telling me what the state of mind of my client was, and if you knew, you probably had some conversations with him in violation of the Code of Professional Conduct. So don't give me that nonsense. I'm—"

"Are you finished?"

"—not going to put up with it."

"Are you finished?"

"I'm finished for now, but I'll put anything on the record I want."

"Okay." I was ready to get back to Simpson. "You put those items in the Bronco?"

"I have no way of knowing." He was continuing to stonewall.

"You deny doing it?"

"Don't answer that." Baker was not finished being steamed. "He's answered the question, and he is not going to answer that. That's argumentative. Don't answer it."

I pressed on. "You don't know what clothes you own, Mr. Simpson?" I asked incredulously.

"Don't answer that question."

"Why not?"

"Because you are arguing."

"I am not arguing." We went on and on. "Do you know for a fact that those items were not in the Bronco?"

"Don't answer that."

"On what ground?"

"I am not going to—You've gone through that. I am not going to allow you—"

"You are not even going to state your objection?"

"No, I'm not!"

"Okay. Well, we will just have to let the judge take a look at these objections."

"I think you should."

Finally I finished with the clothes. From there I moved to the examination of Simpson's body by Drs. Robert Huizenga, Henry Lee, and Michael Baden the week after the murders. I asked him if he knew why they were examining him. Baker advised him to exclude any conversations that he had had with his lawyers about the reason. Simpson said, "No, not really." Apparently, with three highly accomplished experts hovering around him, Simpson had no clue.

"Did they find any injury marks on your body?" I asked. Simpson was a professional athlete; he had been cut and scratched weekly for more than a decade. Surely he had some scars.

"I don't recall," he told me. "Whatever they examined, they examined."

"You don't recall?"

"I don't recall."

Putting aside old football injuries, which apparently did not register with him, I asked, "Did you have any recent cuts on your body on the seventeenth of June?"

"On my finger I had a recent cut." Of course he did. This had been well documented in the criminal trial. Simpson had a significant cut on the middle finger of his left hand. An extremely incriminating cut. He had never been called upon to explain it under oath. Now was the time.

"On the seventeenth of June, you had a recent cut on the middle finger of your left hand?"

"I would say five-day recent, possible." Simpson's voice was getting lower. He once again picked a spot on the table and stared at it. Whatever eye contact we had made was over. He began to tighten up. I leaned closer to him.

"I want to know about cuts that you had on your body on the seventeenth of June when the doctors were examining you that had been caused within the previous seven days." The murder occurred on June 12; I wanted him to go back to June 10, just to see if he would say he cut himself before the murders.

Baker tried to give his client some breathing room. "So, is there a question in there?"

"Yes," I answered. The time for playing with Baker was over.

"Regardless of what you want to know?" he persisted.

"Yes."

"Where is the question?" Simpson, meanwhile, was trying to maintain his composure.

"I want to know what those cuts were."

"Then ask him a question."

"I just did."

"You didn't. You told him what you wanted to know."

This colloquy reminded me of a prizefighter's manager haranguing a referee about a phantom low blow while his guy, having been knocked around, goes to a neutral corner for a couple seconds' rest.

"Describe it to me," I told Simpson.

"Describe any recent cuts that you had that were of five days' duration or less," Baker advised him.

"The only one that I was aware of—"

Did he think he'd get away with that? "I said seven days," I told him.

"The only one I was aware of is the middle finger one," Simpson said lowly. He reiterated that he was "aware of." He was covering himself. He knew photographs and notes existed, some taken by the police, others by his own doctors, that showed and described other cuts.

"You were aware of no other cuts. Correct?"

"I wasn't aware of any cuts, no."

"When you were examined by Dr. Huizenga on the fifteenth of June, had any recent cuts or abrasions or wounds that you may have received been fully healed?"

"I don't believe so, but I'm not sure. You'd have to ask the doctor."

"What did you tell the doctor on the fifteenth as to how the cut on the middle finger was caused?"

Baker again guided his witness: "If you told him anything."

"I don't recall if we talked about it, but we may have. We may have. I don't recall."

"What did you say?"

Baker objected. "There is no foundation for that question if he doesn't recall—"

"You don't recall what he said?"

"No."

Baker told me, "He doesn't recall even talking about it."

I focused on Simpson. "I thought you said earlier that you discussed how the injury was caused."

"I may have, but I don't—I may have, yes." He was getting spacier and spacier.

"What did you say?"

"I don't know if I did."

"And you can't recall. Right?"

"I must have, but I don't recall. I don't recall any specific conversation." He seemed right in the middle of not recalling.

"Do you recall on the seventeenth, any discussions as to how you were cut?"

"Not at all."

Finally I asked the question of the hour. "And how did you suffer the cut on the middle finger?"

"I broke a glass when I was in Chicago, and in the process of cleaning it up, I evidently cut my finger." He spoke so softly, John Kelly, sitting only a few seats away, couldn't hear and had to ask him to speak up.

"I said, in the process of cleaning—not cleaning it up, but scooping it up, I evidently cut my finger."

Evidently? "Did you remember cutting your finger?"

"I remember bleeding," Simpson answered.

"Do you remember cutting your middle finger?" I repeated.

"I remember bleeding and seeing that I was bleeding, so . . ."

Now he was not even saying that he remembered cutting himself, just that he saw the blood. This monumental memory lapse, at a critical time in the chain of events, was an obvious sign of deceit. Rather than hammer at him, I decided to break the events down moment by moment and make him tell his lies in painful detail.

"Exactly how did you cut it with the glass?"

"I was trying to scoop the glass into the sink with some toilet paper and, I believe, a towel."

"You were at the sink of the hotel room?"

"Yes."

"In the bathroom?"

"Yes."

"What were you doing at that time?"

"I don't know. I was trying to pack. I was trying to brush my teeth. I was in and out of the bathroom."

"And at some point you did something to a glass?"

"Yes."

"A drinking glass?"

"Yes."

Although his voice was hollow and he never looked at me, I had him trace his movements in the hotel room, from taking his toiletries out of his kit bag to putting his toothbrush into the glass on the bathroom counter. I asked where the glass was, whether there was a towel or napkin underneath the glass, where his toothpaste was, what motions he made with his hands. "And describe what you did to break the glass and cut yourself," I asked again.

"I don't really know."

I asked him again, "How did you cut your finger?"

"Cleaning up the broken glass."

"How did the glass get broken?"

"I don't know. I was—I don't know. I was out of it, and I was doing a few things and the glass broke, and I was going back and forth to the phone, and maybe I slammed it down. Maybe I knocked it over. I really don't know."

"You are saying you do not know how the glass broke. Is that right?"

"Yes."

"At some point you saw that there was a broken glass. Correct?"

"No. At some point I was trying to get my toiletries together." Chin down, eyes averted.

"And you saw there was broken glass around. Correct?"

"Yes."

"And where was the broken glass, Mr. Simpson?"

"Mostly on the counter, and I think one big piece was on the floor."

"And was any of it in the sink?"

"I don't know. Probably some of it. Maybe. I don't know." Simpson grew more and more uncomfortable. His answer to the crucial question was "I don't know." He wanted to deliver that answer once and be done with it. Not today.

"And you then went to pick up the piece on the floor?"

"I was going back and forth to the telephone, and I was trying to pack, and I was trying to get it out of my way as I was packing."

"And you saw the broken glass, and you wanted to get it out of the way. Correct?"

"Correct."

"Were you on the phone at the time this was happening?"

"I was going back and forth to the phone, so I can't tell you exactly. I wasn't really, you know, trying to remember everything I was doing at that time, so . . ."

"I am trying to focus on the point in time when you saw the glass. Okay? . . . When you saw that there was broken glass on the—"

Simpson was getting impatient with me. "At some point after I was told that my wife was dead"—he took a deeply exaggerated breath—"or that Nicole was dead, I broke the glass." This was a litany. "In the process of going back and forth to the phone and trying to get packed, I cut myself trying to move the glass out of my way. Somewhere in that, that happened."

So this was the Simpson story. I don't know what his lawyers said when he told it to them, maybe they thought he could plow through it in one breath and no opposing attorney would slow him down. Maybe they couldn't get any better explanation when they asked. But this was clearly a monumental hole in Simpson's alibi. He had no credible explanation for the cuts on his fingers and hand. What are the chances of Simpson's innocence when he cannot explain cuts on his hand received at the same time his ex-wife and another man are found knifed to death and there is a trail of Simpson's blood found on Simpson's property leading from his car right up to his bedroom. I wanted to plunge Simpson deeper into this grave of lies.

"Now, how did you break the glass?"

"I don't know. I think I answered that already. I don't know."

"But you do remember breaking the glass. Right?"

"I remember the glass was broke, yes."

"But you don't know how you broke it?"

"No."

"But you are confident you broke it."

"Yes."

"And when you broke it, where was the glass?"

"In the bathroom."

"You went into the bathroom and then, while you can't remember how, broke the glass."

"Yes," he told me.

"Correct?" I made Simpson repeat that response.

"Yes."

"Why did you break the glass?"

"I had no purpose in breaking the glass."

"Did you throw the glass?"

"I don't recall." This is the most common answer of people who lie under oath, because there is usually no way anyone can assail it. The only one who knows what a witness actually recalls is the witness himself— who else knows what is actually in a person's memory?—therefore, there is little room to impeach him.

"Did you squeeze it?"

"I doubt that, but I don't recall." So there was a glimmer of recollection after all.

"When you broke the glass, were you on the phone?"

"I don't recall."

He said he was not on the phone with detectives when he broke the glass. He knew, and I knew, there was no telephone in the bathroom of his hotel suite. I asked him what his next movement had been immediately after breaking the glass. I wanted to slow him down.

"I don't know," he said. "As I told you, I was going back and forth to the phone. Sometimes they had me on hold, sometimes various people I was talking about was trying to find me a flight, and I was just going back and forth trying to pack, and . . . in the midst of all that this glass broke, and in the midst of all that I was cleaning up the glass, and in the midst of all of that all of this happened."

"Do you believe you were on hold when you went to the bathroom and broke the glass?"

"I don't know."

How long was he in the hotel room from the time the police informed him of Nicole's death to the time he went downstairs to catch a cab to the airport? Possibly a half hour. Did he cut himself when he broke the glass? He didn't think so. Which hand did he use to clean it up? He didn't know. Did he know if he used his left hand to break the glass? No. Did he know which hand he had used? No. Did he throw the glass against the wall? At first he said no, then, "I don't recall."

Simpson said he didn't believe he threw the glass in the sink; he might possibly have slammed it down on the bathroom counter. "Picked it up and then slammed it down. Is that your best recollection of how you broke the glass?"

"No, I didn't say that. I said that was a possibility."

"You say it's a 'possibility.' Does that sound like what happened?"

"That's a possibility."

"Are there any other possibilities that you know of?"

"Obviously, a myriad of possibilities."

"Do any come to mind besides slamming the glass down on the counter?"

"I may have knocked it over. I may have hit it with my bag that I use to pack. . . . I don't know. . . . I was sort of out of it at the time."

"Did you break the glass accidentally?"

"Yeah. I believe so, yes." This was a yes-or-no question. How could there be some question as to his intent?

I don't know why Simpson created this mess for himself in the first place. Why didn't he simply come into the deposition and say, "I went into the bathroom and threw the glass in anger. One of the shards went into my finger"? Or, "I broke the glass. I was so shaken by the news, I cut myself when I was picking up one of the pieces"? His ex-wife had just been murdered, both of those would have been plausible responses. Perhaps the reason was that the hotel bathroom was virtually untouched, and he knew we had police photographs of the vanity counter with all the other standard-issue hotel bathroom items in place and intact. The room had been the scene of no wild rampage. Perhaps the reason was tied to his decision not to show emotion at any point in the trial, as if any rampage would lead to the one that killed Nicole. Of course, Simpson would have to answer for the coincidence of his getting a deep cut on his finger the same night his wife and her friend were slashed and stabbed to death, but that question was open either way. Instead he was all over the map and obviously making up his answers. It was strange—but Simpson was a bad liar.

Simpson hadn't thought his story through carefully. He hadn't been grilled on it in sufficient detail and didn't anticipate that he would have to face three hundred questions on the cuts alone. I never let up. What was he wearing when he picked up the broken glass?

"Probably naked," he told me.

"Did you put any clothes on before you picked up the pieces from the floor?" He didn't recall. He thought he got dressed before packing.

"There were no cuts on your left hand at that time, either. Correct?"

"Correct."

"And when you picked up the piece of glass—"

"Not that I know of, I should say."

Before returning to Los Angeles, did he shave? Did he shower? Did he wash his face? Did he brush his teeth? Did he use underarm deodorant? Did he use cologne or aftershave? Did he take any medication? With water? Did he eat anything? Did he drink anything? Did he drink water? We went on for about ten minutes, turning tiny, tedious details of that night over in our minds.

"Now," I asked him, "at what point in this process did you cut your finger?"

"Again?!"

Simpson got visibly upset. He was faced with repeating his entire litany of lies. Would this never end? We had moved away from the broken glass, the cuts had been handled, he was in the clear and running for daylight when the question caught him from behind.

"Yes," I told him.

"Somewhere in between going back and forth to the phone, trying to pack, trying to get dressed, at some point in there I cut my finger." The story sounded even more hollow now than it had the first time he'd tried it.

"Did you cut it on one of the broken pieces of glass?"

"Yeah."

"On what piece?"

Sitting directly beside him, I could see the veins at his left temple begin to pulse and the muscles in the entire side of his face bunch and flex. He couldn't take it. Simpson reached to his face and wiped what appeared to be a tear from his eye. *"Can we take a break?"* he demanded.

"Yeah, sure," Baker told him.

He glanced in my direction. Still no eye contact. *"Jesus Christ!"* he spat. Simpson stood, fumbled to undo the microphone clasped to his golf shirt to record the audio for the videotaping process, threw it on the table, and hobbled out.

Fred Goldman raced out of the bowling alley, across the narrow hallway, and into the conference room where Patti and Kim were waiting to tell them what happened. I had not seen them get so excited before. They wanted to see Simpson in as much pain as possible, and they enjoyed his anguish.

The defense was upset that Simpson had lost his cool. I've had witnesses lose control and fly into complete outbursts, screaming at me in depositions. Simpson's behavior was nothing, in contrast. But this is O.J. Simpson, who is never supposed to lose his cool. This was a man accused of wife-beating and stabbing one man to death and slitting a woman's throat in a state of rage. Simpson and his defense had apparently decided he must never express any emotion, never get angry, never express even the first flash of rage, never lose control.

Frankly, I thought that was silly. If Simpson were innocent, he and his lawyers shouldn't have any problem with him expressing anger. Who doesn't have rage? Everybody, at one point or another, has been in a state of rage. There shouldn't even be a question about that. The question is:

Do you kill when you get there? Do you pick up a knife and put it in the throat of the woman you have been with for seventeen years? Are you capable of *that kind* of rage? The thought occurred to me, these guys don't trust their client! Maybe, if their client does get enraged, they're not sure what he's going to do!

We were not surprised at Simpson's difficulty in dealing with the questions about his cuts. He might have said, "I was cutting my steak and I accidentally nicked myself with the knife," but instinct told him to stay as far away from knives as possible. So, if you exclude a knife, what other ways are left to cut your finger? How about glass shards! The problem with the "broken glass" theory, however, is that it does not explain how Simpson got cuts on the backs of his fingers. How do you cut the backs of your fingers while throwing a glass, picking up glass shards, or sweeping them into the sink? The story defied reason.

And what about timing? Simpson didn't want to say he had cut himself before he left for Chicago, because he didn't bring it to anyone's attention in the limousine, he didn't tell Kato on the way to or from McDonald's, he had no witnesses. He couldn't say he cut himself during the airplane trip because he had no easy explanation how that might occur; he also had no passenger or stewardess to confirm it. He figured, wisely, that it was too unbelievable and incriminating to claim he independently cut his finger at the very same time the murders were being committed, so the only open time slot was the few hours he spent in Chicago. None of the story rang true, but it was the best he could do on short notice. It had been cooked up and presented to Vannatter and Lange of the LAPD when they interviewed him on Monday, June 13.

What was clear was that Simpson was lying about it all; he had not, in fact, accidentally broken a glass and cut himself on hearing the news of Nicole's death. He cut himself while killing his ex-wife and Ron Goldman. When he realized he had to come back from Chicago with an explanation for the gashes on his fingers, he looked around, saw the drinking glass in the hotel bathroom, and broke it. He squeezed a little blood on a hand towel, and left it on the counter to be seen. He left shards of glass on the counter and in the sink. He staged all of this—to camouflage his guilt.

Witnesses commonly ask to take a break from testifying, but for Simpson to blurt out his discomfort so bluntly was very damning.

Simpson's cuts were the source of all the blood and DNA evidence placing him at the murder scene and identifying him as the killer. I had not
been accusatory or confrontational, merely insistent that he provide a
clear, complete explanation. He displayed a total inability to deal with this
line of questions, and we attorneys stored that in our memory for later,
when we got to trial.

His break lasted nine minutes. When he came back in, he appeared
more sedate. Maybe he thought I would move on to something less
intrusive.

"You requested a break, Mr. Simpson. Correct?" I said to him.

"Yes." If he was not the charismatic personality of his $29.95 video,
he was at least a bit refreshed.

"And you wanted to talk to your lawyers?"

"No."

"You requested a break because you were uncomfortable with the
subject matter?"

"No."

Baker objected to my inquiring into his state of mind.

"Why were you unable to continue with the examination?"

Baker said, "Don't answer that. That assumes he was unable to continue with the examination. He is entitled to take a break."

I asked him directly, "Why did you request a break during that part
of the examination?" I was hoping to provoke him again.

"Don't answer that," Baker insisted again. Simpson mouthed something to his attorney. It was, "I can answer it."

"Excuse me?" I said to Simpson.

Baker thought I was talking to him. "I said, 'Don't answer that.'"

"He whispered something," I said.

Like a kid caught in the cookie jar, Simpson said, "No, I did not."

"You mouthed something," I told him.

"I think I'm allowed to mouth something to myself, aren't I?"
Sophomore high school petulance.

After his momentary blackout about how he broke the bathroom
glass, Simpson's memory returned in full force as to how—and why—he
tried to clean it up. He said he took some toilet paper and a towel and
tried to scoop the shards off the countertop so he could "put the stuff in
the travel bag."

"You remember that distinctly?"

"That's the only reason I took the time to sweep the stuff out of the way."

I asked him to demonstrate how he balled up toilet paper and disposed of the glass pieces. Baker objected. "On what theory?" I asked.

"Because he doesn't have to. This is not show-and-tell time. This is just tell time."

Obviously, a demonstration would have made an already cockamamie story even more absurd, and Baker refused to permit his client that humiliation.

EIGHT

"Those Ugly-Ass Shoes"

ownstairs, the media was getting restless. Simpson and his people, who would have liked this entire case tried inside a dark
cave, wanted no part of them. It was up to us to meet the press.
I was still uncomfortable talking about a deposition in progress. Mike
Brewer typically would go down and brief the reporters on what had happened during the sessions. Mike wore his hair in a striking pompadour and,
some members of the press corps told me, strode to the podium like a head
of state, so the press nicknamed him "Pompidou." He also spoke at length,
giving commentary, detail, and ambiance even when there was not a lot of
news to break. The press appreciated his presence for its informational content—in fact, they appreciated his just showing up each day to give them
something to report—but cynics that they are, they could not refrain from
commenting on his lack of brevity. His alternate nickname was "Brouhaha."

John Kelly got another nickname. He was born John Quinlan Kelly,
John Q. Kelly, but when members of the press divined his appetite for ink
and airtime, some of them began calling him "John Q. Public." Plus, even
though there were ample sweets and refreshments on the tenth floor, at
some time each day Kelly usually found it preferable to take the elevator
downstairs, walk through the gauntlet of reporters to the magazine shop
across the Trident Center courtyard, and buy a candy bar from Nick, the
proprietor. He would then turn around and walk back. The media, shut

out of the deposition room and desperate for images to show on that evening's broadcast, would surround him both ways, constantly training their cameras on him and throwing questions, following Kelly back and forth across the plaza in a newshounds' scrum.

This daily routine wasn't lost on Bob Baker, a man with an appealing if acerbic sense of humor. "Kelly," he would call after him. "Hey, Candy Man! Going down for a candy bar, Candy Man?" Somehow the press got hold of that name, too.

One of my concerns about talking to the media at the end of the day was that the defense might use the press conferences as an excuse to ask the court to revisit the issue of sealing the depositions. So for a while I left the press conferences to Brewer and Kelly. The defense, except for the constant barbs, seemed to accept it. Several days into Simpson's deposition, a reporter for the *New York Daily News,* Michelle Caruso, called me late at night. Caruso had been sent out to cover the criminal trial on a day's notice with only the clothes on her back and had stayed for two years, reporting, developing leads, and becoming an unofficial Simpson trial expert; everything there was to know about the Simpson case, Michelle was on to. Her sources were wide, varied, and reliable, her insights were sharp and apt, and her sympathies were with the prosecution.

I had been introduced to Michelle by Kim Goldman, who buttonholed me after one of the first hearings before Judge Haber and assured me that Michelle could be trusted: "She's a good guy and she's on our side."

Being on our side was an important attribute. I was always extremely careful if I was talking to a journalist who I thought believed Simpson was not guilty. They had access to the defense, and whatever I might say, they could go tell Simpson and his lawyers. If I gave a reporter a piece of information based on confidential communication and said, "This is in confidence," I never knew if they were going to keep their word. The system is built on honor, and some people have more of that than others.

Off the record, on the record, confidential source, without attribution, deep background—all these phrases have specific meaning to journalists, and I had to learn the rules of the game quickly in order to play with the media. I was still new to this field, and although a fairly quick study, this was a complicated business. I tried to find out, if they would tell me, each journalist's own leanings. Whenever possible, I wanted to make sure I wasn't dealing with the enemy.

Journalists have private leanings like everyone else, but it is their job, when reporting on the case, to separate those feelings from the facts. As I got to know them better, I found that most members of the media believed Simpson was guilty. They had to check themselves constantly when reporting, to make sure that they presented their stories in a fair and balanced fashion. In their attempt to balance, they often overcompensated and gave Simpson too much leeway.

Michelle Caruso thought Simpson was dead guilty. She also thought I was being far too reticent with the press. In the eyes of the public, she said, the only lawyer they saw on TV discussing the deposition was Mike Brewer, therefore Brewer must be the man in charge. I was doing the questioning, but he—and his client, Sharon Rufo—were being identified with the case. Michelle told me on the phone, "Rufo is a very unpopular figure. You really ought to start going down there or the Goldmans' face on the case could get eclipsed. The reporters are calling you a mystery man. Why don't you come down, talk, and set the record straight?" I thought her point was sincere.

So I began meeting the press each afternoon at the end of the deposition sessions. I was careful in my remarks, because there are ethical rules establishing the parameters of what lawyers are permitted to say concerning pending cases. It would, for example, be inappropriate to misstate the testimony for the purpose of prejudicing a possible jury. I didn't want to give the defense any chance to delay our trial.

At the same time, I recognized I was smack in the middle of one of the most high-profile cases in our history. The public not only wanted, but demanded, information. There was no way we could keep information from them, even if we'd wanted to. They were going to get it in some form or another. By giving it to them ourselves, we had a better chance of controlling how it came out.

As my role became more visible, reporters would seek me out at every chance, sometimes even phone me in the conference room at the end of the deposition day. "Are you coming down?" That was going too far, but I realized and came to accept that working with the media was an important part of this case. They were the eyes and ears of the public, they were here to stay, and they could not be ignored. Halfway through the deposition process, someone at my firm provided a lectern for the daily press conference, with my firm's name—Mitchell, Silberberg & Knupp—

emblazoned on its front, to publicize our efforts. I was always scolding reporters for not mentioning the firm's name in their reports. That was a big joke in the press corps, Caruso told me. Apparently, they didn't see it as their job to drum up business for MSK. "Can you believe that guy? He thinks we're going to put the name of the firm in every story, and he bawls us out if we don't!" Media, I learned early on, could be an invaluable source of information about your case. Michelle was a tremendous help in this regard, and we built a relationship of trust and confidence. She gave me leads, information, and gossip she had heard around town, as well as facts and insights that I had not gleaned from the criminal trial. I spoke and met with her often just to pick her brain. She was a walking compendium of the case, and while our purposes were somewhat different— she was trying to write stories for her newspaper and I was trying to win the case—she was extremely valuable.

After the first couple of days, the atmosphere in the deposition room got less tense. I made a conscious effort to pursue a more friendly approach with Baker. I smiled, even made small jokes, and didn't fight on issues I thought were pointless. It appeared that the better way to elicit information from Simpson was not to piss off his lawyer, so I pulled back a little. Baker backed off, too, and things began to run more smoothly.

Simpson, having now gotten used to the sessions' pace and tenor, eased up as well, if not during the deposition itself, then certainly when he was off the record. He would come in after the breaks, singing pop tunes. Songs like "Blue Moon." He couldn't carry much of a tune, but he had a deep baritone voice that he used to effect. He was putting on a show, as if to say, "I'm not nervous. This means nothing to me." Whistling past the graveyard.

When the video camera was off and Simpson was waiting for the lawyers to file in, the legal pads to come out, and the testimony to resume, he and his guys would sit around and talk sports, mostly golf, which was at the top of Simpson's interests. He and Baker would draw pictures of golf courses, designing holes, discussing various golfing stances. Brewer and Kelly are both good golfers, so they would join in occasionally. They were more at ease in dealing with Baker and Simpson than I was. At times, there was quite a bit of kibitzing across the table. Simpson once said we could settle this case right now with an all-or-nothing golf match. "Hey, you want to settle this case? Me and my lawyer against the two of you," he said to Brewer and Kelly. Though he was kidding, you could see the glimmer of hope on his face that they just might accept the challenge, and this whole thing would go away. I tried not to join in. I was uncomfortable engaging a killer in personal banter. Besides, I was lousy at golf.

Baker, like many of Simpson's friends, called him "Juice." "Juice, what do you think about that?" "Juice, that play you made was amazing." "Hey, Juice, I can't believe the picture of you on the cover of *Sports Illustrated,* where you were in that position and your body's contorted in a way I didn't think it was possible!" He treated Simpson with complete adulation. Their side of the table was always lighthearted, as if two people hadn't been killed, as if this was all a big joke. "Juice." I hated hearing that name. It was a reminder that he had gotten away with it.

Still, Simpson tried to seduce us with his personality. It was no secret that I am a big sports fan, and I had once told Baker that I had been a big O.J. Simpson fan. Perhaps Simpson thought he could use his charm to his advantage; if I liked him, maybe I wouldn't have my heart in it. He didn't make conversation with me, but he would make comments to others in the room, knowing I would hear.

He and his lawyers would trade sports trivia questions. I am as guilty, if not more guilty, than anyone of building up sports heroes, idolizing them, and living vicariously through them. I have been watching and reading about sports all my life, and I'm pretty good at sports trivia. Despite my deep antipathy for the man, part of me wanted to be part of that conversation. And I'm sure Simpson knew it. It would have been easy to join the crowd, call him "O.J.," sit there and bullshit with a Hall of Fame athlete. The scary thing is, I could see how difficult it was to resist him. *How would a jury be able to resist him?*

Dan Leonard, one of Simpson's lawyers and a likable guy, said to me half kidding, half not, "You know, if you wanted to come over to Rockingham after work one day, I don't think O.J. would mind. I think he'd like it."

As they say in the locker room, this case was a gut check.

Even if he were serious, I never would have accepted such an invitation. I had become too immersed in the case and my client's anguish to hobnob with a double murderer. But the idea of going over there, hanging out, and talking sports was tempting, and I knew there were many people who would like nothing better.

For all his chuckling, when the banter was over and the videotape went back on, Simpson once again lost eye contact and slipped back into his somber, trancelike, robotic mode.

By day three it was abundantly apparent to Baker and Simpson that the deposition would drag on for some time. Any hopes of it lasting just a few days were dashed. Early that day I was asking questions about Paula Barbieri and whether she had wanted to go to Simpson's daughter Sydney's dance recital on June 12. "Did you invite her to go with you?" I asked.

"No."

"Did she ask to go?"

"No."

"Why didn't you invite her?"

"Because I didn't invite her."

"She was your girlfriend then. Right?"

"True."

"You had a monogamous relationship with her at that time. Is that right?"

"With who?"

"Paula."

"Monogamous?"

"Yeah," I said. "She was the only woman you were dating. Correct?"

"Yes, correct."

"How long had you been in a monogamous relationship with her as of June 11?"

Baker interrupted. "I assume you mean by 'monogamous' that that was the only person he was dating? Because that's what you just said."

"Only person you were romantically involved with," I clarified.

"Okay. Fine," said Baker.

I couldn't understand how his gloss changed my question at all. I had the feeling he had won a point, but I didn't know what it was. "Am I missing something, Mr. Baker?"

"Sir," Baker said with a jaunty smile, "I don't think you've missed a hair on Mr. Simpson's face so far. You have redefined tedium."

"The truth is in the details," I replied. Then, to Simpson, "You may answer."

He may actually have looked at me. "What was the question? I'm sorry."

For the life of me, I couldn't remember. "I forgot," I told him. "So did I."

The court reporter repeated the question: How long had the relationship been monogamous? Simpson answered, "She's the only girl I had sex with . . . for probably the previous four weeks."

"When you say 'girl,' you mean girl or woman?" He always referred to women as "girls," and I decided to call him on it.

"Woman, yes." He stood corrected.

"Previous four to six weeks?"

"Not four to six weeks. Three to four weeks." His period of monogamy was shrinking as we spoke.

The night following day three of Simpson's deposition, he gave his first television interview since the murders, on the cable network Black Entertainment Television. He had such media power, and had lately been so cloistered, that whenever he spoke about the case he received tremendous attention, much more than any of us attorneys could amass in a month of press conferences. On television, being thrown softball questions, he sounded reasonable. He looked sincere. He worked the Simpson charm and came off, if you listened only to him, as a man with answers. I decided the scales needed balancing. I contacted the top legal affairs editor at the *Los Angeles Times*, Henry Weinstein, and offered him and his paper an exclusive on the Simpson deposition transcript.

Judge Haber had emphasized that all lawyers in the case should be mindful of the ethical proscriptions, that we should not take any action that would have the effect of tainting or prejudicing the jury pool. There was some concern in my mind that presenting the transcript to the *Times* might cross that line. However, I was also aware of a provision in the ethical rules allowing one side to respond to public utterances made by the other. I felt we were well within our rights, and our clients' rights, to release these transcripts in response to Simpson's radio and television appearances in which he pled his case. I had also seen Simpson's $29.95 video, being prepared for imminent release, in which he misled and lied to viewers for two and a half hours about the facts and evidence of our case. I knew that video would have wide distribution and considerable effect, and it was important to me to be very aggressive in leveling the playing field. After all, this was Simpson's own testimony I was releasing, not some phony video.

Weinstein and I negotiated. To counter Simpson and ensure maximum coverage, I wanted them to give us the front page. Weinstein couldn't commit to it but told me it was very likely. (What but a shooting war was going to knock O.J. under oath off the front page in Los Angeles?) I wanted the issues analyzed seriously and pointed out sections of the deposition to which I felt they should pay close attention. I told them they could call me if they had any questions; I had nothing to hide, and I wanted to make sure Simpson didn't put his spin on it. I exacted a commitment that they would read and analyze the examination substantively, rather than simply scanning the transcript for the print equivalent of sound bites. That was why I went to the *Times* in the first place. The *National Enquirer* might have paid $100,000 or more for these pages, but I knew the *Times* would do a smart job of analyzing them, and I knew their analysis would be good for us.

Another stipulation was that my firm's name be prominently mentioned. As the lawyer who took the deposition, my name would be plastered all over the transcripts and the articles, but I asked that MSK also be recognized. As a matter of general policy, Weinstein told me, the *Los Angeles Times* did not ordinarily engage in what they called "promotion" of law firms. However, this time they raised no objection whatsoever. I was approaching them with the first look inside the Simpson depo, and they wanted it badly.

Everybody was dying to know what was going on inside the deposition room. While this was not the dispositive cross-examination of Simpson, it was the first time hard questions had been put to him by an adversary, under oath. The *Times* accepted, acquiescing to our terms. Now everyone could be a fly on the wall.

The *Times* ran the edited transcripts and several lengthy articles, plus sidebars, on Saturday and Sunday, after the first week of Simpson's testimony, and it was big news. As I expected, the paper did a fair and balanced job of analyzing and critiquing the deposition. Once it hit the newsstands, the examination was also closely dissected by so-called experts, TV pundits, lawyers, and regular readers. After the excerpts came out in the paper, the transcripts themselves showed up on the Internet;

then other media sources got them, and they started to get flyspecked. As I feared, some people did not get it.

That Simpson did not have good explanations for much of the damning evidence did not resonate. The pundits focused on the moments he walked out of the room, or didn't listen to his lawyer's advice, or talked over his lawyer's objections. They were looking for little dramas rather than the actual substance of his answers, which was next to nonexistent. In their sniffing out sizzle, they missed the meat of the exam. He had answered all the questions and, if he hadn't been forthright, at least he had not gotten stumped; he hadn't blown up, he hadn't confessed, that was mostly what they seemed to care about. The examination *was* damning for Simpson, many people in the press gave him relatively good marks.

I wished he had gotten hammered, but I tried not to dwell on it. I understood that all they had was the cold, hard transcript. They couldn't see the vacancy in his eyes or hear the hollowness of his voice. They didn't understand that his answers could be shown to be provable lies.

On day five I was discussing Simpson's shoes. I asked him whether he had ever bought shoes at Bloomingdale's in New York. He said, "Dress shoes, and at one point I think I bought some winter boots."

How clever. He knew from the prosecution of the criminal case that it was our theory that the murder shoes, which had been identified by their unique soles as Bruno Magli, had been bought at Bloomingdale's. He knew they were a casual shoe, so to exclude the possibility of his having bought the murder shoes, he told us the only shoes he ever bought at Bloomingdale's were dress shoes and winter boots.

"Winter boots?" I asked.

"Yeah."

"What kind of boots?" If he was going to give us a run, I'd let him run and see where he went.

"I don't know."

"You don't know the name?"

"No."

"You're familiar with clothing manufacturers, aren't you?"

"Yes."

"You're a fashion-conscious person. Right?"

"Yes."

"You're in the public eye. Right? That's part of your career. Right?"

"Being in the public eye?"

"Yes."

"Yes."

"You like to dress nicely. Right?" I was playing to his vanity.

"Yes."

"And you can't tell me the name of the company that made your winter boots?"

"Exactly." Knowing there was no way I could prove he was lying, Simpson was free to be obstinate. Apparently, he didn't care whether his answer was believable, as long as it couldn't be *proved* false.

"Were they a brand name?"

"I don't know."

"What about your dress shoes?"

"What do you mean?"

"Were they brand-name shoes?"

"I don't know."

"What kind of dress shoes did you typically buy?"

"Loafers."

"Who made those loafers?"

"I don't know."

"You don't *know?*"

"True."

"You can't name a single company that made loafers that you owned?"

Simpson tried a little sidestep. "I've never walked into a shoe store in my life and asked for a pair of shoes by name, unless they were tennis shoes."

I pulled him back. "I didn't ask that."

"Well—"

"I didn't ask whether you asked for it by name. I asked whether you knew the name of any of the dress shoes that you have ever purchased." Any fashion-forward man about town would know that.

"I believe I've worn some Ballys. I believe I've had shoes called Ferragamos. I don't know if they would have been called Stacy Adams. I didn't know if wing tips are a brand name or not, or a style."

I went on, drawing this out. Finally I asked, "Have you worn shoes that you did not know the manufacturer of, or the brand name of?"

"I would assume so."

"The answer is you have?"

"I don't know. I would assume so. Since I don't know the names of the shoes, they could have been those. They could have been some other name."

"Including Bruno Maglis. Correct?" Simpson knew from the criminal case that there was no evidence directly linking him to purchasing or owning such shoes. No witness had seen him in them, no photographs had surfaced showing him wearing them. He was very comfortable with that. There was no way he was going to tell me, "Yes, I've owned Bruno Maglis. Yes, I owned the murder shoes." So the best I could do was get him to acknowledge that he *could not exclude* having owned Brunos. And so far, I was doing very well. If he didn't know his shoes' brand names and manufacturers, he was for all intents and purposes admitting that he might have had them in his closet.

"That would be in there, yes." If he had stopped right then, we would have been celebrating in the conference room next door. But he went on and messed it up. "I wouldn't know. I've never seen a pair of Bruno Magli shoes in my closet, and I've never looked for them." Was he saying he wouldn't know if he had Brunos or that, while he didn't know all his shoes' names, he knew none of them were Brunos? The meaning was fuzzy, and I had to make a quick command decision to stop or keep going.

"But Bruno Magli shoes would be in there. Correct?"

"I don't know. I've never—the only pair of—"

"Bruno Magli shoes would be included in shoes that you have worn that you did not know the brand name of."

"That's not correct at all! That's not correct at all! That's not what you asked, either. That's not what you asked, either!" Obviously, I had touched a nerve.

"Let me see the testimony, please," I asked the court reporter. "Let's not get excited."

Baker and I then got into a big argument over what had been said. We had the court reporter read it back and still could not agree on what was meant.

I rephrased the question. "There are shoes that you wore prior to Nicole's death that you did not know the name of the manufacturer of, or the brand name. Correct?"

"Yes," he said. "Correct."

"So, you would not know whether such shoes, that you did not know the name of, were Bruno Maglis. Correct?"

Answer: "Yes." I was satisfied with that. At least I got him to acknowledge, on the record, that some of the shoes in his closet might have been Brunos.

I asked him whether anyone had bought shoes for him. "USC," he said. He was being cute. He hadn't left Trojan cleat marks at Bundy. "The Buffalo Bills, and I can't think of anyone else."

Baker joined in. "Forty-niners, Juice."

Juice. Affectionately. Baker was behaving like another of the sycophants who had surrounded Simpson his entire adult life and who would ignore everything, including murder, so they could be his pal, the celebrity athlete.

Simpson contradicted him. "No. By then I was supplying my own shoes."

"No one but you bought shoes for yourself. Is that what you're saying?" I asked.

"Yes." He was trying to exclude any possibility that Nicole bought the shoes, just as she had bought the gloves that Simpson wore when he murdered her.

"Was that true for five years before Nicole's death?"

"Yes."

"Did you ever buy shoes that you knew were Bruno Magli shoes?" Having gotten him not to exclude owning the murder shoes, I was trying to take it to the next level by asking whether he'd ever bought any like them.

"No."

Next, a very simple, but always effective question. "How do you know that?" Simpson not only had to deny owning the murder shoes, he had to come up with a reason why he would not buy them.

"Because I know, if Bruno Magli makes shoes that look like the shoes they had in court that's involved in this case, I would have never owned those ugly-ass shoes."

It was another colloquial lapse meant to mock the formality of the proceedings, an especially colorful phrase that could get a laugh; a little ambiguous, very conversational. "Those ugly-ass shoes."

But I wasn't in a conversation, I was creating a record. I knew that, later on, we (not to mention all the pundits and analysts) would go back and dissect this record one hundred thousand different ways to see where Simpson lied and how we could prove his lies and this required that my questions be precise and specific. On an issue as important as this, I did not want Simpson to have any room to offer a different or embellished answer at trial. So I bore in on the "ugly-ass" shoes.

"You thought those were ugly-ass shoes?"

"Yes," he smirked.

"Why were they ugly-ass shoes?" When I said it, I was deadpan. Already the phrase seemed to embarrass him.

"Because in my mind they were."

"What about them was ugly, Mr. Simpson?"

"The look of them, the style of them."

"What about the style?"

"I don't know. They were ugly to me." He seemed to get impatient. "Aesthetically, I felt they were ugly, and I guess beauty is in the eye of the beholder, and to me they were ugly shoes."

I tried to pin him down deeper. "Was there anything about the color of the Bruno Magli shoes that you saw in court that you said made them ugly?"

"I don't know. They were a bluish green, I believe, but no—maybe." He couldn't make up his mind how to play this. Why would he never have bought Bruno Maglis, aside from the fact that they were the murder shoes and to admit owning them would have put one more nail in his coffin? "I guess aesthetically, it was the whole thing together, they were not really attractive shoes."

"It wasn't the color, necessarily. Right?"

"No."

"It wasn't the style of shoe?"

"For the most part, yes."

"And what about the style?"

"Just aesthetically. I don't know. I looked at it. I didn't like it. . . . To me, aesthetically, I didn't like the shoe. Nothing specific. I didn't study it. I looked at it, and I didn't like the shoe."

Good. I didn't want him to base "ugly-ass" only on the shoe's color, I wanted him to exclude the Bruno Magli type and style of shoe across the board. He was on record: He would never own "those ugly-ass shoes." He could never withdraw or change this position without suffering devastating impeachment on a crucial piece of evidence. He would have to stick to this position until the bitter end. And we would have to prove that he was lying through his teeth about it.

After five days, on Friday, January 25, Simpson's deposition was nowhere near being completed. I needed at least another two days to complete my questioning, and both Brewer and Kelly needed time to do their questioning. The court had ordered the deposition be held day by day, which meant it would be carried forward from one day to the next if it was not completed, but Baker played hardball. He wanted to put the deposition off for a while. "And let's keep this on the record," he told us. "Mr. Simpson is not going to be here, I'm not going to be here, Mr. Leonard's not going to be here, nor is Mr. Blasier going to be here, so you can take whatever solace you want in that. . . . Mr. Brewer, you can be unreasonable and obviously tell the press anything you like."

"First of all," Brewer told him, "we don't need those comments on the record, Mr. Baker."

"Well, I wanted to put them on the record."

I think Simpson may have had other commitments the following week, and rather than simply ask to reschedule, Baker pulled his usual macho routine and walked out at the end of the fifth day. We went to court to bring Simpson back, and it wasn't until February 22, almost a month later, that the deposition resumed.

By the second day of round two of Simpson's deposition, Bob Baker was more than restless. It is routine for the videographer to ask the counsel present to identify themselves and state whom they represent at the beginning of each day.

"Daniel Petrocelli for Plaintiff Fred Goldman."

"Arthur Groman for Plaintiff Fred Goldman."

"Michael Brewer for Plaintiff Sharon Rufo."

"John Kelly for Plaintiff Brown."

"Phil Baker for O.J. Simpson."

"Dan Leonard for Mr. Simpson."

"Bob Baker, held hostage, day 7, for O.J. Simpson."

After Simpson's deposition, things really loosened up with the media. During the criminal trial, Geraldo Rivera had devoted his hour-long nightly cable TV show, *Rivera Live,* to the case, discussing not only the sensational and titillating aspects, but also the law. Geraldo had a reputation as the King of Tabloid Television, and his daytime show seemed calculated to expand that title. His nighttime show, though, was completely different. I had tuned in occasionally during the criminal trial and been impressed with the commentary and analysis of the case. Discussing the case for an hour every night, Rivera was able to delve into it in great depth and detail. Now, even in this lengthy pretrial period, he was showing every inclination of continuing that trend on our case.

Rivera Live had a good pipeline to Mike Brewer, who seemed to be giving them almost real-time reports on the inside goings-on at the depositions. One of their producers, Linda Sittenfeld, didn't want to wait for the transcripts to come out, she would call at the breaks for updates.

Watching the show, I found that Rivera had good instincts when analyzing the facts and issues in the case. He also believed Simpson was guilty and said so—repeatedly.

He was also pretty funny. When the show would receive copies of the transcripts in printed miniscript form, four pages of transcript to one printed page, Rivera would have the camera zoom in on the text. He called this "depo cam." We thought that was hysterical, but apparently the Simpson camp didn't find it so amusing. I was told that Simpson was glued to the set. He and his attorneys—Phil Baker was over at Rockingham all the time, and Dan Leonard and Bob Blasier practically lived there—were beside themselves, sitting there, alternately cursing at the screen or laughing at Rivera himself.

Either way, the defense was clearly obsessed with Geraldo. They began calling him "Retardo" and insulted us for giving him information. "Why don't you call Retardo right now and tell him what happened?" Of course, the more it bothered them, the more we did it. I once had counted the references to Rivera in all the deposition transcripts, and they totaled more over 160, most of them by the defense. I wish there had been more.

Simpson was deposed for eleven days, total, and his testimony was the launching pad for our case. We fleshed out in detail his story about the events of June 17, including whether he contemplated killing himself, the writing of his "suicide" note, the contents of his black bag and how they came to be found on his person, the Xanax pills, the key to Nicole's condo, the green towel with blood on it, the underwear, and the clothing found in the back of the Bronco. We nailed down his version of the Bronco chase. None of his explanations was believable.

We grilled him on all the items of physical evidence, starting with his own body: all the cuts he had on his fingers and his inability to explain how they got there. I asked him hundreds of questions on the cuts alone, and he didn't have one satisfactory answer.

We explored his ownership of the leather gloves, shoes, hat, and sweatsuit used in the murder. He said he didn't own even innocent examples of any of them; he had given his gloves away and he never owned a dark sweatsuit. He said he didn't know if he had ever worn Aris Leather Light Isotoner gloves, the murder gloves found at the crime scene and at his home on Rockingham. "I could have."

"You wore warm gloves that fit snugly. Right?" I asked.

"If they fit, they fit. If they don't fit, they don't fit. I don't know what 'snugly' means."

"Seems like I've heard that before," I said.

"Then you must acquit," Baker beamed.

"You must acquit," Simpson echoed.

"I have a different theory about that," I told them.

Later in the deposition, Simpson said he routinely gave away clothes in New York at the end of each football broadcasting season. "And whom did you give them to?" I asked.

"Some to a guy named Fuhrman, believe it or not, and then other guys in the building. You put them in big bags and you take them downstairs. I don't know if they go to Goodwill, or the doormen go through them, or what."

"You're not saying you gave away a pair of Aris Light gloves to Mr. Fuhrman, are you?"

Baker broke in immediately. "Don't answer that!" He looked at me. "That's a great question, though."

"I couldn't resist it."

"I understand."

We questioned Simpson extensively about his ownership of guns and knives. To no one's surprise, he collected guns, not knives.

We questioned Simpson exhaustively on his relationship with Nicole, their history and chronology: their first meeting to their getting together, breaking up, getting back together, getting married, divorced, separated, reconciled. We grilled him about his history of domestic violence and his beating of Nicole, which he denied completely across the board. We confronted him with Nicole's diaries, which he disputed—"Why would she say such things?"—and he accused Nicole of manufacturing it all at the behest of her lawyers to cheat him in divorce proceedings. We questioned him about a written agreement he made with Nicole after the New Year 1989 beating, saying if he ever hit Nicole "hereafter" she could rip up their prenuptial agreement, which at the time would have cost him approximately $5 million. We spent a long time detailing his activities and interaction with Nicole in the last several months of her life: who broke up with whom, what happened on various days, how their relationship broke off for the last time just before her murder.

We asked about his relationship with Paula, how she came in and out of his life. He swore they were back together after his final split with Nicole.

Simpson was questioned about his activities on the days leading up to the murders: Thursday in Connecticut at the Swiss Army Company board of directors meeting; the free promotional knives he obtained there (which he denied), his encounter with a limousine driver concerning those knives (which he also denied); Friday, returning to Los Angeles, spending the night and next day with Paula Barbieri, not going to bed with her Saturday night, the two of them going back to separate homes. He denied they fought or argued, but first thing the next morning, Paula leaves an eight-minute message on his answering service telling him it is over between them. He denied receiving it. It all led to the events of Sunday, June 12. We covered everything he did that day. We went over all his actions and emotions of the night, blow by blow, from the time he went to his daughter's dance recital to his return to Rockingham, to the hour and a half between 9:30 and 11:00 when no one saw him and the murders were committed. He said that around 10:00 he took "three, four, five" used golf balls from the trunk of his Bentley and practiced his golf game there by the light from his garage. He had everything up to and including the brand of ball ("Maxfli 100s") and his choice of clubs (a Callaway pitching wedge, "I was looking for a sand wedge") down to a mantra. "I chipped a couple . . . five or six yards, brought them back, then I hit a couple into the sand . . . when I say 'a couple,' two or three one way and then whatever was left the other way. . . . I sculled one of them and it hit [his children's playground] equipment, I don't know where it went. . . . One or two I tried to hit over my tree into the yard across Ashford." He remembered the ball traveling between "forty and seventy yards, I would say."

Simpson said he got his cell phone from his kitchen, walked outside, and called Paula Barbieri from his driveway. He got no answer and left a message on her machine. He took four to six golf balls and a windbreaker from the trunk of the Bentley, put them in a blue-gray bag, put other golf balls in a white bag, and left both on the ground behind the car. With a three-wood in his hand and his cell phone in his pocket, he then went out the Rockingham gate and walked his dog Chachi ("She took a dump"). Considering his vagueness surrounding the breaking of the glass in Chicago, his detailed recall of the most minute details during this critical time was remarkable.

We covered everything Simpson said happened when he got into the limousine, arrived at the airport, got on the plane, and arrived in Chicago. Minute by minute. He was questioned about all his items of luggage he took to and from Chicago—the Louis Vuitton bag, a suit bag, his black grip, the golf bag, and the mysterious bag that Kato Kaelin and limo driver Allan Park saw but has never been seen again. Exactly which pieces went to Chicago, how they got there, which pieces came back, how they returned. We asked about the clothing he wore to Chicago and the clothing he wore back.

We made him recount his activities the entire time he was in Chicago—his arrival at the airport, the limo drive to the hotel, his room, his being informed by the Los Angeles police of Nicole's death, his subsequent flurry of phone calls to lawyers and friends, his conversations with the limousine driver who could not pick him up on time, his deep interest in his golf bag. We asked him about his flight back to Los Angeles, his conversations and contact with the LAPD, his meetings and conversations with friends and advisers. We asked him everything, often more than once.

For his part, Simpson probably thought he had done well. He had gotten through the deposition without having been forced to throw a fit or confess or do something obviously incriminating. I'm sure he felt he had handled me without difficulty and thought he would have no problem facing off at trial. Good. We chose not to confront Simpson with his many contradictory statements to Detectives Vannatter and Lange. Confrontation was not our goal. We were obtaining the raw materials, laying the groundwork to build our case for the jury, later, at trial, when it counted.

In the end, what emerged was that, despite his denials, Simpson did not have good explanations for the incriminating evidence. He didn't have credible explanations that pointed to innocence. No believable explanation for the cuts. No explanation at all for why there were pictures of him wearing the same gloves worn by the murderer, and no idea where "his" pair might be. He didn't know exactly how he cut himself, how "a glass broke," yet he knew exactly what he did every second between nine-thirty and eleven, when the murders were committed, including the sequence of golf clubs he used while supposedly sculling balls in the dark on his property. He acknowledged there wasn't a single living human being who could account for his whereabouts between 9:30 and 11:00 that night.

He gave embarrassing denials of ever having hit Nicole; these would make it easy for us to prove he was a liar. He previewed his Trashing of Nicole defense—pointing the finger at her, her lifestyle, and her friends as the cause of her death—but was unable to provide a shred of evidence to back it up. He couldn't point to any individuals with whom she had any serious conflict or problems in her life, other than himself.

There was nothing in his deposition that remotely pointed to the identity of any other possible killer. Simpson told the world, in a prepared statement read by his son on the occasion of his acquittal of criminal charges, that he would devote a great part of his life to finding the "real killer." He couldn't point to one thing he had done, from that moment to the time of this deposition, to find such a person. He couldn't point to a single piece of solid evidence that said, "Look, this shows I am innocent." Nothing. Nothing at all.

On top of that, Simpson did not live up to his billing as a charming, seductive communicator. He didn't look good as a witness. He slumped in his chair, stared vacantly, delivered answers robotically, and showed no energy, no punch. He did not take this deposition as an opportunity to sell his innocence.

He also called Mike Brewer an asshole. Brewer had been grilling Simpson, again, on the cuts he said he received in Chicago, and the defendant still couldn't remember at what point in the process he had received them. Brewer asked if Simpson had been "a little squeamish" when he saw the blood. "No," said Simpson. "My mind was on other things that was more pressing."

"That was Nicole, the loss of your ex-wife?"

Baker admonished him, "He's gone over that fifteen times."

"Well," said Brewer, "I don't know whether it's his travel arrangements or his ex-wife."

At which point Simpson said, "You're really being an asshole right now."

Ten minutes later, Baker got in the spirit of things and called him an asshole, too. "Well," Brewer said, "that's two of you."

For the next two days, Brewer got to wear the curses as a badge of honor. He was proud, I was jealous. I told Mike, "I wish he'd called *me* an asshole!"

This was not the charismatic "Superstar in a Rent-a-Car." This was a lying witness, a lying murderer.

So while he didn't confess, lead us to the murder weapon, break down, or throw anything at me, my verdict was that he was vulnerable as a witness at trial. I felt that with a carefully constructed cross-examination and all the facts in our hands, he could be beaten. Provided we could build the case to show that most of what he said was lies.

Demonstrable lies. Not lies because we *said* they were lies, or lies because they were improbable; we had to prove Simpson told *demonstrable* lies. We needed witnesses to contradict him and documents to impeach him. If you sat and listened to Simpson's story, it was completely unbelievable, it made no sense. We needed a jury who would rely on their common sense. And before that, we needed a jury who would listen.

NINE

Faye Tells the Truth

During the twenty-six-day hiatus between Simpson's deposition sessions, the case kept rolling. The defense deposed both Fred and Kim Goldman. Their purpose, I suspected, was to try and find dirt on Ron.

To the Goldman family, this case was about one thing: the life and death of Ron Goldman. It would be a witness, in some sense, to his life—to what he accomplished and what he was, how he died—and why he was not here with us anymore. So it was vital that Ron be portrayed honestly. This was the only case he would ever have. Because he had been killed with O.J. Simpson's ex-wife, an ordinary citizen crumpled next to a celebrity's spouse, he initially became known as "the second victim," when he was mentioned at all. This infuriated Fred and the family; Ron had a name, they wanted him to be called by his name. He was not just some other person.

Ron had been the subject of ludicrous rumors regarding his sexuality and supposed drug use; it was very important to the Goldman family to set the record straight. I wanted to see how far Simpson and his attorneys were willing to go to try to muddy his name.

Not far. And rightly so. Ron led a very clean life. He didn't drink, and he didn't use drugs. He was a healthy, handsome, twenty-five-year-old guy who worked out, watched what he ate, then walked in on a murder and was himself killed. To the best of both Kim's and Fred's knowledge, he was friendly with Nicole, but they did not have a romantic relationship. There was really nothing more to tell.

I, of course, was very protective of Ron, his reputation, and his family. As I grew closer to the Goldmans and to the case, I shared more of their loss and grief for this young man I never knew. I had listened to the messages left on his answering machine June 13, as word of the murders leaked out. His friends first heard rumors that he might be a victim, then they learned the truth. The messages were heart-wrenching. Ron's outgoing message said, "Hi, this is Ron. I've stepped out. You can page me at 888-5241. Thanks. Have a good day." The background music was Tears for Fears.

His friends kept calling:

"Hey, Ron. It's about 10:45. I was curious if you wanted to come to work today. So, talk to you later. Bye."

"Ron, Ron, what's going on? Where are you, Ron? I hope it's not you, Ron."

"Hey," it was his girlfriend, Andrea Scott, "I'm coming home tomorrow. I don't know if they're playing a joke because you have the car and the keys and everything, but call me. I'm going to try paging you." His pager must have buzzed a moment later, somewhere in the property section of the morgue.

"Hi. It is Patti. I—I—I—I—I need to talk to you. I'm not sure if what I'm hearing is right."

"Ron, this is Jeffrey. If you are dead, man, you'll hear from me up above. I love you, man. I just heard on the news right now. My fingers are crossed and I'm hoping it's not you. Trying to get ahold of your parents. Love you, man. Take care."

"Hey, Ronnie, I don't know if you're ever going to get this or not. Oh, man, please call me. Let me know what's going on."

Listening to those messages brought the reality of this tragedy to life for me.

At the very end of Kim's brief deposition she was asked, "You believe O.J. Simpson murdered your brother?" Her response was, "Yes."

"You have a lot of hate for him, don't you?"

My first reaction was to object. I instinctively did not want her to answer. One way to attack a witness's veracity is to show he or she is biased against your case or client, then you can argue that the witness has a reason or motive to fabricate or lie. The defense was simply trying to get her to admit she was biased against Simpson. I asked for a break.

In the conference room Kim told me, "Dan, I do hate him. He murdered my brother. I hate him more than anything in the world."

She stopped me cold. I said, "You're absolutely right." She had every reason to hate him, and whether they wanted to charge her with bias was beside the point. I was reminded for the thousandth time that this was not a case about lost profits. She was being totally honest. Of course she hated him. "Go in and say that," I told her. "That is how you feel."

"I absolutely hate the man," she said on the record when we returned.

"And you'll say anything to make sure that he is found responsible for that death, true?"

"No," she said simply.

Simpson and Baker always berated Fred Goldman. They thought he was a publicity hound. They were always taking shots at him, things like "He hasn't met a microphone he didn't like" or "Okay, Fred, time to go down and hit those microphones." They couldn't stand him. The reason, of course, was that he was relentless in telling the world their client was a killer. He hounded Simpson for being a killer who got off, and he embarrassed his attorneys for representing him.

Which is why I was quite surprised that Fred's deposition was even more brief and perfunctory than Kim's. He was questioned mainly about the monetary damages part of the case, which, if Simpson lost, would require him to pay a sum of money representing—put in cold legal terms—the lost value of the relationship that Ron had with each of his parents. I had counseled both Fred and Kim not to use their depositions for venting anger and feelings of disgust toward Sharon Rufo. The defense would have loved that. But even here, the defense questioning was brief and superficial. Fred's and Kim's depositions were over in three hours. I surmised they had elected to save their best attacks for trial and not preview them in deposition. We would not be caught off guard at trial, I told myself.

Faye Resnick became the poster child for Simpson's criminal case defense. Rather than testify, she had written a book for money. The book described the tumultuous relationship between her close friend, Nicole, and O.J.

Simpson—how Simpson degraded, beat, stalked, and threatened to kill Nicole, revealed many inner secrets shared by Faye and Nicole, including a purported lesbian episode between them. Faye never testified under oath. The prosecution, believing the book had destroyed her credibility as a witness, never called her. The Brown family was upset with the book and initially denied its assertions. The defense tried her in absentia, savaged her, saying she was a druggie, an unsavory person, a bad friend to Nicole, and the reason for Nicole's problems. Simpson, over and over in print and television interviews and in his video, went so far as to say the answer to Nicole's death "lies in the world of Faye Resnick." He and his surrogates relentlessly and successfully assassinated her character to the point that, as far as the public was concerned, anything she said was suspect.

I was still reading massive amounts of material from the criminal case: interviews, reports, documentary materials, diaries, letters. The prosecutors and police detectives had interviewed the entire roster of Nicole's family and friends, as well as all of Simpson's friends who would speak to them. Then I read Faye's book, and it was dynamite. The essence of it rang true. Her stories about Nicole matched much of what I was reading; they confirmed Nicole's side of the story, while entirely eviscerating the spin Simpson was putting on everything.

I spoke with some of Nicole's friends about Faye, including Kris Jenner and Cynthia Shahian, and they told me Resnick was telling the truth. They quibbled with some of her comments and thought that others were exaggerated—they didn't know about the purported lesbian episode—but the gist of it, they told me, "It's true. Nicole would tell us the same thing." I decided I needed Faye's story told under oath for the first time. I decided to take her deposition.

Normally, a lawyer will not take a deposition of a friendly witness. Assuming the witness resides within the subpoena power of the trial court, lawyers will generally learn what the witness has to say from private conversations with her, and then call the witness to testify at the time of trial. If, before trial, the other side with whom the witness is not cooperative wishes to find out what she knows, they are the ones to request and take the deposition. So because Faye lived in Los Angeles and was extremely cooperative with the plaintiffs and despised Simpson and his lawyers, conventional wisdom dictated we keep her in our camp as a friendly witness and wait to see if the Simpson side took her deposition.

But this was not a conventional case, and Faye was anything but a conventional witness.

In the criminal trial, rather than testify, Faye holed up in Vermont, writing her book, and was out of reach of subpoena. Now, she had just completed and was about to publish her second book about the Simpson saga. I didn't want to take the chance that she might get spooked and elect not to testify for us. I wanted the option of using her testimony, because if she stuck to what she had said in her book, I was confident it would be helpful.

On the other hand, there was considerable risk associated with deposing Faye. After my questioning, the defense, I fully expected, would come after her with everything they had, to demonstrate she was a liar with a personal vendetta against their client. If Faye did not hold up well under fire, her testimony might end up being more harmful than helpful. Once I put her story on record, if she was not available to testify at trial, the defense could present their own edited portion of her videotaped deposition to the jury.

The rap on Resnick was that she was drug addled and, by writing a book rather than testifying, had "sold out." Baker and his boys constantly vilified her. "Oh, can't wait till you call Faye Resnick. Make my day. Please call her." But if they were trying to bluff me off deposing her, there had to be a reason.

I had met Faye at a fund-raising party for the Ron Goldman Justice Fund about a month earlier, and when I got her on the phone to discuss testifying, she balked. I said, "Look, this is the last chance we're ever going to have in a court of law to find Simpson responsible as the killer you think he is. It's now or never. You didn't testify at the criminal trial—okay, that's past, that's behind us. Now we have the civil trial. This is the last chance."

It turned out she was not averse to going on the record, but she was concerned for her safety. She said she was getting threatening messages and phone calls, and she feared getting harmed, maybe even killed. So she wouldn't stay in one place, she was moving all around, in and out of California. Whether or not she was actually in danger, these were her fears, this was the reality I was dealing with. After several calls I said, "We don't have to do it in L.A. We can do it anyplace in the country."

"Oh, we can?" That surprised—and seemed to please—her.

The next time we spoke, she said she had talked with Geraldo Rivera. She said Rivera would put her up in a hotel in New York, pay her expenses and airfare, and provide security. Faye, in turn, would appear on Geraldo's daytime and nighttime shows. I said, "Well, if that's the deal you made, that's fine. I don't really care, so long as none of this interferes with your testimony in the deposition, and there are no conditions or strings attached. In other words, you're not promising to say certain things just to make the television appearances more entertaining."

"No," she said, "absolutely not."

I made plans to take her deposition in New York City and arranged for Leonard Marks, a prominent New York attorney, to represent her.

The night before the deposition, we talked on the phone again. I was confident that if she simply testified to what she had written in her book, she would do fine. She was terrified at the prospect of Simpson sitting there in the room with her. I explained he had a right to be there, and likely would be. "Just ignore him, Faye. Don't even look at him, not one time," I counseled her. She was also concerned about how the defense would treat her. "Don't expect them to ask you about the facts of the case," I told her, "they're going to try to destroy your character. They're going to ask about your history with drugs. Just tell them exactly what happened." I had done my homework and learned that, contrary to public opinion, she had not been irresponsible. On the contrary, she had been to several treatment centers in an attempt to rid herself of drugs. Unfortunately she had a history of relapsing.

I thought her story was sympathetic and compelling. She had been clean for several years, from 1991 until a month before the murders, when she had had surgery and begun taking medication for the pain. That started her back on cocaine, a month or so before Nicole's murder. She said her cocaine addiction weighed in at $20 a day, and in her relapse she had spent a total of $200 before Nicole and her other friends organized an intervention and she went back into a treatment center several days before the murders. We were talking about minuscule amounts of cocaine in a town where people—including, according to his friends, Simpson himself—used that drug and others in significant doses. Far from dealing with some exotic and dangerous drug pusher, Faye had bought her small amounts of cocaine from a Brentwood real estate agent.

During the criminal trial and continuing through the civil case, the defense flew ridiculous rumors and theories involving Colombian drug lords. This was the fabled "in the world of Faye Resnick" solution. Somehow these murders were supposed to be tied to a drug hit by cartel hit men ordered on Faye (who, by the way, looks nothing like Nicole), even though Faye was in a treatment center the night of the murders. Cochran went so far in the criminal case to suggest in his questions that Nicole was killed by a knifing maneuver called the "Colombian necktie." It was laughably absurd baloney, but the defense would shout these theories, the press would repeat them, and they would be argued on national television so people would hear this nonsense and ascribe it some weight.

Anyone who knew the facts knew it was a joke. The Cali cartel hardly was sending professional killers to slice up Brentwood thirtysomethings over $200 worth of blow.

I told Faye, "Go ahead, tell the truth and don't worry about it. You've got nothing to hide, let them trash you, but just tell it all; it looks worse if you're evasive."

For all their hot talk, the only defense attorney who showed up to examine Faye Resnick was Dan Leonard. Simpson was also a no-show. They knew this could be their one and only shot at her, that she easily could make herself unavailable to show up at trial; whatever cross-examination would have to be done here. The fact that they never made any attempt to take her deposition signaled to me that, while they took every opportunity to attack her in public, they didn't really have anything on her. If she had information damaging to our case, they would have raced to find her and put it on the record. Their sparse showing at the deposition told me they were shooting blanks.

Faye arrived at the deposition accompanied by two very large, husky men who waited in the reception area while she testified. She wore a beige wool sweater ensemble, with a matching scarf tied around her neck. Her bangs hung over her eyes. She looked like a movie star.

I began the questioning and had her tell her whole story. To preempt much of the anticipated cross-examination, I brought out that in the over two-year period covering her accounts of Nicole and O.J.'s problems, she was sober the entire time and only started taking drugs in the last few weeks prior to the murders. This would enable us to argue that the effects of cocaine did not have any impact on her ability to perceive and recollect the events she was relating.

Faye did a great job. Many witnesses in the criminal case had been evasive and uncooperative, didn't want to get involved, lied to the police, were vague, indirect and difficult, hedged their bets, and were otherwise annulling prosecution witnesses. Many, even though they deep down thought Simpson was guilty, didn't want to alienate him. Others sold out, most notably Faye herself. But this time, Faye came through. Once she got in that room she was unwavering in her testimony. She had been Nicole's best friend during her last years with Simpson, she knew who he was and what he had done. She told it like it was. I admired her for that.

Faye and Nicole became close, she said, while Nicole was separated from and going through her divorce with Simpson in 1992. They confided in each other.

Faye had seen Simpson in a rage. At a sushi restaurant in Hermosa Beach, she recalled, Simpson had gotten so incensed over Nicole's simply mentioning the name of a man she had dated, that he lost control and started screaming at her in public. "It was as if a different person just took over," she said, "and it was like watching a man possessed. . . . His jaw would protrude, his teeth would clench, sweat would come pouring from his head. . . . He would perspire through his clothing. His eyes would get narrow and black. He became—the only way to describe it is—animalistic when he would become angry at Nicole. . . . It would happen within minutes. . . . He just became bigger than life. . . . I felt very small and insignificant. I felt afraid for myself."

The description illuminated the other side of Simpson, the dangerous counter to the smiling icon. And here was someone alive who had seen it. The vivid description had the ring of truth—it coincided exactly with one Nicole had told police when she summoned them to her home during one of his rages in October 1993. The police had surreptitiously taped both her and Simpson that day, and she had said, "When he gets this crazed, I get scared. . . . He doesn't even look like himself. All his veins pop out, his eyes are black, and he's just black and cold like an animal. I mean very, very weird." The parallels were eerie. Nicole told the police she called them to the house as a "precaution, more than anything. I think he wouldn't hit me again because he had to do community service and stuff like that for it." That was his punishment for the New Year's 1989 spousal abuse conviction. "I just got scared. I don't totally think I believe it would happen, but I get scared. I think if it happened one more time, it would be the last time." Eight months later, she was dead.

Faye said she met Ron Goldman twice, once when she and Nicole went dancing with him and his friends, and another time in front of a Starbucks. At Starbucks, Ron and his friends and Faye and Nicole were talking together when Simpson drove up in his Bentley, got out, walked over, and said to Goldman, "This is my wife!"

"O.J. used to get upset whenever Nicole was around any guys," Faye added, "so it was normal to us." She confirmed that Nicole and Ron were not romantically involved.

Marcus Allen was another story. Allen, an all-pro football player for the Oakland Raiders and Kansas City Chiefs, had followed Simpson as a star running back at the University of Southern California and approached his level of skill as a pro. The first time Nicole and Simpson separated in 1993, Nicole and Allen had a fling. Faye said Nicole had admitted this to Simpson after they reconciled later that year. This much was relatively widely known. Few people, if any, knew about a second affair. Faye testified, "Nicole started seeing Marcus Allen in the end, right before she died. . . . I was driving past Nicole's house and I saw Marcus's car parked in front of her house. . . . I called her and I asked her if that was his car, and she said it was, reluctantly. I told her . . . I felt she was setting herself up for murder."

"You told her that?"

Faye's eyes started to tear. "Yes, I did."

According to Faye, in the two weeks before Nicole died, she said that she was no longer seeing Simpson and that she loved Marcus Allen.

Allen was married at the time.

As a former drug user, Faye was very attuned to Simpson's drug use. She recounted under oath how in 1993, at the opening of the Harley Davidson Cafe in New York City, Simpson had pulled out a vial of cocaine at the table and snorted drugs in her presence. I asked her, generally, about Simpson's drug use. I did this to send a message that if he wanted to play the drug card, we could play it, too. "He said to me if I ever needed any coke, he always had it."

I asked what Nicole said about Simpson's drug use. "Nicole had said that O.J. was addicted to, from when he was a football star, that he became addicted to every pill there was, to uppers, to downers. She said he had a

'Christmas tree' jar full of every kind of pill. . . . He called it his 'Christmas tree' because it was every color of the lights that we would see on a Christmas tree. She said he needed to have pills to go to sleep, he needed to have pills to wake up, he needed to have pills for pain, he needed to have a lot of speed during the time that he was playing pro ball. She had essentially said that he was addicted to every kind of pill there was."

Nicole, she said, "took drugs once in a blue moon."

For all the talk of narcotics, in my analysis, Faye's, Nicole's, and Simpson's drug use were pretty much irrelevant to the case—unless Simpson was taking drugs the night of the murder and we could prove it.

The last few years, Simpson and Nicole's relationship had been rocky. Having been together some seventeen years, married for eight years, and separated and divorced in 1992, they had reconciled for a year, beginning in the spring of 1993. In April 1994, they took a trip to the Mexican resort Cabo San Lucas with Faye and other friends. Before the trip there had been talk that Nicole planned to move back into Rockingham. In anticipation of her return, Simpson had fired his longtime housekeeper, Michelle Abudrahm, who did not get along with Nicole, and replaced her with a woman named Josephine "Gigi" Guarin. Perhaps he was entertaining thoughts of remarriage. According to Simpson, the trip to Cabo with Nicole was wonderful. "We were like lovers. We were planning to be together. She was planning to move in. You know, we had the best sex," he said.

Apparently not. Faye recounted that Simpson had left Cabo for Los Angeles to shoot the television movie *Frogman,* in which he played a Navy SEAL adept at killing with knives. Nicole and Faye stayed behind with their children. In his absence Nicole had a quick fling with a guy named Bret. (Faye claimed she didn't know his last name. I was never able to track down this Bret.) Far from deciding to move in with Simpson and perhaps get remarried, Nicole told Faye in Cabo their relationship was finished. For good.

Faye described a long talk she had with Nicole at a restaurant called Palmilla just before returning to Los Angeles. For the first time, Nicole opened up and described in detail the full extent of Simpson's threats, mistreatment, and beatings. "From that night on," Faye said, "Nicole was a different person. She remembered all of the abuse. She had broken through that pearl that she had formed around the abuse and was now having a catharsis by telling me about it. . . ."

"[He] had threatened her life many a time, threatened to take her children away from her. He had beaten her too many times to count, he had locked her in a closet and beat her with wine bottles. He had bruised her, broken her ribs, sent her to the hospital, made her tell the doctors that she had fallen off a bicycle; . . . he beat her, kicked her, slapped her, pulled her hair, threw her in the closet and left her there for fifteen minutes, and then he came back and opened the door and she thought he was going to let her out and he started beating her again, and he continued doing that all night long. . . . She thought that he was going to beat her to death that night. . . .

"She told me about pregnancy beatings, when he used to kick her in the stomach and tell her that she was worthless. . . .

"Nicole said that she had been at a party with O.J. in Las Vegas and there were a lot of important people there, and she had embarrassed him in some way in front of Dean Martin. . . . And when he came to the room she was in her panties, getting undressed, and he just attacked her because he said that she embarrassed him, and viciously beat her that night, and he threw her outside in the corridor of the hotel and left her there. That's what she said."

Faye testified that on May 2, 1994, Simpson called her, beside himself, because after having such a great time in Cabo, Nicole was acting distant toward him and wasn't returning his calls. He was ranting. "I tried to calm him down," Faye said, "because at this point I was now afraid that he was going to harm me also, since he was blaming me and since he was screaming at me. . . . He didn't understand why Nicole had wanted to leave him, and I said—I couldn't keep it back any longer—I said, 'Because you have beaten her in the past, you have threatened her. She's afraid of you!'

"That's when he said, 'You lied to me! I know she's seeing another man, and if I catch her with another man before August, I will kill her.' Because she had humiliated him in the past . . . he would not let her humiliate him again in public by leaving him, especially because she begged him to come back. . . . [He said] that he couldn't take it and that he would have to kill her."

When Faye got off the phone, she told her fiancé, Christian Reichardt, that Simpson was very angry, that he had threatened Nicole's life, and that she was afraid he would go through with it.

Now, this was powerful evidence. But it was hard to tell whether and to what extent these accounts were exaggerated, whether in her zeal to make the point, Faye was adding hyperbole. I had heard most of these stories from other sources, with different details or variations—the celebrity was Frank Sinatra, not Dean Martin, for example. It was like the game of "telephone," in which you tell someone one thing and they tell someone else, and by the end the story is out of whack.

Unfortunately, because she had been attacked so viciously and often, I think she had become an advocate for herself as well as for Nicole. Nevertheless, I believed the core of what she was saying was true, and it was consistent with a great deal of other evidence I had seen. The message was right, the messenger had problems.

True or not, it would take a Herculean effort to get even 20 percent of what Nicole said to Resnick into evidence. Faye's personal observations were admissible, and she did see Simpson get verbally abusive and lose control, but she never saw him commit any physical abuse. Simpson's statements to Faye were admissible, but the statements made to her by Nicole were all hearsay—the only person who could verify her recollections of these conversations was dead—and I knew I would have to struggle very hard to get those before a jury.

On cross-examination, Dan Leonard did little to undercut her testimony. For sure, he tried to show her drug use was substantial and sustained, but he had no ammunition and scored few points. He pointed to some inconsistencies in various drafts of her book manuscripts, in an effort to suggest she was making it all up, but these were explained by the editing process. In the end, it was not a strong cross; they were not able to confront Faye with anything solid that would show she was lying. They had nothing on her.

In fact, the cross was so weak, I half suspected they were sandbagging me, trying to pretend they had nothing substantial in hopes of baiting me into calling Faye as a witness, then unleashing a furious attack. If so, that was a very risky game to play. If Faye Resnick were not available to be subpoenaed to attend trial—as was quite likely—the defense was stuck with her deposition.

Faye testified for three days, each time wearing a scarf, and with each successive session her bangs moved more and more off her forehead until on day three her face appeared totally open. When she was done, she left to do *Rivera Live* and try to get on with her life.

T E N

Katospeak

There was more controversy swirling around Kato Kaelin than anyone else but Simpson. People took sides. Most were angry with him, thinking that he knew the closely guarded inside story of what actually happened on Nicole and Ron's last night and that he withheld it to curry favor with his benefactor. Others felt he wasn't loyal enough. I read his criminal trial, grand jury, and pretrial hearing testimony, plus various police and press interviews. I also heard the audiotapes from the book he prepared with a writer, from which he ultimately walked away. Through it all, I found his story to be fairly consistent. I thought he was getting a bad rap.

As with Faye, I debated whether to take Kato's deposition or wait to see if Simpson would. Because I didn't know which way the winds might blow, I decided we should take the offensive and get him on record, so we had him subpoenaed. But before I took his deposition, I arranged to meet with him. I wanted to judge for myself whether he was holding out with crucial evidence as so many speculated.

Kato was represented by an experienced L.A. entertainment lawyer named Michael Plotkin, whom I respected. (He was also the father-in-law of a lawyer in my firm.) In his mid-fifties, Plotkin had been with Kato through all the ordeals from day one and was very loyal to his client, something of a father figure. He preached over and over to me that Kato was innocent of all the speculation and rumors people were saying about him.

The rumors surrounding Kato were far-reaching. I got a call from a New York journalist trying to run down one particularly popular story alleging that on the night of the murders, Kato drove Simpson in the Bentley to a Burger King, where they met a man named Ron X, who gave Kato some crystal methedrine for Simpson, who ingested it in the car. Of course, the toxicology report showed no such drug in Simpson's system, and Kato told me the story was completely false.

Kato said he himself had never even touched a drug, never took a hit of a joint, never did drugs whatsoever. As I learned more about his background, I concluded that, in spite of the California beach bum looks, he was a rather naive, relatively clean-cut goodhearted kid from Wisconsin. A thirtysomething basketball player with a twelve-year-old daughter. Not the brightest guy in the world, certainly not the most courageous or the most responsible, perhaps something of an opportunist, but not a druggie and not a dishonest person. More like a kid who never grew up.

He told me his story.

Kato met Nicole in Aspen, Colorado, in December 1992 shortly after Nicole's divorce from O.J. became final. Kato's friend Grant Cramer was attracted to Nicole, and he succeeded in winning over her affections. Kato tagged along, a kind of court jester who liked to have fun and party. Comic relief. Returning to Los Angeles, Nicole asked him if he would help out with baby-sitting her kids in return for staying in the guest house at her rental at 327 North Gretna Green Way, plus a little rent. Kato agreed.

He lived at Gretna Green throughout 1993 and became good friends to Nicole and her two small children, Sydney and Justin. He was very playful, and the kids loved him. Nicole often would invite him into the main house to talk. They would drink tea together, and Nicole would invariably turn the subject to her life with O.J. and the problems they had. One day she said, "I know how O.J. would kill me. With a scissors. If O.J. would ever kill me, he'll get away with it because he's O.J. Simpson."

Once, after double-dating—Nicole with Marcus Allen, Kato with another woman—they came home and, to Kato's surprise, Nicole said, "I think I'm falling in love with you."

As Kato described it: "I said, 'No, no, no, you're not. We're friends . . .'
I thought it was just she had said because I was good with the kids. And I
was on a date when it happened, and she said I was polite opening the door
and all that stuff, and I went—and I had the date in the room, so I said,
'No . . . I could not be romantic with you, and I think at this moment
you're just saying that,' because it was a night that we had gone out and had
drinks. . . .

"I took it as not a joke, but it wasn't plausible. I wasn't attracted to
her in a romantic way, and I think that's pretty much where it stopped. . . .
And the period after that, it was like no talking for a week because I had
said that."

Nicole moved out of her Gretna Green home when she bought the
condo at 875 South Bundy in January 1994. The place did not have a guest
house, but because Kato was so good with the kids and they had become
such good friends, she wanted him to move into Bundy, in a separate room.

By this time, Simpson and Nicole were in the middle of an
attempted reconciliation, and Simpson didn't want Kato living under the
same roof with his ex-wife and children. He offered Kaelin a better deal:
a bigger, nicer room in a separate guest house at Simpson's estate on
Rockingham—for free. Kato took it. Nicole was unhappy to be abandoned in favor of her ex-husband. Although she knew Kato moved out
because of Simpson's manipulations, she took it out on Kato, and their
friendship came to an end.

On the morning after the murders, Kato was awakened in his guest-
room on Simpson's estate by the four police officers who went over the
wall at Rockingham: Tom Lange, Phil Vannatter, Mark Fuhrman, and
Ron Phillips. He was briefly interviewed and then driven to the police station where he was interviewed by Detectives Paul Tippen and Brian Carr
in the morning and afternoon. He was not told Simpson was a suspect,
he had not spoken with any member of Simpson's entourage, and he had
no idea he was on the verge of becoming a key witness in the Trial of the
Century. Although the interview was not comprehensive—a consistent
problem I found when reading the LAPD's work—it gave essentially the
same details Kato repeated throughout the case.

I was heavily influenced by Kato's first statement. It seemed like the
purest evidence of what he really knew. If I fault him for anything, it's for
not going far enough, for not volunteering everything he knew to the

police at the very beginning. He had two choices: he could tell every little detail he remembered from the night before, or he could simply answer their questions. He chose the latter. I guess he didn't want to get involved or he was afraid he might become a central figure, which would have put him very uncomfortably on the hot seat. Courage was not one of his primary virtues.

Still, I formed the judgment that Kato was not implicated in any wrongdoing, that he had not seen Simpson in the act of killing Nicole and Ron, or, as some suspected, covered with blood, burying the murder clothes.

I was also influenced by the fact that Kato turned down about $1 million in offers from various tabloids and other media. Although he signed on to do a book, he pulled out at the last minute because the manuscript was, in his view, not accurate. The book was published anyway without his permission. But from what I could gather, he was *never* paid for information about the case. He received a few radio and television jobs, and although they came because of his newfound visibility, they did not focus on the Simpson case. He was not a wealthy man, yet he turned down $1 million. I don't know anyone else—not Simpson, not witnesses, not the lawyers, and not me—who did that. I think that says something about the guy.

Because he had testified extensively under oath and would be subject to impeachment if anything was significantly altered, I was stuck with either accepting or rejecting his previous statements. And because that testimony had been so tortured, if we had to rely on Kato to any considerable degree to prove Simpson's guilt, we were in trouble. Nevertheless, Kato was a high-profile witness, and if we did not call him to testify, the jury might perhaps wonder where he was and view us with suspicion. More important, Kato was one of two witnesses—Allan Park was the other— who could help destroy Simpson's alibi. He was indispensable, and I knew we would have to call him at trial. So it became necessary for me to learn Kato's whole story and figure out how to best present it.

But before I could get his testimony, I had to get him to speak English.

Kato speaks Katospeak. He does not go from subject to verb to direct object, he just starts throwing out ideas and leaps from one to the next, off-road, with no verbal road map. "Was Nicole afraid? Did she express any fear of Simpson?" I asked him. His reply: "Fear—you know, um, you know—O.J.—Nicole with the scissors." I couldn't get a simple answer out of him.

He also had trouble understanding what someone was trying to get at. He reminded me of the old TV series *Get Smart.* Maxwell Smart would tell one of his agents, "Kill the lights," and the guy would pull out a machine gun and shoot the chandelier to smithereens. That's the way Kato answered questions. This may have caused problems with Marcia Clark, who asked questions for a purpose and expected the answers to line up exactly. Kato and Plotkin made a point of telling me that his communication problem was exacerbated by Clark's needling. First, they said, she was not particularly polite to him. The way they described it, she treated him like a dog. They said that at one meeting she sat across a desk from Kaelin, and every time she got what she felt was the right answer she'd flip him a pretzel.

The difficulty came to a head on the witness stand, when Clark called Kato to testify for the prosecution. After a few too many days on the stand, Kato was nearing completion of his testimony. Clark thought Kaelin had previously emphasized that when Simpson returned from Sydney's dance recital on June 12, he had told Kato how upset he was about Nicole wearing a short, tight, sexy dress. Now Kato seemed to be saying that Simpson was more upset about Nicole's not letting him see their kids. After fighting him on the point, Clark got frustrated and in open court asked the judge to declare him a hostile witness.

In fairness to Ms. Clark, Kato was no picnic to question, and her frustration with Kato's verbal meanderings had built up over several days of testimony, but it was ill-advised to declare him a hostile witness over this. First, if anything, Clark had the emphasis on the wrong issue. Tight skirts can send a jealous husband into a rage, and that is clearly what the prosecution was striving for, but Nicole was a beautiful woman who made a practice of dressing provocatively, so that was nothing new to Simpson. What was new, and went far deeper, was that Nicole would not let Simpson see Sydney that night. She was playing hardball with the kids. This was a power play that infuriated him; she was taking something Simpson felt belonged to him, betraying his control. This was a real sore spot with the man. That was the *real* issue.

Second, and even worse for the prosecution, the blowup occurred at the tail end of Kato's testimony, after her examination and cross-examination, on redirect. Declaring him a hostile witness only served to make Kato, and his testimony, lose credibility with the jury.

Declaring someone a "hostile witness" simply means the lawyer is now permitted to ask him questions in leading form. Clark compounded her error by asking to treat Kaelin as a hostile witness in the presence of the jury, instead of quietly at side bar, to the considerable ire of Judge Lance Ito. To the layperson, the jurors, the entire nonattorney world, Clark's declaration made Kato appear to be hostile to the prosecution.

This continued to haunt Kato's image long after he stepped off the stand. Now everyone assumed he was a turncoat who played ball with the defense and refused to tell the truth. There would be potential civil-trial jurors coming in with preconceived notions about his honesty, about whether he was a flake. He had a couple of strikes against him. Before he even uttered a word on the witness stand in our case, he would have to be rehabilitated.

Kato, when I asked about his difficulty with Clark in court, claimed he had no clue what was happening. He said he was just trying to answer Clark's questions as best as he could understand them.

To be sure, I realized that, in the aftermath of the criminal verdict, Kato knew which way the wind was blowing—heavily against Simpson. We were the good guys, and Kato badly wanted to be perceived as a good guy, too. But I did not want to put him on the stand and have him be accused of hitching a ride on our wagon. I didn't want to reform his testimony, I wanted to clarify it and then figure a way to limit it as much as possible.

I most definitely didn't want to encounter the same problems with Kato's language, so I tried to work with him. Kato could state facts; it was when you asked him to characterize something that you got into trouble. How could I make Kato understand what I was asking and answer it directly?

I had him repeat my questions. "Okay, Kato. When I ask you, 'Did Nicole express any fear of Simpson?' you answer the question either 'Nicole did express fear of Simpson' or 'Nicole did not express any fear of Simpson.' I want you to repeat my words in your answer, so you'll be anchored to the question. It'll help you stick to it. Just repeat the words I say and put them in your answer."

Kato got it. He kind of laughed at me for being so surgical, but he and Plotkin realized this was exactly the right medicine.

Kato's knowledge about the case was divided into two large subject matters: his familiarity with the relationship and problems between Simpson and Nicole, and his observations of Simpson the night of the murders.

Kato was deathly afraid of Simpson. The night after the murders, he told me, he had gone to stay at a friend's house, where he was tracked down by Simpson's assistant, Cathy Randa. Simpson and his attorneys got on the phone and began to question him. He felt they were trying to secure him, to bring him into the fold right away. Damage control. They literally brought him in, had him come to the house at Rockingham that night. He arrived to find a large group of business associates, family, and friends gathered in the living room. Simpson hadn't seen his kids yet— their mother had been murdered less than twenty-four hours earlier—but he was hunkered down with his inner circle.

Simpson was on the couch, yelling at the television. He had three sets in a row—probably to watch three football games at a time—and they were all tuned to the news. Simpson was sitting there screaming at the screens. Kato saw Simpson's finger with a big, bloody bandage around it and at that moment was scared for his life. I think he realized right then that Simpson did it.

"Kato knows where I was." Simpson turned to him. "I was home. Kato knows where I was."

Kaelin walked into the kitchen. Simpson came in, and he found himself alone with O.J. "You saw me go into the house after we got back from McDonald's," Simpson said. "Right? You know I was in the house."

Kato mustered the courage to tell him the truth. "No, O.J., I didn't see you go in."

Simpson walked out. Kaelin was terrified.

The next morning, Kato was taken to the office of Simpson's adviser and attorney Leroy "Skip" Taft to be interviewed by Simpson's lawyer, Robert Shapiro. As he was leaving Rockingham he passed the inner circle, gathered in the main house again, who knew where he was going and why. Kato said it felt as if he were passing a Mafia den. A Simpson acolyte named Mark Slotkin called to him: "Get it straight. It's O.J. It's the Juice, man. Get it straight."

Kato was interviewed by Shapiro, came back, got his stuff, and got the hell out of there. He moved out of his room that day and hadn't spoken to Simpson since. He told me, "I thought something might happen to me."

I think fear greatly influenced him at the criminal trial, and I know it affected him at our deposition. He, like Faye, was fearful Simpson would attend. You should expect Simpson to be there, I told him. "One way I want you to deal with it is to block him out. In fact, I want you to rotate your body and look at me on the other side of the table, so you do not even see him. You cannot be looking at him when you are answering questions because it will affect your testimony. Turn your body and look at me. You and I will have a conversation. It will be just you and me."

The deposition started. Simpson was present. The afternoon before the murders, Kato had returned to Rockingham after going for a run. His room was located in a wing of the guest house adjacent to and across from the main house's back doors leading to the pool. To get to his quarters he had to take a path around back. As he walked between the house and the pool, Simpson called to him. This in itself was unusual. Simpson and Kato weren't pals, they didn't hang out together, Kato was a houseguest and did not enter the main house without invitation. He walked inside.

Simpson was sitting in the den, watching television. The movie *The World According to Garp* was on. They chatted for a few minutes, Simpson telling him about the people he knew on TV shows. "Watch this part here," Simpson told him. It was a scene in *Garp* in which a woman is giving oral sex to a man who is not her husband. As they watched, Simpson then told Kato that he had seen Nicole giving oral sex to a man named Keith in the living room of her Gretna Green apartment.

I had questioned Simpson about this at his deposition. Simpson said he had run into Nicole and a restaurant manager named Keith Zlomsowitch at a Brentwood restaurant earlier in the evening. He claimed he just came over to visit later that evening when, through the front window and open blinds, he saw Nicole performing oral sex. He had no good explanation for why he was making this nighttime visit after he saw her out with another man, and denied he was stalking his ex-wife. He said he was so stunned by the sight of Nicole having sex that he stopped and watched for five to ten seconds. The image of that scene, Simpson standing there in the dark, spying on his ex-wife in the act, was unsettling. The next day Simpson returned to Nicole's house, while Nicole was giving Keith a back rub. Simpson put a polite spin on that encounter. Zlomsowitch, when interviewed, described a more aggressive confrontation.

This had happened two years earlier but had such a profound effect on Simpson that he was still recounting the story to Kato the day before Nicole was killed. Kato was uncomfortable with the entire subject.

Simpson, as he always does, talked on and on. He told Kato he and Paula Barbieri were going out that night to a black-tie function in honor of the First Lady of Israel. Paula, he told Kato, was "incredible in bed."

Kato said, "Not that I need to set him up on dates or anything, but . . ." he told Simpson of a friend, Tracy Adell. "This is a really cute girl. You should meet her." Simpson asked what she looked like. "She's in *Playboy* right now," Kato answered. "I can get an issue," which he did, at Simpson's request. Kato drove to a local outdoor market, bought *Playboy,* brought it back, and pointed out his friend. She was the centerfold. Simpson said she was "a great-looking girl" but not his type. "I like blondes."

Nevertheless, Kato and Simpson called Ms. Adell long-distance. She was not in, so they left a message.

Kato said the next day, Sunday, June 12, he first saw Simpson around noon. As he passed the kitchen's breakfast nook, Simpson saw him— "Hey, Kato!"—and beckoned him inside again. Kato was expecting to see Paula as well, but she had not spent the night.

Simpson had already had an active Sunday. He had woken early to play golf and had an angry confrontation on the course with one of his golf partners, a movie producer named Craig Baumgarten. Simpson spent about an hour talking to Kaelin. He told him he didn't think Paula was the woman to marry; she wanted children, and he was finished with that. He said she wanted to go to Sydney's dance recital that night, but he had told her he didn't want her there. Paula had taken it badly. (This directly contradicted and impeached Paula's and Simpson's disclaimers that they had fought about this.)

Tracy Adell returned the call from the day before and Kato overheard Simpson say, "Trace, I'm a single, successful guy, I've got pretty much everything. I've got a huge house, and I would want the white picket fence and the family. . . ."

Simpson and Kato talked about the NBA playoffs, which made Kato want to play some basketball. Simpson told Kaelin he was taking a red-eye flight that night and had some packing to do. Kato went off to play ball.

Kato came back after Simpson had returned from the recital. For the second time that day, the third time that weekend, Simpson called to him. This was extremely unusual; Simpson had never paid that kind of attention to him before. Simpson, Kato recalled, was wearing a dark sweatsuit. (Simpson had denied owning any dark sweatsuits.) He talked for almost a quarter hour about how frustrated he was with Nicole at the recital, how the minidress she had worn was inappropriate, club wear at a family occasion. "How can they wear those miniskirts?" Kato recalled Simpson saying. "What are they gonna do when they're grandmothers? They're gonna have to learn how to dress."

"I believe it was during the dress conversation," Kato testified, "that [Simpson said he] was going to, I don't know, call the IRS, do something with the IRS where she'd get in trouble. What exactly, I don't know, but some kind of trouble."

"Did he appear to you to be upset about Nicole not letting him see the kids?" I asked.

"Yes," Kato answered.

Simpson had been reacting with obvious disapproval to much of Kaelin's testimony. He had not attacked Kato, had even been somewhat kind in his treatment of him, when I questioned Simpson in his deposition. I suspect Simpson came to this deposition expecting Kato to return the favor and hoping to see a replay of Kaelin's performance in the criminal trial. I could see and hear Simpson beginning to complain to his lawyer about answers that he didn't like.

"Kids?" Simpson sputtered. Kato blanched.

It is not appropriate for anyone to comment audibly about a witness's answer during a deposition, and I told Phil Baker, there until his father arrived, that I wanted to hear no more of that from his client. My greater concern was whether Simpson's tactics would intimidate Kaelin and affect his testimony. Kato immediately asked for a short break, which he was granted. I reminded him to ignore Simpson. When he regained his composure, he testified that Simpson had said Nicole was "playing hardball with me. . . . They're my children, too." She had arranged a post-recital family dinner and pointedly not invited Simpson. Kato said, "I don't know why you'd be upset. You've got everything."

Kato was uncomfortable during that hour-long conversation with Simpson. They didn't have a close relationship, and he didn't want to get involved in anything heavy. Kato was a fun-loving guy who liked to keep everything light, and Simpson kept talking about serious personal issues. To escape the conversation, Kato asked permission to use Simpson's Jacuzzi, which was at the north end of the estate's swimming pool.

Kato was out of the Jacuzzi and on the telephone in his room when Simpson came to his door and reprimanded him for not turning off the Jacuzzi jets when he had finished. This was odd. Simpson had never come to Kato's room before. He turned back toward the house but, five or ten minutes later, while Kato was on the phone long-distance to San Diego, Simpson came again. This time, he asked for money. He said he was going to dinner, all he had was hundreds, and he needed to borrow some cash for the skycap at the airport later that night. Kato fished in his drawer and gave him a twenty.

This episode was even more strange. Simpson had never before reported his comings or goings to Kato, who was a nothing to Simpson. Simpson had gone out of his way to emphasize that point at his deposition. (The criminal case prosecution team, in order to give weight to his testimony concerning the Simpson-Nicole relationship, presented Kato as an insider. I did the opposite; I said he was treated like a dog, which he was, making it very suspicious that Simpson would go to his room and make a point of saying that he is going out to dinner.)

After having played basketball and hitting a fast-food sushi shop to down a quick California roll, Kato was hungry. He got up the nerve to invite himself along for dinner. The way he described it, the words just popped out of his mouth. Simpson mumbled, "Sure," and Kato instinctively felt he had overstepped his bounds. They had never before shared a meal alone.

Simpson didn't bother to tell Kato where they were going. He just started walking into and then out of the house, as Kato followed behind. They got in the Bentley, headed out of the driveway at about 9:10 P.M., and took a left onto Rockingham. He felt awkward, and neither man said much during the ride. About ten minutes later Simpson pulled into a McDonald's drive-through and ordered either a Big Mac or a Quarter Pounder. Kaelin, who ate more healthy food and did not ordinarily go to

McDonald's, would have preferred eating elsewhere but ordered a chicken sandwich, fries, and a large orange soda. He paid. "It was one of those gestures," he told me. "I gave him another twenty."

In the Bentley, Simpson said, "Sorry about doing this to you." No bag, no tray, he tossed the food in Kato's lap. He also gave him back the change. Then he drove off. Kato ate a couple of French fries. "It was his Bentley, and I wasn't going to eat in the car." He didn't want to risk getting the expensive automobile dirty.

Simpson inhaled his burger. "I think he ate it before we left McDonald's. It was, like, immediate. . . . It was right out of the parking lot and it was gone."

Listening to this, Simpson suddenly couldn't take it anymore. "Oh, Jesus!" he exclaimed. I immediately complained to Simpson and his lawyer that we would not tolerate any more outbursts. We took a break to let things cool off.

I think Simpson got upset because Kaelin more likely than not was mistaken about the speed with which Simpson gobbled his hamburger. This is vintage O.J. He murders two people and lies about it with impunity. He is righteously indignant, though, when someone gets their facts wrong about a hamburger.

Back at Rockingham, after returning from McDonald's, Kato exited the Bentley and headed toward the main house, thinking Simpson was following and would sit with him while he ate. When he turned around, he was surprised to find O.J. standing next to the car. Kato, realizing Simpson was not coming inside with him, kept walking around the house, to the back, and into his room. From the time Simpson had come to his room to the time they got back, it was twenty-six minutes. A very short trip for dinner. Why would a guy announce "I'm going to get something to eat?" if he was only to be gone so short a time?

This bizarre sequence of events strongly suggests Simpson came to Kato's room as a pretext. He wasn't planning to go to dinner as he announced, and he could have gotten change for a hundred in any of a thousand places. He was setting up an alibi. He had made up his mind to go to Nicole's and confront her, to teach her a serious lesson, to show her who was boss. He may have even decided he would kill her.

There was nothing much to do in Kato's room. Kato routinely either watched TV or talked on the telephone. An hour and fifteen minutes later he was sitting on his bed with his back against the headboard against the wall, chatting on the phone with his friend Rachel Ferrara when he heard three loud noises. Kato felt the vibrations through his body. "A thick noise," he testified. The sound moved from his right to left, "as if a body hit the back of the wall." A picture on the wall tilted.

These three "thumps" were important; they were the sound of Simpson returning from the murders at Bundy. Directly opposite the back of Kato's room was a five-foot-high wire chain-link fence with enough space between its top and the thick foliage above it for a man to climb through and over. The ground on the property next door was a couple of feet lower than it was on the Simpson side, so if an agitated man were scaling the fence and jumping down in the dark, he might well misjudge the fall, lose his footing, and bump into the building before he righted himself. He could easily drop a glove.

When we were preparing for his deposition I had said to Kato, "Get up and demonstrate what the noise sounded like." Kato stood, went over to the conference room wall, and crashed against it three times. It sounded, indeed, "as if a body hit the wall."

From what little I had heard during the criminal case, that was not my impression of the "thumps." When he had testified, Kato had demonstrated by knocking three times on the witness box. The sound had been thin and hollow, a knuckle against a rail; it sounded nothing at all like a man returning from a killing.

"Why did you knock on the witness stand three times?" I asked incredulously.

"Well," he explained, "they were asking me to demonstrate the rhythm of the sounds. *Bah, bum-bum*. I just thought they wanted to know, sort of, the pattern, or the rhythm. No one asked me to go and demonstrate how it sounded, or did it sound like someone falling against the wall." And Kato, for his part, had not volunteered.

When Kato demonstrated these sounds at his deposition, Baker and Simpson snickered. I could tell they were going to spin this big-time: Fortunes had changed, the winds had shifted, and Kato was blowing right along with them. That was their way of explaining any unfavorable witnesses. Any time testimony hurt them, they fostered and fed the illusion that it had been given by problem witnesses. They would go to the press and say things like "Everybody knows Resnick is a liar. Everybody knows Kato is a flake." They would act as if these were givens.

But I would not let them get away with it. I would not accept their assertion that Kato Kaelin was a damaged witness whom I could never use. "Who's everybody?" I would say. "I don't agree with that. You are the ones who have been saying that. You are the ones who made that up!" As an advocate, you can never give an inch. You can never let the other side get away with anything; you cannot let them pull even the first fast one.

Back in his room, still on the telephone, Kato asked Rachel Ferrara, "Did we have an earthquake?" She said no, and he hung up. He looked for a flashlight in the nightstand drawer, and took the path to the front of the house to see what had happened. This took about two or three minutes. (The police never pursued this point. Simpson's attorney Bob Shapiro did. He tape recorded his interview with Kaelin in which Kato laid out the time frame. When I went to Rockingham and timed it, the walk from Kato's room to the front of the house took approximately thirty seconds.)

As Kato walked from the back to the front of the house, he was seen by the limousine driver Allan Park, who had arrived early to pick up Simpson and take him to the airport, but who, strangely, was still outside the gate waiting to be let in. Kato didn't stop, he went past the gate, and he kept going around the side of the house until he came to a dark pathway that led to the back wall outside his room. Then he stopped. It was real dark back there. He took a few steps forward, got scared—whoever made that noise might still be hiding—turned around and came out.

Kato proceeded to walk back in the direction of the white limousine still parked outside the gate on Ashford, went to the nearby gate control box, and let him in. Chachi, Simpson's arthritic old dog, crossed slowly in front of the limo as it entered and lay down in his favorite spot in the grass. The limousine pulled up to the two benches outside the front door, and the driver got out. Kato asked Park, "Did we have an earthquake? I felt this thing." Park had felt nothing.

With Park on the property, Kato felt, as he described it, "more nervy." He ventured again behind the house down the dark pathway. Not very much farther than the first time, however. Again, he got scared and came back.

A few minutes later, while Kato and Park were loading Simpson's luggage into the car, Simpson came out of the house. He was wearing a blue jean pants-and-shirt outfit, loafers, no socks. Kato saw a small knapsack-like bag across the driveway near where the Bentley was parked. As Kato went to retrieve it to put in the limo, Simpson overtook him, saying, "No, no. I'll get it." Simpson grabbed the bag and put it in the car. That bag has never been seen again. Kato told Simpson about the noises he had heard, and asked Simpson for a flashlight. Simpson took him into the house and into the kitchen to find one, then abruptly said it was late, got into the limo, and left.

During our long interviews, while I was piecing this all together, Kaelin was consistently fuzzy on a couple of important details. He said at some point he saw Simpson, dressed in a dark sweatsuit, walk into the house. Unfortunately, he could not remember whether it was after his first trip behind the house when the limousine was still parked outside, or after the second trip when the limo had been buzzed inside already. This was crucial. Kato distinctly remembered Simpson wearing a sharp-looking, dark sweatsuit with a white or light silver zipper in the Bentley on the way to and from McDonald's, but when Simpson came down to the limo he was wearing a blue jeans outfit. If he saw Simpson on his second trip, when the limousine was inside the compound, it didn't mean much; in his deposition Simpson claimed he had come out of the house and gone down the driveway to his Bronco to retrieve his cell phone equipment. He would claim that Kato had simply seen him on his return, and that Kato was mistaken in saying Simpson was wearing a sweatsuit.

If, however, Kato saw Simpson dart into the house after Kato's *first* trip to the pathway, when the limousine was still outside, it was extremely incriminating. According to Simpson, he had been asleep, then gotten up and taken a shower. Kato had just passed the front door; how would Simpson have gotten outside his house? What was he doing there? Why was he going back *into* the house, and where was he coming from? Why was he wearing a dark sweatsuit when, according to Simpson, he had showered and changed into his travel clothes? If Kato saw Simpson after his first trip to the dark pathway, Simpson had no innocent answers to these questions. Kato would have seen Simpson in the murder clothes returning home from the murders.

I had been going over and over this chain of events with Kaelin during our preparation sessions and getting nowhere with him. "I can't recall whether the limo was inside or outside the gate," he kept telling me. "I just can't remember." But that made all the difference in the world.

When we got into the deposition he still could not give a definitive answer. As we were about to delve into the topic on the record, under oath, we took a break. In the conference room with Kaelin and Plotkin I said, "Kato, we're getting to the end of the deposition. I'm telling you, something is wrong with your testimony. If you saw him with the sweatsuit on, it had to have been while the limousine was parked outside." This had not been dissected and presented to Kaelin before. Now that it was, he understood and acknowledged the importance of his recollection at this single, defining moment of time.

Kato paced the room. He clenched his fists and closed his eyes, trying to re-create the scene in his mind, trying to remember. There was a desk in the room; Plotkin was sitting behind it in the lawyer's chair, and I was sitting in one of the two guest chairs. Kato collapsed into the other. A tear edged its way down his cheek. Then he began to talk to me. Quickly, Plotkin cautioned him.

"Kato, think about what you're saying. You have consistently said 'You don't remember. You don't remember.'" As Kaelin's lawyer, Plotkin was doing the right thing, reminding his client of his consistent prior testimony. He wasn't telling his client not to speak, he wanted to make certain that Kaelin understood the consequences of what he might say. Kato being Kato, Plotkin wanted him to understand that if he were to testify now that he, in effect, saw Simpson coming back from the murders, this would constitute a dramatic change, and he would be vilified.

Kato stopped. I could see the decision get made. To this day, I don't know whether he recalls exactly what he saw and when he saw it, has blocked it, or legitimately can't remember, but at that point he simply wasn't saying.

"Okay," I said, "fair enough."

I was never able to get Kato to admit what I believe he saw: Simpson returning from the murders. He didn't know it at the time, but he should have suspected it after the police knocked on his door and interrogated him about Nicole Brown Simpson being killed. He should have been more clear, concise, and complete about what he saw while the events were still fresh in his mind. But he was not, and that is something he and we will have to live with.

Kato testified that Simpson called him later, he didn't know from where, and directed him to turn on the estate's alarm system, which was hooked to a private security firm named Westec. Kato had never done this before, either, and Simpson had given him the code to punch in on the keypad inside the main house's front door. Kato turned on the alarm and secured the house, then went back to his room.

The evening's events had scared him and he couldn't sleep. He lay there, reading the "Calendar" section of the *Los Angeles Times,* and at about one-thirty in the morning heard the clicking of ladies' heels on the path. He assumed it was Simpson's daughter Arnelle, who lived in another part of the wing, coming home. Some time after that, he fell asleep. He woke up when the police banged on his door.

Kato testified for three days over the course of a week. He did quite well on direct examination. Then, near the end of day two, he came up against Bob Baker. Baker did not attend the first day of Kaelin's deposition. He sent his son instead. Again, I wondered about the defense team's priorities, but I was just as happy not to have him across the table.

Bob Baker is everything Kato isn't: tough, combative, focused, aggressive, snide, self-possessed. Kato is, by nature, a person who tries to please. He is anti-confrontational. In order not to do battle, he is apt to agree with whoever is asking him the questions, even when he is being misled into saying things that convey an inaccurate impression. Faced with Bob Baker, Kato was overmatched and began to fall apart.

Kato is easy to intimidate, and Baker did a good job of it. The lessons we had worked on about answering questions directly and not wandering were slipping away. He was not backing up his testimony, but, rather backing down when challenged, he was allowing points he had made previously to be undermined. Before day three I told Kato, "Wake up! You are being led all over the place. You are not here to please. You've got to do a better job, now dig in and be a little tough!"

On the third day, Kato rallied.

In the final analysis, Kato did a creditable job and buoyed my confidence that he would be a witness we could work with and use at trial. Having spent almost a week with him, including two days of preparation and three days of deposition, it was clear I would have to keep Kato's testimony narrow and confine it to only that information we could get nowhere else. He was not a hostile witness by any means, simply a difficult one.

Simpson, for his part, couldn't control himself and rarely showed up at another deposition.

I came to learn that our access to the public through the media could be used to great advantage. We were having trouble serving deposition subpoenas on several witnesses, including Al Cowlings, Bob Kardashian, and Simpson's two adult children, Jason and Arnelle. I asked Simpson's lawyers if they would accept service of the subpoenas, but as usual Baker said no. When, after a while, we were still unable to find and serve them, I went to a bank of microphones out on the Santa Monica courthouse lawn and made a public plea for help. I asked if anyone knew the whereabouts of these witnesses to please give my office a call. That afternoon and evening and all during the next day, my voicemail was flooded with messages pinpointing the locations of all four witnesses. It was almost comical; their movements were being reported to me in real time. The next day, Simpson's lawyers called and agreed to accept service on behalf of Jason and Arnelle Simpson.

A few days later, we were in the process of completing the second phase of Simpson's deposition. I went to the restroom during a break, and Simpson was there with his lawyers. The lawyers filed out and once we were alone, Simpson came up to me, pointed his finger in my chest, and said, "I don't care what you say about me, but leave my kids out of it!" It gave me a momentary glimpse of what he really must be like when things don't go his way. When I recovered my composure, I told him that he should talk to his lawyers, since they were the ones who forced me to do what I did. And with that, I walked out.

ELEVEN

Everybody's Talking

The lines had been drawn clearly during the criminal trial: Nicole's friends knew Simpson did it, and, with some notable exceptions such as Faye Resnick, were willing, though reluctantly, to testify. Simpson's friends, in my view, also realized he was guilty, but with one exception—Ron Shipp—were prepared to look the other way. In order to fully understand Nicole and Simpson's relationship and how it broke down, I would have to talk to both sides.

I don't think this area of the case was handled well by the prosecution in the criminal case. Yes, they were confronted with far more direct incriminating evidence—Simpson's blood and DNA at the crime scene—and were working feverishly to identify, analyze, and prepare their evidence while the defense lawyers rushed the case through pretrial proceedings to trial. Clark and Darden also had the crush of the media in their path every step of the way. Still, having decided to put on a motive case, they needed to work harder and dig deeper to piece together a cohesive, compelling case. They fell short.

As I began to meet and talk to the witnesses, a recurring criticism I heard was that police and prosecutors had not treated them too well. A large segment of Nicole and Simpson's stratum of society—the powerful, status-conscious wealthy—expects deference and knows a snub even before it feels one. These were affluent people used to getting their way. Being hauled

down to the grungy Los Angeles courthouse amid the bustle of alleged perpetrators, ambulance chasers, and the irate wrongfully accused to answer
questions as if they were suspects didn't sit right with them.

Moreover, it's intimidating to go to the police station or district
attorney's office in the first place. You're in the criminal justice system,
maybe you have a few secrets of your own you'd rather not discuss. People
can go to jail. For a rare moment you're out of your element, and you're
talking about the grisly murder of a woman not unlike yourself or your
wife. Many witnesses reported to me they were not made comfortable,
and they didn't like it.

District attorneys and police detectives, on the other hand, deal with
criminals every day. They have seen one too many bona fide lowlifes proclaiming their innocence to take any story at face value; they have a limited tolerance with outsiders to begin with, and are not reticent about
showing it. They tend to demand rather than request—and usually have
the power to back it up—and are not above strong-arming people when
they need to move things along. They are the ultimate pragmatists who
have seen murdering rapists go free, and they don't like to lose. They have
their own set of rules, which they insist others follow.

I made it clear up front to the people I met and interviewed that I
was not a prosecutor, I was not a criminal lawyer, this was not a criminal
case, and they would not be hauled down to the DA's office or Parker
Center. I had the advantage of a nice office in a building owned by my
law firm on the well-regarded west side of town. I would bring these people into our offices and pay for their parking. Lunch was served. All in all,
the event was as comfortable and unintimidating as possible. Then I told
them, "Look, you have to tell me *now* what you know or it's going to the
grave with you. Nicole's already in her grave, and she's entitled to have the
truth known. This is her last chance for justice."

I began to get some results. David "Pinky" LeBon had met Nicole
in 1974. After she dropped out of high school, she came to Los Angeles
and moved into his apartment. In 1977, LeBon said, Nicole was a wait-
ress at a nightclub named Daisy's, where she met Simpson, who although
married at the time, asked her on a date. The first night they went out,
LeBon remembered, Nicole arrived home at two in the morning with the
front of her pants ripped open. Nicole told LeBon that Simpson had tried
to be forceful in his Rolls-Royce.

LeBon remained friends with Nicole for the rest of her life. He was very protective of her. When she caught Simpson cheating and told LeBon about it, which was frequently, LeBon finally confronted O.J. directly. "Why are you screwing around on Nicole?" he demanded.

Simpson said, "Well, I'm O.J. Simpson. You don't know what it's like to be O.J."

LeBon said Simpson bought Nicole off with a Ferrari.

LeBon's wife, D'Anne, said that after Nicole's divorce from O.J. in 1992, Nicole once confided in her that she felt Simpson was going to cut her up in pieces and throw them over the freeway.

Because of hearsay problems, much of this would likely never appear at trial. But I was trying to educate myself, find out as much as I could to make my own judgment about what was true and not true about this complex relationship. I didn't know what I was going to do with the information, I just kept asking questions and stockpiling the answers. The more people I spoke to, the more I heard similar stories, the more I got a sense that much of it *was* true. It all fit.

Robin Greer was a woman whom Simpson despised. She took credit for helping Nicole leave him. Greer said she had not seen Nicole for about a month prior to the murders, but on Thursday night, June 9, they had talked at length on the phone about Nicole's problems. Particularly about "the IRS letter."

I kept hearing about the IRS. In the criminal trial the prosecutors had admitted into evidence a letter from Simpson to Nicole, dated June 6, 1994, telling her to stop using Rockingham as her legal address. The prosecution used it in an attempt to demonstrate Simpson's hostility toward Nicole at the time of her death, but, as I began to discover, there was more to this letter. They hadn't developed its full import.

Simpson had given Nicole a condo in San Francisco as consideration for her signing a prenuptial agreement in 1985. She kept that condo, along with a lump-sum payment of approximately $400,000, in the property settlement in their divorce. Nicole tried her hand at interior decorating, but was making little or no money on her own, and had rented out the San Francisco condo to earn income. When she split from Simpson and moved out of Rockingham in 1992, she rented an expensive Brentwood townhouse condominium on Gretna Green. Realizing she was paying a considerable amount in rent, she sold the San Francisco condo and combined the money from that sale with the cash she got in the divorce to buy the condo on Bundy. That left her with approximately $90,000 in the bank.

The sale of the San Francisco condo had achieved a significant profit, which ordinarily would have been subject to capital gains tax. That tax would not arise, however, if she rolled over the profit into another rental unit. Bundy had been purchased in January 1994, at a time when Simpson and Nicole were attempting a reconciliation with an eye toward Nicole's moving back in with O.J. at his Rockingham estate and possible remarriage. Nicole's thinking was, "I'll list Rockingham as my home address because I will be moving in there, and we'll just say that 875 South Bundy is a rental unit and avoid all this capital gains. But since I'm not ready to move into Rockingham yet, I'll move into Bundy with the kids and wait until the time is right." She and Simpson agreed to handle it that way. All her mail came to Rockingham, and she used that address on her bank statements.

(Simpson claimed in his deposition he agreed to this deal only if she put the expected taxes into a bank account to pay if the government did not accept this arrangement. He had no way of verifying this.)

When Nicole broke up with Simpson, he wrote her a letter.

On my visit to the LAPD's SID physical evidence storage facility, I had seen a May 30 fax cover sheet, which the police had found sitting on Simpson's Rockingham desk when they executed their search warrant. In it, long-time friend, lawyer, and business adviser Leroy "Skip" Taft told Simpson that he had "made changes you wanted but did not get revengeful." This told me there had been a prior draft, most likely one that Simpson himself had prepared, and that Taft, upon reviewing it, tried to tone down. Simpson had downplayed the letter at his deposition, saying he simply wanted to protect himself with the IRS, but the import was devastating.

Simpson's letter put Nicole in the untenable position of remaining at the Bundy condominium after having received full knowledge that she was in violation of IRS laws. If she elected to stay, she would have to pay the capital gains taxes she had been avoiding, perhaps $90,000 to $100,000. It would wipe out her savings to do so. She had no income, no prospects, an expensive lifestyle, and only enough funds to last a limited amount of time. Simpson knew Nicole would have no choice but to move. So she would be out on the street. And her children—O.J. Simpson's children—who had already moved twice in the previous two years, would be out on the street once again.

The letter was pure retaliation for Nicole's dumping him for good. He would hit her where it hurt the most. In a radio interview before the civil trial, Simpson said that, next to his mother, Nicole was his favorite person. His favorite person, yet he was going to throw her and their children out on the street or turn her in to the IRS.

The final draft of that letter was hand-delivered to Nicole on June 6, six days before the murders. She went wild.

According to Robin Greer, Nicole told her that Simpson was going to have her arrested for tax violations and take the kids, and she was "freaking out." Nicole thought, Why would you do such a thing to me? Just to be vindictive? Just to retaliate? To punish me? To control me? I'm not going to let you get away with it! She was livid, and though she and the children had just settled into the condo, she called a real estate broker and started looking for a new place to live—this time out of Brentwood and away from O.J. Simpson. For Nicole, O.J.'s letter was the last straw.

Greer told me about a conversation with Nicole concerning Bret, the man Nicole had met in Cabo San Lucas. She said Cabo was where Nicole decided she would end her reconciliation with Simpson. Nicole had been out dancing and had a fling with a younger guy, and she liked it. She started seeing other younger men. This was the kind of behavior that would cut Simpson to the core. He took credit for molding and sculpting Nicole into the woman she was. He got her new breasts—from the "titty fairy" as he would put it—put her in fancy clothes, introduced her to the ways of a new world. And on his arm, she was an eye-catching trophy wife, the ultimate Heisman Trophy. But now Simpson was nearing fifty. He was an older man being left for younger ones. It must have eaten at him.

At Nicole's wake, Greer said, Simpson had wept and said, "I'm sorry." He kept repeating it: "I'm sorry." She thought it odd that Simpson was apologizing. She said it was understood by everyone that he had killed her.

In the days after Simpson was jailed, Greer told me, his teammate on the Buffalo Bills and his friend for life, Al Cowlings, had gone on a witness round-up, trying to do damage control by gathering Nicole's friends into the fold. Cowlings, a large man and an intimidating physical presence, did Simpson's scut work all his life and continued to do it while Simpson was in jail. He called Greer and suggested they meet in a secluded place.

The two met at the Brentwood Country Mart and then drove in Cowlings's car to a residential neighborhood. There A.C. asked if Nicole was using drugs. Greer said, "No." He asked if she knew whether Faye Resnick was in rehab. Greer said she was. He then asked if she knew if Faye or Nicole had had any dealings with cartel drug lords. "Sure," Greer told him, "she was dealing with those drug lords in between taking Justin to karate and Sydney to ballet class. Stop off at the old Colombian drug lord's."

"Who could have done the murders?" he asked.

Greer replied, "It was either O.J. or you." This was a woman who took no shit.

"What about one of Nicole's jealous boyfriends?" Cowlings asked. "Couldn't he have killed her?"

"What about one of O.J.'s jealous girlfriends?" She replied derisively. "Unless someone framed him," Greer told Cowlings, "O.J. is the only one." Cowlings realized he was getting nowhere, and that was the end of the conversation.

Greer gave me rundowns on various people in the case, including Simpson's family and Nicole's social circle. Jason Simpson, O.J.'s oldest son, she said, was hyperventilating at the wake. He was not very smart or athletic, not his father's favorite, but Nicole had always gone to bat for him. Greer believed he would break if questioned. Arnelle, she told me, was militant and would do anything for her father. The same was true for Cathy Randa: "You'll never get through to them." Kato, she said, was very shaken by the events. She said she told him, "If you do not go forward, it will be between you and God."

There were four women Nicole confided in, Greer told me: herself, Faye Resnick, Cynthia "Cici" Shahian, and Cora Fischman.

"Who else might know things?" I asked.

She named tennis pro and sports agent Joe Kolkowitz, "a worshiper," and Allen and Pam Schwartz. "Be careful," she said, Allen Schwartz was linked to Skip Taft.

Faye Resnick had become their crowd's front person in the Nicole defense, Greer said, gobbling up all the credit and publicity because of her book. Cora, jealous of the attention, had slammed Faye on the Barbara Walters show. In her anger with Faye, Robin told me, Cora Fischman had turned and was now in Simpson's camp.

I knew I would never call Robin Greer as a witness. She could not testify to any threatening statements made directly by Simpson, all her information was hearsay. Simpson claimed she had a drug problem, and was sure to mount a Faye Resnick–like attack on her. Her intense feelings were mixed with a degree of exaggeration and hyperbole, and some of the details were wrong. But she was a valuable resource and helped me to understand Nicole's feelings of shame and embarrassment about her abuse and how obsessive and possessive Simpson was toward her.

The same day I interviewed Robin Greer, I spoke with Cynthia Shahian. She had moved to Houston since the murders, but was back in Los Angeles on a business trip. She was very proud of the fact that although she had been asked, she had declined to write a book about her relationship with Nicole and had not made a penny off the murders.

Shahian was Bob Kardashian's first cousin. During the first week after the murders, she told me, Al Cowlings had called her on his witness round-up. She had just moved and changed her phone number, but he had tracked her down. She didn't return the call. He'd called again at the end of the criminal case, but again she had not responded.

In contrast with the Hollywood affectations of Resnick and Greer, Shahian was more down-to-earth. She and Nicole had known each other, through Bob Kardashian, for approximately thirteen years. They went to dinner together a couple of times a week, jogged together, were close. Cici said Nicole told her that Simpson hit her repeatedly. She specifically mentioned the Las Vegas incident. Simpson thought Nicole had been flirting and threw her out of their hotel room naked. Nicole also talked about the New Year's Eve incident. She told Cici O.J. and she were drinking, and got into a fight over Tawny Kitaen, an actress with whom Simpson had an affair. He got enraged and beat Nicole. His housekeeper, Michelle Abudrahm, would not help her. The police came.

Nicole recounted another incident and said, "Cici, he was kicking my stomach and he was punching my face." Nicole and Cici started to cry. Cici had never heard anything like this from Nicole and was shocked. She said Nicole was not the type who shared her private life, but this time Nicole just opened up by herself. Cici asked, "What did you do?" Nicole told her O.J. and she went to the hospital and told the doctor she had fallen off a bike.

Cici told me it took Nicole three years after the 1989 beating to muster up the courage to actually leave Simpson. When I asked Cici why Nicole went back to him a year later, she told me that Nicole said she was dependent on Simpson, that she could not live without him, and she wanted to reunite her family. As Shahian described it, one day in March 1993 Simpson and Nicole took a long walk around the block at Rockingham, and Nicole told him she wanted to come home. This took Simpson by surprise, but by the end of the walk they were reunited. They made ground rules for dating: they would be monogamous. She would also take up golf. Nicole got to keep her girlfriends, except Robin Greer, whom Simpson forbid her to see. They would give it one year.

When Nicole called Cici to tell her the news, she said that she had felt, by walking out on Simpson, she had hurt both her immediate and extended family. The benevolence was over. When she left, Simpson had fired her housekeeper Maria. Maria's husband, Juditha Brown's nephew Rolph Bauer, also lost Simpson's support, and as a result, lost his Pioneer Chicken franchise. The Browns loved Simpson and were not happy with the divorce. O.J. pulled the plug on Lou Brown's car dealership, and Judy Brown's travel agency went down the tubes. Nicole's sister Denise was no longer able to live in one of Simpson's Monarch Bay condos. Nicole had given her father $10,000, but still felt responsible for all of these financial problems.

Nicole had a strong sexual appetite, Cici said, and her sex life with Simpson was very active. During their split she had a number of relationships, and Shahian named the men, including the mysterious Bret from Cabo and Marcus Allen. Upon their reconciliation, Shahian told me, Simpson gave Nicole two ultimatums: "I'll kill you if I catch you with another man" and "If I can't have you, nobody can." He insisted that they identify the lovers they'd had in the interim. When Nicole told Simpson about Allen, he got extremely upset.

Cici told me that she and Cora Fischman both supported Nicole's decision to return to Simpson. Cici felt profoundly guilty for having encouraged her.

Cici confirmed Nicole's outrage when she got Simpson's IRS letter. She'd said, "This is it. He wants to see me on the streets, to take my kids. This is the last straw."

The last time Cici saw Nicole, June 11, they jogged their usual six miles together down San Vicente Boulevard to the Pacific Ocean and back to Brentwood. Nicole mentioned in passing that the extra set of keys to her condo were missing. Cici said sarcastically, "I wonder who could have taken them." They both knew it was Simpson. Nicole told Cici her relationship with her ex-husband was over and done with, 100 percent, but that he would make sure her life was miserable. Nicole repeated something she had told Cici previously. "He does not love me," she said, "he is obsessed with me. He is going to kill me, and my friends are going to sell me out." The next night she lay in a pool of her own blood.

Cici believed in her heart that Nicole and Simpson fought on the telephone on the night of June 12 and that this triggered his final fury and rage on her. There was an unsheathed knife found on the Bundy kitchen table, and Cici felt Nicole was afraid.

As I studied the evidence and learned more and more about what happened in the last weeks, days, and hours of Nicole's life, I, too, believed that Simpson called Nicole after she returned from her daughter's dance recital and dinner with her family, and that they spoke about 9:00 P.M. I believed that there were raw, ugly words exchanged in that conversation, words that convinced O.J. Simpson that he had to do something to take control of this problem, once and for all. The LAPD had not acted quickly enough to obtain telephone records of local calls between the two of them and such data became irretrievable within days after the murders. Strangely, knowing such records didn't exist, Simpson actually admitted in his deposition that he called Nicole's condo around 9:00 P.M. the night of the murders, but only to speak to his daughter. He denied having any conversation, let alone an argument, with Nicole. This, in my view, was a lie, but whether I could ever prove it remained to be seen.

Simpson said many times in his deposition that *he* was the one who broke up with Nicole, *he* went back to Paula, *he* was in control of everything. People like Cici Shahian, Faye Resnick, and other friends of Nicole told me Simpson was lying: Nicole ended the relationship and Simpson was furious. But their testimony of what Nicole said was hearsay and would be difficult to admit into evidence. I wanted a witness who would say, "O.J. Simpson said Nicole broke up with him." The law calls that kind of testimony a "party admission," and it is directly admissible. That was the kind of evidence I was looking for. I wanted to show that Simpson was dumped, he was rejected, he was abandoned. Having been cast aside and divorced once already by Nicole, it had been a painful and new experience for him to get on with his life. Then, she had pulled him right back in, kept him on a string for a year, and right when he thought things were working out great—by which he meant "great sex" in Cabo—he was out in the cold again. Cast aside again. I wanted to find out what happened. What took him from that point to murder?

Our research told us that people who kill their spouses often have recently been estranged, rejected by the spouse they then kill. I was in search of a witness who would tell me that O.J. admitted he was rejected by Nicole. I wasn't likely to hear that from Nicole's friends, he wasn't talking to them. I needed to get it from Simpson's circle, people who spoke candidly with him. Unfortunately, the people he had talked to weren't talking.

Kris Jenner, Bob Kardashian's ex-wife who had married the Olympic decathlete Bruce Jenner, was in an awkward position. The Kardashians and the Simpsons had been very close friends. After Kris divorced Kardashian, Nicole left Simpson; it may have been Kris's example that gave her the confidence and courage to make that move.

Kris stayed in contact with Kardashian, they still had four children to raise. Immediately after the murders, at her house, she had asked him whether Simpson did it and how he could remain the man's friend. She wanted to make sure he wasn't brainwashing the kids into believing Simpson was innocent. Kardashian summoned her out of the house and into the street so they would not be overheard and told her that, so far, only Simpson's blood had been found, and they could deal with that. If they found Ron Goldman's blood in the Bronco, however, that would be a big problem. Of course, they did later find Ron Goldman's blood in the Bronco. Nonetheless, Kardashian remained at Simpson's side.

Kris laughed uproariously when I mentioned Simpson's fake goatee and beard. She and her children had gone to Disneyland with the Simpsons, and she said O.J. had worn sunglasses, apparently to avoid being approached. However, when he saw a tour bus emptying, Simpson conspicuously took them off. Kris recalled there was a camera crew in the area when O.J. flashed his smile. The suggestion that he would disguise himself was absurd to her. Simpson loved to be recognized. He loved being O.J.

Kris Jenner and Nicole spent a lot of time together after their divorces, and became close friends. Kris introduced Nicole to Faye Resnick and Cici Shahian. She gave me good leads. She pointed me toward Nicole's friend Ron Hardy, who had some important information that was buried in the police reports. Ed Medvene searched out his name in what the LAPD called its "Murder Book," the main repository for the case's evidence, and there he found a police interview in which Hardy confirmed he had hosed down and helped wash blood off the back gate at Bundy on June 14, two mornings after the murders. This was an important piece of evidence because it showed the blood had not been planted there later, as the criminal defense so loudly charged.

"Who saw any abuse?" I asked Kris. "Who would know about hitting?" The gold mine would be if there were persons who actually saw Simpson hit Nicole, a lesser success would be if they heard O.J. admit it, third best would be if Nicole had told them about it. She said Simpson's longtime friend Allen Schwartz might have firsthand knowledge. She also mentioned Cora Fischman.

"Well, Kris, who do you think would know about what happened in the last week or two? Who was O.J. hanging with?" Kris shrugged, she had been somewhat left out of Nicole's circle of friends in the month prior to the murders. She said Nicole was acting "kinda funky," which she attributed to neverending problems with Simpson.

Kris and Nicole also used to go running together on a regular basis. (They were supposed to go out in the late morning on June 13. Kris had called and left a message on the answering machine that afternoon, wondering where Nicole was.) Nicole once said to her while jogging, "He is going to kill me and get away with it." Nicole had said this before, Kris told me, but this time she had said it with urgency. Kris had heard about the phone call Faye had received on May 2 from Simpson, threatening to kill Nicole if he saw her with another man. Kris felt Nicole was not joking and suggested she get some protection, someone to stay with her.

Kris emphasized how deeply Nicole must have felt threatened to say such a thing, because she was a very private person who ordinarily did not discuss personal problems easily.

"There is another person I think you should call," she finally said to me. "His name is Alan Austin. I think he will talk to you."

This was a surprise. Austin had been one of Simpson's best and closest friends, a regular golfing buddy, one of the four men Simpson played with at the Riviera Country Club on the day of the murders. I never dreamed he'd be willing to talk to me.

"Confidentially," Kris told me, "he's hoping that you'll give him a call. He's asking to be subpoenaed."

Peter Gelblum had had a conversation with Christopher Darden concerning Austin early on, when we were taking over the case. Darden thought Austin had important knowledge that he had been unable to get out of him and thought it unlikely Austin would talk to us. I called Austin and invited him to come see me.

Alan Austin was a successful man, retired, in very good shape. He had white hair, a square jaw, was wealthy-looking and tanned. He had been in the clothing business, with a line of expensive women's clothes named after himself and stores throughout the country, including Beverly Hills. My office and desk were filled with confidential papers and documents, so I met witnesses in a clean conference room across the hall from my office. I brought Alan there, offered him a cup of coffee, and made light conversation. As I prepared to get down to business, I told him I could subpoena him to give a deposition, or he could talk privately to me, either way. He said he preferred to talk.

Austin met Simpson in the 1970s, pre-Nicole, and they had been close friends ever since. They partied, traveled, and, in recent years, played golf nearly every day at Riviera Country Club. He and Simpson had no significant business connections. They had played eighteen holes at Riviera on the morning of June 12.

Finally, I asked him, "Where do you stand? Do you think he did it?" This was a question I put to everyone connected with the case. If they hemmed and hedged, I knew where I stood. Austin was forthright. "Yes," he said, "I think he did it."

"Weren't you one of the guys who stood by him during the criminal trial?" I asked.

"Yes, in the beginning, because I didn't think it was him."

He described a meeting at Bob Shapiro's office soon after Simpson had been arrested. Almost the entire Simpson coterie was there or participated long-distance by telephone, including, in addition to Austin,

Marcus Allen, Kathryn Allen, Joe Kolkowitz, Bill Pavelic, Al Cowlings, Craig Baumgarten, Mike Melchiorre, Allen Schwartz, Skip Taft and his wife, Chris Taft, Cathy Randa, Bob Kardashian, Reggie McKenzie, Bobby Chandler, and Wayne Hughes. The room was full, standing room only around the conference table. A speakerphone sat in the middle.

Shapiro spoke first. He told the gathering, "Don't say anything. Don't talk to the media. Don't talk to anyone. Don't trust the telephone. If you have any evidence or knowledge or information, give it to Bill Pavelic." (Pavelic was one of a number of investigators hired by the criminal defense team.) This was purportedly a support and fund-raising meeting, but it sure sounded to me like a lot more than that: "Don't talk to the police" was the message I suspected. Then Simpson got on the speakerphone, from jail.

"Hey, this is Juice. Are you with me? I love you."

He went around the room, picking people off one by one.

"Marcus, you've been with me all these years. You're with me, baby, you're going to stay with me, we're going to get through this together. I'm gonna fight and you're gonna fight. I love you. You know I love you." It was like a big pep talk, a pregame motivational speech, except his life depended on it.

As far as I was concerned, Simpson was pleading a cover-up to help conceal his guilt. By the time he was done, people were crying.

Austin was moved. Also convinced. "But the more evidence that came out," he told me, "particularly the blood, and he never had an explanation . . ."

Austin visited Simpson in jail often. Simpson said he would take the stand and set the record straight. He'd answer all the questions then. Then he'd reneged. On top of that, Simpson and his lawyers played the race card and cast O.J. as a representative of the entire downtrodden black community and a victim of racial prejudice. It worked. Simpson was acquitted without ever going on the record and answering a single question.

After his acquittal, Simpson made the rounds, going to restaurants in South Central Los Angeles, speaking at black churches. His friends like Alan Austin were offended, because they knew otherwise.

"O.J. doesn't give a shit about the black community!" Austin said sharply. "I've talked to Jim Brown about it." The former Cleveland Brown running back and movie star was Austin's friend. "Brown cares, he does all this work for black youths, he's in there fighting, dealing with troubled kids. O.J. never did this." Far from South Central Los Angeles, O.J. lived the lifestyle of a rich man in a white world.

Austin was very bothered by the fact that Simpson had flown cross-country from New York to attend Sydney's dance recital, and had then the night of Nicole's murder scheduled a night flight to Chicago. That wasn't O.J., he said, he wouldn't put himself out like that. If Simpson had to be in Chicago on Monday morning, he would simply have stayed back east; and if he truly had to be in Los Angeles for the recital, he would not have stuck around all night, he would have flown out immediately.

Simpson wouldn't go out of his way for a dance recital, Austin said. He was constantly away from home, broadcasting from city to city during the football season, playing at golf tournaments and celebrity events, or just generally off being O.J. A month earlier, Simpson had missed Sydney's first communion, a very important event in a Catholic child's life. He had missed Justin's graduation party from elementary school just five days before Sydney's dance recital. That O.J. would criss-cross the country suggested an element of premeditation. "You know," he said, "it doesn't make any sense."

Austin spoke haltingly and I constantly had to pull things out of him. He was still struggling with the issue of whether his friend of twenty years could really have murdered his ex-wife. He would think out loud. "Sure, O.J. was jealous, but he's not going to kill her because he's jealous." Austin ridiculed the prosecution for their evidence on this issue. He was convinced that something must have happened to make Simpson snap.

After a couple of hours, Austin and I sensed a camaraderie. I felt he knew what I was doing and wanted to help, to make sure I didn't go down fruitless paths. But he said he didn't have the crucial answers I wanted. He would talk to others to talk to me and would give me whatever help he could. We shook hands and said good-bye.

A week or so later, we met for dinner. I asked him about Simpson's divorce from Nicole. Alan told me O.J. fought it for a while, lost a lot of weight, and desperately wanted Nicole back. Finally, when Nicole started dating around, O.J. moved on with his life. He met Paula. We then talked about O.J. and Nicole's reconciliation in 1993 and their final breakup in 1994.

In or about April of 1994, he told me, Simpson announced that Nicole was going to move back into Rockingham. The fact that he was allowing her to return to his home confirmed that he wanted her back very, very badly. Then, Alan said, Nicole pulled the plug. Austin told me that a few weeks later, in May, Simpson said Nicole had broken up with him.

There it was. This was admissible evidence. Simpson had told him that he was the one who'd been dumped.

But that wasn't unusual, Alan stressed. He thought there was nothing particularly traumatic about their last break-up, because they were always breaking up, going back and forth. Nicole would constantly change her mind, and this would drive Simpson crazy. Austin also said the idea that Simpson was over Nicole because he had brought Paula back into his life was nonsense. Simpson had been seeing Paula on the side even when he was supposed to have been reconciling with Nicole.

What continued to haunt Austin more than anything is that while he believed that the DNA and blood evidence showed his friend was guilty, he really needed to understand why he did it. In his mind, the motive for the murders had something to do with Marcus Allen.

There was an intense rivalry between Simpson and Allen. Simpson had won the Heisman Trophy while at USC in 1968, Allen won it at USC thirteen years later. Simpson was elected to the Pro Football Hall of Fame, and so, sooner or later, would Allen. Both were attractive men, but Allen was still playing in the NFL, still in the spotlight, and Simpson was not. Simpson was jealous. He always thought he was better than Allen, could run faster, play harder. In fact, once when they were on the beach, Simpson challenged the younger man to a race—and beat him, arthritic knees and all. Simpson bragged about that all the time.

Their rivalry extended to women; Simpson swore he was a better cocksman. The fact that Nicole had an affair with Marcus and admitted it to Simpson—even though Allen denied it ever happened—seemed very important to Austin. If Marcus Allen had come back into Nicole's life, he told me, that was a factor that could have driven Simpson to kill.

Austin told me he learned from a reliable source that Simpson's therapist, Dr. Burt Kittay, may have consulted with Simpson and Nicole regarding a domestic violence incident that occurred after the 1989 New Year's beating. Simpson, of course, swore he never touched Nicole after the 1989 incident (when he only admitted to fending off her attacks of him). Austin would not reveal the source of this information, so we tracked down Kittay, who was living in Corpus Christi, Texas. Kittay refused to testify on the grounds of patient-therapist privilege, and I was never able to verify Austin's report.

"They talked about his blowing up on the golf course the morning of the murders," Austin said. "The prosecutors made a big deal about his arguing with Craig [Baumgarten]. That's nothing. That happens all the time." Austin thought the prosecution placed far too much emphasis on Simpson coming to near blows with his friend. Nevertheless, I felt the golf partners Baumgarten, Bob Hoskins (not the actor), and Mike Melchiorre might have valuable information, and I wanted to talk to them. Austin told me he would help with Hoskins and Melchiorre, but "Forget Craig. It's a waste of time."

Something else rubbed Austin wrong. "O.J. was notorious for cheating at golf," he said. To people who play religiously, cheating at golf reveals the true measure of a man. Golf is a gentleman's sport, with a bedrock reliance on a player's honesty; Simpson would cheat and expect to get away with it. If he hit a bad shot he would complain he was interfered with and was entitled to another. He expected a Mulligan. If he couldn't find his ball, he would drop another. He would improve his lie. Even though his partners were counting shots, he would say he'd shot a six when he shot a seven and expect them to look the other way. Austin was so bothered by this, I used to joke to myself that more than Simpson's blood at the murder scene, his obsessiveness, or jealousy, Austin found it easier to believe that Simpson killed Nicole because he cheated at golf.

Austin then mentioned, almost in passing, that he had hosted a birthday dinner party for his then girlfriend, Gail, on Sunday of Memorial Day weekend in Palm Springs and that Simpson had attended. Simpson sat next to a woman named Donna Estes and her friend Steve Antabee. Simpson had come with Paula, but they got into a fight and she left. This, I recalled, was what Baker had questioned Paula about in her deposition. I pressed Alan for more details. Simpson, he told me, had been complaining to him about Nicole the entire weekend—their relationship was going back and forth and she was driving him crazy—and he spent a good deal of time at that party airing those complaints to Donna. Austin promised to call Donna and ask her to speak to me.

We subpoenaed Allen Schwartz and his wife, Pam. Allen called me up and said he had heard some people were meeting with me in lieu of giving a deposition. I invited him in. He was another of Simpson's wealthy businessman friends, like Alan Austin, in the garment business. Allen owned and operated a company that manufactured and sold women's clothing. He and his wife, Pam, had been social friends of the Simpsons.

Allen Schwartz came through the door looking like James Caan. His face was deeply tanned and deeply lined, showing off blindingly white teeth and ample black eyebrows. In his late 40s, he wore his gray hair short and had the solid look of a man with the time and desire to work out hard. He also had the air of a man who enjoyed his wealth. Pam Schwartz was blond, pretty, shapely, but quiet and troubled.

To earn their confidence I told them what I knew, from the beginning of Simpson's relationship with Nicole through their various breakups, the beatings, the trip to Cabo, the IRS letter, and their troubles at the end. I presented it as if I was arguing to a jury. They were impressed with my command of the facts and how well I understood O.J. and Nicole. "You got it," Allen said. But there was more to get.

I asked them, "How do you feel?" Allen Schwartz said, "Look, I think he did it." His wife, Pam, couldn't say. "I just can't believe it," she told me. "Could he really do it?"

"We don't think the prosecutors really understood what happened," Allen told me, "but you've showed us a lot of evidence and we're confused."

They, too, had been told Simpson would testify in the criminal case and were disappointed when he refused. The race card also upset them.

I asked what they knew about Simpson hitting Nicole. Allen said Simpson had come to their house the morning of January 1, 1989, and said he and Nicole had gotten into a bad fight. Simpson did not say he had hit her, only that they had gotten into a fight and that the police were looking for him. He wanted to pull his car into the Schwartzes' garage so the cops wouldn't see it. Simpson called Skip Taft and Al Cowlings to come over. Taft, at the time, was also a close friend of Allen Schwartz and represented him in his business dealings. Schwartz said Simpson sat on their couch, pulled a blanket over himself, and waited.

The cabal huddled all day, deep in discussion, with Schwartz stepping in and out. "It was damage control," he said. Taft was upset that Nicole called the police and risked hurting Simpson's career as a personality/spokesperson, as well as her own financial security. Taft's own career was involved, as well.

I showed the Schwartzes passages from Nicole's diaries and told them, "I know Simpson was beating her. I know that Nicole was very, very unhappy about it. I need people to step up to the plate and tell me what they know—whether Nicole told them of the abuse, whether Simpson told them, whether they saw anything themselves." I did not know if I was getting through.

Then I read them a long letter Nicole had written to Simpson about the state of their marriage, their relationship, written before Nicole left and filed for divorce. I showed them that it was written in her own hand.

O.J.:
. . . I'd like you to keep this letter if we split, so that you'll always know why we split. I'd also like you to keep it if we stay together, as a reminder.

The letter then went on to recount Nicole's heartwrenching pain and disappointment, as her husband violated her trust, called her names, ridiculed her appearance during pregnancy, beat her, abused her, and destroyed her hopes and dreams.

Pam Schwartz started crying. Allen was wiping away his tears.

Nicole talked about Simpson's "mean streak." When she had been pregnant, she said, rather than reveling in the fact that they were going to have a baby, Simpson had berated her about her gaining weight.

She talked about the time, "you beat the holy hell out of me and we lied at the X-ray lab and said I fell off a bike." She said he criticized her housekeeping and cooking. "I just don't see how that compares to infidelity, wife beating, verbal abuse."

She could have hurt Simpson after the New Year's Eve beating by going public and then prosecuting him, she wrote, but had decided not to.

About the New Year's Day beating in 1989, Nicole said, "I called the cops to save my life, whether you believe it or not . . . But I've never loved you since, or been the same." The beating had made her examine her life, and she hadn't liked what she'd seen. From the outside, it looked perfect, but on the inside she knew it was a sham.

Nicole concluded by saying:

I just believed that a relationship is based on trust and the last time I trusted you was at our wedding ceremony. It's just so hard for me to trust you again, even though you say you're a different guy, that O.J. Simpson guy brought me a lot of pain and heartache. I tried so hard with him. I wanted so to be a good wife, but he never gave me a chance.

Both Allen and Pam were deep in tears by the time I finished reading. They hadn't known the details, they had not understood the depth of Nicole's despair. "Nicole hid this," they told me. "She didn't talk about this kind of stuff."

"Dan," Allen said, "I'm telling you. In my opinion, this involves Marcus. For him to do what he did, I think this involves Marcus." I pressed him for details, but he had none. It was just a gut feeling.

Allen Schwartz told me he witnessed Simpson's aggression firsthand. For several years, he said, he organized July Fourth softball games; he would put a team together consisting largely of white Jewish businessmen, and Simpson would put a team together consisting largely of black professional athletes. It was a big joke, the blacks against the Jews. They would go to a park and play. Simpson's teams routinely triumphed, but it was a fun day.

One year, Schwartz invited some good athletes to try and even the score, and by some miracle his team won.

The next year Simpson put together a stud team and wiped them out, destroyed them. Simpson trash-talked while they piled it on. The game was more than a blow-out, it was an intended humiliation. What had been a friendly outing became tense, edgy, and unpleasant. It was no fun at all.

Schwartz was embarrassed in front of his friends, some of whom had come all the way from the East Coast to play and enjoy the day. As he was packing up his equipment at the end of the drubbing, Simpson continued to give him a hard time. Later, at a postgame party at the Schwartzes' home, Simpson was still ragging on him. Finally Schwartz said, "Will you just knock it off! It wasn't that much fun out there, what you did." Simpson got right in Schwartz's face and started yelling at him. Allen thought Simpson was going to belt him. Finally someone came and broke it up.

Stories like this, while of no significance to proving Simpson's guilt, were nonetheless important to me. They helped me to understand what O.J. Simpson was really about; they helped me see the man and not the icon.

The Schwartzes had arrived at the MSK offices at eleven in the morning. At five in the afternoon they invited me to continue the discussion at their home in Brentwood, not far from Simpson's. I said I would stop by after work.

The house was beautiful, warm, and homey. Simpson had been a frequent guest and would come and go as he pleased, almost like family. We sat down to eat, with the television on, in the same room and at the same table where they all used to eat dinner and watch television with Simpson. "Where would he sit?" I asked. "Right where you're sitting," they told me. They pulled out pictures of trips to Las Vegas and vacations they and the Simpsons took together; here were Simpson and Nicole in what appeared to be happy times. Simpson always wore the O.J. smile; Nicole's was more distant.

Allen Schwartz said that when you went out with O.J. he was always the center of attention, wherever he went. The public adored him. He said Simpson loved the publicity and notoriety, loved being admired and fawned over, loved being O.J. He also said Simpson was insanely possessive toward Nicole, fiercely proud of her physical appearance, and controlling and manipulating toward her. She had to do whatever he said.

Pam Schwartz had been very tight-lipped all day. Allen did all the talking. But over dinner, as we all got to know each other, she began to warm up. When I called her the next afternoon to thank them for their hospitality, she found it easier to talk.

Pam had seen Nicole on the weekend she was killed. That Saturday, she said, Pam and her daughter, Danielle, attended a rehearsal at Paul Revere Junior High School for the next day's dance recital. Nicole was there with Sydney, and the two women spoke for several hours. Nicole told Pam she was finished with Simpson, that the relationship was over once and for all. "This time he really did it," she said, but did not explain what it was Simpson had done. (I knew she was referring to the IRS situation.)

Nicole made it clear that *she* had ended the relationship; she told Pam she would always love O.J., but he would never change. Her decision was final, she said, and she was looking forward to moving in a new and positive direction. There were other mothers around at the time, so she didn't get into details, but Nicole did stress that her future was going to be good. She seemed free, Pam said.

According to Pam, Nicole could be brutally honest and direct. She didn't lie, and she never beat around the bush. She would be kind to a maid at a fancy dinner party and not hesitate to speak her mind to a famous celebrity. Pam believed strongly that Nicole was the one and only true love of Simpson's life; even though he could have many other women, no one could replace Nicole. Paula, said Pam, meant nothing to him. Nicole, however, was haunted by Simpson's infidelity and deceit, and that is what forced her to leave him.

Little by little, I was not only piecing together what really happened but also developing evidence to impeach Simpson's many lies.

Another piece of the puzzle fell into place when I was introduced to Jackie Cooper at one of the dinners at the Schwartzes' home. "I'd like you to meet this guy," Allen said, "maybe he'll be able to help you."

Cooper was a tennis pro at La Quinta Country Club in Palm Springs who had known Simpson for a number of years. Allen Schwartz and Alan Austin told Cooper about me, and he agreed to come to Los Angeles to see me.

At dinner I found Cooper to be a quiet, low-key man. That's his personality, he doesn't say much. He had graying wavy hair and the look of a Boston Irishman who had come west and never gone home. Kind of a closed face. After the meal, he and I walked outside to the Schwartzes' tennis court, and I asked him about Simpson's Memorial Day weekend 1994 in Palm Springs, two weeks before the murders.

Simpson and Paula Barbieri had rolled in to La Quinta in separate cars in the wee hours of Saturday morning. With little or no sleep, Simpson had played an early round of golf with Cooper, Alan Austin, and one of Austin's relatives. Simpson rode with Cooper in the golf cart. Throughout the round, Simpson talked about Nicole. Nicole had split up with him, Simpson told Cooper, and the split was final. He was devastated.

Early that afternoon, Simpson came by Cooper's home wanting to play a second round. Cooper said no, it was 105 degrees outside and he was tired. Simpson asked Cooper to call Paula and tell her O.J. was sleeping on his couch. Cooper said he didn't want to do that. Simpson left.

Around six in the evening, Cooper received a phone call. It was Simpson. He and Paula had gotten into a fight. "If Nicole were here, you wouldn't be playing golf," she had said, "you'd be spending time with her." The fight had progressed. "You still love her," she'd said, "don't you." Simpson told her, "Yes, I do." Paula had taken off.

Simpson spent an hour on the phone with Cooper. They would have gone on longer, but they had to get to Alan Austin's dinner party for his girlfriend, and Cooper still had to get dressed. Simpson spent the entire time lamenting his loss—of Nicole. Paula had just walked out on him but all he talked about was his ex-wife. Cooper confirmed what Austin had told me. O.J. said Nicole was the one who broke off the relationship.

Cooper was a reluctant witness. He was close friends with Al Cowlings, who he said was a decent person. Even though he said he never thought much of Simpson, he did not want to get involved in the lawsuit. I said, "You know, Jackie, what little you have to say is very important, and I would like you to testify at the trial."

"I really don't want to. Do I have to?" he asked.

"Well"—after hearing Cooper share his thoughts I was reluctant to strong-arm him—"the answer is, you don't have to. If I subpoena you, you'll have to, but if it will make you miserable, I won't do it. But you need to think about it."

There was nothing for Cooper to gain by talking to me, and it would have been easy to clam up and say he did not remember. But he knew that talking was the right thing to do; as difficult as it was for him, he did it. There were not enough people like that. People like Cooper were real heroes.

Alan Austin and Pam and Allen Schwartz were even more torn. They had been best friends with Simpson; when confronted with the possibility that their good friend was a murderer, they simply and understandably hadn't wanted to believe it. Intellectually they knew that the evidence pointed to his culpability, but their internal conflicts kept raising questions. "Dan, why did he do it? Did he go there with a knife and gloves? Did he plan it? Could he have done it alone? Do you think somebody helped him clean up? What about the fact that they found this sock on the rug? Why is it there?" I had to convince them of what they already knew in their hearts but didn't want to acknowledge: Simpson was guilty.

Allen Schwartz gave me some other important leads to run down. He said, after the murders, Bob Bender, another of Simpson's close garment business friends, told him that on June 9 Simpson had spent the night at Bender's home in Long Island before returning to Los Angeles for his daughter's dance recital. Simpson was so racked with depression over Nicole having dumped him that Bender could not entice him out of his chair. This, of course, contradicted everything Simpson was saying about being free of Nicole and back with Paula. I asked Schwartz to help me get Bender to say this on the record. I had high hopes that he would come through. Ultimately, when I took his deposition in New York, Bender denied the story, under oath. He claimed Simpson was depressed because his family was not together and not because he had lost Nicole. So, it wasn't all success.

Alan Austin helped set up a meeting with Joe Kolkowitz, a talent agent and Simpson's friend, tennis partner, and an occasional golfing partner. When he walked in I shook his hand and said, "Joe, how's your brother, Dan? How's your father, Hymie?" He looked at me and his eyes got real wide. *"You are the same Danny Petrocelli!"*

When I was in high school I used to go to my friend Dan Kolkowitz's house, hang out, listen to music. He had an older brother, a real hippie. Sure enough, here was Joe, the same guy I knew twenty-six years earlier, but with short hair. We talked about the old days in West Orange, New Jersey, then we really started talking.

Joe told me Simpson was "a complete mess" after Nicole had filed for divorce in 1992, that he must have lost at least twenty-five pounds. "He was a pathetic, sniveling, crying person," Joe told me. This was an important insight, I thought, because it showed, despite the fact that he could have had his choice of women, how emotionally attached Simpson actually was to Nicole.

Kolkowitz had known Simpson for almost fourteen years. He'd stood by him throughout the criminal trial, particularly helping private investigator Bill Pavelic collect evidence against Simpson's friend Ron Shipp (who was a friendly witness for the prosecution). But there were several "blows," as he described them, which made him change his mind and decide that Simpson was guilty. One was that Simpson did not testify. Simpson had told him repeatedly that he *would* speak in court on his own behalf. His old friends believed in him and wanted to hear him clear his name.

The other was Marcus Allen. Joe had heard the rumors of the affair between Nicole and Marcus and asked Simpson about it while visiting him at the jail one day. Simpson denied knowing about it and downplayed the affair. Later, from reading Faye Resnick's book, Joe learned that Simpson knew about the affair all along; he was both upset and suspicious that Simpson had not leveled with him.

Kolkowitz then angrily called Allen, telling him he was out of line. Allen told Joe the relationship was never consummated. As unlikely as that seemed, Kolkowitz thought the whole thing odd; Nicole had told Joe she thought Marcus Allen looked like ET. He suspected she had been with Allen just to get back at Simpson. In his opinion, Simpson's killing Nicole had something to do with Marcus Allen.

Joe ran a talent agency. I was gearing up to depose Marcus Allen but did not know how to contact him. I told Joe I could subpoena the information or he could provide it voluntarily. The next day, via fax, there was Marcus Allen's address. Joe also said he would call Tom McCollum for me. I was beginning to get passed around.

Tom McCollum was another of O.J.'s and Nicole's friends. He was given one pair of gloves as a Christmas gift by Nicole, Simpson was given another. McCollum's gloves were not Aris Leather Light gloves, the type of glove used by the killer. I was concerned that the defense would use McCollum to say the gloves Nicole gave to Simpson also were not Aris gloves. McCollum confirmed to me he did not know what Nicole gave O.J.

Donna Estes was a good friend of Alan Austin's. She had been at the Palm Springs dinner party thrown for Austin's girlfriend, at which Paula had walked out and Simpson was wailing about Nicole. She said Simpson sat next to her and proceeded to bear his soul. "Paula just split on me," he told her. "We had a big fight about Nicole. She just wants to screw around, and I'm trying to settle down in life, and I want to have a nice family life, and she's still not ready for that." Paula had asked Simpson if he still loved his ex-wife and he had answered "Yes." Simpson, she told me, went on about how he couldn't think of a better day than to go to Disneyland with Nicole and the children, it would be the best day of his life. But Nicole, O.J. complained, "would rather go out and wear short skirts and see who notices her ass." He could not stop talking about Nicole. "She is the love of my life," he told Estes.

I interviewed Bob Hoskins in the presence of his attorney, Ron Papel. He had played golf with Simpson on June 12, had visited Rockingham several times over the years and seen Nicole there, and had spoken to Simpson only once since the acquittal. I had been told by a source that Hoskins had once seen Simpson hit Nicole at Rockingham. I wanted him to admit it. He denied it. He gave me no information. A gruff guy with a gravelly voice, he didn't have money like the rest of the crowd, he was just an old-timer playing golf. He was not going to say a word.

Wayne Hughes is a very wealthy man who owns Public Storage. I subpoenaed him for a deposition, and he agreed to meet with me instead. He had been Simpson's friend and mentor since the athlete's days at USC, consulting on his business deals and NFL contracts. He'd been a fatherlike figure for Simpson. The previous five or six years, however, their relationship had been fading. Nevertheless, Simpson had called Hughes from the Bronco during the low-speed chase and asked that he take care of his kids.

I wanted to talk to Hughes about an incident in the early 1980s, in which Nicole had shown him bruises she said Simpson had given her. About ten or eleven at night, Hughes told me, Nicole arrived at his house and said Simpson had hit her. She pulled up her sweater and showed him the marks. Hughes saw a red welt underneath and to the side of her breast. He had never before heard that Simpson abused her. She told him, "I don't understand. He gets so mad. Look at what happened. I'm afraid to go back." Nicole asked if Hughes would cool him down.

Hughes drove to Rockingham, but Simpson was not there. The former running back had a pattern of fleeing. Hughes waited ten minutes, then drove home. He spent the evening talking to Nicole. She left around one A.M. When he called the next day to see if she was all right, Nicole told him not to talk to anyone about what had happened.

On January 2, 1989, Hughes picked up Simpson to take him to the Rose Bowl. In the car, Simpson said he had gone to a party with Nicole on New Year's Eve and gotten drunk. Marcus Allen and his girlfriend, Kathryn, had been there. Kathryn showed Nicole a piece of diamond jewelry Allen had bought her at a discount jeweler. "How do you like yours?" she asked. Apparently, Allen had told Kathryn that Simpson had bought a similar item at the same time. Of course, Nicole had not gotten it. When Nicole and Simpson got back home, Simpson wanted sex. According to O.J., Nicole had said, "Why don't you fuck the girl you gave the diamonds to!" Hughes said that according to Simpson, Nicole had then attacked him. Simpson said he had caught her with a backhand swing.

In his deposition, Simpson had flatly denied ever hitting Nicole. Never swung his hand at her. Just tried to restrain her. Another important impeachment.

After the football game they drove back to Rockingham, Simpson talking about the incident all the way. Hughes spoke with Nicole for quite a while. She was angry and, hoping to get even, wanted to go public. He told her, "If you want to leave O.J., that's your business. But you will need money. If you go public, you will hurt everyone."

"It's not fair," she moaned. "This happens to me, but nothing happens to him!" She was extremely upset.

Hughes remembered looking at the situation logically, like a businessman. He said it was something he now deeply regrets.

TWELVE

The Lethal Paralegal

Not all of Simpson's friends came our way. Many ran in the other direction. It was our job to track them down.

We were using a company that specialized in serving subpoenas, and they were not getting the job done. Witnesses were ducking their process servers, and we were getting large bills for surveillance charges and multiple attempts. While I was annoyed at the time it was taking to get hostile witnesses in the deposition room, I was not paying close attention to the billing. Our paralegal, Steve Foster, looked at the high charges and poor results and came to me, saying, "Let me take a shot at serving these people."

Steve Foster was a godsend, the son of one of MSK's clients who had been working as a summer gofer before heading off to law school. I didn't know him well, but when I would see this tall, lean, redheaded guy around the offices, I liked the spring in his step. This was a kid, twenty-three years old, with a light in his eye. I saw him walking in the hall one day during his last week of work, and on a clear lark said to him, "How would you like to put off law school and work as a paralegal on the Simpson case? We can't pay you much, but you'll have the experience of a lifetime. I'd like you to think about it."

He said, "I just did. I'll do it."

I was concerned that as a process server, Steve would run off like a cowboy and get himself into trouble. I was also worried about his safety; he would be coming into close contact with some powerful people who wanted less than nothing to do with any of us. Still, he talked me into giving him the job and I said, "Go for it."

Craig Baumgarten, one of Simpson's golfing buddies, part of the group Simpson played with on the morning of the murders, had avoided us for a considerable length of time. The process service company had had no luck getting him at his office, no luck getting him at his home. They had run up quite a bill in the meantime. Baumgarten was an artist's manager in the entertainment industry and an aspiring movie producer; his office was not far from ours. Steve paid him a visit.

The secretary outside Baumgarten's suite said, "You need an appointment." Apparently that had stopped the service company.

Foster played on his own youth. "Well, you know, I met Mr. Baumgarten on the golf course the other day with my uncle, and he said he's got a great book that I need to read." Steve was making it up as he went along. "He's not going to remember me, he's going to remember my face. Can I pop in and just grab the book?"

The secretary was charmed. "I'll go see, I think he's on the phone." She walked down the corridor. Steve waited until she turned the first corner, then ran to that wall, pressed himself against it, and peered around like a paratrooper going house to house. She turned a second corner, and he pulled the same maneuver. She entered Baumgarten's office, and Steve followed her in. Baumgarten's desk was off to the left, and he was doing business on the speakerphone, screaming. Steve walked over to Baumgarten. The secretary, surprised to see him behind her, tried to usher Steve out, but to no avail. He took the folded subpoena from his back pocket.

"Mr. Baumgarten, I am Steve Foster and I'm serving you with this deposition subpoena for a personal appearance and production of documents and things. You are served!" He slapped it on the man's desk.

Baumgarten started screaming at him. It was bad enough to get slapped with a subpoena he had been trying desperately to avoid. It was worse to get served in his own office, behind his own security, *in front of business adversaries on the speakerphone.* As Steve reported to me, Baumgarten freaked.

"Get the fuck outta here! Who the hell are you? Goddamn you! Get the fuck out of my office!"

Foster was fearless. Joe Stellini, a restaurateur and Simpson's friend for over twenty years, Sydney Simpson's godfather, had also been avoiding us. He lived close to our office as well, and Steve would drive by his house every night on his way home. Twenty nights he knocked on the door, rang the doorbell, got nothing. On the occasions he looked through the window, he saw pictures of Simpson running up the staircase wall.

Steve basically gave up, figuring they were on different schedules and Stellini would never be there, but out of habit he kept going back. One day, expecting nothing, he parked his car on the wrong side of the street, left his engine running, went over and knocked. As he was getting ready to turn away he saw a glimpse of a head inside the house. "What do you want?" a voice asked.

Steve was unprepared. "Uh, my name is Steve," he began, just to buy himself some time. "I'm your next-door neighbor and I wanted to let you know that some guy is casing your place."

"Yeah?"

"Yeah. He's been looking in your windows, he's been looking in your garage, he's been standing around—"

"Hold on. Hold on a minute." He opened the door and stepped outside. "What does this guy look like?"

Steve whipped out the subpoena. "You're served, Mr. Stellini!"

"You fuckin' prick! You fuckin' little prick!"

Steve walked quickly to his car. "See you at your deposition, Mr. Stellini!"

"I hope you pop a fuckin' tire!"

Steve peeled away.

Mike Melchiorre, another of Simpson's regular golfing buddies, lived in a big house up Mandeville Canyon with a lot of windows. He had a good view of visitors. Foster arrived at 6:00 A.M., while the house was asleep, and waited for Melchiorre to come outside and pick up his morning newspaper. He never did. The paper just sat there. Finally the garage door opened and Foster nailed him. "Damn," said Melchiorre. "Goddamn." He walked away, very upset, then seemed to calm down and came back. He talked to Steve for a few minutes, very unusual for someone who has just been served a subpoena, and Steve felt he was "a really nice guy." He just did not want to get involved.

"Maybe it doesn't have to be a formal deposition," Steve told him. "Maybe you could just come talk to my boss and answer the questions, and if he needs to take your deposition, he can serve you again." Melchiorre seemed to mellow. The next day he had a heart attack and died.

Steve's most notable service was on Dr. Ron Fischman, another of Simpson's close friends. Dr. Fischman's wife, Cora, was part of Nicole's social circle and at the time of the murders was having a secret affair with a bag boy at one of the local supermarkets. A successful endocrinologist, Fischman was avoiding his deposition notice like the plague.

Steve did his homework. He reviewed the LAPD's "Murder Book" and found that the police had also had a hard time serving him. In their files was a detailed description of Fischman's cars. So Steve staked out Fischman's home on North Rockingham for several days. First he would drive by. If the doors to the house were open, he would walk past and see what cars were around. If none were in the driveway, he would sit for hours in his own car behind some bushes a block away and wait for him. For days he saw nothing.

Finally a black BMW pulled in and a man stepped out. Steve recognized him as Dr. Fischman. He dove out of his car and flew down the street on foot.

"Dr. Fischman! Dr. Fischman!" By the time he ran the block he was out of breath and panting heavily.

Fischman turned to face him. He was a doctor, so perhaps he thought it was a medical emergency.

Steve kept his subpoenas folded with a nice crease in his breast pocket so he could pull them out quickly and easily. He reached in, trying to catch his breath and talk at the same time.

"You're served with a . . . You're served with a subpoena."

Fischman immediately ducked his head and put his hands behind his back. He turned and started to run inside his house. Steve threw the subpoena over Fischman's shoulder, and the doctor actually kicked it through the door and into his garage.

Steve called the office and said, "He's served. He's nailed."

Fischman didn't show up for his deposition. He disputed the fact that we had served him. We had to go to court and submit a sworn declaration regarding the facts of the service. Judge Haber issued an order to show cause (OSC) commanding Fischman to appear in court and show good cause why he failed to appear for deposition. But now we had to serve the OSC on him.

This time, Steve took a couple of MSK summer associates with him, law students recruited to work at the firm during the summer in anticipation of possible future employment. They brought a still camera to record the action. As they were driving up the street, the black BMW was pulling out of the driveway. Steve didn't have his papers ready; they were in his briefcase. He pulled his car in front of Fischman's driveway and fumbled for them. Fischman was sitting behind the wheel, waiting for this roadblock to clear, when he realized who Steve was.

Fischman's house was hidden behind head-high shrubs, which protected a manicured lawn and a circular driveway. Fischman threw his car into drive and lurched forward. There was room for him to escape, but he could not negotiate the angle because Steve had it blocked. He jammed the BMW into reverse and tried to hang a U-turn to get to the other exit. Meanwhile Steve had jumped out of the car with his papers.

Fischman was skidding back and forth, trying to get free, when he got stuck between a Ford Explorer and his garage. As he looked over his shoulder to see if he was going to make it, Steve slammed the subpoena on the driver's side window and screamed, "You're served with an order to show cause! You are commanded to appear . . . !" He had the legal wording memorized, and he was screaming. Fischman cranked the wheel all the way to the right, threw it into reverse, and gunned it. The entire front end of the BMW was heading right for Foster. Steve leaped onto the grass. Fischman put it in drive and headed straight for him.

Steve leaped again, and Fischman went peeling across the lush grass of his front lawn, lost control of his brand-new BMW 740 IL, and went tearing broadside into a chain-link fence on the other side of the property. He hit a bolt that scraped and screeched along the entire side of the car, then went barreling out of the driveway. Two tires skidded and Fischman fishtailed across the street, careening into the opposite curb. He just missed a trash Dumpster, almost hit Foster's car, and left rubber down the street of his residential neighborhood at around sixty miles per hour.

The summer associates were snapping away. They got the turn, they got the flight. They got the rubber prints on the pavement and the deep tire tracks chewing up the front lawn. They took several pictures of the run-over subpoena sitting crumpled on Fischman's driveway.

Fischman failed to appear in court for the order to show cause. Judge Haber issued a bench warrant for his arrest, with $25,000 bail. This got Fischman's attention, and he finally showed up for his deposition. He ended up having to pay my firm $4,000 for the fees and costs associated with serving him, including Steve's time. We cashed it happily and tacked a photocopy of his personal check on the wall of the War Room to remind us of who we were dealing with.

When I threatened to depose Craig Baumgarten under oath, he chose to come to the MSK offices and talk. He arrived with his lawyer. Baumgarten was a smart, aggressive guy. He told me at the beginning, "I've got to be up front with you, I don't think he did it." He was still Simpson's friend.

On the morning of the murders, during their golf game, he had gotten into a screaming argument with Simpson at the second tee. This had drawn a lot of attention during the criminal trial because it implied that Simpson began the day in a dark mood. I wasn't so sure. As I had learned from Allen Schwartz, Simpson was apt to blow up in competitive situations, and this may have been nothing out of the ordinary. "Oh, that's kind of been blown out of proportion," he said. But, he proceeded to admit, in response to my questions, they did face off as if they were about to come to blows, which had never happened before. He admitted never having seen Simpson quite so angry, but said they were both competitive guys, and it didn't mean anything.

Baumgarten dismissed the hard evidence against Simpson, saying he believed the blood evidence was planted, and the gloves were not Simpson's. He was just spitting back everything O.J. had told him. They had talked about Nicole's affair with Marcus Allen, and Simpson had said he wasn't jealous. He told me that after Simpson's divorce, it was Nicole who pursued Simpson to get back together. She started taking golf lessons and brought their kids to the golf course to see him. She began coming to Rockingham unannounced.

I asked Baumgarten about Simpson's infidelity. He was tight-lipped, but did admit that Simpson had had an affair with Tawny Kitaen, who was one of Baumgarten's clients.

Baumgarten acknowledged Simpson was sad at his and Nicole's final breakup, that Simpson had hoped they could get back together in the future, but at the time Nicole had to go her separate way. I sat there, realizing this guy had no intention of helping me and was not, in my view, forthcoming.

"What did he say about Paula?" I asked him.

"They had a big fight at the party the night before. Paula was pissed off because she couldn't go to the recital." This was a big slipup, a wonderful nugget, but I remained stolid. The fact that he had just badly impeached Barbieri and Simpson on a key fact was lost on him. Baumgarten told me Simpson said it wasn't right, that Paula's presence would make everyone uncomfortable and he didn't want her there. Paula had gotten very upset.

"Are you sure about that?"

"Yeah," Baumgarten chuckled. "I'm so sure that when I heard about Nicole's murder, I thought Paula did it!"

Cora Fischman was among Nicole's closest friends. They had gone running together, discussed their husbands, confided in each other about their affairs with younger men. When Barbara Walters came looking for someone to go on-camera and tell Nicole's story, Cora filled the bill. Walters elicited some good information from Cora. Cora admitted that Simpson had been following Nicole, that he would lose his temper, that Nicole said Simpson beat her, and that Nicole was scared of him. She told Walters that Nicole was not into drugs, her life was not spinning out of control, and that actually Simpson was her problem. Cora was a firm Nicole supporter.

Then Faye Resnick wrote her book and cornered the market on attention and notoriety for their little circle. Cora was left out. She didn't like Faye; she called her the "drama queen." At that point, Cora did an about-face. During the criminal trial, she sat down with a couple of reporters from the *National Enquirer* and Michael Viner, who had published the Resnick book, and tried to develop a proposal of her own. Michael gave me a taped copy of that interview, and it was pretty tawdry. The reporters were looking for exploitive sex secrets. Did Nicole have sex with other women? Were there threesomes? With the Nicole's Best Friend slot filled, Cora sidled over to Simpson. By the time she showed up to be deposed, there was no question where she stood.

Cora Fischman was a petite woman of Filipino descent who wore her black hair past her shoulders. In her thirties, she was thin-fingered and aerobicized without actually being attractive. When she entered the room for her deposition there was no sense that she wanted to be there. The only person who wanted to be there less was Simpson himself.

I established that since Nicole's death, Cora and Simpson had had long conversations reminiscing about the last years of Nicole's life. Never once had Simpson offered a single idea or suggestion about how he believed Nicole was killed. Never once did he say the LAPD was biased against him or had treated him unfairly in the past or that he'd been framed. He offered no explanation for the evidence in the case.

In May and June 1994 Cora and Nicole had kept in close contact. Then they'd had a falling-out. Though she tried to deny it, there was clearly tension between the two. It seemed to arise from the fact that Cora used Nicole to cover for her in keeping her affair a secret from her husband. At midnight on the Saturday before the murders, Cora was at the home of her lover. Her husband—Dr. Ron Fischman, the motorist who tried to run over Steve Foster—called Nicole looking for her. Fischman and Nicole had a long conversation that grew heated. He thought she was lying to him, thought she knew where Cora was and was not saying. Nicole got off the phone, upset, and called Cora's lover, who also lied and said Cora was not there.

Sex was an important element of Cora's testimony. As part of the "Trash Nicole" defense, she swore Nicole told her she and Faye had participated in a threesome with a man. However, Cora was not present during this reported tryst, and I pointed out that when she was interviewed by LAPD detectives Cliff LeFall and Bert Luper, she did not tell them anything about Nicole's alleged solicitation of men.

She tried to avoid admitting the obvious. She had told Barbara Walters that Simpson had a violent temper, but when I said, "You told someone that O.J. Simpson had a violent temper. When you did so, were you telling the truth?" She answered, "I don't remember."

"You don't remember if you were telling the truth?!"

"Well, you know, there was a lot of confusion. . . ."

"You were confused about whether O.J. Simpson had a violent temper?"

With each evasive answer, the examination grew more contentious and aggressive, and I began to get answers damaging to Simpson. I established that Simpson was a jealous and controlling man when it came to Nicole. We went around and around over whether he was obsessed with her. "They were both obsessed with each other," she insisted.

"Was O.J. Simpson obsessed with Nicole? Yes or no?"

"'Obsession,' what do you mean by 'obsession'?"

"Ms. Fischman, you just told me they were both obsessed with each other. Correct?"

"Right."

"Now I am just asking you: Was O.J. Simpson obsessed with Nicole? Do you have trouble answering that question?"

"I never really saw the obsession."

"Never saw any evidence of obsession?"

"No."

"And never told anybody that O.J. Simpson was obsessive towards Nicole. Is that right?" She had said exactly that in the Viner interview, which she did not know we had. I pressed on. "When you say, 'They were obsessed with each other,' by that you mean that O.J. Simpson was obsessed with Nicole and Nicole was obsessed with O.J. Simpson. Is that right?"

"It's—"

"Is that right?"

"I would say so."

I ran Cora through the history of Nicole's original breakup with Simpson and how adamantly opposed Simpson had been. He would call Cora and ask, "Is Nicole having an affair?" She was. Cora said that six months before she moved out of Rockingham, in response to Simpson's constant womanizing and his many absences, Nicole had an affair with a man named Alejandro. Cora had covered for her. Simpson was not convinced. "Well, someone is eating the caviar and champagne every time I leave," he complained.

Cora had told Viner that Nicole was even afraid of Simpson's voice. She said, "He's really got a very bad temper." As of June 1994, Cora related in the deposition, Nicole was physically afraid of Simpson. "I'm so scared of O.J.," she'd said. The only person Nicole ever said she feared was Simpson. Once, when they were jogging together, Cora showed Nicole bruises she had received. Nicole was not impressed. "That's nothing compared to what I had," she'd said.

According to the Viner tape, age was also an issue between Simpson and Nicole. Cora said Nicole wanted to live a younger lifestyle and threw it in Simpson's face. "She had this fear of aging," Cora told me. "She said, 'I'll be sixty years old and nobody's gonna look at me. O.J.'s gonna be sixty and O.J. will still find a twenty-, thirty-year-old wife, and I'll be sixty; nobody's gonna look at me." Nicole was only thirty-five and wanted to take advantage of her looks while she felt she still had them. She was looking at younger men. Simpson wasn't getting any younger. He told Cora, "Hey, listen, I'm forty-seven years old. My knees start cracking. I've worked hard. When I was twenty-nine I was all tight."

Cora had told the detectives that Nicole wasn't seeing anyone at the time of her death. She had supposedly stopped seeing Bret from Cabo. "Well, you know," she told me at the deposition, "she was still seeing Marcus Allen."

One afternoon over coffee, Nicole told Cora she had seen both Bret *and* Marcus Allen the same day. "Why?" Cora asked. "O.J.'s out of town again?" Cora testified that, "Marcus calls Nicole when O.J. is out of town."

Two weeks after returning from Cabo, Cora confirmed, Nicole dumped Simpson. Simpson called Cora, very upset. "What's going on here?" he pleaded. "We were planning to be together. She was planning to move in. . . . What happened? What happened?" He was confused; Nicole kept going back and forth like a yo-yo. "Cora, I feel like a battered husband here. . . . I want to have my own life, and then when she sees that I have my own life, she comes back. What does she want? Tell me what she wants! I don't know what to do. I'm on the back nine, you're on the front nine. I'm forty-seven years old!"

Cora also confirmed that at the end, Simpson and Nicole were fighting. Nicole was furious with Simpson and said she didn't want to have anything more to do with him. There were two reasons.

She told Cora, "O.J.'s trying to steal all my friends. He's trying to buy my friends." Simpson gave Faye Resnick's fiancé, Christian Reichardt, $5,000 and invited Faye to an elegant sports celebrity event. Nicole called him and said, "How dare you buy everything. You took my friends away, took my family away." (When they had first split, years before, Nicole had confided to Cora how very bad she felt that many of her friends had abandoned her. Cora mentioned Faye in particular.)

Nicole also told her how angry and scared she was about the IRS letter and the fact that Simpson was going to have her and the children thrown out of the house, onto the street. "That's the last money I have!" she had screamed over the phone. "He wants me to go to jail!"

But none of this came easily. Cora appeared wary and uncomfortable during the entire deposition; she consistently tried to soft-pedal Simpson's behavior and inject unflattering sexual innuendoes into Nicole's portrait.

The more time I spent with Cora Fischman, the less I liked her. I believed she was a traitor, trying to help Simpson, trying to distinguish herself in some way, any way, no matter how perverse. I hammered her for two days and would not let her get away with spinning Simpson's side of the story. I kept bringing her back to her earlier statements, the ones she'd made before she turned. She kept trying to incriminate Faye, but when asked for specifics, she didn't have any firsthand information. Even though they were extremely close, she had never seen Nicole use drugs. The same applied to the supposed threesomes. I could use these admissions to neutralize Cora from testifying against us in the "Trash Nicole" defense—that was becoming more clear with each defense witness I spoke to.

The best thing that came out of Cora Fischman's deposition was her testimony that Simpson had been dumped by Nicole, not the other way around, and that Simpson had been very unhappy about it. This destroyed the entire scenario Simpson and his lawyers had been trying to sell. Conversations between Nicole and Cora were hearsay and therefore troublesome; I probably could not get them into evidence. But we had also unearthed some excellent conversations between Cora and Simpson which would serve our purposes very well.

As I did with several pro-Simpson witnesses, I showed Cora entries from Nicole's diaries detailing Simpson's physical abuse and cruel treatment. This frazzled the defense, who could do nothing about the effect it had on people. I showed them because I wanted these people to see and hear Nicole's own words. I wanted to make Cora see how Nicole really felt, to make her feel guilty for hiding information or holding back. Cora was moved to tears by the diaries. "Nicole never told me any of this," she said softly.

For all her attempts to aid Simpson, Cora failed.

Christian Reichardt had been engaged to Faye Resnick at the time of the murders. He was a chiropractor in his forties who wore his long blond hair in a ponytail. With his piercing blue eyes, chiseled chin, and big smile on his face, his engaging appearance had been a little bit of a hit at the criminal trial.

Reichardt was the male equivalent of Cora Fischman. Directly after the murders he made a statement on Barbara Walters's show confirming Faye's account of her phone call with Simpson in which he threatened to kill Nicole. However, in the intervening months he had been seduced by O.J.'s celebrity and had clearly joined forces with him. Now, although he had not heard Simpson's voice on the telephone that night, he was saying the threat had been a misunderstanding, a figure of speech, that the whole thing was a joke. I disliked him immediately. He never lost his cool, never showed emotion, he could look you in the eye with a penetrating smile and just lie to you. I called him the "Ice Man."

At their depositions, I always asked the Simpson allies about their interaction with the defendant. "How many times did you see him? Did you see him in jail? Did you talk to him on the phone in jail? Since he got out of jail, have you seen him? How many times? At his house? Your house?" They were under oath and had to answer. They tried to downplay their contact by saying things like "I've seen him a few times," but I wasn't going to take "a few times" for an answer. "How many times? When was the first time? How long was it? Who was there? What was said? What was the reason you were there? How did you get there? Who invited whom? What were the circumstances?" Then we would go to the second time, then all the phone calls. I just kept going through it, and as I deposed Reichardt it was clear he was trying to become Simpson's good buddy and attach himself to O.J.'s world.

Simpson had called Reichardt at 9:00 P.M. on June 12, only about an hour and thirty minutes before he committed the murders. They were not particularly close friends, they had not spoken in ten days, but there was O.J. Simpson chatting him up. Reichardt remembered hearing a television in the background and asking Simpson if someone else was in the room. He assumed it was Kato. We knew Kato was in his own room at that point.

Reichardt said Simpson sounded more relaxed and jovial than usual and talked about how happy he was to be seeing Paula, which we knew could not be true because earlier in the day she had dumped him. Simpson didn't sound gloomy, didn't say anything about Sydney or the dance recital or having flown all the way back from the East Coast to attend. He indicated he was packing and getting ready to catch a red-eye out of town. He said he would be back Wednesday.

Reichardt may not have been lying on this point. This seemed to me to be a transparent attempt by Simpson to establish an alibi, to paint himself as an improbable person to go out an hour later and kill Nicole. If he did stage this conversation, it was pretty clever on his part.

Reichardt's function in the defense was to come in and slam Resnick. He was going to use her drug experience to suggest that all her observations, testimony, and perceptions were tainted. If this was going to be his position at trial, I would use the deposition to get admissions from him that would blunt his ability to damage us.

"Have you spoken to any members of Mr. Simpson's entourage?" I liked using the word "entourage," it was a little dig at the shameless faithful in Simpson's wake.

"I talked to Dan briefly on Wednesday evening."

"And by 'Dan,' you are not referring to me, of course. You're referring to Dan Leonard."

"Yeah," Reichardt said. He didn't like being made fun of.

"Attorney for O.J. Simpson?"

"Yes."

I was just playing with him. The court is a place of ceremony, and I was contrasting that formality with Reichardt's implied familiarity with Simpson's attorney to show he was biased. He made it sound as though the two men had been palling around, so from that point on, whenever I asked further questions about his conversations with Leonard, I referred to the lawyer as "Dan."

"And why don't you tell me about your conversation with *Dan*. . . . *Dan* called you? . . . When was your meeting with *Dan* and O.J. Simpson?"

"I am going to object to that. It wasn't a meeting," said Leonard.

"Excuse me, *Dan.* Let the witness testify. Okay?"

In the body of his deposition, Reichardt was prepared to admit next to nothing. "Nicole Brown was a dear friend of Faye Resnick's," I said. "Right?"

"That's right."

"You don't deny that, do you?"

"No."

"And Faye Resnick was very upset over Nicole's murder. Correct?"

"Well, that's where I'm trying to let you know." The condescension was dripping. "If somebody goes to drug rehabilitation, everything gets amplified significantly. . . . Was it because she lost a friend or she was going through drug rehabilitation?"

I was offended by that answer. First of all, Resnick was taking relatively small amounts of drugs and went into rehab because her friends intervened to prevent a minor binge from exploding into a major one. But putting drugs aside, who wouldn't be distraught over the loss of a friend? It was a simple question, but Reichardt was not only being obstinate, he was blindly using every opportunity to throw drugs into the situation.

"I move to strike the answer as nonresponsive," I said. "I would like you to answer my question."

Dan Leonard began to defend his client, and I cut him off. "Maybe Mr. Leonard can ask you those questions. Can we get back to my question, please?"

Leonard got his back up. "There is no reason for that kind of a comment, Mr. Petrocelli."

The whole bunch of them annoyed me. "Mr. Leonard, if you want to examine your witness at the appropriate time, you may do so. I am examining this witness, and I am not getting answers to my questions, and I am going to press for answers."

"I think he is answering your questions."

"So what do you want me to do? Agree with you and move on?"

"Why don't you ask another question."

"You want to take the deposition?"

"It's your deposition. Go ahead."

"Exactly. It is my deposition. That's my point." I read Reichardt the question once again: "And Faye Resnick was very upset over Nicole's murder. Correct?"

Reichardt refused to act reasonably. "I don't think that's a question I can answer with yes or no because I don't know Faye's state of mind at the time."

This was unmitigated bullshit, and I wasn't going to let him get away with it. I immediately punched a hole in it. "Did you think Faye had the kind of relationship with Nicole Brown that when her friend was murdered, she would have been upset about it?"

"Yes."

"Were you on drugs at the time?" He was Faye's fiancé, he was part of "the world of Faye Resnick," I wanted to hear him answer that question.

"No," he swore.

"Were you upset?"

"Yes."

"Over Nicole's murder?"

"Absolutely."

"Were you grief-stricken over it?"

"Absolutely."

"Did Faye have a closer relationship with Nicole than you did?"

"Absolutely."

"More than you?"

"Absolutely."

"Irrespective of drugs. Correct?"

"Excuse me?" He must have been thinking, I really want to slam Faye, but I'm looking silly now, so he bought some time.

I simply repeated the question. *You heard it.* "Irrespective of drugs. Correct?"

"Yes."

"Thank you. That's all I want to know."

That was an issue of control. I didn't really need the answer to that question, but once I asked it, and Reichardt tried to spin his response like a Simpson advocate, I went out of my way to crush him.

This was a recurring pattern with Simpson's witnesses. Rather than be fair and neutral, come in and tell the truth, they chose to be advocates for him, and I wasn't going to put up with it. I sat there and wore them out until they had been disciplined. Some fought me more than others, but ultimately it wasn't a fight they were going to win. I had a right to get my questions answered, and I wasn't interested in their advocacy.

As Faye's fiancé, Reichardt was a very important window into that world. He was intimately involved, so one would think he might have inside knowledge if Faye was cavorting with dangerous people. He certainly was sympathetic to Simpson, and if he had such knowledge, he would have used it to impugn Faye's credibility.

Reichardt had told Christopher Darden that he spoke on the phone with Simpson several weeks before the murders. I took Reichardt through that interview. "What I just read to you was true, right? That wasn't a lie, right? You're not making that up, right?" Reichardt agreed. Simpson had told him, "I'm splitting town, I don't want to deal with this anymore, I'm getting out of this."

"And O.J. Simpson told you in substance that Nicole was driving him crazy. Correct?"

"Yes."

"Excuse me?"

"Yes."

This was powerful evidence coming from the mouth of a Simpson supporter.

Most important, I questioned him regarding Simpson's threatening to kill Nicole. "Who was the person that Faye said would kill Nicole?" I asked.

"I think I understand what Mr. Petrocelli is leading at."

"I am sure you do."

"That's why I say it's not a question that could be answered with yes or no."

"Oh, please try your best."

"If I answer yes, then it would be construed one way. If it's not—"

"You don't need to worry how it will be construed," I told him, "because there are lots of very talented lawyers, far more talented than I, who will make sure that it doesn't get misconstrued. So answer my question, please. Had anyone ever told you that someone had said he or she would kill Nicole, as of June 12, 1994?"

"As a figure of speech or as a—"

"Kidding around, figure of speech, dead serious, in the middle of a confession to a priest, any statement in any context."

"Kidding around, figure of speech, yes, Faye Resnick told me that O.J. had said to her once he's gonna kill her."

"Okay. So Faye had a conversation with O.J. Simpson, and O.J. Simpson told Faye that he was going to kill Nicole, and Faye told that to you. True?"

"Yeah."

This was confirmation of Faye's report by an uncooperative witness staunchly trying to help his murdering buddy. Of course, Simpson had denied ever making that threat. Even his advocates were being forced to impeach him.

In the last several weeks of Nicole's life, I asked Reichardt whether Nicole and Faye were having intimate relations together. In threesomes? Or whether they were going around with dangerous people who might be a threat to their safety? Or had threatened anyone, or had received threats on their lives? No, he said, he had no such information. So much for Simpson's drug-related, Colombian-hit-man, "World-of-Faye-Resnick" theory. Reichardt had nothing on Faye.

At the end of his deposition, Reichardt, the Ice Man, walked out as unapologetically fervent as he had walked in. He had made a fool of himself.

Why did people blindly support Simpson? Why did they choose to ignore the truth—the blood evidence, the fiber, the hair—and drape themselves in rationales? Simpson's hangers-on never confronted him. Nobody asked him specifically to defend himself. When he refused to take the stand at the criminal trial and, under oath, explain the concrete incriminating evidence against him, after assuring his friends he would, not one confronted him and said, "You murderer! You lied to me! You lied to everybody else, and you killed two people, including my good friend!" And later, when he got out, nobody told him, "You said you were going to find 'the real killer' and you've done nothing! Why aren't you doing anything, you son of a bitch? You did it, didn't you? You lied!"

Some decent people, like Alan Austin and Allen and Pam Schwartz, Joe Kolkowitz and Tom McCollum, quietly left the scene, but nobody stood up to him. Not even his lawyers; they were having too good a time playing with "the Juice."

Why did no one hold Simpson accountable? Why did they let him get away with it?

The more of them I encountered, the more disgusted I got. These people were weak. They wanted to be *with O.J.* He was the closest they would get to fame and fortune, and these wannabe's wanted to be part of his life, they wanted to be *O.J.'s friend.* For others who were closer to Simpson, they didn't want to admit that this celebrated man with whom they had played golf, talked, partied, and had so much fun was a double-murderer. What did that say about their own lives? "How can I feel good if I am consorting with the man who murdered my friend Nicole?" This was a real dilemma, she was their friend, too. They strained to justify their choices and minimize their guilt. On one side there was Simpson, their contact with world-class fame, on the other was their conscience and the ability to get up every morning and look in the mirror without shame. So many of them lied to themselves, to each other, and to me.

If they had said, "Look, I am a coward, I don't want to ask him. I'm afraid," at least that would have been honest. Simpson is an intimidating man. "I want to be O.J. Simpson's friend, and you know what? I'm willing to write Nicole off. She's dead, I can't bring her back. I don't want to lose him. He's been acquitted, so, hey, the system worked. I'm gonna be his buddy, I don't know the answers to those questions, I don't want to know, and I'm not going to ask." That's even more honest.

But to defend him, to shade the truth, to lie for the man in the face of overwhelming evidence that he slit his ex-wife's throat, that was despicable.

After five days of Cora Fischman and Christian Reichardt, I needed a shower.

THIRTEEN

Fuhrman, Fuhrman, Fuhrman

Mark Fuhrman and the race issue were joined at the hip.
At the criminal trial, the LAPD detective had been
caught in an outright lie, denying under oath that he had used
the offensive and incendiary word "nigger." If Mark Fuhrman became the
major issue in this trial, we would lose. If we could keep Fuhrman's presence minimal and focus the case on the evidence of Simpson's guilt, we
stood a much better chance of winning.

In the criminal trial, Simpson's "Dream Team" exploited Fuhrman's
prejudice and created an atmosphere in which they could argue that
"everybody knew" Fuhrman was a bigot, therefore "everybody knew"
everything he said was a lie. We had no doubt the defense would employ
the same strategy against us, when examining him on the witness stand,
as well as the other witnesses: "Where was Fuhrman? What did Fuhrman
say? How about Fuhrman?" Fuhrman, Fuhrman, Fuhrman.

We had to live with that. However, what many people had forgotten in the wake of Fuhrman's "N-word" testimony, was that before he
came undone, he was a star witness. F. Lee Bailey, a formidable courtroom
opponent, had not laid a glove on him.

Assistant District Attorney Bill Hodgman told me Fuhrman had
done the best detective work at the crime scene on the night of the murders, had used good police instincts, and been very observant. Outside the

gate at Rockingham, after Simpson's two small children had been brought to the police station and the cops were looking for Simpson to break the news of his ex-wife's death, Fuhrman saw a parked car and noticed a small spot on the driver's side door. He pointed it out to the three detectives with him, and they all recognized it as blood.

When no one inside Rockingham answered the phone and the detectives decided to go on the property, they found Kato Kaelin asleep. Fuhrman shined a light in his eyes, checked his shoes against the bloody footprints found at Bundy, questioned him, asked if he was on drugs, and treated him as a possible suspect. When Kato reported the loud noise, on his wall, Fuhrman went around and looked where the sounds had come from. He found a bloody glove, immediately summoned his colleagues, and pointed it out to the other officers. At Bundy he had taken hand-written notes documenting various pieces of evidence, including blood on the back gate. For the brief time he was involved he did a good job of police work. If we kept Fuhrman and the evidence he found out of the trial, we would lose some important evidence.

The prosecutors claimed they tried to prepare Fuhrman for the "N-word" line of questioning and that he refused to cooperate. I don't know how he was actually prepared. But when Bailey asked Fuhrman if he had used "the N-word" in the previous ten years, the course of history was changed. The question should never have been permitted in the first place. Ito should have granted the prosecution's request to exclude this evidence. The answer was not relevant, it didn't prove or disprove anything concerning the evidence. It could only inflame the jury and fuel their own prejudices. But Judge Ito let it in. And then Fuhrman lied and sealed his fate—and with it the fate of two innocent murdered people. Required to answer, he should have told the truth and said, "I use the word all the time, I'm sorry to say. It is unpleasant language, but it is the language of the streets and the language of where I work. I use all kinds of racial epithets for all kinds of people. That language is directed at me and we direct it at other people. We use it among ourselves, even among police officers. I'm not proud of it, but of course I've used that word. Are you trying to embarrass me, Mr. Bailey?"

Ed Medvene was our man in charge of Fuhrman. Putting aside the racial epithet, Ed's investigation confirmed that Fuhrman was telling the truth. Fuhrman had not been specially assigned to the case, he was still sleeping at the time critical evidence was found—therefore it would have been impossible for him to have planted it. We all knew that the issue of race had nothing to do with Simpson's guilt or innocence, but Fuhrman had destroyed his credibility with that one answer. We did not want to lose Fuhrman's honest and important contributions, but we didn't want to give the defense another chance to use Fuhrman to take down the case. The decision to use him would be a difficult one, but not one we had to make now. We would keep our options open.

The defense rang the Fuhrman bell first by requesting his deposition. Fuhrman had moved to Sand Point, Idaho, and, therefore, could not be forced to attend the trial in Santa Monica. This meant his pretrial deposition would likely be the only examination the civil case would ever see. There is a jury instruction stating that if one side does not call a witness at trial, the other side can argue the inference that that witness would hurt the first. To negate that potential argument, we decided to request Fuhrman's deposition as well. We also wanted to signal to the defense that we were not afraid of Fuhrman and would not back away from him.

Ed traveled to Idaho for Fuhrman's deposition. When he got there he was struck by the signs taped up in many store windows on the main street, reading "We are not racist," "We don't hate people." Medvene had grown up in the East and lived in many multiethnic neighborhoods; he had never seen such signs. At his motel there was a similar flyer, distributed by the Sand Point Chamber of Commerce. Apparently there were several neo-Nazi militia outposts nearby, which the local inhabitants found troubling and disturbing. Fuhrman's presence only added to the unsettled atmosphere.

After the criminal trial, the California Attorney General's office began an investigation into whether Fuhrman committed perjury—a felony under California law—by his "N-word" testimony. Since the investigation was still ongoing, we all anticipated Fuhrman would invoke his Fifth Amendment rights against self-incrimination rather than answer anyone's questions. Fuhrman's lawyers had not allowed Medvene to meet with their client prior to the deposition, so Ed was not absolutely certain what Fuhrman's position would be. He was prepared to examine him fully.

The media was out in full force, presenting Sand Point with a rare traffic jam. Medvene drove to the compound where the deposition would take place, with a press caravan trailing. The "compound" was actually a country club that could be secured from the public; its caretaker was the daughter of Fuhrman's lawyer. The media was not allowed to follow Ed onto the grounds.

Outside the room in which the deposition was held, Medvene was introduced to Fuhrman and chatted briefly with him. Small-talk. "What are you doing in Idaho?" kind of talk. "He did not have the horns he had been portrayed with," Medvene says. In the wake of the Simpson case, Fuhrman had retired from a successful career as a LAPD detective and was working part-time, learning to be an electrician, trying to rebuild his life. It may not have been politically correct, but Medvene, despite himself, kind of liked the guy.

At the deposition, the defense was represented by Bob Baker and Dan Leonard. They were loaded for bear, but Fuhrman would not be a target. He took the Fifth to all their questions. To laypeople, if a witness is asked, "Did you plant the glove?" and he answers, "On the advice of counsel, I invoke my Fifth Amendment rights against self-incrimination," it means, "Well, gee, he must have done something wrong with the glove." To lawyers, it does not mean that at all; if a witness chooses to answer some questions, he must answer all the questions, so a Fifth Amendment refusal simply means that regardless of the content of the question, the witness will not answer anything. After the defense heard enough of these refusals to answer, Medvene asked Fuhrman some questions of his own. He fully expected Fuhrman to take the Fifth—which Fuhrman did—but Ed wanted to make clear on the record that we had tried ourselves to get Fuhrman to testify rather than happily accept his refusals to answer. This might prove useful later in responding to defense criticism that we were not interested in obtaining his testimony. Ed then asked one question which we hoped would make it clear that Fuhrman was not refusing to answer because he had done something improper, but because he had been advised by counsel not to respond. Fuhrman answered that he would, indeed, like to testify.

During a break, Medvene found himself outside on a balcony with Baker and Leonard. They were excited.

"I think he waived the Fifth!" one said.

Standing in the April Idaho air, the three of them debated whether by admitting he would like to testify, Fuhrman had, indeed, testified. Baker and Leonard took the position that Fuhrman had waived his rights and they could now ask a court to require him to testify fully. The argument went back and forth for a while. Eventually Baker and Leonard, for their own tactical reasons, decided against pursuing it.

Fuhrman's deposition ended. He had said nothing. We chose to leave the decision about how to handle the "Fuhrman, Fuhrman, Fuhrman" defense for later, at trial.

When we took the case in October 1995 we thought there was a chance we'd be ready by the April 2 scheduled trial date. However, it quickly became apparent that this was not realistic. At a pretrial hearing in February, Judge David Perez, the presiding judge in the Los Angeles Superior Court West District, housed in Santa Monica where our proceedings would take place, told us there was no way we were going to trial in April; there was still too much to do. I pleaded for Judge Perez to set as early a date as possible, and worried that he might kick it a full year, to the next April. I thought we won a great victory when he scheduled us for September 1996.

Nevertheless, Fred Goldman was very upset. He showed his frustration at a press conference on the courthouse lawn; the process was starting to wear on him. He understandably wanted his day in court, and I had to calm him down. "Fred," I told him, "it is going to work to our benefit, believe me. We will have more time, and we need more time to develop the facts and prepare our case. We will benefit from this delay, I promise you."

Although I was as anxious as Fred to get going, the extra six months were critical for us. In the criminal case, the defense lawyers had jammed the trial down the prosecutors' throats, forcing them to present their arguments while they were not yet prepared. While we were all raring to go, we were nowhere near ready.

Curiously, the defense lawyers wanted more time, too. Bob Baker had planned to try the case in conjunction with F. Lee Bailey, but Bailey was sitting in the pokey in Florida on a contempt charge. I told the judge, "You know, Judge, if there is a problem with Mr. Bailey still being in jail come September, I don't want this trial date to move because he is sitting in the slammer." I enjoyed needling the defense with that argument. Their co-counsel was in the hoosegow for disobeying a court order; what kind of a statement did that make about the people trying Simpson's case? To

Baker's credit—sometimes he surprised me—he didn't disagree with me. Maybe he was glad to be rid of Bailey. Sure enough, even after Bailey got out of jail he never came back into the case. His partner, Dan Leonard, assumed his role.

Having spoken with a number of Simpson's former friends, I now dove into the heart of his cadre, inside the bunker of the defense. In the course of two months we took the depositions of Allen Cowlings, Robert Kardashian, Jason Simpson, Cathy Randa, Skip Taft, and Arnelle Simpson. My own opinion was these people would say anything for their man.

Cowlings, a one-time defensive end known among his crowd as "A.C.," was Simpson's football teammate at the City College of San Francisco as well as at USC and a first-round draft pick of the Buffalo Bills when Simpson was their star running back. He is a big, physically imposing man. John Kelly wanted to handle some "marquee" witnesses, and he took the lead during the first three days with Cowlings.

Because Cowlings was still vulnerable to be charged for his role in the Bronco chase, he elected to take the Fifth and refused to answer any questions about anything that transpired from the time Simpson returned from Chicago, approximately eleven on the morning of June 13, to several weeks thereafter.

No one in Simpson's entourage ever admitted to asking Simpson whether he had killed Nicole, but Denise Brown herself had asked Cowlings days after her sister's murder whether O.J. did it. His answer was vague. "At that time, I didn't know anything," he testified. "I don't know for sure what I said."

"Did *you* know at that time whether or not Mr. Simpson had murdered Nicole?" Kelly asked.

"I don't remember."

He doesn't remember? What kind of an answer is that? When *did* he find out that Simpson killed her?

Cowlings and Simpson go back a long way. They met in third grade and grew up together in San Francisco. They were in a "social gang" called the Superiors. Simpson met his first wife, Marguerite, when she was Cowlings's girlfriend. Good buddy that he was, he stole her away. Cowlings is the godfather of Simpson's son Jason. The two men were, and still are, very close. The world had watched Cowlings chauffeur Simpson along the Southern California freeway system during the Bronco chase, and we had the unshakable impression that he would do anything to save him. There was no expectation of our getting anything damaging from Cowlings, unless he slipped up.

"When Mr. Simpson was playing with Buffalo," Kelly asked, "did you ever see him run right over three-hundred-pound linemen?"

"On some incidents you have no choice. I mean, he has taken some licks." Even in this football context, Cowlings tried to turn Simpson into a victim rather than the victimizer. Kelly wouldn't let him.

"Have you ever seen him give some licks, too?"

"Yeah, you got to. You know, you got to be able to defend yourself."

"I am asking, did you ever see him run right over a defensive lineman?"

"O.J. was more elusive than bowl somebody over. That wasn't his style."

"Did you ever see him do it, though?"

"I've seen goal-line situations, short-yard situations where you only need two or three yards, where he'll go up the middle. It wasn't too many people that could take him on one-on-one in the open field."

This whole line of questioning about Simpson's demeanor and performance on the football field was obviously a metaphor for his actions on the night of June 12. Cowlings knew what was being asked and was pretty clever in not giving much away.

Could Simpson talk himself out of situations? "O.J.," Cowlings recalled, "he could talk."

This was a familiar refrain. No matter where people stood on the question of Simpson's guilt, everyone who knew him said he could talk, talk, and talk. He would go from one subject to another, a steady stream of O.J.–speak, without waiting for a response or ever caring if anyone was listening. Judy Brown, Nicole's mother, said she would doze off on the telephone with Simpson jabbering nonstop, only to wake up and still hear him going a mile a minute. Dan Leonard, who lived in Simpson's house while working on the case, told me the same thing. Dan once quipped to me, "I'm convinced that O.J. didn't do it, because if he did, he would have had to tell somebody." "Maybe he did," I said.

Cowlings met Nicole in the late seventies when Simpson began dating her. At first, he said, she was shy. As Simpson and she spent more time together, Cowlings was often around, and when Simpson was out of town he would visit Nicole and help her out. Nicole, he said, was fun-loving, athletic, liked to dance. It was obvious that he cared for her deeply.

Cowlings was questioned about all the beatings and abuse Nicole suffered at Simpson's hands, and to no one's surprise, he denied knowing about any of it, with a couple of notable exceptions. Cowlings confirmed an incident described in Nicole's diary that he witnessed between Simpson and Nicole when living together in San Francisco in 1979. It was nighttime, and Nicole had come out of the bedroom looking upset. Cowlings asked, "What's wrong?" but she was tight-lipped and just shook her head. He then heard "a commotion," went into the bedroom to investigate, and saw that Simpson had thrown her clothes out the bathroom window. "I looked out and her clothes were three stories down, laying over her car." Cowlings asked Simpson what he was doing. He responded, "None of your business." Cowlings said, "You're crazy." He went downstairs, gathered everything, and brought it back up into the apartment. "I folded them, tried to put them neatly back in the living room. When I got back, the two of them were in the bedroom together. . . . The door was closed." He denied, of course, that Simpson beat or hit Nicole.

In the period between 1980 and 1985, before they were married, Nicole and Simpson broke up regularly, mostly over Simpson's incessant womanizing, and Cowlings was always the one called upon to move Nicole's belongings. "I told them, if they kept that up, I was going to go into the moving van business."

Cowlings thought of Nicole as one of his closest friends. He took her to the hospital after the 1989 New Year's Eve beating. He had been awakened by a phone call from Simpson's housekeeper, Michelle Abudrahm, saying Simpson and Nicole were fighting. "I dropped the phone and jumped in my car and drove up there," he testified. He lived five minutes away.

When he arrived, Nicole was in the kitchen, angry but not crying. Simpson entered. "If you don't get outta here, I'm gonna call the police," she shouted at him. He went out the back way. Cowlings embraced her

and asked if she was all right. "If you need me. . . ." he said. She cursed
Simpson and said she just wanted to be left alone. Cowlings went home.

Simpson called soon after. He was at Allen Schwartz's house and
wanted Cowlings there. "I threw on some sweatpants and, I guess, a T-shirt
and jumped in the car." When he arrived, in five minutes, he found
Simpson sitting on the couch under a blanket, "babbling." Cowlings then
told us a story that was so convoluted and unbelievable as to be laughable.
Sitting in Schwartz's house, Simpson said that the police were coming after
him, Cowlings explained. When he'd left Rockingham earlier, "He went
one way, they went the other way, so he lost them." Apparently Simpson
had gone to the Schwartzes' home in his Bentley, put it in their garage to
avoid its being seen by the police, then driven *back* to Rockingham in
Schwartz's souped-up black Buick muscle car. Simpson told Cowlings that
while in his house he had taken Nicole's jewelry, put it in a black velvet
bag, and hidden it outside in a next-door neighbor's garbage can. In the
process, he said, he had lost Allen Schwartz's car keys. Apparently, he had
climbed over the neighbor's wall and walked back to the Schwartzes. He
asked Cowlings to go find the keys and the jewelry bag, which Cowlings
dutifully did. Cowlings told us he never looked in the bag.

The story, as told, was comical. We thought the bag, of course, contained dope. Why else would anyone go back into a house to which the
police were coming and from which Simpson had been expelled, take a
bag of *something,* and then place it in a garbage can? Why would Simpson
take Nicole's jewelry? Even assuming Simpson wanted the jewelry, why
would he put it in a garbage can, why not simply take it with him? Of
course, if he had drugs in the house and knew the police were coming, the
reason becomes obvious. When Cowlings returned with the bag and the
keys, Simpson "was nervous."

Cowlings then returned to Rockingham to see how Nicole was doing.
When he arrived at Rockingham, she was in the kitchen, feeding the baby,
Justin, who was under a year old. Nicole told him she and Simpson had
had a fight because "she wouldn't fuck him." He said he didn't notice any
scratches or bruises. Her head hurt, and she was rubbing it. She said
Simpson had hit her, but she didn't want to go to the hospital.

Cowlings said he had planned to go to the Rose Bowl game with
Simpson and Wayne Hughes. USC was playing. As Cowlings remembered it, he was so upset by the fight that he went back to see Simpson at

Schwartz's house and canceled. Cowlings watched the game with Schwartz. Simpson went anyway.

(Cowlings had his days confused and the story telescoped. The Rose Bowl was the next day, January 2. Simpson would try to seize on this error to demonstrate that Cowlings was wrong on other facts as well. Despite the fact that Cowlings got his days mixed up, this did not seem likely.)

Cowlings drove Simpson back to Rockingham. Nicole's head was still hurting. "Nicole," he told her, "why don't you let me take you to the hospital."

"No."

"You may have a concussion, and the worst thing you can do is to go to sleep." As a former professional football player, he knew about concussions. He asked her again. "C'mon, Nic, let's go."

Cowlings drove Nicole to St. John's Hospital in Santa Monica. Simpson did not accompany them.

In the car, Nicole did most of the talking. Simpson had hit her, she said, and "I want him to pay for this." "Nicole," Cowlings told her, "if you're gonna do it, you got to go all the way." Cowlings was as much as advising her to press charges. He was "letting her know that I was not trying to talk her out of it. I felt what he did was wrong and it shouldn't never have happened, and I was supporting her. . . . I don't think any man should hit a woman."

Nicole also told him she felt her family would side with Simpson, and that "disturbed her a great deal."

"When we went down to the hospital, I stood by her," he said. "[When] the lady said, 'How did you sustain your injuries?' . . . Nicole kinda hesitated a little bit, she mumbled something, and she looked at me, and I said, 'Nicole, you got to tell them the truth.'

"Finally she said, 'I was hit.'"

Cowlings admitted that Simpson had hit Nicole. This was surprising to us. Simpson had denied it up and down. Cowlings was Simpson's alter ego, but unlike Simpson, he felt some compassion for Nicole, and something inside must have forced him to tell the story as he truly remembered it.

Cowlings, I'm sure without realizing it, impeached Simpson when he said he never had a key to Nicole's condo at Bundy; Simpson had implied that the key found in his bag when he was arrested on the seventeenth after the Bronco chase was one Cowlings had gotten from Lou Brown to help move Nicole's belongings out. Cowlings did have a key to Rockingham.

Cowlings talked to Kelly relatively easily. He had a quick temper, yet at times exhibited gentle feelings. He cried at times when talking about the beating Nicole took in 1989 or about her death. I wasn't certain what triggered his emotions, be it the loss of a friend, guilt, or both.

Cowlings and I did not hit it off so well when I examined him a few weeks later. I went at him more aggressively, which he did not appreciate, and he treated me with sullen disrespect. He made no eye contact, he was surly, obstinate, monosyllabic, as if trying to make me feel his hatred through his attitude.

Cowlings had just returned from visiting someone in the hospital, and he was in no mood to be pushed by me. At one point, his anger boiled over, and he shot up, yanked off his microphone, slammed it down on the table, and towered over me menacingly, about to squash me. His lawyer escorted him out for a break and things calmed down after that.

Cowlings was very coy about Marcus Allen. This was apparently a very sensitive area, and they were all protecting each other. Cowlings had previously admitted that several weeks after the murders he had pulled Allen aside at the home of Wayne Hughes and said he was aware of Allen's affair with Nicole. Cowlings said Allen was "bothered, upset, probably confused" over what to tell his wife. Cowlings had seen Allen the afternoon of the murders, after which Allen and his wife had left for a vacation on the Cayman Islands, where they were at the time of the murders. Though he called often, Allen chose not to return to Los Angeles for Nicole's funeral. Simpson apparently told him to stay where he was.

Based on the evidence I was accumulating, it seemed that Marcus Allen had resumed seeing Nicole when she broke up with Simpson just before her death. He was attracted to her, and I think she used him to lash out at Simpson. She knew having an affair with Allen would enrage Simpson more than anything else she could do. This is what many of Simpson's friends believed, and they were probably correct.

"When was the last time that you saw Marcus Allen in person?" I asked Cowlings.

"I don't remember," he intoned, slouched in his chair, eyes averted.

"Have you seen him in the last thirty days?"

"I don't remember."

"In the last two weeks?"

"I don't remember."

"In the last week?"

"I don't remember."

He was disgusted and responding robotically, without regard for his obligation to answer truthfully. He was stonewalling and the whole room seemed in a torpor. I decided to seal it by asking the absurd.

"Did you see him yesterday?"

"I don't remember."

"Did you speak to him yesterday?"

"I don't remember."

Robert Kardashian was another longtime friend of Simpson's, dating back to USC days. He had been a lawyer, then had entered the business world and run a music business trade magazine, a radio network, and a company that piped music into movie theaters. Cathy Randa had been his secretary before moving over to serve Simpson.

Kardashian had taken a lot of heat in the press as the man seen walking off with the luggage. After Randa and Skip Taft delivered Simpson from the airport to the Rockingham estate when he returned from Chicago the morning after the murders, a film crew had caught Kardashian walking away from the house, carrying Simpson's Louis Vuitton garment bag. Police were swarming over the property, and Kardashian was seen walking in the other direction with what could have been crucial evidence. Tragically, we will never know what was in that bag: Bloody clothing? The murder weapon? Speculation abounds. What we do know is the bag went to Kardashian's house, where Simpson stayed for most of the week leading up to his arrest. It remained there for months before finally being brought to the courthouse—empty. But, of course, there is no guarantee that it was brought intact.

Kardashian looked sinister. He had a Bela Lugosi hairline, low forehead, black and bushy eyebrows, and he wore his outsized head of black hair slicked back like a mobster's. A startling shock of white hair streaked back from his widow's peak. In our crowd he had developed the nickname "Skunkhead."

Kardashian was a staunch Simpson supporter. His law license had been inactive, but he reactivated it in order to join Simpson's defense team and to cloak all their conversations in the attorney-client privilege. He put his business on hold, went and lived in the O.J. Simpson defense camp, and sat at the counsel table in the courtroom for a good part of the criminal proceedings. A short man, he favored dark, fancy suits not often seen in sunny Southern California. The persona "Skunkhead" Kardashian projected was that he brought not only Simpson's luggage, but his own personal baggage to this case.

One image seared into my mind was of Kardashian's face when the criminal verdict was read. The video clip was played over and over on television and had become a seminal media moment. At the moment of decision F. Lee Bailey didn't respond, he was implacable. Johnnie Cochran breathed a huge sigh of relief and rested his cheek on Simpson's shoulder. Simpson had an awkwardly pained smile on his face. (I have watched that clip many times, and his reaction does not appear to me to be one of a man who just found out he had gotten away with murder. It is too much of a performance, and he is not a good actor. There were reports that the result of the verdict had been leaked to him in his jail cell by the deputy sheriffs the previous night, when the jury was celebrating in their hotel rooms. In my opinion, he knew in advance.)

But Kardashian wore his feelings on his face. When the words "not guilty" were announced, his was a look of pure, unadulterated astonishment.

By the time he showed up for deposition in the civil case, Kardashian was a pariah in some Los Angeles social circles. At one point during a break in the deposition, as I was standing up and stretching my legs, he came over and we spoke. He was polite and gentlemanly and in the deposition was always well-mannered and never lost his cool. Skunkhead told me, "This has been so hard on me. I'm having a difficult time. I can't get reservations in restaurants. People avoid me. I can't understand why my reputation is so tarnished."

I looked at him in utter amazement. "You've got to be kidding me, Bob. Every time you turn around, you're seen holding a piece of O.J. Simpson's luggage. What do you mean, you don't know why?"

Simpson, Kardashian, and their lawyers took an overly expansive view of attorney-client and attorney-work-product privilege when it came to questioning Kardashian. That privilege is supposed to protect confidential communications, generally meaning legal advice and strategy. It is not intended to cover physical observations—for instance, whether a guy has one cut or ten cuts on his hands. How is that observation a privileged communication? Nevertheless, Kardashian asserted it throughout the deposition to avoid answering the hard questions. When we later took the issue before Judge Haber, he ruled in favor of Kardashian. I think they were both wrong, but judges will bend over backward to protect the lawyer-client privilege.

As a lawyer, I understand there are compelling reasons for upholding claims of privilege. The theory is if the privilege is not vigorously protected, people will lose confidence that their confidential communications with their lawyers will remain totally private, they will be inhibited from speaking frankly, and the entire system of justice will be sabotaged. The theory holds. So does the Fifth Amendment privilege against self-incrimination. I don't fault lawyers or parties for asserting these privileges.

However, in the case of O.J. Simpson, when the defendant and his lawyers consistently went before the American public and adamantly asserted his innocence, when he writes a book and markets a video professing his innocence and calls it *I Want to Tell You,* then why not waive the Fifth Amendment privilege and testify in the criminal case. He claimed he was an innocent man falsely accused of heinous murders, his life was hanging in the balance, and he repeatedly insisted that he wanted to proclaim his innocence. Okay, do it. Take the stand and testify! He chose not to.

The same was true in the civil case. Simpson had his lawyers assert the attorney-client privilege left and right. Cowlings took the Fifth, although, granted, he had his own backside to protect. But then Cowlings had his lawyer trotted up to the microphones and said, "We would love to tell our side of the story." If they wanted to shine in the public eye and convince the public they had nothing to hide, why wouldn't these witnesses testify? Simpson had the right to waive his privilege. He could have said, "I've got nothing to hide, I'm innocent. Tell them, A.C. Tell it all, Bob." Again, he chose not to.

One reason Kardashian's claim of privilege was so untenable was that immediately after the criminal trial he made major appearances on national television. Barbara Walters asked him, "Listen, you are one of O.J. Simpson's closest friends. Did you ever say to him, 'O.J., did you do it?' " Kardashian answered solemnly, "Yes, I did. I looked him straight in the eyes. He was in jail and I said, 'O.J., I am going to ask you a question.' He said, 'What?' I said, 'Did you commit these crimes?' He said, 'I did not. I am innocent. I did not commit these crimes.' " And then Kardashian started to weep.

Kardashian made much the same presentation three days later on CNN's *Larry King Live,* also on *Dateline* and *48 Hours.* The guy went on a media spree.

First of all, no criminal lawyer worth his salt asks his client these questions. These are not questions you want to risk hearing answered in the affirmative. Maybe Kardashian didn't know better because he was not a criminal defense lawyer. However, I don't think he ever asked. And even if he did, that is about the most privileged conversation you could have with your client in the eyes of the law, and yet Kardashian goes on national television and tells the world about it.

Technically, a lawyer cannot waive a client's privilege; only the client can do that. If a lawyer sneaks around secretly revealing information that is confidential without the client's permission, that does not waive the privilege. That gets the lawyer disbarred. However, this was no secret; Kardashian made these statements on national television, at least twice. I asked him, "Did you ever get any objection from O.J. Simpson? Did he sue you? Did he report you to the bar? Did he take any action against you?" He did not. Our position was that Simpson waived his privilege by permitting Kardashian to make these statements, not once, but twice, possibly even more, without complaining. Unfortunately, Judge Haber disagreed.

Kardashian had a meeting in Simpson's Brentwood office sometime on Tuesday, June 14, at which it was decided that he would join the team. He had spent time with Simpson earlier that day, before the privilege kicked in, and he had to answer questions about what he saw and heard during that period of time.

In his deposition, Simpson had testified that he and Kardashian were just driving around the San Diego Freeway to relieve the tension on the afternoon following the murders, when they happened to approach LAX. On the spur of the moment, Simpson had said, he'd decided to go to American Airlines and retrieve his golf clubs. He had left the clubs in his golf bag in the trunk of a car in Chicago, for use at a Hertz golf outing the next day. When he'd had to jump on a plane to return to Los Angeles, the driver had been too far from the hotel to pick him up on such short notice and the bag had missed the flight back. It had been placed on a later flight and was being held for him.

Putting aside the fact that if you're driving around trying to reduce stress in Los Angeles, you do not go anywhere near the 405 Freeway or LAX, Kardashian did not back Simpson up. Simpson, he said, called Hertz to locate his clubs, then asked Kardashian to accompany him on the drive to get them.

"Either Mr. Simpson or Mr. Taft called Hertz to find out about his golf clubs," said Kardashian. "I believe Mr. Simpson did, and got the individual, whose name I don't know, on the phone and asked him where his golf clubs were." Simpson had testified that he did have his assistant, Cathy Randa, call Jim Merrill, the driver who had picked him up from Chicago O'Hare and took him to his hotel a few minutes away. According to Simpson, however, he called not to inquire about his golf clubs, but to apologize for Simpson's being brusque to him the day before.

"O.J. asked me if I would drive him to the airport to get his golf clubs," said Kardashian.

"What did you say?" Kelly asked.

"I said, 'Sure.'"

"Where did you tell Skip Taft you were going?"

"To the airport to get O.J.'s golf clubs."

"What happened next?"

"We went to American Airlines. I think it was American—"

"You drove the Rolls-Royce?"

"Yes, drove the Rolls-Royce."

"You and Mr. Simpson?"

"Yes."

In the car, Kardashian recalled, Simpson "was pensive. It was quiet. Which is unlike him. . . . I think he just said, 'Let's go get my golf clubs.'"

This testimony directly contradicted Simpson's feeble account. There is no good reason why a man whose ex-wife has just been murdered, who hasn't yet seen his grieving young children, is going to drive to Los Angeles International Airport to get his golf clubs. *See my kids/Get my golf clubs? I'll get my clubs.* His credibility was in tatters. Simpson's sworn testimony that he had been driving around to relieve tension and just happened by the airport was an obvious lie. His explanation that two days after the brutal killings, with police crawling over everything and the media ablaze and himself a suspect in the horrific murders, Simpson would track down a driver he had met only once, the day before, and apologize to him—for anything, let alone brusqueness, was a laughable lie. Simpson was tracking his golf bag, he wanted to get to it before the police got to it. O.J. Simpson isn't a man who runs out to the airport to pick up his bags, he has them delivered. American Airlines would do that for him in a heartbeat. Failing that, Cathy Randa could get any messenger in the city to go fetch. But no, this time Simpson had to get them himself.

Why? To inspect the bag for telltale blood or trace evidence, to destroy or clean up what was there. I don't think he was dumb enough to have kept the murder weapon inside, though I suspect it was in the bag in the baggage compartment of the plane when Simpson flew to Chicago immediately after the murders. Once he arrived and retrieved his golf bag, and before putting it into the trunk of the waiting car, I believe Simpson removed the knife and put it in one of the bags he took with him into his hotel room. When he was dropped off at the hotel, the driver kept the golf bag in the trunk of the car with instructions to come back in a few hours to take Simpson to a celebrity golf event. When Simpson's plans abruptly changed and he was summoned to return to Los Angeles, the driver could not pick up Simpson or meet his flight in time, so the golf bag was put on a later flight. I believe the bag might have had blood in it from the knife or from Simpson's bleeding cuts, or perhaps a bloody towel. There was something about that golf bag on which Simpson was fixated, and it wasn't golf clubs.

Kardashian tried to walk the line. He remained loyal to Simpson, but he wanted to regain his social respectability. It was hard to appear respectable when he was defending a murderer.

When I asked Ron Fischman about the accusations of sexual harassment against him, he looked like he was about to swallow his tongue.

This doctor, whose job it is to save people's lives, had almost run over Steve Foster in his zeal to avoid this deposition. He had paid $4,000 for that maneuver, and I was looking forward to squelching any other moves he might throw our way. I invited Steve to sit next to me at the deposition just so Fischman would see him.

Fischman had not testified in the criminal trial. When the prosecutors interviewed him he had shown up with a lawyer, been very short with them, and provided little information. He apparently had exhibited no such reticence toward Simpson's defense team, meeting with Robert Shapiro and providing a picture of a smiling O.J. at the dance recital for their use. I would show him no mercy. The stocky little man had indeed been sued by an employee in his medical office for unwanted sexual advances. Now he knew that I knew; if he couldn't hide that, he couldn't hide anything. He was in for a rough ride.

We went at it pretty good for a while. Fischman was a wealthy man with a full-blown sense of his own worth. His stupidity in avoiding subpoena service had been mocked all over the newspapers. He was a physician, he had a practice, yet he had made himself look like a nutcase. This was a chance to rehabilitate himself. My approach was to accuse him of being a toady for Simpson and dare him to disprove us.

Fischman and Simpson were friends, as his wife, Cora, and Nicole had been. Their children were friends. They vacationed together, went to the Super Bowl together, and when Cora was sleeping with a grocery clerk Simpson was the person Fischman confided in. Simpson and Fischman were an unlikely couple, united in their failing marriages. I questioned him about Nicole and Simpson's relationship "getting physical from time to time."

Fischman began to rise to the challenge. He acknowledged, "Their relationship was, you know, it was volatile. The whole time, not just towards the end. And fighting . . . could include some times where they both got physical with each other."

"Do you know how he felt about her as of the time of her death?" I asked. His lawyer objected and we went around a few times, but ultimately Fischman answered the question.

"I believe I have some understanding as to how he felt towards her, yes."

"On June 12, 1994. Correct?"

"Yes."

"Tell me what it is."

"He was confused and frustrated."

"Tell me on what you base that opinion."

"The conversations that we had prior to her death." This was important. I needed people to tell me what O.J. Simpson said; words spoken to
them by Simpson would be considered "admissions," an exception to the
hearsay rule, and directly admissible evidence.

"Confused and frustrated," I reiterated.

"Over the failure of their reconciliation, yes."

"And tell me what he told you about feeling confused and frustrated
over the failure of their reconciliation." Fischman's lawyer and Dan
Leonard interposed some silly objections, and I got impatient. "These
objections are frivolous," I told them, "you can make them all you want.
We are going to get to it." I said to Fischman, "You may be confused to
think that because Mr. Leonard objects, that you are to somehow change
your answer. Okay? So you understand that you are to not listen to his
objections?" I made my point. Fischman continued.

"He found her behavior to be very erratic during that time," he said,
"and he didn't understand how she was relating to him. . . . There were
times where she was loving and everything was going quite well, and then
there were other times where she was angry, short with him, rejecting."

"Rejecting him?"

"Yeah."

Finally! Simpson had insisted that he was completely unfazed by
Nicole, that he no longer cared about her, that *he* had rejected *her* and
now was with Paula and had moved on with his life. Johnnie Cochran
built his closing argument around that statement. I knew it was a lie, but
I had no admissible evidence to prove it in court, I was being stonewalled.
I had been banging my head against the Simpson circle's wall of silence
for eight months and the very first witness who tells me under oath specifically that O.J. Simpson *said* he was feeling rejected by Nicole turns out
to be, of all people, Ron Fischman.

"And he indicated to you that that was frustrating and confusing
to him?"

"Yes."

So Fischman broke. Simpson, he told me, said he was frustrated
because he couldn't get Nicole on the phone, she wouldn't return his calls,
she was abrupt and short and unavailable to him. Simpson, he said, had
been looking forward to having Nicole and their children living with him

at Rockingham again. When that did not occur he became "very sad about his inability to reconcile with a woman who I believe he did love. . . . His sadness was something that some other people can relate to. . . . He was a middle-aged man, had had two prior marriages, both of them failed. He had two families, four children, and the level on which we communicated was sadness over the deteriorating situations in our families."

I'm sure Fischman felt this soliloquy humanized Simpson's image and was helpful to him, but it was only digging him in deeper. "The last few months were, as I recall, very tumultuous, and I think by the time it ended he was just very frustrated and confused about the way Nicole was behaving. On the one hand, she would want to be in the relationship; on the other hand, she wouldn't, and that seemed to dominate the conversation."

Mike Brewer took over and elicited important testimony about Simpson's demeanor at the dance recital just hours before the murders. Fischman said he saw no communication between Simpson and Nicole; Simpson was tired, withdrawn, not "his usual bubbly self. . . . I'd never seen him quite like that."

Much had been made of a videotape in which Simpson had been seen laughing after the recital with Fischman, who was also there to see his daughter, and members of Nicole's family. The defense in the criminal trial used it to prove that Simpson was carefree and unconcerned, even as his family was going off to a special celebratory dinner without him. The rhetorical question being: How could he smile and laugh so easily and be capable of killing Nicole a few hours later? "I think I made a joke," Fischman explained. "I believe he had asked me something about dinner, and I said, 'I'm going out to dinner with the wife.' And he said, 'Good luck.'" Wry humor, at best, and the only smile out of Simpson all night. Not only had both Nicole and Paula rejected him, now even Ron Fischman was turning down his dinner invitation.

So much for Simpson's denials, and so much for Dr. Ron.

I love the *Godfather* movies. If the Simpson family was the Corleones, Jason Simpson was Fredo.

O.J. was attractive, sculpted, athletic, a leader. Jason was beefy, soft, not particularly good-looking, and anything but dynamic. He was the ugly duckling who didn't live up to his father's expectations. He had not testified in the criminal trial, and we had heard from numerous people that he'd had a troubled relationship with his father. Several friends of the family reported that he had taken a baseball bat to a statue of Simpson in their backyard. We also heard that Simpson beat him. We deposed Jason to see if we could pry him open. Early in the deposition he admitted, "I kind of messed around a lot when I was a kid" and that his father had hit him "with a belt on my butt . . . maybe ten, twenty times. I don't remember exactly."

Among the rumors that kept the fires of this case roaring was one that held Jason had committed the killings or helped his dad clean up. My partner Peter Gelblum was particularly enamored of this theory. Jason didn't do it, his blood was not found anywhere in the crime scenes, and there wasn't a shred of evidence to indicate he was involved. Still, it became a running joke. Whenever we came to a stumbling block, I would say, "Well, maybe Jason did it." Robin Greer, Nicole's friend, believed Jason knew what happened and would break if questioned.

Jason and Nicole had been only about ten years apart in age, and they had been friends. She was like a big sister to him, often taking his side in disagreements with O.J. After she and Simpson divorced, Jason would go to Nicole's house on Gretna Green where they would hang out and listen to rock and roll. At her wake, he had been very shaken.

It didn't take five minutes with Jason Simpson to get a sense of him. This was a twenty-six-year-old kid who was never going to live up to his father and who had given up trying, probably for the better. Although he had played football for USC and had played in the 1989 Rose Bowl, he was not a gifted athlete and had not been a star. I felt sorry for him almost immediately. As one might expect, he would not say anything harmful about his father and he wasn't about to help our side. But he looked at me directly and actually seemed to consider the questions he was being asked, rather than plot ways to subvert them. I tried to dig out information about Simpson's violent temper, and whether Jason had seen him hit anyone, but I got nowhere. Still, I had to ask. Jason Simpson had never testified or been examined under oath, and I had to do my job and probe everything.

It was very difficult to ask him these questions, and I didn't have the heart to press hard. Jason was guileless and seemed a sad person. This was not a kid who needed someone else giving him a hard time. I felt sorry that he had to be O.J. Simpson's son. O.J. was not the perfect creature he projected himself to be—Jason, of course, knew that—and I wondered whether some part of the son might feel almost relieved that his father's dark side had been exposed to the world. I am a father, this case was about a father losing his son; the relationship between father and son was at the core of this tragedy.

"Is it fair to say that you love your father?" I asked. I just wanted a son's presumed bias on the record.

"Yes," he answered.

"Is it fair to say that you don't want to see him lose this case?"

Jason seemed actually to consider the question. "I wouldn't want to see him lose it, no."

"And is it fair to say that even if a jury were to conclude that he killed Nicole and he killed Ron, you would stand by his side?"

"It would be kind of hard."

I was surprised. "You wouldn't abandon him, would you?" This was a switch. In order to affirm bias, it seemed I was encouraging a young man to back up a killer.

"It would be really hard. He is my father." It was clear to me that Jason's loyalty wasn't blind, that he had given this some thought.

I asked, "At any point in time, from the moment you learned of Nicole's death to the present, did you ever form a belief that your father might be responsible for these deaths?"

"I never formed a belief, no," he said softly.

"Did you ever form a suspicion?"

He let out a noise that in normal conversation is understood as "Of course." Then he said, "I formed a suspicion."

"And did you ever share your suspicion with Arnelle?"

"Probably, but I don't remember." Consider the scene of two grown children discussing whether their father slashed the throat of their stepmother.

"Did Arnelle ever tell you that she, too, formed a suspicion that your father might be responsible?"

"Never."

If Jason is Fredo Corleone, Arnelle Simpson may well be Michael. Smart, attractive, accomplished, Arnelle must make O.J. proud. She was another witness I did not expect much from.

In the criminal trial Arnelle testified that she had not been inside the main part of the house at Rockingham at all on June 12, having left her guest room around ten A.M. to go to church, coming back at eleven, going out again at twelve-thirty in the afternoon, and not returning until after one the next morning. I established that when she returned, rather than walking through the main house, she walked the outside path directly to the backyard and to her room. Kato remembered hearing her footsteps. The last time she had been inside the main house was between nine and ten o'clock on Saturday night. Her father hadn't been there; he was out at a function with Paula Barbieri.

Questioned by Marcia Clark at the pretrial hearing and again at the criminal trial, Arnelle testified that when the police woke her in her room at five-thirty A.M. and asked if she knew where her father was, she said he was out of town. This is in direct contradiction of the police, who say she said, "Isn't he inside?" On the basis of that answer and some other statements, they had been able to obtain a search warrant for the premises. Johnnie Cochran and the defense team vehemently attacked the police and prosecution on this issue, saying these were all lies fabricated in order to gain entry to search and seize Simpson's home; the police knew Simpson was not home, they argued, because Arnelle had told them; therefore the search was illegal and all evidence obtained thereby should be excluded. They did not prevail on that point.

The Constitution prohibits unreasonable searches and seizures, and through the years courts have held that when police violate that rule, the penalty shall be that all seized evidence plus other evidence that is "fruit from the poisoned tree," will be excluded and not used against a defendant. This is the so-called exclusionary rule.

However, the courts have also decided that the exclusionary rule does not apply in civil cases. We made this clear in briefs at the beginning of our case: From a legal standpoint in *Rufo, et al.* v. *Simpson,* whether the police had probable cause to go onto or search the Rockingham property was utterly irrelevant. So I was not very concerned with what occurred between Arnelle and the cops on this issue.

In the criminal trial, Cochran put Arnelle on the stand and she testified that she and Detectives Lange and Phillips had entered the house by circling the property to the front and going in the front door. She said two other officers were still interrogating Kato Kaelin in his room at the time.

In her version, she said she chose the front entry because she wanted to turn off the alarm system, using a keypad that was located outside that door. Now, one might wonder why she would care about the alarm system; she was in the company of police detectives, why worry about tripping a house alarm? The alarm could be deactivated once inside the house. She said in her deposition that she was "nervous and scared."

Kato and four police officers all testified that Arnelle's version of the facts was wrong. There is a back door into the main house, just yards from Arnelle's room. Kato said this back door was not routinely locked, that it was usually left unlatched, so that people could come inside from the pool area and the backyard. He and each of the four detectives distinctly remember entering the house with Arnelle, all six together, through the rear door. There's no question, they went in the back.

Why is this important?

Simpson had called Kato from an LAX airport pay phone a little before midnight on June 12 just before boarding his flight and asked that he set the alarm system. This was the first and only time Kato had been asked to do this job. He had not previously been entrusted with the code, so Simpson recited it to him. Not wanting to screw up, Kato wrote the code down on a piece of paper, went to the front of the house, punched the numbers on the system's keypad, set the alarm, walked back to his room, and went to bed.

This was incontrovertible. Simpson and Kato testified to it, there was no dispute. The house was secured.

But when they entered the rear door with Arnelle, Kato and the police detectives were positive that no alarm went off, no beeping was heard, nothing.

So why did the alarm system not go off?

Under Simpson's alarm system, from the time a secured door opens until the proper code is entered on the keypad and the system is deactivated, a beeping noise will sound, giving you time to turn off the alarm. If it is not promptly deactivated, the alarm starts to ring. There was no keypad either directly inside or outside the back doors, you had to go into the house near the bar area to find the closest one. Nobody saw Arnelle go into the bar area to deactivate the system. There was no record of an alarm having registered at Westec, the company that provided security for the estate.

Were Kato and four detectives all lying when they said they entered through the back door together? They would have no reason to lie about this fact—it didn't help the case against Simpson to say they went in through the back. Kato would never have been capable of making that kind of sophisticated calculation in the first place, and he would have had no reason to. Neither would the cops. Even if you have a jaundiced view of the LAPD and believe there are bad cops who fabricate evidence or concoct incriminating scenarios, it would be nearly impossible to get four police officers to lie about a seemingly minor detail when any one of them could turn on the others and rat them out. At the time it was an innocuous fact.

But that innocuous fact leads to an incriminating conclusion: after Simpson left, someone else was in that house.

Between the time Kato turned on the system at midnight and when he, Arnelle, and the four police officers entered just past five-thirty A.M., that system had been disarmed. Someone who had the code was in there and did it.

If Arnelle was not telling the truth and she did, in fact, go through the back door with the four officers and Kato Kaelin, then that tells me someone definitely was in the house. That someone might have been Arnelle, and if it wasn't Arnelle, she may well know who it was. Why otherwise would she create the fiction of her journey to the front door?

What was the person or persons who deactivated the Rockingham alarm system doing in the house?

The police found a load of wet laundry sitting in Simpson's washing machine, apparently including some of Arnelle's underwear. The housekeeper, Gigi Guarin, hadn't run it. She had been away that weekend and had testified in the criminal trial that she had left Friday with all the laundry dried and folded. In any case, she didn't do Arnelle's wash. When shown a video of the contents of the washing machine while testifying in the criminal trial, Gigi identified the laundry basket as Arnelle's. Arnelle said she hadn't done any laundry from June 9 through June 12, nor had she been inside the main house, which included the laundry room, since Saturday night. She said she had gotten home Sunday morning and gone straight to bed. Simpson didn't do the laundry, that night or any night.

So, who did this load of laundry? Why was it still in the machine? To what end?

The most striking possibility, of course, is that Simpson had returned home from the scene of the crime and bled all over it. In his haste to seal his alibi and meet the limousine and catch his flight, there's no telling what condition he may have left the place. He made at least one phone call—to Kato—just before boarding his plane from a pay phone at the gate. He could have made other calls then, or even when he landed at O'Hare. He could have asked someone to clean up after him, to give the place a once-over, to check and see that he didn't leave any incriminating evidence where it could be found. Quentin Tarantino would have a field day with this scene. Who might Simpson call? Who were the people closest to him? Who could he trust? Cowlings had returned from a party and was at home alone. Arnelle was in her room alone. Cathy Randa was at her home alone. All were familiar with Simpson's home and property.

Whoever he might have called, he or she or they gained access and turned off the alarm system when they entered. They would not have risked turning on the lights; Kato was in his room, neighbors might notice, some stray motorist might remember lights blazing in the mansion late at night. So they picked up whatever they could find, and wiped up the rest. It's not impossible to surmise that, in the dark, they might have missed the few small blood drops that were still there when the police entered early in the morning, or dropped something, like socks on a carpet.

They took their load—a sweatsuit? towels?—and ran it through the washing machine, then ran a load behind it as camouflage. Knowing what they knew, think about waiting in that house, at that hour, for the spin cycle to finish.

In their haste on the way out, whoever did this clean-up job forgot to reset the system.

What had needed washing so badly that it was done in an empty house after Simpson was gone? What had been washed? How many loads? Who ran them? These remained unsolved mysteries of the Simpson case.

So, do we have an accessory after the fact? I think so.

Who routinely cleans up after Simpson?

FOURTEEN

Help, Help Me, Randa

C athy Randa was totally invested in O.J. She had been working for Simpson for more than twenty years, she ran his office, ran his life, kept his calendar, was the center of his business universe. And he was the center of hers. She was financially dependent on him.

My image of Randa before I met her, from people in and around the Simpson case, was of the villainous Machiavellian manipulator, pulling all the strings, doing all the dirty work. She took care of the details. Because she was so attached to Simpson and had given over so much of her adult life to him, protecting and exonerating his life served to validate her own.

When she walked into the deposition room she looked as she should have looked: short, heavy, with a pinched mouth and a tight, hawklike, angry face. A short stretch of barbed wire. She had worked as an ad hoc assistant to the criminal defense team. Simpson would call her from jail, and she would use her conference line to route calls for him like a command center. To destroy Simpson would destroy her, and as far as she was concerned, nobody was going to get away with that.

A crucial early task of Simpson's criminal defense team was corraling everyone who could be counted on to support Simpson, and Randa was at the heart of that effort. She came up with names, called people and urged them to stay in O.J.'s corner. She was instrumental in arranging the witness round up at Shapiro's office. As I envisioned it, Randa had a tally sheet, like in political campaigns or on the Senate floor; she was lining up the states, counting the votes.

Randa also masterminded the mundane. She put together Simpson's wardrobe for court each day, choosing his outfits, placing them in a garment bag, and giving them to Kardashian to pass to O.J. in jail.

By the time I deposed her, in early May and again in early June, I was versed on almost every detail. I knew the evidence cold. I had no illusions that I would get anything incriminating from Randa; instead, I used the opportunity of her deposition to gather additional details about a wide variety of facts—the mechanics of Simpson's office, how his business was conducted, the workings of the telephone system at his house, his voice mail, his cell phone, travel issues, his schedule in normal times, his itinerary and activities during the days preceding and following the murders, basic information that was not disputable. Also, I had been told that Randa had never liked Nicole but did respond well to Paula and used to jot down notes of their various conversations. I wanted to see those notes.

Simpson had shared office space with Skip Taft but in January 1996, to save on expenses, he had Randa move his operation to a room adjacent to Kato's old room in the guest house at Rockingham.

I, again, did not expect to get anything damaging out of Randa and assumed she would be obstinate, evasive, pugnacious, untruthful. I was not mistaken.

While Simpson was running around the 405 Freeway in the Bronco with Cowlings on June 17, Randa and Taft paid a visit to Simpson's safe-deposit box at Union Bank. Michelle Caruso, the *Daily News* reporter, gave me this lead. Randa, whose name was on the bank's signature card, giving her access, said, "Mr. Simpson was going to be arrested, and he asked me to get his papers out of the safe-deposit box"—she had made a telling mistake and quickly corrected herself, "have *Skip* get the papers out of the safe-deposit box, or anything in there that would be for his children." She denied even seeing the contents, leaving them to Taft, who as Simpson's lawyer conveniently could refuse to reveal them by the attorney-client privilege.

Those contents are another unsolved mystery. An employee of the building complex where Simpson had his office said he had been asked by Taft and Randa to stand guard outside the safe-deposit room. He said he saw them take what Michelle described as "thousands . . . piles of cash that had hundred-dollar bills visible, and stuff the cash into a leather satchel." Randa denied this up and down. Caruso told me, Randa said that the employee made up the part about cash being taken from the vault to gain media attention, although the employee avoided the media like the plague.

Michelle called this "Skip and Cathy's Excellent Adventure."

The first time the LAPD searched Simpson's office they observed an information pamphlet on spousal abuse, which they were not sure was covered by their warrant. When they returned three weeks later with a warrant asking specifically for this document, Randa indicated she had put it in the trash and shredded it *the same day the detectives had originally arrived,* without speaking to Simpson about it—because it was old and "I don't know, the paper just looked yellowish to me."

(The office had only recently acquired a shredder. The media had surrounded their building and begun looking through their trash. When asked about the shredding of this document at the Al Cowlings grand jury, Randa took the Fifth.)

At one point during a break, after she had given me a series of answers I found completely unbelievable, I got up and rolled my eyes at Dan Leonard. He said, "What do you expect? Go knock yourself out, you're not going to get anywhere with her."

One of the documents that was produced was a single page entitled "Re Nicole Physical Rage," which had three entries:

- 4/18/89—Nicole hit O.J. with scripts regarding Ron Shipp evicting her tenant in Laguna.
- 9/3/89—Nicole physical confrontation with O.J. re legal document—NBC contract. O.J. refused to sign. Nicole grabbed and hit O.J. Cursed him repeatedly saying, "You asshole." O.J. replied, "Nicole, you are spoiled."
- 2/7/91—Nicole punched O.J. 12 times re postcard from Hawaii.

These were notes Simpson had asked Randa to make after the 1989 New Year's Eve incident to memorialize beatings Simpson is supposed to have received *from Nicole.* Simpson liked this document, because it showed him being "abused," not doing the abusing. I liked the notes even more, because they showed that theirs was a volatile, physical, and violent relationship. I tucked that one right away.

In his deposition, Simpson said Nicole had made up diary entries to defraud him in their divorce case. Randa was someone Simpson would have discussed this with, so rather than getting anything good from her, I wanted to make sure she couldn't hurt us by corroborating Simpson's lies. "Did O.J. Simpson tell you that Nicole was making things up about him?"

"No."

"Did he ever tell you that Nicole was inventing stories of spousal abuse against him?"

"No."

"Did he ever tell you that Nicole was attempting to defraud him?"

"No."

"Did O.J. Simpson ever tell you that in his divorce with Nicole, that Nicole had been asked to attempt to cheat or defraud him?"

"No."

Since Simpson instructed Randa to keep notes of Nicole beating him, he certainly would have confided in her about Nicole's inventing stories against him if that had occurred, but of course he didn't tell her anything of the sort. If Simpson was going to trash Nicole on that issue, I had one of their own to testify against him.

Randa had told the police she got a call on her answering machine from Simpson on the night of June 12. (I suspect she told them not out of civic duty, but because she thought it might show up on his or her phone records, and to deny the call would then be very incriminating.) Simpson later told her he had made it at 7:30 P.M. Might have been. Might also have been at 11:30 from a pay phone in the airport. We'll never know; the next morning, despite the fact that she knew Simpson was wanted for questioning by the police in the matter of Nicole's death, Randa made no attempt to save it. "I never even thought about it." The message was taped over.

If you believe your boss, to whom you are entirely devoted, is being unfairly implicated in a murder, you don't expunge exculpatory evidence, you save everything that might point to his innocence. She was on the phone with Simpson in Chicago and from the airplane many times that morning, she made his travel arrangements, called Skip Taft to pick him up at the airport, and had spoken to Simpson from Chicago and from the airplane about finding a lawyer—a criminal defense lawyer—but when she had the one piece of evidence that could conceivably exonerate him, she didn't save it. Now, perhaps amid the anxiety and grief over Nicole, she simply forgot to pop the tape out of the machine. More likely, that call either didn't exist or included information they didn't want anyone to hear. To me, it doesn't add up.

She recalled the message as: "Hi, Randa. I'm home, getting ready to go, nothing important." There is the possibility that he said, "Randa, I need your help. You've got to go take care of some things."

She and Taft picked up Simpson when he arrived from Chicago and drove him back to Rockingham. They drove there directly. "Did you make any stops?"

"No," she answered.

"Did Mr. Simpson touch any of the luggage?"

"No."

"Did he change his clothes?"

"No."

Whereas Bob Kardashian was protected by the attorney-client privilege and Al Cowlings was taking the Fifth, Randa had no such hiding place from our questions concerning the week of June 13. I had been blocked, so I used her as much as possible to get information about Simpson's activities during that week. Randa, I learned, prevailed upon Paula to come back from Las Vegas to be with Simpson. Paula, it turned out, was driven to Kardashian's house by Allan Park, the same limo driver who had picked up Simpson on the night of the murders. Cathy liked Paula and had stayed in contact with her during the time Simpson was supposed to be reconciling with Nicole. "She did keep in contact with me," she said.

"And with Mr. Simpson, right?"

"No. Not necessarily."

"What does that mean, 'not necessarily'? Did she keep in contact with Mr. Simpson during the time that he was purportedly reconciling with Nicole?"

"Yes."

So, it appeared that Randa was setting up these little meetings on the side.

This only underscored how hopeless and scorned Paula must have felt on the day of the murders. Simpson had broken her heart a year earlier when he had dumped her and gone back to Nicole. Now, even after he and Nicole had broken up again and he had asked Paula back into his life, Simpson did not find her suitable to bring to a family function like the dance recital. One could understand why they had fought bitterly over Nicole, the feelings were still raw. Having gone down that road before, it must have been heartbreaking for Paula to get so deeply sucked in once again. This gave legitimacy to the assumption that Paula's early-morning phone message, far from the ordinary talk that Simpson would try to make it out to be, was in fact a painful, agonizing breakup call. Simpson was a man in intense personal turmoil. On the morning of June 12 he'd had two women close to him, and he had struck out miserably with both of them.

It was increasingly clear that I had not done a very good job of deposing Ms. Barbieri. Had I better understood the history, dynamics, and details of this love triangle, I could have confronted Paula more forcefully and confidently and, perhaps, gotten more forthright answers. I wrestled with the thought of taking Paula's deposition again; to do so would have required court permission. But there was so much else to do, and time was running out.

Cathy Randa's Excellent Adventure running mate, Leroy "Skip" Taft, was a tall gray-haired man in his sixties. He was Simpson's business manager, and while he had other clients, Simpson was his main draw. He controlled Simpson's financial world, O.J. didn't do anything concerning money without Taft taking care of it for him. Taft's life was to exploit the name and image of O.J. Simpson for the benefit of O.J. Simpson, Simpson's family, and people like Skip Taft. He was a loyalist to the end. If O.J. was indeed guilty, then Taft had staked his whole life on a double-murderer.

I took Taft through the panoply of issues: the relationship between Simpson and Nicole, the 1989 New Year's Eve incident, and the letter he drafted for Simpson stating that if Simpson thereafter hit Nicole, the prenup would be ripped up. I questioned him about the events of the last year of Nicole's life and focused on the sequence of facts surrounding the IRS letter to Nicole that Taft had helped Simpson write. Taft danced around some and completely denied there was anything "vengeful" in its original draft (although he himself had described it as such in his cover letter to Simpson) or in Simpson's motive for sending it. Taft claimed not to know of any conflict between Simpson and Nicole at the end, which I found utterly unbelievable.

I asked if he was present when Simpson asked Kardashian to take him to the airport and pick up his golf clubs. "It was discussed on Tuesday morning, whether he was going to go get those golf clubs at that time or not. I wasn't sure whether they were going to go pick them up or wait for another day." Can you imagine that? Simpson saying he wanted his clubs, Kardashian and Taft saying, *"O.J., do you know how terrible that will look?"* Simpson responding, "Bob, are you going to take me to get my clubs or am I going to go myself?" I'm sure that was the gist of the "discussion."

I asked Taft whether, when he picked Simpson up at the airport and drove him to Rockingham (or later at the police station, after his client had been interviewed by Lange and Vannatter), he had observed Simpson's fingers and hands, whether he'd seen any cuts.

"It was his middle finger. I think on one hand he had a cut." This was part of the Simpson story. No news so far.

"What was he wearing?"

"It was a white golf shirt, I think. It even could have been like an Izod with an alligator as an emblem, and some dark slacks."

One of the unfortunate pieces of evidence was the selection of photographs taken by the LAPD that day. Although there was a big gash on the fourth finger of Simpson's left hand, they only took pictures of his middle finger. There were two cuts on his middle finger, and Simpson cleverly kept his fingers pressed together in an attempt to hide all others. Very bad piece of evidence, which the defense was going to jam down our throats. Vannatter and Lange had testified that they got a fairly good look at his hands and noticed only cuts on the middle finger. Now they were stuck. They weren't about to say, "We're stupid, he had all these cuts and we didn't notice them." The best we could do was get them to concede that they did not thoroughly inspect each and every digit. Nevertheless, this was a problem for us.

Two days after being photographed by the LAPD, Simpson was examined by a Beverly Hills physician named Dr. Robert Huizenga, who reported in his notes that Simpson had ten cuts or scratches on his left hand and one on his right. Where did he get them? Simpson had no answer at his deposition. Obviously he had gotten them during the commission of the murders, but we had no witnesses to say, "I saw all of the cuts on Monday."

I pulled out big blowups of other photographs of Simpson's hands, taken on June 17 at Kardashian's house, and showed them to Taft. Either he couldn't think quickly enough and didn't know all of Simpson's cover stories or I caught him off guard, because, to my astonishment, he conceded that he saw several of those cuts—two and perhaps three—at the police station *on Monday,* including the cut on the side of the fourth finger. I pointed to Simpson's fourth finger and asked, "Did you see that cut on him during the week of June 13?"

"I may have," Taft said. "I may have seen it down at Parker Center."

Baker was getting worried. "Don't speculate," he told Taft, whom he was also representing. Instead of taking the hint—"Don't speculate" is lawyer's code for "Don't say it unless you're absolutely 100 percent sure, *and you're not sure, right?"*—Taft, himself a lawyer, came right back and said, "Yeah, I think that's probably where I saw it."

This was an absolutely devastating admission. I could not believe he said it, and I moved immediately to lock it in.

"And for the record, we are pointing to a photograph that shows a cut on the side of his finger. Correct?"

"Yes."

Just to juke them a little, I asked a question about Simpson's last will and testament, to which Baker objected. I was buying precious time, during which I considered whether to go back to the cuts. I decided to go for it.

"I have a better picture of Exhibit Thirty, the cut on the side of the finger, that's Exhibit Thirty-eight."

Baker blatantly cut in, "Don't guess or speculate if you've seen that before." I came right back.

"You said at the Parker Center."

"Yeah, I believe I saw that cut at the Parker Center."

"On what day?"

"The thirteenth."

He asked me if it was on the fourth finger. I said it was. "I saw that cut," he asserted, "and then I saw the cut on his knuckle, on his left knuckle." All by himself he admitted seeing two cuts!

"Let me show you that cut," I said agreeably. I was happy to let him examine it. "And you see a cut above the knuckle?"

"Yes," he replied.

"And then one a little bit lower than that. Right?" I was going for cut number three!

"Right."

"So you saw a total of three cuts at Parker Center on June 13 on Mr. Simpson, on the fingers of his left hand. Right?" The key here was that the pictures I showed him were taken on Friday, June 17. He was telling me he saw these cuts on the previous Monday, within eighteen hours of the murders.

"I saw two for sure. I'm not sure of that third cut that you pointed out in that picture."

"The third cut you are referring to is the one at the top of the ring finger?"

"Yeah," said Taft, "I don't have any clear consciousness of that cut as I do of the one on the fourth finger and the one on his middle-finger knuckle." His words! I didn't lead him, I didn't ask whether he had "a clear consciousness" of those cuts; he was a lawyer and he volunteered that language!

If Simpson had those cuts on June 13 at Parker Center—putting aside the one he claims to have gotten when "a glass broke" in Chicago—then he murdered those people. Plain and simple. He had no explanation for how he got the cuts; he claims they occurred later, but his lawyer and friend, having looked at his hands that Monday, was telling me, "I have a clear consciousness of that cut on the fourth finger."

Taft had just buried Simpson on one of the most damning pieces of evidence in the case. The guy didn't know it, but Baker sure as hell did.

FIFTEEN

Breaking Ranks

The Geraldo Rivera people called with a lead for us. They had been approached by a psychotherapist named Dr. Jenniefer Ameli, who claimed she had been treating both Nicole Brown Simpson and Ron Goldman in the months leading to their murders. She was in possession of notes on her sessions as well as copies of bills to each of them, and they needed permission from the estates of each to use them on the air. Were we willing to waive the psychotherapist-patient privilege? No, we weren't, and I scuttled her appearance, but we were interested in talking to Dr. Jenniefer Ameli now that she had been brought to our attention.

She came to my office and met initially with John Kelly and me, and later with Peter Gelblum. Dr. Ameli informed us that she had treated Ron beginning in October 1993 and into 1994. I questioned her in detail, figuring if she got things clearly wrong, we would find out immediately that she was a fraud. She had her facts and nuances reasonably straight: family background, childhood, sister, father divorced from natural mother, how Ron and his sister felt about it; closeness to sister and father, some unresolved guilt about feelings toward mother abandoning them; said he was seeing someone, didn't want to talk about it.

Ron had introduced Ameli to Nicole, whom she saw more regularly up to and including three days before she died. She brought with her several documents, including the notes and bills. We read them. The notes

289

of Nicole's sessions were remarkably consistent with the events transpiring in her life; the notes pertaining to Ron were more amorphous.

For example, in a session on May 26, 1994, Ameli's notes indicated Nicole talked about being ill with pneumonia, and how her husband had been nice and helped her. Except for referring to Simpson as her husband, this was all accurate. An entry for June 3 had Nicole quoting Simpson as saying, "You hung up on me last night, bitch." This matched exactly what Nicole had written in her diary.

The entry for June 9 was explosive: *"Patient extremely upset about her relationship with husband. Fear of getting hurt. Today Nicole seemed extremely frustrated and fearful of husband. Patient stated that during the past few days he had threatened her by saying, 'Stop this nonsense or else.' Then other subjects were brought up: M. Allen, Ron G., and government money."*

The notes went on to say: *"At this point Mr. O.J. slapped her and kicked her. When she fell on the floor he pulled her hair and then wanted to have sex with her. Nicole is determined to leave him forever even though she believes he will try to kill her."*

This was serious stuff; three days later Nicole was dead.

The issue immediately was: Is this some wacko or is Jenniefer Ameli for real? If she was legitimate, she possessed extraordinary evidence. Throughout the criminal trial and our investigation, no evidence had ever surfaced suggesting Simpson had beaten Nicole right before the murders, or that she was seeing a therapist. The notes had enough in them to appear accurate and authentic, including little details that were not known generally to the public.

I had never heard of Dr. Ameli, but when we began investigating we found the LAPD had a large file on her. She had not come forward in the criminal trial until three months after the murders, September 1994, when she reported a break-in at her office. The police had arrived to find file drawers open, papers strewn around, a real mess—and some notes from her files on Ron and Nicole lying on the floor. At that point, although she claims she was coerced into revealing this, she told the police she had been receiving threatening phone calls and messages. She felt someone was trying to shut her up because she had evidence that would bury Simpson.

The police looked into Dr. Ameli's information long and hard and concluded that there just wasn't enough for them to feel comfortable with.

There was the sense that the break-in might have been staged. When they basically wrote her off, she disappeared from the landscape.

Kelly didn't believe her from the get-go because there was no evidence of payment, she didn't have checks from either of them. We looked at Ron's bank account and could find no checks to her, but she said Ron paid her in cash from his tips as a waiter at Mezzaluna. Nicole, she told us, had never paid her, preferring to put the bills through her medical insurance, which she had not yet done at the time of her death. I have to confess, the whole story was wild.

The Goldmans were convinced Ameli was not authentic because Ron would have told them if he was in therapy. Kim, in particular, who was very close to Ron, believed he would have mentioned it to her and said it wasn't like Ron to be seeing a therapist about issues of self-growth and improvement, as Ameli claimed. Still, young adults have been known to keep secrets from their families, particularly of a psychological nature.

Aside from the fishy story about the break-in, the one detail that really bothered me was the fact that when the police began their investigation, she didn't tell them everything she knew, the information came slowly in dribs and drabs. The reason, she explained to us, was that she had spoken with an attorney for the California Association of Marriage and Family Therapists who had told her she was not permitted to identify her patients or talk about them to anyone. Even so, one would have expected her to have contacted the victims' families. But she never did.

Nor did she level with us at first. When we met her in February and asked to be told everything, she gave us some information; when we met with her a second time we were presented with more information, new documents began to emerge, new notes she hadn't mentioned at our first meeting.

She produced several witnesses to confirm that she had treated Ron and Nicole. Her daughter, Chantelle Ameli, a pleasant twenty-year-old college girl, told us she had arrived at her mother's office for lunch one afternoon and found her mom running late. As she waited downstairs in front of the Santa Monica office building, she saw a large black man shaking a blond white woman very hard. He was yelling at her and she was shouting right back. Chantelle was about fifteen feet from them and turned away in embarrassment. She did not recognize the couple at the time, but after the murders she realized it had been Simpson and Nicole.

We interviewed two of Ameli's assistants, both young students with no reason to tell anything but the truth, who confirmed Ron's and Nicole's visits and provided substantiating details.

As our meetings with Dr. Ameli and her witnesses increased in frequency, so did her story increase in drama. The kicker came when she told us for the first time that she had called Nicole from a pay phone at a Persian restaurant on Santa Monica Boulevard on the night of the murders. She knew Nicole had been going to see Sydney dance, she said, and that Simpson might be there. According to Ameli, she told Nicole, "I was worried about you. How did your recital and dance go with the family?" Nicole told her, "I told him to 'f' off today"—the doctor was not a natural user of profanity—"and I am relieved. I am happy on one hand, but I'm frightened. He's not going to let me get away with it."

If she had presented this story to us at our first meeting, I don't know how I would have reacted. To hear such important evidence so late in the game was too much to accept.

To expose that she was a fraud, the defense subpoenaed her for deposition. Ameli needed legal representation, and I referred her to Peter Lesser, an attorney I respected. I asked him to do his own investigation and decide for himself if she was real or not. The last thing I wanted was to vouch for a witness who was not genuine. I said, "The best service you can do for all of us is to check her out thoroughly. You have the attorney-client privilege, I don't want to know things that are privileged, but go ahead and do your investigation and let me know."

Lesser got back to me. "Dan," he said, "I have now verified this whole story with at least eight people."

There was enough private fact and detail in Dr. Ameli's story to make it seem plausible, even true. For her to have made it up would have required her to have read and digested an overwhelming amount of information. Only an absolute trial junkie might have pulled it off. There were such people, and even if Dr. Ameli was one of them, how had she involved all these other people in this intricate bizarre scheme? And why?

If this woman was a fraud, what was her motive? Money? She never sold her story, though in the O.J. Simpson market at the time, this was a $100,000 tabloid deal and she'd had the entire run of the criminal trial to pursue it. Social policy, to bring the issue of domestic abuse to the forefront? Could all of Ameli's witnesses possibly have been driven by the same deep-seated motive and been prepared to go to court and commit felonies right and left? That wasn't plausible. People don't make things up out of whole cloth, en masse, especially in a case of such intense scrutiny.

My ultimate decision was not to use her at trial. Neither the Goldmans nor the Browns believed her, there was no evidence of payment, but there was nothing about her story I could flatly contradict— nothing I knew was absolutely false—only the way it was delivered was completely incredible. Plus, even if Dr. Ameli were telling the truth about everything, as devastating as this evidence was, she would have been subjected to three or four days of cross-examination. Baker would have hammered her: She didn't give the police her information immediately, she didn't tell *anybody* immediately; then there was the question of whether the break-in was staged, and the fact that her story came out in evolutionary stages.

Whether or not she was telling the truth, we could not allow her testimony to turn the proceedings into the trial of Jenniefer Ameli. The defense would have loved that: *If Jenniefer Ameli is not telling the truth, then O.J. Simpson is innocent. If she's a nitwit, you must acquit.* This was not acceptable. We had a better case against Simpson than we did defending Ameli.

Nevertheless, if Jenniefer Ameli is telling the truth, what happened is far more horrific than we realized, and Marcus Allen is at the center of it. Simpson found out Nicole was seeing Allen. She called the Sojourn battered women's shelter on June 7, looking for help. He was beating her again.

I kept telling the defense that I fully intended to use Ameli. It is part of the game lawyers play to try and juke the other side. I put her on the witness list, just to make them worry about her. Her story was long and detailed; they would have to be prepared for it and they had to be concerned. I would always look Baker or Leonard straight in the eye and tell him, "First witness is Resnick, second witness is Ameli. Get ready. You guys don't think I'm calling them? You just wait."

We took our show on the road. In Chicago we deposed James Merrill, the Hertz employee who picked Simpson up at O'Hare and whom Simpson called the next day to apologize for brusqueness; Raymond Kilduff, another Hertz employee who drove Simpson from his hotel back to the airport;

and Mark Partridge, a passenger who sat next to Simpson on that flight. All three had been called as witnesses by the defense in the criminal trial supposedly to establish that Simpson did not carry himself like someone who had just committed a double homicide. Partridge, a copyright attorney, had gone so far as to take notes of his observations that night and put a "c" with a little circle around it on the bottom. We also deposed Chicago police detective Ken Berris, who had been summoned to investigate Simpson's hotel room on the morning of June 13. All would figure prominently at trial.

In St. Louis we observed as Dan Leonard took Sharon Rufo's deposition. We were prepared for a bloodbath—"Oh, you haven't seen your kid in sixteen years and you've just come out of the woodwork for the money"—but Leonard treated her rather gently. He got out the basic facts, but in trying to be sensitive to the fact that she was a mother who lost a son, no matter how removed, he opted to go easy on her. She cried a couple of times, and he hardly grilled her at all. I thought under the circumstances Rufo did quite well. We didn't ask her a single question.

In Kansas City, for our deposition of Marcus Allen, we retained a local firm and they laid out a conference room with comfortable accommodations and a beautiful spread of food. It was a big day for the firm; the secretaries all wanted to meet the Kansas City Chief all-pro running back. Because Allen was such a big deal in Kansas City, they asked if he would be kind enough to sign some autographs. An impressive array of hats and footballs and sports memorabilia was arranged respectfully on a table, and like a total gentleman, Allen went in there and signed everything.

The deposition was a big local event, the Simpson case was coming to their town, and a gaggle of reporters and cameramen showed up. Usually the press is kept downstairs, but in Kansas City they were allowed right outside the office; you opened the door and there they were between you and the elevator. The crush was so great, I felt as if we were at a rock concert or on the road with a political campaign.

Marcus Allen was a wild card. He and Simpson had been close friends, but they had a difference of opinion about the facts.

In his deposition, Simpson said Nicole told him she'd had an affair with Marcus in 1993, and that they'd had sex. She said, "He is still calling me." Simpson said the following week he confronted his friend on the telephone: "Marcus, do me a favor and ease up on Nicole, because whatever is happening with you guys is really screwing her up. She is, like, going bonkers." To Simpson's knowledge, he said, the relationship stopped at that point. About a week after that, Simpson was taking a nap when Allen walked into his bedroom and apologized. Some months later Allen was permitted to use Rockingham as the site of his wedding, hosted by Simpson and Nicole. Simpson used this scenario to show that, far from a raging and murderously jealous madman, he was serene and forgiving.

In Marcus Allen's version, none of that happened; there had been no affair, no sex, no romantic relationship at all. "Nothing happened," he testified, they were just friends.

Allen wanted no part of our deposition and would not cooperate in accepting a subpoena. We had to hire a Kansas City process server, who went out to the Chiefs' practice facility to serve him. All the players parked their cars in the driveway except Allen, who hid his around back. Our guy got him on the way out. The story got big coverage in the *Kansas City Star*.

Marcus Allen had a clean image. He was handsome, powerful, talented, well-spoken, a true crossover celebrity with endorsement deals and a bright future in business or the media whenever his NFL playing days came to an end. It was a valuable franchise to protect, and anything associated with the Simpson case was a negative. The last thing he wanted was to admit sleeping with his best buddy's ex-wife, who was then murdered. There was no plus for him in getting involved.

In the criminal case, Christopher Darden had flown to Kansas City and interviewed Allen at length, although not under oath, and he had stuck to his story. The police had spoken to him over the phone, same denial. I assumed when we deposed him that he would not depart from that line, let alone admit he had an affair with Nicole directly before the murders occurred. Nicole had told both Faye Resnick and Cora Fischman that she was seeing Marcus again, and Faye had seen his car outside Nicole's house, but that was as close as we could get to confirmation. Then again, I didn't know how Allen would react to questions under oath, whether he would commit the felony of perjury or tell the truth.

It was worth a try. A large part of the Simpson defense was based on the premise that the whole investigation and trial was a big white conspiracy against O.J. The idea of Marcus Allen, a successful black athlete, a respected man in his community, testifying against Simpson could also serve to defuse a claim of racial bias.

Allen walked into the deposition room wearing slacks and a white T-shirt under a blue button-down work shirt, quiet, reserved. It was his word against about a half dozen other people, but it was obvious from the start that he was sticking to his guns, though he didn't speak with any sense of conviction. The sense he gave was "Just let me get through this."

When he'd heard of the murders, Allen testified, he was on the golf course in the Cayman Islands. He called Simpson at Rockingham to see if he was all right. "He said he couldn't even grieve because they are accusing him." When Allen asked, "Do you want me to come back?" Simpson said no.

If true, I found that suspicious. Given that he just lost his ex-wife, the mother of his children, herself a dear friend of Marcus, and was being questioned and investigated about his role in her death, Simpson would want the help and support of his friend, and would beckon him to come home. But he didn't; perhaps Simpson thought it best that Marcus stay as far away as possible.

I find it equally incredible, whether Simpson encouraged him or not, that Allen did not immediately come home, to be with Simpson, and attend Nicole's funeral. Whether or not Marcus and Nicole were lovers, they were friends. If a friend dies, you don't stay on the golf course, you attend her funeral.

At the deposition, he said he and Simpson were no longer friends. He had refused Simpson's request to write a letter to *Time* magazine contradicting their coverage and supporting him, and had refused again when Simpson asked him from jail to testify that he and Nicole had had an affair. After that second request, they never spoke again.

There is the possibility that Marcus simply never owned up to O.J. about his affair with Nicole. Though it seems clear that they *did* have an affair, Allen may have steadfastly denied it to Simpson. If that's true, then Simpson made up Allen's contrition in order to make himself appear even more beneficent by hosting Allen's wedding. The weight of the evidence supported Simpson's version.

Allen sometimes gave me the Al Cowlings shut-down, but in between he admitted he had visited Nicole's place on Bundy on several occasions, "just stopping by to say hello." She lived at Bundy for only six months, he was married, he popped over a few times, the last only a few weeks before her death. The last time he spoke to her was Friday the tenth.

"She said she was busy, or 'Call back.' I don't think I ever called back. . . . She said she was looking for a home, or something like that."

He spoke to her on Friday, he's married, she's broken up. Why was he doing this? Just good friends? Perhaps. But I suspect it was more.

Simpson had seen Nicole giving oral sex to Keith Zlomsowitch while looking in the window of her condo. He had stopped, stared, and then dropped in on them the next day. But Marcus Allen was different. He was a good-looking black celebrity athlete on his way to the same Hall of Fame that housed O.J., but he wasn't pushing fifty, he was still active, very active. Alan Austin and Allen Schwartz said Simpson didn't care about Nicole being with anybody else. Only Marcus. I believe that.

But there is a vast legal difference between being convinced of a fact and presenting it as acceptable in a court of law. Even if we could prove that Allen was seeing Nicole, we could not establish that Simpson knew it. Without that hook, and without a witness who would tell us, "I talked to O.J. about Marcus," or, "I heard Nicole tell O.J. about Marcus," this was just another lead we could not pin down conclusively enough to use.

Plus, even though I desperately wanted to know, understand, and be able to show exactly what drove Simpson to kill, there was no legal requirement for us to prove a specific motive in order to win our case. We didn't have to prove the killing was motivated by Nicole's relationship with Marcus Allen; and if we set that as a standard and failed to meet it, the whole case could topple.

So if Marcus Allen was the final straw for Simpson, we did not have enough evidence to prove it. Nicole's friends—Cora, Faye, Kato, Cici, and Kris—believed it was, but their information wasn't admissible. Simpson and Cowlings and Allen knew, but they weren't talking. It was very frustrating. We could not get at the whole truth. We were getting parts of it, pieces, but we weren't getting the entire story because people were lying. Simpson was lying, Marcus was lying, Nicole wasn't talking, she was dead.

Whether or not Marcus Allen was an element in the killings, I think the cause was more complicated than that. Simpson was entering his late forties and had the fantasy of settling down with a family, the house with "the white picket fence." Nicole, a much younger woman, finally realized she didn't want Simpson anymore. She was not done spreading her wings, going out with younger men. Simpson felt abandoned. He lashed out by punishing her financially. She retaliated. She swept the kids away from him at the recital and showed him up in front of her own large family, who had lionized him and with whom he had become close. She was taking away his kids, she was taking away her family, she was rejecting him because of his age. Plus she cost him his relationship with Paula and was screwing around with his rival friend Marcus. He was losing his life. *Enough's enough. That's it. She can't get away with this. She can't destroy me.*

Allen Schwartz gave me the names of some other people to talk to. Two, in particular, were Louis Marx and Frank Olson. Marx was a principal stockholder of the Forschner Company, maker of Swiss Army watches and Swiss Army knives. Frank Olson was chairman of the Hertz Corporation. Simpson was a spokesman for both companies.

"You've got to go after those people," Schwartz told me. "They probably are going to talk and tell you things because they don't want to be associated with him anymore, they don't want to be identified with him, they don't want to have anything to do with him. Simpson will hate it because those are the money people, those are the people he's trying to hang on to. Don't let them off the hook. You've got to shame them."

I thought it was a good idea. Simpson was making the rounds, asking people to contribute to his defense fund. How could a guy who was worth around $10 million at the time of the murders possibly put his hand out? He spoke at churches, where people who made less than $20,000 a year were rushing to take money out of their pockets and put it into his. Why? So he could continue to live at Rockingham? It's one thing to ask rich people to support you, but to ask poor people for money? That was abhorrent.

By speaking with Simpson's wealthy friends, I could find out if they were financially supporting his defense, unless they were prepared to lie about it. If they were giving him money, I did not want them doing it quietly. Allen Schwartz had it right, I was going to shame them.

Simpson had attended a Forschner Company board meeting in Connecticut on June 9 and visited their warehouse, which also housed the Sabatier line of French-made cutlery that Forschner distributed. Simpson left with a shopping bag full of watches and cutlery. The limousine driver who picked Simpson up, John Upson, had given a statement to the

Connecticut State police and passed a lie detector test indicating that Simpson had brandished some large knives in the backseat of the limo and said, "You can really hurt somebody with this. You could even kill somebody with this." I spoke with Upson on the telephone and he confirmed those facts.

Louis Marx had known Simpson for twenty years but had not spoken to him since Simpson got out of jail. I wanted to find out if Marx could testify that he saw Simpson get the knives when he attended the board meeting. At his deposition held in New York City, Marx was extremely guarded and cautious in his testimony, not helpful at all on this particular point. He admitted that Simpson and the other directors had received bags of promotional watches and other items on visiting the company warehouse after their meeting. He admitted this same warehouse housed knives. But he claimed not to know whether Simpson received any knives. The last thing in the world he wanted to do was give me evidence that Simpson committed the murders with one of *his* knives. That was not the kind of celebrity endorsement Forschner had been looking for when it hired Simpson.

I asked Marx about the 1989 New Year's Eve incident. Simpson's employers would have been the ones most disturbed by the negative publicity, and Simpson obviously would have gone into deep damage control to maintain his image.

Marx had seen photographs of a beaten Nicole on television, and I asked him, "Were the observations of those photographs consistent with what Mr. Simpson told you about the incident in 1989?" I couldn't lose with that question; if he said yes, it showed that Simpson admitted he beat her, if he said no, Simpson lied.

Marx cleverly answered, "I drew no conclusions of what either of them looked like after the incident. . . . It is correct to say he did not say to me that she looked like she had been battered."

"He didn't say anything to you to indicate that she had been physically battered, correct?"

"That is correct."

"So when you saw the picture of Nicole battered, you did not immediately relate that to the incident in '89?"

"No, I did not." So, plainly, Simpson lied to him.

I stumbled onto another Simpson lie when I asked if Marx had ever seen Simpson with Paula Barbieri. He had, several months before the murders, at his office in New York. Simpson and Nicole were supposedly reconciled and monogamous at the time.

Skip Taft had approached Marx about contributing to Simpson's defense. Marx said he decided not to make a contribution.

I deposed Frank Olson at the Hertz corporate offices in New Jersey. He had known Simpson since Hertz hired O.J. to do television commercials during his days with the Buffalo Bills in the mid-seventies. Simpson was Hertz's chief spokesman, and Olson had been instrumental in turning him into their "Superstar in a Rent-a-Car." Olson counted Simpson as one of his personal friends. But the last contact he had had with Simpson or anyone from Simpson's organization, he said, was June 1994.

Olson said O.J. was superb at his job. "He was extremely popular as a personality," he explained, "and he would play golf with our customers. He would share with them anecdotes from his professional football career or his film career, and he would just, in general, socialize with our customers." Simpson was an effective speechmaker for Hertz, Olson affirmed; he was popular, well received, entertaining, witty, charming, a good communicator; he could tell a good story.

I was glad to hear it. Simpson was witty and charming and persuasive—all the attributes of a functioning con man—and was a very effective salesman. Now, at trial, if Simpson put on the charm on the witness stand, I could argue to the jury, "Look, his best friends, the people who know him well, will tell you he's a professional salesman, and his bogus story of innocence is what he's selling you. Don't buy it."

Simpson had done a lot of work for Hertz. In mid-May 1994, he attended an important sales event for Hertz, requiring him to miss Sydney's first communion. On the Monday following that outing, after a round of golf, Simpson told Olson that his reconciliation with Nicole hadn't worked and that he was thinking of getting away from Los Angeles and moving to New York. "He was very upset that it hadn't worked out. . . . I changed the subject to discuss something else, and he came right back to that same subject. . . .

"O.J. was not his usual outgoing, effusive self. I mean, he was signing autographs for kids and talking to a mother [who] came up to him about her son [who] had graduated from law school, and he wrote a note for her. And he did all those things like he normally did, but he was more melancholy than anything."

Even when he was hurting inside, Olson testified, Simpson was always able to be "O.J." "From time to time," I asked, "did Mr. Simpson share personal problems in his life with you?"

"Yes."

"Do you think that Mr. Simpson, so far as you were able to observe him, was able to project a very positive and friendly image on behalf of Hertz even during times when he was under personal stress?"

"He was consistently the same whenever he did work for us."

So much for the defense's much ballyhooed witnesses who saw Simpson at LAX and on the plane and said his demeanor was friendly.

Olson had talked to Simpson about his reputation for womanizing. "I said to him that if this was true, this was not good for us or for him." Then Olson said something very significant. "Everything about O.J. was his image."

The last thing Hertz wanted, said Olson, was to have a situation in which Simpson was not faithful to his wife. Simpson denied the infidelity. "He'd always laugh it off, joke about it, say that they were just rumors, they weren't true. . . . Well, there wasn't any place that you would go that women wouldn't go up to O.J. and were constantly—almost throwing themselves at him. And many of these women were very attractive. . . .

"There were always rumors about O.J."

Olson said he never knew whether these rumors were true. Simpson "had a way about him that would always give you the impression that people are always saying things about him that aren't true. . . .

"The only concern that we had about O.J. was his popularity with the customers. If his popularity had declined, we would not have renewed his agreement."

Hertz had been profoundly concerned about the 1989 New Year's Eve beating incident. They had been in touch with Simpson almost immediately upon their learning of it, and Simpson had put Nicole on the phone with Olson himself to minimize the damage. Allen Schwartz had told me Simpson and Skip Taft immediately went into damage control. "I had the sense of feeling that both of them were going to try to protect the Hertz relationship. . . ." Olson said. "I think he was nervous about his relationship with Hertz, and so he wanted to explain it to me before the publicity occurred."

"Why were you concerned?" I asked.

"Because O.J.'s image was that of a clean-cut, all-American, kind of a perfect personality. . . . Men loved him, women loved him, children loved him. And something like this would damage his image with the consumer, and therefore, since he was a personality working for Hertz, would damage Hertz."

Simpson had given Olson great, yet insignificant detail, about his argument with Nicole, ending with the tale that "one of the assistant district attorneys, who was a woman, was the president of some association about things like this, and he was being used as a scapegoat to identify this kind of situation."

Olson had learned the actual details of the 1989 beating during the criminal trial. "I was not only stunned," he testified, "I was embarrassed."

"Why were you embarrassed?" I asked.

"That I had believed him. That I had believed what he told me."

"Why did you believe him?"

"Because he was so convincing and because Nicole supported him. I wanted to believe O.J."

"Why did you want to believe him?"

"I wanted to believe Nicole because I had known him for so long. It was just so out of character. If I had any idea at the time that this was the circumstance that it was, O.J. Simpson would never have worked another day for Hertz."

Olson was refreshingly direct and seemed completely honest. He was coming clean about this. He had his own company's interest to protect, certainly, but he wasn't pulling any punches. I asked him the same question I asked Louis Marx: "Were the bruisings and markings on Nicole's face that you saw on the photographs consistent with what O.J. Simpson told you about the event in 1989?"

I got a much straighter answer. "No, no," Olson exclaimed. "No, no, that is ridiculous. It is ridiculous. Of course not."

Among the correspondence we found when we subpoenaed Hertz's files on Simpson was a letter he wrote to Olson dated January 14, 1992, following negotiations over renewal of his contract. In the letter, Simpson complained sardonically that Hertz was getting him dirt cheap. Near the end of the letter, Simpson wrote:

> *Frank, in the words of my wife, 'I've given you the best years of my life and all you want to do is control me.' Okay, it's alright. I'll just have to raise the stakes in our gin game so I can recoup some of my losses.*

In the words of my wife? Over ten days of his deposition, Simpson vehemently denied trying to control Nicole, but here, three years earlier, it slipped out in a letter. I'm sure that's exactly what Nicole said to him, that's what it was all about: control. When he could no longer control her, he killed her—the ultimate act of control.

There was another part of the letter that was more telling to me. Simpson told Olson:

> *. . . Once again, you've been able to get the best deal in the world today for a celebrity endorsement. Every time I read about this crippled Bo Jackson, and not to mention Magic Johnson (incidentally, I've tested negative on all recent physical exams) getting paid millions for limited involvement, it amazes me. . . .*

We were never going to get these offensive remarks into evidence; even if he were joking, they were too inflammatory and prejudicial and not legally relevant. However, those words spoke volumes about the man O.J. Simpson really was. The "clean-cut good guy" image cultivated over his lifetime was revealed as a false facade. The real O.J. Simpson was brutal, blithely calling Jackson a cripple and demeaning Johnson for being HIV-positive. He was not only a killer, Simpson was an ugly human being.

After Simpson's arrest, Skip Taft negotiated a buy-out of Simpson's contract. Hertz wanted nothing more to do with Simpson after he was put in jail. He was done.

Olson was deeply disillusioned because he was so misled by O.J. The irony is that his company paid Simpson all this money over all these years to sell an image to the American public, and Olson, like all the millions of other O.J. Simpson fans, bought that image. Olson helped create the fantasy, he fashioned it, he styled it. He fell in love with it. Then he was deeply crushed when he realized it was just an image after all.

SIXTEEN

The Brunos

Have you seen the *National Enquirer?!*"
Of course I hadn't. But when I opened it up, there was this grainy photograph of O.J. Simpson wearing what the *Enquirer* was insisting were Bruno Magli shoes, the same style of shoes that left the bloody shoe prints near Ron's and Nicole's bodies, the shoes the killer wore. The team gathered. We shook our heads. No chance. A photograph like that doesn't fall into our lap, things don't happen so perfectly in this life. We pored over the photo. It was dark on the newsprint, but, you know, whatever Simpson was wearing on his feet sure did *look* like the Brunos.

The photograph was big TV news that night, and already Simpson's attorneys were scoffing that it was a fraud. I had the same suspicions. The photo had not surfaced at the criminal trial, before and during which there had been a frenzied hunt for everything having to do with Simpson and shoes, gloves, hats, clothing. Perhaps the only hole in the prosecution's case was their inability to show through a photograph, witness, or other clear proof that Simpson owned and wore the Bruno Magli murder shoes. I assumed it was much too late for this spectacular new evidence to be untainted, there seemed to be no way something this vital would have been overlooked.

The photo credit was Gamma-Liaison, and we began tracking down the photographer through that agency. That day a lawyer from Buffalo, Mike O'Connor, called John Kelly in New York to tell him he represented Harry Scull, Jr. Now we knew who the photographer was and now we had a contact. John spoke with O'Connor, and then I did, and he assured us both that, "Harry Scull is no flake. He's no fraud." Kelly flew up to Buffalo to meet with them.

Scull turned out to be a thirty-year-old college graduate with a degree in criminal justice, single, kind of a heavyset guy with a happy, chubby face. Appearances can be deceiving, but he certainly did not appear devious enough to manufacture evidence in one of the biggest trials of the century and think he was going to get away with it.

Kelly saw the original photograph as well as the negatives. There was Simpson, wearing a blazer, shirt, tie, slacks, and Bruno Maglis, striding across the end zone at Buffalo's Rich Stadium before a Buffalo Bills–Miami Dolphins game. Now Kelly started to get excited. The photograph looked authentic to him, but Kelly was no photography expert.

Ed Medvene had been working with Bill Bodziak of the FBI on studying the killer's shoes. Bodziak was the ultimate authority, *the* expert on the forensics of footwear. He wrote the definitive book *Footwear Impression Evidence,* everything there is to know about footprints. He had testified in the criminal trial and presented definitive proof that the bloody shoe prints were made by a killer wearing size 12 Bruno Magli shoes, Lorenzo style, with a Silga sole. He told Medvene he had a general knowledge of photography in his field but that the man Ed wanted to talk to was Gerald Richards.

Jerry Richards looked like a middle linebacker, except bigger. He had been head of the FBI special photographic unit and still taught at the Bureau but was now a consultant in private practice. He came from the best tradition of the old agents. He looked like a rock, had a big speaking voice, excellent projection, and he looked at you when he spoke. He was just a big, powerful guy who exuded honesty and confidence. Medvene hired him on the spot.

Kelly took Richards to Buffalo to meet Scull, review his photos, negatives, and equipment, and discuss the circumstances under which the photograph was taken. It turned out that the equipment Scull used to take the photograph had been stolen from him. Only in the Simpson case.

As an expert, Richards was aware of the possibilities of altering photographs. In the old days, doctoring of images had to be done cut-and-paste style, physically handling one negative and then reshooting it to create another. With the advent of the computer and digital imaging, doctoring has reached levels of sophistication never approached before. Richards was the expert in this field, and he examined the negative closely.

After an intensive review, Richards found no evidence of fraud; he determined that the photograph was genuine and authentic. Further, he suggested he take an exemplar of the Bruno Magli shoe and match it up point by point, characteristic to characteristic, to the shoe Simpson was wearing in the photograph, which would be the photographic equivalent of having Simpson try it on.

Scull had taken a marvelous picture of Simpson. In a phenomenal stroke of good luck for us and rotten luck for Simpson, the paint in the end zone reflected up from the ground and revealed the pattern on the sole of the right shoe. After receiving permission from the FBI we gave the print to Bill Bodziak. Using high resolution photography techniques Bodziak was able to blow up the photo and actually see the Silga sole treads, the same pattern as the bloody footprints leading down the footpath away from Nicole's and Ron's bodies. The photograph also clearly showed that Simpson was walking pigeon-toed; the bloody footprints were pigeon-toed as well. "This thing matches like a fingerprint the sole at the crime scene."

Now I got excited. We had a picture of Simpson in the murder shoes! This one photo destroyed every myth, deception, and lie the defense threw at the judge, jury, and public in the criminal case. Not one of their clever concoctions about police conspiracies, planting of evidence, racial animus, and police incompetency could explain away this evidence. The criminal defense team couldn't challenge Bill Bodziak's conclusion that the murderer wore size 12 Bruno Magli shoes. They just said there was no evidence Simpson had such shoes—no photograph, no witness, nothing. I wondered how they all felt when they saw Scull's photograph, an image that singlehandedly exposed their complicity in perpetrating the most reprehensible miscarriage of justice seen in an American court of law.

At this point the civil defense team woke up and realized they would have to deal with this photograph, they couldn't just scoff it away. They noticed Harry Scull for deposition, which was held July 1 in Buffalo. I went up there with Kelly. Bob Baker and Dan Leonard represented Simpson, and they brought with them a photo expert named Pat Clark of Hy Zazula & Associates in New York City, who sported a handlebar mustache. Scull was represented by Mike O'Connor. We decided we would question Scull as well, anticipating that we would elect to use the videotape of his deposition at trial rather than calling him as a live witness. We didn't want Harry Scull to be a star witness, we wanted his photo to be the star evidence.

Scull showed up for his depo in a dark suit, showing respect for the proceedings and an unfamiliarity with the process. He could have come in jeans, for all we cared. He seemed nervous in this big-time atmosphere, didn't want to get anything wrong. Clearly, he took this very seriously.

Scull was a photo enthusiast and had been taking pictures his whole life. He loved sports and had taken thousands of pictures at football games played in his hometown Rich Stadium in Orchard Park, right outside of Buffalo. Simpson was a star on the Buffalo team for years, and then later, showed up regularly to broadcast games there for the television networks. Scull had taken scores of photographs of O.J. Simpson over the years.

On September 26, 1993, Scull was working as a stringer—a freelance photographer—for the Associated Press. He had done his prep work, then gone out to shoot warm-ups. He took a couple of rolls, including shots of various cheerleaders, as well as Bills and Dolphins players and coaches such as Marv Levy, Don Shula, Brian Cox, Dan Marino. O.J. Simpson, on hand as a broadcaster, was on the Bills sideline, doing a stand-up for the pregame show. After playing in Buffalo for a decade, Simpson was still a local hero and when Scull saw him walking across the end zone, he snapped him.

Baker grilled Scull on why he hadn't come forward with his photograph in the criminal case. Scull said he hadn't thought he had anything of value. During the criminal trial, he had contacted the *National Enquirer* about the photograph, but they weren't interested, saying they were "O.J.'d out." This sounded questionable to me only because I couldn't imagine the *Enquirer* ever being "O.J.'d out." Still, Scull hadn't pursued it further.

After Simpson's deposition in the civil case, having heard the hullabaloo about the "ugly-ass" shoes, Scull's friend, an agent and businessman named Rob McCelroy, had been rummaging through Scull's photos and found the head-to-toe shot of Simpson. He had never before represented Harry Scull.

"How come on this particular occasion Rob McCelroy acted as your agent?" Baker asked.

"He asked if he could," Scull answered. "He said, 'Maybe we can make ourselves each a couple hundred dollars.'"

Trying to prove the photo was a fraud, Baker questioned Scull about the weather at Rich Stadium, whether it had rained that day, was the field dry, was it windy, what was the temperature. This caught me by surprise, and I worried if they had something up their sleeves. It did rain in Buffalo that day, but the photograph showed Simpson in a blazer and slacks, no overcoat, dressed for relatively warm weather. Was this the silver bullet? You didn't see any water on Simpson in the photograph, and if it was raining, why would Simpson be wearing casual suede shoes like the Brunos? It made no sense; therefore, deduced the defense, the shot was a phony.

What had actually happened was that the photo was taken around 11:00 or noon, the game started at 1:05 P.M., and it rained later in the day. Sharp questions, commonsense answers.

During a break, Pat Clark examined the negative. When a month later it came time for the defense to designate expert witnesses at trial, Clark disappeared off the radar screen. I surmised he had nothing to tell Simpson's defense team that they wanted to hear.

Scull performed well in his deposition. He came across as naive and earnest, fine for our purposes, hardly the conniving photographic felon the defense wanted him to be.

In fact, Scull was so offended by being accused of fraud that he and his very capable attorney, Mike O'Connor, mounted a counterattack. In autumn 1993 Scull had submitted the Simpson photograph and some others to *Pro Football Weekly* hoping they would buy the photos for publication. The magazine was not interested. Now Scull contacted the magazine to find out whether the picture was still in its files. If so, all this talk that he had fabricated the shot to incriminate Simpson and make some dough would be proved a lie.

Sure enough, one week before his deposition, Scull called the magazine's offices in Ohio and spoke to the art director, Bob Peters, who received the photos from Scull in September 1993. Peters confirmed the photos were still on file.

This was dynamite. I told Kelly, "You get in touch with Peters at *Pro Football* and see if he'll cooperate with us."

Kelly tried.

But Peters got cold feet. Maybe the pro football community supported its own, maybe he was concerned about retribution, maybe he was concerned about sales. I don't know. What I do know is he said, "I don't want to get involved. I don't recall exactly when we got the picture." Peters knew how to keep from getting involved. If the photo arrived after the murders, his testimony was worthless; if it arrived before, he verified its authenticity. I told Kelly, "You've got to get him to come out. You've got to convince him!" Kelly tried and kept on trying right through the trial. When the deposition period elapsed, he tried to convince him to get on a plane and come to California and testify. He still refused.

Let me jump ahead for a moment. This was July. In December, with the trial drawing to a close and Peters still not budging, we got a tip out of the blue from a Jacksonville, Florida, attorney named Hank Coxe. Coxe represented the NFL's Jacksonville Jaguars. He told me one of his clients had worked at *Pro Football Weekly* in October 1993 and was with Peters when Scull's photograph came into the office. The client had heard on the *Rivera Live* show that Peters didn't want to step up to the plate, and although he didn't want to get dragged into the frenzy of the Simpson case, he was willing to come out and testify at trial that he had actually seen the photograph at that time.

I was ecstatic and thanked Coxe profusely. The only hitch was that the witness was working full-time and would have to wait until after the football season to testify. That was okay, Jacksonville was a new franchise, even if they made the playoffs, they were sure to get knocked out early.

But this was the Simpson case, nothing came easily. The Jaguars went on a tear with quarterback Mark Brunell and went all the way to the AFC Championship game, where they lost to the New England Patriots. By that time, other more stunning developments in the trial made it unnecessary to call this witness. Still, when someone with nothing to gain and a lot to lose volunteers to do the right thing, it makes it all worthwhile.

Bob Peters, on the other hand, had critical information that could have led to the conviction of a killer but refused to get involved. He should be ashamed of himself.

Because Simpson had been advised by counsel not to answer so many of our questions during the first ten days of his deposition, we went to court to overcome those objections. By this time, I had little interest in most of those questions. I'd gotten the answers from other sources, or didn't need or care about them anymore. But I did want Simpson back in the deposition chair for one more hour—that's all I needed. I had a few questions for him about his prior statement under oath that he'd never wear those "ugly-ass" shoes. Accompanied by Bob Baker, his son, Phil, and Bob Blasier, Simpson was not pleased to be back with us, for his eleventh day of deposition.

The 1993 NFL season was Simpson's last as a broadcaster before the murders. I asked if he recalled working as a commentator at Rich Stadium on September 26, 1993. "I recall being there from time to time," he said. We were early in the deposition, but he had reassumed his normal depo demeanor, eyes fixed on the table, unwilling to make contact with me. "I don't know if that was a date I was there, but—"

Was he going to be so foolish as to quibble with dates? "Do you recall covering a game early in the 1993 season between the Buffalo Bills and the Miami Dolphins?" I asked.

"I've done games for Miami and Buffalo." He hadn't answered.

"Including in that year?"

"I'm pretty sure I would have in that year."

Harry Scull took three photographs of Simpson that day. I picked up one of him talking to the Miami running back Keith Byers. "Are you in that photograph?" I asked.

"It appears to be me, yes."

"And do you recall the circumstances under which you were with Mr. Byers that is depicted in this photograph?"

"It looks like it's at a football game."

"Do you remember interviewing him at a football game?"

"Not particularly."

"And on September 26, 1993, do you recall the time that you went to the sidelines at Rich Stadium?"

"No, not at all."

Baker interrupted. "There is no foundation that he has any recollection of being there on that day."

Okay. "Do you have any reason to believe you were not there on that day?"

"No."

I showed him another photo. "What does that picture depict?" I said.

Disinterested. He hardly glanced at the photo. "It appears to be me with a mike in my hand."

"Do you recall what you were doing when that photograph was shot?"

"No."

"When you would give color commentary before a game, would that be when the television coverage began? Or would you be doing interviews, filmed or taped interviews, before the actual live coverage began?"

"I could have been."

He just did not want to answer the questions. No surprise.

"Do you recall this specific occasion?"

"No."

"Now, are you saying that you don't recall being in Buffalo for a game with the Dolphins on September 26, 1993?" I asked it incredulously. You wouldn't let a teenager get away with this kind of obtuseness.

"I'm saying I know I've been in Buffalo for games and I know I've been in Buffalo for games with the Dolphins, but when you give me a date like September whatever-it-is, I don't recall any particular dates."

It was apparent I would have to do this the hard way. "Do you recall the first game of the 1993 football season—"

"No."

"—between the Bills and the Dolphins?"

"No."

"Do you recall covering any games in that football season between the Bills and the Dolphins?" If he thought he would get away by not recalling that it was the *first* game, now he had nowhere to hide.

"Not really, but I'm sure I've covered a lot of Buffalo games, and the Dolphins may have been one of those games."

"Now, looking at the two photos that I've shown to you, does that refresh your recollection that you were covering the game between the Bills and the Dolphins?" Anybody who felt any semblance of an obligation to tell the truth would say, "Now that I see the picture, it obviously refreshes my recollection that I was there, yes." What does Simpson say?

"No."

"It does not?"

"It doesn't refresh my recollection."

"It doesn't cause you to remember that you did?"

"No."

"Do you have any reason to believe that you did not cover the game?"

"No."

He didn't want to put himself in the same state as that photograph, let alone the same end zone. I could have moved along to the photograph; now that he had told me he had no reason to believe he wasn't at the game, I really didn't need to press on. But I didn't want to let Simpson get away with this kind of behavior. I didn't have much left to ask him, but I was going to play this game right along with him and keep him there as long as he and his lawyers played it. He was lying, we all knew he was lying, I just didn't want to make it easy on him.

"The last football game you covered was the Super Bowl in January '94. True?"

"Yes."

"And the last time you covered the Buffalo Bills and Miami Dolphins was September 26, 1993."

"I don't know."

"Don't answer that," jolted Baker.

I paid no attention. "True?" I asked again.

Baker scolded me. "[The judge has] allowed you to go into the Magli shoes, the Randa documents, and the questions that are set forth in your motion, not to reopen the deposition." Then, to Simpson: "So don't answer that."

I talked right past him. "That is the last time you were in Rich Stadium covering a Bills-Dolphins game, September 26, 1993. Correct?"

"Don't answer that," Baker repeated. "You are supposed to be talking about Magli shoes."

"You're the one who's talking about no foundation, and I'm trying to jog the witness's recollection." Then to Simpson: "It's the last time that you were in Rich Stadium covering a Bills-Dolphins game. Correct?"

"I don't know."

"Do you remember the last Bills-Dolphins game—"

"Don't answer that!"

"—you covered as a sports commentator?"

No lawyer likes to be treated as if he's not there. "That's enough," Baker spat. "Don't answer that."

I pressed on. "Do you recall that, yes or no?"

Baker: "Don't answer it just because he said 'yes or no.'"

"Do you recall the last time you were in Rich Stadium covering a game?"

"No."

"Was it after September 26, 1993?"

Baker was boiling. "Don't answer that." He warned me, "If you don't move on, we're gone."

A lot of lawyers, constantly intervening to disrupt and frustrate an examination, stop their clients from answering damaging questions with the idea that it is better than the alternative, which is for their client to get walloped. Most cases don't go to trial, so often the questions never get answered and the tactic works. But there was no doubt where we were headed, and ultimately Simpson would have to respond. "I don't care what you do, Mr. Baker. I don't control you."

"Fine. Let's go. Depo is over." He stood up to walk out.

I sat there. "I am not finished with my questions."

"You are now," he sneered. "If you can't abide by the court order, you are finished." This piece of hyperbole demanded a response; you don't want to leave an accusation like that hanging.

"I was given full opportunity to examine the witness about these photographs and about the Bruno Magli shoes, Mr. Baker. There is no limitation, and I am trying to get—"

Simpson was still seated and looked confused. Baker looked down at him. "Let's go, Juice."

"—the witness's testimony, and we will just have to take it up with the judge."

They got up and left. Mike Brewer asked, "Does this mean that we'll have to go to the judge—"

Still on the record, with the chance to get in the last word, I said, "We are going to because the court has ordered us to do so, and I intend to abide by the court's order."

Simpson and his entourage stormed out. Brewer and I stretched our legs. They had no case. If Simpson wanted to be so obstinate as to refuse to admit he was even in Rich Stadium the day the photos were taken, of course I would have to pursue him, and I had done so. More than anything, I think Baker was upset at being ignored.

Three minutes later, Phil Baker, whom we called "Little Baker," came back into the room. Once the heated words had subsided, the room felt oddly silent. "Look," he said apologetically, "I can maybe talk him into staying." He was talking about his dad; Simpson had stood up in resignation, not anger. "I can try to get him." As if he hadn't been sent in there with marching orders. "Will you please get to the picture?"

"I'm trying to." Little Baker was a soldier, having been sent in to fight his father's lost cause. I had made my point. "O.K. Bring him back and I'll ask about the picture," I told him. They filed back in.

I showed Simpson the Scull photo. "First of all, do you know where in Rich Stadium you are standing?"

"Judging by the field, this looks like it could be the end zone." Okay, he had implicitly agreed that he was, indeed, standing in Rich Stadium during the taking of this picture.

"And that is a picture of you. Correct?"

"It appears to be me, yes."

"And the jacket you're wearing, could you describe it?"

"No."

He couldn't describe the jacket. "Do you remember owning that jacket?"

"No."

"What about the shirt?"

"Looks like a white shirt."

"Nothing stands out about that white shirt?"

"No." He looked at it a little closer. "I like the collar." Now we were into fashion design.

"What do you like about it?"

"I don't know. It looks nice."

We went through the whole day's wardrobe. Tie, jacket, pants, a belt with a silver buckle. "You haven't laid the foundation that he has ever had that belt," Baker objected.

"Did you ever have that belt?"

"I can't tell."

"How did it get on you?"

Baker: "Well, that assumes that it was on him, that the photo isn't doctored, an assumption that we don't buy into."

Finally we'd gotten to it. "Well, let me ask you that question," I said to Simpson directly. "Do you think this photograph is doctored?"

"Don't answer that, because he has no expertise in the area."

Again, without responding to Baker, "Let me ask you this question: Do you know of any reason why you believe this photograph may be doctored?"

"Don't answer that, either."

I asked one more time: "Is there anything about your appearance in this photograph, Mr. Simpson, or the clothing that you're wearing or anything about the depiction of you in this photograph that leads you to believe that this is not a true and accurate photograph of you?"

Baker again objected, frivolous objections. He didn't want his client to answer because, as I saw it, he would have preferred Simpson to take a different position. At the deposition, during the "ugly-ass" shoe discussion Baker clearly didn't want his client to back himself into a corner. Never say never. Should something untoward happen, he wanted the wiggle room of being able to say, "My client never said he didn't own them." Simpson's stubbornness and arrogance permitted no wiggle room. He would go down swinging on this one. Realizing he would get nailed if he kept on objecting, Baker said Simpson would answer "as a layperson."

Okay. "As a layperson," I agreed. "I am not asking for an expert opinion."

Simpson took another look at himself crossing the end zone. Looking directly at the photograph, he said, "Everything looks a little big."

"Excuse me?"

"Everything looks a little big."

"You mean the body parts?"

"I mean the clothing."

Anything other than that?

"I don't recognize the shoes, obviously."

SEVENTEEN

How Do We Deal with O.J.?

I was working twenty-four hours a day. I was on the Simpson case in
my sleep. I barely saw my family. I'd leave for work while they were
still sleeping and get back when they were already in bed. I couldn't
stop thinking about the case. My only diversion was an occasional
Saturday night movie, and no matter what movie it was, something in it
brought me back to the case. By now, a fair number of people recognized
me from the steady stream of television reports as the trial date drew near.
While people who approached me only had good things to say, usually
exhorting me to "get the bastard," this only served to increase the already
enormous pressure I felt. Look at all the people depending on me. What
if I lost? How would they feel, how would my family feel? How would my
client feel?

The fellow members of my team were deeply immersed in their areas
as well. We circulated memos daily, and talked to one another constantly.
I'd go into Tom Lambert's office ten times a day, reporting on the depositions, passing along new information, determining areas that needed
more work, testing ideas. We began to hold frequent team meetings. The
case had become our life.

In late July we held a big trial-prep team meeting to map our overall strategy. Opening day was only two months away and we still had a
tremendous amount of work to do.

In our team's shorthand, I had plunged myself in the "motive" side of the case: O.J. Simpson's world, what drove him in general, and what drove him to commit the act of murder in particular. At trial we were scheduled to present our case first, and since Simpson himself was at the center of the case, I had always assumed that we would put him on the witness stand. I went into our meeting with that assumption. "The jury will want to hear from him," I said. "He is what the case is all about, and we need to tell the motive part of the story anyway." I did not expect any disagreement. To my surprise, I found my assumption was not widely held.

Ed Medvene was very concerned. He didn't want to call Simpson at all. "The physical evidence proves that he did it," Ed began. "We've got all this good hair and fiber evidence. Tom's got the blood evidence. We've got the shoe evidence. We now have the Scull photo. That is the guts of our case. Simpson really doesn't matter.

"We win our case without Simpson, with the forensics. We don't need Simpson to say anything or do anything on the witness stand to prove that he committed these murders. We don't need to prove that he is a liar, that is not our burden. If we take on that burden and don't meet it, we are in trouble.

"Plus, Simpson is a larger-than-life guy. Not that you wouldn't do a bang-up job on him, but, you know, he could really charm the jury. He could take the ball and just run away from us. I don't know why we would call him. The defense will certainly call him. Let 'em, and we can cross-examine him at that time." Ed had clearly given this issue extensive thought.

"If we call Simpson," he said, "the defense gets a chance to cross-examine their own witness in our case. He'll tell his whole story *in our case,* then they can go back in their case and tell his whole story *again.* The jury will have heard Simpson twice. *He gets a double shot.* I'm really worried about the double shot."

It was a very persuasive argument, and he made it with conviction. The thought of giving Simpson two opportunities to argue his case was troubling. As Ed was speaking I thought, Geez, he is making some excellent points. I haven't even considered that. What have I been thinking? I was simultaneously glad and relieved that Ed was working with me; this was the kind of experienced analysis we were going to need to win this case.

He was making very powerful points, and no matter what the ultimate decision, I could not move forward without thinking them through.

"But how's that going to look?" I asked. "We could have all the perfectly sound legal reasons in the world for not calling Simpson, but we all know it would signal to the jury that we're afraid of him. We can't be afraid of Simpson."

Ed said, "We also really ought to think seriously about why you want to put him on."

Unstated, but in the air, was the issue of my entire focus. I had assigned myself the motive part of the case and become completely enveloped by it, and who was the most important motive witness? O.J. Simpson.

During the discovery phase, it made sense to do everything I could to pursue Simpson; it was the only time anyone would have to compel him and others to talk under oath. There is nothing remotely parallel in the criminal process. A good civil litigator will take many depositions, usually constrained only by cost. By this time, we had thrown that constraint out the window and were deposing every witness who wouldn't talk to us voluntarily.

But trial is a different story. Every decision, every step, had to be carefully considered. Every witness to be called had to be essential to winning the case. Was O.J. Simpson an essential witness? Certainly Fred Goldman thought so, the public would agree, and the media were panting to see him on the stand. What more dramatic moment in a courtroom could there be. And whoever examined Simpson was guaranteed his place in history. Did I want to be that lawyer? You bet I did. But for the right reasons? That was the question still hanging in the air.

As lawyers, we often argue among ourselves from a variety of standpoints, to ensure we have considered all sides of an issue. Were my partners playing devil's advocate or actually questioning my motives? Had I really thought this out or was I planning to put on Simpson just to get massive media face-time? I tried not to take it personally, but in the heat of the moment that was difficult.

"The jury needs some sense that Simpson was capable of killing her," I said. "They'll need that to pull the trigger." I was committed to the belief that the body of our case had to consist of more than blood and DNA. I outlined my feelings about motive. "The only witness we have who can tell the story of Simpson and Nicole's relationship is Simpson. I recognize that it will be a fight, and that he'll spin everything his way, but we can at least get from him the general picture of what was happening between them: together, broken up, back together, reconciliation, final break. Some of those things he really cannot argue with. Otherwise we have no witness to get it out."

Lambert said, "Yes, but do we really need to get into that at all? We don't have to prove motive, and motive proves nothing." He had said that to me several times privately, but in this open meeting it took on more conviction.

"However," he continued, "if we don't call him there's no question that they will. I suspect they will put him on in their case last or first. If I were Baker I'd put him on first. I'd have him up there three or four days, asking him softball questions and letting Simpson give twenty-minute answers, if the judge lets me. Then we've got to overcome all that.

"The risk is, we put him on, we really can't do much with him, and he hurts us. Then they get to put him on in their case. We've not only not gained anything, he gets the double shot, as Ed said, and our case has been damaged during our presentation. Do we have enough on him that we're going to make him look bad in front of the jury?"

I thought Lambert made some good points, too. I said, "If we don't call him and *they* call him, then he testifies under Baker's friendly examination on their turf in their ballpark. The jury's first exposure to Simpson is in that circumstance. Whereas, if we call him, the jury sees him on our terms for the first time, confronted with hard questions, and then *they've* got to rehabilitate him. Maybe by that time we will have succeeded in doing enough damage that they can't.

"Plus, guys, look, without trying to stroke myself here, he doesn't have good answers. Forget the motive part of the case for now. Where are the gloves? Why are you wearing the murder gloves in those pictures? What about the shoes? What about the picture of you in the shoes? How did you cut yourself? Why is there blood all over your house and car? These are incredibly damaging areas for him, and *he does not have good answers!*

"If we don't call him and wait for Baker to call him, maybe he won't ask him those questions. Maybe Baker stays away from all the physical evidence and just asks him softball questions, then we *never* get a chance to ask him the hard questions. Never!" In cross-examining a witness, one is limited by law to the scope of the direct examination. "If I'm Bob Baker, I don't go near the physical evidence, I don't go near the cuts or the shoes. I talk about Nicole and what a great guy I am, I won the Heisman Trophy. Then, I'm forced to cross-examine Simpson about the strength of his case, where he can lie most effectively."

There was an awkward silence. I had made good points, and Peter, in particular, seemed persuaded. Ed and Tom were not. We were not ready to decide this issue today, so I moved to a different topic.

Mitchell, Silberberg & Knupp's senior partner Arthur Groman was my mentor. When I joined the firm in 1980 he was a man in his mid-sixties and took me under his wing. He had been with the firm since 1944 and represented many important people, among them Howard Hughes (he tried one of the few cases in which Hughes appeared in court), Al Jolson, Edward G. Robinson, Jack Warner, Jack Kent Cooke, Paul Newman, Mick Jagger, and Warren Beatty. He was Armand Hammer's personal lawyer for over thirty years. I studied under Arthur and tried cases and worked with him. In 1990, he showed supreme confidence in my abilities by turning over to me a suit involving hundreds of millions of dollars against the Hammer estate. I think I made him proud by winning.

When I think about what it means to be a lawyer, I think about what Arthur Groman possesses: complete commitment to the practice of law, total dedication, total preparation, a great legal mind, unblemished and unimpeachable ethics. In Arthur's legal world you don't cheat, you do everything aboveboard, and you zealously devote and dedicate yourself to your client and your client's cause. He never went into a courtroom unless he was more prepared than his opponent. I had watched as he sat and, in hand, wrote and rewrote a question over and over until it was perfect.

When I took on the Simpson case, Arthur was in semi-retirement. I went to him and asked him if he would help me on the case. I wanted his help brainstorming legal issues and tactics, but more so, I needed his counsel, wisdom, and unfailing confidence in me to help me get through what would surely be the biggest challenge I would ever face. Arthur immediately agreed. And with that, he became something of a spiritual adviser to me. I would consult with him on tough decisions and delicate situations, especially when I needed advice on handling sensitive issues involving my partners or other lawyers on the case.

Arthur was not present at the meeting about whether or not to put Simpson on the stand. Afterward, I went to him, summarized the discussion, and asked for his opinion. Without hesitating, Arthur looked at me intently and said, "Dan, don't even think about it. You've got to call him, and you'll destroy him." That's why I loved Arthur Groman. He knew what was right, and what I needed to hear. Arthur said he felt so strong that he insisted on putting his views in a memo and sending it to the team. Here is what he wrote:

> RE: Calling Simpson As Our Witness.
>
> I understand a discussion is under way as to whether or not Simpson should be called as an adverse plaintiff witness. I submit there are numerous advantages for so doing, with hardly any disadvantages. . . . I don't think this is a subject for debate because the risk of not calling him is so enormous.
>
> We already have the example of the criminal case in which Simpson was not put on the stand by the defense despite the overwhelming prosecution evidence of guilt. I think we have to conclude, on the basis of his performance so far, that Baker is a shrewd and highly experienced attorney. He is as aware as we are of the devastating and numerous impeachments of Simpson, developed in his depositions, and additional facts such as the statements of witnesses like Fischman, Cowlings, and the photo of Simpson wearing the Bruno Magli shoes. . . .
>
> Baker may very well conclude that he will not put Simpson on the stand and subject him to what will certainly be a powerful and devastating cross-examination, and rely on what has proved to be a successful defense in the criminal case, attack the police department, Fuhrman, and prate about "contamination." If we don't put Simpson on, and Baker doesn't put him on, then we have totally lost Simpson as a witness and all the points we can make only from him.
>
> My point is, we cannot afford to take any chance that Baker will not put Simpson on the stand, even if it's only 10%. Personally, I think it is better than 50–50. If we don't put Simpson on, and Baker doesn't put him on, and we lost the case, we would go down in legal history as worse lawyers than Darden and Clark.

Arthur made a convincing case, and I knew what my decision would be, but there was no need to make it now. There was ample time to continue the debate.

John Douglas was the former FBI's renowned criminal personality profiler. His success and ability in profiling serial killers and other murderers made him so famous that a character in *Silence of the Lambs* was based on his work and career. I went to Virginia where Douglas lived and discussed the case with him. I then sent him crime scene photographs, autopsy photographs, and reports and asked him to give me his opinion about the killings. Douglas came out to see me a month later and told me we had a classic case of a rage killing. In this case, the rage was directed at the female victim, Nicole Brown Simpson.

We drove to 875 South Bundy so that he could see the crime scene for himself. It was a strange and eerie feeling seeing Douglas in action. He walked slowly up to the front gate where Nicole's body was found in a fetal position at the base of the stairs. He surveyed the tiny dirt area where Ron's slain body was found crumpled next to a tree and walked the long, narrow alley to the rear gate and out to the driveway, the route the killer used to escape. We then strolled around the block, stopping at Dorothy Street around the corner from Nicole's condominium. I pointed out where the car Ron Goldman had borrowed was found parked on the street.

We then retraced Ron's steps from the car up the short block to Bundy, where we made a left and walked back to Nicole's condominium. It felt to Douglas that Ron had walked up to the front gate, pressed the buzzer, and Nicole had come out to let him in (Tom Lange's crime scene report indicated that Nicole's inside buzzer was inoperable). Simpson, we visualized, was sitting in his Bronco on Dorothy, ruminating, thinking, getting increasingly aroused, not able to make up his mind, until he saw Ron pull up. He recognized him—he'd seen him talking to Nicole and others in front of Starbucks. When he saw Ron headed toward Nicole's condo, it was the last straw. She was flaunting it right in front of him, with this young "boy toy," with his kids in the same house. Simpson had his gloves, hat, and knife with him as he sat there in that car, not knowing whether he actually could do what he'd come there to do. But seeing Ron Goldman sent him over the edge. He now had no choice. He got out of his car and began walking. He saw Ron at the front gate, Nicole coming down to greet him. Douglas was convinced that this was how Simpson approached the two of them, and this was how he attacked them. From behind. He shoved Ron quickly and violently into the area, which is probably when Ron yelled "Hey, hey, hey!" Simpson punched Nicole, knocked her down, perhaps even unconscious. He then turned to Goldman, who was stunned and defenseless, and overpowered him with rapid, furious thrusts of his knife. Ron was trapped in a tiny area knocked against a tree, had nowhere to run, and had no room to even fight back. When he collapsed, Simpson turned to Nicole—perhaps she stirred—stabbed her in the head, then in the neck, then delivered the last gaping wound that nearly severed her head. Unable to contain his rage, he was frantic and disoriented. He dropped one glove, his hat came off, his finger was cut. He walked toward the back of the condo so as not to be seen, went to his Bronco, drove away from the crime scene, and was home within five minutes.

Douglas, as it turned out, was unavailable to be called as a witness during the trial. I doubt if the judge would have let him testify anyway.

Do I agree with Douglas's scenario? For the most part, yes. Other scenarios are plausible as well. Minor details can vary. But there is one thing that can never vary: the only living person who can tell us is O.J. Simpson.

EIGHTEEN

Mock Trial:
The Question of Race

O ne month before the trial was to begin, we conducted a day-long jury research session, a mock trial. With so much preparation and work still ahead to get ready for trial, I debated whether we had the time for the mock trial. But we didn't want to leave any stone unturned, so we made the time. DecisionQuest was renowned for their work in compiling jury research—to help trial lawyers better understand the issues in the trial, how to best present those issues, and how to identify jurors most receptive to both your case and your opponent's. There is a large segment of lawyers who scoff at jury research; they believe in picking juries the old-fashioned way—by experience and instincts. Jury research is, by no means, a substitute for a trial lawyer's skills; rather, by giving the lawyer information that is more than anecdotal—data that is scientifically and statistically determined—it enhances his skills. Don Vinson, DQ's founder, urged us to do a series of the research sessions, and assigned two of his top people, Steve Patterson and Norma Silverstein, to head up the work.

To conduct the mock trial, DQ recruited thirty-three people off the street, divided them into two groups and paid each person $100 to act as a juror during our presentation and then discuss the case afterward. Because most of these individuals were either not gainfully employed or were retired or between jobs, as a group they were a little skewed. But this

325

was DecisionQuest's business, they assured me this was a representative sample of the Santa Monica jury pool we could expect at our trial, and we were satisfied with their methods.

Each "juror" was asked to sign a confidentiality agreement. They were not told they would be hearing the O.J. Simpson case, but once they got inside and began to fill out our questionnaire, they figured it out pretty quickly.

The mock trial was held in a relatively large rented conference room. Fortunately, its location had been kept secret and no press was aware of our actions. When we pulled up to the parking structure next to the building where it was to be held, I said, "I can't believe this." We were right next door to Bob Baker's office building. I worried that he would see us, the word would get out, and the press would hound us about our results. We wanted to perform this exercise in private, absorb the lessons it would teach us, and not give the defense anything good to play with.

We had collaborated with DQ on a 106-question questionnaire very much like the ones given to a real jury prior to a trial. This was given to the mock jurors to complete before hearing the mock trial. It is used to ascertain the jurors' perspectives, opinions, and points of view before they hear the presentations by the lawyers.

Before we began the "trial," the jury was polled on whether each of them thought Simpson had killed Ron and Nicole. I was stunned when their pretrial verdict came in: Only 55 percent thought Simpson was guilty. A full 45 percent—fifteen out of thirty-three people—thought he was innocent.

How could that be? It was one thing for the criminal trial jury to acquit him; they were under tremendous pressure, they weren't in possession of all the facts, they had been racially inflamed, they were sequestered, they were dazzled by a powerful defense team with a dizzying display of smoke and mirrors. But the mock jurors had had the opportunity to hear it all, they could read the newspapers and hear the commentary—and still they voted to acquit. I had to hand it to Cochran and that crowd, they had done such a brilliant job of sewing confusion that, despite clear and powerful evidence, even *now* Simpson's obvious guilt was in doubt.

The "trial" was to unfold in two hour-long presentations, first our case and then the defense's. The jurors sat in a room much like a classroom and were asked to respond to the lawyers' arguments by turning dials at their desks, in much the same way market research is handled for movies and television shows. Their responses were recorded in lines that ran across the bottom of a bank of video monitors in an adjoining control room; we could watch the lawyers argue and see the effectiveness of each argument immediately as it was being made. The jury's responses were broken down by racial group, and we could see exactly where and when an idea made an impression on the blacks, whites, Hispanics, and Asians. A blended line gave us the jury as a whole. We videotaped the entire proceedings.

I gave the presentation for the plaintiffs' side of the case. Ed Medvene, Tom Lambert, Peter Gelblum, Yvette Molinaro, Steve Foster, and the folks from DecisionQuest watched from the control room. I had asked Ed Medvene to present Simpson's defense; he had a professional lifetime's experience in front of a jury and I thought he would be a formidable opponent. If you're going to scrimmage, scrimmage against the best.

I began by introducing myself and told the jury whom I represented. I explained the difference between a civil case and a criminal case. I talked about Ron and Nicole. Then I went through all the evidence. I put up the still photographs that had been used at the criminal trial and then started to lay out the timeline evidence, the time of the murders. I introduced the Bundy crime scene and reviewed all the evidence that had been found there. I summarized the evidence found at Rockingham, then the evidence found in the Bronco. I punctuated my points with photographs projected on a television monitor through an "ELMO" machine; I was so inexperienced in the use of the ELMO that I put the first photo in upside down. There I was, talking to the jury, and the photo was upside down, and I didn't know it. I had a lot to learn about high-tech equipment.

I talked about the shoe evidence and went into the whole Bruno Magli/Harry Scull photo scenario. I talked about the cuts on Simpson's left hand that he could not explain. I talked about the dark sweatsuit, about the DNA.

With each piece of evidence, I demonstrated in commonsense terms how it all related back to Simpson. I made it very simple by dressing Simpson in the killer's clothes. Bloody shoe prints: Here's a picture of Simpson wearing the same Bruno Magli shoe. Check. Blue/black cotton fibers: Kato sees dark sweatsuit. Here's a picture of Simpson wearing a dark sweatsuit. Check. Gloves found at the murder scene: Picture of Simpson wearing the gloves.

I drew all the obvious and direct links to Simpson. Blood from a cut on his left hand (it was to the left of a bloody left shoe print): Picture of Simpson with a cut on his left hand the day after the murders. Blood found in the Ford Bronco: Whose Bronco was it? O.J. Simpson's Bronco. Blood found at one other house in the entirety of the Brentwood area. Whose house was it? O.J. Simpson's house.

Then I picked apart and debunked the two main defense arguments: planting and contamination of blood evidence. The defense in the criminal trial had claimed that Simpson's blood at Bundy, the glove at Bundy, the blood on the back gate at Bundy, the blood at Rockingham, the bloody glove at Rockingham, the blood on the socks in Rockingham, and the blood found in the Bronco had all been planted. This was preposterous and I explained why it could not have happened. They had no access to Simpson's blood to plant, even if they wanted to. All the blood was observed by numerous investigators *before* he returned from Chicago. As far as the glove was concerned, not one of the many officers at the Bundy crime scene *ever* saw a second glove there. Hence, there was no second glove to pick up and plant on Simpson's Rockingham property. Nor was there a plausible reason to plant evidence against Simpson, because the LAPD *liked* O.J. and had always treated him with the kid gloves and reverence usually accorded celebrities in Los Angeles. They had no reason to frame him. They also did not know where he was at the time of the murders, he was not at Rockingham but could have had an airtight alibi, in which case these perceived attempts to frame him would have backfired and implicated the cops in a serious felony.

I dealt with the issue of contamination quickly and summarily. No witness ever stood up and testified, "Look, I spilled the blood. I scattered it all over the place. I mishandled it." There is no evidence that anything happened to ruin the blood evidence in collecting and testing it.

Then I got to motive. I began by deemphasizing the entire area. "Two thousand relationships each year end in murder. Of course, most do not. But what separates those that do? People always ask, 'What is the motive?' That is a good and important question, but we don't have to prove motive, the law does not require us to do that.

"But when there is a motive on the part of the defendant, that motive helps us identify him as the killer. And here, Simpson had a motive to kill Nicole."

I wanted to give a little scientific underpinning because there may have been people in that room who had been beaten but were not dead. What made Nicole different? I explained, as our behavioral science experts had explained to me, that the relationships that end up in murder proceed along a path as prescribed as the Stations of the Cross: history of abuse, history of rage, estrangement, jealousy, rejection. It's common sense.

I described how stormy, turbulent, and abusive was Simpson and Nicole's seventeen-year relationship. I did not go into the many physical beatings we suspected occurred because we were on shaky evidentiary ground, but I talked about the 1989 spousal abuse plea. "He hit her and she hit him and the relationship was violent both ways by both people."

I zeroed in on the last year of Nicole's life, then sped to the last few months, then went through the chronology of the murder night. Simpson, I established, was the only person in the world with a reason to kill Nicole, and to kill Ron because he was a witness. I reviewed how "a glass broke" in Chicago, then demolished his cuts alibi. I talked about the Bronco chase, his fleeing the police indicating a strong presumption of guilt. I brought to their attention Simpson's suicide note. Why would Simpson kill himself and orphan his kids if he were innocent?

I thought I had done pretty well. The jury was polled again: 86 percent voted to convict. I had pushed them from 55 to well past the necessary 75 percent needed to win a civil trial.

Then Ed took over.

Ed and I hadn't cheated. We hadn't compared notes before we began, we wanted this test to be legitimate. His only advantage was that I asked him to include all the defense arguments, even those that we would fight to keep out of the trial, such as the race card. A lot was riding on it.

"My name is Edward Medvene," he began, "and I am proud and privileged to represent O.J. Simpson." He then began hammering us big-time. Cuts? What kind of an issue is that? Nobody saw any cuts on his client. O.J. Simpson was supposed to have slashed two people to death. Oh, yeah? Where are all the marks on his body? There is no way one person could have done all that hacking and not have a single mark on his body.

Ed took us apart on the timeline and length of struggle. We had said the killings happened in a few minutes. He scoffed. "It's impossible for two young, healthy people to be butchered like they were in a matter of minutes," he proclaimed. "This was a long, fierce, violent, ongoing, sustained struggle. There was blood everywhere. The man doesn't have a speck of blood or a mark on his body and you can't tell me he did it!"

Pretty quickly he made the inevitable segue. "You know, Mark Fuhrman, this bigoted officer filled with racial venom, couldn't wait to get Simpson. He was lurking around the crime scene by himself. All of a sudden he insists on going along to Rockingham with the officers. Then, lo and behold, guess who finds the most incriminating piece of evidence, the glove? Fuhrman. Fuhrman finds it! Fuhrman is all over this case. Fuhrman finds the glove, Fuhrman finds blood on Simpson's Bronco. This is all about Fuhrman, and guess what, my distinguished colleague representing Mr. Goldman doesn't want you to hear about Fuhrman, they want to hide Fuhrman, they want to pretend Mark Fuhrman doesn't exist!" Fire in the eyes. Rage, anger, fury. Race. *Fuhrman, Fuhrman, Fuhrman!*

The Bruno Magli photo? A fraud. Where did we find it? That monument to integrity, the *National Enquirer.*

He hit hard on the planting of evidence. "What is Detective Vannatter doing running around town with a vial of O.J. Simpson's blood? *What is he doing with O.J. Simpson's blood?* How many officers do you know carry blood from Parker Center all the way to Rockingham, when all he had to do was go next door and book it? Five minutes away, all he had to do was drive five minutes. Instead he puts the vial in his pocket and races all the way across town! You're trying to tell me he didn't make a pit stop, sprinkle that blood?"

Lawyers can be really deceitful, we can make powerful and passionate arguments that are just totally false. The idea that Vannatter took a vial of blood to Bundy, overflowing with media, and—"Coming through, gotta plant some blood!"—sprinkled it here and there is wildly out of the question. Aside from the fact that no one saw such a thing occur and that it just didn't happen, Vannatter has big, thick, meat-hook hands. The idea of him tinkling fine little blood droplets around like fairy dust was truly absurd.

Contamination? It was all over. "You know," Medvene told the jury, echoing John Gerdes, a prominent DNA expert for the defense in the criminal trial, "the LAPD testing lab is a cesspool of contamination." Ed pulled out all the criminal trial's most memorable catch phrases—Fuhrman and Vannatter, the "twins of deception"—and strung them together to encourage this jury to come to the same verdict.

Medvene pooh-poohed the motive case. "Hey, people have problems in their relationships all the time. They don't get killed. The young lady was spreading her wings and going out with other men, doing all kinds of wild things. We mean no disrespect to her, but she was reckless." He refrained from further trashing Nicole and risking a backlash of sympathy for her, which was smart. He was scoring.

I had asked Ed, as part of his presentation, to play about fifteen minutes of Simpson's *I Want to Tell You* video, in which he delivered a monologue advocating his own case. We watched from the control room as the mock jury reacted to it.

Something unexpected happened. We assumed, from news reports and widespread anecdotal material, that Simpson was fully supported by the black community. Conventional wisdom had it that he was their champion. The sight of Howard University students erupting in cheers when he was acquitted was an image that didn't leave me. Why, then, when Simpson was seen clearly lying on his self-produced video, did the lines indicating blacks and whites come closer together? (The black and white responses were the two key lines we were monitoring.) Peter Gelblum, who was watching the proceedings intently, wrote in his notes: "The only time those lines moved together is when Simpson's own words impeach him." He told me, "When you said he was lying, the black and white lines were miles apart. When you read a few quotes from his depo, the lines got closer. But when the lies came out of Simpson's own mouth, the lines converged."

We felt that perhaps this was a chink in his armor; blacks were defending Simpson as a representative of their race, not as an individual human being. They were offended that the system appeared to be attacking a celebrated black man; it was now beginning to seem they were less attached to O.J. Simpson personally, particularly when he showed them disrespect by lying to their faces.

Ed did a very good job of presenting the defense case. He was impassioned, witty, forceful, and smart. When he had finished, the jurors were divided into two groups, ushered into separate rooms, and instructed to begin deliberations. We sat behind two-way mirrors and watched them.

The rooms were down a hall from one another, so we could not see and hear both at the same time, but the deliberations were videotaped and we all had the opportunity to watch two separate juries at work.

As a lawyer, you constantly wonder how juries function, how the group dynamic is established, and how you can influence them—so this was fascinating. At the same time it was an eerie feeling watching people who don't know you're watching them. For the past several hours they had been sitting and listening to us, now they were talking, scratching themselves, interacting. I felt I was invading their privacy.

Not only did I feel like a voyeur, I was doubly apprehensive because these strangers could easily say something embarrassing or humiliating about me in front of my peers. Indeed, at one point a juror, talking about Medvene, said, "You know, that old guy"—Ed just hung his head in both hands—"he was good." Ed brightened.

"Yeah," said another panel member, "and that well-dressed guy"—I started to get excited—"I didn't buy what he said at all." You've got to have a lot of self-confidence or a couple of sedatives to put yourself through this.

Despite the fact that civil cases may be decided by as little as a 9 to 3 vote, in order to find how their thinking might develop, these juries were asked to deliberate to unanimity. At the beginning of their discussions, each took a straw vote. This time, 57 percent voted guilty, 43 percent for acquittal. After all the arguing, all the forensics and motive, after dressing Simpson in the murder clothes, we had only managed to move the jury two percent. Ed and I had knocked each other out, and the jurors ended up right where they started. Maybe the deliberations would change their minds, I hoped.

On the jury panel I watched the most, the forewoman was a pro-plaintiff juror. A white woman, she was quite strong and did a lot of the arguing for our position. It is an enormous, usually decisive, advantage to have the foreperson in your corner; by directing the flow of discussion, he or she is able to swing people in ways that a regular juror cannot.

The other white women on the jury were quiet, reserved, almost intimidated. The Hispanics were open-minded but leaning more toward the defense. The three blacks were adamantly, vociferously, powerfully pro-Simpson. No matter what the foreperson brought up, they would knock it down. They sounded all the defense themes: "Where did the blood go? . . . You heard that guy say Fuhrman got all the important evidence. . . . That blood was planted on the sock, it was pressed on there. . . . You know, the cops hate blacks."

The accusations of tampering with evidence, by which I mean planting and deliberate manipulation, carried a lot of weight with this mock jury. As lawyers we knew there was an argument open to us that held that, even if there had been some tampering with evidence, this in itself did not mean Simpson didn't commit the murders; plenty of untainted evidence said that he did. That argument didn't sit right with this jury, however. If there was tampering, there were dishonest cops on the scene. If you've got dishonest cops, that throws the entire investigation into question and you're not going to get a conviction. Clearly we would have to negate all such hints or implications, because there would be no finding Simpson guilty or responsible if there was any evidence of tampering.

The jurors had been instructed to base their discussions and decisions only on what they had heard the lawyers say in their presentations, but that went right out the window. People quickly began talking about what they'd heard on *Rivera,* what they'd read in the *Globe,* what they had seen on *The Charles Grodin Show.* They took as gospel Johnnie Cochran's TV punditry. They could not separate what they'd been told in the past two hours from what they had heard for the previous two years; popular wisdom and their own convictions about the case had become part of their basic consciousness. How were we ever going to get an untainted, unbiased jury?

There was not much discussion of Simpson, or of his relationship with Nicole. The jury wanted to talk about police frame-ups, conspiracies, racial bias. The black jurors in particular were extremely interested in planting and contamination and whether the LAPD had "followed procedures." If the LAPD didn't get the warrant right, Simpson walks. If they didn't pick up the evidence "according to procedure," he walks. It was like a game. In that room we discovered something in the jurors' minds akin to a legally recognized exclusionary rule: If the police didn't follow "procedures," O.J. gets to kill two people.

We all expected a racial divide; that was the legacy of Simpson's criminal defense. But to see and witness the racial chasm was quite another thing. It was painful and sobering. Although there were only three black jurors in the room, they dominated the discussion. They were fervent, angry, zealous. To the blacks, this was not the case of determining who murdered Ron Goldman and Nicole Brown Simpson on June 12, 1994, this case was about what happened *after* June 12, it was about the LAPD and its investigation. Deeper still, it was about paying back the LAPD, the legal system, and society in general, for years of mistreatment. They overwhelmed, even intimidated, the other jurors who were arguing to make a decision based on the physical evidence. They wouldn't have anything to do with supporting the police, or even considering the possibility that the cops had done their job. No, none of the standard measures of justice applied. This ran much deeper.

To the white, Hispanic, and Asian jurors the case against Simpson did not have the same meaning or the same stakes. They were arguing logic while the blacks were aroused by passion. Reasoned advocacy versus a visceral rage over two hundred years of victimization and oppression. Which do you think will carry the day?

It was no contest; the nonblack jurors were getting blown away. The less educated blacks, in particular the women, were the most vocal. While other jurors would not put aside their individual reasoning and agree, after several hours they got tired and couldn't keep up. They had no stomach to combat such heated intensity, the case didn't mean that much to them. It was getting toward the end of the day, they had made their hundred bucks, they wanted to go home. Imagine how a sequestered jury must feel.

We polled the jury again. Simpson picked up a few more votes. We were losing ground. Still failing unanimity, we sent Steve Patterson of DecisionQuest into the jury room to pose some final questions.

"Put aside all the debating and the deliberations and the evidence," Patterson said. "Forget all that. How many of you think he did it?" Ten out of fifteen hands went up, including one of the most vocal blacks. This was profound, I thought. It told me there was a segment of people, blacks included, who believed Simpson was guilty, but who would not vote for guilt. There was a gap between these two ideas, and we had to find a way to bridge it.

Patterson asked what they had thought of Simpson on the videotape. One juror said he didn't look caring, another said he looked coached, another that he was acting. One woman said Simpson's lawyer, Medvene, had made several good points but that Simpson had then messed them up; they would have been better off if they hadn't played the tape in the first place. She commented on how smart the criminal case defense lawyers had been not to call him. Even the blacks on the panel said he was not very convincing. This, to me, was another profound observation.

Tom Lambert had not been seen by the jury and went in without their having a preconceived notion about him. "Would it make a difference to you to know that up to twenty officers were at the crime scene before Mark Fuhrman ever got there? Between midnight and two-thirty there were male, female, white, black, Hispanic, people of all races were there and none of them saw a second glove. Would that make a difference in your thinking?" He was told it would.

"Would it have changed your mind if it had been proven that the blood at Bundy had been collected by the criminalists before Mr. Simpson gave his blood to the LAPD officers?" he asked.

"That is an important point," said a pro-plaintiff juror. "If that was true, of course, that would really undercut all these planting arguments."

"That's not true!" accused a middle-aged black woman sitting near Tom. "You're not saying that's true, you're just making it up!"

"No," said Tom, "I'm just hypothetically asking you, would it have made a difference if that was the case?"

She said no and continued to attack him. "Are you that lawyer representing the Goldman family?" snapped the black woman.

Peter Gelblum went into the other jury room and asked, "Assume these facts are true: There are three hundred pairs of this make and model Bruno Magli shoe in the world. We have a picture of him wearing that shoe a few months before the murder, and there are his size shoe prints at the scene. Would that be something that was important to you?"

Without hesitation, a black woman at the end of the table said, "No, because somebody could have stolen his shoes and done the murders." Others joined in. The degree to which the pro-Simpson jurors, especially African-American women, would discount, disregard, or dismiss evidence damning to Simpson was mind-boggling. It was clear that, no matter how strong the evidence, some jurors would simply not convict. It was clear that we had little or no chance with such jurors.

I was devastated. I'd been sheltered in my cocoon of depositions, legal research, and interviews. We were winning arcane battles in court, we were getting good evidence from a wide variety of witnesses, we'd had no major setbacks and were feeling very good about ourselves. Now, all of a sudden, I saw our case unraveling.

The technicians were unplugging the machines, shutting down the monitors, and packing up the videotapes. Ed left, so did Yvette and Steve. Tom and Peter and I were paralyzed.

All our hard work had meant nothing. The case was only one month away and it was coming down to the confusion and lies and racial animus the defense had sown in two years of constant public disinformation. We'd thought we were winning, but it turned out we were getting drubbed. It was very sobering. We had a loser.

"I can't go home after this one," I said. "We've got to go out and talk. Let's get a drink."

We went to a bar next door, and sat on bar stools, discouraged and demoralized. I ordered bourbon. "What just happened?" I asked out loud.

"You got your ass kicked," Tom told me, "that's what happened."

"I might have gotten *my* ass kicked, but we are going to get *our* ass kicked soon if we don't do something to change this." We were too shaken to do anything but moan about our fate: Our jurors were weak, theirs were strong; instead of judging Simpson against all the evidence we presented, they were talking about criminal trial defense issues—the LAPD, conspiracy, planting, contamination. We had answers for all their questions, but the jury wasn't hearing them, *and we couldn't do a thing about it.* We sat there for two and a half hours, doing a step-by-step postmortem and crying into our beer.

I drove home that night woefully depressed. What am I going to do? I told myself, You can't just fold your tent and run away. You are in this thing, you're going to have to brace up and face it and just get going. I allowed myself an evening of abject misery, woke up the next morning, and started to rethink and retool our case.

At the office I got a call from Bob Baker. "Next time you go to a bar and spill out your whole trial strategy," he chuckled, "you guys ought to keep your voice down." Baker explained that a couple of secretaries from his office were sitting in the bar and overheard our conversation. I was mortified, but recovered quickly enough to tell him we were there to plant misinformation and was delighted to hear our mischief worked. He replied, "Yeah, sure." As soon as I got off the phone, I tried desperately to remember everything we'd said in the bar, but found no comfort. Then I ran up to Lambert's office and told him what happened. "Were we really talking that loud?" He shrugged and said, "Yes." Always one to find the silver lining, Tom added, "Don't worry about it. It'll just make them over-confident." Tom was forever my emotional regulator. Now, feeling better, I could get back to work.

DecisionQuest analyzed the data and prepared their report of the mock trial. Those jurors who voted for the plaintiff cited as their major reasons the blood evidence and DNA, the preponderance of evidence; the testimony of the limousine driver Allan Park, who picked up Simpson at Rockingham on the night of the murders; and the glove, shoes, and hair samples. Those who voted for Simpson cited not enough evidence, their feeling that the blood had been tampered with, poor police work, and a perceived lack of time for the defendant to commit the crime. Our strengths, said DQ, were that most people were persuaded by the evidence, most people thought he "probably" did it, and the fact that even the defense jurors found Simpson hard to believe. Our weaknesses were that the defense jurors were far more committed to their positions than the pro-plaintiff jurors; "political correctness in the jury room," which meant that some white jurors, rather than punish Simpson, bent over backward to find reasons to understand him; the perception of sloppy police work, and the feeling among some jurors that Simpson had been victimized.

DecisionQuest recommended four "key themes" to sound at our trial:

- Different case—different legal standard.
- Simpson is not credible and is a liar.
- There is no evidence of a conspiracy.
- The evidence is overwhelming—Simpson caused the death of Ron and Nicole.

We then commissioned DQ to conduct a telephone "Community Attitude Survey," from which we developed a better sense of the prevailing mood and opinions of a wide cross section of some 600 people. The results mirrored the conclusions drawn from the mock trial and underscored the deep racial divide.

To try and better understand the views of blacks, we also decided to have DecisionQuest conduct an all-black focus group. They recruited sixteen African Americans, eight men and eight women, to sit around a table in a nondescript conference room and discuss race. The sample was, again, designed to approximate the blacks in the jury pool we could expect at trial. DQ's Steve Patterson posed an opening question and then left the room.

We videotaped the proceedings from behind a two-way mirror as the discussion unfolded. The panel members had been told they would be observed, but they didn't know by whom, and after a while they became so engrossed in the discussion they forgot about it.

To disguise the fact that our interest was in their thoughts on Simpson, the first hour was a general discussion of race in America. Observing this discussion was a rare opportunity for me, as I suspect it would be for the vast majority of white Americans. It is undeniably the state of race relations these days that blacks and whites do not routinely talk candidly to one another. There is so much distrust, ignorance, and enmity between the races that open dialogue is next to impossible. While, of course, people have friends of both races, by and large the opportunity for extended conversation is hard to come by; as opposed to several decades ago, when there appeared to be some common goal around which the races could unite, now there is little blacks and whites can point to that brings them together. Sad but true.

Which made this focus group all the more significant for me personally, and vital for our team. Race was an issue that had been injected into the criminal trial and would play a part in ours, and we had to be prepared to deal with it.

What made an immediate impression on me was how differently the African Americans in this group and I viewed the world. Without having to say it out loud, there was a common bond in that conference room that, whatever their personal differences, *We are all black people.* This meant that, in some core way, they *were treated by and understood the world* in ways other people did not, ways white people would never grasp. The words "brother" and "sister," which I had thought of as mere rhetoric among African Americans, gained new meaning. Everyone in that room assumed that each other person, no matter their differences in education or wealth, had lived through similar experiences. What was important for me to recognize was that, at trial, African Americans would bring these specialized experiences and perspectives to bear in the jury room.

Theirs was a black view through a black prism. It did not take long for the group to begin sharing stories of their own experiences with police, none of them positive. Everyone seemed to have been treated badly at one time or another simply because they were black. "The police beat the hell out of my brother for no reason," one woman volunteered. "All cops are gonna lie," said a man, "you can't believe a word they say." After the Rodney King case, and the race riots that followed, the LAPD had a very poor image. Unless you caught them abusing people on videotape, the focus group felt, they were going to lie about it. The general consensus was that white police officers would lie in order to get black suspects, and the biggest fish of them all was O.J. Simpson. Black man, black hero, black role model; the cops would do anything to take him down.

Similarly, there was a uniform feeling that the judicial system was stacked against racial minorities and that the court system had done nothing to improve the treatment of blacks or alleviate the racial problems they suffer. There was an overwhelming consensus that the judicial system—in fact, the entire economic and political system that runs this country—was rigged against them. This was more than a shared belief, this was accepted as an undeniable truth.

One man was convinced that the court system was in cahoots with the prison system to jail blacks for money. His theory was that whoever runs the prisons makes, let's say, $40 per inmate per day. The more people they put in jail, the more money they make; the longer the better. Who's the most available target? Black people.

They felt purposely abandoned, particularly as far as discrimination was concerned. Blacks had been held back since they were slaves, "but when there is a crisis in this country that's not just blacks, like the AIDS crisis, all of a sudden everybody pulls together. They pass legislation, they raise money, they solve that problem." They felt left out of the American equation, which made them resentful.

When the subject of O.J. Simpson was introduced the level of intensity rose immediately. Voices got louder and faster, opinions were voiced more strongly. There wasn't any overwhelming degree of sentiment in favor of Simpson, in fact many of the men were quite critical of him as a person. "I think he did it," said a man who looked in his early thirties and said he had spent time in prison. "He's O.J., man, he got the money to get off, that's all it was. It takes long paper to get off like that. He shouldna got off, I don't care what nobody says."

They objected to his lifestyle. "Yeah, O.J. was gifted," said an older man. "He had talent and skill. Then when he made it he said, 'I don't need these people anymore.'"

"O.J. was never a community-minded person until after the trial," another man added. "He's a fake, a fraud, a phony. Why does he go to the AME Church now? Because he can't go to the white places in Westwood anymore, where he used to go. They don't care about the Juice. Now he finds out how they feel about him."

"Yeah," said a woman at the far end of the table, *"he found out he was black!"*

Another woman defended him. "You never heard of the prodigal son?"

So O.J. Simpson, the man, was vulnerable. But the black man, the black race, the black culture, was not. As a symbol, they almost all supported him.

"This was one time the police didn't get their way."

"I didn't expect the race card to be played," said one middle-aged woman. "Of course, that's what got him off."

One college-educated woman, who had expressed herself very articulately on a number of issues, had been raising her hand for a long time, trying to be heard. I was interested in what she would have to say. "When I saw the verdict," she finally said when she got a chance, "I was excited! We were pumped because he got off. And, to this day, I don't know if the man did it or not. I have no idea, and I'm not going to sit here and try to figure it out. But I do know this, I was happy because throughout our history white people do it all the time, paying judges off, things like that, and nobody says anything. But when you have this brother get off, the whole world stops. 'Wait! Something is wrong with the justice system. We've got to do something!'"

Another woman added, "I can speak for a few of my friends, we feel bitter towards a lot of things that have happened. When we first found out about the trial we did some research and [found "in the history of the judicial system"] it is rare that a white person gets convicted for hurting a black person. But ninety-five percent of the time, a black person is convicted of killing a white person. They go down." This was received without contradiction, as common wisdom. "The first time you have it [the other way around], the world is in a rage. Oh, yeah, it's about O.J., but there is a whole 'nother reason. And I'm just not with the whole O.J. thing, let's deal with the system as a whole."

She was applauded. "That's right!"

No one in the room appreciated that when O.J. Simpson was acquitted in the criminal trial it did not mean he did not murder two people. Of course, the acquittal only meant that the State of California failed to prove that Simpson committed the murders beyond a reasonable doubt—nothing more. There was no finding that he didn't do it.

But far beyond their unfamiliarity with that legal nuance, there was uniform incomprehension about the purpose and legality of the civil trial. They said it was against the law, that it was double jeopardy, that we didn't even have the right to bring this case. Almost everyone saw it as vendetta. Someone stated, as though it were a known *fact,* that a special law had been passed to let the Goldmans bring the suit *just to get Simpson.* One woman was so angry she could almost spit. "Because he is a black man, and a black man of power, they've got to bring him down." She got no argument.

Our research showed that the black women in the mock trial, focus group, and telephone survey, and by extension in the black community at large, were the most protective of Simpson. Men seemed to have a more realistic appraisal of the man, but African-American women—particularly those without extensive education—seemed to have almost a maternal instinct to keep him from harm. Theirs was a clear bias, one that would be very difficult, if not impossible, to overcome. There seemed to be no realistic chance of getting such a juror to vote in our favor.

After losing the mock trial there was no doubt that to the black population, the trial of O.J. Simpson hinged on a far larger issue than whether or not he killed two people. What was at stake to so many African Americans was the history of prejudice, discrimination, mistreatment, and abuse with which they alone were intimate. They had very little power in this world, but they were using what little power they did have to send the white world a loud, unmistakable message: We will defend our race.

"Send a message." That is what Johnnie Cochran told the jury in his closing argument. A classic case of jury nullification. In their minds, O.J. Simpson equaled the black community. Never mind that he had nothing to do with the black community, that he had made a conscious choice to live the celebrity life in the white world. He didn't accept them, but they still took him to heart.

I thought it was tragic. Race had nothing to do with the reality of this case. Nothing. But it might have everything to do with the result.

I lay this wedge in the racial divide squarely at the feet of Simpson and his lawyers. In one of the most disgraceful, cynical, and socially irresponsible defenses ever used to set a guilty man free, they created the race issue and exploited it. *White people are out to get this black man.* Using false arguments and a gospel cadence, Johnnie Cochran blinded a largely African-American jury with such intense and fervent feelings of racial pride and passion that they let a killer back into their community.

Racial pride is important. Blacks have every right to be angry at their treatment in American history and proud of their accomplishments in spite of it. What is so disturbing is that, in defending O.J. Simpson, black America has embraced a liar, a cheat, a womanizer, and a butcher.

NINETEEN

Something Wrong

D
r. Henry Lee had been a big hit at the criminal trial. America's best-known forensic scientist, he had examined the wrapped samples of blood—bindles—taken at the crime scene and found one that had not dried. Being led through his examination by Simpson's attorney Barry Scheck, himself an expert in the field of DNA, he had looked at the bindle and told the jury darkly, "Something wrong." According to Larry Schiller and James Willwerth's book, *American Tragedy,* Lee and Scheck had worked on the exact wording for weeks.

Scheck had taken that phrase and run wild with it. In his closing argument to the jury, he had railed, in reference to Dr. Lee's testimony, "There is something wrong. There is something terribly wrong about this evidence . . . you must distrust it. You have to distrust it. You cannot render a verdict in this case of beyond a reasonable doubt on this kind of evidence, because if you do, no one is safe. No one. The constitution means nothing."

In charge of cops and coroners, Ed Medvene was scheduled to take Dr. Lee's deposition in Connecticut, where Lee lived and worked. I would be there to assist. A few days before we were to leave, Ed tore a hamstring playing racquetball. He was bedridden, black and blue up and down his leg, barely able to walk, but Baker refused to postpone and the judge upheld him. Like the trouper he is, Ed popped a lot of painkillers, hobbled onto a plane, and we flew east.

We knew Dr. Lee was not going to appear at trial; his testimony supporting Simpson in the criminal case had been controversial and it was apparent that he didn't want to relive it. So the videotaped deposition would be the defense's only chance to parade their star witness in front of the jury, and our only chance to rain on their parade. As a result, we expected Baker to conduct a comprehensive direct exam of Lee on a wide array of issues related to the forensic evidence, and Ed would then have to conduct a careful cross-examination. This would be no fishing expedition. Baker had shipped in his oversized exhibit boards and we had done the same. This was going to be show and tell.

Ed had dissected and digested the doctor's criminal-case examination and told me, "He's charming, he's charismatic, he's magnetic, he says all these cute things, but in the end he really says very little that actually pertains to this case." Ed's strategy, which was extremely effective and correct, was to make it clear what Lee was actually saying, which was very little.

About a month earlier, Bob Baker had told me that Barry Scheck would be representing Simpson in handling the Lee deposition. So, who shows up representing not Simpson but Dr. Lee? Barry Scheck. Dr. Lee is being billed as a world-renowned *independent* expert; why is he now being represented by O.J. Simpson's criminal defense lawyer? How independent is that? Not very. Clearly, Lee and Scheck were still working very closely as advocates for Simpson.

Dr. Lee was trying to have it both ways. Professionally he had put his reputation on the line when he advocated Simpson's position in the criminal case, and he had no choice but to defend that testimony. However, because of the flack he took for his role in lending his awesome skills, experience, and reputation to help acquit Simpson, he no longer wanted to be perceived as a paid Simpson hand, particularly now that Simpson was such a pariah. *Let me stick to my guns, but let me do it quietly.*

I had a problem with Barry Scheck. He received a lot of acclaim and kudos for his performance at the criminal trial, but I was disgusted that he sold out his formidable skills. Scheck has a reputation as a smart guy, a brilliant lawyer who not only mastered the field of forensic DNA, he built a career using it to acquit innocent people. In the Simpson case, he applied those special talents to fool a jury. They placed great stock in what he said. He was probably the most potent of Simpson's advocates because he professed to impart science to the jury as he led them astray.

Scheck knew that Dr. Lee's "something wrong" with one evidence swatch did not mean something was wrong with *all* the evidence. He and his colleagues could not have rationally believed that every single piece of evidence showing their client's guilt was planted or contaminated. They spent endless hours reverse engineering ingenious arguments to account for and explain away each drop of damning blood evidence, and then delivered them to an unsuspecting jury draped in the mantle of scientific authority. They were hired and paid to get their guilty client off, and that is what they did.

I had never met Scheck before. When we shook hands he tried to convince me that, like Dr. Lee, he was no longer associated with Simpson. He made a point of telling me, "I haven't been involved in this case at all. I'm completely out of it." He was representing Lee, yet the night before the deposition he and Bob Baker had met at Lee's laboratory and they had all gone out to dinner. How surprised would I be if Barry Scheck were ghosting Baker's examination? This whole thing was a charade.

I saw them huddling during a break and started in needling Scheck right away. "Hey, what're you guys talking about? I see you're not helping him, Barry, you being so independent and all." He looked at me sheepishly, as I walked by without waiting or caring to hear an answer.

Dr. Lee, for his part, was everything they said he was. Before he began to testify he took out a little .35 millimeter camera and asked if he could take a group picture for his scrapbook. He gave Medvene a gift. He gave me a ruler with his name on it.

Lee is a very charming guy, incredibly smart. He is a very glib speaker, with a friendly smile, and an Oriental accent that plays well, but he is deadly. He exudes mastery of his field and passion about his work.

Baker began his examination with approximately forty minutes of what I called "A Monument to Dr. Henry Lee . . . by Dr. Henry Lee." It seemed like his entire *curriculum vitae,* from birth. On the record! It finally ended when Baker asked him, "Now, Doctor, putting modesty aside, have people indicated in your presence that they believe you are the number one criminalist in the world?"

Lee ho-ho-hoed and said, "I don't consider that," but Baker's point was clear: since Lee was the foremost authority and supported Simpson, all others should bow to that authority and do so as well.

Baker did an effective examination. He was on top of his game, he knew the material and took Lee through it expertly. Dr. Lee did the same dog-and-pony show he performed at the criminal trial—the spattering of red ink showing all these neat little patterns indicating height, distance, velocity of blood as it shot out of a body. He testified powerfully, giving a course on how to read blood stains.

Lee discussed at length all the brilliant techniques and equipment he and his lab customarily employed in documenting, collecting, and analyzing evidence. He contrasted this with what he characterized as the shabby equipment, poor techniques, and lack of expertise of the LAPD; they don't measure blood properly, they move pieces of evidence, they don't pick things up the right way, they shouldn't have put blood swatches in plastic bags, and on and on and on. Very impressive. But it had nothing to do with the case. Just as we expected, he did *not* say, "And therefore you cannot use any of this evidence; it is not trustworthy." While he didn't come out and say that, he had the uncanny ability to create that impression anyway. We were determined to make him say what he meant.

Lee spent a very long time going through all the crime-scene photographs—blood here, blood there, blood on the ground, the pager is here, the glove is there—the idea being that such a detailed chaotic scene must have taken a long time to create.

Of course, we were waiting and waiting for the climactic moment. Toward the end of the day, sure enough, Baker got to it. "Now," he said dramatically, "what does the fact that there was wet transfer in at a minimum three of the seven swatches indicate to you?"

"Get ready," I whispered to Medvene. *"Here it comes! Here it comes!"*

"I really cannot give you a conclusion. I only can tell you that's a wet transfer. And if in fact the report said complete dry, then"—Medvene and I started to grin—"something's wrong."

Baker tried to lock it in. "Something's wrong at the LAPD crime lab, right?"

Ed wouldn't let him. "Objection. Leading and suggestive, and counsel's testifying. That's not what the witness said."

Lee volunteered, "What I say, something is wrong with this particular evidence. . . . That's all I can say."

Ed had been concerned about cross-examining Dr. Lee. There were areas of data and nuance we had not yet fully absorbed. Usually a lawyer gathers all his information and finds full focus just as a trial is about to begin, but here we were forced to face a truly formidable opponent weeks before opening day. This wasn't a deposition where we could make a mistake, this was like a full day in the trial.

In preparation, Ed had consulted with a former Oregon homicide detective named Ron Englert, who had worked with the criminal prosecution team, particularly on the issue of the length of time it took for the killings to occur, but had not testified. At the criminal trial, Dr. Lee supported the defense pathology expert, Dr. Michael Baden, in his contention that the death struggle was not short. If it did actually take the murderer some fifteen to twenty minutes to kill Ron and Nicole, we lose. Because the murders likely began around 10:30, and because Simpson was heard and seen at his house by 10:50 to 10:55 P.M., there was little or no likelihood that he could have done it; he didn't have enough time. As Ed saw it, "If he says twenty minutes, we've got a problem. Ten minutes, it's possible, but still too tight. I've got to push him back to a minute."

Englert gave Ed a crash course in criminalistics. The Bundy crime scene looked chaotic and covered with blood, but Englert explained that during a fight a person can drop his glasses, keys, and pager in a split second, and one stab wound can cause hundreds of blood drops. "Your battle, confined to a six-foot area, could have taken only a minute. Don't be thrown off by all the blood in different places, no one can tell you how long it took to get there." Englert gave Medvene the courage and confidence to challenge Dr. Lee's expertise.

Ed then went in and completely shut Dr. Lee down. Rather than encourage the good doctor's speculation about what pieces of evidence *might* have revealed had they been found—the third button on Ron Goldman's shirt, the piece of paper that was photographed but not picked up, one of the lenses in Juditha Brown's glasses—Ed established that, in their absence, Dr. Lee could not state anything about them with scientific certainty.

"You're not saying any of the evidence *not* collected was in any way going to exculpate Mr. Simpson," Ed asked Lee, "because you don't know that as a matter of scientific fact. Isn't that true?"

"True."

Baker had done a good job guiding Dr. Lee through testimony designed to imply that the struggle had taken a prolonged period of time.

Ed went right at him. "You don't know how many actions anyone took to cause those particular drops or spatters or patterns. Isn't that correct?"

"Correct."

"And you made no scientific study of any kind to estimate how long it would take for one, by particular action, to cause the blood drops, spatters, or patterns. Is that correct?"

"Yes, sir, that's correct."

"So it's obvious, then, is it not, Doctor, that you're not able to tell us with any scientific certainty, based on your examination, how long it took for the encounter between the assailant and Mr. Goldman and Ms. Brown?"

"Based on my experience," Dr. Lee said, "cannot be one second." Ed hadn't asked whether the killings took one second, but okay, it wasn't one second.

"Is it true that because you did not perform any scientific analysis or tests to show how long it would take for various spatters or patterns to be created, or one to drop their glasses, that you don't know if it's forty-five seconds or sixty seconds or seventy-five seconds or what?"

"Nobody can reproduce that kind of an experiment." He returned to his assertion: "I know definitely not going to be one second."

"So it would be fair to say, then, Doctor . . . whether it was sixty seconds, give or take fifteen seconds one way or another, you really don't have a scientific opinion?"

"I cannot come here to tell you exactly how many seconds." Ed was doing well. Minutes were no longer in play, Dr. Lee was now counting seconds. "Not going to be short time." Ed then went for the gold ring.

"So whether the murders took sixty seconds or thirty seconds or two minutes, there's really no way you could say with any scientific certainty from the scene that you were presented. Isn't that fair?"

"Maybe ten minute, maybe twenty minute. Okay. Anything is possible. I cannot come here to tell you exactly the time. I do know have a struggle. That's a scientific fact. . . . [Goldman] did not, as described, throat cut in one second. . . . *Anything above minute, I don't know.*"

There it was. According to Dr. Henry Lee, the killings could have taken one minute and one second. In the criminal trial, Dr. Lee said the struggle "was not a short struggle." But now Ed got him to admit it could have been as short as sixty-one seconds.

"So whether it was a minute more or less to do the killings, you really don't know with any scientific certainty? Is that a fair statement?"

"Yes, sir."

A masterful job. Lee was locked in tightly.

As for Dr. Lee and his organization doing a better job collecting the crime-scene evidence than the LAPD: "If you would have taken better pictures, there might even have been more evidence showing Mr. Simpson committed the murders than has been presented; isn't that true?"

"Something wasn't there, I cannot make a comment on it."

"So you don't know if anything that *wasn't* done would be favorable to Mr. Simpson. That would just be speculation. Isn't that true, Dr. Lee?"

"Anything can be favorable or disfavorable. We don't know. I don't want to speculate."

Ed then established that Dr. Lee did not challenge the DNA testing results or the hair and fiber evidence amassed against Simpson. He had given the impression at the criminal trial that there were footprints other than the Bruno Magli at the murder scene, but we established that he had no evidence that any prints were made at the time of the murders. Concerning the bindle with which "something's wrong": "Is it fair to say that the simplest explanation . . . would be that the swatches were not completely dry when they were put in the bindle?"

"I offered that explanation from day one." So he had, indeed, been talking about one individual bindle, for which there was a totally innocent and obvious explanation.

". . . You're not saying you have any scientific fact to show that any LA police officer planted or did anything, cheating with any evidence; isn't that correct?"

"Correct."

Something was wrong all right; something was terribly wrong with the injustice perpetrated by Simpson and his team.

In California, each side in a civil suit has the option to automatically disqualify one judge assigned to them—one judge, one time. In mid-July, Superior Court Presiding Judge David Perez organized a conference call among all the attorneys, and told us Judge Alan Haber, who had been handling the case from inception, would be the trial judge, and gave us twenty-four hours to decide whether or not to disqualify him.

Haber had been doing a good job. Unlike Ito, he did not allow the crush of media and public interest to affect his rulings. He called them exactly as he would had there been no outsiders sitting in the courtroom. My only gripe about the judge was that he tended to give the defense more leeway than I thought they deserved. Then again, I thought they deserved *no* leeway. I thought they won some rulings that they shouldn't have, particularly in upholding the claims of privilege asserted at Kardashian's deposition. But we had no intention of disqualifying Haber. He was a seasoned, smart judge, fair to both sides, courteous to the lawyers and amiable. Baker, on the other hand, had been complaining about him for months. "That guy is gone," he'd told me one day over the deposition table. "Don't bank on him, we're going to ding him."

"You're not going to ding him." I figured Baker was just doling out more disinformation.

"How much you want to bet?"

"I'll bet you a hundred bucks you don't ding him." We shook on it.

If you disqualify a judge you'd better have done your homework and found out who his replacement might be; you can't disqualify two judges in a row, and you might get stuck much worse off than if you'd stood pat. Of course, you can't call up a judge and find out who's next in line. The best you can do is dig around, talk to lawyers and others around the court, inquire about which judges are occupied and which are available and try to get a handle on who you are likely to draw if you disqualify the one at the plate.

Mike Brewer had heard that Baker's firm had, in the past, repeatedly disqualified one particular judge who was available as a possible replacement. The conventional wisdom is that if you keep doing that, sooner or later you will end up in front of that judge, who just might take it out on you. I figured my hundred bucks was safe.

Baker dinged Haber early the next morning.

There were four or five remaining Santa Monica Superior Court judges. I was told later that some of them let it be known that they didn't want this case under any circumstances. Others were more receptive to it. This case would be highly controversial, hugely public. The judge would be in a fishbowl. Depending on each individual ruling, one side or the other would always be unhappy; worse, one side's pundits and commentators were certain to loudly criticize the judge. He would be like an umpire at a sold-out ballpark, someone would always be booing him. We were all scrambling to find out who we might get.

Judge Perez named Judge Hiroshi Fujisaki. Now it was our turn to decide whether we would keep him.

Fujisaki was sixty years old and a veteran trial judge. During World War II, he and his family had been forced to live in an internment camp. His first job as a lawyer was for the Los Angeles public defender's office. Eight years later he entered private practice and four years after that he became a judge. He was no stranger to high-profile cases. Three years earlier he presided over a defamation trial that pitted Elke Sommer against Zsa Zsa Gabor.

I had been before Judge Fujisaki on some minor pretrial matters in previous cases. Although he'd ruled in my favor, I'd found him rather abrupt, impatient, and ill-tempered. Other lawyers in my firm had been called on the carpet and also treated harshly by him. We called the district attorney's office, whose lawyers were in and out of his courtroom every day, and their reviews were decidedly mixed. No one told us to drop him, but no one told us we had been particularly lucky, either. Because Judge Fujisaki had been in the public defender's office when he'd gotten out of law school, we worried he might be too pro-defendant.

But when we checked with other attorneys, the overriding consensus was that Judge Fujisaki did not meddle in *how* lawyers conducted a trial; he called balls and strikes and moved things along quickly. I phoned a lawyer who had tried a case in front of him the year before, who said, "He lets you try your own case but he doesn't put up with any bullshit." Having dealt with Bob Baker for almost a year, that was at least good news.

Deciding on the right judge can determine whether you win or lose. If you come before a judge who does not see things your way, you can be at an extreme disadvantage throughout the entire trial, one that is difficult to overcome. The judge controls the courtroom, it's his home ballpark, he decides the ground rules. Even before we had started, the game was on the line.

Peter, Tom, Ed, and I sat around my office. We just did not know what to do. Baker had spent his, but we had one more bullet in the chamber. Tom said, "This is probably the most important decision of the case. If it's the wrong decision, it's *your* decision." He started laughing. "And if it's the right decision, it's mine!"

"Okay, let me make it clear to you, guys," I chuckled. It was getting late and we were getting giddy. "If everything goes wrong, you can blame me. If everything goes right, you can take the credit."

The phone rang. It was Bob Baker.

Fujisaki, it turned out, was the judge whom we had been told Baker's firm had repeatedly disqualified. He said, "You know, Dan, put aside the jockeying and let's talk man-to-man." Alarms started sounding, red flags went up. Whenever you get one of those "man-to-man" calls from your adversary, you know you're in trouble. "You gotta ding Fujisaki. We can't try this case before him."

I immediately started to pull his chain. "I don't know, Bob, I'm hearing some good things about him. I think he might be a great judge for the case."

Baker said, "Dan, do what you want. But it would be malpractice for you not to ding this judge."

"Bob, it was malpractice for you to ding Haber." I hung up and turned to the guys in the room. "That cinches it," I said. "It's Fujisaki." I sent Baker his hundred bucks.

After we advised the court of our decision, there was a flurry of speculation in the media that Judge Perez had deliberately chosen another Japanese American, neither a black nor a white, to preside over this trial specifically to defuse the race issue. I don't believe there was any basis for this. Although Lance Ito, also a Japanese American, had worked the criminal case, it was just a coincidence. I had heard Judge Ito wanted the criminal case, lobbied for and hustled it; Judge Fujisaki, I've been told, did the opposite. He was preparing to retire and did not need or want the attention or stress of such a high-visibility trial at the end of a solid career. Nevertheless, he was a paid employee, they gave it to him and he accepted the responsibility.

Shortly after Fujisaki was appointed, I went to his courtroom to catch a glimpse of him in action. He had just concluded a trial and the courtroom was empty except for his staff. I introduced myself to the judge's court clerk, Erin Kenney, and his bailiff, Vicky McKown, and ended up speaking to them for over an hour about how the judge ran his courtroom. I learned real fast that Fujisaki and his staff ran a no-nonsense, tight ship. Pleased, I felt that this was just what we needed.

For about a month, our discovery matters were heard in front of Judge Jack Newman because Fujisaki was booked; Haber, once booted by Baker, could not have anything else to do with the case. Newman wrapped up the remaining pretrial matters in rapid style and handed the case off to Fujisaki in early September. Meanwhile, on August 5, all the lawyers in the case were summoned into Judge Perez's chambers and introduced to our trial judge.

Judge Hiroshi Fujisaki was a tight man with a taciturn way about him. Right away it was clear that he had very firm ideas about how he would run this case. He started laying down the ground rules. There would be only two lawyers for each party at the counsel table. The parties (Goldman, Simpson, etc.) could not sit there; they would have to sit elsewhere. Our side alone had three parties and at least a half-dozen lawyers. Adding to the logjam, John Kelly had just asked a prominent New York City lawyer, Paul Callan, to work with him at trial. So we knew we had some convincing to do if we wanted Fujisaki to make room for all of us.

Baker's opening gambit was to float the idea of a gag order. This is an order issued by the judge prohibiting all the lawyers and parties in the case from commenting on the trial to the press or public at any time of its duration. This, I saw, was a clear attempt, as we were being introduced, to poison the judge against the plaintiff's side, and in particular against MSK and me, by implying that we were publicity hounds and would be out there pitching our case to the public rather than arguing to the jury in the courtroom. Baker was playing to Fujisaki's strength right off the bat. I was impressed. He was getting ready for battle, the pretrial process for which he exhibited little patience was drawing to a close, and he was getting his game face on. He would be, no doubt, one tough opponent in that courtroom. To my surprise, the judge made no decision on Baker's request for a gag order.

Three days later we were in chambers again, this time to hear Fujisaki lay down more ground rules. Once again, Baker took the initiative and brought up the gag rule. The judge said, "Fine. Does anybody object?"

I wanted to object, because Baker was trying to send a message to the judge that we (I) would not act professionally. But I had trouble coming up, on the spot, with a good reason *not* to have a gag order. We had no intention of leaving the courtroom each day and running up to a bank of microphones, as Simpson's defense had done during the criminal proceedings; I didn't think that was appropriate. The jury would not be sequestered, they would be going home each night, and I thought press conferences would be prejudicial. In any event, I didn't think they would be permitted. As long as both sides abstained from talking, I could see nothing wrong with a gag rule. So I agreed to stipulate to it. Boom, we had a gag order.

What later came to concern me was that Simpson had an aggressive band of surrogates who would constantly advocate his position and we did not. These were not people working on the case, and were not covered by the gag order. For example, there was Leo Terrell, an attorney and rabid Simpson supporter in close contact with Simpson and his lawyers, who was consistently on the air zealously advocating Simpson's side of the case. Terrell was a civil rights lawyer who became a fixture on *Rivera Live,* screaming, yelling, always making race the center of every issue. No matter what the topic was, he raved and ranted and got it back to race. It made for good television—and he parlayed that *shtick* into appearances on other TV shows and to a radio show of his own—but it violated the spirit of the gag order something fierce.

On another issue, Bob Blasier, who would head up the DNA and science side of the civil defense, used state-of-the-art computer technology and wanted to plug into the court reporter's stenography equipment to get real-time transcripts of the daily testimony. The judge said there would be none of that. Court reporters review and correct their notes before the transcript becomes official, and the judge didn't think it would be fair to tap into them until the court reporter completed and signed off on the transcripts.

Judge Fujisaki's legal assistant assigned to the case was a young attorney named John Byrne. He had helped Judge Ito during the criminal trial, had an excellent background in the case, and would help the judge handle the mountain of paperwork we all would generate. The judge disclosed to us that John Byrne and his family were neighbors and good friends of the Bakers. He asked if we had a problem with Byrne.

I wanted to say yes. While I didn't know Byrne and had no reason to distrust him at all, I was nonetheless bothered by the Baker connection. Why, of all the people in the world to help the judge decide important legal issues, did he have to be Bob Baker's neighbor? Why did we need that?

On the other hand, the issues would be decided on the strength of our papers, and I knew we would do a much better job than the defense on briefing matters. If the judge said he needed this guy and we dinged him and he was unable to get a replacement, he was not going to be very happy with us. Who knew what that could mean?

All this theorizing was going on in nanoseconds. I sucked it up and said, "That's fine, Your Honor."

I asked if we could use a big-screen projection television to display our graphics in the courtroom. "Naw, I don't want that." We would have to go with a standard monitor. I had to fight just to get an ELMO projector to show the jury close-ups. It was clear Judge Fujisaki wanted a good old-fashioned trial. He didn't look kindly on the large displays we created to demonstrate everything from the layout of the Rockingham estate to the pattern of the Bruno Magli Silga sole. "You better have a place to put them," he said. "They are not going to go in the jury room. When the jury deliberates, they're not going to have boards in there. You're going to have to have your exhibits in books."

The judge made it clear that he was having nothing to do with the media. "I am not going to be in charge of assigning seating. Judge Perez has agreed to do that." It had been one of the conditions under which Judge Fujisaki had accepted the assignment. (To accommodate the press and public interest, the trial would be moved from Judge Fujisaki's usual courtroom into a larger one. There were eighty seats in the courtroom, and Judge Perez did indeed assume responsibility for seating.)

After this day of judicial housekeeping, the press was waiting for us outside the courtroom. We walked right by them. "Can't talk." I was nervous even to say, "There's a gag order"; I didn't want to violate one of the judge's first orders and get him annoyed with me.

The press was furious at being shut out of the process. With no one giving them information, a gag order would make their lives infinitely more difficult. They filed a motion asking Fujisaki to eliminate the gag order, and requesting that cameras be allowed in the courtroom, as they had been at the criminal trial. On August 23, Judge Fujisaki heard these arguments.

A powerful array of media attorneys—including those representing radio, network and cable television, the press, the *Los Angeles Times,* noted free-speech attorney Floyd Abrams for Court TV—plus the plaintiffs' and defendant's lawyers made an appearance. The judge told us, "Make your arguments one by one." We paraded before him and he sat there patiently watching, listening. Didn't ask one question.

I had discussed these issues at length with Fred Goldman. We decided we didn't have a problem with the gag order, we just wanted to make clear what the order's actual language meant. On the issue of cameras in the courtroom, we had some disagreement.

Fred very much wanted this trial televised. He felt strongly that the public should see Simpson testify. Not just the American public—the world. Simpson had been acquitted in full televised view of the nation, and then taken his case to the public in his $29.95 video and his post-criminal trial publicity spree. Now it was time to face the music. Simpson had no answers. The man had killed Fred's son, and Fred wanted him confronted with the whole world watching.

Tom Lambert was opposed. He felt that unpredictable things would happen if we allowed the trial to be televised, and the greater the degree of unpredictability, the worse it was for us. Pundits would be buzzing around, flyspecking everything, getting in our way. Cameras could scare off helpful witnesses or scare up wannabes with made-for-TV revelations. Either way, nothing good would come of it.

All that was true, I couldn't quarrel with it. What bothered me was that Simpson and his lawyers didn't want the proceedings televised. I pay close attention to the rule that states, *If your adversary wants something, you don't.* Baker and Simpson weren't doing us any favors. They had reasons to keep the trial off TV: They wanted to bury everything. Both to win the case and, looking down the road, to rehabilitate his image, Simpson didn't want to see another second of Nicole's beaten face on national TV, he didn't want that 911 tape played on television one more time.

Ultimately, I agreed that it was in our tactical best interests not to have the case televised. I listed our other various reasons to Fred: We wanted to keep a tight, fast-moving trial, and TV causes problems; lawyers play to television and the arguments become unnecessarily longer; witnesses play to television, and testimony changes in unforeseen ways; the judge might cut the defense's silly arguments more slack, causing huge risks. Everyone saw what cameras did to Lance Ito.

However, Fred was the client, and he was very clear in his feelings. He wanted the trial televised to the public. Believing that Fujisaki would not allow television to enter his courtroom under any condition, we decided to take a moderate position in favor of the cameras. We didn't make an impassioned argument, we didn't file a long brief. We argued that news shows would play criminal trial footage after each witness appeared at the civil trial, confusing jurors who happened to watch inadvertently.

The media representatives were much more vociferous, of course. They argued the First Amendment, they argued precedent, they argued the public's right to know. One guy went in asking that only radio be permitted. As in *Inherit the Wind.* Radio, he said, is the truest form of communication: "You can't play to the radio microphones."

Baker argued that they didn't want to see this trial on the 6:00 news. The civil justice system has worked just fine for two hundred years without TV, he said, we don't need television. That must have been music to Fujisaki's ears.

The judge said, "I'll have my ruling at two o'clock" and walked off the bench.

Packed courtroom at two o'clock. Judge Fujisaki had written a five-page ruling. Regarding the gag order, he modified certain language, but left it in place.

No cameras. He concluded that the criminal trial had become a circus, that television had contributed to that unfortunate atmosphere, and that he would not permit a repeat performance. The media had requested, as an alternative, that a closed-circuit TV feed be established to a satellite room where press who could not gain access to the courtroom could observe the proceedings. Barring that, they asked for an audio feed. The judge rejected it all.

They took him up on appeal. The California Court of Appeal affirmed Judge Fujisaki's rejection of cameras in his courtroom. It modified the gag order making it slightly less onerous, and reversed the judge on the issue of the audio feed. Much to the media's satisfaction, a trailer was parked in the courthouse lot, inside which the audio portion of the proceedings was broadcast live for members of the working press, and a bailiff supervised under courtroom rules: no tape recorders, no video cameras, reporters were only allowed to sit there and listen and write.

The defense pulled a couple of quick stunts shortly before the trial began, serving notice that they intended to sow confusion and wreak havoc in the civil trial as their predecessors did in the criminal trial. They arrived in court with a long list of extra names they were adding to their witness list—Marcia Clark, LA District Attorney Gil Garcetti, a Mafia informant, some blond and mustachioed serial killer: goofy names with no real connection to our case. They claimed these people were important witnesses whose identities only recently became known to them from the LAPD "tips" file which they charged we had been sitting on for months and never made available to them.

Before I had a chance to respond, Judge Fujisaki said, "Mr. Petrocelli, I do not think you are acting very professionally in this case." These are frightening words from a judge to a lawyer and they really got me steamed. Baker had succeeded in getting me off to a bad start with Fujisaki, encouraging the judge to think I was playing fast and loose with him, the last thing I could afford. No lawyer wants to go into trial with the judge distrustful of you; it can only spell disaster.

I asked for twenty-four hours to set the record straight.

Peter Gelblum, Yvette Molinaro, Steve Foster, and I worked through the night, going page by page through the defense material books on each of these witnesses. By morning we had an extensive brief showing, one by one, how each of these so-called hidden witnesses had, in fact, been known to the defense all along, and that most were not legitimate witnesses and had no business being called at all.

Fujisaki looked at our brief and excluded every single one of the defense's new witnesses. From then on we knew how to approach him. Fujisaki was the "Show Me" judge. You didn't tell him anything unless you could back it up. We were accustomed to writing at length, but Fujisaki said, "If you can't say it in five pages, I don't want to hear about it." Make a statement, give him the proof, he would deal with it.

This first encounter ended up giving us credibility with the judge and showing the defense could not be trusted. From then on, he knew we were prepared. In this way, trial practice is not unlike baseball. A pitcher who is constantly wild is not going to get the borderline strike. We were like the Atlanta Braves' Greg Maddux, always around the plate. Umpires and judges like that sort of thing, and sooner or later they'll give you the close call.

Jury Selection

We were going to trial, so we needed a command post from which we could run our operation, prepare for the day's events, talk with witnesses, discuss strategy. The MSK offices were only a ten-minute drive away, but I didn't want to deal with the distractions of returning to the office each day. I wanted to hunker down right next to the courthouse. After canvasing the surrounding hotels, we rented a two-room suite at the DoubleTree Guest Suites one long block across the parking lot from the Santa Monica Courthouse where the trial was to be held. I turned over the running of the place to Tom Lambert's secretary, Carolyn Walker.

In the days when I used to coach my son Adam's youth baseball teams, the mother of one player on each squad took on the task of organizing that team's practice schedule, contacting the players, arranging transportation, providing refreshments, and generally seeing to the children's well-being. This was no small undertaking, involving thoroughness and patience, and was usually handled with the grace and good spirits a good mother must possess. She freed up the coaches to do their jobs. Her invaluable position was lovingly known as Team Mom.

Carolyn Walker was our Team Mom. She had worked at MSK for twenty-seven years and had served this same function for me and Lambert during the Armand Hammer case several years earlier. She whipped our

DoubleTree suite into shape. One of her first triumphs was the negotiation with the hotel to install discrete and secure telephone and fax lines, including voice mail, directly into our suite. Speed and security were both of the essence. We didn't need our incoming calls and faxes being routed through the hotel switchboard, where they could grind to a halt, get lost, or be monitored by outside forces. We also didn't need the hotel's normal surcharge of $2 per outgoing long-distance call. With that move alone, Carolyn saved us many, many thousands of dollars.

Carolyn hired a locksmith to remove the hotel's standard card-operated security system and install dead bolts and special coded locks. The hotel insisted that we give them a key to be used in case of fire. We said, Absolutely not. In an emergency they would have to break out the window or knock down the door; we were not giving them a key.

We pulled most of the furniture out of the rooms and replaced it with office equipment. At first, concerned that some enterprising reporter or defense snitch would set up shop across the way and spy on us through the hotel windows, we didn't even want the curtains open. The room stayed dreary until, little by little, we got acclimated and the place lightened up.

Carolyn supervised the installation of our computer system, getting the bugs out and making sure no one could hack their way in. We ordered the trial transcript right off the Internet. It would arrive on-line at around three each morning, and Carolyn arranged with MSK's word-processing department to have it printed out so each of us could have a full transcript in front of us when we arrived for work.

Carolyn served as secretary for all the partners when they were at trial, organizing information, typing memos. Nothing was too large or too small for her attention. When it became clear that Simpson and his crowd were planning to eat lunch every day at the DoubleTree's atrium restaurant, she organized with the restaurant kitchen to have our meals served in the second-floor lounge, down the corridor from our suite. She went as far as to order our meals.

I am a big pretzel and M&M's fan, and she hustled down to Costco and came back with $150 worth of snacks. The hotel coffee tasted terrible because of the poor quality of the Santa Monica water, so the firm ordered us bottled water to make our own, which she personally rolled in. The bathtub was filled to overflowing with bottles of soda, water, and juice. We stuck a refrigerator in the bathroom as well.

They say an army travels on its belly. Well, we felt like we were under siege in there, so Carolyn tried to keep our stomachs full. Not only did she think to provide salami and crackers, bagels and cream cheese, spreads and crackers, she went so far as to vary the menu day by day, week by week, to keep us from getting bored. She gathered DoubleTree coupons for discounts on meals and obtained passes for free valet parking. She was so amiable and wonderful to work with that if the hotel wasn't fully booked, the management gave us free rooms in which to make phone calls, hold conferences, or simply get away for a few hours and think in peace. Carolyn Walker was a great team mom.

The DoubleTree became our office/control center/locker room. A television was always on, often with the sound turned down, playing CNN or the local news or, as seasons passed from one to another, the ball-game. I commandeered a favorite chair in the back room, Tom had his desk set up exactly the way he liked it. This would be our home for as long as it took, and we had a strong feeling that it was going to take quite a while. People became very territorial.

By this time, I had practically become a total stranger to my family. My daughter, Rachel, had just left home for the first time, to begin Georgetown University in Washington, D.C. My son, Adam, was starting his first year of high school. My wife, Marian, was left to deal with these important, difficult transitions on her own. I was now totally immersed and lost in a world of my own; I was unable to deal with anyone or anything not connected to the trial.

My secretary, Maria Johnson, was taking care of my MSK home front. Maria was an extremely competent, highly professional woman with a twenty-five-year career as a legal secretary. She was feisty and quite funny once you got to know her, but she could be a very efficient and formidable gatekeeper. She was also fully capable of telling me when she thought I had screwed up. In the years she had been working for me, we had developed a friendly banter and a lot of mutual respect. The fact that she was an African American had never been an issue between us.

During the criminal trial, Maria had told me she had a connection to Johnnie Cochran. Her boyfriend's brother, an accountant, was married to Cochran's sister and worked in the same suite of offices as Cochran. He was also Maria's accountant, and she had visited him there occasionally. She didn't know Cochran well but had been to his home and had also attended family functions at which he was present. She showed me snapshots of the family in which they both appeared smiling.

When I accepted the case, given the severe split along racial lines, I wondered whether Maria would be troubled by my working on it. I never asked her. I didn't want to make her uncomfortable, she was entitled to an opinion different from mine, and I did not want to damage our relationship. I did consider whether her relationship with Cochran, however removed, would pose any problems. I knew Maria was completely trustworthy, but could she somehow be duped or tricked into providing information to the other side? Did her intimate access to our computer files make her a possible target for espionage?

I decided to ask her whether working on the case with me would cause any difficulties. I didn't ask whether she thought Simpson was guilty or innocent, but if the situation made her in any way uneasy, I said, she could be transferred to another attorney in the firm for the duration, after which she could return to work for me.

Maria did not want to transfer. She said she had no intention of speaking to Cochran or anyone else about what she learned from my involvement in the case, and she understood that everything was to be held in the strictest confidence. She did tell me, however, about some of her own experiences.

Her father, she said, had been pulled out of his home and spread-eagled in the front yard by the LAPD because they had gotten a call about a burglary and thought he was the suspect. Her father was over the age of seventy at the time, and even a cursory look at him would reveal someone highly unlikely to be running around stealing things from houses. Yet and still, they had laid him out on the ground. It turned out the cops had the wrong address.

Maria did not approach the LAPD with the same confidence that I did, and to her the idea of a police conspiracy was not at all unthinkable. Her brother had been the victim of several instances of police brutality. She considered this disrespect and physical intimidation part of her normal life experience.

Maria became emotional when she told these family stories. I just shook my head; I don't know what I would have done if the cops had put my father facedown in the street. She knew I had no idea what black people really thought. I thought it spoke well for both of us that we could have so forthright a conversation, and I was glad she was staying with me.

I also mentioned Maria to Fred Goldman, who showed not the slightest trace of concern. He told me, "If you feel comfortable with her, that's fine."

The single most important phase of this trial was jury selection. Much had been made of the makeup and character of the criminal trial jury and the prosecution mistakes that led to a panel capable of sitting through nine months of testimony and then rendering a unanimous verdict in under three hours. Each side knew the stakes this time and that the fate of the trial might well rest on jury selection.

California civil case juries consist of twelve members of the community. To win, one side must convince nine of those twelve jurors. If four hold out, that's a hung jury; you declare a mistrial and start all over. The number of alternate jurors is left to the judge's discretion, and in consultation with the attorneys Judge Fujisaki decided eight would suffice. We had to choose twenty people to hear this case.

As opposed to the criminal case, the civil suit was to be tried in Santa Monica. Under normal circumstances, because of residential population patterns, one would expect the Santa Monica jury pool to be more predominantly Caucasian than the downtown jury pool, which was dominated by African Americans and Hispanics. Although not a single juror had been seen, the defense was already complaining about an "all-white jury." That phrase in itself, conjuring images of Jim Crow verdicts and the segregated South, did nothing to foster civil discourse. They went into the process trumpeting bias by this as-yet-unseen "Santa Monica jury."

Because of the anticipated length of the trial and the contentious battles expected over the selection of this jury, some one thousand juror summonses were sent out to fill the twenty spots. However, rather than draw heavily from the largely white areas in the immediate vicinity of Santa Monica, the large number of summonses were dispersed on a more widely geographic and racially diverse basis. When we learned how many summonses went out and where they went, we knew we could expect a significant number of blacks, Hispanics, and Asian Americans. The majority would still be white.

Because the racial issue seemed almost outcome-determinative, we were very concerned about whether we would be able to impanel a fair jury. Our mock jury research had showed us how difficult it would be to convince people of color to vote solely on the evidence. We would have to question each and every prospective juror in detail, ferret out the biased ones from those who could be sufficiently impartial to sit as fair, objective jurors. This was sure to be a tedious, time-consuming process, and I worried if Fujisaki would have the patience for such an ordeal.

Not all one thousand summonses were answered. About a hundred people a day showed up in the jury room to be interviewed. They were not told this was the Simpson case, only that the trial was likely to last many months. Cameras outside, press gathering—it didn't take an advanced degree to figure it out.

In the criminal case, selecting a jury had taken several months. To better organize the process, Judge Fujisaki established a three-stage selection process. Stage one consisted of a hardship round conducted by the court. Jurors would be excused if they could prove that serving on this jury over an extended period of time would be a financial or other burden. The self-employed, for example, would find it difficult being unavailable for work for several months. Some companies pay their workers' salaries while they are on jury duty, but those workers whose companies do not pay or that severely limit the payment might be excused.

Our research seemed to indicate that the better education the jurors possessed, the better plaintiff jurors they would be; more discerning and analytical, more receptive to DNA arguments and the reliability of intricate scientific evidence, and less likely to be influenced by claims of wild conspiracies, racial bias, or other emotional concepts having nothing to do with the reality of the case. These were exactly the people who were being excused for hardship.

So right away our jury base was radically diminished as well as essentially shaped. People who are unemployed or work in government jobs usually comprise a large percentage of the available jurors. The county government pays fully for extended jury duty, the federal and state governments pay, a few big corporations pay. The post office pays.

Judge Fujisaki believed that people should be jurors. Even people who were taking care of sick relatives were asked, "What about your brother or sister, do you have anyone else in the family who can care for them?" He didn't let them off easily.

Stage two was the publicity stage, an investigation to determine how much each prospective juror had been influenced by the publicity surrounding the Simpson case. This, far and away, was the single most important part of the selection process. Never before had there been a case with the media coverage and publicity of the Simpson criminal case. Never before had our nation become so transfixed by a crime. And never before had a second trial had to follow such unprecedented publicity. How could we ever expect to find people to comprise a fair and impartial jury in these circumstances? We were in uncharted waters. The battle would be fought and won in the publicity round.

To begin, each prospective juror who survived the hardship round was given a sixteen-page questionnaire to fill out. Prepared by the judge based on suggestions and input received from the lawyers, it was an attempt to save time in oral examination. No personal background information was asked—no name, race, sex, age—just exposure to the case.

Normally, several dozen jurors are brought into the courtroom, twelve names are chosen out of a hat, and those people are put in the jury box while the rest sit in the audience. The lawyers for both sides ask the first twelve jurors questions: "Who here believes they do have a problem sitting on this jury?" "Is there anyone here who cannot be fair?" "Why not?" The problem with that approach in our circumstance is that people were expected to have very strong views about the case and we did not want one person's statement affecting anybody else. Although it was extremely time-consuming, the judge ordered a sequestered *voir dire,* or jury examination process, under which each juror would be questioned separately from the others, one at a time, in the jury box.

As the jurors completed and turned in the questionnaires, copies were made and given to the lawyers. Fujisaki wanted the *voir dire*—or questioning—to begin right away. Tom Lambert and I immediately began reviewing and analyzing the responses.

The questions were far-flung. Prospective jurors were asked which commentators they watched on TV and whether they had seen or heard anything about the Bronco chase. They were asked if they had formed and/or expressed opinions in regard to: media coverage prior to Simpson's arrest, the slow-speed pursuit and arrest of Simpson, the relationship between Simpson and Nicole, the day and night of the murders, the Bundy and Rockingham crime-scene evidence, the police investigation, DNA and blood-matching evidence, the overall conduct of Simpson himself, the conduct of the attorneys trying the criminal case, the jury, the jury's deliberations for their verdict, jurors' comments about their experience on the case.

They were asked how accurate they felt the media had been in reporting the case. (Our research showed that people who thought the media coverage was inaccurate were typically pro-defense jurors, which made this a good question because it was so disguised.) They were asked for opinions they had formed about numerous witnesses who testified in or became known during the criminal trial.

"Based on all you have read and heard about the criminal case, do you have an opinion about whether there has been a police frame-up or a police conspiracy in this case? Yes or no. If so, what is your opinion?" "Can you set aside and disregard this belief?"

"Do you have an opinion about whether any evidence in this case was contaminated? Yes or no. If so, what is your opinion?" "Can you set it aside and disregard?"

They were asked directly, "Have you ever expressed an opinion about the guilt or innocence of O.J. Simpson? Yes or no. If yes, what have you said?" "Can you set it aside?"

There were some follow-up questions as well. "Have you purchased or otherwise obtained any commercial item relating to this case, such as a T-shirt, book, video, or trading card? If so, explain." Someone who had paid for, or even watched, the $29.95 video could hardly be categorized as unbiased, to say nothing of a person who would wear an O.J. Simpson T-shirt. "Have you or has anyone you know made a financial contribution to any organization involved with the relatives of the victims in the case or the defense of O.J. Simpson in the criminal or civil case? If so, explain. If not, have you received any request from them for contributions? In what form?"

"Have you ever driven by O.J. Simpson's Rockingham estate or Nicole Brown Simpson's condominium on Bundy?" This was to eliminate that stream of gawkers Simpson called the "looky-loos." They might have seen something that might be evidence in the case, and in any event the mere fact that they were interested enough to drive over there made their objectivity suspect.

We really didn't want anyone on the jury who actually wanted to be there; neither side could be sure of their motives. They might have a social agenda of their own, and what better platform than the Simpson jury. They might try to exploit their involvement in some way, perhaps base their decision on what might yield the most money. If a juror campaigned to get on the jury, he got bounced. On the plaintiff side, we had no reluctance to have jurors with as blank a slate as possible because we thought we could win on the evidence. We didn't need biased jurors to win—only the defense did.

The bottom line. Question #21: *"Based on what you have read, seen or heard about the murders of Nicole Brown Simpson and Ronald Goldman, do you believe that O.J. Simpson is: 1) definitely guilty; 2) probably guilty; 3) not sure/not enough information; 4) probably not guilty; 5) definitely not guilty."* We fought with the defense over that question; we didn't want to include it because we thought the answers would not be good for us. We were right, they weren't. More people thought he did it than didn't, and we had a hard time keeping them.

The tough ones to analyze were the 3's, which were the majority of the responses. Both "definitely"'s were automatic dismissals. When jurors answered "probably guilty," we fought like crazy to rehabilitate and save them. We tried to predict the poisonous questions Baker would soon fire at them like darts, and innoculate our jurors against them.

"If you were to sit as a juror in this case and you were to listen to all the evidence, and hear all the witnesses from the witness stand, and have a chance to size them up one by one, you think you could do that?" *Yes.* "Do you think you could make your decision based on seeing and hearing all this evidence in the courtroom for the first time, and disregard any of the stuff you've heard before, put it out of your mind and set it aside. You think you could be fair and impartial?" *Yes, yes, yes, yes.* "Thank you very much."

Then Baker would get up and ask some killer questions. He was very good.

"You checked 'probably guilty,' right?" Baker would ask. "You had a choice of checking 'not sure.' You didn't check 'definitely not guilty,' you checked 'probably guilty,' right, and you think my client did it, don't you? You think he did it, right? Be honest, you can tell us. You think he did it. You think he killed two people, right?" *Yes.* "So you would agree with me, you wouldn't be a fair person to sit on this jury." *Yes, Mr. Baker, I'd agree with that.*

After both sides exhausted their questions—and the judge's patience—the juror was asked to go into another room. Then we would argue each juror's case to the judge. Each of us would emphasize the best or worst position a prospective juror had taken.

For instance: "She said that cops planted evidence, Your Honor. That is an extreme position for anybody to hold. How many times in the history of this country can anybody come up with an example where a police department framed an innocent man for murder? I'm not talking about salting a little extra cocaine on a dope suspect for probable cause or to get a warrant or to justify getting into a car. I'm talking about framing one of the most famous men in the country for a double murder! That's absurd, and she thinks that happened!"

I made the argument that it was more unreasonable for a person to think that the police planted evidence than to believe Simpson did it. The belief that the police framed Simpson, I argued, was such an extreme point of view that it indicated a deep-rooted and pernicious bias that would be all but impossible to put aside and constituted grounds for dismissal. I think that scored some points with the judge.

Jurors whom we knew were pro-Simpson—from their answers to all the other questions—routinely marked "not sure" about his guilt or innocence. We attributed this to a variety of factors: a disinclination to express an opinion out in the open, a desire to get on the jury, a propensity to accept defense theories explaining away the evidence of Simpson's guilt, and a refusal to disclose a clear bias in favor of Simpson. Many people who checked "not sure" about Simpson's guilt or innocence also said they had never expressed an opinion on the matter. I found that hard to believe. They also had no stated opinion about most, if not all, of the people involved in the criminal trial; in fact, many pro-Simpson prospective jurors simply did not respond to that part of the questionnaire at all. Our judgment was that the vast majority of the "not sures" were Simpson jurors.

The judge would not disqualify a person who said she had no bias simply because we on the plaintiff team had a feeling she wasn't telling the truth. Failing a compelling reason, he would pass them through to the next round. Our job was to see whether or not these jurors were being truthful. This was the most difficult and disturbing part of the process for me. I didn't enjoy it at all. I was essentially telling them, "Hey, you're not telling the truth."

No opinion about Mark Fuhrman? "Come on," I would cajole the juror sitting alone in the jury box, "you've heard of Mark Fuhrman, haven't you?"

There was just no way a juror could plausibly deny that. "Yeah, I may have heard something about him."

"Well, you know he's a police officer, right?"

"Yeah, I know that."

"You know he had something to do with a glove, right?"

"I heard something about that."

"Like he dropped the glove, right? You know that he's accused of planting evidence against Mr. Simpson, don't you?"

"Well, yeah, I kind of heard that."

It was like pulling teeth, and at times the judge himself got disturbed by the juror's obvious reluctance to provide even rudimentary information. A number of times I was able to get a pro-Simpson juror disqualified not only for having bias but for trying to hide it.

DecisionQuest told us to stay away from black women, we couldn't win with black women. It was clear to me, on a statistical basis, that this pro-Simpson bias did exist. But if there was no other indication of bias, and the prospective juror seemed honest and straightforward, I would say to myself, "The only reason for going after this person is because she's black." I wouldn't do it. I let them continue. Then, I questioned whether I had done my client a disservice. When a white person got up there and said they had no opinion, I'd think, "Is he lying? Do I care? Should I bring that out?" That's how much race dominated the agenda.

Jury selection is all about bias. Lawyers are looking to excise bias against them, and if race causes the bias you can't ignore it. But it is the bias not the color of skin that informs the decision. For example, a well-educated black man with a job in city government, a guy who seemed like a real leader, indicated on his questionnaire that Simpson was "probably guilty." A black woman law clerk also indicated Simpson was "probably guilty." They were biased against Simpson, and we would have been happy to accept them both.

We were engaged in serious battle, and the judge tried to cut through all the clever lines and leading questions. He was not certain the jurors understood where they were being led, whether they were agreeing with the attorneys because they were being put on the spot, intimidated, or because the answers seemed logical. At one point he refused to excuse a juror, saying to Baker, "Well, you led her right down the primrose path." Baker was furious. Later in the day, he asked to see the judge in chambers.

Fujisaki is a tough guy, not a judge to push around. Just prior to that comment he had made some remarks critical of Dan Leonard in the presence of a juror. In chambers, outside the presence of the court reporter, he took off his robe and sat behind his desk. "Your Honor," Baker said heatedly, "I wanted to have this conference because I am unhappy with some of the comments you are making about my partner, Dan Leonard, in front of the jurors." The more he spoke, the angrier he got. "I don't think it's appropriate." Then he shook his finger in Judge Fujisaki's face. "And I don't appreciate what you said about me. If it happens again, I'm going to call you on it. And I won't do it back here, it will be out there."

I was dumbfounded. Some judges might have called for the bailiff and thrown him in the slammer for demonstrating such disrespect for the court. Lance Ito would have done it *in public*, to show how tough he was. I wouldn't have dreamed of talking like that to a judge. I waited for Judge Fujisaki's reaction.

To my surprise, he said, "Okay, Mr. Baker, you are right." From that point on, even at times when Baker scowled disrespectfully in the courtroom in front of the jury and the entire media, the judge seemed extra careful to be deferential and polite to him and his colleagues.

For a while the incident troubled me. I admired Baker for his ability to stand up to a judge whom he felt was hurting his client's case; he would not back down to anyone. As a lawyer, that is a powerful quality to possess. I also wondered about the judge. The trial was in its second day of jury selection and already it seemed Baker had intimidated him. Would that spell trouble for us for the whole rest of the way?

As I thought about it, though, I realized Fujisaki was right. He refused to be baited into a battle of egos with Bob Baker and risk having it become an issue in the trial itself. He wanted this case tried on its merits and would not interject himself or his personality into the proceedings. For that he deserved a medal.

Simpson was in the courtroom for several days during this stage of jury selection. The defense clearly thought their guy, attractive and celebrated, could charm the prospective jurors, particularly younger women. We could tell just from his demeanor that they apparently thought he had a way with blondes.

Then he left. The press speculated that Simpson was upset at seeing blacks being disqualified. I believed he absented himself because his lawyers felt some of the African-American jurors, wanting to bond with him, were reluctant to say anything negative about Simpson in his presence, and their positive shows of support were getting them bounced. During questioning, I would glance over at Simpson from time to time, and he would be making the same exaggerated faces he made during the depositions—shaking his head in agreement, pleading for understanding, or huffing and puffing when anyone said something against him. He continued to be a bad actor. I think his lawyers encouraged him to leave the courtroom not to calm his moral outrage, but to make it easier to retain jurors they thought would get him off.

The press kept telling me the ladies loved Baker. I could see why. He was a handsome older man with wavy gray hair and a way with him. It worked to the defense's benefit, because their research, like ours, must have shown that white women were Simpson's least desirable juror. Personable, funny, owner of a great smile, Baker was very good at walking up to a juror, making her feel at ease, and then cutting her head off.

Baker must have felt the issue of domestic violence would turn white women in their thirties and forties against Simpson, because he went after them aggressively. "You think my client's a wife beater. You believe he *hit* Nicole and you think there's some link between hitting Nicole and murder, don't you? A person who hits a woman has a predisposition toward greater violence and escalation of violence, isn't that right?"

I was amazed at how confrontational he became with them. "You think my client did it, don't you?" It was angry, hostile cross-examination and most of the women were cowed by it, but some fought back. What was he, crazy? What if he didn't get that juror disqualified? Now he's made an enemy *who is on the jury.* The strategy must have been successful for him in previous cases because it was definitely part of his game plan, but I couldn't figure it out.

The process went on for days, then weeks. Whites favored our side, blacks favored Simpson, we were face-to-face with America's unyielding race problem and it was very demoralizing. Here, in front of our eyes, the case was degenerating into a racial contest, our worst fear.

I would get to the DoubleTree first thing in the morning and just feel exhausted. In a normal trial jury selection takes a day or two and you don't have a decision until the end, so with a little concentration you can stave off your anxiety. Here the judge was constantly ruling for or against us, we were winning or losing ten to fifteen times a day. We were engaged in trench warfare, and it was grueling.

Then, right in the middle of the process, Mark Fuhrman pleaded *nolo contendere* to perjury. He had sworn in the criminal trial that he had not said the N-word in the past ten years, and he had lied.

This was a devastating development. We had been working so hard every day to find jurors who would not buy into the defense theories of police corruption and racial conspiracies, and now the defense had an open shot to destroy most of what we'd been working for.

The plea was all over the news that morning and the defense was preening. The judge ruled that, since Fuhrman was still potentially a witness in our case, the jurors could be questioned about him, so Baker jumped right in. "Have you heard that Mark Fuhrman has pled *nolo?* You understand that's a conviction of guilt in the eyes of the law?" Now we had to worry whether a juror could separate perjury from the planting of evidence. Fuhrman had already admitted one; therefore, in the defense's scheme of things, he must be lying about the other. Both perjury and planting were sneaky, dishonorable, and criminal acts, and Baker used the perjury plea to give substance to the planting idea, "He pled *nolo* to perjury, he *must* have planted that evidence." Look what we had on our hands: a key player who was a convicted felon. It was like a blow to the stomach. It knocked the wind out of us.

Baker showed up in court the next day grinning and said, "Hey, did you hear the news?"

"What?"

"Vannatter's pleading next!" He was pulling my chain, but obviously he was going to try to paint all our people as liars and cheats. And he was having a good time. The entire defense side of the courtroom was all smiles. We were grim-faced and quiet.

We had to find a way to turn this devastation to our favor. Finally, we had a brainstorm. We took what the defense gave us.

"You heard Detective Fuhrman pled *nolo* to perjury, right?" we asked pro-Simpson jurors. "You heard he admitted he lied. You're going to have a hard time believing anything Mr. Fuhrman says, right?"

"That's correct."

"It's going to be really hard for you to accept things that he says, because you think he's a liar."

"Right."

"You think he's a perjurer?"

"Right." The animus could not be contained.

A guaranteed disqualification. The judge could not accept a juror who has made up his mind about a witness's credibility before even hearing his testimony. We got several difficult jurors knocked off that way.

One hundred and three people cleared both the hardship and publicity rounds and made it to Stage Three, the general and final round of examination.

Baker and his boys looked over the list of upcoming jurors and Dan Leonard told me, "We like this jury. We'll take all of them!"

Of course, that would never happen. In this round, both sides would seek to dismiss jurors who evinced any previously undisclosed bias. In addition, this was the time when both sides would exercise their peremptory challenges. These are automatic challenges and do not require lawyers to state or prove a reason for them. Lawyers exercise peremptories when, even though they lack the ability to demonstrate bias or good cause, they still do not think the juror will be helpful to their side.

The one hundred and three finalists were given a second questionnaire, this time running 23 pages and 120 questions. This was much more detailed and intensified than the first. Background information included age, sex, marital status, occupation, children, occupation of children, how

long they had lived in Los Angeles County, the neighborhood or community in which they lived, where else they had lived. Was English their
first language? Level of education, schools attended, specific training
skills. Military service. Were they football fans? Did they follow professional football? What was their contact with law enforcement? Did they
have any friends or relatives who worked for law enforcement (with a list
of government agencies including the police department and district
attorney's office)? Would they tend to believe or disbelieve testimony of a
law enforcement officer? Any experience, or members of one's family's
experience, with crime? Domestic violence? How did they rate their satisfaction with the legal system? The justice system?

Lambert and I again did most of the work analyzing the answers.
Norma Silverstein of DecisionQuest, and Joe Rice, a jury consultant
working with John Kelly and Paul Callan, assisted in ranking the jurors.
We rated fifty-eight of the one hundred and three as "neutrals." The
remaining forty-five were pretty much equally divided between pro-
defendant and pro-plaintiff.

Trial lawyers make careers out of trying to ascertain how a juror will
think and vote, to determine who will be a good juror for your case and
who will be a bad one. Most lawyers would deny this, but all this talk
about simply wanting a fair and unbiased jury, that's nonsense; you want
jurors who are biased in your favor. You want to win.

We particularly wanted to win with African Americans on the jury.
A "guilty" verdict from an unbiased racially diverse jury would go a long
way toward blunting attacks on its credibility.

Unlike the one-on-one questioning of jurors in the publicity round,
the final round of questioning took place with twelve jurors sitting in the
jury box, with those next in line in the audience.

Baker, who liked how the initial group lined up, passed on the first
twelve jurors in the box. This means he did not seek to challenge any of
the jurors and was prepared to accept the panel as is. If we then passed,
the process would be over, and we'd have ourselves a jury. But Baker knew
we had to challenge several of the jurors; he was forcing us to start using
up our peremptories—and each side only had eight. A smart move. But
pretty soon he joined the fray.

One prospective black juror was dismissed because she admitted that
she "hoped and prayed" every morning that O.J. Simpson was innocent.

Another one, an older black man, had disobeyed the judge's instructions and gone out and done his own DNA research. Another woman—also black, a postal worker—was in the midst of suing her supervisor. The claim? While she was celebrating Simpson's victory after the criminal trial, the white supervisor allegedly called her a racial epithet. The judge found all three exhibited strong biases against us.

In the meantime, the peremptories started flying back and forth.

We anticipated that any person who had been the subject of domestic abuse would be knocked off by the judge, but Fujisaki had to be persuaded that each individual showed bias. One young woman from a tough neighborhood in Washington, D.C., had grown up in poverty, witnessed murder, been attacked with a knife, and then turned around and beaten up her attacker. She had joined the military, gotten out of the ghetto, was now out of the military and had a grip on her life. This woman had been through ten lifetimes, and our sense was she would think what Nicole went through was nothing. This was a woman who might not give us too much understanding, and we were concerned that she would not make the link between Simpson's violence and Nicole's murder. The judge liked her because she was so honest about her feelings, and it took a lot of convincing for us finally to persuade him to excuse her for cause.

It wasn't long before the defense played their race card. Under *People v. Wheeler*, they moved for a mistrial, arguing that, in using our peremptory challenges, we had been systematically excluding African Americans from the jury.

This was an all-out attempt to make us look like a bunch of bigots. It played big on television, yet again poisoning the black community against us, and it gave commentators one more opportunity to discuss something other than the facts of the case. It also told me Simpson and his lawyers were hardly confident about their case; they were willing to scuttle the process before it even started. But we were prepared for it. We knew we weren't excluding people because they were black, we were excluding them because they were biased.

Tom Lambert defended in open court—on multiple grounds—the challenge of *every single* black person we struck. He showed how, in answer after answer, each challenged juror had exhibited significant bias in favor of Simpson and against our clients. It wasn't even close. The judge denied their motion wholesale.

With that, the selection process quickly drew to a close. Twelve jurors and eight alternates were seated. The process had taken fifteen working days, three weeks, shorter than we had expected.

Of the twelve sitting jurors, one had said Simpson was "probably not guilty," two said "probably guilty," the rest were undecided. Tom took down the ugly hotel artwork at the DoubleTree and hung a "map" of the jury box, a single-page typed profile of each juror, in the position they were seated, that took up half the wall and showed us who we were talking to.

Juror #1: 33-year-old single male, born in Kingston, Jamaica, who described his ethnic background as Asian/Black. A letter carrier for the post office (not downtown) with a B.A. in math from Cal State Fresno.

Juror #2: 67-year-old white female, widowed, with three grown children. Formerly a bank teller. Graduated from UCLA with a degree in art.

Juror #3: 30-year-old white male, living with nonmarried partner. Listed his background as Mexican-Irish-English-Dutch. Airline flight attendant.

Juror #4: 25-year-old white woman, married a year and a half. Manager of a jewelry store. Graduated University of California at Santa Barbara with a degree in drama and literature. Interested in musical theater.

Juror #5: 40-year-old single white woman. Background: Greek-Asian. Free-lance set designer and stage manager. B.A. in theater arts, post-graduate work in theater design.

Juror #6: 39-year-old Mexican-American man. Married three weeks. Postal worker. Some college. Associate's degree in art.

Juror #7: 62-year-old black woman. Widowed, mother of three grown children. Two years of vocational school, some college. Formerly a dispatcher for a telephone company.

Juror #8: 35-year-old single man. Background: Italian. College graduate in history. Supervisor for a museum.

Juror #9: 55-year-old white male. Married but separated, with three older children. High school graduate. Unemployed in the construction business.

Juror #10: 63-year-old white woman. Listed her background as Norwegian. Married 35 years. Six children. High school graduate, some college. Worked in the legal department of a large corporation.

Juror #11: 27-year-old white male. Married a year and a half. Some college, vocational school for optics. Worked as an optician.

Juror #12: 62-year-old white male, married 33 years, two older children. Vocational school and some college. A technical illustrator, retired, doing handy work and odd jobs.

As a group they ranged widely in age, were relatively well-educated and professionally responsible, seemed willing to listen, and, best of all, didn't hate us. We had dodged that bullet. We had a chance to win.

TWENTY-ONE

Opening Statements

The entire jury selection process, like the mock trial before it, had been focused on defense themes. We had spent the better part of a month talking to these jurors about race, and police conspiracy, incompetence, and misconduct. At the same time, our team had been meeting to hone in on exactly what it was that we would present as our case.

What it came down to was this: This was the trial of O.J. Simpson. This was not a malpractice case against the Los Angeles Police Department, this was not an investigation into the evidence-gathering capabilities of its crime lab or the racial preferences of its members; the LAPD was not on trial here at all.

We wanted to establish from the beginning that unlike the criminal proceedings, this would not be a trial of smoke and mirrors. The mere verbal suggestion of improper actions, we argued before Judge Fujisaki, was not sufficient reason to bring them before the court; under law, such suggestions must be supported by facts or else are not admissible and cannot be mentioned. In our pretrial *motions in limine,* or motions "at the threshold" of the trial, we asked the judge to preclude the defense from arguing that evidence against Simpson had been planted by the police because there was no evidence to support such a claim. In discovery we had asked the defense to present us with any and all such evidence, and they could not. Therefore, none existed for trial.

The judge compromised. He barred the defense from telling the jury in their opening statement that Simpson's blood was planted in his Bronco, on the Bundy trail, and on the Rockingham trail. During the course of our trial, witnesses could be examined, if appropriate, concerning these matters. The criminal trial had been consumed by postulations and suppositions and wholesale fabrications about what *might have happened.* Well, what might have happened was not at issue in our trial.

We expected Baker to make a splashy attempt to muddy the waters and confuse the jury in the cross-examination of LAPD criminalist Dennis Fung and the other people involved in collecting the evidence, who had been abused by excessive questioning at the criminal trial. But evidence collection, particularly in regard to blood evidence, is relevant only to show that the evidence being offered against the defendant was picked up where it was found, was brought to a safe place for storage, was not damaged or destroyed, and was the same evidence that was ultimately tested and brought to court. This is called "chain of custody."

We found a California statute that states that regular, routine work done by state employees is presumed to be done correctly. With that in hand, we could walk all the evidence through with no witness testimony about the collection process if we so desired. If the defense could demonstrate that evidence was somehow contaminated or tampered with, they could put that on in their case. We did not want them confusing and distorting our presentation of the evidence.

Along the same lines, we made a separate motion *in limine* to prevent the defense from arguing or asking questions about the kinds of techniques and procedures of evidence collection employed by other law enforcement agencies. This was a crucial part of our plan to keep the issues in our trial confined to what happened in our case. We didn't want witnesses such as Dennis Fung to be examined ad nauseum about what he should have or might have done. Nor did we want the defense to play hours of Dr. Henry Lee's deposition attacking LAPD for their sloppy techniques and lousy equipment and touting how he and others would have done a better job.

Fujisaki agreed. He explained it better than we did. "This is not a malpractice case [against the LAPD]. It does not matter how the evidence was collected," the court said in granting our motion to limit Dr. Lee's testimony. "The fact remains that the evidence was collected, examined, and the evidence cannot be attacked because of the collection procedures unless that attack establishes some defect, incompetency, or lack of foundation in the chain of evidence. . . ."

For the same reasons, we also pointed out that the defense should not be allowed to argue about blood and other evidence that they contended should have been collected and tested but never was. We explained that such evidence was not relevant because we were not relying on it or offering it against Simpson. Furthermore, we argued, the suggestion by the defense that such evidence would have exonerated Simpson was foolish; the defense couldn't prove that. If anything, the LAPD did Simpson a *favor* in failing to collect every stain of blood evidence at the crime scene, since undoubtedly that would have only yielded more evidence of Simpson's guilt.

The judge concurred with this reasoning. "The argument of the experts should be directed to the evidence that was, in fact, collected, why it's good or why it's not good, examining about that, whether it was accurate or inaccurate. The fact that there could have been more blood taken or collected—that doesn't go to the weight of the evidence itself that was collected and the examination and opinions of each expert thereon. So the court doesn't want this case to get lost in an argument about who has better collection procedures."

We also succeeded in preventing the defense from arguing about other killers. In discovery, the defense could produce no evidence pointing to any other killer and, unless such evidence surfaced at trial, we did not want them misleading the jury with talk of Colombian drug lords and Mafia hit men. Again, the judge agreed.

These motions and the judge's positive response sent an early and loud signal to the defense that this was not going to be a replay of the criminal trial. We would doggedly press to confine the case to the evidence that showed Simpson was guilty and not allow the trial to explode into a free-for-all against the LAPD, the coroner's office, or anyone else connected to the investigation.

What was this trial really about? We hashed it out constantly. The trial was upon us, yet we were by no means in agreement. We knew we had to focus on Simpson, but how? How were we to get out of the morass of police issues? What *was* our case? What was the theme and message of our case?

I thought we should fight for justice. Fred Goldman, our client, had lost his son. "This is a case about justice," I said to my partners. "It is not about money, it is not about compensation, it is about justice. Fred Goldman's last chance for justice."

Tom had some trouble with that. "You are wrong," he told me. We knew each other well enough that we didn't have to pull any punches. "People aren't going to buy that. He *is* suing for money, and I think we should make it clear and not be elliptical about it. Fred is suing in the tort system for compensation for these harms he has suffered, and the only compensation you can seek in this system is money. He's not doing it *for* the money, but we are asking for money." I think to Tom, the whole battle for justice sounded a bit pretentious and candy-ass. In the real world, people sue for money; nobody sues for justice. Tom was not at all certain the jury would agree with my proposition, particularly at the beginning of the case, and we might come off as disingenuous or worse.

Ed had been concerned about the issue of money for some time. Fred Goldman is Jewish, and there was anti-Semitism to consider. Ed, himself a Jew, was worried that Fred would be stereotyped: *Everybody knows Jews like money. If he denies he's in it for the money, he's lying.* Goldman, gold man, man of gold. Money was important, it was the only recompense available to us in the civil justice system, but it had to be touched on lightly.

I thought both their points were well taken, so rather than focus my opening statement on "justice," I decided to let the trial take its course and see where we came out. We would go with the evidence and establish our extremely formidable forensic case. The mock trial had shown that we needed more, however. We would have to put Simpson on the stand. Of course, he would lie as it suited him, so we would make him tell demonstrable lies, attack him on the stand with firsthand evidence of his lies, then follow him with a parade of impeachment witnesses who would reveal the rest of his lies. We would then close our case with Ron's and Nicole's families.

We all committed to one guiding principle: Less Is More. We would avoid the pitfalls of the criminal trial, in which the prosecution introduced too much detail, from tracing every police footstep from Bundy to Rockingham, to educating the jury about evidence collection techniques and the intricate science of DNA. We would focus our witnesses just on their individual pieces of the puzzle and get them off the stand in a hurry. Every witness, every piece of evidence must be essential to our case. Once we put it all together, the portrait of the killer would be revealed. It all would lead to Simpson.

We arrived in the courtroom on the first day of trial, nervous but ready. Each of the parties came loaded with their full contingent of lawyers. We had six from our team; Kelly and Callan were for Nicole's family; Brewer was there with his partner for Rufo; and Simpson had five lawyers. To accommodate the anticipated crush of observers, the proceedings had been moved from Judge Fujisaki's usual courtroom to a larger one, and the judge was very particular about our housekeeping in his borrowed space. He wanted to return it in the same shape in which it had been received.

To deny any lawyer access to counsel's table in the courtroom would have been unfair, but the judge was notably unenthusiastic about seating us all. For one thing, the original courtroom table had been wide and short, much too small to accommodate everyone. To make sure there was room for our team, I volunteered to supply tables with sufficient space to allow everyone to sit. Baker agreed because he would get more room for his team as well.

We came up with a two-tier approach, one long front table for each side, with a long thin table behind it, thus seating twice the number of interested parties in the same amount of space. Unfortunately, such tables were not available for rent, so we had to have them made. As of the night before jury selection, they had not yet been fabricated. On top of worrying about meeting our first jurors, I was faced with the possibility of looking like a fool in front of Judge Fujisaki and the world's assembled media when they walked into an empty courtroom. Fortunately, thanks to Team Mom Carolyn Walker's good offices, the tables arrived that morning, about a half-hour before court was to begin.

We called the second row "the kids' table." The Goldmans sat in the first row of seats behind the bar, the Brown family behind them. Simpson's friends and family sat to their immediate left, in the first two rows. The rest of the courtroom was packed, mostly with media.

From the beginning, I had hoped Simpson's original Dream Team would remain on the scene and represent him at trial. We would have liked to try this case against Johnnie Cochran, F. Lee Bailey, Barry Scheck, and the rest of them. I thought nothing would be better than to bring them down along with Simpson. Ed, being a gentleman, said, "It would be a real challenge to go up against them, and it would be fun." I said, "Nah, I just want to kick their ass."

We expected, of course, that a principal defense strategy would be to try Mark Fuhrman in absentia, to put racial prejudice on trial instead of O.J. Simpson. It had worked once, it had been previewed throughout jury selection, and even as close as five minutes before the start of the trial Simpson and his lawyers were still attempting to incorporate Fuhrman into the proceedings. Fuhrman now lived in Idaho where he could not be subpoenaed, and there was no realistic possibility of his coming to California to testify. In his stead, the defense wanted to read Fuhrman's criminal-trial testimony into the record so they could impeach it with his inflammatory statements about race. Their problem was that if Fuhrman did not testify, there was no such issue and they would be left without their primary smokescreen.

We filed a motion to prevent the defense from introducing that testimony and also from referring in their opening statement to Fuhrman's recent plea of *nolo contendere*.

"Where I come from," said Dan Leonard, "this is called a sandbag, Your Honor." But the judge ruled that without our having access to Fuhrman, his prior testimony was inadmissible. Because Fuhrman could not be guaranteed as a witness in this case, the judge also precluded them from mentioning his plea and his criminal testimony in their opening. Fuhrman was not at issue here, and so long as we kept him out of our case, they could not refer to him. This was a big victory for us; it went a long way toward preventing the defense from prejudicing the jury with rhetoric having nothing to do with whether O.J. Simpson murdered two people the night of June 12, 1994.

It was finally time to begin.

Everyone on the team contributed to the preparation of my opening statement. I decided that the opening should be relatively brief and would be most effective if delivered by one lawyer, rather than splitting it up as Clark and Darden had done. I worked with Kelly and Brewer to carve out discrete areas they could talk about that would not break up the flow and force of the comprehensive presentation that I would deliver. Ed gave me material on police, FBI, and coroner witnesses; Tom prepped me on the science; Peter helped work up relationship and domestic violence issues; Yvette Molinaro and Steve Foster plugged in details and coordinated the graphics. I wanted to use just a few photos and exhibits, preferring to keep the presentation simple and to the point. I sat down and wrote out the first several minutes and committed it to memory because I wanted to get started with something clean and dramatic. The rest I worked on from notes.

When we read a good book, it tells a compelling story. When we go to the movies, we want a story that engages us. Life is a series of interlocking stories that happen to people we know and people we don't. In my opening statement, in plain, simple terms, I tried to tell the jury a story they could understand easily. It was a story about two people and how their lives ended tragically, together, in murder.

I stood up, opened my notebook on a lectern placed in front of the jury, and began. "On a June evening, the twelfth of June 1994, Nicole Brown Simpson just finished putting her ten-year-old daughter, Sydney, and her six-year-old son, Justin, down to bed. She filled her bathtub with water. She lit some candles, began to get ready to take a bath and relax for the evening.

"The phone rang. It was nine-forty P.M. Nicole answered. It was her mother, saying that she had left her glasses at the restaurant nearby in Brentwood, where the family had all celebrated Sydney's dance recital over dinner, just an hour before. Nicole's mother asked if Nicole could please pick up her glasses from the restaurant the next day. Nicole said, 'Of course, good-bye,' and hung up.

"Nicole then called the restaurant and asked to speak to a friendly young waiter there. Nicole asked this young waiter if he would be kind enough to drop off her mother's glasses. The young man obliged and said he would drop the glasses off shortly after work, on his way to meet his friend in Marina del Rey. The young man's name was Ron Goldman. He was twenty-five years old.

"With the glasses in hand, Ron walked out of the restaurant, walked the few minutes to his apartment nearby, to change. He left the restaurant at nine-fifty P.M. After Ron changed, he got into his girlfriend's car parked in his garage and drove the short distance to Nicole Brown Simpson's home at 875 South Bundy Drive in Brentwood. Ron parked the car on the side street, walked to the front of Nicole's condominium, and turned up the walkway to the front gate. Just past the front gate were steps leading to Nicole's condominium.

"Ronald Goldman never made it past those steps. It was at that front gate that Ron spent the last few savage minutes of his life. It was there that his brutalized body was found next to Nicole Brown Simpson's slain body, with her mother's glasses lying next to him on the ground in an envelope.

"Ron Goldman's young life ended because he agreed to do a friend a favor, only to come upon her rageful killer and his. He might have run from danger, but he did not.

"Ron Goldman died, ladies and gentlemen, with his eyes open." The attorney and TV journalist Star Jones had mentioned to me that Ron's eyes were open when he died—the clouded blindness of death—and that soulful image had stayed with me. "And in the last furious moment of his life, Ron saw through those open eyes the person who killed his friend Nicole. And for that reason, he too had to die. The last person Ron Goldman saw through his open eyes was the man who took his young life away: The man who now sits in this courtroom, the defendant," I turned and pointed at him, "Orenthal James Simpson."

I am usually a pacer, inside the courtroom and out, but I was pretty still. I was nervous and a bit stiff. But from the beginning, I wanted to import a serious, if not somber, tone to the proceedings. Even though Simpson's life was not on the line, I wanted the jury to fully appreciate we were talking about the murder of two people, and we were here to decide who was responsible for killing them. It was different from money all right.

I summarized the physical evidence in plain English, avoided scientific terms, then moved on to Simpson's lack of an alibi, his power and rage, the short time it would take for such a strong man to overpower and kill two weaker people.

I outlined what we would present in our case, told them that all the evidence identified Simpson as the killer, and there was no one else in the world with an apparent motive for killing. "The house was not ransacked . . . Expensive automobiles in the garage, one being a Ferrari, they were not taken . . . No breaking and entering, no burglary." This was no rape, no stick-up, no drive-by shooting. This was a single-minded, rageful murder.

"We will reveal to you lies and deceptions in the sworn testimony of Mr. Simpson when questioned under oath for the first time," I told the jury. Baker objected, trying to break my flow and the jury's concentration. The court overruled him. "We will prove to you that when asked all the important questions about his involvement in these murders, O.J. Simpson could not, would not, and did not tell the truth."

I was playing with Simpson's own words. He had stood up in Superior Court when he'd entered his not guilty plea and told the judge, "I could not, would not, and did not commit these crimes."

"Your Honor, I'll object again. This is argument."

Lawyers have to think long and hard about whether to object to opposing counsel's opening and closing arguments in front of the jury. Juries do not like the interruptions when someone is talking to them. If your objections are overruled, they may think you don't know what you're doing, particularly in the beginning when they don't know you, or that you're trying to hide something behind a legal technicality. Baker defied convention, he didn't pay any attention to these rules, he was going to do what he wanted.

"Overruled," said Judge Fujisaki.

"And finally, ladies and gentlemen, we will show that when faced with the truth of his blood, his hair, his clothing, his gloves, his shoes, his Bronco, his rage, his motive, his words, and his actions, you will see how Mr. Simpson in this trial will resort to theories of police conspiracies, frame-ups, cover-ups, and incompetence, to try to explain away all of the incriminating evidence. And we will show you that there is not one ounce of evidence, not one ounce of proof, and not one ounce of truth to any of these things.

"We will demonstrate to you that far from these theories, born out of desperation, there is only one—"

"I object! Again, this is simply argument theory. 'Born out of desperation' is argument!" The court sustained him. Unlike closing argument, opening statements are not supposed to include the lawyer's arguments about the evidence and what it means; the lawyer is just supposed to state what the evidence will be. I was cutting it pretty close.

To preempt Baker, I wanted to deal with his conspiracy and contamination defenses. Who was supposed to be involved in this conspiracy to fabricate incriminating evidence? At 1:00 in the morning when the crime scene was discovered, I said, "Mark Fuhrman is in bed. Detective Tom Lange, who later got involved, he's in bed. Detective Phil Vannatter, he's in bed. Dennis Fung, the criminalist who got involved later on, he's in bed. His assistant, Andrea Mazzola, she's in bed. The lab technician who did a lot of labwork, Collin Yamauchi, he's in bed. His boss, Greg Matheson, he's in bed. The head of the lab, Michele Kestler, she's in bed. So you get the picture.

"Now, while all these people are in bed, the first officers on the scene see all the basic evidence. . . . When the other teams of officers came and finally the detectives arrived, everybody was pointing out the basic evidence so they wouldn't touch it or interfere with it." The so-called twins of deception, Fuhrman and Vannatter, did not get to the crime scene until after four. Fuhrman was never alone with crucial evidence. This "conspiracy" to create incriminating evidence would have to involve dozens of people, most of whom didn't even know each other, none of whom had the opportunity.

As for their motive, far from being a target, in a town full of celebrities Simpson was a police favorite. Lange and Vannatter went to Rockingham to notify Simpson of his ex-wife's death personally not because they wanted to frame him, but because he was a VIP, *they were giving him preferential treatment.*

One of the arguments the defense would make was that the LAPD waited eight hours before processing the Bundy crime scene. The insinuation was that there was something sinister about this.

I explained that the actual reason for the delay was that when the cops learned one of the victims was O.J. Simpson's ex-wife, the original detectives from West Los Angeles—Fuhrman, Phillips, and Roberts—were replaced by the big guns from downtown Los Angeles's Robbery/Homicide Division, Lange and Vannatter. That's a two-hour delay right there. When Lange and Vannatter went to give Simpson the news, they expected to return right away, the last thing they expected was to encounter another crime scene at Rockingham. The detectives called in one evidence-collection team to cover both scenes, on the theory that one team would have a handle on everything. Thus, minus a conspiracy, the eight-hour wait.

Contamination? I explained to the jury that criminalist Collin Yamauchi would testify that he didn't spill anything, that he conducted himself carefully in working with Simpson's blood sample as well as all the other samples collected at the scene. There had never been any testimony that blood actually had been spilled, nor would there be. Forensic bungling or incompetence—in the defense shorthand, "contamination"—was a theory completely unsupported by any facts.

I closed by saying we would present "a compelling case of liability against Mr. Simpson." I had spoken for about three hours.

Judge Fujisaki warned our side not to overlap in our presentations. He didn't want each attorney duplicating efforts just to pile up time with the jury. Mike Brewer's opening focused on the Bronco chase and the car's contents, plus Simpson's suicide note, to demonstrate consciousness of guilt. Kelly reviewed the domestic violence incidents between Simpson and Nicole and their "complicated, dynamic, and passionate relationship of extremes." He turned flowery, telling the jury they would go "beneath the polished veneer to a sometimes dark and violent and frightening world of uncontrollable rage." I thought that sounded a bit overwrought, but as much as I tried to orchestrate and coordinate every last detail, I could not control everything.

At the end of the first day, outside the presence of the jury, Baker once again tried to inject Fuhrman deeply into the case. He told the judge I had told the jury three things "that had come from Mark Fuhrman's lips": that Fuhrman was asleep, that he alone found the glove at Rockingham, and that he had interrogated Kato Kaelin. "I think he has opened the door to the issue, and I think I ought to be able to do it in my opening."

No chance. I had been very careful to confine my remarks about Fuhrman's actions to evidence that would be elicited from other witnesses. "For example," I told the judge, "Mark Fuhrman was asleep. He was called by Officer Ron Phillips, and Phillips will so testify."

"Okay," said the judge. "Order remains."

The next day, Baker opened.

"As you know by now," he said, smiling to the jury, "my name is Bob Baker." He called himself Bob, never Robert. He was already their friend. Baker was in full trial mode, and he was good. He spoke with confidence in a voice that rose and fell with impressive range, far from a monotone. Rather than use the lectern, he leaned casually against the empty witness stand and spoke to the jury as if he were talking to a neighbor over a back fence. For all his feistiness, he appeared extremely likable, and in a courtroom likability generally translates into a winning persona with a jury. No doubt about it, Baker was very good.

"It's my privilege, and indeed an honor, to represent Orenthal James Simpson." Medvene had nailed it before the mock jury. This rhetorical flourish was the exact right thing to show he believed in his client as he would a lord under siege.

It didn't take thirty seconds of Simpson's personal background before he was into football. "At San Francisco Junior College, O.J. Simpson *smashed*"—he said the word with emphasis—"every junior college record in the book known for running backs."

I was startled. Why was he saying any of this? "And he then left after two years at San Francisco Junior College and went to USC. That was in 1967. And in 1967, he immediately started as a tailback for the University of Southern California and led that team to the national championships." You've got to be kidding me. This is relevant? "He also in that year ran the four-by-one-hundred relay, and along with his teammates at USC, set a world record." That's it! Don't say anymore! Get this guy out of the courtroom and sanction the Goldmans for suing him.

"He continued at USC. In 1968—well, let me go back just a second." This was a Baker technique, moving around, then doubling back to pick up pieces. Baker had a general command of his material, but precise details weren't his specialty, he made many little mistakes in areas like dates and times.

"Nineteen sixty-seven, first semester, he goes home to San Francisco and marries Marguerite, his high-school sweetheart. And there are two children born of that union. There's Arnelle, who was born on December 4, 1968." We were waiting for this because we had heard it in the criminal trial. I sat at the counsel's table, trying not to be impolite, but I shifted in my seat toward Tom Lambert and said, "Here comes the Heisman Trophy." "That happened to be the day that O.J. Simpson was named and received the Heisman Trophy for being the most outstanding football player in the United States in 1968."

Baker replayed Simpson's pro football career: three-time MVP, seven-time All-Pro, first player to rush for over two thousand yards in one season. Mind you, we don't have a lot of people interested in sports on the jury. "At the time O.J. Simpson retired from football, ladies and gentlemen, he was a sports hero. He was a celebrity; he was a personality. Make no mistake about it.

". . . O.J. Simpson went to the podium on the day of the ceremony that he retired and he said, 'Fame is a vapor, popularity is an accident, money takes wings. Only one thing, only one thing endures, and that is character.'" I'm sure Simpson wrote that himself. "And he walked away. He never carried a football again. . . .

"He never spit in the face of an umpire. He never, ever told a fan he didn't have time for an autograph. . . . And nobody, nobody had a bad word about O.J. Simpson because he treated everybody as a human being."

This was the last tack I'd thought Baker would have taken. We were involved in the equivalent of a murder trial, Simpson's life would be ruined if he lost, there was overwhelming, highly incriminating evidence against him, and I'd thought Baker would start with a direct assault on that evidence, something more sharply on point.

I looked at the jury. Were they buying this? Did Baker believe they were foolish enough to think that because Simpson was a great football player, he didn't commit murder? Because he was among the greatest of them all in the most violent of American sports, he was not capable of violence?

The jury was stone-faced. Some were looking down. *Mr. Baker, could you please get to the facts of the case?*

"I want to go back for just a moment. . . .

"After O.J. Simpson had separated from his first wife, Marguerite, he and Nicole became an item."

False! He dated Nicole while he was with Marguerite, cheating on her.

Baker tried to stake out more territory for Simpson than his client had actually been willing to admit in deposition. He said Simpson probably bled on the driveway at Rockingham. He said, "I'm not here to suggest to you that Mr. Simpson never touched her [New Year's Eve 1989]. I'm not here to suggest to you that she didn't touch Mr. Simpson that night. That was a physical encounter that O.J. Simpson was appalled about. . . . He takes full responsibility now; he took full responsibility then." As early as opening statements, Baker was trying to cover for his client.

Then he started to trash Nicole. "Simpson became, and was Nicole's confidant. . . . She had many boyfriends, and men loved her. She was gor-

geous, and they loved to be with her. And she was with a lot of them."
Here was the "Trash Nicole Defense" in full roar. Nicole the Tramp. "And
when she had boyfriend problems, she went to O.J. Simpson." Saint O.J.

As if he were sharing a secret with the jury, he lowered his voice so
they almost had to lean forward to hear him. "Let me tell you how much
of a confidant O.J. Simpson was to Nicole.

"In the summer of 1992, she became pregnant by one of her
boyfriends. And she turned to O.J. Simpson for moral support. She told
two people in the world; she did not tell her mother, she did not tell her
sisters. She told her best friend, Cora Fischman, and she told O.J.
Simpson. And then she decided to terminate what was apparently an
unwanted pregnancy. That was how deep the relationship was in terms of
being a confidant."

Baker was trying to show that Simpson was not insanely jealous, that
in fact he could talk to his ex-wife freely about her being impregnated by
other men. He hadn't killed her when he saw her giving oral sex to Keith
Zlomsowitch in her living room—"Lights on, draperies open, kids in the
house"—had he?

"Now this man, who is supposedly a raging, violent human being,
didn't . . . like the fact that Nicole was having parties, visiting people . . .
who were prostitutes, inviting drug users into his house"—he corrected
himself—"into her house with his children there." Baker added, "And
when you hear the tapes, you'll hear the name Heidi Fleiss, you'll hear
'prostitute,' you'll hear 'drugs.'" And still, Simpson had had the self-
control not to murder her.

Artfully worded—the jury would hear all kinds of words on those
tapes having nothing to do with the case—but dead wrong. Nicole never
consorted with Heidi Fleiss girls, and as for Simpson complaining about
her seeing drug users, that was low irony.

"Her mood swings were enormous. Incredible. One day she was
warm and loving to him, the next she was out of control . . . She was
drinking excessively when O.J. wasn't around. And in fact, the evidence
will show when, well . . ." he paused slyly. "Wait till I get there."

The whole approach was shameful. Baker was trashing this poor
dead woman without any regard for the effect it would have on her children—Simpson's children—whose friends could hear about it on the
news and torture them in school, or who would grow up and read these

transcripts or hear these stories of all the men Nicole had sex with and all her abortions. And there was Simpson, sitting at his table, with a face that read, *Tell them, Bob. It was her fault, the bitch, she deserved it.*

Baker was freewheeling, talking about the case in no ordered or logical sequence. Perhaps that was his style. He was obviously a very powerful courtroom personality, but as he jumped from topic to topic I found him hard to follow. So, I would expect, did the jury.

He floated the theories of police conspiracy and malfeasance. He said the crime scene was not rapidly enough or properly processed, leading to evidence contamination, which would be detailed by Dr. Henry Lee. He told the jury Simpson had agreed to take a polygraph test, which the prosecutors refused. That stunned me. I was about to object, but then thought better. That admission opened to us an entire topic of discussion—the lie detector test that Simpson had failed miserably—which we would otherwise have been prohibited from pursuing.

Baker said Nicole was trying to win Simpson back. "She was the pursuer." This was so important to Simpson's narcissistic ego. Baker read the jury a letter Nicole "hand-delivered" to Simpson in March 1993 in an attempt to reinvolve him in their relationship. It was a pathetic letter, filled with self-loathing—"I never stopped loving you, I stopped liking myself," she had told him—but it served Simpson's purposes. "She was pursuing O.J. Simpson," Baker declaimed. "She sent tapes of family movies. She would come over to his house day and night. She sent cookies to his house."

It was music to Simpson's ears, even if it was his own hired troubadour doing the crooning; women want O.J., *he* never begged, *they* pursued *him* around the world. In the first fifteen minutes of Baker's opening statement he had established what a great athlete Simpson was, what a great person he was, and just how big a tramp the dead mother of his children had been.

But that letter was written more than a year before her death, and it resulted in their getting back together. Even then, according to Simpson, it was he who called the shots. "O.J. agreed to try to reconcile, but he put some conditions on the reconciliation."

Baker was leading the jury to believe the letter reflected the state of affairs just before and leading up to her death. Again, he was trying to portray Simpson not as a jealous, obsessive controller in a smoldering rage, vengeful and threatening at the time of her death, but as a calm, cautious, and caring man being pursued by his troubled ex-wife, just trying to help her out of her boyfriend difficulties and her abortions.

In the letter, Baker said, she revealed "basically what her state of mind was." Lawyers don't usually leave that kind of opening; Baker may not have realized or meant to do so, but as far as I was concerned, he had opened the door for us to present evidence of what Nicole's *true* state of mind was at the time of her death. This would help immeasurably to introduce important hearsay evidence, such as Nicole's diary entries and her statements to friends.

Who ended their relationship in May 1994 after their trip to Cabo San Lucas? "It wasn't she who broke it off," said Baker, "it was O.J."

A major theme of the Simpson defense held that Nicole was no longer important in his life. Why would he kill her, the theory went, when he was through with her? He had moved on. He had Paula. "[Nicole] was not being pursued at all by O.J. Simpson at the time," Baker asserted. Johnnie Cochran had assured the criminal trial jury that Simpson and Paula were a loving couple at the time of the killings.

In her deposition, Paula said she had called Simpson at seven A.M. June 12 and broken things off. There was no way to prove that statement, so according to Baker, "He doesn't know that Paula had called his cell phone answering service, and he never picked it up when she says that she was breaking up with him—which she did not do. . . . O.J. never picked up this call that they say starts him smoldering."

Baker mocked the LAPD's efforts to find the murder weapon and the killer's bloody clothes. "They enlisted the Boy Scouts. . . . They went in the sewers, ladies and gentlemen. They enlisted the Chicago Police Department . . . and, of course, they found nothing. They found nothing at all."

Ultimately, he got to the Bruno Magli shoes. Baker admitted that the killer wore size 12 Bruno Magli shoes. "Mr. Simpson didn't produce any Bruno Magli size 12 shoes . . . because he doesn't have any and never had any."

The Harry Scull photo? Baker admitted it depicted the Bruno Magli murder shoes. "It's not given to any police department, it's not given to any prosecutorial agency, it's not even given to Mr. Petrocelli. It's given to the *National Enquirer*—for money. . . .

"This photograph is a phony. It isn't real. It was doctored!"

More than anything else he said, these few strong words buried Simpson. Baker was staking Simpson's entire case on proving the photo was a fraud. He left no room to wiggle. If Baker failed on this one issue, by his own reasoning and his own words, his client, O.J. Simpson, was a killer.

In closing, Baker encouraged the jury to deny science ("You can't trust the blood evidence"). Then he leaned on his one major asset: O.J. Simpson. "Mr. Simpson will take the stand and he will be here as long as Mr. Petrocelli wants to examine him. And if you believe Mr. Simpson, *if you believe O.J. Simpson*"—he was making a direct appeal to celebrity and image; I thought that was fine, since I intended on separating the man from the myth—"you must find him not responsible."

I could live with that equation. The other side of it was, "If you don't believe him, he's a murderer."

TWENTY-TWO

The Case-in-Chief

We decided to start our case-in-chief with the chain of events leading to Ron's and Nicole's murders. I wanted the jury to have a sense of the victims' last hours. Our first witness was Karen Crawford, the Mezzaluna manager who fielded Nicole's call, probably the second-to-last person other than Simpson to talk to her. Next came Stewart Tanner, who had been tending bar that night and had plans to hook up with Ron later in the evening down in Marina del Rey.

From there we went straight to Robert Heidstra, a wild card who had been called in the criminal case by Johnnie Cochran and had been quite antagonistic to Chris Darden. Heidstra was walking his dog near Bundy at about 10:30 or 10:35 in the evening when he heard what he recognized to be Nicole's large Akita "barking like crazy, like he was confused and panicky." Baker moved to strike, "No foundation."

"You want to lay a little dog foundation?" the judge asked. The courtroom broke up in laughter, but I don't think Fujisaki was joking. "The man's had a dog for twenty-six years. He can distinguish it," he ruled.

To avoid risking a dogfight, Heidstra cut through a nearby alleyway. About two minutes later he heard "a clear, young" male voice say, "Hey, hey, hey!" A deeper male voice followed, "very fast, sounded like an argument." Heidstra was probably an earwitness to the murders. "It didn't last no more than fifteen seconds, I would say. Then I heard a gate slamming."

He continued walking his dog and a few minutes later saw "a white kind of Jeep with tinted glass" stop under the streetlight on the right side of Dorothy Street "for one moment" and then speed away south on Bundy, away from the murder scene. Reconstructing his movements and adding up the time each took, rather than simply accepting his estimates, I put the time at between 10:35 and 10:40. Baker used Heidstra's criminal trial testimony ("It must have been in that time exactly when I came to the alley. Exactly. Around that time.") in an attempt to move him closer to 10:45, which would make the timing tighter. Heidstra was on and off the stand before lunch.

Louis Karpf, who lived next door to Nicole, went outside to his mailbox and saw her Akita roaming the street, "barking profusely" enough to frighten him, between 10:45 and 10:50 at the latest. He heard no struggle going on at that time. His original police statement had put the time at between 10:50 and 11:00, but when neighbors had first been interviewed neither they nor the police had an appreciation for the precise timing that would be necessary to resolve this case, and the estimates had been fairly broad.

Stephen Schwab had been surprised to see a dog on the street without an owner. It was about 10:55 P.M. He'd patted its head and noticed it was wearing a collar. When he'd looked down he noticed there was blood on its back legs and paws. There was a combination of blood and mud on its chest. "It was red and shiny." He took the dog to his neighbor, Sukru Boztepe. The dog took Boztepe to the dead bodies.

Mr. Boztepe ran to a neighbor and asked them to dial 911. It was shortly after midnight.

We had established the timeline. Ron and Nicole were dead by around 10:40. We were essentially accepting the criminal defense's timeline because that was the time we thought the murders actually occurred.

In the criminal trial, the timeline witnesses took fifteen hours on the stand. Heidstra alone was up there for five. Our six witnesses were on and off by 2:15 in the afternoon on the first day of testimony. We had planned to follow with our police witnesses, but this was Friday and we had not scheduled them to come to court until after the weekend. I thought we had done a good day's work, but when I asked to resume on Monday, Judge Fujisaki got cranky. "Ladies and gentlemen, that's all the witnesses that they have for today. I have asked them to tighten up the witness scheduling so that we may have full days, so hopefully we'll be able to utilize our time a little more efficiently." Fujisaki, bless him, cut nobody any slack.

On Monday we went right to work with the police. We debated long and hard about this part of the case. On the one hand, we needed the police to testify about their discovery of the victims' bodies and the evidence the killer left behind at the scene of the murders. They also needed to testify about the evidence found at Simpson's Rockingham estate and in his car. On the other hand, putting these witnesses on in the second day of trial was walking right into the teeth of the defense's strategy. Their goal was to try the case of the Los Angeles Police Department and keep the attention off their client. The last thing we wanted was to serve up a full menu of police witnesses and give the defense weeks of counterattacks in our case-in-chief. We decided we would use a minimum of individuals to lay out the police evidence, and would keep it very tight. There would be no duplication, no two cops telling the same story, no opportunity for Baker to pit one against another. In addition to laying out the physical evidence, we would spend a little time preempting the defense's planting and conspiracy case. But we would keep the witnesses brief, and object persistently to the defense attempts to cross-examine our witnesses outside the scope of their direct testimony. We were armed with the judge's rulings on our motions *in limine,* and these would help to block the defense's cross-examination and limit their ability to insert their case into ours.

We started with Officer Robert Riske, the blond patrolman who, with his partner, Miguel Terrazas, was the first to arrive on the scene, shortly after midnight, June 13. It was very important that we show the jury that all the evidence was found before Detective Fuhrman arrived, thereby limiting the damage the defense could inflict.

In the criminal trial the prosecution went overboard establishing the professional background and knowledgeability of their police witnesses, sounding defensive and giving Simpson's lawyers many openings for attack. We just established that Riske was a cop. That was plenty good enough.

With John Kelly doing the direct questioning, Riske laid out the basic crime scene evidence, including the one glove that was found, the hat, the pager, the various items lying next to the bodies, the blood droplets along the alley going away from the two victims and toward the back of the house, the blood in the back driveway, the blood Riske and Terrazas both observed on the back gate. Officer Riske described his actions in securing the crime scene and calling the LAPD for investigators. Riske's direct was done in about an hour.

The cross-examination by Bob Blasier ran according to their game plan. He asked whether Riske had received any training in crime scene processing. What's the point? Riske didn't process the crime scene, he only secured it. Had Riske received any training in collecting evidence for DNA training, Blasier asked, suggesting that this officer, who did nothing but observe the evidence, might have tainted it. "Did you have any training at all in the area of how evidence might be contaminated with other biological fluids?"

Finally Kelly objected. "Relevance."

The court: "Sustained."

Period. End of story. Move on. In the criminal trial, that would have been a half hour right there. The prosecutors would have objected and Ito would have overruled them, and that was how the defense made mincemeat out of so many of the police witnesses. Unlimited cross-examination on arcane and irrelevant and confusing issues. Not in Judge Fujisaki's courtroom.

"Was there ever a canine unit called out to determine whether a path could be found of the perpetrator or perpetrators leaving?"

"Objection, Your Honor. Relevance."

"Sustained."

They had no witness who saw a perpetrator walking away at that time, this was idle speculation. Smoke. So the judge blew it away. Officer Riske's crime scene observations were what was relevant, not actions he might have taken but didn't. Thanks to Fujisaki, we avoided another half hour following police dogs down some blind trail.

"When you went in the house, had you conducted any kind of inspection for possible trace evidence in the house?"

"Objection. Relevance."

"Sustained."

Riske was a patrol officer, inspecting for trace evidence was not his job. If he had, he'd have been pilloried. "You're a patrol officer, you're supposed to be securing the premises. What else was going on while you were playing Sherlock Holmes?" There was no winning. This was straight out of the defense play book from the criminal trial, only this was a new game.

Judge Ito was weak. No guts. He appeared very worried about how he would be perceived by the public, and he didn't want to get reversed. If he'd been judging our trial, we might still be going at it. Judge Fujisaki was impressing me more by the minute.

True to form, Blasier ran the Fuhrman game. "Give me your best estimate of when Detective Fuhrman arrived. . . . Where did Detective Fuhrman go first? . . . When you got to the alley, what did Detective Fuhrman do? . . . When you went to the rear gate, you went with Detective Fuhrman? . . . Did you show Detective Fuhrman upstairs?" The answers, of course, were irrelevant. He was just using the witness as a prop to shout *Fuhrman, Fuhrman, Fuhrman!*

Officer Terrazas followed. He had been the first to see the blood on the back gate, at 12:15 A.M., while Fuhrman was sleeping. The criminal defense had argued that because no close-up pictures of the gate had been taken that day and criminalist Dennis Fung had not taken that blood until three weeks later, that there *was* no blood on the back gate, that it had been planted after the fact by anti-Simpson conspirators.

Ed Medvene quickly took Terrazas through his investigation of the crime scene, including the blood on the back gate. Terrazas explained that he specifically noted these blood spots in his written report. Unfortunately, when the defense asked him to circle those spots on a grainy, blown-up long-shot photo of the gate, he circled a rust spot as well as the blood.

Baker got excited. *Ahhh, the guy is lying, he circled rust, there was no blood on the back gate.* I didn't think it was a big deal; Terrazas had made a mistake, it happens.

I was wrong. After the officer left the stand the press surrounded me in full cry, as if we'd had a major fiasco. "What are you going to do? He circled the wrong blood. He messed that point up. He screwed up! You are in trouble now!"

I thought I knew the media by this time, but apparently I didn't. They were so sensitive to even the most arcane facts, they were such aficionados, such *trial junkies,* that even the littlest mistake was magnified into a verdict-threatening blunder. I thought, Boy, these people are intense. One little mishap in otherwise flawless testimony and it overshadows everything. We better not make any mistakes, ever.

Plus, some of these reporters had become my friends, and I got pretty defensive. "So what? He made a mistake. What am I supposed to say, 'Oh, he screwed up, Simpson is innocent'?" They laughed at me. "I love talking to you," one reporter told me. "All I have to say is one thing and you go off for a half hour." We were only three days into the case-in-chief and my hide was raw. I knew I'd better toughen up if I was going to last.

The first several police officers were presented mostly to introduce the basic evidence and establish the facts that there was blood on the back gate and that everyone saw only one glove at Bundy. We hammered those points home repeatedly. It was a dance; we produced evidence and the defense portrayed us as being in bed with the LAPD.

Ed then called Police Officer Donald Thompson to the stand. Thompson, for some reason, had not been called by the prosecution at the criminal trial. A powerful six-foot-six African American, in uniform he cut an imposing figure in the courtroom. He had been sent first to Bundy and then to the Rockingham crime scene before Simpson arrived home. With a pointer, Officer Thompson pointed out to the jury the drops of blood he had observed in the street outside the Bronco and on the driveway inside Simpson's compound. It would have been hard to plant blood evidence while the blood was still in Simpson's arm in a hotel room in Chicago.

While we hoped the jury would not think LAPD officers would lie, we certainly hoped they would not think this black LAPD officer would lie. I sat and thought, Here is a terrific, articulate witness carrying himself with great bearing and honesty, showing what is so obviously true: after returning from committing two murders, O.J. Simpson dripped blood all over Rockingham. Doesn't this just debunk in one fell swoop the whole notion of a racial conspiracy. Thompson was magnificent.

Ed had prepared an extensive chronology of each officer who arrived on the scene, when they'd arrived, what they had done. He spoke to virtually all of them, and we then discussed and selected those best suited to testify. After Thompson, Ed called Detective Ronald Phillips.

Phillips was our Fuhrman surrogate. As head of the West Los Angeles Homicide Unit, he was Fuhrman's superior. He could vouch for the information Fuhrman had provided. Solid and unassailable, he was our pre-emptive answer to the defense strategy of *Fuhrman, Fuhrman, Fuhrman.*

In the criminal trial, Lee Bailey had tried to establish that Fuhrman had been alone at Bundy for some period of time during which he saw and grabbed the bloody glove that every other police investigator comb-ing the crime scene for evidence had somehow overlooked. Bailey's theory was that, after getting knocked off the case in favor of higher-ups, Fuhrman invited himself over to Rockingham to plant that glove, frame Simpson and thus take down a black man and become a star. This twisted theory caught the public's imagination and remained a sinister shadow over Fuhrman and the LAPD up to and during our trial. It continues to be a pervasive accusation, even to this day.

The theory is absolutely preposterous, and I prepared a long list of points demonstrating exactly why. Just for starters:

- No one *ever* saw a second glove at Bundy. Cops were crawling all over this crime scene *for two full hours* before Fuhrman arrived. They found one glove only, not two. There was no second glove at Bundy to plant at Rockingham.

- For many hours after the discovery of the bodies, police were can-vasing the Bundy neighborhood, knocking on doors, asking what people had seen or heard. How did Fuhrman know what this would reveal? What if someone had said, "I saw four short men with ski masks come tearing out of the condo and go running south on Bundy at 10:45"? Or, "It was three white guys. One had red hair, one was blond, the third was six-foot-eight and had rings in his nose. Their car was blocking my driveway and I got the license plate"? Where's his frame job then? How did Fuhrman know an eyewitness would not walk right up to the police and say, "I saw the murders"? If he'd planted the glove at Rockingham and they'd caught a different killer, Fuhrman would go to jail, conceiv-ably for life.

- The crime scene was swimming in blood. How did Fuhrman know whose blood that was? The real killer could have dropped gallons all over the garden. It could have been anyone's blood. The killer would have been positively identified by this blood, clearing Simpson and leaving Fuhrman exposed.

- What if the glove Fuhrman supposedly planted at Rockingham was covered with someone's blood other than Simpson's? To frame Simpson, you need Simpson's blood *at* Simpson's home. How could Fuhrman possibly know the blood on the glove was Simpson's?

- What if Simpson had an air-tight alibi? Fuhrman was sleeping when the cops caught the call. How did he know Simpson wasn't on an airplane or at a restaurant or making a television appearance at the time of the murders?

There are no answers to these and many, many more questions, except to say that this theory of the planted glove is absurd and discredited. It didn't happen. The glove was found at Rockingham for one reason: O.J. Simpson dropped it there falling against a wall in the dark when returning from killing Ron and Nicole.

As well as the theory being absurd, Detective Phillips explained that Fuhrman was not out of his sight the entire time they were at Bundy. Ed took him through the events leading from the Bundy crime scene to going over the wall at Rockingham. "[The commander] wanted to make sure that I notified Mr. Simpson in person . . . [He] did not want the news media to make that notification or have him find out in any other way." (From the start, O.J. Simpson was getting VIP treatment.) Phillips recalled events from waking up Arnelle and Kato to seeing the blood drops and the bloody glove.

We allowed the jury to hear this chain of events for the first time under friendly circumstances rather than in the hostile environment of cross-examination. Although we tried very hard not to involve ourselves in the story of the police investigation, we had to explain why the officers went to Simpson's home and what they found there. Baker had said in his opening statement that the police had gone to Rockingham to frame Simpson, and we had to respond to it sooner or later.

Phillips had been the man who notified Simpson by phone in Chicago of Nicole's death. He had made this death notification several hundred times over his thirty years on the force. "There is initial shock when I tell them," he testified, "then they always want to ask questions about how, why, when, where, am I sure, how do I know."

"Were any of these questions asked by Mr. Simpson?" Ed asked.

"No."

On cross-examination, Leonard tried to impeach Phillips by contrasting his testimony with his original notes and typewritten report. Police are notoriously poor note takers, preferring quick terseness to detail so as to shorten the writing process and leave little room for contradiction. Unfortunately, when it comes to trial and they flesh out their stories with facts they didn't originally enter, they invariably get hammered with the defense question: "Why didn't you write that in your report? Are you making it up now?"

Baker had warned from day one of jury selection, "You understand that this is not a place for the faint of heart. You are not going to be offended by tough questioning of police officers, are you? You understand it's not dinner talk?"

Detective Tom Lange was our next witness. He had recently retired from the force and was working for a private investigation firm. The defense had put Vannatter and him under siege in the criminal trial and he felt the LAPD had not backed them up. One day when Ed and I were preparing him to testify, I'd said, "Tom, aren't you going to miss being one of the top detectives in the city of Los Angeles? Aren't you going to miss all the big cases, miss your work?"

"Of course I am," he told me, "but I had no choice. They put a bullet in my back and Phil's." It was heartbreaking to see two guys who had put so much of their lives into their job go out on such bitter terms.

We limited Lange to three basic topics: the Bundy crime scene evidence (the only evidence we discussed was that which was collected and upon which we were relying. By excluding all other items, we were trying to prevent or limit the defense from questioning him about them), the decision to go to Rockingham to give personal death notification to Simpson, and Simpson's flight from arrest.

Under Ed's questioning, Lange explained the positioning of the bloody footprints and the Bundy blood trail. He confirmed the blood on the back gate. To correct Terrazas' error in circling the wrong blood spot,

Lange explained that the June 13 photograph of the walkway leading to the gate that Terrazas used was a general orientation photo and had not been intended to document the blood.

Baker's aggressive cross started by snidely pointing out that the Goldmans had attended both Lange's and Vannatter's retirement parties (since the murders, both men had retired from the LAPD). He tried to establish a sinister pro-plaintiff bias by getting Lange to admit he had spent nearly twenty hours with us in preparation for his deposition and trial testimony. Sure Lange cooperated, he felt bad that a guilty double murderer was walking free on his watch.

Baker belittled Lange's reasons for initially going to Rockingham, suggesting it was ridiculous to try "to establish some rapport" with Simpson, as Baker put it, at such a traumatic and tragic time. He tried to impeach Lange's statements that he was not aware of Simpson's prior domestic violence incidents when he went to Rockingham, but on redirect we established that he found out about them only later. (Fuhrman had been summoned to Rockingham once before in 1984, when Simpson took a baseball bat to Nicole's car. Baker was trying to suggest that this information was used to define Simpson as the prime suspect.)

Baker got Lange to admit that he had created a possibility of contamination by dispatching Officer Thompson to put a blanket from inside the house over Nicole's body. They were trying to lay the groundwork to argue that Simpson's hair and fibers came from previous contact with that blanket. He would not allow Lange to state his reasons for doing so. On redirect we brought out that he had asked for the blanket (Thompson found it folded clean in a linen closet) to prevent the media, with its sophisticated long-range equipment, from taking pictures which would have had the effect of compromising the investigation. Lange explained that key information is often withheld from the media in order to ferret out whether leads are genuine or fake. Lange also said he wanted to prevent the invasion of the dead woman's dignity and privacy.

Baker was very hostile to Lange, suggesting by the tone and tenor of his questions that the detective was dishonest. Unfortunately for Baker, Lange wasn't giving him the answers he wanted and came back at him pretty aggressively as well. "I'm trying to give you an honest, straightforward answer that's to the best of my ability," Lange said.

"Can you answer my question and not give us what you want? Can you just answer my question?"

The best Baker could do was point out some inconsequential errors here and there and second-guess the detectives for failing to retrieve the blanket, or not getting the criminalists and coroner to the scene quickly enough, or not picking up certain individual pieces of potential evidence at the scene. He would have to make the case that a bunch of small errors equaled one totally corrupt and incompetent investigation.

Baker's style was to ask long, argumentative, accusatory, leading questions. When the witness answered, "No, that's not true," he would go on to the next. We had to point out to the jury that the harsh tone, snide manner, and loaded content of Baker's questions were not evidence. Only witnesses' answers are evidence, and Baker rarely got the answers he was trying to get.

Lange's performance at the criminal trial had been criticized for being too soft. This time the press said Lange, in his new feisty made-over mode, went too far the other way. When asked yes-or-no questions with obvious implications, he tried to offer his own interpretations so as not to allow the jury to be misled. Baker kept insisting that he answer yes or no, and for the most part the court backed Baker up. I thought, I hope he does the same with Simpson. Judge Fujisaki was quite insistent on making witnesses answer lawyers' questions, I just hoped he would not bow to the pressure of celebrity and make an exception for O.J. As skilled as Simpson was at answering his own questions rather than mine, that could lead to a long and difficult fight.

When Baker was finished with Lange the defense probably thought they had done pretty well with him. But if you put aside Baker's performance, they got nothing helpful to their case. Baker was in fine form but they got nothing.

Lange was followed to the stand by Phil Vannatter, who had retired to a farm in Indiana earlier in the year. As we were getting ready for the examination, Baker passed by and said, "It's gonna be a bloodbath."

Vannatter was one of Johnnie Cochran's twins of deception who was used to decimate the criminal case. He was the guy who, with his meathook hands, was supposed to have gone on a blood-sprinkling spree all over Rockingham and Simpson's Bronco. It was a disgrace for Judge Ito, even while upholding the legitimacy of the LAPD's search warrant, to throw the defense a bone and call Vannatter's conduct in obtaining it "reckless." That made the detective a sitting duck for the wildest and most vicious accusations. He'd been hung out to dry. Our research showed that many people questioned his honesty and still wondered whether he had planted blood evidence.

What were we to do with him? If we didn't use him at all, we would be admitting to the jury that his testimony concerned us. Baker would not fail to ask in his closing argument, "Where's Vannatter?" and paint the omission in the worst possible light. If he did testify, we ran right into his credibility issue. John Kelly was assigned to question Vannatter, and I met with John and Paul Callan to finalize the gameplan. The initial thought was to severely limit Vannatter's testimony; have him testify mainly about drawing Simpson's blood and transporting it to the criminalists who were still working at Simpson's house. Callan made the good point that it would look very bad to the jury if we took this important witness who had played an integral role in the investigation, and put him on as if he were just a messenger. The flip side of that argument, however, was that the more we limited his testimony, the less the defense would be able to cross-examine him on all the dicey areas in which they ate him up in the criminal trial.

We talked it out. Ultimately we decided to limit our exposure. "Very narrow. Just the blood." The lead detective in the case was reduced to testifying as a chain-of-custody witness.

Vannatter testified he saw Simpson give a blood sample to police nurse Thano Peratis at around two-thirty on the afternoon of June 13. The blood was drawn into a syringe, and the syringe was then injected into a purple-top container. The top was never removed. Vannatter then saw the vial put into an "Analyzed Evidence" envelope, which he took upstairs to his office. He stayed in his office until he left for Rockingham at about 4:00 P.M., except when he went to get a sandwich and a cup of coffee. At no time did he open the envelope. At no time did he put the envelope in his pocket. He drove to Rockingham and at about 5:15 delivered the envelope containing the vial that held Simpson's blood to Dennis Fung. That's it.

While testifying, Vannatter—hardly the picture of a deceiving devil—was calm and sincere, he came across as easy-going and made a good impression. He had spent days on the stand in the criminal trial; we had him on and off in fifteen minutes.

Baker was typically hostile in his cross-examination but was unable to go beyond the scope of these facts. "You looked at Mr. Simpson's fingers . . . and his hands . . . didn't you?" he asked.

"I looked at his hands, yes," Vannatter answered.

"And he had one cut that was on the knuckle or the middle joint of his large finger, long finger on his left hand. Isn't that true?"

Kelly: "Objection. Beyond the scope."

The court: "Sustained. . . . I'm just interested in taking of blood. That's all that was examined of this witness. You want to use him for some other witness, call him as your witness at your time."

Significantly, at no time did Baker ask Vannatter, "Did you take that blood vial, leave Parker Center, and go to Bundy and put blood on the back gate?" "Did you drip blood anywhere at Rockingham?" "Did you drop blood anywhere at Bundy?" Those questions were available to him, but he never asked. It was one thing to imply conspiracy, but they had no evidence to back it up and they knew it.

Baker got frustrated. Out of the presence of the jury he complained, "They're making this a compartmentalized case instead of having this lawsuit tried." I just shook my head. What a ridiculous point. The only thing wrong with our strategy, as far as Baker was concerned, was that it was working.

TWENTY-THREE

The "Gag-Free Zone"

Judge Fujisaki was getting hammered by the pundits on television. The print media tended to be a bit more balanced in their coverage, but the TV people jumped on the pro-plaintiff angle, and they were having a field day criticizing the judge's rulings.

It started as far back as jury selection, when they charged him with booting the blacks and "stacking it" with whites. The dismissal of prospective black jurors couldn't be attributed to the fact that those particular jurors exhibited bias or could not honestly and fairly set aside their beliefs, it couldn't be that the plaintiffs' lawyers were making good and proper arguments or that the judge was making his decisions based on the law and the merit of each side's position. No, it was the judge out to get Simpson. Now, by not allowing Baker and his boys to question our witnesses outside the scope of their examination, Judge Fujisaki was supposedly taking the defense away from the defense.

Who were these pundits? Most seemed to be professional defense lawyers, but whoever they were, they pretty much all shared one common characteristic: They knew very little about our case. They didn't know the evidence, they didn't know the issues, they didn't understand the arguments. They'd been fed wire service clippings concerning the day's events, placed in front of a camera, and asked to contribute to an intelligent discussion. Everyone was looking for an angle, and the angle was that the judge was tilting the playing field to even out the scales. Somehow the conspiracy had reached into the judicial chambers. *Okay, Simpson won one, he's not going to win this one.*

I heard Johnnie Cochran, who of all people should know better, say on national television, "We call this case 'O.J. Lite' because the judge is leaving out all the evidence."

What an irresponsible, uninformed comment. That just burned me. I'm a great one for talking back to the TV screen, I do it all the time. I said out loud, "The judge is excluding irrelevant and prejudicial evidence, Mr. Cochran. Evidence that should have been excluded from your case!"

Assistant District Attorney Bill Hodgman had warned me not to follow the coverage or watch it on TV. "Just ignore it," he had advised. "It will frustrate the hell out of you." It was good advice, but it was difficult to live up to. I could not resist reading the *Los Angeles Times* in the morning, and I was not particularly happy with their coverage. In an effort to balance the reporting of the day's events, they and most news outlets would create a distorted impression.

For example, on a day in which we scored 95 percent of the points, the media would give plaintiffs and defense equal time. We would present devastating and incontrovertible testimony, and we would hear, "Baker grilled the witness on why the police went to Rockingham with four detectives. He further asked whether there were, in fact, eight unidentifiable fingerprints at the crime scene, indicating the presence of another killer." Readers were told about his derisive, sneering cross-examination— but what about the answers? He got no good answers. Evidence counts, not posturing. I know the media did not want to be accused of favoring one side over another, but if you're calling a ballgame and the visiting team is ahead 16–3, no responsible broadcaster reports it as an even game.

Most of the reporters believed Simpson was guilty, and many of them struggled over how to report the trial properly. To counter this bias and guard against their feelings interfering with their work, I felt reporters tended to compensate by leaning too far toward the defense. I would grouse about it to them.

"Look, just report what happened," I'd say. "If it was a 100 percent day, report it as a 100 percent day."

"Well, you know the way editors are," the reporters would tell me, "they like the articles to say something about the plaintiff and something about the defense."

"Yeah, but if you devote equal space it looks like the trial is going 50-50, and it's not!" They would just end up laughing at me.

Our team would come back to the DoubleTree after court and watch the 5:00 TV coverage. I, of course, would start yelling at it. "Wrong! You are full of shit! The testimony was exactly the opposite!" The TV broadcast channels all did a two- or three-minute segment and didn't have enough time to do too much harm. I tried not to tune in to shows that regularly covered the case, such as *Larry King Live* or *Burden of Proof*, for fear I'd get even more frustrated. Thankfully, the DoubleTree did not get CNBC and its *Rivera Live* and *Charles Grodin*, or MSNBC, Fox Cable News, and all the other cable stations covering the trial. Occasionally, when I got home and got into bed with the next day's reading material, I couldn't resist catching a few minutes of *Geraldo* or Larry King reruns. When I did, I generally regretted it. Not that the shows were bad. It's just that I was working obsessively hard to maintain control of the case in the courtroom, and I couldn't bear to watch and listen helplessly while others talked, theorized, dissected, and digested my case to pieces.

The jury was not sequestered, and although they had been instructed not to read the newspapers, you never knew. The newspapers I was really concerned about, in terms of affecting our jury, were the *Los Angeles Times* and the *Daily News,* the San Fernando Valley newspaper, which for the most part picked up Associated Press wire stories. The jurors weren't going to read the out-of-town papers.

The print media press corps had taken a room on the second floor at the DoubleTree directly across the atrium, about thirty feet from ours. No one sat guard duty, but they kept an eye on us, watching who was coming and going. At first we were anxious; I was worried they would see and report on what witnesses would come by to visit and prepare for their testimony. The other lawyers took to preparing their witnesses at MSK's offices or other locations. But I would only speak to the witnesses at the hotel. I had vowed not to return to MSK until the verdict was in. Until then, I was a self-imposed prisoner of the DoubleTree.

The judge had issued a gag order that restricted us from commenting on the trial, so our contacts with reporters were circumscribed. These were seasoned Simpson hands, veterans of the criminal trial wars, but they didn't always understand what our role was, they kept calling us "prosecutors." Although most knew the facts cold and were more than on top of the nuances, not as many had covered lengthy civil trials. The entire concept of "wrongful death," and what the damages were, for example, was murky to the media.

Often the reporters had questions concerning trial procedure: what was happening, why was it happening, what would happen next? If someone was pushing a deadline, he or she might knock on our door and ask. Such questions were not covered by the gag order. We did not allow them inside our war room, but would stand in the doorway or block up the hall and answer their questions if we could.

Down the hall and around the curving corridor, halfway between the press room and ours on the mezzanine level, was the hotel bar. Five o'clock was Happy Hour, and each night they put out different hot hors d'oeuvres, from batter-fried shrimp to chicken fingers to fried cheeseballs to salsa and chips. Monday was hot dog night. At first we were wary of crossing the line; a gag order is a serious piece of legal business and we did not want to jeopardize our case by violating it. However, as time went on, we found ourselves taking a break from our work and heading off to the bar to unwind. At first it was only on Fridays, at the end of a hard week, when we didn't have court the next day and they didn't have to write. But after a while we got to congregating nightly.

Ed Medvene usually drove home early, but at about 6:30 or 7:00, one by one, Peter, Tom, Yvette, Steve, Carolyn Walker, and I found our way over. There was a big-screen TV always tuned to the news. The reporters, having just filed their stories, were generally too tired to go get dinner and were content to chow down on the cheeseballs.

We called the place the Gag-Free Zone. If the reporters wanted to chat us up, this was the spot. No notebooks, nothing on the record, just a place to relax and talk. They never once violated our trust.

Our conversations often involved hard-core Simpson arcana among the cognoscenti. "Yeah, but it can't have happened that way because Nicole bled out on the second step, and the blood went down to the first step, yet on the final wound her head is turned towards the street and all the blood runs down there. . . ." Work was finished, but the mystery was still enveloping.

In fact, we got as much information from the media as they did from us. Of the dozen or so reporters who were at the bar nightly, most had sat all the way through the criminal trial, knew the players, knew the witnesses, knew what each had said, and in many ways knew the facts as well as, if not better than, we did.

We would take media soundings. "Do you think this proves what we're trying to prove or not?" "How do you think this witness was perceived?" "Was that cross-examination good or bad?" They were journalists, a particularly cynical breed, and intimately involved Simpson journalists at that, so we took their reactions with a grain of salt. They didn't have a juror's perspective, but they had a lot to say about the rest of the country's perspective on the trial, so we listened when they spoke. The majority were convinced Simpson was guilty. However, having lived at close hand to the criminal trial, they were less convinced the case was winnable.

It didn't take long for the reporters to figure out how to get me going. All they had to do was point out to me their doubt about one of our witnesses or question the soundness of one of our positions, and I'd launch into a twenty-minute closing argument to prove how wrong they were. Then they'd just smirk, ask a new annoying question, and order another round. It took me months to realize they were not on the jury and didn't have a vote. Invariably, the conversation would degenerate into a free-for-all about the lawyers, jurors, the judge, and, yes, even themselves. Reporters can be cruelly funny, and you need a thick skin to survive. I'm sure they had all sorts of nicknames and one-liners about me, and I pressed to find out. But for my own well-being, they never told me.

David Gregory, a talented TV journalist, was an excellent mimic, specializing in the personalities of the Simpson world. He did a killer Cochran and perfect cock-of-the-walk Baker, with his theatrical voice, and not a bad Medvene, but he broke the place up imitating Bob Baker's son, Phil. Phil was forever stumbling over something. "Here's Phil Baker," Gregory said. He walked two steps and tripped on his own feet. Two days later, as Phil was negotiating his way to the lectern to interview a witness, he kicked a juror's leg in the tight aisle and almost went sprawling. Phil's dad and the rest of us had a good, affectionate laugh about it in court, but back at the Gag-Free Zone, David Gregory's legend was secured for eternity.

Seasons don't change much in Southern California, but I knew it was autumn because the Fall Classic, the World Series, was in full swing.

I am a diehard Yankee fan, have been all my life, but things were looking grim for the home team. The Yankees were down two games to nothing to the Braves and going back for three games in Atlanta against the best pitching staff in the majors, perhaps the best staff of all time. I told Lambert, "If the Yankees win this series, we will win this trial." (Of course, I never said if they lost the series we would lose, too. Losing wasn't in my plans.) When the Yanks won four in a row and were World Champs, Lambert thought I had called it, like Babe Ruth pointing with his bat before hitting a home run.

We needed those breaks because the rest of our time was spent trying to avenge two murders. But even these rare breaks couldn't ever get me completely away from the case.

My best friend, Lew Goldstein, was getting married in mid-October. He was planning a big wedding in Santa Barbara, and I was the best man. This would be my first weekend off in months. I tried to put the case out of my mind, but it was all I could think about. Then, while greeting guests arriving for the wedding, I saw John Byrne, Judge Fujisaki's law clerk, walk in. My mouth dropped. "What are you doing here?" I asked. He was a relative of the bride, he said. I assiduously avoided him the rest of the day and evening, and told Fujisaki and Baker about the incident on Monday morning. I was taking no chances. That was my last weekend off until after the verdict.

Tom Lambert had spent months preparing voluminous and very detailed "Requests for Admissions," which we served on Simpson's lawyers before trial. These were documents requiring Simpson to admit or deny key facts about blood evidence found at the crime scenes, including all the samples from which conventional blood tests and DNA testing were done. Simpson had to admit, of course, what his blood type was. He admitted the victims' blood type, as well. And importantly, he had to admit that the laboratory test results for the various blood stains were valid and proper. In all his admissions, however, he insisted on the following disclaimer:

"In admitting this Request for Admission, the defense will adopt the plaintiff's definition as communicated to the defendant as that point in time when an item was tested by an outside laboratory, as opposed to the time of collection or any other point in time."

Essentially Simpson was challenging the chain of custody. He was saying it was his blood tested at the lab all right, but it wasn't his blood at the crime scene. Okay. We had now established, and Simpson had admitted, that the outside labwork was accurate. If we can show the blood arrived there without being tampered with, they lose.

Our next witness was Greg Matheson, the LAPD scientist who supervised the conventional blood tests. He was solid and sincere, not an advocate but a straight-shooter. In the criminal trial he had spent 17½ hours on the stand, but Tom got right to the point.

Matheson worked for the city as supervisor of the serology trace and field units and was assigned to oversee the fieldwork and coordinate the case. He described the technique by which blood was collected. Cotton swatches, not unlike small pieces of gauze, are used to soak up blood and then stored in plastic envelopes. Criminalists use as many swatches as it takes to absorb the blood, as many as six or seven per drop. Swatches of the surrounding area, with no blood on them, are also taken as controls. Back at the lab, the blood-soaked swatches are put into a test tube and left to dry overnight. The next day they are taken out of the test tube and put in a folded piece of paper—the by-now notable bindle—then wrapped, numbered, and initialed. The bindle is then put into a coin envelope for safekeeping. It was one of these bindles with which Dr. Lee found "something wrong"; some of the swatches hadn't dried sufficiently.

Matheson did some experiments, trying to replicate Fung's experience, and found if he crammed six or seven swatches into a test tube, as Dennis Fung was wont to do, some dampness would still exist for as long as 36 to 48 hours.

Matheson testified that upon initial visual inspection of Simpson's famous dark socks found on the rug at Rockingham there was no blood "obvious" but indicated in his notes that they should be examined for blood at a later time. They were then put into evidence. When they were ultimately tested, the socks came back showing Simpson's and Nicole's blood. From this normal, innocuous circumstance, the defense, of course, argued that the blood had been planted. But Matheson made clear his original inspection had been cursory, while the later one had been intensive. The jury could decide whether Matheson was another in a long line of perjurers or a man doing his job.

There were other key pieces of evidence that were observed during the initial investigation but not tested until some time later. In addition to

Simpson's socks, there was the blood on the back gate, and the blood found in a second evidence collection from the Bronco. Whenever evidence was not collected or analyzed immediately, the defense claimed it was part of the sinister plot to get Simpson. At the same time, whenever the work was performed promptly, it was part of the "rush to judgment" against Simpson.

Matheson explained that the first DNA tests had been performed to "see if we could exclude the parties that were associated with the case at that point." What he was saying, in the formal language of law enforcement, was that they didn't want to risk embarrassing Simpson. That's why he wasn't arrested immediately. Many people under similar circumstances would have been arrested on the Monday after the murders, rather than four days later. *He comes back, he's got a cut on his finger, he can't answer even the most basic questions about where he was at the time of the killings. Get the cuffs out. Okay, buddy, you're going to jail.* The cops, not wanting to mess with a celebrity, figured, "Let's do a quick DNA test, rule him out, and start finding out who the killer is. We don't need to be harassing this guy." Then the tests came back. "Whoa, wait, not so fast, we can't exclude him."

The blood found at the Bundy murder scene was either the victims', or O.J. Simpson's. No one else's blood was found there. DNA tests performed by three different laboratories confirmed this. The defense claimed contamination that supposedly infected the sensitive DNA testing, but not even they could come up with a contamination argument, however fanciful, that applied to the conventional blood testing that Matheson also had performed. Matheson's conventional tests showed that Simpson's blood type, found at the murder scene, was matched by only one person in 588. Rather than the astronomical numbers of DNA testing, this made things a little more understandable and still pointed strongly at Simpson as the killer. It was also uncontested by the defense.

When Simpson's Bronco was impounded, several blood stains inside the case were collected and tested for DNA, and the results showed Simpson's and Nicole's blood. In September, a second collection of blood from the vehicle revealed Ron's and Simpson's DNA mixed together. This was powerful evidence; according to Simpson, the two had never made physical contact, so what was Ron Goldman's DNA doing in Simpson's Bronco? There was no innocent explanation.

The second Bronco collection had presented a problem at the criminal trial, however. A witness named William Blasini, who worked for a company that bought impounded cars, swore he had examined the inside of the Bronco and seen no blood. From there, the defense leaped to the theory that, needing more conclusive evidence, the prosecution had spiked the Bronco before reexamining it.

Tom spoke to Blasini on the phone and said the guy was sticking to his story. Maybe there wasn't good light, maybe he had missed the blood altogether, but he said he saw what he saw and wasn't budging. It didn't make sense that blood would be planted and then allowed to sit in the car for three months, but Baker was going to hammer us with Blasini. Tom and I had a tough discussion at the DoubleTree one hour before Matheson was about to take the stand. Should we open this topic to defense examination by presenting it on direct?

After going back and forth on the issue, I finally said, "The hell with Blasini. He's just wrong." The blood wasn't planted and one minor witness wasn't going to scare us off. Tom had Matheson put the second Bronco blood collection into evidence.

(It turned out that Blasini never showed up at trial. The defense asked if I would agree to their reading his criminal trial testimony into the record and I jumped at it. Whether he was mistaken or just willful, Blasini was one person I did not want to see in the courtroom.)

Greg Matheson was followed onto the witness stand by LAPD criminalist Dennis Fung. Fung was the witness who made Barry Scheck a famous lawyer.

When Tom Lambert had originally gone to meet Fung, he came back and told me, "Now I know why Barry Scheck had such a field day with him. Fung is a sweet man, a great person, but he's a sitting duck for any kind of clever cross-examination." When I met him, it didn't take ten minutes to figure out that was true. Fung was naive and totally guileless. He will not fight with you, he will not even try to figure out where you're going with a question. He is easily led, and, as a result, is fully capable of saying things he does not mean.

Fung was in charge of gathering and preserving blood and other physical evidence at the crime scenes and transporting it to the lab for analysis. Because of an expansive direct examination (ten hours with Hank Goldberg) and the unlimited scope of the 21-hour cross, Barry Scheck had eaten him up. He had asked questions like, "Do you agree it was a mistake to put the blanket on the victim's body?" Instead of saying,

"I don't know if it was a mistake, I didn't put it on," Fung would oblig-ingly give answers like, "Yes, it was a mistake."

"You agree it was a terrible mistake."

Fung was thinking, *I guess if it was a mistake, and this is a murder case, and I shouldn't make* any *mistake, then any mistake is a terrible mistake.* His answer would become: Yes, it was a terrible mistake.

The defense pulled out picture after picture, along with crime scene notes and videos, and nitpicked Fung to distraction. He didn't use pro-tective gloves. He left blood evidence in a plastic bag for hours in an evi-dence truck with a broken refrigerator, so the blood "cooked." He did not examine the socks at Rockingham closely before putting them in an evi-dence bag. He didn't sterilize his tweezers after picking up each blood swatch. In his notes, Fung said "I" picked up certain pieces when, in fact, his assistant Andrea Mazzola had; "I" and "we" seemed interchangeable for him. Throw all these little errors into a pot and stir, which Scheck did brilliantly, and you have a contaminated stew.

Fung was not a professional witness, adept in framing his answers to best effect. He was a working criminalist, who did his best work out of the presence of lawyers and jurors. The problem was that now an exten-sive record had been made of his testimony that was inaccurate as to numerous little details—but not in important respects. "Cooked" blood, for example, would not change its DNA, it would simply degrade more quickly, leaving less of it to test. The defense should have been thanking Fung, otherwise the blood would have been even richer in DNA content, showing more definitively that Simpson committed the murders.

Our motions *in limine* would have permitted us to enter Fung's evi-dence through documents, eliminating his presence entirely, but we needed to make the jury understand how the evidence was collected, and to disabuse them of the notion that it was tampered with. Plus, Baker would have called him in the defense case, leaving us the more difficult task of rehabilitating him. We thought a fair-minded jury would see Fung was not a sinister or evil conspirator. They would understand his innocent mis-takes, see that he was not perfect but just a guy doing his job, and appre-ciate his sincerity under our friendly questioning. Much as I had worked with Kato to frame his answers, Tom did yeoman's work with Fung.

Fung explained that he and Ms. Mazzola worked as a team, preempt-ing the Scheck-type "I/We" cross-examination questions. He described how the blood swatches were dried and bindled and how he came into the lab the next morning to complete the processing. The criminal defense had argued that the Rockingham glove was wet, suggesting Fuhrman had picked it up wet from the murder scene (and somehow preserved its wet condition while transporting it to Rockingham to be planted). Fung described the glove as dry but glistening.

Bob Blasier's cross-examination was "Scheck Lite." First, our examination had been very limited. Second, this judge was not going to let him get away with far-ranging hypotheticals. Dennis did very well and we were relieved. I congratulated Tom on a magnificent job with a difficult witness.

We had started with Ron's and Nicole's last hours, then talked about the timeline. We had the officers finding the bodies, securing the premises, and processing the crime scene. We had the evidence taken to the lab and with Greg Matheson even had the first blood test results. Under normal circumstances, our next move would have been to follow the evidence straight to the DNA labs, explain how it was analyzed, and get the full results identifying Simpson.

However, the DNA material was very complicated and the witnesses Gary Sims, Collin Yamauchi, and Robin Cotton, were all to be handled by Tom Lambert. I wanted Tom to do them immediately, but having just finished Matheson and Fung, he needed more time to prepare. "Don't ask me," he said. "I cannot do it. Ask Ed. Put on one of Ed's witnesses." People's nerves were beginning to get frayed by the pressure being put on them, because everyone wanted to do so well.

Medvene was working furiously. Having been in front of the jury for most of the first week with the cops, he was facing the coroner and hair-and-fiber witnesses back to back. He couldn't go, either. But if we had dead time the court wasn't going to say, "Mr. Petrocelli, I know you want your case to flow beautifully, so we'll wait four days for you to properly present the next witness in your game plan." No, Fujisaki wanted to keep this trial moving.

We began to have scheduling conflicts. Our witnesses were coming from out of town, they had other commitments, they couldn't hang around and wait for an opening. It was a nightmare, and Yvette Molinaro and Carolyn Walker were working around the clock sorting out the logistics. I scrambled to find witnesses to plug the gap.

We played for the jury the videotaped deposition of Brenda Vemich of Bloomingdale's taken earlier in the year in New York City. Vemich authenticated a sales receipt showing that Nicole purchased two pairs of Aris Leather Light gloves, extra large, at the New York store on December 18, 1990. Based on her examination of the murder gloves as well as photographs, she testified that they were, in fact, Aris Leather Light gloves, extra large, the type sold by Bloomingdale's in December 1990. We showed her various photographs taken of Simpson wearing gloves at football games, and she said those gloves appeared to be Aris Leather Lights.

We then introduced testimony from the photographers who took the photos of Simpson wearing the Leather Light gloves while broadcasting football games. The photos showed Simpson wearing both brown and black gloves in rainy weather, which could be used to help explain the gloves shrinking. None of us had forgotten Simpson's glove scene at the criminal trial.

Richard Rubin was the former general manager and vice president of Aris and an expert on the gloves. Rubin was prepared to say positively that the gloves found at the murder scene and at Rockingham were the same glove type as those Simpson wore in the photos. Rubin had been on the stand when Chris Darden had Simpson try on the murder gloves during the criminal trial. Many people believed this was the irreversible turning point of the trial. Rubin explained to us that those gloves had been sitting in evidence for a year and a half, they hadn't been stretched, they hadn't been warmed or worn.

Simpson, he said, had an extra-wide palm but not long fingers. It was easy for a person with such a hand to make a glove look like it didn't fit, just stretching out the palm and fingers would make putting them on very difficult. "Imagine trying to put a pair of pants on a crying infant," he told us. That, combined with the drag created by the latex gloves Simpson had been wearing, make it almost impossible.

"The gloves will fit him. There's no question they fit at the criminal trial. It's not a perfect fit, it might not even be a good fit now, because of the shrinkage. It's the *quality* of the fit that's in question, but the gloves fit." The problem was the big show Simpson had put on, the mugging and the grunting.

We decided to talk to the judge. We didn't want any stunts in front of this jury. We told the judge at sidebar that if Baker intended to have

Simpson try on the murder gloves, we wanted no latex gloves underneath. That would distort the fit. We also wanted Simpson to put the gloves on his hands outside the presence of the jury, so he wouldn't be able to put on another misleading show; once the gloves were on, the jury could be brought in. Fujisaki agreed Simpson could not use latex gloves, and said he would decide how the gloves would be put on if and when Baker got to that point in his cross-examination of Rubin. Anticipating that Baker would not put the gloves on Simpson, especially since the judge would not permit the latex gloves, we asked the judge to prohibit Baker from showing a video replay of the glove demonstration from the criminal trial. Judge Fujisaki would not bar the defense from playing the video, but he made them delete the sound.

John Kelly handled the direct examination. Rubin testified that two hundred to two hundred forty pairs of Aris Leather Lights, brown, extra large, were sold in the United States, exclusively through Bloomingdale's. Kelly handed the two gloves found at the crime scenes to Rubin, who looked at the cutter number on each and verified that they were mates. They were a fit, he said, but they were "one inch short in the wrist."

"May we ask the witness not to pull the gloves," said Baker.

"Don't pull the gloves," instructed the judge.

Rubin started to handle them. It was natural, the man was a glove expert, his whole life was gloves. "It's really just that they hadn't been used in a long, long time."

"So when you put gloves on, you—"

"Work them out a little." He pulled the fingers one by one. Kelly began buying time, bending down to ask Medvene a question, while Rubin continued to work out the leather. With the court's permission, Rubin inserted his hand. In the criminal trial, everyone had used rubber gloves in handling these; here, he just tried them right on. Rubin continued to work these dried-up-bloody gloves right there on the witness stand, just sitting there idly refurbishing them as he testified. This went on for a while, and we had a pair of nicely warmed and pliable gloves in hand before Baker made him take them off. Simpson wasn't going to be wearing *these* at trial.

We followed Rubin with the edited video of Harry Scull, Jr.'s deposition. This established the fact that Scull had taken the photograph of Simpson wearing the Bruno Magli shoes, and explained the circumstances under which it was taken. Now we had pictures of Simpson wearing the murder gloves and the murder shoes.

Thursday, November 7, was Cut Day. I called Dr. Robert Huizenga to the stand. In the criminal trial, he'd been called by the defense to talk about Simpson's arthritis, the idea being Simpson was so lame he couldn't have killed two people. Well, the idea was so lame that not even Baker, who wasn't shy about advancing positions, abandoned the argument in the civil trial. I called Huizenga and had him explain the photographs he took of Simpson at his office on June 15 and at the Kardashian house on June 17, which I had projected on the television monitor. He acknowledged having observed three cuts or lacerations and seven abrasions on Simpson's left hand, and one paperlike cut on the right hand. He gave me a whole page of very serious-sounding doctor talk—"a slightly deeper, but actually more of an avulsion-type laceration, or the more proximal half of that lesion"—which made these injuries seem very bad. Simpson had told the police that he was always getting "nicks and stuff" from playing golf and that "I bleed all the time." I asked Huizenga whether all these cuts were of recent vintage and, more to the point, whether they could have been received on Sunday, June 12. Huizenga said yes.

Dr. Huizenga was followed by the videotaped deposition of Chicago Police Detective Ken Berris, who had investigated the hotel room in which Simpson claimed to have cut himself when "a glass broke." His photographs showed the bathroom virtually untouched, all the soaps and amenities neatly in order on the countertop, except for a few pieces of broken glass in the sink.

Berris told me several pieces of important information I could not get into the trial because of hearsay laws. He learned, for example, that Simpson had ordered his calls held and that he not be disturbed when he arrived. Two laundry bags, which had just been placed in the room, were missing. On the way out, Simpson had made a scene, banging on the front desk demanding a Band-Aid. This was uncustomarily loud and angry behavior for Simpson, who was known for never losing his cool in public. He was clearly trying to make people notice his cut—the one he'd just gotten from a glass that broke.

But Berris also offered testimony for the record. Simpson supposedly broke the glass while he was on the phone, but that was proving difficult to do. There was no phone in the bathroom; the phone was bedside. Berris also depicted the layout of the room in detail and established that nothing except the bed had been used. In Simpson's version of events, he got there, hopped in bed, was awakened, showered and left. But there was absolutely no mess in the room. Nothing.

Berris found a blood spot in the center of the bedding. Simpson, of course, would say he had sat on the bed facing the headboard and supported himself with his newly bleeding left hand while he was talking on the phone. But one normally sits on a bed with one's back to the wall, and the telephone sat with a short cord on a night table to the right. Simpson would have had to rotate and contort his body to land his left hand in the middle of the bed. More likely, he bled from his cut left hand onto the sheet when he lay down waiting for the inevitable phone call.

This took us to the lunch hour, at which time Simpson walked out and didn't come back. His people reported to the press that Simpson had to go play golf, but members of the media told me he was upset. He had struggled with the cut testimony at his deposition, now this.

The judge threw out our behavioral scientists and almost derailed Peter Gelblum.

Dr. Donald Dutton and Dr. Park Dietz were our experts in spousal homicide and domestic violence. I had begun to involve myself in this topic, but as other things consumed me turned it over to Peter to develop and present at trial.

Dr. Dietz is a renowned and experienced specialist in forensic psychiatry and crime scene analysis. As part of the U.S. Government's National Center for the Analysis of Violent Crime, he headed the FBI Academy's profiling unit. He had evaluated President Reagan's attempted assassin, John Hinckley, on behalf of the U.S. Attorney's Office and worked for the prosecutors on the Richard Allen Davis, Colin Ferguson, and Susan Smith cases. He was a clinical professor of psychiatry and biobehavioral sciences at UCLA. His *curriculum vitae* ran thirty-nine pages. He's a brilliant man. We had planned to use Dietz in tandem with John Douglas, the FBI profiler. When Douglas had to drop out, Dietz had to assume the full load.

Dr. Dietz was tall, thin, sort of spooky looking. Some people called him "Dr. Death." After examining our files, he came to the conclusion that Simpson was narcissistic in the extreme. "Individuals like this require excessive admiration," he said. "They are preoccupied with how well they are doing and how favorably they are regarded by others. They constantly fish for compliments, often with great charm. A sense of entitlement is evidenced in these individuals. Unreasonable expectation of especially favorable treatment. They expect to be catered to and are puzzled or furious when this does not happen."

After reviewing the autopsy and crime scene photographs, and notes and diagrams prepared by the LAPD and the coroner's office, Dietz concluded that the killer knew, and had recently experienced intense emotions toward at least one of the victims. In his opinion, the nature and extent of Nicole's wounds—focused, as they were, on the scalp and neck—indicated the principal emotion exhibited was rage. Ron's wounds were more diffuse and included some that were defensive in nature.

Dr. Dietz found indication that this was a revenge killing. He pointed to the fact that the killer was sufficiently calculating and organized to bring with him a hat, gloves, and a weapon. Because there was a rapid exit from the scene, as indicated by the abundance of evidence left behind—the hat, gloves, hair fibers, blood drops, bloody shoe prints— Dietz found that things had gotten out of control. The fact that there had been no attempt to "stage" or mask the crime to make it appear either accidental or natural indicated the killer was not a professional—so much for the Colombian hit man theory—but someone who had come seeking a particular victim.

He analyzed the scene's "victimology" and found Nicole's background pointed to problems with Simpson.

Dr. Dietz originally believed the killer had had to exert himself to perform the killings. But after further consideration, and consultation with Douglas, he concluded the killings were evidence of "sustained aggression," not "physical exertion," and may not have "even constituted an aerobic workout."

Douglas believed that, by the time of trial, Simpson would have dealt with the trauma by actually believing he was innocent. Douglas had said to me, "Watch out. Don't fall for their trap of offering to have him take a polygraph test; by having convinced himself he didn't do it, Simpson could probably pass." Dietz, while seeing how such a thing was possible, was not prepared to agree.

Dr. Dietz's conclusions were all well within the realm of common sense, but he was arriving at them through behavioral scientific analysis. We wanted the jury to have the benefit of Dietz's analysis.

Dr. Donald Dutton was also a research psychologist with a specialty in forensic psychology, specifically in spousal violence. He had worked in the field for twenty-two years. Dan Leonard quickly stipulated that Dr. Dutton was an expert. Dutton gave us two opinions: Simpson fit a behavioral pattern of spousal homicide, and his demeanor following the murders was not inconsistent with someone who had committed spousal homicide. We planned to use his latter opinion in rebuttal to answer the question, "Does this look like a man who just killed his wife?"

Dutton had conducted research on men recently convicted of spousal homicide. Among the several factors causing that special kind of killing, he explained, were a history of prior violence, reports of jealousy made to third parties, and recent estrangement. The *modus operandi* one typically sees, he testified, was overkill: the use of knives, for example, which is up close and personal as opposed to the more distant use of a gun; also the fact that far more wounds are inflicted than are necessary to effect the killing. The site is frequently the victim's home, which is not typically the case in nonspousal killings of women.

Dr. Dutton's research also showed that a great percentage of all femicides involved spousal killings; women are usually killed in their homes, with a knife, because of problems with their husbands or boyfriends, and in situations characterized by overkill.

All of these factors, of course, were present in the Simpson killing.

There are approximately 1,800,000 battering cases reported in the United States each year, and about two thousand homicides of women. We expected Dutton's opinion to be attacked as follows: "Do the math. Only about one tenth of one percent of batterers ultimately go on to kill their wives." That was the methodology of the criminal trial: If you start with batterings and move to killings, it's .1 percent.

However, we turned the statistic around and looked at it from a different direction. Start with the dead body. That's what our case started with. When a woman gets murdered, who does it? What percentage of women who are murdered are killed by an intimate batterer? It is between 50 and 70 percent. That is a very high correlation. It may be difficult to predict who, among battered women, is going to get killed, but once a woman is dead it is significantly less difficult to find her killer. Look to the spouse.

We gave Dutton a detailed summary of all our evidence and he came to the very firm conclusion that not only did the murder fit the characteristics of spousal homicide, but based on his analysis, Simpson "fit" the pattern of the spousal killer. He also concluded that Simpson's post-homicide demeanor was not inconsistent with a person who had killed. The popular image of a man who has just killed his wife is a sweating, nervous, wild-eyed guy who shows guilt all over his face, but that turns out not to be the case. Based on his conversations with and examination of spousal killers, Dr. Dutton found them to be relatively tension-free after the act, which they described as extremely cathartic and a great release of tension. Simpson had been signing autographs in the airport.

Gavin de Becker is the nation's leading expert on threat assessment and pre-incident indications of violence. He consults on security for high-profile people and institutions such as the U.S. Secret Service, the FBI, and the Supreme Court. De Becker had created a computer program called MOSAIC, which he used to predict the people most likely to commit violence. His program basically answers the questions: "Is this person a threat?" "Is this person likely to commit violence?" De Becker worked behind the scenes for the prosecution in the criminal case and helped us as well. He fed Simpson's information into his computer program and O.J. came back off the charts. Of the twenty-three characteristics associated with husbands who kill their wives, Simpson demonstrated twenty-one. While convincing to me, I didn't want the jury to think we needed a computer to find Simpson guilty. Baker would have had a field day with that. We wisely decided to forgo MOSAIC.

A hearing was held outside the presence of the jury to determine whether Drs. Dietz and Dutton were acceptable witnesses. Dan Leonard argued for the defense that both doctors' testimony was "profiling," giving the jury a set of predictive criteria, a formula by which to judge the defendant. If the defendant fit the formula, he was guilty. "That's precisely the kind of evidence that has been found to be inadmissible time and again," argued Leonard, "for the very important reason that it does invade the province of the jury. . . . [Dr. Dietz] was trying to tell this jury that Mr. Simpson did it because he's the kind of person who *would* do it. . . . Propensity is something that is absolutely barred."

But Dietz and Dutton had extensive credentials, and we argued that they should be treated no different than any other experts. The law states that expert testimony is appropriate if it is helpful to the trier of fact in an area that is beyond the normal realm of one's life experiences. We argued that spousal homicide is well outside that realm.

Judge Fujisaki was no fan of experts. If it were up to him, they would be outlawed from trials. He was easy prey for the defense's position; he struck both Dietz and Dutton from our case. Considering Dietz and Dutton's extensive credentials, he was concerned that the jurors would feel their testimony was infallible and would therefore feel committed to accept it rather than use their own independent judgment. In the judge's view, the jury had over five hundred years of life experience and could decide for themselves what constituted the characteristics of this particular homicide. Dietz and Dutton were out.

Peter Gelblum was very disappointed. This was to have been his big moment at trial, he had spent considerable time and effort shaping this testimony to our best advantage, and now he was out in the cold. I had promised Peter a significant role in this trial, so I approached Ed Medvene and asked if he would relinquish the examination of photography expert Jerry Richards and the cross-examination of Baker's photography expert Robert Groden, to whom he had previously been assigned. Peter, the former stage and TV actor, was very well-versed in the area of photography, and Ed agreed to step aside.

With behavioral science ruled out, we went directly to forensic science. We needed to know how Ron and Nicole died.

TWENTY-FOUR

"More Degrees Than
a Thermometer"

On one level, the answer was obvious. In lay terms, Nicole had
died because her throat had been cut almost to the spinal column, and Ron had been stabbed to death. At the criminal trial
this had been established in testimony by the Los Angeles County
Coroner, Dr. Lakshmanan Sathyavagiswaran, who was on the stand for
eight solid days of direct examination explaining the many embarrassing
missteps of his department, and then had to endure a full day's brutal
cross-examination from Robert Shapiro. Dr. Sathyavagiswaran had concluded that Ron died from having his jugular vein slashed.

Medvene, in charge of the coroner's testimony, went looking for
someone with considerably less baggage to present the cause of death. The
defense's expert, Michael Baden, former New York City medical examiner,
had praised a Dr. Werner Spitz as one of the dominant figures in the field
of forensic pathology, as had Deputy District Attorney Brian Kelberg,
who had examined Baden.

Spitz was editor and chief writer of the definitive forensic pathology
textbook, *Medicolegal Investigation of Death*. He was a university professor of both pathology and chemistry. In his forty-three-year career, he had
performed or supervised more than fifty-five thousand autopsies and had
served on the U.S. Government committees investigating the assassinations of President John F. Kennedy and the Reverend Martin Luther King

Jr. He had testified at hundreds of trials, was familiar with our case, and agreed to testify. When he examined the evidence he came to an entirely new and different conclusion about Ron's cause of death from anything heard at the criminal trial.

One of the major problems the prosecution had encountered was the question: "Did Simpson have enough time to commit the murders?" Baden, testifying for Simpson, had estimated the length of struggle between the victims and their killer at from ten to fifteen to as long as twenty minutes. Dr. Henry Lee had not quantified the time but implied there had been a protracted struggle. As Ed said, we had to beat them both.

Robert Heidstra heard Ron Goldman shouting, "Hey, hey, hey!" at around 10:35. Kato Kaelin heard three loud thumps on the outside of his wall at approximately 10:51. Limousine driver Allan Park saw Simpson at Rockingham at 10:54. These were markers, and if the struggle took more than ten minutes, that would effectively rule out Simpson as the killer; he simply would not have had sufficient time to do it and get back to Rockingham in time to be heard bumping into a wall at 10:51 and seen at 10:54. This was one of the reasons Marcia Clark and the prosecution had gone with an earlier time of death.

Knowing that Simpson *did* commit the murders, we had to reveal a timeline in which he left Bundy by 10:45 *at the latest.*

We called Dr. Werner Spitz to the stand.

Medvene had worked long hours with Dr. Spitz prior to his pretrial deposition, visiting the Bundy crime scene, studying the medical evidence, attempting to re-create the murder scenario. Spitz was ready.

Most witnesses are overwhelmed by the event of a major trial; they give their testimony and are absorbed into the mix. Los Angeles Deputy Medical Examiner Dr. Irwin Golden had seemed like a ferret caught in sunlight when testifying about the same material. By contrast, Dr. Spitz glowed with confidence. Whether detailing his professional background or explaining how he handles requests for testimony or discussing the case materials he reviewed to arrive at his opinions, there was not a shred of doubt, not a thread, that he was presenting the truth.

Dr. Spitz was a compact man, seventy years old with a white crew cut and the personality of a grumpy professor. A grumpy, brilliant, German professor. He spoke impeccable English with a German accent, not confusing the jury with medical terminology but using conversational language with surgical precision. Spitz commanded the stage, a pathology Einstein. As I watched Ed begin to examine him, I could see the jury rivet their gaze on him. They liked him.

Ed was very cagey. He knew Spitz was a winner, and he got out of his way. Very early in the examination he put a metal pointer in Spitz's hand and invited him to leave the witness chair and demonstrate his conclusions. This was a dynamic man you wanted as close to the jury as possible.

We had blown up the autopsy photographs and mounted them on boards so the jury could see the extent of the wounds. To protect the families' privacy, these photos were never shown to the courtroom at large; they were placed with their back to the gallery, facing only the jury; nor did we want anyone in the courtroom to write about or exploit these horrific images. The crime scene photos were bad enough, but these autopsy photos, so cold, were much more difficult to look at. On the occasions we had to display them, I would signal Fred, Patti, and Kim to avert their eyes. They couldn't look.

Fred had seen just a few of the crime scene pictures, and I cannot imagine what he must have felt. Ron is crumpled against a tree, one shoe kicked off, his eyes open; Nicole lies in a fetal position in a river of her blood. See those pictures once, and they are burned indelibly into the mind. If the picture is of your son—I just can't imagine. When people knock Fred Goldman or question his motives in his pursuit of O.J. Simpson, all I can think of are these photos. After seeing them, one could never question Fred Goldman's desire to bring the killer to justice.

Spitz began by showing a bruise on Nicole's scalp. "The brain in the skull is like Jell-O in a cup," he explained. His use of language was extraordinary. "And when you rattle it very sharply, the brain strikes; or when you inflict a blow to it, the brain moves and strikes the skull under the blow, and then it moves opposite and strikes the inside of the skull on the opposite side. Either way, it would get a bruise." Nicole had been punched. She may have been dazed.

Dr. Spitz scrunched up his face and used his hands so descriptively he was mesmerizing. He took over the courtroom, standing with his pointer in front of the board as if he were teaching a class. Some lawyers might have coveted the spotlight, but Ed wisely let the professor take control. He was like a referee in the ring letting the fighters go at it, and Spitz began to pummel the defense case.

Spitz explained that several wounds to Nicole's scalp had not penetrated; the right-handed killer had hit the bone in her neck in a vertical line *one-two-three-four-five*, in rapid succession. The stabs were so close together, they could not have been inflicted slowly. Whoever did this did it fast. The fifth entrance of the knife began the gaping wound to her throat.

"The assailant was in back; and the slash runs from left to right."

"With the court's permission," Ed asked, "could you just demonstrate on me quickly how that would happen?"

Dr. Spitz stepped behind Ed and put his left hand over Medvene's chin, his right hand to the left of Ed's neck, and ripped the metal pointer straight across. The courtroom was more than silent.

Ed asked the important question: "Dr. Spitz, from the first mark or wound on Ms. Brown to the slashing of the throat, do you have an opinion on how long it took before the assailant slashed her throat?"

Dr. Spitz spoke readily. "I think the slashing of the throat was the terminal event, and I think the entire scenario, from the first wound to the last, was less than fifteen seconds."

Ed asked which way the blood would flow. "May I use you again?" Spitz asked. Ed accommodated. Spitz explained that the blood would spurt away from the killer, into the ground.

Definitive and assertive, Spitz did not believe in equivocation. Lawyers always like a little room to work so their witnesses do not get unnecessarily impeached, but Dr. Spitz would have none of that. He was not guessing; he was presenting his clear view of the events. He spoke in the present tense, as if he were narrating. The effect was as if we were watching the murder.

"The cut occurs very rapidly. The hand holding the blade moves away from the source of the bleeding, so the body of the victim shields the assailant, and the bleeding occurs after the hand has moved away." As he pulled his hand from left to right across Ed's throat, the jury could see how close the blade would come to the fingers on the killer's left hand, the fingers on which Simpson had his cuts.

"The blood is coming from the two carotid arteries, which are each the diameter of your little finger." Spitz had pulled back Medvene's head from behind. The neck was taut during the murder, he said, and the blood was shooting down, "a pulsating hemorrhage that would go up to a twelve-foot ceiling."

Judge Fujisaki abruptly ordered a ten-minute break.

When he returned, the judge spoke to the courtroom. "Okay. The audience, first row by the jury box"—this was media row—"there's a complaint that the jurors are able to hear your comments. If you continue to talk and peer around that barrier, I am going to clear that first row."

Spitz continued. He said Ron Goldman died of blood loss, as had Nicole. He grouped Ron's wounds: various superficial, defensive-type wounds to both sides of the body, including a wide and gaping cut on his left thigh; a stab wound to his internal jugular vein; two penetrations in the right side of the chest and the lung; and a wound in the back side of the left flank.

"There's movement. Sometimes the victim presents the right side and sometimes presents the left side." Spitz turned one way and another, arms protecting himself as if warding off an attacker, as he described how Ron received the superficial wounds. The effect was painful. "That's how it started."

The wound to the jugular, he said, was not the ultimate killer. What was?

"The wound to the left flank. I cannot say exactly when it happened, but it occurred early on." Spitz spoke with absolute clarity and authority. He said this was an unimpressive wound, but the fatal one. The killer's knife, he said, cut through skin and muscle and severed the aorta. "The aorta is a garden-hose-diameter pipe, tube. The aorta comes directly out of the heart, makes a curve called the arch, runs to the left of the vertebral column, and then comes down into the lower abdominal area and bifurcates into each leg." He sensed his language was getting technical, and he made an adjustment.

"When there's a hole in the aorta, the blood gushes out at fantastic speed. . . . [The] pressure drops, exactly the same as would happen if you make two half-an-inch or two five-eighth-inch holes in your garden hose; you could not expect that the sprinkler at the end of the garden hose is going to generate a lot of water, because the water is running out before it gets to the sprinkler."

Spitz said Ron bled inside. "All other wounds combined caused lit-tle bleeding. The bleeding from the aorta was overwhelming, and is, in fact, what killed him."

Again Ed asked the key question: "How long did the struggle take between Ron Goldman and the person who killed him?"

"It is my opinion that this struggle took around a minute, give or take." With a near immediate fall of blood pressure, Spitz said, there was not enough blood to reach the brain. "A person loses ability to stand up, loses ability to think, becomes woozy, and, in very short order, disabled." No one with a slashed aorta could remain standing, let alone continue to fight for ten, fifteen, twenty minutes.

The defense's theory held that Ron Goldman died from blood slowly escaping from his jugular vein. This was the essence of Michael Baden's testimony in the criminal trial. As the blood oozed down his shirt and pants, Baden opined, Ron had remained upright, battling a man with a knife for a quarter of an hour until he bled out and died.

Spitz was completely certain it hadn't happened that way. "There is only one cause of death here, and the cause of death here is cuts in the aorta."

Ron's blood did not escape, Spitz continued, it stayed inside him, collecting in a space in the lower back called the retroperitoneum.

Ed pursued another devastating attack, asking if the assailant would have any injuries or marks on him as a result of the struggle.

As well as inadvertent cuts from the murder weapon as the killer wielded it, "Injuries from fingernail marks are likely to be inflicted," Spitz testified. As it happened, Dr. Spitz's definitive text included an entire chapter on fingernail marks, or "gouges." Ed showed Spitz a close-up of Simpson's left hand, taken on June 12, sometime before the dance recital. There were no marks. As of around seven on the night of the murders, Simpson had no fingernail marks on his left hand. Ed put up a photo of Simpson's cut finger, taken by the police on June 13. There were gouges visible. "Could those marks be from a cut glass?" he asked. No, Spitz answered. They were from the victims.

We had ended with Ron and Nicole clawing for their lives on Simpson's hands. It was about as close as you could get to identifying a killer. Ed sat down. He had done a phenomenal job.

Baker sprang right up. This seemed to be his cross-examination trademark. Boom, he was ready. He liked to whack the first pitch down the line for a double.

"All those [gouge] marks you've circled, Dr. Spitz, are about the size of the head of a pin or less, right?"

Dennis Fung would likely have said, "I guess so." Spitz was no Fung.

"I don't know," he said. "I can't tell you whether they are the size of a head of a pin or less, depending on the pin. I suppose there are pins with little heads and big heads. There is no scale on this. I could say that they are small, but I cannot tell you how small." Oh, this will be fun, I thought. Spitz is not going to back down to anyone.

Baker was an experienced medical malpractice attorney and he demonstrated his versatility by going toe-to-toe with our expert. He didn't treat Spitz with the derision he had displayed to the police, he showed him respect, but even there he, too, was giving no ground. "You have more degrees than a thermometer, right?" The jury busted out laughing, and I determined to use that line if I ever examined a doctor. Baker was not to be intimidated.

Ultimately his main theme was that Spitz couldn't know exactly how the murders had happened because he hadn't been there, that his opinions were merely educated guesses, not to be taken as gospel. He tried to get Spitz committed to such a precise and certain sequence of events that his credibility could be brought into question.

"I get the impression, sir, from your testimony in the last few hours in this courtroom that you had done, in your mind, a complete reconstruction of how these murders took place, how these defensive wounds took place, and how these wounds were inflicted, to come up with your opinion that within fifteen seconds from the time the first wound was inflicted, Ms. Nicole Brown Simpson was deceased or had a fatal wound inflicted on her; and within less than one minute from the first wound of Ron Goldman, he had a fatal wound inflicted in him. So, is that correct? You did a full reconstruction of how these murders took place, in your mind, that you're willing to sit here and tell us about? Yes?"

"Yes."

Here it comes, I thought. Baker is painting Spitz as a Quincy wannabe, not just doing his job, but solving murders. Werner Spitz as Jack

Klugman. This was not good. The jury would be left wondering, "Can anyone know that?" Would they think he was pushing his point of view too hard, devolving from expert to advocate? That would ruin his testimony, just as Baker wanted. We didn't need Spitz to tell the jury each and every blow that was struck; that was a burden we neither wanted nor had to assume. He could give his important opinions on the length of struggle, on the gouges, and leave it at that.

Baker drew him deeper into the details. "In your reconstruction scenario, after she takes a couple of defensive wounds to her hands, she is then knocked or loses her footing to the extent that she takes this blow to the head, correct?"

"Yes."

That answer was supportable by the forensic evidence. But then Baker tried to dramatize his point. He put on the monitor a diagram of the closed-in area in which Nicole was killed, and asked whether Ron had been there during the fifteen seconds in which she was killed. He was implicitly putting Spitz at the scene as an eyewitness.

Spitz could not resist. "I think he probably was."

In Spitz's mind he was just drawing logical inferences and conclusions from the nature of the wounds. Ed and I, however, sitting at the attorneys' table trying to show no emotion, were cringing inside. We had based our presentation of this case on the credo "Less Is More." We were not planning to tell the jury exactly how Simpson got to the property; we were not planning to tell them exactly which route he took home. We were not planning to detail how the murders went down or how he disposed of the murder weapon or where the murder clothes were. We didn't have to prove any of those things in order to win our case. Those were details we would never know, details that Simpson was keeping to himself.

But Spitz wasn't there to play ball; he was, in the truest sense, an independent expert. I whispered to Ed, "Does Spitz know how to say, 'I don't know'?"

Baker, having gotten what he wanted, said, "Okay," but Spitz, to his credit, caught himself.

"I really don't know that he was, but I think he probably was, or was arriving at that time." He paused. "Well, I'm not sure." He had gotten a grip just in time. "I'm not sure."

Baker jumped on him. "You actually don't know 'cause you certainly weren't on the north side of the fence, looking. This is your *opinion,* based on *reconstruction,* is it not?" The implication was that he was making all this up. Spitz had to answer yes.

"Now, Dr. Spitz, in terms of the gate, that is the front gate, sir. Do you know whether that gate was locked or unlocked before you rendered the opinion that Mr. Goldman was in the closed-in area at the time the altercation with Nicole Brown Simpson took place?"

Now he had Spitz locking and unlocking the gate. Medvene jumped in to try to get our guy out of the jam. "Objection, Your Honor. It misstates his testimony. He didn't say he was in the area or not. He said he didn't know." *Get it, Doctor: You don't know!* This was a speaking objection, but Ed got away with it. The court sustained him.

Baker pressed his case. "Do you believe that Mr. Goldman was in that area when that altercation and struggle and ultimate demise of Ms. Brown Simpson took place?" Ed objected again, but the judge let Spitz answer.

"I personally believe that he may have been there, but I'm not basing that opinion on any scientific evidence or any material evidence that I really have. My area of expertise is injuries." Spitz had gotten the message, but Baker came right back at him.

"But you've opined here not only about injuries. You opined about how long it took to get the injuries. You've opined about what angles the assailant was at. You've opined about how the knife wounds were inflicted. And you weren't there when you opined about all of those things, correct, sir?"

"No," said Spitz. "All I testified to is appearance of injury, types of injury, how injuries were inflicted, how long it took to inflict the injuries, how much blood was lost from injuries, and this kind of thing." Then he let Baker have it. "Every time you want to characterize my testimony, you'd have to submit that it is intended to convey information about wounds, about injuries, not whether who was present or how long interaction took place before the first wound was inflicted. That, I do not know."

Baker had had Spitz cornered, but now he could feel him getting away. He tried to bring him back by asking what distance Nicole had been from Ron if and when she had let him in the gate. Ed objected, and the court sustained. Baker started getting angry.

"Well, you've testified as to where you thought the assailant was. . . . You've testified that Nicole Brown Simpson was killed first, because if she wasn't killed first, she would run away. Those are all your opinions, correct?"

"Yes," Spitz answered.

"And in your opinions, and you sure don't know whether Nicole Brown Simpson were to run away or not—you weren't there and you've never met her, isn't that true?" He was fairly shouting at Spitz now, questioning him angrily.

"That's correct."

"And you've testified that the assailant was in front and then around behind, and you weren't there and you don't know whether the assailant was or wasn't in front of her, do you?"

Spitz was not pleased to be challenged in his field of expertise. "Yes, I do know," he said gruffly.

"And you don't know that it took any fifteen seconds from the first defensive wound to the last, because you weren't there, isn't that true, sir?" Baker's anger was now getting the better of him.

"No," Spitz argued in return. "I know that to sustain the type of injuries that Ms. Simpson had would take less than fifteen seconds."

Baker was pacing in front of the witness stand. "I mean, you sat up here and you demonstrated—*umpf, umpf, umpf*"—he stabbed the air with his hand three times in a gesture I found both highly graphic and extremely insensitive—"about three times with your hand, and you know, do you, Dr. Spitz, that's how fast the assailant did it because you were there and you saw him, right?" Medvene objected. Baker continued, "You don't know, sir, how fast the wounds were inflicted, do you? Now, do you?"

Spitz put his foot down. "Yes, I do know."

Dr. Spitz became a star overnight. When court adjourned Friday afternoon, he still had to face the remainder of Baker's cross as well as our redirect, so he stayed in town. Despite the gag order, his dynamic presentation and feisty presence made the press thrust their microphones at him and shout for comment. He said nothing publicly.

Over the weekend, taking breaks from his preparations for the rest of his testimony, Spitz and I went to a Santa Monica Bagel Nosh and got to know each other. We talked about his background for a while, but I was so intensely involved in the case that the conversation never strayed very far from it.

"You know, Doctor," I said, "I'm curious. If Michael Baden is so smart and talented, one of the top pathologists in the country, how can you and he be so diametrically opposed on the length-of-struggle issue?"

Spitz pulled no punches. "He's just wrong. He is giving them what they want to help make their case, but he is wrong."

I already knew the answer, but to hear Spitz say it reassured me. Simpson had been on trial for double murder. It was a "reasonable doubt" case in which the law allowed the defendant to latch on to anything that could possibly suggest a different explanation for the deaths than his guilt. By this time I was familiar with the experts in the criminal trial who had given testimony that didn't add up and the lawyers who presented and supported this testimony. I felt that if these people had been contacted by an independent commission, presented with the same evidence in a hypothetical case, without its being attached to O.J. Simpson, and told, "Bring your special talent and knowledge to bear on this and tell us: Was there contamination of evidence? Was there planting of evidence? Was this a long struggle?"—clearly their answers would have been "No." What was it about the Simpson case that brought out the worst in otherwise honorable professionals?

The intoxicant was fame, notoriety, celebrity. Far more than money; most of Simpson's experts didn't need the money. But the lure of instant recognition—unprecedented media coverage and cameras in the courtroom ensured the ability to become an American household name overnight—overcame whatever qualms they may have had about helping to set a murderer free.

Monday was Veterans Day, and court was not in session. I spent it at our command post at the DoubleTree, preparing Spitz for cross and redirect. Ed was getting ready for our next witness, Doug Deedrick of the FBI, a hair and fiber expert. At around 6:00 P.M. Spitz was on the phone with his secretary back east when he said, "Baden is on TV now. He is talking to Geraldo Rivera about the case. He is talking about what I said."

"No way!" There was a gag order, Baden was a very important, high-profile defense witness, this was way out of line.

The hotel suite didn't get CNBC. "Tape it. You've got to tape it!" I insisted. I called someone local and asked him to tape it as well. Fortunately I got home before nine that night and could watch the rerun. Sure enough, there was Baden commenting directly on Spitz's Friday testimony. This was an absolute outrage. Suppose a juror caught it! I couldn't wait to tell Fujisaki.

The next morning we asked to be heard in open court, before the jury was brought in. I told the judge, "We have here an expert witness consultant retained by the defense, paid by the defense, on television last night commenting specifically about the testimony of a pending witness *whose testimony is not even concluded.* [Dr. Baden] is going to be in court testifying for the defense, talking about Dr. Spitz's testimony in court. I don't think it's appropriate that witnesses under the control of a party, retained witnesses who are thereby agents and representatives of counsel or a party, be talking about the proceedings." Fujisaki declined to hold Baden in contempt but ruled that if he or any witness pulled that stunt again, they would be barred from testifying at this trial. Baker, who didn't even argue the point, had dodged a big-time bullet.

Baker and Spitz became loudly argumentative on this second day of testimony, Baker trying to muscle Spitz into specific testimony ("Can you answer my question for a change?") and Spitz resisting ("I'm not in agreement with you because what you are doing is misleading!"). I was watching the jury during all of this, and they were rooting for Spitz!

Baker, a real showman, was questioning Spitz about the fingernail gouges. Because Ron Goldman had short fingernails, Baker was attempting to make the point that such marks were not possible. Over the weekend Spitz had dug his nails into his own skin and showed me the results: marks similar to those found in the Simpson photographs. On the witness stand, Spitz asked Baker, "Would you like me to show you how this works?"

"Sure," Baker said. "Gouge me." The jury laughed.

"You may be sorry."

"Go ahead!"

"Well, take up your sleeve."

Baker, sensing a put-up job, tried to change the venue. "No, go ahead. Do it right on my hands. . . . Go ahead."

"You want me to scoop? Tear you out?" Spitz was just making sure. He didn't want to be accused later of battery.

"I want you to scoop," Baker dared him, "tear it out." Tough guys, both of them. The courtroom roared.

Judge Fujisaki had had enough of this little evidentiary S&M. "Mr. Baker, I'm not going to have any gouging out of flesh in my courtroom." He got a laugh, too.

Ultimately Dr. Spitz took off his suit jacket and dug his nails into the fleshy part of his own left arm. Despite his short nails, the marks were there.

Try as he might, Baker could not shake Spitz's testimony. Spitz was too tough, too smart, *and he was right.* "Regardless of whether a hole was dug, regardless of whether keys were flung . . . you can opine that all of those wounds were inflicted first to last within less than sixty seconds, true?" Spitz remained adamant.

We'd thought this might happen and we were prepared for it. On redirect, Ed asked Spitz to mark off sixty seconds on his watch.

Spitz banged his hand on the witness box like a gavel, and the courtroom fell eerily quiet. We hadn't warned the judge we would be doing this, so Ed spent the minute worrying Fujisaki would be irritated that we were wasting the court's time and would interrupt and embarrass us. The judge, however, like the rest of the courtroom, remained silent and still.

Sixty seconds passes very slowly when you are quiet. I became aware of my own breathing, I could hear my pulse. The silence contrasted profoundly with the scene I think everyone had in their mind: the thrashing brutality of one minute on June 12 when Ron Goldman, fighting for his life, was being stabbed to death by O.J. Simpson. There was more than enough time. One minute seemed like an eternity.

When Spitz banged his hand on the witness box again, it was as if the whole courtroom came back to life.

Dr. Spitz was the high point of the trial. So far.

TWENTY-FIVE

Blood Simple

E verybody wanted to know when O.J. was going to get called.
Television reporters approached me in the courtroom, wanting to
know when they should send for camera crews; media people in
New York wanted to know when to send their operation out; media representatives were calling from around the world, saying they were coming
in, where should they stay, when would he be on?

I didn't know. In the grand scheme of things, Simpson would be
called after we had concluded presenting the rest of our case. We had
determined that the forensic case would be complete, and completely
unassailable, before Simpson took the stand.

We were nearing Thanksgiving, and the press wanted to know our
plans in the worst way because some of them wanted to take time off
around the holiday. "Please, I won't tell anybody. Off the record. Don't
worry, I won't tell Baker. I just don't want to miss it." I told them all, "I'm
not one hundred percent sure, but don't make any plans."

Baker kept trying to smoke us out so they could gear up. "When are
you going to put him on?" he asked me. "When are you going to put the
Man on?" By court ruling, I had to give him three days' notice.

He went to the judge to smoke me out. "Mr. Simpson is only available the next couple of days," he told him. "If they don't use him then,

it's going to be December because he's going to be testifying in the child custody case and I can't have him testifying in both at the same time."

Simpson's attempt to gain legal control of his and Nicole's children, handled by a different set of lawyers, was also before the courts. Simpson shuttled between that trial and this one, and I suspected from the start that he had timed those proceedings to coincide with ours. He knew he would win the custody battle; he had been judged "not guilty" in the criminal trial, and the Browns had no legal leg to stand on. He must have believed that a favorable judgment, handed down during the middle of the civil trial, would help him. The idea being: No judge would give the kids back to a father who was a murderer, he must be innocent.

I wasn't having any of these tactics. "Judge," I said, "Mr. Simpson is not going to dictate when he testifies in this case. He's just playing games." I gave the Court the approximate date we planned on using him. "We're going to have him here for a couple of days. They can't pull the rug out. This is a transparent attempt to get him not to testify at all, or to control when we put him on so we're not ready or out of sequence."

Judge Fujisaki said, "I'll settle this." He called the judge who was handling the custody case, worked out a schedule, and cleared the days. Simpson would begin testifying on Friday, November 22, the week before Thanksgiving.

We put on our next witnesses in rapid succession. FBI expert Douglas Deedrick indicated that twelve hairs found in the knit cap at the murder scene were consistent with Simpson's hair. To rebut the notion that these hairs might have been flying around Bundy or been transferred from the blanket used to cover Nicole's body, he pointed out that several were embedded in the fabric, meaning they had not simply floated in but had been worked into the cap through contact.

Deedrick noted that samples of the same blue/black cotton fiber were found on Ron's shirt, Simpson's socks, and the glove at Rockingham. This was vital evidence, one common element linking three objects in different locations. There was no innocent explanation.

Deedrick also explained that a rare type of carpet fiber found on the Rockingham glove and the Bundy knit cap matched the carpet fiber in Simpson's Bronco. This directly linked the murders to Simpson's car and, hence, to Simpson.

Dan Leonard's brief cross-examination of Deedrick sought to characterize Deedrick's work as more of an art form than science. There was nothing else he could do. Deedrick's conclusions were very damaging to Simpson, and the defense had no answer to him.

We then turned to the even more damaging blood evidence. We had decided long ago that we would not take this jury to DNA school; we would not attempt to teach them science. Instead, our goal was to make them feel confident in our experts' credibility and stature, explain that DNA is used in making life-and-death medical decisions, and assure that it is just as reliable in forensic applications.

Tom Lambert's exams are like smart missiles: targeted and to the point. Lambert had the DNA lab witnesses Robin Cotton, Renee Montgomery, and Gary Sims on and off in no time. Cotton had spent twenty-six and a half hours on the stand at the criminal trial, in our trial she was done in five hours. Montgomery, five hours in the criminal trial, about one hour with us. Sims, twenty-seven-plus hours down to about half a day.

The blood drops that were sent out for testing included evidence from the trail at Bundy, the back gate, Rockingham, Simpson's socks, and his Bronco. Whether they were sent to the California Department of Justice lab in Sacramento, or the nation's leading private lab called Cellmark, or the LAPD's own lab, the results were all consistent: the blood belonged to O.J. Simpson. This much had already been admitted by Simpson in response to our Requests for Admissions.

Tom's work with Robin Cotton concerning the blood found on Simpson's socks was startling. Cochran *et al* had claimed the conspirators planted Nicole's blood there to frame Simpson. Dr. Cotton explained that when blood is drawn for testing by labs, it is preserved with the chemical EDTA, which stops the DNA in the blood from degrading. (Degradation is simply the breaking down of a chemical into its component parts over time.) But when she compared the degradation levels of Nicole's blood on Simpson's sock with a sample of blood taken from Nicole's autopsy vial, Dr. Cotton found the autopsy vial contained the *more* degraded blood. The blood on the sock was fresher and richer in DNA content than the blood in the vial.

Once blood has degraded, it is impossible to raise its DNA count; you can't pony it back up. Under the conspiracy theory, the blood used to plant on the sock came from Nicole's autopsy vial, but that blood had a lower DNA count than the blood on the sock. Nicole's blood was fresher when it spurted out and splashed onto Simpson's sock as he was killing her than it was two days later when the coroner collected it. This completely destroyed the notion of any planting; it is *impossible* for degraded blood to become fresh again. Nicole's blood on the sock could not have been planted.

I will never forget Johnnie Cochran's righteous indignation about these socks. "Then we come to those socks. Those socks. They just don't fit. They just don't fit. They just don't fit" he preached in closing argument. Powerful rhetoric. But nothing more. How I wished he were in this courtroom instead of some far off TV studio to see how "those socks" now fit.

Our presentation not only identified the blood at the murder scene, at Simpson's house, on his gloves, and in his car as *his* blood, but at the same time destroyed any notion that it was planted along the way. We were leaving the defense defenseless before they even started their case.

With our Requests for Admissions, Tom had forced the defense to admit the legitimacy of the test results. During the discovery period, we had also forced them to admit there had been no planting of Simpson's blood at either Rockingham or Bundy. If they wanted to pursue that line of inquiry at trial, the laws of discovery demanded that they produce all evidence that would lead to the conclusion that planting of Simpson's blood had occurred, and they had produced none. And so far, they had come up with nothing at trial, either. They were running out of time.

We showed that all crime scene blood samples had been collected *before* Simpson returned from Chicago; there was none of his blood *available* to scatter around. All Rockingham blood samples had already been collected, too, before he got back to L.A. (Because the blood on the back gate had not been collected until some time later, however, they still clung to that one. But with our short and sweet examination of Vannatter, they struck out in suggesting that he took some blood from Simpson's arm, brought it back to Bundy, and sprinkled it on the gate; not even Baker could get up the nerve to ask Vannatter that absurd question.)

Now they were boxed in. By chopping off the planting theory at both ends, we squeezed them down to one final argument: the planting of

Simpson's blood had to have occurred in the lab, sometime between the moment the "real killer's" blood was brought in from the Bundy crime scene and the time it was sent out for testing. Somehow a massive switch occurred. Of course, it didn't happen, and they never came up with a single shred of evidence of such a switch. Not one. For all their talk about what might have or could have happened, when called upon, they had no facts to back up their conspiracy theory. For all their suspicious rhetorical questions— "Where was Vannatter? What happened to the rest of Simpson's blood?"— they had no answers. None. In the criminal case they had very effectively, very recklessly, very cynically spread doubt. The prosecution had not been sufficiently prepared to counter that doubt with factual certainty. We were. The planting argument, which had billowed so menacingly amid the criminal defense's smoke and mirrors, just disappeared into thin air.

Which left their contamination argument.

Collin Yamauchi was the LAPD lab analyst who handled the blood samples. He explained under oath the technique he used to test the blood for DNA. When working on Simpson's blood, he said, he stood on the far side of a laboratory bench, away from the evidence, which lay in evidence envelopes on a table in the middle of the room. (Tom had visited the lab and had a visual image of the layout from which to work.) It was important for us to have Yamauchi explain exactly where he performed his work so the jury could see that he could not have contaminated any of the blood samples. He presented his information cleanly.

"Did you spill the blood at all when you were doing this process?" Tom asked directly.

"No," Mr. Yamauchi answered.

"Did the blood go flying out of the vial and go across the room and land on the evidence envelopes that were ten or fifteen feet away?"

"No."

"Did the blood in any way at all contaminate those items of evidence during this process?"

"No."

That was the end of the contamination argument. Right there. Unless he was lying, which no one had reasonably suggested.

But putting aside honesty, let's look at the facts. Each blood-soaked swatch was wrapped in a bindle of pharmaceutical paper. Also present, in their own bindles, were control swatches: swabs taken from the ground around the blood drops but containing no blood, routinely used to show there are no interfering substances in the area that could cause anomalous results. Each bindle, both blood sample and control, sat inside an evidence envelope. When blood-stained swatches are tested, so are the corresponding control swatches. Every single control swatch tested in the Simpson case came up negative, meaning there were no anomalies, the control swatches were clean. Assume, for a moment, that Yamauchi was committing perjury, and that he had slipped on a banana peel and the blood he was testing had flown through the air like cartoon liquids. In order to contaminate the evidence the blood would have had to work its way inside these sealed envelopes, slide inside the pharmaceutical paper, and then somehow land only on the swatches that contained blood, and on none of the controls, which were as clean as a whistle. Impossible!

Tom took Yamauchi very carefully through all the processes, including his safety procedures, and obliterated any notion that the testing was compromised. End of contamination theory.

Before wrapping up, Tom had Yamauchi explain why the blood stains were not discovered right away on Simpson's socks. Yamauchi was with Greg Matheson and Michelle Kestler, who was in charge of the LAPD lab, on June 29 when they had looked cursorily at Simpson's dark socks without noticing any blood. They made a note to inspect them more closely later on. They were put in a secure location. On August 4 Yamauchi examined them closely for the first time, did a quick test, and found the presence of blood. Thereafter, DNA tests confirmed the presence of Simpson's blood and Nicole's blood.

Mr. Yamauchi had been on the stand for fifteen hours in the criminal trial. Tom examined him in under two hours. Bob Blasier did his best to cast doubt on Yamauchi's testimony but the confusion sown in the criminal trial simply did not sprout in this one. They went nowhere with their innuendo.

I watched with great satisfaction as Tom sailed through his witnesses as Ed had done before him.

It was very gratifying to work with such talented lawyers at the top of their form. All the defense's masks, disguises, distortions, and concealments from the criminal trial were being peeled away, and the truth was unfolding in the courtroom. Their unsound arguments, like a flashy mansion built without a foundation, were collapsing under the weight of the facts, and we were there to cart away the debris.

We had presented the main physical evidence—hair and fiber, gloves, blood, the victims' wounds—all except for the shoes. Our next witness should have been William Bodziak, the foremost footprint expert in the country, who would have testified about the Brunos. Unfortunately he was not available for several days, so we followed Yamauchi with a string of police witnesses put on by John Kelly to testify about Simpson's history of domestic violence.

This was the start of the assault on Simpson's character. We wanted to condition the jurors to this side of Simpson, to show what kind of a man he was, before calling him to the stand. More than simply arguing, "He hit her, so he killed her," we were preimpeaching the defendant. We knew Simpson was going to lie, so we laid a trap for him; first the jury would hear several credible witnesses telling the truth, then they would hear Simpson lie in their face, then they would be presented with an impeachment parade in which his lies were identified and countered again. Now it began.

Police Officer John Edwards testified about the 1989 New Year's incident in which he responded to Nicole's 911 call. Nicole, wearing only a bra and sweatpants, "ran across the driveway from the bushes to the control box," he testified. "She yelled several times to me, 'He's going to kill me, he's going to kill me!'" When the gate opened, she collapsed in his arms. "She was crying, she was hysterical. . . . I said, 'Well, who's going to kill you?' And she responded, 'O.J.'" The gate closed behind her.

Now, this is hearsay. Why did this come into evidence? There is an exception to the hearsay rule called "spontaneous statements," which are statements made when someone is extremely excited or agitated. The law says this is credible and trustworthy evidence because a person in that state of mind would not have the opportunity, incentive, motivation, or wherewithal to fabricate. Nicole, scared to death, was clearly being "spontaneous."

Nicole was cold and shivering. Edwards was a supervisor at that time, training a new officer, and he quickly asked his trainee, a woman, to lend Nicole her jacket. He noticed a bruised swelling on the right side of Nicole's forehead. She told him that Simpson had pulled her hair and hit, kicked, and slapped her. Standing right next to Nicole, Edwards noted the specifics of her beating, "and I saw a human handprint on the left side of her neck. I could actually see at least three finger outlines." He put her in the backseat of his black-and-white patrol car.

Nicole said, "You guys come out here, you talk to him, and then you leave. You've been out here eight times before, you never did anything. I want him arrested, and I want my kids back." She signed a crime report. She was still crying.

Then Simpson showed up, bare-chested, wearing a robe and his underwear, no shoes. He was yelling. "I don't want that woman in my house anymore. I got two other women, I don't want that woman in my bed anymore!"

"His face was in a rage," said Edwards, "he was very excited. There's two veins on his head, one on each side of his head, up before you got to the hairline, and they were pulsating rapidly, you could see them very clearly."

"I didn't hit her," said Simpson, "I just pushed her out of bed." Officer Edwards told Simpson to go inside and change clothes, it was his duty to place him under arrest for spousal battery.

Simpson went inside. Next out of Rockingham was his loyal house-keeper, Michelle Abudrahm, who opened the back door of the police cruiser, grabbed Nicole's arm, "started pummeling on her," and tried to pull her out. Nicole resisted.

About three minutes later Simpson reappeared. "Now he was wearing a dark jogging suit or running suit," said Officer Edwards, "either blue or dark blue, I couldn't be sure about the color."

"What makes you so special?" Simpson challenged Edwards. "Why do you want to make a big deal of this?"

When Edwards turned his attention to his own supervisor, who had just arrived on the scene, Simpson bolted. He jumped into his Bentley, exited out of the Rockingham gate on the other side of his house, and gunned it down the road. With Nicole crying and hysterical in the backseat, Edwards and his trainee ran to their car and gave chase. They put out a car-to-car bulletin that they were in pursuit of a blue Bentley with O.J. Simpson driving. (They refrained from putting it on the city frequencies, where anyone monitoring police activities might hear it; even then, the cops were protecting Simpson.) "[We] started searching through the area for the Bentley and never did find it." (They didn't look in Allen Schwartz's garage.) They lost him.

Edwards and his trainee then took Nicole to the West Los Angeles police station, where he photographed her.

Sharyn Gilbert, who had fielded Nicole's 911 call, took the stand. Kelly played a tape of that call in court, and she authenticated it. The night of the disturbance, she had changed its designation from "unknown trouble" to "screaming woman" when she heard Nicole get slapped.

Next came Mark Day, of the Westec alarm company, who testified about a 1984 incident in which Nicole summoned security because Simpson took a bat to her Mercedes. "The glass was shattered and the front hood of the car had several dents in it as well. On the ground, I observed the baseball bat." In his deposition, Simpson testified that he swung the bat playfully, and nothing broke or shattered.

Police Sergeant Robert Lerner responded to an urgent "code 2 high" domestic violence call at Nicole's residence on Gretna Green at around ten at night on October 25, 1993, less than eight months before her murder. We played that 911 tape, in which Nicole had locked herself in her bedroom and Simpson, who had broken her back door, could be heard screaming in the background. (Simpson blamed the broken door on his small kids.) Nicole, Sergeant Lerner testified, was "very scared." Simpson "was pretty much enraged. He was pacing back and forth and talking very loudly."

One of the officers on the scene had surreptitiously taped both Simpson and Nicole talking to Sergeant Lerner. We played part of this "surreptitious tape" for the jury. Nicole, clearly shaken and upset, says, "When he gets this crazed I get scared. . . .

"He doesn't even look like himself. He gets a very animalistic look in him. All his veins pop out, his eyes are black, and he's just black and cold like an animal. I mean, very, very weird. And when I see him, it just scares me." It was remarkable and chilling, the number of witnesses who independently described Simpson in such similar terms.

"[The 911 call] was precaution, more than anything. I think he wouldn't hit me again because he had to do community service and stuff like that for it. I just always believed that if it happened one more time . . . I don't totally believe it would happen, but I get scared. I think if it happened once more it would be the last time."

Nicole as much as predicted her own death.

The next witness, Michael Stevens, was a Los Angeles County DA's Office employee who supervised the opening of a bank safe-deposit box that contained photos of a battered Nicole in an envelope marked "Open Only in the Presence of an Attorney." Also inside was her will. Why would so young a woman make out a will? In safeguarding these photos and her will, Nicole had again presaged her death.

So now we had incidents showing a continuum of violence and rage by Simpson toward Nicole from 1984 to 1989 to 1993.

Meanwhile, back at the DoubleTree, Bill Bodziak rolled into town, and Ed was working hard to get him ready. Tom, breathing easier now that he had finished up with his blood witnesses, wanted to know what he could do to help on Simpson. We were all gearing up for the Simpson examination. I said, "Why don't you pull together the testimony on the cuts and blood as a nice little package. Break-outable." He went to work.

The issue of Simpson's blood was very important. We debated among ourselves whether to ask if he had an explanation for his blood found at his Rockingham home and inside his Bronco. Simpson, of course, wasn't going to ever concede bleeding at Bundy, but when push came to shove, what would he say about Rockingham and the Bronco? In his deposition, he said he momentarily saw a speck of blood on his pinky just before getting into the limo, but did not remember bleeding or seeing blood anywhere else. This was Simpson's clever way of explaining why there might be his blood in his house, on his driveway, and in his car, without having to admit he cut himself at the exact time his wife was being cut to death. Simpson wanted to say to the jury, "Yes, I was bleeding, but just a tiny bit, and no, I wasn't at the murder, and I didn't cut myself on a knife, and nobody scratched or gouged me. But, jeez, I just don't know why I was bleeding and how all these blood drops got there." I had no intention of allowing Simpson to be vague or equivocal.

Frankly, I wanted to hear Simpson categorically deny he dripped blood that night. His blood was on the driveway, in the hall, in the kitchen, in his car. If Simpson wasn't the killer, what's his blood doing all over the place? If he didn't drip the blood there, who did? The "real" killer? Why would the "real" killer, after murdering two people at Bundy, show up at Rockingham to drip blood? And how could he drip Simpson's blood? It was no one else's blood but Simpson's; it had been collected while he was returning from Chicago, so the police had no sample of his blood to plant. Tell me again: It's not your blood? You didn't drip it there? It was laughable, a complete lie, and I hoped he said it. The blood at Rockingham was a huge problem for Simpson.

If he denied dripping blood at Rockingham, we wanted Simpson to admit he had no explanation for all the blood found there. "I have no idea." That would be fine because we had an explanation that the jury would find believable: he cut himself while killing Ron and Nicole and dripped all over on his return. Tom and I carefully worked out our questions, but we worried that if I asked the wrong one, or posed it in the wrong way, I might open the door for Simpson to say, "The reason blood is there is because someone planted it," and then go on to argue his case.

Now, "Someone planted it" would not be a proper answer, because he does not have any personal knowledge of such planting, but I didn't want to give him the opportunity to argue his case in my examination. I wanted to avoid that.

We decided to see how we were positioned as the examination progressed; I would get a feel for our momentum and make that call at the line of scrimmage.

But before we got to Simpson we had two key witnesses to present: Kato Kaelin and the limousine driver, Allan Park. Between them, if handled properly, they could decimate Simpson's alibi.

The results of jury questionnaires were not generally positive about Kato. Our jury pool believed he was "flaky," he was perceived as a person who, rightly or wrongly—and most felt, wrongly—had used his position in the Simpson saga to gain publicity. They thought he knew more than he was telling, and there were unlimited rumors swirling around him: Kato and O.J. bought drugs together; Kato saw Simpson strip down to the murder clothes; Kato knows where the murder weapon is. The facts didn't come into play here, people just had strong feelings about him. To counteract those feelings and still get his information into the record, we would have to keep his testimony as abbreviated as possible.

In the days before he was to take the stand, I had given Kato a linguistics refresher course to deal with the Katospeak problem. I told him, "When I ask you something on the witness stand, just stay with my question. Don't think out loud, don't talk in fragmented sentences. Your testimony will be a lot shorter and a lot easier than last time, and don't worry, I will not declare you a hostile witness."

I prepared him for the expected unfriendly cross-examination by Bob Baker. "Whatever you do," I told him, "don't lose your cool. Don't argue with him." That didn't seem likely; Kato never loses his temper, he doesn't seem to have that emotion in him. In fact, he goes the other way; when confronted, Kato wants to accommodate and please to an extreme. "Don't let him rattle you," I said, "but at the same time, don't let him put words in your mouth."

The crucial issue was time. I said, "Kato, this is what you've testified to: You estimated you heard the thumps against your wall between 10:40 and 10:50. You've testified that way before the grand jury, in the preliminary hearing, at the criminal trial, in our civil deposition; you gave police statements to that effect. Baker is going to want the thumps at 10:40 because he wants to exclude Simpson, and under our theory, Simpson is probably still at Bundy at 10:40. If the thumps occurred at 10:40, the killer is not Simpson.

"I'm more than happy to live with all this because you've not really wavered in your most critical testimony: you've always made clear that you didn't have a watch, but that when you heard those thumps you got off the phone right away and went out and checked. You've always estimated it took you just a couple of minutes to get back there." Kato had even given a statement when he was brought into Robert Shapiro's office two days after the murders, saying he had investigated the sounds within between one and five minutes of hanging up the phone.

Kato's lawyer, Michael Plotkin, was present at our prep sessions as well. Kato, a fidgety guy at the best of times, was nervous. I tried to be calming, but I had to tell him straight, "Understand, you're going to be grilled. They will try to have you move those thumps earlier. It's the key to their case. Just say what you've always said and everything will be fine."

I put Brian Kaelin on the stand on a Tuesday morning. He had become a cult figure, a genuine momentary pop icon, one of those one-name people—"*Kato.*"

Kato wore a tie and sported a shorter haircut for the occasion, and looked a little less like the prototypical California airhead. We had decided to limit his testimony to the 1993 incident in which Simpson kicked in Nicole's Gretna Green door and his time with Simpson on the weekend of June 11 and 12. This would also limit the defense's ability to delve into his relationship with Nicole, to confuse Kato with a vast array of details, and to involve the police.

On the stand he started perfectly, giving me simple answers to simple questions. He has a good memory; if you ask him for facts like "What happened next?" and "Was that there?" he will respond quite ably. It's when you ask him to characterize things that his testimony gets to be a disaster.

We wanted to present his relationship with Simpson for what it was, an acquaintanceship, not a friendship. This was true; they weren't best buddies, and Kato didn't know any of Simpson's intimate secrets. I liked the fact that they were distant. It made Simpson's trip to his room to announce, "Hey, I'm going out to dinner," all the more suspicious.

I also couldn't resist the Chachi questions. Simpson had testified in his deposition that he had not let the limousine into Rockingham on the night of the murders because he was afraid once the gate opened, his dog, Chachi, would run out. (In fact, Simpson didn't let him in because he wasn't home.) In taking the depositions of many people who were in and out of Rockingham regularly, I routinely threw in a seemingly innocent Oh-by-the-way: "Did you ever see Chachi run out the gate?" "Did Chachi run around a lot?" Nobody ever recognized the significance of my questions, and they all said no. I asked Kato, "Could you describe the physical condition of Chachi?"

"I think Chachi had arthritis in the leg," he said. "It was always hobbling, kind of arthritic."

Baker jumped right in. "Move to strike on the basis of no veterinary foundation." Laughter bounded around the courtroom like a puppy.

Fujisaki answered, "Overruled. Lay opinion as to a dog's condition is common." He got a laugh as well.

Kato said he had never seen the dog run out of the gates when they were open; he had never seen Simpson walk the dog or even take him outside the property. "Chachi," he said, "usually stayed in one spot on the grass."

To show that Simpson, on the weekend he killed Nicole, was ruminating about her and dwelling on her being with another man, I ran Kato through Simpson's conversation on Saturday, June 11, while they watched *Garp* on Simpson's TV, and the talk of a white picket fence and "the sound of having children around."

Kato did lapse into Kato-speak on occasion. "There was talk of the IRS," he testified, "and he was mentioning how he was going to do something with the IRS, with changing Nicole's address, and somehow that would cause some sort of financial damage to her." But "there was talk" does not introduce admissible evidence. In order to put the testimony in acceptable legal form, I asked, "Is that what he said?" Kato said yes.

Kato said Simpson mentioned that "Paula probably wanted to get married and have kids, and he was fine, because he had enough kids now and he didn't want any more kids. And he wasn't sure that she was the one for him to settle down with." Why did Simpson not want Paula at the recital? "He thought it would be a family thing, and he didn't want Paula to be there." Simpson would deny this, but Craig Baumgarten was on record saying the same thing; now I had two witnesses to impeach him on the point.

After the dance recital, Kato testified, "[Simpson] said that Nicole was playing hardball with him because he wanted to see his daughter, Sydney." What was Simpson wearing at the time of his conversation with Kato at about 7:00, Sunday, June 12? "I thought it was a sharp-looking sweatsuit, dark, white zipper. . . . Like a jogging outfit."

The more detail we included about Simpson's dinner trip to McDonald's, the more vivid the picture we would paint that he was setting up an alibi, which would suggest he had already made up his mind to kill Nicole. But we didn't need to prove premeditation, we only had to prove that Simpson killed her, and I didn't want to open up an issue if I couldn't nail it down definitively. I toyed with leaving the McDonald's trip out altogether. I could have asked whether they had gone and at what time they had returned and left it there. In the end, though, I decided, "It is suspicious behavior; either he was going over to confront her or to kill her. We'll argue it." Also, I needed to establish that Simpson was last seen by Kato at around 9:30 P.M. in order to start the clock ticking.

The important part of Kato's testimony began when they had returned from McDonald's and Kato headed inside. When he turned around, Simpson was still "at the front door of the Bentley, just standing there." I preimpeached Simpson by asking whether Kato saw him walking, bending down, scooping out lettuce from the driver's side of the car, all as described by Simpson in his deposition to come up with an explanation why he remained behind at his Bentley while Kato walked toward the house. The answers were all *no*.

The three thumps, Kato said, were "like someone falling back behind my bedroom wall." (In fact, I tried to stay away from the word "thump" altogether; it had become an infamous term, and it was misleading because it didn't fully describe the actual sound made by the crashing impact.) He hadn't said that in the criminal trial, and I did a little preemptive strike by having Kato pound the witness stand with his fist and explain the "rhythm and volume" of these noises, knowing he would be slammed in Baker's cross by his several prior testimonies. Then I homed in on the crucial timing issue.

"How long were you on the phone with [his friend] Rachel from the time you heard these noises until the time you got off?" I asked.

"About two to three minutes."

"Approximately how long did that take, from the time you got off the phone with Rachel until the time that you arrived around this point right here?" I pointed to a spot on the diagram of the Rockingham estate, inside the compound and toward the front of the house, where Allan Park had first seen him.

"Thirty to forty seconds."

I now had a total of two and one-half to three and one-half minutes. If I could fix the time Park saw Kato and subtract those minutes, I could establish exactly when the thumps occurred. "Do you have an estimate of the time that you heard these noises?"

"In between the 10:40 to 10:50 hour."

I decided not to question Kato about having seen Simpson walking toward the front door in a dark sweatsuit; he had equivocated at doing so in his deposition as to the sequence of events in which he made this observation; I wanted him to testify as to facts that no one would dispute and on which he could not be fairly challenged. I also wanted to keep Kato and Park in agreement on the essential points, so I concentrated on those points only and tried not to get greedy.

As Simpson was about to leave, he said, Kato saw a small dark bag across the driveway behind the Bentley. He started to walk toward it.

"No, Kato, I'll get that. I'll get that!" Simpson had brushed by him to handle the bag personally. I picked up a blue bag the defense had offered as the bag in question.

"Do you see this bag?" I asked.

"Yes."

"Is this the bag that you saw behind the Bentley?"

"No."

Kato then testified about Simpson calling him from the airport to set the house alarm. I moved from there to his being summoned to Simpson's house the next night, where the cabal had gathered. I heard Leonard say to Baker, "He's skipping the police stuff!" I caught Baker's eye. He shook his head and kind of smiled.

Damn right I was skipping the police stuff. Kato had been interviewed by Fuhrman. That didn't prove anything; our story was not the police, and we were attempting to seal off Simpson from the *Fuhrman, Fuhrman, Fuhrman* defense.

"Were you interviewed by any lawyers?" I asked. Yes, he said, by Skip Taft and Robert Shapiro. "Mr. Shapiro, here in the courtroom today?"

"Right there." Kato pointed.

Robert Shapiro had begun covering the trial that day for the local CBS affiliate, KCBS. Regular members of the media were upset because he got special treatment, sitting up front in seats designated for Simpson's family. That morning, as we were waiting for the judge to enter, he and I had made eye contact. In full view of the jury, I walked over and we shook hands. Shapiro had made a well-publicized break with the defense team, and I figured, by making that gesture, I would signal to the jury that even Simpson's lawyer thought he was guilty.

"And what did you tell Mr. Shapiro?"

"In my interview I said I heard it between 10:40 and 10:50."

If Baker beat up Kato badly on cross-examination, I was toying with the idea of calling Shapiro to verify this testimony. I had him right there in the courtroom; he could have walked right out of the gallery as on *Perry Mason* and been forced to corroborate our timeline. That would have been a scene.

Shapiro didn't last long. The press made a big commotion. After being such an integral player in the case, Shapiro's role as an objective journalist was called into question. Combine that with his special access to the defendant, and his tenure in the fourth estate was very short-lived. He showed up in court the next day but not again after that.

The cross-examination was vintage Baker: snide and sneering.

"Now, Mr. Kaelin, you are an actor, right?"

"Correct."

"Kind of a wannabe actor, would that be fair?"

Kato, I'm sure, wondered at Baker's sense of fairness. Others might have shown annoyance, but Kato simply said, "I studied. I don't know."

"And you have your attorney here in the courtroom?"

"Yes."

"Is your agent here?"

Baker spent considerable time trying to show that Kato was a publicity hound, that he had spent a lot of time with me, preparing for the testimony. They had all his prior testimony and statements up and running on computer, ready to go, and they began by impeaching him on little details, then tried to move into areas we had not covered in our examination. I objected, but to my surprise, Judge Fujisaki overruled and let him continue. This was unlike the judge; he was usually quite a stickler for confining cross-examination to the bounds of the direct exam.

After we broke for lunch, the judge called me and Baker up to the bench without the court reporter. He said, "With all the media surrounding this witness, I prefer not to have him come back to the courtroom, so," he told Baker, "I'm going to let you go beyond the scope."

Fujisaki was always concerned about elements out of his control that would affect the integrity of the trial. He did not want the jury hearing evidence or analysis or even coverage of the trial outside the courtroom. Kato presented a problem. He was not subject to the gag order, and Fujisaki, I presumed, assumed Kato would talk to the cameras when he got out of court. Kato was simply a witness, not a party to the suit, and no one involved had any control over him.

"Your Honor," I complained, "he's not that bad of a guy, and I object to this."

"Well," said the judge, "I know you object. Your objection is noted, but I want to get it over with today so he doesn't have to come back."

Kato was known as "America's houseguest," and the judge didn't want him to become his personal judicial houseguest. A cartoon ran in one of the newspapers showing Kato reclining on the witness stand and Judge Fujisaki saying, "Bailiff, please inform Kato that he can't live here." Fujisaki was taking no chances.

Over lunch I pumped Kato up, "You were absolutely perfect." Kato smiled. "Just magnificent." He started to beam. He was very proud of himself, and he should have been. "Now, just don't get rattled during cross, stay focused, stay on target. You're doing great."

With his new freedom, Baker used Kaelin to try to show that Nicole pursued Simpson to reconcile in 1993, that Simpson knew she was socializing with Marcus Allen and wasn't jealous, that Simpson had been tired but not angry on June 12. He constantly attacked Kato for bias and for courting the press, the idea being that he shifted his entire testimony to be received favorably by the public. Even though he wasn't getting the right answers, he was still making his arguments to the jury.

I constantly worried whether this tactic was effective with the jury. If the jury placed more credibility in Baker as a lawyer than in Simpson as the defendant they might begin to believe what the questions implied rather than what the witness answered. Pitting an effective speaker like Baker against an elliptical guy like Kato did not show our case to our advantage. Still, Kato held his ground. He respectfully, and not confrontationally, refused to roll over.

Of course, Baker spent a long time exhuming Mark Fuhrman. Kato's testimony presented no problems for us, but the entire subject was a diversion. I wanted to destroy Simpson's alibi, now all of a sudden the jury was presented with an hour or so of Vannatter and Fuhrman. Baker asked ominously whether there had been a window in Kato's Rockingham bathroom. "Right," Kato answered, "it is a wind-up window." Baker was trying to plant the idea that Fuhrman went in and dropped the bloody glove through it onto the back alley and then went around to "discover" it. Of course, that didn't happen; Fuhrman never went into Kato's bathroom. It was all nonsense, and it was a pain to listen to, and we would not have been subjected to it if the judge wasn't hellbent on bidding a final farewell to Kato.

On redirect, I relieved my frustration by prancing around the courtroom batting back Baker's attempts to undermine Kato's testimony, reha-

bilitating Kato on all the key points. Yvette Molinaro had helped to organize and pull all of Kato's previous testimony together. She sat at the counsel's table and whenever I needed documentation, she was right on top of
it. John Kelly said, "She's a machine." The bathroom window? It was covered by a screen and Kato had never seen that screen removed. The timing of the noises? Simpson's own lawyers could confirm his testimony.
Kato's supposed exploitation of the saga for gain? He had never received
a dime.

"How much money have you been offered to talk about the facts of
this case?" I asked.

"Between five hundred thousand and a million dollars."

"And you turned it down?"

"Yes."

Despite the harangue about Kato being in this only for profit, he had
been offered more than almost anyone else in the saga and had turned it
all down. For all his flaws, Kato was honorable; he didn't take blood
money.

For the first and only time, the judge extended the session ten minutes, and Kato was gone.

TWENTY-SIX

The Alibi Buster

llan Park is the single person who destroys Simpson's alibi. If you believe Allan Park, O.J. Simpson is a murderer.

Park was the limousine driver who picked Simpson up on the night of June 12 and drove him to the airport. Twenty-five years old, with wavy light brown hair, he was short, kind of stocky, just a very normal-looking young man.

The pickup had been called for 10:45, but Park was a late replacement for his boss, had never driven Simpson before, and arrived well before he was expected so as not to be late for his new celebrity client. At around 10:20 that evening, driving a white stretch limo, he rolled up North Rockingham looking for number 360. He had not been given directions, so he was moving slowly. It was a clear night, not raining, and Park had good vision. He was watching for the numbers painted on the curb in front of each house. "Did you have your driver's-side window open as you were looking at the numbers?" I asked.

"Not that I recall."

That was a slip-up. I normally won't ask a question when I'm not absolutely certain I have a positive answer.

Park noticed the street numbers were leading in the right direction, and he sped up to reach 360. "I was going just a little bit too fast, so I slowed down immediately and noticed that he was on the corner lot." He

saw the number 360 on the curb next to the Rockingham driveway as he
drove by.

"Is there *any* doubt in your mind that you saw the number 360?"
I asked confidently.

"No," he answered, that was the only way he knew it was Simpson's
house.

I put up a big board schematic of Rockingham, showing the location of all buildings, pathways, driveways, entrances, and exits. I then
asked Park a very important question: "Was a vehicle parked there when
you saw 360?"

"No," he said firmly, "I didn't see one."

Park took a right onto Ashford, made a U-turn, came back, and
parked directly opposite Simpson's Ashford driveway. He had not yet
made a decision whether to use the Ashford or Rockingham gate to enter
Simpson's property. He looked at both his watch and the dashboard clock.
It was 10:23, 10:24.

I put up a large police photograph of Simpson's Bronco, parked
where the police had found it the next day, on the street in front of the
Rockingham gate. In the photo, the number 360 was clearly visible to the
north of the vehicle.

"When you were driving up Rockingham, you were driving in the
same direction that that vehicle is facing, right? . . . You were sitting in the
driver's seat, and the 360 was to your right, is that correct?" I was trying to
re-create the image for the jury, let them ride shotgun with Park. "Now,
did you see that car parked there at 10:23, 10:24, when you drove by 360?"

Baker objected feebly, "Asked and answered," and was immediately
overruled.

"No, I didn't."

That was the alibi buster. Simpson had said in his statement to the
police and in his deposition testimony that his car had been parked in
front of the Rockingham gate from approximately 7:30 or 8:00 at night
until the police found it there after the murders. He and Kato had driven
to McDonald's in the Bentley, after which, he said, he had come home,
packed, made some phone calls, hit some golf balls, walked the dog, taken
a nap, "took a dump," taken a shower, gotten dressed, finished packing,
and hit the road. The Bronco, according to Simpson, had never been
moved.

But at 10:23, 10:24, the Bronco was not there. Where was it? Simpson—the only person who drove that car, the only one with the keys in his pocket—had no innocent explanation. If the Bronco was not at Rockingham, neither was Simpson. He was lying, he had no alibi, he was guilty.

Park got out of the limo, sat on the curb, and had a cigarette. "Did you see O.J.Simpson walking a black dog around the block?"

"No."

As part of his alibi, Simpson had said he was walking Chachi. He didn't have a clear idea when he'd walked that dog, but one thing he knew, even though he wasn't looking at a watch at any time that night: It was absolutely before 10:23, 10:24. Why did he know that? Because he'd been sitting in jail learning all the evidence; he knew when Park had arrived, so he knew he couldn't be walking that dog at 10:23, 10:24.

For my part, I kept bracketing the time up until the witching hour. "During the time that you smoked your cigarette and the time that you started to take off again," I asked Park, "during that five- or six-minute interval, did you see O.J.Simpson?"

"No."

Park got back in the car and listened to the radio. At around 10:39 he started it up, took a left, and drove to the Rockingham entrance. He came to a complete stop directly in front, with his window parallel to the gate. He turned his head to the left and looked up the driveway. He was trying to decide which entrance was most convenient for a stretch limousine. This was a big thing for him, this was his first time, this was O.J.Simpson; he didn't want to screw it up.

"Did you see the number 360 again?"

"Yes." He was directly in front of it, on the other side of the street. He was looking right at it with a clear field of vision.

"And did you see any vehicle parked there at that time, 10:39, 10:40?"

"No, I didn't."

Again, the alibi buster. The Bronco wasn't there, and neither was Simpson.

"Now, by the way, when you drove down Rockingham to assess the situation, and when you stopped in front of the Rockingham gate, did you see O.J.Simpson?" I loved asking those questions.

"No, I didn't."

The angle into the Rockingham driveway was too tight for a stretch limo to negotiate, so Park decided he would stick with Ashford. He backed down Rockingham, then turned and pulled the limousine to within inches of the Ashford gate. The gate was closed. He got out of the car, went to the intercom call box, and rang the buzzer. It made a loud noise, but there was no answer.

The house was dark. On his $29.95 video, Simpson had stressed that Park could not possibly have known that all the lights were off downstairs because one cannot see into the family room and other parts of Simpson's house from the Ashford gate, and when we had gone to Rockingham to investigate, that appeared to be true; certain downstairs lights could be turned on without being visible from the Ashford gate. I asked a very specific preemptive question, knowing that Baker would try to hammer him on cross. "When you say you noticed there were no lights on downstairs, what you're saying is that from what you could see, you couldn't see any lights?" Park said that was correct. But he could see right through the bars of the gate, he testified. I was setting up his field of vision for an important sighting.

"You have a cell phone in the car?" I asked. He did. Phone records revealed that Park had made and received a series of calls during that time frame, and DecisionQuest had developed a large graphic showing them all. Park's cell phone records from then on became the timekeeper for all the action at Rockingham.

At 10:43:44 P.M., Park called his boss Dale St. John's pager. After that, at about 10:45, he said he got out of the car and rang the buzzer a few more times. From 10:46:30 to 10:48:50 Park was on the phone with his mother, getting St. John's home number. (What he didn't know was that at 10:48:13 and again at 10:48:38, St. John was responding to his page; in a burst of modern technology, the cell phone log showed "incoming call received busy signal.") He called St. John's home at 10:49:07, letting the phone ring for fifty-nine seconds, but got no answer. (Again, St. John was calling Park and getting a busy signal.) He put the cell phone down, got out of the car, and rang the Ashford gate buzzer a few more times. Still no answer.

Park was standing next to the buzzer at 10:52:17, when he heard the cell phone ring inside the car. He hurried to the car and got back in. The radio was on low, the driver's-side door was open, the other doors were closed. It was St. John. Park said he didn't think there was anybody home; there were no lights on downstairs but that there was a light on upstairs. His boss, Simpson's usual driver who had chauffeured him more than a hundred times before, was not handling this job only because he was busy picking an all-star team for his son's little league team. St. John said, "O.J. usually runs late. Go ahead and wait until 11:15. If he's not there by then, go ahead and come on home."

"Somewhere in the conversation, that's where I saw the white male come out from the back of the house." Park described him as a blond-haired male, five-ten, 170 pounds. "Somebody's here," he told St. John. Thirty seconds later, at 10:55:12, he hung up the phone. Park had seen Kaelin at approximately 10:54:30.

Kato had testified that it was between two and a half and three and a half minutes between the time he heard the thumps against his wall and the time he reached the front of the house. Using simple arithmetic, we had now pinpointed the times those thumps occurred: 10:51 to 10:52.

We were coming to a very important part of Park's testimony, one that caused us consternation. Park had testified before the grand jury that he had seen "a black male" walking across the driveway. There were two issues of contention: what he had been wearing and where he had been. Park had originally said the man was wearing "all black clothing, dark pants, dark top" and had "crossed the driveway."

As early as June 15, Simpson had concocted an alternate wardrobe. When Park was interviewed by Shapiro and described the clothing, the lawyer asked, "Could it have been a robe?" Park, having been told by Simpson that he'd just stepped out of the shower, said it could have been. Cochran seized on this in his questioning and turned "dark clothes" into "a hem of a robe swirling around." I had digested all this when I asked Park, "At that moment [when he first saw the man in dark clothes], did you believe that you were seeing that person wear a robe?"

"At that time, no," Park responded.

"Did you believe that you saw a swirling hem of a robe?"

"No."

"Did you believe you saw a belt of a robe waving and flipping around, and so forth?"

"No."

"Before you learned anything else or talked to any lawyers or any-body else, at that point in time, you believed, when you said 'dark cloth-ing,' that the person was wearing what?"

Baker knew what I was doing and objected, but he was overruled.

Park had testified that the man he saw cross the driveway in dark clothes was African American, six feet, 200 pounds. I was disappointed I couldn't put the number 32 on his back.

At the criminal trial, Marcia Clark had Park use a Telestrator to define the exact spot that Simpson crossed. I was under the impression that Park had manipulated the Telestrator himself, but in our interviews he explained that a technical person in the courtroom held the controls, and Park had told him, "Move it, move it, move it. Okay, there." The tech person had marked the spot with an X.

The placement of that X was not on the side of the driveway where Park had actually seen Simpson, but on the other side, near some benches, leading to the front door. Now there was a difference, a conflict, in Park's testimonies.

The night after Simpson's acquittal, Johnnie Cochran had appeared on *Larry King Live* and Simpson had called in. Among his major points was that Marcia Clark had misled the jury by saying Park saw him cross the driveway. Simpson explained that Park did not testify at the trial that he saw Simpson walking across the driveway, as Clark argued. Rather, Simpson insisted Park said he saw the figure five feet from the front door. At his deposition, Simpson gave the fuller version of this attempt to explain Park's incriminating observations. According to Simpson, Park saw him after he had come down from upstairs. He had changed, had a robe on, had pants on, and had no shirt. That explained "a figure with dark clothing." Simpson claimed he had come down to check his golf bag for shoes, saw the limo driver out there, actually waved to him, then walked back inside. Park saw Simpson walking back inside after looking in the golf bag, not coming back from the murders.

Before we met, I struggled with the question: Why had Park put the X in two conflicting locations? When I asked, Park explained it simply. He had always said he saw Simpson "walking across the driveway," but he did not appreciate the need for such a high degree of precision in defining exactly where. Surely that precision was necessary; the one piece of evidence the criminal jury had asked to review in their brief deliberations was Park's testimony. One of the jurors who held out—if three hours can be considered a hold-out—relied heavily on Park.

Park was going to get hit by Baker full force on this discrepancy, so I decided to deal with it first. I had Park walk up to a diagram and point exactly to the place where he first saw Simpson, in the driveway near the Bentley. Then, he explained how the *X* came to be misplaced at the criminal trial. Park also impeached the statements Simpson had made during his deposition: he never saw Simpson nod or gesture in any way; never saw Simpson signal to him or hold up a golf bag.

After Park saw Simpson enter the house, he figured the gate would open. Fifteen, thirty seconds went by without response. Then, he stepped out of the car and pushed the intercom button. This time it was answered. Simpson said, "Sorry, I overslept. I just got out of the shower. I'll be down in a minute." Park went back to the car. Another half minute passed. Finally, not Simpson but Kato opened the gate for him.

To review: Park saw Simpson go inside. He got out of the car, called him, talked to him, went back to the car, and still was not let in. What was Kato doing all that time? Still checking behind the house? Probably, but we don't know for sure. It's a hole that has never been filled.

The dog didn't bolt. When Kato opened the Ashford gate and Park's stretch limo pulled slowly in, Chachi stayed put.

Kato asked whether Park had felt an earthquake, then started talking about the sounds he'd heard against his wall. He started to go around the house to investigate, but after walking halfway down, thought better of it, and returned.

By then, Simpson had come out of the house. He was wearing stone-washed blue jeans and a white polo shirt and carrying "what we all know now is the Louis Vuitton bag," said Park. He set that down next to a suit bag and his grip, which were already sitting on the porch. Park remembered that, "He just seemed to be in a very big hurry." Simpson proceeded on foot down the driveway toward the Rockingham gate. I followed that trail.

"And did he then leave your field of view or vision for a while?"

"Yes, he did."

Park didn't know it, but Simpson was going to get his cell phone, which was sitting in the Bronco. He had told the police he had used it to call Paula. The only record of such a call was at 10:03 P.M. That was another alibi breaker; if the cell phone is in the car at 10:03, then Simpson is in the car and not at Rockingham. To cover for this devastating fact, Simpson said he did not go down the driveway to get his cell phone but to get his cell phone *accessories.* It was a bad joke, but he stuck to it.

As Park was loading the Vuitton bag and Kato was putting the golf clubs into the limousine trunk, Park saw a small, dark bag lying on the edge of the driveway, to the rear of the Bentley. "Kato said, 'I'll go get that bag for you,'" Park testified. "Simpson jumped out and said, 'No, no, no, that's okay, that's okay, I'll get the bag, don't worry about it, I'll get it.' So Simpson went and grabbed the bag." Park could not remember where he put it.

I showed Park the blue bag Simpson had brought to court as the bag in question. "Is this the bag that you saw there?" I asked.

"No," he said.

Park put the suit bag and Simpson's grip in the front seat. There were five bags in all.

Another trouble spot for Park in the criminal trial was the fact that he had not recalled seeing the Bronco parked on Rockingham as he left for the airport. This was an observational mistake, because the Bronco was there by then. Park also thought he saw a second car inside the Rockingham property, which Kato says was not there. Cochran linked these two errors and claimed that therefore none of Park's testimony was reliable. I tried to rehabilitate him on these points. "You didn't look for parked cars; is that what you're saying?"

In the limo on the way to the airport, Park said, Simpson "seemed to be bending down, working with the bags." At the airport, by the time Park produced a luggage cart, there were only four bags to load. The dark blue carry-all was not in sight. Simpson claimed during his deposition that he put it in the golf bag while consolidating luggage.

Park shook hands with Simpson when he left. Expecting the defense to ask whether he had seen cuts on Simpson's hands, which Park had not, I made it clear that he didn't touch, examine, or even look closely at Simpson's left hand.

I was extremely pleased with Park's testimony. He was rock solid. He had no reason to lie about anything. The defense could quibble about his recall of inconsequential details, but the essence of his story was completely irrefutable: The Bronco wasn't there and Simpson wasn't home; he saw Simpson go into the house and all of a sudden Simpson was home. The mock jury had been extremely persuaded by my discussion of Park's testimony, and I felt the real jury reacted the same.

Baker's defense relied on their recapitulating parts of Park's criminal trial testimony. He cherry-picked it and found an unfortunate moment between Park and Marcia Clark. "When you were looking at the curb and you say you saw this address," she had said, "you indicated earlier that you did not see a white Ford Bronco."

"I wasn't looking for it. I didn't see it," he said.

"Are you sure you didn't see it?"

Now, that is a dangerous question from a prosecutor trying to elicit a "yes" to one of the single most important questions in the trial. Rather than demanding the correct answer, it projected uncertainty. You're going to get burned with that question; you're planting a seed of doubt in the witness's mind. *I can't be 100 percent sure of anything.* Park didn't see the car, he never saw the car, but he answered, "I wouldn't say I'm positive. I wasn't looking for a car, I was looking for an address." That answer was a disaster.

Baker pulled out Cochran's examination and read as the skilled attorney led the witness regarding the clothes he saw on the man entering the house:

"It could have been a robe, is that correct?"

"It seemed to be dark clothing. It could have been anything."

"It could have been anything because you don't know, isn't that true?"

"That's true."

"You just got a fleeting glance, isn't that right?"

"Yes, sir."

"You just got a fleeting glance, isn't that right, sir?"

"Yes."

This is how trials become word games. The witness saw what he saw, and yet a good lawyer could change that. Now Cochran had Park saying he didn't know what he saw. Park, for his part, was not a strong fighter, but even the strongest witnesses told me they had been frightened and intimidated when they got on the stand at the criminal trial. They had seen the proceedings on the tube every day and now *they* were on television, the media surrounded them, this was the Trial of the Century, they were not about to get into a fight with some sharp attorney and get embarrassed. The pressure on witnesses was nerve-wracking, and after a while they just gave in.

Baker scored some points. He pointed out that Park could have corrected the placement of the X at any time during his examination, and didn't. He noted strongly that Park had never before testified that he had seen Simpson "round the corner" to get into the house, "and yet, you've been asked about this incident under penalty of perjury, now, at least four times." He was trying to suggest fabrication because Park's testimony had never before been so damaging to Simpson.

In redirect I had a little rehabilitation to do. I pointed out Park's very first statement to Shapiro on June 15: "I saw somebody cross the driveway and go into the house." Shapiro was still in the courtroom and it must have been difficult for him as I used his own interview to destroy his own case. "The person was dressed how?" Shapiro had asked. "They were wearing a lot of dark clothes." He said nothing about a robe. In fact, outside the presence of Simpson's attorneys, Park had told the grand jury, "It was just a dark shirt and dark pants."

Finally I wrapped it up. "Is there any reason, Mr. Park, you would have to come into this courtroom and tell anything but the truth?" I asked him.

"No reason at all." Park had emerged from his day on the stand with his honor thoroughly intact that both question and answer were mere flourishes.

"How much did you get that night for all your trouble?" I asked.

"Possibly about forty bucks."

We finished up the physical evidence case with the FBI footprint expert William Bodziak. He explained the method by which he determined that the shoe prints at the murder scene were made by Bruno Magli shoes and their Silga sole. He recounted the international search that successfully concluded in the small town of Civitinova Marche, Italy, where the Silga soles were made. Bodziak had done a brilliant job; all he'd had to work with was a few bloody shoe prints and every shoe in the universe, and he had made the match.

Bodziak and Medvene had organized an exhibit showing a blowup of the bloody shoe print and an acetate overlay of the Silga sole, revealing them to be a perfect match. Ed demonstrated for the jury by flipping the acetate: shoe print, overlay, shoe print, overlay. The images were identical. In one moment it was completely clear.

Bodziak had testified at the criminal trial, but Ed refined and high-lighted the most persuasive points of his testimony. We blew up the crime scene photographs and let Bodziak use his expertise to analyze them specifically. This was a man who knew what he was talking about. He was a very powerful witness.

Bodziak also established that a bloody pattern in the driver's side car-pet of the Bronco was consistent with the Bruno Magli Silga sole, but he could not identify it positively because there were not enough points of comparison to make the identification absolute.

But we had more. We had the Harry Scull Jr. photograph of O.J. Simpson walking through Buffalo's Rich Stadium, the sole of his shoe reflecting the bright red paint of the end zone. Bodziak explained how he used eighteen points of comparison between the shoe in that photograph and a Bruno Magli exemplar and found them to be exactly the same.

This was the clincher. Testifying in the criminal trial, Bodziak had only been able to identify the type of shoe worn by the killer and state that there were only 299 pairs of these shoes, size 12, sold in the United States. Other than the shoe size, he had not been able to tie the shoe to Simpson because there was no direct evidence—no receipt, no eyewit-ness—putting Simpson in the shoe. Now we had Simpson wearing the murder shoes.

Ironically, Bodziak's potent testimony was largely unnecessary. In his opening statement, Baker had admitted Bodziak's two main points: One, the shoe prints at the crime scene were made by Bruno Magli Silga soles, size 12; and two, the Scull photos depicted such shoes. So basically we didn't need Bodziak, but he was such an impressive witness that we wanted the jury to feel the scientific certainty of his findings.

There was one other reason we gave so much attention to the shoes: It was untainted testimony. The blood evidence had been so effectively attacked at the criminal trial with accusations of planting by the twins of deception and wild talk of a "cesspool of contamination," that it carried significant baggage. The gloves, also very damaging evidence—I don't know how much more damaging you can get than to have a photograph of the defendant wearing the murder gloves—suffered from being linked to Mark Fuhrman, and put on by Simpson grimacing in front of the jury, as he struggled to make sure the gloves didn't fit.

The shoe evidence, however, was pristine. The criminal defense team had not found it necessary to devise and mount an attack to destroy it because it hadn't existed. We could just see Simpson and his team of experts breathing a sigh of relief: "At least we don't have to come up with a planting argument for that." Because the issue of shoes posed so little threat—just say "No, I didn't own any"—they had been able to largely ignore it. Had photos of Simpson wearing Bruno Maglis surfaced during the criminal case, you could have counted on a cockamamie theory of how some nefarious conspirator had gone into Simpson's closet, pulled out these shoes, hightailed it over to the crime scene, and started tromping around in them. Indeed, Lee Bailey couldn't resist suggesting a hypothetical shoe switch by the real killer in his pointless cross-examination of Bodziak in the criminal trial.

So, now they were unprepared.

To my surprise, young Phil Baker rose to cross-examine Bodziak. It seemed to me they were throwing in the towel on this one, given big Baker's opening statement concessions. Phil, whom we called "Little Baker," asked a couple of tough questions and hit Bodziak hard about the placement of the shoe print in the Bronco, trying to show its location was improbable, and suggesting that the stain wasn't a shoe print at all.

Phil did a good job, and afterward I told him, "You know, I didn't think anybody could cross-examine Bodziak, and you made him breathe hard a couple of times." I patted him on the back. Phil was a nice guy. I told his father, "You should be proud of your son. You fed him to the wolves and he did just fine." Baker liked that. Whenever you told him anything good about his son he beamed.

I could not help but notice Baker's face as he watched his son work in the courtroom, it was full of a father's pride and pleasure. Everybody saw it. Even in the midst of this intense battle, Baker could step aside for a quick moment like a soldier stopping for a smoke and watch his kid performing like a champ. He was just so proud of his boy. And rightly so.

TWENTY-SEVEN

Examination Day

Bodziak finished up and we all took a big breath. We had proven through the blood, the hair, the clothes, the gloves, the shoes, the photographs, the alibi witnesses, and the domestic violence witnesses that Simpson was the killer. We had one major job left: Dismantle the man. I had to put Simpson in front of the jury and let them feel what I had come to feel, what I had come to know over the previous twelve months: He was a despicable man, a liar, a cheat, a fraud, a murderer. The jury would see for themselves, something Simpson made sure the criminal jury never had the opportunity to do. O.J. Simpson was going to take the stand the next morning.

Lawyers don't like to make decisions until the last minute. We like to keep our options open, not unlike a good running back watching for holes in the line and then darting through. But as the trial unfolded and our case drew closer toward conclusion, the issue became settled in my mind: we would call Simpson to the stand and question him about all the important issues in the case: his relationship with Nicole, his history of abuse, his motive, his alibi, all the physical evidence, and his last minute flight from the police. Two months of trial had given us a strong impression of Judge Fujisaki, and we were convinced that if we put Simpson on and told the entire story through him, the no-nonsense judge would not permit Baker to repeat that information during the defense case. The jury would be left with our presentation, our direction, our analysis, our verdict.

More than anything, I wanted Simpson's first appearance before the jury to be on our terms, a confrontational, accusatory examination in which we would throw everything we had at him. We would damage Simpson, injure and wound him as much as we possibly could. We would be getting two for the price of one; not only would we be arguing our case through Simpson, but we would also be impeaching him, demonstrating at every turn that he was a liar. After days of Simpson lying to the jury, we were willing to let the defense take their shot at putting him back together again. I didn't think it could be done.

The examination had one guiding rule: I would ask questions that forced Simpson to give us an answer helpful to our cause or tell a demonstrable lie. I would then impeach his lies with documents, statements, tapes, photographs, and his own previous deposition testimony—and I would do it right then, right there. I would not allow him into any area in which we did not have the evidentiary bullets to shoot him down. When he was done, we would run a parade of witnesses in front of the jury to finish off the impeachment, but at all moments we would reveal Simpson to be the liar he was. There was no final team meeting or discussion to conclude our year-long debate of this issue. It was clear to everyone.

I asked Peter Gelblum to work with me in preparing the outline for my examination. I said, "I want to attack him hard. I do not want to let up for one minute." He agreed completely. For the entire first month of the trial, while I was in the courtroom, Peter was working fifteen-hour days back at his office, at the DoubleTree, and in the courtroom itself. He organized all of Simpson's information into several hundred different files, created a subject matter index—alibi, bag, Bloomingdale's, gloves, luggage—and had virtually every piece of evidence at the ready. From that universe he created a cohesive outline, plucking Simpson's statements and pairing each with an impeachment, moving seamlessly from point to point. Peter was the only one of the partners who knew how to use the computer, and he walked around with most of the trial information in his laptop; but more than that, he was an excellent writer with a tactician's sense of development and a performer's sense of pace.

We started with day one, the day Simpson first met Nicole, and ended on June 17, the day he was arrested for her murder. We would tell the whole story.

We were at it for a solid month, meeting after court, at night, on weekends. Peter's work was brilliant. He could pull out obscure witness statements, find exactly the proper place and moment to juxtapose them against Simpson's assertions, and insert the conflict into the chronology. He would sit at the keyboard and put things together on his own, then I would read it, enjoy it, change it. We would argue points and discuss pacing, then I would go back to court and he would keep moving forward. We did this for days and nights and weeks, working, focusing, shaping this body of work. We created a steamroller of impeachment.

A term had been coined at the criminal trial for impeaching a witness, to hang someone out to dry: to "Fuhrmanize." The paradigm was: "I didn't say the N-word in the last ten years"—*boom,* here's the tape of you saying it. We were going to "Fuhrmanize" Simpson.

Peter had also recently come up with a piece of gold. The defense had subpoenaed from the district attorney's office all the phone records they had accumulated, including Simpson's records. They showed up during jury selection, a stack of bills and printouts three feet high. Both sides were permitted to examine the originals and make whatever copies we saw fit. Over lunch, Peter was rummaging through one bundle while Phil Baker and another defense attorney, Melissa Bluestein, flipped through the others. This was not easy going. The computer printouts had row after row of raw data, run-in fine-print numbers, no spaces. The numbers ran the length and width of the page, a cinderblock of digits. Hard on the eyes. Pacific Bell meets *The Andromeda Strain.*

Peter found something. Looking at a computer printout for Simpson's Rockingham home phone, he noticed listings of a 999 number. Gelblum knew every call on Simpson's phone bill by heart, but he had never seen this number before. What the hell was it? According to the records, Simpson called it several times on Sunday, June 12. Peter tabbed the listing, then tabbed some others to camouflage his interest from Little Baker and Bluestein when they flipped through.

It turned out to be Simpson's message manager, the number he called to pick up his cell phone voice mail. And there, on the printout, was a listing for a five-minute call from Rockingham to the voice mail on

Sunday, June 12, at 6:56 P.M. This was exactly the time—after the recital, after talking to Kato—when Simpson had said he'd been on the phone. *Simpson had picked up his messages.* Peter was certain we now had documentation that Simpson, despite his adamant denials, had indeed received Paula's "Dear John" call.

I was petrified that the information wasn't what Peter surmised it was. Peter was excited, bubbling, "Look, here's Simpson's phone number, here's the time, here's the date, here's the duration! If he denies, we can bring in someone from the phone company to authenticate it and verify it."

Peter sat at the keyboard while I paced the floor and read his drafts, and day by day we built the examination. In the process of talking the outline out loud, I learned it inside out. I did not want to be surprised by any answer Simpson might give, so I kept on preparing. I was so consumed with working on the outline, constantly reorganizing and remodeling it, that I never sat down and practiced cross-examining Simpson. From casual conversation to individual excerpts, Peter and I had gone over it a million times, but we never had a dress rehearsal.

Gelblum and I hammered out the 105-page outline. Peter, Yvette, Carolyn Walker, Steve Foster, Maria Johnson, and I commandeered the DoubleTree suite as the final drafts came off the printer. We each kept a copy in our black, vinyl-covered three-ring notebooks. Inside, the topics were laid out in order, point by point. There were no specific questions to pose, just the points to be covered, but the structure of the examination was between those covers.

Also the cues. As well as being the text of a tragedy, this outline was a stage manager's script. Every time a demonstrative exhibit was to be used, Steve would be on his mark. When a document was mentioned, Yvette would have it ready for me like a scalpel for a surgeon. A photograph? Cue Steve on the ELMO. Steve and Yvette were vital to the examination's smooth operation.

By this time I had an encyclopedic command of the details and facts of the case. They had invaded my life. The digital clock would show "10:03" and I would say, out of nowhere, "Simpson's calling Paula." I was more than ready.

I took a room on the eighth floor of the DoubleTree that night. I didn't want to have to get up early and fight traffic. I was settling in when Fred Goldman called.

"So how do you feel, Dan?" he asked. Fred was excited. He was doing his own prebattle preparations.

"I'm getting ready." I deliberately tried to keep my feelings low-key.

"I know you're going to kill the son of a bitch!"

As the Simpson examination approached, Fred had been asking me for several days, "Now, you're going to go after him, right? You're going to get in his face, aren't you?" This was his way of reminding me.

"Fred," I promised, "you can bank on it." From the first day I'd met him, Fred had made clear what he wanted. He was battling Simpson vicariously, through me. We knew that. I accepted that mantle.

Fred and I had become very close during the past year, and I had changed in quantum leaps from the lawyer and person I was when I'd first taken the case. I no longer had any ambivalence about Simpson; he was a cold-blooded killer, a liar, a cheat, a fraud. I would no more shake his hand than salute him. I felt Fred was almost like a brother, and I felt like a second father to Ron, even though we had never met.

Patti and Kim were on the phone as well. They had become my family in this small private world I was occupying. They joined in the pep talk. "We know you're going to do a great job. We can't wait! We've been waiting for this day for a long time."

I didn't think I would be able to sleep. I am usually pretty wound up the night before a big day in court, so add to that the fact that I was in a strange bed and was facing a day in which the whole world would be watching me. But surprisingly, I didn't even feel the need to work through the night. I was confident and relatively calm. I watched ESPN SportsCenter for an hour, as I usually do, then clicked off the light.

I woke up around five-thirty, showered, put on my suit and the UNICEF lion tie that my wife had given me, tucked my black-vinyl outline notebook under my arm, and headed down to the DoubleTree dining room. The room was dark; it didn't open until six-thirty. The waiters were ambling around, setting things up for the morning rush, but they let me in, opened a booth, and turned on a light for me so I could work. When the coffee was fired up, they brought me a cup. I was in there turning pages as the place opened for business.

Usually the DoubleTree was quiet in the morning, with people straggling down for a casual breakfast. But that day the crowds arrived early and with a sense of urgency. This was it!

The hotel had filled with media. Many reporters, seeing me poring over my notebook, came by briefly to offer words of encouragement. I appreciated the good will but it was too distracting to get any work done so I just ate my Raisin Bran and bananas and read a couple of newspapers. I was upstairs in our suite at about seven o'clock when the team began to arrive.

Fred bustled in as if emerging from a scrum. "It's a zoo down there!" The hotel's atrium lobby had swelled with camera crews, and the Goldmans had been mobbed as they tried to go upstairs. Patti and Kim hugged me when they came through the door. Patti's mother was there, too. Tom came by, patted me on the back. Ed did the same. The firm had hosted a dinner the night before, which of course I didn't attend. "I told everybody you couldn't be there because you were preparing for the 'Cross-examination of the Century,'" Tom laughed.

Many on the team brought family and friends to court for the big day. Peter's wife, Sian, arrived, as did Ed's; Team Mom Carolyn Walker had the taxing task of securing them all seats. I could not get involved in that kind of Super Bowl distraction. I didn't have anybody there—no relatives, no friends; I didn't even make arrangements to bring my wife or my kids. Nobody. I was separated—physically, emotionally, in every way—from everything except this trial and this day. I was alone.

Finally it was time to go. I put on my jacket and made sure I had my daily supply of Certs. (I am a superstitious man, and it was one of Steve Foster's tasks in the struggle to see that I had a fresh supply each day.)

We gathered in the lobby, a big, big group now. Me, Tom Lambert, Peter Gelblum, Ed Medvene, Yvette Molinaro, Arthur Groman, Steve Foster, Carolyn Walker, Fred Goldman, Patti Goldman, wives, friends, associates, secretaries. There must have been twenty of us. I said, as I said every day before walking over, "All right! Time to rock and roll!"

We walked through the DoubleTree doors into the middle of a firestorm.

I had seen this kind of mob scene in movies, on television, in news footage of Vietnam protests or Rolling Stones concerts. People were lined up thick and deep the entire two hundred yards between the hotel and the courthouse, and it seemed as if they were all screaming at us. The closest were the reporters and their camera crews, all civility gone, elbowing each other for position and shouting questions: *"How do you feel?" "What are you going to do to him?" "What is your first question going to be?"* This was no time to answer; I felt that if we stopped for a moment we would get overrun.

Our Los Angeles County deputy sheriff escorts had put up barricades in the parking lot and cleared a path for us, but people were straining over them, reaching, shrieking. This exceeded anything I'd seen so far. The walk to court was usually a pleasant stroll by the media and groups of onlookers. That morning I heard some new exhortations: "You're our hero!" "Petrocelli for President!" But there was also more than a little jeering, some of it anti-Semitic, most of it pretty ugly: "Goldman, you gold-digger," "Go in and get your money." I don't know that anybody actually called Fred a "Jew bastard," but that was the idea.

The crowd was hysterical and actually kind of threatening. It made me feel like I was in the middle of a 1960s civil rights march. I never expected to see such a whirlwind, let alone be at its center. The scene was something out of a dream, like it was happening to someone else. Our team walked through the screaming, side by side.

Rather than enter through the main courthouse lobby, our usual procedure had been to duck into a side door and take the back stairs up to the courtroom. This day, we were very thankful for that sanctuary. Once those doors shut behind us we were in a different world. Somehow serene. We walked up one flight of stairs, past institution-green walls that still showed the effects of the most recent earthquake, and through the metal detector, which looked like an old-time phone booth with the back taken out.

A large corner of the second-floor hallway had been cordoned off for the principal players, and from the floor-to-ceiling windows I looked outside and saw the entire courthouse lawn packed like a carnival midway. What looks on TV like a reporter's unique perspective is, in fact, a thigh-to-thigh camera setup. Some stations had erected platforms for their coverage, as if they were doing a pregame show. Thick cables were running from light stands to generator trucks, technicians were plugging things in, pundits trundled from one station to another like traveling salesmen, while reporters were talking to everyone and each other. The press had called the congregation outside the first Simpson trial "Camp O.J." This was "Camp O.J.-by-the-Sea."

We were searched and patted down by courthouse security, then allowed inside the courtroom. I opened the door, and, though the room

was empty, was hit with a blast of uncontainable energy. I put my outline
on the lectern, spread out my materials, and began to arrange the blocking. I installed Peter in my seat, where he could work with his notebook
and laptop; I didn't figure I'd sit down. The counsel table was full, and I
had made a special point of asking Arthur Groman to be present.

A few minutes later, the press—the lucky ones who had been able to
wangle credentials for that day and were not relegated to the media trailer
for the audio feed—were ushered in. Seating was assigned. Usually before
court was in session, one or two reporters might come up and have something to say, but on this day they weren't about to intrude or even come
near me. They waited for my lead. I was trying to keep things as natural as
possible, so when I came visiting they were more than happy to chat.

The aura of expectation was high. There were no casual observers in
the room, everyone had some vested interest: the parties, the lawyers, the
families, the media (who wanted to see a good fight). Certainly the few
members of the public on hand, who had invested considerable time and
energy by lining up in the wee hours of the morning for tickets, felt personally involved. Courtroom decorum maintained that noise be kept to a
minimum, especially in Judge Fujisaki's court, and people were keeping it
down to a hum.

There had been times in the past, both as a trumpet player before a
big solo and a lawyer before an important argument, when I'd gotten a
bad case of the butterflies, but I was so focused on what I had to do that
I was strangely calm. I moved straight into tunnel vision. I looked up and
the crammed courtroom was overflowing with emotion. It was as if hope
and anger, fear and aggression, and honor were all physically present and
making the walls bulge.

Court was to be in session beginning at eight-thirty, and I figured
I had better make a trip to the bathroom. I didn't want to find myself
in the middle of an intense examination and have to excuse myself for
a pit stop.

I took a left out the large courtroom doors, took another left, and
there was O.J. Simpson. He and a group of friends and family were
crowded in the hallway in a tight circle, saying prayers. Praying to Jesus.
I heard, "Lord, give him strength," and, "God be with him."

What I found striking about this prayer vigil was how uninvolved
Simpson appeared. All the others had their heads bowed, their eyes tightly

shut. From their body language I could tell they cared with a passion, that it was important to them that this man win. They were intensely engaged, convinced that Simpson was innocent, that he didn't do these terrible things, and that God would prevail on his behalf.

I didn't get that feeling looking at Simpson. Although a part of the circle, he seemed apart from it, almost as if he were going through the motions to make his followers happy. Their heads were down in supplication, his was up and looking around. He saw me catch him in his disinterest. He knew that he had killed two people, he knew this prayer was a fraud, a farce, a charade. He knew he was taking the name of the Lord in vain. But Simpson would do whatever he had to do, including pray to whichever God was expedient, to continue to be O.J.

I thought, "What are you praying to God for? God won't bless you and give you strength to lie; he doesn't do that kind of work." I walked on down the hall.

When the jury filed in I noticed they were dressed more nicely than I'd ever seen them. On some days the men didn't shave, just threw on jeans and a sweatshirt, but this day everyone seemed freshly spruced up. Even Judge Fujisaki took the bench with a particularly somber demeanor.

Before I could get at Simpson, the defense tossed up a silly motion to stop us from using reference to the Schiller book *American Tragedy* in our examination. It was frivolous, and we swatted it away easily. I was glad to get in a couple of practice swings. Tom Lambert kept a copy of the book, face up, on the counsel's table just to rattle him.

This was the moment I and a great many people had been waiting for, the moment O.J. Simpson was called upon, under oath, to answer for his actions. It was the defining moment of the trial, the focal point of the world's media. There were no cameras in the courtroom, but I could feel the eyes of the world peering down on us. The trial would be won or lost depending on what happened between me and O.J. Simpson.

I could not ignore the pressure. Fred Goldman was sitting in front of the bar, next to Ed Medvene, Patti and Kim behind him, all of their hopes and expectations resting on me. This was his last chance for justice; they would never have the opportunity to confront Simpson again. I owed it to them. I owed it to Ron and Nicole.

I was comforted by the presence of my team: Arthur Groman, Tom, Ed, Peter, Yvette, and Steve. John Kelly, Mike Brewer, and their colleagues. Everyone had worked endlessly, in superhuman ways, to bring this case to this moment. They had put their trust in me, now it was up to me to deliver. But in addition to their support, I was also aware of their demands and expectations. Their professional lives and careers were at risk. We had come from nothing—no information, no visibility, no money—and we now had the opportunity to both showcase our skills—and to obtain justice.

The case had already taught me about the fallacies, flaws, and deceptions that are involved in building people up to be something they truly are not. I'd had my vision of American heroes smashed, but my sense of the possibility of American justice was still intact—for the time being. As I faced Simpson, that was at risk, as well.

And then I had to consider myself. Not only my career but my life was going to be judged very publicly—in the next half hour.

I did not want to blow this case. Christopher Darden had put gloves on O.J. Simpson and changed his own life forever, not for the better. I was fully capable of asking Simpson two or three inopportune questions and getting walloped. What if I flopped? What if he dominated me, or he controlled the examination, or I wasn't tough enough? *What if I just plain wasn't a good enough lawyer?* I might be in over my head; what then? People on television, on every station every two minutes, were dissecting and destroying careers in thirty-second sound bites; they would not fail to mention mine. What if I failed miserably?

For weeks the crowds and the pressure had grown exponentially. Both civilians and the media had been telling me, "You've got to get him to lose his temper. You've got to get him to throw a fit in the courtroom, to throw something at you, to break down." They expected me to bait Simpson into a full raging tirade, then a full confession, and have him walk us out of the courtroom directly to the place the murder clothes and murder weapon are buried.

I tried to put this all out of my mind. *Look, you know what you're doing. You know how to question this witness, you've questioned him for ten days already. You are prepared. You are more than prepared, you're obsessed. In the witness stand, he's no superstar. Just treat him like any other witness and you'll be okay. Don't get sucked into other people's expectations. Don't try to make history, don't try to hit the ball out of the park. No theatrics. You don't have to make him rant and rave, all you have to do is make him answer your questions. His lies will come out. The truth will emerge. Just go and be yourself.*

It took Arthur Groman to get to the core of the matter. "You know," he told me, "O.J. Simpson is just a man who is particularly adept at dodging tacklers while running."

TWENTY-EIGHT

"A Pack of Lies"

S lowed by bad knees and the forty pounds he had put on since the criminal trial, Simpson lumbered to the witness stand. His blue suit was small on him. He was pigeon-toed, just like the footprints leading away from Ron's and Nicole's bodies, and he rolled in the manner of so many athletes who have lost more than one step.

He was all alone. Simpson had stood mute when he was on trial for his life, he had been comforted by the security of his lawyers at his deposition and by his producers in his $29.95 video. But now, for the first time, he had no blockers. His family and friends sitting in the front row would have to hear him testify. His lawyers, try as they might, couldn't help him. He was up there by himself. To his right was a fair and impartial judge, to his left was a jury of his peers waiting very anxiously to hear what he had to say for himself. I stood at a lectern directly in front of him, at most four feet away. Behind me, Fred Goldman sat, glaring.

I was surprised at how nervous Simpson was. Even after all this time, I expected to confront the "Superstar in a Rent-a-Car." I was prepared for the game face, the aura. I was looking for "O.J.," and he did start off cocky, but after about ten minutes of courtroom discipline, I got Orenthal Simpson's attention.

After I had challenged him to show me how he had gotten "physical," to put me in the same headlock he'd put Nicole in, I quickly homed in on the 1989 New Year's Eve incident. In Simpson's lexicon, "getting physical" meant beating the crap out of someone. "You would agree that you had some type of physical confrontation with Nicole in that bedroom downstairs," I said accusingly.

"I wouldn't describe it as that, but we probably touched." *They probably touched!* She was banged up, black and blue! "But I wouldn't describe it as physical."

"The police came out, right?"

"Correct."

It must be said that after about two questions, all sense of nervousness in me disappeared. I was so completely joined in the pursuit that nothing could break my concentration. I was aware of my surroundings, but the edges were blurred. What was in sharp focus was Simpson.

"And you've heard the testimony that Nicole told the officers that you had punched her, and pulled her hair, right?"

"Yes."

"And those were true statements by Nicole, were they not?"

"No." When Simpson became ill at ease he would tilt his big head back slightly, chin up, and grind his teeth. I could see his jaw moving, and the veins on each side of his forehead begin to pulse. With his mouth pursed he would fill his upper lip and cheeks with air, as if trying to keep some explosion inside. When this bubble would burst, the microphone on the witness stand picked up a great roar of frustration. Simpson's eyelids fluttered. He was forty-five minutes into questioning and already he was laboring.

"Nicole had to go to the hospital, right?"

Exhale. *"Had* to go?" In other words, *I didn't beat her that bad, she could've stayed home, she could've handled it.*

"Went." I didn't argue the point. Let the jury pick up his pettiness for themselves.

"Yeah, I asked her to go."

"I asked you if she *went* to the hospital." I didn't want Simpson arguing to the jury that he, out of the goodness of his heart, was responsible for Nicole getting treatment.

"Yes." But, of course, Simpson would not give a concise answer. He added, "We asked her to go." That was a lie; Cowlings alone made her go. I came back at him more forcefully.

"I didn't ask who asked her; I just asked you if she went!"

"Okay, okay." He wanted me off his back.

"Okay?" I had no intention of getting off his back.

"Yes."

Without letting him argue with me again, I went to the real point. "Did you go to the hospital, by the way, for any treatment?"

"No."

"Did you fall down in the mud and get all muddy and dirty that night?"

"No."

"Were you shaking with fear that night?"

"No."

"Were you injured that night?"

"I mean, not really, not what I would call an injury."

He's such a coward. He was still trying to suggest that somehow Nicole, this well-conditioned woman, abused him. Why didn't he just say no? If he were a man, he'd say no. I kept after him. "Did you have marks all over your face?"

"No."

"Did you have bruises under your shoulders?"

"No."

I moved on to another picture of Nicole, this one taken a few days later and still showing the damage he had inflicted, and I let that sink in. I watched the jury's faces, and they were mesmerized. Here was the dead mother of his children, obviously beaten by someone—*obviously beaten by him!*—and for half an hour all he had done was tell one lie after another about her. His credibility was being shredded in front of him, and he refused to admit it.

Simpson couldn't tell the jury how Nicole got the bruises they were seeing, he would *"assume"* it was when "I was being physical with her." "I physically attempted to get her out of the room, and I was wrong in doing that." He was, once again, trying to take responsibility without admitting guilt. *Only thing I did wrong was try to get my crazy, drunken, trashy wife out of my room.*

"So, in your mind, you weren't battering her that night, were you?"

I thought I couldn't lose with that question. If he admits it, it's a great answer; if he denies it, that's probably better.

"At the time," he said, "I would have said no. But what I know now, I would have said yes." This was Simpson's way of acknowledging awareness of the issue of spousal battery. Of course, on June 17 in his "suicide note" he said he was a battered spouse and didn't mention Nicole. You've got to hand it to the guy, he was sly.

Nevertheless, I was setting him up. Simpson had sent Nicole several handwritten letters after the incident, apologizing profusely and trying to win her back. Steve put one of them on the ELMO. (Many words were misspelled in the letters, and Dan Leonard told me during a break, "You shouldn't show those letters to the jury, they'll get offended at you. Don't make fun of O.J.'s poor spelling.") In the letter, Simpson said he was "thinking and trying to realize how I got so crazy. . . ."

"When you said those things, you were apologizing to Nicole for hitting her, were you not?" There was only one obvious answer: Yes.

"No."

Anyone with half a brain could tell the letter was an apology, but Simpson was hell-bent on not admitting it.

Simpson wrote two other letters expressing great concern over losing Nicole and how he would change if only she would stay. He went so far as to amend his prenuptial agreement. The amendment, cleverly written by Skip Taft, said Nicole would be entitled to half Simpson's net worth if he ever hit her "hereafter." Had Taft used the word "again," it would have constituted a clearer admission of abuse, but the protective attorney had covered Simpson's back by refraining. I had no such mandate.

"You were so concerned about losing Nicole," I told him, "and you were so concerned about what you had done, you agreed to tear that prenuptial agreement up if you ever hit her again, true?"

I braced for his quibbling about the difference in wording, but either he couldn't think quickly enough or was unaware of the good care his attorney had taken to protect him. Instead Simpson said, "That's right." He had admitted he beat her.

I moved to another point: Simpson's obsession with his own image. It was time to attack the persona.

"You were also concerned, were you not, sir, about the damage that this incident might have to your public name, reputation, and image. True?"

"I think I always would have had those concerns, yes," Simpson admitted.

"And you were concerned about it at that time, right?"

"I don't think that was a concern at that time." So, he denied it.

"Your image has always been important to you, sir, has it not?"

"Who I am, yes." This was not difficult for him to reveal. But he was wary.

"And you always have been aware of your image, right?"

"Yeah. I always know people like me, yes."

"You wrote, when you first began your football career, back in the first book that you authored, 'I have been praised, kidded, and criticized for being image-conscious, and I plead guilty to the charge.' True?"

Simpson was not prepared. He looked startled, as if things were going too fast. "At that time, yes." Always the qualifier.

What a stroke of good fortune, to be able to present the jury with a piece of evidence in which Simpson said directly, "I plead guilty." The quote came from a book written by Simpson and Pete Axthelm, now deceased, called *Education of a Rich Rookie,* which was out of print, but which we had found in the library. Chapter One was titled "A Question of Image."

"And you wrote, 'I tried all the images.'"

"I don't recall that, no."

"It's in your book," I challenged him.

"I didn't *write* the book." Again, he was trying to quibble. If he demanded to look foolish, I was more than happy to oblige.

"You approved the book, right?"

"Yes."

"You wouldn't allow anything in there about you to remain in it if it were false, would you?"

Again, Simpson was prepared to cut corners. "I think that's a certain license people take when they write books—"

"And did you also write that 'The ghetto makes you want to hide from your real identity from cops, from teachers, and even from yourself. And it forces you to build up false images—humble, swaggering, casual, or tough—in order to handle your enemies and impress your friends'? That's what you wrote."

He heard how damning that sounded. Here it was, under his own byline, in his own book. Whatever image has to be erected, no matter how false—you've got to say what you've got to say, and do what you've got to do. That's *exactly* what he was doing now!

"I didn't write that." Again.

"It's in your book, true?"

"It's in my book, but I didn't write it."

"Now you disavow that, right?"

"I happen to believe a lot of that sentiment, but I didn't write that, no." Fine with me.

"You agree with it?"

"A lot of it, yes."

"You agreed with it at the time, and you agree with it now, true?"

"In the ghetto, I agree that you have to, at times, hide behind a tough exterior. Yes, I do agree with that." A modified race card; he was trying to use African-American culture as a cover for his lies. I was not going to let him keep away.

"Mr. Simpson, you're not saying that you don't agree with what was put in the book under your name, all about you, first book ever written? You're not saying *that* to this jury?"

He caved. "In general, I okayed the book."

"Okay."

I was prepared to move on, but Simpson couldn't get enough of a beating. "I agree with a lot of the sentiment in the book, but I didn't write those exact words."

I resumed rubbing his nose in it. "You didn't take any legal action to prevent this book from being publicly issued?"

"No."

"Or take it off the market, did you?"

"No."

These were not confident *No*'s. He wasn't making eye contact with the jury, he was sitting stiffly in the witness chair, looking straight ahead—at me but through me, as if almost in a trance—with his eyes bugged wide open. He was huffing and puffing, a human heavy bag while I was whaling away.

"Okay." I paused. *Want to continue?* I did. I had saved the best shot for last. We had found another great quote, with which Peter Gelblum had wanted to open the entire examination. I'd said, "No, no, no, I want to keep it for the right moment." That moment was now.

"By the way, in that book, you also wrote, 'I think I lie pretty effectively,' did you not?"

Simpson about blanched. "No."

"You are aware that that quotation is attributed to you in your book, are you not?"

"Now I am, yes." It was a measure of the respect we had drummed into him that he didn't doubt the source.

I repeated the quote, slowly. " 'I think I lie pretty effectively.' " I continued reading from the book, in which someone is talking to Simpson: " 'You look so serious and intent on what you're saying, it gives you away. When you're saying something and you're laughing, that's the only time I can tell you're telling the truth.' And you said, 'I figured that it was something to keep in mind for my acting career.' Right?"

Eyes fluttering, Simpson seemed befuddled. He had prided himself on knowing all the details of his trial and his alibi; he'd thought he knew all the angles. "I don't know. I don't recall saying that, but—"

I shook my head. "You *are* a pretty effective liar, aren't you."

Baker shot out of his seat. "Object, Your Honor. That's argumentative!"

I proceeded to tie things up. "You lied to cover up the 1989 incident with Nicole, true?"

"No."

"You told [journalist] Roy Firestone, on a national television interview on ESPN, the following: 'We were both guilty. No one was hurt, it was no big deal, and we both got on with our lives.' You said that on television, did you not?"

Everywhere he looked, I had something on him. I had his book, I had a videotape of him saying exactly what I'd just read, which I would be happy to play if he wanted me to.

"Yes." Even Simpson couldn't deny videotape.

"And that was absolutely false. True?"

"I disagree with you on that."

Simpson had to stick to his story or admit he had lied. Both were intolerable for him. He couldn't get out of this. He couldn't win. I moved in.

"Did Nicole get hurt?"

"She had some bruises." There they were, blown up, in color, facing the jury.

"Are you minimizing her injuries now, sir?"

"I'm not minimizing my action, but we got on with our lives."

"I'm talking about your statement, 'No one was hurt.' That was a false statement, true?"

"Technically." *Technically?!*

"It was a lie!"

"I disagree with you."

"It was false!"

"I disagree with you."

"It was true?"

"I disagree with what you are saying." Simpson was obstinate, but he had nowhere to go.

"Was it true or false that no one was hurt? Answer my question!" We were almost shouting at each other.

"Nicole, yes, she was." Simpson broke.

"So Nicole was hurt, right?"

"Yes." Having shown him to be a liar in front of the jury, I made him admit it again.

"And you did not tell the truth about it, and you attempted to minimize the incident to cover it up, true?" He did it then, he had tried to do the same thing now.

"This was a sports show," he tried to explain, "and, yes, I most definitely on this sports show minimized what happened in my personal life. Yes. But not to the police officers, I didn't minimize it." Simpson himself was making the very connection I was trying to make to the jury.

"And in trying to minimize, you did so in order to try to protect your interest, correct?"

Simpson tried to say he was protecting, "first and foremost," his family. "So you were not trying to protect and hold up your good name and image?" I looked at the people watching him. "Is *that* what you're telling the jury?"

"*I'm* part of my family." He would quibble forever.

"You don't have any problem admitting you were trying to protect yourself, right?" It was a rational thing to do; self-preservation is universal, a hard trait to deny. He realized, *Okay, I'm trapped.*

"No," he finally admitted.

"You have no problem saying that, do you?"

"You're correct."

"And when you were trying to protect yourself, and it was necessary to lie, you lied. Right?" I brought him back to his lies on videotape. "You told another lie, too. You said it was 'no big deal,' true?"

"As far as the country was concerned," he said, "I thought it was no big deal."

"It was a big deal to Nicole, right?"

"I would think so." Even there he refused to admit the obvious.

"And you said she just got some bruises, is that right?"

Simpson spoke very softly. "That's what she got."

I spoke softly, too. "Not a big deal, some bruises, right?"

"To me and to Nicole it was a big deal. To America—I didn't think it was any of their business."

I didn't think quickly enough on my feet, and I missed an opportunity here. Ed Medvene mentioned it to me at the break. Simpson justified lying to America—and he didn't even consider what he'd done lying—because it was none of their business. Well, America was out there in the gallery, in the media's audience, on the jury. If it was, indeed, none of their business, he would feel free to continue lying. *Which is exactly what he was doing:* Lying to all of us because it's none of our business. I wish I had thought of that at the time, but I didn't, and I wouldn't get another opportunity.

"And Nicole was hurt, wasn't she, sir?" I continued.

"Yes, emotionally she was hurt." Even now, such relentless evasion. Did he really think he would get away with it?

"And physically?"

I forced him to spit it out. "And physically she was bruised and hurt, yes."

I showed the jury Simpson's letter agreeing to tear up the prenup at the potential cost to him of $5 million and then moved on to further cover-ups. It was important to show the jury how Simpson lied to protect himself in all areas of his life: his personal life, his image, his finances.

He told Frank Olson, chairman of Hertz, that charges concerning the New Year's incident had been filed because "they were using you as a scapegoat. True?"

"I still believe that, yes." He was his own worst enemy. After beating his wife and lying in their faces about it for nearly an hour, he could still tell the jury the only basis for bringing charges against him was that a bunch of rabid, zealous feminists wanted to make an example of him. *There were seven women on the jury!*

One year of hard work was coming together. We pulled two or three lines from Olson's deposition and plugged them right in. The prenuptial letter, plugged right in. The rookie book, plugged right in.

Simpson had severely minimized the same New Year's incident to the Forschner Company's Louis Marx. "I think I told them the truth." I just let that sit there, then set him up for impeachment.

"You had an altercation with Nicole in the parking lot when you slapped her in the face and knocked her glasses off to the ground, true?"

"No." We had a witness who saw it.

"And there was another incident . . . out near your place in Laguna, out on Victoria."

"I don't have a place in Laguna." Now he was quibbling about the exact name of the town.

"There was a time *on the sand* when you and she got into an argument and you slapped her and she fell down to her knees?"

"Absolutely not." We had a witness.

"Then there was an incident in the late eighties when you were having an argument with Nicole in the back of the limousine and you struck her in the back of the limousine?"

"Absolutely not." We had the limousine driver.

"Didn't you tell Wayne Hughes after the 1989 incident you caught too much of a backhand in hitting Nicole?"

"I don't believe so, no." Hughes would confirm it.

We took a break. Simpson sat in the witness stand while the jury filed out. Then he got up. As he limped by, he said to me, "Pretty good. Pretty good"—as though his perjury were just a game.

Yvette had an open tin of Altoids mints sitting near the corner of the kids' table, and as Simpson passed he stuck his hand in, grabbed a handful, and chucked them in his mouth. Yvette was appalled. "His murdering hands," she told me.

My team surrounded me. "It's going great! Keep at it." Fred Goldman put his arm around me and said, "You're doing a great job. Get the bastard! Get the bastard!" Patti told me, "Dan, it's incredible!"

The defense sent someone, I think it was Dan Leonard, to change the angle of the microphone. They were apparently concerned that Simpson's loud braying would influence the jury against him.

Some in the press raced from their seats to call in their first stories. As I walked by press row on the way to the lobby, others shook their heads and rolled their eyes.

The criminal case prosecution had not documented sufficient domestic violence incidents to make a case that they had led to murder, and that line of reasoning had ultimately been rejected by the jury. We did not want to make that mistake. We used the domestic violence testimony, which I had covered in the first hour, to demonstrate Simpson's lying more than we did to establish a progression to murder.

After the break I picked up the chronology in 1992, when Nicole left him, leading to their divorce. I had him admit how upset he was about losing Nicole, then detailed his involvement with Paula. I directed him through the episode when he saw Nicole and Keith Zlomsowitch having sex, during which he trashed her a little, then reached the beginning of their reconciliation.

"Were you pursuing her?" I asked.

"No! She was incessively pursuing me!"

"Excuse me?"

"Incessively!"

"Now, are you sure you were not pursuing her this time?"

I was tweaking his vanity, but there was more to it than that. I wanted to make clear to the jury in the strongest terms that Nicole had, indeed, pursued Simpson. It helped set up Simpson's extreme rejection when, after he finally gave in and abandoned this great new life he was extolling to return to Nicole, *she* dumped *him*. It helped establish the motive (rejection) for the consequent revenge.

"No." Simpson was adamant. "I think everyone, including our family, knows it was her pursuing me."

As I asked for details of how Nicole tried to win him back, and let Simpson's responses become more expansive, he began to rebound and gather strength. I showed him a March 1993 letter in which Nicole wrote, "I want to come home, O.J. I want to come home." Two months later they were reconciled.

"And you broke Paula's heart?"

"Yes." I liked that answer. It helped set up the breakup call on the morning of the murders.

Simpson and Nicole put a time limit on the reconciliation. "I gave her a year," he said.

"You gave *her* a year?" I repeated. "Is that what you're saying?"

"Yes."

"You gave her a year to do what, sir?" I was relatively convinced this cocksure certainty would not sit well with the seven women on the jury.

"She had a concern at one point that if we argued, that I would just stop, and I said, 'Okay, I'll give it a year.'"

"Before, you said you'd give *her* a year. Was that a slip?"

"No, that's how I felt."

One of the issues that particularly upset Simpson during their year of reconciliation was a *National Enquirer* article that said he had begged Nicole to get back into their relationship. "And that *really* upset you?"

"Yes, it certainly did!"

"And it upset you because it was false, right?"

"EXACTLY!"

"*She* begged; you did not beg her?"

"EXACTLY RIGHT!" Such total conviction. This was clearly important to him, and there was no question that he was telling the truth. Simpson didn't beg anybody; he was O.J. Simpson! The jury could contrast that certainty with his other, less impassioned answers about the truly important issues in the case.

I decided to push his button one more time. "It upset you because you didn't want America to think that you were begging another woman, correct?" I didn't much care about the answer, the jury understood the point.

"I didn't want an inaccurate thing to be written in the paper, and I didn't think it was right that one of her friends would go to a tabloid and make any characterizations about anything that was going on between Nicole and I."

Simpson didn't mind lying under oath to the American people, but he went apoplectic if the *National Enquirer,* which so many thinking adults rely on as the newspaper of record, reported one detail of his life inaccurately.

Simpson lied about the 1993 incident when eight months before her death, Nicole called 911 because Simpson would not leave her home. I played both the 911 and the surreptitious police tape, and he said Nicole had lied to the 911 operator when she cried, "He's going to beat the shit out of me!" The jury could hear her voice and determine for themselves whether they thought she was afraid. It was more than obvious.

I asked whether, when he became enraged, he would acquire an animal-like look. He came up with a wise-ass answer: "I can never recall being mad and looking in a mirror."

"You knew she was frightened that night."

"Not that night! I will debate forever that she was not frightened of me that night."

"Debate with whom?" I challenged. "You think this is a debate, sir?"

"Pardon me?" Simpson had launched into one of his programmed sound bites and I had interrupted.

"You think this is a debate?" I chastised him.

"No."

I took him through his final weekend with Nicole in Cabo San Lucas when Nicole made up her mind to end the relationship. He tried to argue that she was caught up in the dark underworld of Faye Resnick, but he had no proof, no witnesses, and the court would not hear it.

This was a difficult road for me. I was using the most adverse and hostile witness to introduce the basic facts of the case. For example: "You and Nicole were having sort of a difficult time the first week or so of May, right?"

"I was, she wasn't. She had said she loved me and she was sorry about the way she acted and she picked me up at the airport. But I, at that point, wanted out."

But the facts were: They reconciled, there were problems in the relationship, the reconciliation failed, the relationship was over, a conflict developed near the end, and she wound up dead. It took time and effort, but the facts emerged. He kept trying to sell the jury his story, but that was the price I had to pay to use him as my narrator; extreme vigilance was required to keep his spin to a minimum.

Simpson was also overselling. It appeared to me he was offending the jury by continuing to bash Nicole: He wanted out, she lied to the 911 operator, he's right, she's wrong. It was unseemly.

Simpson said he had dumped Nicole on May 10. Without showing the document to him, I quoted Nicole writing in her diary on May 22: "We've officially split."

"That's *absolutely* wrong!" he huffed. His story was that they broke up on May 10; he wanted to put as much time as possible between the breakup and the murders to undermine the clear inference of motive. When I attempted to enter Nicole's diary into evidence, Baker jumped up. This was a critical argument.

Before trial, the defense had moved to keep Nicole's diaries out of evidence, arguing they were hearsay. The judge refused, ruling that Nicole's state of mind at the time of the murders was relevant. In fact, Baker's opening statement opened the door wide by making direct reference to her state of mind. I argued that the whole fabric and nature of the relationship was at the heart of the case, and the issue of who was breaking up with whom was critical: "There's a buildup of intense anger and hostility between the parties which we say proves the motive Mr. Simpson has denied."

Under California law, a person's state of mind is relevant not only to show how she was feeling, but also to show how she acted in conformity with that feeling. For example, if Ms. Smith writes that she is "really scared" of Mr. Jones and then is killed the next day, it would be permissible to introduce that document to show it was reasonable to believe Ms. Smith did not go out voluntarily with Mr. Jones.

The judge listened, reviewed the law, and ruled in our favor.

This was a big victory. Now the jury could see how Nicole felt and acted, from her own incendiary words.

After laying out the entire IRS situation, in which Nicole either had to fork over $100,000 or move out of her home, I introduced Simpson's letter threatening to report her to the government for tax evasion. I said, "The two of you had some very vile arguments about this issue prior to your sending the letter, true?"

"That's absolutely wrong."

"And you threatened her that you would be sending this letter, didn't you?"

"No."

"And on June 2, Thursday, you had a telephone call with Nicole and she hung up on you in that call?"

"No."

"When Nicole hangs up on you, you get angry and you want to retaliate, true?"

"No." He was having trouble again. The one-word explosions were back, the fluttering eyelids.

"Let me see the entry." On cue, Steve flashed a page from Nicole's diary up on the ELMO. The dead woman had had neat, schoolgirl's handwriting. I read the first four sentences, which Simpson agreed were accurate. Then:

"You said to her, 'You hung up on me last night. You're gonna pay for this, bitch.' True?"

Simpson was gruff. "Absolutely false!"

"'You're holding money from the IRS. You're going to jail, you fucking cunt!' Did you say that?" I was shouting at him.

"I have never used that phrase, ever, with anybody, in my life!"

"And you certainly didn't use it on this occasion?"

"Absolutely not."

"Nicole just made all this up?"

"Absolutely. And this is not true."

The jurors, those who could tear their eyes off the sight of me and Simpson screaming at each other, could read along with me on the ELMO. "'You think you can do any fuckin' thing you want. You've got it coming. I've already talked to my lawyers about this, bitch.' Is that all untrue?"

"Yes."

"'They'll get you for tax evasion, bitch, I'll see to it. You're not gonna have a fuckin' dime left, bitch.' You said that, didn't you?"

"Absolutely not."

"And three days later, you hand-delivered the letter to Nicole, true?" Several witnesses were on record to confirm this.

"I think the next workday, Cathy may have sent it." Vintage Simpson, always blaming someone else.

"We're talking about you, not Cathy Randa."

"No. That's absolutely false."

"So you're saying the fact that this letter was sent on Monday the sixth, by hand delivery, had *absolutely nothing to do* with a conversation you had with Nicole on Friday, June 3. Is that what you're telling this jury?"

"Yes. That's what I'm telling this jury." He had no credibility left.

Simpson confirmed the accuracy of Nicole's June 4 diary entry. "So in other words," I added, "everything in these diary entries that we just showed you is true, except where Nicole reports what you said to her?"

"Yes."

"And that's all a pack of lies, right?"

"Yes."

I turned my back on him in disgust and just let his answer hang in the air.

Denying the Undeniable

S impson denied his conversation with Donna Estes, he denied his conversation with tennis pro Jackie Cooper. He denied having an argument with Paula before Alan Austin's party at La Quinta; "she just said she was leaving." Nicole did, however, call and yell at him and accuse him of stealing her friends; that he remembered clearly. He didn't mind admitting their fights when Nicole was out of control, which was fine with me; I was interested in showing the escalating conflict that went on between the two.

I started moving day by day toward the murders.

Monday, June 6: The IRS letter was delivered to Nicole. Picked up the dog Chachi at Bundy. Saw Nicole on the balcony. She wouldn't talk to him.

Tuesday, June 7: Denied he told Alan Austin that he and Nicole were over once and for all. Flew back east to go golfing. His son Justin graduated from Sunshine School. Simpson missed it.

Wednesday, June 8: Had another letter delivered to Nicole, stating that she was not to use his housekeeper, Gigi, as "an emergency cook, baby-sitter, or errand runner." Things were getting more hostile.

The entire week before her murder, Simpson admitted he had no conversation with Nicole on any subject outside the kids and the dog. The truth, I believed, was they had ugly, fighting words, escalating in anger and intensity with each day. On the East Coast, he flew from a golf game in Virginia to a meeting of the Connecticut Swiss Army knife company, then limo'd down to his friend Bobby Bender's home on Long Island. (We decided not to tell the limousine driver's story of Simpson stabbing the air with a large knife; although it provided compelling anecdotal evidence, we couldn't tie it up by proving any of those knives were used in the murder. It was a mystery that was not our problem to solve, and I didn't want the jury worrying about it.)

Simpson denied being so depressed that Bender couldn't get him out of his chair to play golf. "That was about my knees and hands being swollen from flying and playing golf," Simpson insisted. He wouldn't even admit being upset about breaking up with his ex-wife; he adamantly denied what would be a normal human emotion. This was his paradox: In order to be someone who was not ruled by emotion, he was compelled to portray himself as a man with no emotions at all. This put the lie to him in a big way.

Despite his swelling, Simpson played golf Wednesday and Thursday, as he had played golf every day for about two weeks straight.

Friday, June 10: Played golf in Long Island. Got on a plane. Flew to Los Angeles. Was picked up by Paula, who drove him to Rockingham and had dinner with him before they went to bed. "I think she may have left in the middle of the night," he testified.

Saturday, June 11: Got up at about six A.M. to play golf. Spent the afternoon at Rockingham. Commiserated with Ron Fischman about their failed relationships, talked to Kato while watching *Garp* on TV. (He denied mentioning Keith's oral sex with Nicole.) Went out with Paula to a dinner honoring the First Lady of Israel. Denied having a fight with Paula over her desire to attend Sydney's dance recital and be included with the family in Nicole's presence. Went home alone.

Sunday, June 12, the day of the murders: Played golf at the Riviera Country Club with his buddies Austin, Baumgarten, Hoskins, and Melchiorre. Denied telling Austin and Baumgarten that he and Paula had had a "beef" the night before. Denied picking up her "Dear John" message. Denied Paula dumped him at all. Denied having a near physical confrontation with Baumgarten on the golf course.

Drove his Bronco home from Riviera. We went through his car phone calls and established that he called Paula at 2:12 P.M., and again at

2:23, 2:24, and could not get through. He made repeated calls to her number all day. He called Nicole at 2:18 P.M. and they spoke for four minutes. Simpson said he offered to take care of Justin for the day, but we don't know what they actually said. He made all these calls from his cell phone while driving in his Bronco. He parked it in his usual spot on Ashford near the mailbox.

After getting home, Simpson spent twenty minutes on the phone with Kato's *Playboy* centerfold friend, then dozed off. "You were taking a 'red-eye' that night and you wanted to make sure you could sleep on that 'red-eye,' right?" Nobody takes a nap before hopping on a transcontinental flight, and I wanted to show that it wasn't sensible for Simpson to be dozing off between 10:15 and 10:45, which was a major portion of his alibi.

I moved to the dance recital, and Simpson started talking. "The thing was standing room only, and where Nicole had saved my seat was two seats from her, with only two seats between us. That was for the kids, and directly in front of me was her sister and Cora Fischman, and directly in front of them was her mother, Ron Fischman, and her father. . . ." According to the renowned threat expert, Gavin de Becker, a liar will fill his answer with a jumble of unrequired details to create a buffer of credibility and truth around a core lie. This was a classic case.

I put up a photograph, taken that night, showing Simpson with his arm around his daughter. The criminal defense had loved this picture; Simpson was smiling and really didn't look like the popular image of a man about to commit a murder. But we weren't afraid to show it to the jury; we established something quite different. We zoomed in on his fingers. No cuts. I had him admit that, as of then, he hadn't seen a single drop of blood come from his body all day.

As his family drove off to dinner without him, Simpson put on a brave face and told Ron Fischman he was "glad to be out of the mix." Simpson drove home alone.

"When you got to Rockingham, using your home phone, you picked up a message from your cell phone voice mail system, true?" I was beginning my assault on Simpson's lie that he never picked up Paula's message dumping him on account of Nicole. Simpson knew how much Paula's rejection contributed to his murderous state of mind. That's why he was so insistent about denying it.

"No," Simpson said firmly, "I never picked up a message." That was his story, and he was sticking to it.

I had him explain the workings of his system. If no one answered his cell phone, incoming calls were transferred to his voice mail, from which Simpson could retrieve them.

"And at 6:56 P.M. on June 12, after you got home to Rockingham, you called your message manager and you retrieved a message spanning five minutes?"

"That's incorrect."

"Correct?" I gave him the opportunity to bow out gracefully, but as far as he was concerned he had no reason to concede.

"That's incorrect." Now he was firmly on record.

"And the only message that had been left on that machine all day was one at about 7:00 A.M. from Paula Barbieri, right?"

Simpson wasn't budging. "Since I never picked up any messages, I don't know."

"And if phone records indicate, sir, that that 6:56 call was placed from your home, would that refresh your recollection?"

"No, it wouldn't, because I know at about that time I was in my kitchen, talking to Kato." Simpson was on top of his alibi; he thought he knew everything there was to know about the available evidence.

"At exactly 6:56, you can remember that specifically, can you?" Now, you'd think Simpson would have sensed a trap; there had to be a reason I keyed in on this time. But, no, he kept rolling out his alibi.

"I believe I came back home, and I was trying to make those calls again, and Kato came in and we were talking."

We had three independent pieces of evidence verifying that he picked up the long message from Paula that day: he admitted it in his June 13 statement to Vannatter and Lange, and he told criminal defense domestic violence expert Dr. Lenore Walker, which she had duly noted on paper, when she came to examine him in jail. Paula, too, had testified in her deposition that Simpson had picked up her message and responded on her answering machine. Still, Simpson was denying it.

I asked if he recognized a phone number. It was his home phone on June 12, 1994. "It may have been one of my numbers," he said. He was equivocating about his own home phone. I showed him the computer printout.

Simpson looked quizzical. He had created his alibi to cover all the known physical evidence and by this time must have been comforted by the assumption that nothing new would appear. But the piece of paper he held in his hand was genuinely new, and I watched as he scanned the rows of numbers and tried to take it all in.

"So," I asked, "does that help you remember that at 6:56 P.M., from your home phone number, you called and picked up a five-minute message?"

Simpson denied the undeniable. "No, I didn't pick up any message."

"The records, then, are incorrect?"

"I don't know about the records. I know I was at home. I know I checked my home message machine. And I know Kato came in, and Kato and I was talking."

I stopped there. I wanted to be one thousand percent certain of everything I said, and I was not entirely confident with my understanding of the printout to push it further, so I moved to the next piece of impeachment on this point.

"You told Detectives Vannatter and Lange that you *did*, in fact, pick up the message from Paula Barbieri, true?"

"Yes."

A devastating admission! On the witness stand he had just said he did not pick up the message, but hours after the murders, while being questioned by the police, he said he did. I read that testimony: "'And then I checked my messages. She had left me a message that she wasn't there, that she had to leave town.' And you made that statement." I pointed straight at Simpson. "Right?"

"Yes."

"And that statement was true when you made it, correct?"

"Yes."

After he heard the message, Simpson had called a former model named Gretchen Stockdale and told her that he was "unattached" for the first time in a long time. Simpson denied there was a connection between getting dumped and making that call ("I don't think Gretchen knew about Paula"), but that denial was not credible. I was starting to drive the points home. On the night of June 12, two women, Nicole and now Paula, had dropped him. When Nicole rejected him, Paula had been his emotional parachute. When Paula cut the strings, he was in free fall.

Simpson was reaching out to other women and not getting through; he was emotionally aroused; Nicole was having dinner only a mile or two away with *his* kids, his family, paid for by *his* money, and *he wasn't invited.*

The phone records showed that Simpson tried calling Paula a few more times, both her home and cell phones. He called his message manager again and retrieved the same message. He'd been trying to call her all day long, but she had put herself out of his reach.

"I don't recall doing that. I don't believe it happened," he said.

"Well, your phone records show that." I was pacing, up to the witness stand, back and forth in front of the jury, down to the counsel table, over to the ELMO. I never stood in one spot.

The procession to murder continued. Simpson's housekeeper, Gigi, called him to say that she wanted to stay away that night, and he let her. Simpson testified that Kato was the only one on the property.

At about 9:00 P.M., Simpson called Nicole at Bundy. At his deposition, Simpson claimed he called only to talk to Sydney, his daughter. The best we could get from him was that "absolutely nothing" was said to Nicole. In my view, this was a conversation that led to murder. Nicole had it with him—throwing her and their kids out of her home, jeopardizing her financial security, pulling every string and using all the power he held over her—the IRS threat was the last straw. Nicole was known for her unrestrained ability to speak her mind; one can only imagine what she said to him.

Within a few minutes Simpson was in Kato's room. He said he was going to get a burger. He borrowed twenty bucks to tip the sky cap. Kato asked if he could come along. Although the Bronco was his favorite car— "I'd rather drive it than any other car"—they went to McDonald's in the Bentley. He didn't tell Kato where they were going.

"I didn't have a date with Kato; I was going to get a burger." The jury laughed, and it bothered me. We were talking about my client's son and Simpson's ex-wife being killed in about an hour, and he was clowning around.

"Do you think this is funny?"

"No, they laughed, not me."

"Do you think this is the time to make jokes?"

Baker objected and was sustained. Simpson answered, "I don't think any of this is funny. I wish I was anywhere but here."

At McDonald's, Kato paid. "It was very nice of him," said Simpson. This time no one laughed.

I established that by the time they got back, 9:35, he had not bled at Rockingham or in the Bentley.

In Simpson's reconstruction of reality, before going to McDonald's he drove the Bronco from where it was parked on Ashford to where it was found the next day on Rockingham. His story was that he needed his golf clubs, so he walked to the car, opened the gate, drove into the compound, unloaded, drove out the other way, walked back, and closed the gate behind him. Of course, that was a longer trip than simply going to his Bronco on Ashford and carrying the bags back, and he could easily have backed out and left the car in the more convenient spot where he usually parked, on Ashford. I went through that little exercise with him in front of the jury. I was trying to let the jury see that Simpson's explanation for why the Bronco ended up on Rockingham—where Simpson rarely parked it—was illogical and not credible.

In his deposition, he'd claimed he'd done it because he wanted to make sure his dog, Chachi, didn't run out and get away. I could not resist pinning him. It was such a playful, funny point, and he was so obviously lying about it. Chachi, the Chia pet, the lawn ornament of pooches. By this time I had brought up the subject enough that Simpson had crafted a response. Chachi, he said, was trained and lame *now,* but had not been *then.* The man was shameless.

This whole scenario never happened; he didn't bring his car in. He had to come up with a reason for the Bronco being on Rockingham, other than the fact that he drove it to Bundy, committed the murders, and parked there on his return.

Finally, we were at the critical time. "Now," I began, "between 9:35 P.M. and 10:55 P.M. on Sunday, June 12, there is not a single *living* human being"—I underscored the word—"who you can identify, that saw or spoke to you; is that true?"

"That's absolutely true, unless somebody drove out and saw me when I was outside—" He was heaving again.

"Excuse me." I didn't want him filibustering, I wanted him to answer my question. "Is that true, that there's not a single living person that you know of who saw or spoke to you between 9:35 and 10:55? Is that true?"

"No one was at my house. Unless they were driving by when I was in my yard—"

"Sir, I'm not asking about things that you don't know about."

Baker objected and was overruled.

"It was a very simple question. Nine thirty-five P.M. to 10:55 P.M., you cannot tell this jury the name of a single person—*living* person—that you saw or spoke to you in that time. Is that correct?"

He had nowhere to go. "That is correct." The eyelids fluttered overtime.

I lowered my voice. "And the reason why you didn't get in that Bronco [to go with Kato to McDonald's] is because you used that Bronco to go to Nicole's condominium that evening after you came back from McDonald's. True?"

"That's not true." He was puffing big-time now.

"You had gloves, you had a hat, you were wearing a dark sweat outfit, and you had a knife. And you went to Nicole Brown's condominium at 875 South Bundy, did you not, sir?"

"That's absolutely not true!" His eyes grew wide.

"And you confronted Nicole Brown Simpson, and you killed her, didn't you?"

Simpson did something extraordinary. Between heavy breaths, he rotated his large body, and as if on cue, pointed himself toward the jury. It was so obviously different from anything he had done during the course of the examination. Someone must have told him, "When he asks you 'Did you kill them?' you've got to look the jury in the eye and tell them . . .'"

"That's absolutely not true!"

This was a scary moment, one the entire team had worried about. If, despite a day full of lies, when O.J. Simpson turned to the jury they thought they saw truth in his eyes, that would be the end of our case. Reason or star power; it came down to this moment.

But Simpson is a bad actor, and the line was delivered poorly. He got nothing in return. The jury just stared at him.

"And you killed Ronald Goldman, sir, did you or did you not?"

"That's absolutely not true!" He remained glued to their faces. Nobody moved.

"And then you got in your Bronco and you drove back the very short distance to Rockingham, and you parked on Rockingham because you knew that there was a limousine waiting at Ashford for some time. True or untrue?"

This time he didn't look at them. He looked at me.

"That is absolutely not true!"

"And you got on your property, sir, and you bumped into the wall of the side of your house at 10:50, 10:51 P.M. True or untrue?"

"That's absolutely untrue!" The answer was so mechanical, so contrived, so clearly rehearsed—as if "absolutely" were going to be the key sales word. No innocent person would repeat such a mantra; he'd be screaming with outrage. Simpson, straining for sincerity, delivered his empty line and failed.

"And you dropped one of your gloves there, you put other items in a bag, and you left that bag behind your Bentley to be picked up later. True or untrue, sir?"

"That's absolutely untrue."

"And you walked from the Bentley into your house at 10:55 P.M. and were seen by Allan Park. True?"

Simpson knew his plot line. "I believe when I came out, at one point, I thought whoever the limo driver was would have seen me, yes."

"You were walking from the side of your house diagonally to the Bentley, so you would not be seen by the limo driver, and then you skipped into your house. Is that true or untrue, sir?"

"That's absolutely untrue."

"And you dropped the bag right here?" I pointed to the correct spot, where both Kato and Park had actually seen it. "And you went inside at 10:55 P.M. Yes or no?"

"No."

"And you dropped a piece of blood near a cable in the back, near the wall, where you ran into the wall. Correct?"

"That's incorrect."

"And you bled on that cable wire, didn't you, sir?"

"That's incorrect."

"And you bled on that air conditioner, didn't you, sir?"

"That's incorrect."

"And you bled all over that driveway and in your Bronco, didn't you, sir?"

"That is *absolutely* incorrect."

I'd had enough of him for one day. "Eight-thirty, Monday morning," said the judge. He gave the jury their standard admonition, and court was adjourned for the day.

My examination was the lead story on all the news shows that night and the next morning; it was all anybody I knew talked about. I got calls from people I hadn't heard from in years, friends and acquaintances around the country who saw my name and had to get in touch. If the trial had been high visibility before, the scene of Simpson on the stand made it inescapable.

Peter Gelblum and I ripped our outline apart and put it back together over the weekend. As well as the first day had gone, I wanted to destroy him on the second. This would be the fun part, the physical evidence; we had an encyclopedia of damning facts, and Simpson had no innocent explanation for any of them. We wanted to make sure the dominoes were in order. Actually, the way things were lining up, they were falling more like bricks.

I was told that one of Mike Brewer's partners had said, "Dan should turn up the heat. This is not a deposition." That annoyed me. I confess to paying too much attention to criticism, but the more I thought about it, the more it motivated me to ratchet it up. I entered the courtroom on Monday determined to be tougher and more confrontational.

I assumed Simpson would do the same. They'd had a weekend to retool him, to tell him, "Argue with him. Don't give him his pat answers. You're giving in too easily. Fight with the guy!" Of course, I didn't think the judge would not let him take that tack, and if Simpson tried, it would just be a matter of time before I regained control.

So I was surprised when Simpson dragged himself to the witness stand that Monday. He looked tentative. His physical presence, usually among his strongest assets, exuded no confidence or certainty. For a moment I thought he might be playing possum. Where was "O.J."?

Peter had checked with the phone company about the printout showing Simpson's calls. Now that I fully understood it, I could hammer Simpson with confidence. We put a big exhibit board in front of him that detailed his phone calls on the murder night. He refused to admit what they meant. Now, it's one thing to argue with your wife's diary, which may be hearsay, but no one disputes the phone company. We accept their records, we pay our phone bills every month, we believe them.

"You do see '6:56, message manager,' true?"

"Yes."

"And you also see it again, '8:55, message manager,' true?"

"Yes."

"And 'CF' stands for 'call forwarding,' right?"

"I would assume so, yes."

"And the reason those entries are on your bill is because you twice picked up messages from your house at Rockingham. True or untrue?"

"That's untrue." Apparently GTE was in on the conspiracy.

"And by the way, do you see that you called at 8:58 and 8:59, the number of Paula Barbieri, a 305 cell phone number?"

"That's correct."

"So you made all those phone calls at the times shown on these cell phone records, didn't you?"

"I would assume so, yes."

"You'd include picking up messages from Paula, true?"

"That's incorrect."

It was like asking a kid with chocolate all over his face, "Did you eat chocolate?" and having him look you straight in the eye and say, "No."

"You told that to Dr. Lenore Walker, didn't you?"

In a remarkable moment while deposing Dr. Walker, Peter Gelblum had asked for the contemporaneous notes of her sessions with Simpson, taken while he was in prison. Not only did Dr. Walker have them with her, she turned them over to Peter immediately. It was like uncovering sunken treasure. Among other findings, Dr. Walker freely admitted Simpson was a spousal batterer and Nicole a battered spouse. Simpson had also told her that he had, indeed, picked up Paula's message and that he had called Paula on the night of June 12 *from his car.*

"Incorrect," said Simpson.

I had her notes in my hand. "Did you not tell Dr. Lenore Walker on February 25, 1995, the following: (from her notes) . . ." I paused. "She was taking notes, correct?"

"Yes."

"You saw her taking notes, right?" I didn't want him denying that, too.

"Yes."

I started reading Walker's notes to the jury: " 'Called Paula, not home. Call forward on car phone message from Paula. Whole long message about golf. Don't see you. He's not sure if in Arizona or Las Vegas, or if angry with him. He listens to message. Kato goes by house.' " I stopped and looked at him. *Come on, admit it. How painful does this have to be?* He did not respond. "You told all of that to Dr. Lenore Walker, didn't you, sir?"

"That's correct."

"And you told Dr. Lenore Walker that you got a whole long message about golf from Paula Barbieri. True?"

"That's untrue."

Simpson, by now, lacked even the faintest pretense for obeying the oath. The lies just came pouring out. I became very loud and challenging.

"Your story is that you—"

Baker whined an objection to my calling it Simpson's "story." I used the word quite purposefully. I was going to show the jury not only the lie itself, but how Simpson went about fabricating his lies.

The judge was sitting right next to this man, as close to him as anyone except me. He had to be offended. This defendant, who had put the court and the country through the wrenching fiasco that was the Simpson saga and who should be in jail for the rest of his life, was sitting in his courtroom trampling on the oath. Sometimes the lies were so blatant, I could see the disbelief storm across Judge Fujisaki's face. The judge, quite legitimately, gave me all the room I needed.

"Overruled."

I began to read from Simpson's statement to the police, only hours after Nicole's death, "I checked my messages. *[Paula] had left me a message that she wasn't there,* that she had to leave town." I let his words sink in with the jury. It could not have been clearer. Now he denied he was referring to the message he picked up from his voice mail at 6:56. "Untrue," he said. To explain away his admission to the police, he concocted a story that he had been referring to the outgoing message on Paula's telephone answering machine. As if Paula Barbieri would leave an eight-minute message detailing the reasons she was breaking up with Simpson on her answering machine for the most casual acquaintance or telemarketer to hear when they called. "Like when you call my house and I say, 'We're not home right now, please leave a message,' right?" I asked him.

Baker could see his client completely coming apart and was willing to try anything to stop the bleeding. "He wouldn't call your house," Baker interjected, desperately trying to rescue his lying client. I ignored him.

"You want to tell this jury under oath, that when you called Paula's machine, the number anybody could call, there was a whole long message about you and about golf and about her being unhappy and so forth. Is that the story?"

"I believe it was directed more to me, but it wasn't about golf, no."

"So when Lenore Walker wrote in her notes a 'whole long message about golf,' you say it's all false, right?"

"That's—"

"False?"

"Yes, it's false, yes." This renowned expert, who spent sixty-plus hours in Simpson's jail cell, her notes were false. Simpson's phone records were false, his police statement was false. It was all false. Simpson was sticking to his naked lies.

This was a long trial, and I wanted to make certain the jury understood the significance of this testimony, so I asked a string of questions for their benefit:

"The truth of the matter, sir, is that you were desperate to get in touch with Paula because she had left you. True?"

"False."

"And you were trying all day to get in touch with her, call after call after call. True?"

"That's not necessarily true, no."

I didn't care what his answers were at this point.

"And the reason you were trying to get in touch with her is because you were feeling alone on that evening, weren't you?"

"That's not true."

"And you blamed Nicole for feeling alone, sir, didn't you?"

"No."

Nobody cared what he was saying.

I established quickly that he had gone to McDonald's with Kato, then asked about the call he placed to Paula at 10:03 P.M. that night. "When you spoke to the police detectives on June 13, hours after Nicole's murder, you told [them] that you made a phone call to Paula driving over to her house in your Bronco, from your cell phone. True?"

He wouldn't answer the question, so I read the police statement: "[After the recital] I came home, *I got in my car,* I was going to see my girlfriend, *I was calling her* and she wasn't around. . . . The Bronco is what I drive, rather drive it than any other car. *And as I was going over there I called her a couple of times,* and she wasn't there and that she had left a message. And then I checked my messages, she had left me a message that she wasn't there, that she had to leave town. Then I came back and ended up sitting with Kato."

According to Simpson's phone records, the only cell phone call *after* the recital was made at 10:03 P.M.

"You told the police you drove to Paula's after the recital in your Bronco and made a phone call to her from your cell phone. True or untrue?"

Obviously he has to admit that; I had just read to the jury the statement in which he said it. "True," he answered.

"The only time after the recital that you have any cell phone calls to Paula is at what time?" I pointed to the big board. "Looking at your cell phone records." I want him to state the time.

"Ten oh three."

"So, sir, you were in your Bronco calling Paula at 10:03, just like you told the police. True?"

If he answers yes, it's tantamount to a confession. Allan Park had established conclusively that the Bronco was not at Rockingham at 10:03; therefore if Simpson was in the Bronco, he was not at home. It was that simple. If he was not home at 10:03, he was committing the murders. It followed as night the day; the physical evidence put him at the scene and he had no other explanation for his whereabouts. If he had, he would have told us where he was. If Simpson called Paula from the Bronco, Simpson killed Nicole and Ron.

"That's incorrect."

"Ohhh"—as sarcastic as I could be—"so you lied to the police."

"No."

I stood in front of him, just shaking my head. "You have a different story now. It's different now, isn't it."

"I think it is more accurate now."

"It's different! Isn't it!"

"Yes."

"*NOW* you say you didn't get in the Bronco and drive to Paula's and call her from the phone. True?"

"That's true."

Normally I would stop there. He'd been impeached, he'd been shown to be a liar over and over—and in this case, more than a liar: a killer. The damage had been done.

But my next step was to tell the jury what his newly created story was going to be. When I sat down and Baker stood up to rehabilitate him, they surely would spin that yarn, so I wanted Simpson to weave his patchwork of lies and then I would unravel it myself. I would impeach him, unwind his story, and impeach that. If, later, he tried to weave another, he would look absurd.

This was what Peter and I had spent the weekend constructing: an examination that moved from one damning impeachment to the next like mobile artillery, blasting each of his alibis right up out of the water. We were still in the first ten minutes of the day's examination, and Simpson was defenseless.

"And *now* you say that—of course, after meeting with teams of lawyers and investigators and defense experts, and seeing that there are cell phone records at 10:03 putting you in the Bronco. True?"

"True."

Simpson really didn't have a lot of fight left in him. He could have said, "Mr. Petrocelli, you are trying to mislead the jury." He could have said, "I was in a great deal of torment, my ex-wife had just been brutally murdered and I was doing the best I could. After further reflection, I find I misspoke." He could have said a lot of things. But Simpson was a defeated man, the best Simpson could come up with was, "True."

"So your story *now*, then, is that you didn't make this call from the Bronco, right?"

"That's correct."

"And your story *now*, sir, is that, in fact, your cell phone wasn't even in the Bronco at 10:03, right?" I was co-opting their examination, stealing it right out from under them. How were they going to argue any of this when I had already destroyed it?

"That's correct."

"You're *now* saying that you took it out of the Bronco hours before?"

"That's correct."

He had fallen into another trap. I pulled out the June 13 police statement, in which Simpson had been talking about leaving in the limo for
Chicago. "'The *last* thing I did before I left, when I was rushing, was went
and got my phone out of the Bronco.'" The cell phone was still in the Bronco
a little past 11:00 P.M., right where it was when he used it at 10:03 P.M.,
right where he left it when he returned from the murders. "Remember
saying that to the police?" I demanded.

"I don't think that's complete."

"Do you remember saying that to the police? Yes or no?"

"I remember saying that and more to the police," he tried.

"Do you think the transcript is wrong? Is that what you're saying?"
I started getting heated.

"I know it is."

"Had no problem with it on Friday, did you?"

Baker objected, and the judge sustained him.

"You told the police that the last thing you did, sir, before leaving
for the airport, you went out and got your cell phone from the Bronco—
because it was in the Bronco at 11:00, true?"

"That's incorrect."

"Now you are trying to say the police statement is wrong because
you don't want the phone to be in the Bronco at 11:00. True?"

"It wasn't in the Bronco!"

"You don't want it to be there because if it was there at eleven, it was
there at ten; and if it's there at ten, you're in your Bronco and you're not
in your home, and it destroys your alibi?!" I yelled it at him in outrage. It
was a summation for the jury.

Baker was screaming. "It's great final argument and great sound
bites, Your Honor, but it's not a proper question!"

"No speaking objections," I snapped at him.

"I don't take legal advice from my adversaries!" We were yelling at
each other across the courtroom.

The court sustained his objection, but the point was slammed home.

"What's your story now?" I demanded. Baker objected, but this time
he was overruled. Forced to invent yet another lie to explain away damning evidence, Simpson delivered a set piece about his cell phone *accessories,*
insisting that he had already taken his cell phone out of the car earlier in
the day, that it was the *accessories* he was collecting for this overnight trip

to Chicago. Try as he might, he could not present this tale with notable confidence or conviction; the word or concept of accessories had never been mentioned before his deposition and had clearly been added after the fact. Simpson was kind of rocking back and forth uncomfortably. He wasn't looking the jury in the eye. I let him give his spiel, filled with all the telltale unrequired details, then immediately confronted him with another part of his police statement.

"'When I was leaving, [Kato] said something to me and I was rushing to get *my phone. . . .*' Remember telling that to the police?"

It was crystal clear. The phone was in the Bronco at 11:00.

Establishing that every other time he had used the cell phone that day it had been in the Bronco, and that "the only call you would like this jury to believe that you made from your cell phone not in the Bronco, but in your driveway, is at 10:03, right?" Right.

"You were calling Paula, driving in your Bronco to Bundy, calling Paula, 'cause you were desperate and you were alone that night, true?"

"Untrue. . . . If she was still in town, it was still not too late for her to take me to the airport," suggesting he was trying to reach Paula at 10:03 P.M. to get a lift to the airport. This was pitiful. He had told both the cops and Dr. Walker that he knew she was out of town; plus, a limousine had been ordered by Cathy Randa, as always, to be at his house at 10:45.

Simpson was an embarrassment. Here's where I wished cameras had been allowed in the courtroom. If the world had seen Simpson rocking, puffing, and blinking as he told his litany of lies, there would be no doubt in anyone's mind about the depth of his guilt.

And imagine what Simpson saw when he looked at me. I knew everything! I had absorbed every piece of evidence, every line of deposition or interview testimony, every sound bite, every incriminating statement and nuance of this case, and was able to call it up at will. I had total command of the material, and it must have been intimidating for Simpson to see me spitting his own words back at him verbatim without looking at a note.

Simpson's story was that he made the 10:03 call from his cell phone while standing in his driveway on his way to scull a few golf balls. While I was eliciting the defense's story, I thought I might as well get the golfing mantra out of the way. "Go ahead," I said dismissively with a mocking grin, "tell us."

"I grabbed a three wood."

"Give us as much detail as you can." I kind of waved him on as I walked away.

"I grabbed a three wood, and I looked at the face of it and I swung it a bit. And I went to the trunk of my Bentley, where I had another set of clubs, 'cause the purpose of going into the garage was to get a sand wedge, which is a special league club, and I was playing with a new set of golf clubs that I had just got from the Callaway people the previous week . . ."

Simpson knew more about those golf clubs than anything else in the case. His memorization of the unrequired detail was amazing: The MaxFlite 100HT, the old sand wedge, the new sand wedge, the pitching wedge, non-scuff balls. He produced a story that accounted for all the evidence: *I covered the bag, I covered the 10:03 call, took care of the downstairs lights. . . .* If only for the fullness of its coverage, the story was very impressive.

I stood by my podium, idly flipping the pages of my outline, shaking my head occasionally as if to say, "You can recount every second of your alibi time, but you can't tell us how you cut yourself and bled all over the place." I gave him as much time as he wanted, and he spoke uninterrupted for several minutes. When he was finally through, I said, "Mr. Simpson, if I asked you to repeat that, you could do it word for word, couldn't you?"

"I—I may be able to come relatively close to that." He admitted it!

"You memorized it, have you not? You've sat down, rehearsed it, and memorized it?"

"I don't think I've ever rehearsed it."

I pulled the story apart. Had he told any such details to the police when they had questioned him? No. Had he gotten it straight in practice sessions in jail with lawyers who came down from San Francisco for precisely that purpose? Baker yelped. I wanted the jury to understand that this had been a staged performance. "And you told that story in your deposition after you heard all the witnesses testify, and all the evidence, correct? . . . You knew exactly what you had to say to meet and defeat all the witnesses and evidence that was against you, true?"

"Great sound bite. Horribly argumentative," Baker told the court.

I wasn't taking that from Baker. "If he has a legal objection, make it. But this stuff about sound bites is showboating!"

Judge Fujisaki said, "Excuse me?"

Baker threw up his hands. His witness was destroying everything he had worked for, and he was unable to contain himself. "*This* is showboating!" He pointed to me. "Right *there* is showboating!"

The judge said, "Excuse me. That answer is overruled." He meant "question." Even Fujisaki was flustered.

I ran Simpson through his supposed tour of the neighborhood with Chachi. It was absolutely crystal clear in his mind, he said, that he was back inside Rockingham before 10:20. No response. "And the reason it is," I accused him, "is because you know that Allan Park is sitting out there at 10:23, smoking a cigarette, and he would have seen you. True?"

Baker objected, "Argumentative, Your Honor."

"Sustained."

Simpson continued, oblivious. "If I would have been there at that time—"

Baker called, "It was sustained, Mr. Simpson. *O.J., it's sustained!*"

"I'm sorry."

Simpson was coming apart. I, meanwhile, was smelling blood.

At the break, Simpson was breathing hard, like a fighter between rounds, while his corner men were trying to stem the flow. Baker was the cut man, while Simpson simply looked dazed. The defense tried to put on good faces because the press was watching every second of interaction for even the most minute signs of significance. The reporters were scribbling madly, trying to catch a trace of what was being said. The lawyers, of course, were being very careful not to say anything that could be reported. I looked over there and didn't see any back-slapping, there was no smiling going on.

I was in control of the courtroom. Simpson and Baker were undoubtedly trying to make adjustments, but we had them all covered. It was an extraordinary feeling. In this case that had obsessed our country, with the eyes of the world upon us, we were finally pulling out the truth. I felt powerful and prepared.

THIRTY

No Explanation

We had caught Simpson retrofitting his testimony. There is nothing so incriminating as being able to actually pinpoint a witness changing his testimony before a jury's eyes. It's like videotaping a pickpocket.

"Isn't it true, sir, that you told Dr. Lenore Walker, your own hired expert, that you went into the Bentley for the black shoes, which Bentley was parked across the driveway?"

"I heard many things. We were trying to figure out the evening when I spoke to her."

I couldn't believe my good fortune. I jumped at him. "Figure out?"

Simpson immediately denied it. "No."

I had spent the course of the trial trying to show that this was exactly what he had done: figure out an alibi to explain the world of incriminating evidence and facts against him. The whole thing was a "figure out"!

"Why did you have to figure out anything?" I asked.

"Trying to figure out what took place," he backtracked.

"Trying to figure out what to say, is that what you said? 'Figure out the evening'?" I approached him.

"No," Simpson insisted. "Incorrect."

"You didn't just say that you tried to 'figure out the evening'?" I wouldn't let him off, I was milking it. I was two feet away and we were arguing intensely.

"I was trying to figure out what happened that evening, and I had heard Allan Park long before February."

"Excuse me." In his preliminary hearing and grand jury testimony Park said he'd first picked up Simpson at the Bentley located across the driveway from the front door of Simpson's house. I believe Simpson had crouched behind the car, laid down his bag containing the bloody murder knife and probably the shoes, and darted across the driveway to get into the house. That's when Park saw him. To explain this guilty predicament, Simpson told Lenore Walker he went to get his golf shoes from the Bentley and Park simply saw him as he was coming into the house. Nothing sinister. It was *after* the Walker sessions that Simpson heard Park give his trial testimony placing Simpson at the benches, much closer to the front door. Simpson seized on this fortuity and refined his story in case he ever had to tell it—like now. He would say he came out of the house to look inside his golf bag resting on the benches, and that is where and why Park saw him. In Simpson's mind, it looked less guilty to be seen closer to the benches than the Bentley. He was adapting his story to the evidence; when the evidence changed, so did his story.

"Is it your testimony under oath before this jury that you heard Allan Park testify long before February that he saw you only at this point," I marked a spot near the benches at the entrance to the house, "and not across the driveway?" I looked him straight in the eye and, with homage to Barry Scheck's examination of Dennis Fung in the criminal trial, raised my voice. "Answer *that* question, Mr. Simpson!"

Baker started screaming. "Just a minute, Your Honor, this is in-your-face!" He was yelling. "Maybe Mr. Petrocelli can go back and get at the podium, since he's not doing anything over there except pointing at my client!" I *was* pointing at his client, and I continued to point.

"Mr. Simpson—"

"Would you direct him to get back to the podium!" Baker shouted.

The judge refused. "You've done the same thing with other witnesses, Mr. Baker." Baker sat down and fumed.

Simpson tried to duck and run, but I pursued him. He tried to say he went outside twice, but that was not reflected in Walker's notes.

Simpson finally did what he usually did when confronted with incriminating facts: He denied them. He contradicted Dr. Walker's notes directly.

"Is it the Bentley or the benches that you went to?"

"The benches."

"Not the Bentley?"

"Not the Bentley."

"The benches?"

"The benches."

Dr. Walker would join in the impeachment parade.

It was while he was gathering his belongings and preparing to leave for Chicago that Simpson claimed he saw blood on his left pinkie. Why the pinkie? Because he wanted to distance himself from the cut on the middle finger of his left hand which he claimed happened when "a glass broke" in Chicago. He would have liked to say he dripped blood at Rockingham before he left, but at his deposition he had said he didn't remember dripping it in the driveway; if all of a sudden he had a flashback recollection, he knew I would impeach him badly. I figured he was going to try and get away with saying, "I didn't see blood, but that doesn't mean I didn't bleed."

His blood had also been found in the Bronco, and I wanted to exclude the possibility that he dripped it there on his way to or from getting his cell phone (or cell phone accessories). If Simpson could not account for innocently dropping blood in the Bronco, there was only one other explanation. Assuming we could eliminate planting—which, of course, we could—the only remaining possibility was that he dripped it there on the way back from the murders.

We retraced his steps to the Bronco and the motions he made climbing in. Simpson tried to resist my efforts to pin him in. He vividly recalled looking at the face of his golf club, but could not remember how he entered the vehicle, or whether he got inside it at all. "You didn't bleed in that Bronco?"

"If I did, I would have no knowledge of it."

He didn't get in, sit down, close the door, and then remove the cell phone accessories, he said; he didn't touch the headlight button, didn't see blood on the light switch or the inside door handle, where his blood had been found. He said it was not possible that he left a bloody footprint in the car.

We had debated how far to go with this line of questioning. Simpson had proved adept at designing plausible after-the-fact explanations, and we did not want to give him the opportunity to insert an innocent explanation for the presence of his blood into a scenario in which there was none. We had decided to play it by ear. I went for it.

"You have no explanation for that blood, do you, sir?"

"That's correct."

"You have no explanation for how blood matching your blood, and DNA matching your DNA, were found in that Bronco the next morning, true?"

"I don't know if it was found the next morning, but—"

"What do you mean, you don't know?"

"I don't know when they took it out. I didn't think they did that the next morning." Simpson was quibbling with the fact that the blood in the Bronco was collected not the next morning, but the morning after. He added childishly, "I'm sorry that I may be ignorant to that." I decided to keep going.

"And you have no explanation for how your blood was found in that Bronco, right?"

"That's correct."

"And you have no explanation, sir, for how the blood of Nicole's was found on the carpet of the driver's side, do you?"

"No."

"And you have no explanation for how Ron Goldman's blood got in your car that night, do you?"

"Me personally, no."

"Have no explanation for this jury, do you?"

"No."

"None?"

"None."

With no innocent explanation, Simpson's blood was in the Bronco either because it was planted there or because he killed two people. We could show it wasn't planted, which left only one other explanation.

As opposed to the immaculate cut on his pinkie—according to Simpson there was no cut, only blood—Simpson told the police the cut on his middle finger occurred at Rockingham on the night of the murders, and that he "opened it again" in Chicago. (In other words: *I cut myself at the same time my ex-wife was getting her throat slit. But I didn't kill her.* Which is why, I suspect, Vannatter and Lange thought they had a slam dunk of a case. What cop wouldn't?) I went right up to him and pointed to his hand. "Now, the cut on your middle finger is the one that still bears a scar, does it not?" Simpson carries a physical reminder of his murdering two people everywhere he goes. He is, quite literally, scarred for life. He looked at it.

"Left hand middle finger." I pointed to it, almost touching it. "Right across the knuckle."

"Yes," he answered. I let that hang for a moment.

"How did that mark get on your finger between 10:00 and 11:00 on June 12 in Los Angeles?"

"I didn't see that or any mark on my hand between 10:00 and 11:00 on June 12."

"How is it, then, that you *reopened* that cut in Chicago the next morning?"

"It was an assumption on my part."

"What do you mean by 'assumption'? You assumed—"

Baker: "Let him answer the question!" I ignored him.

"You assumed—"

Baker: "He asked you what?"

"Would you answer the question."

Baker: "What do you mean by 'assumption'?" He obviously wanted Simpson to answer that particular question, so I cut him off and withdrew it.

"You *assumed* you reopened the cut; is that what you're saying?"

"Yes," Simpson said, "because I did not see any cut, as I emphasized to the police *on numerous occasions,* the night before. And I guess I did the wrong thing by trying to *assume.* . . . I assumed that if I was cut the night before, *maybe* it was the same cut, because there was no other cut on my hand." Were we supposed to believe this? The gash on his finger was long and deep, and he didn't notice it until it was *re*opened—*if* it was reopened?

"Well, the cut that you were talking to the police about, was this the one that still bears the scar?"

"That's correct."

"You told the police, sir, that you reopened that in Chicago. True or untrue?" I posed it very simply. "Just answer the question."

"I can't answer that question 'cause I think I said 'may have.'"

"You *may have* or *did?*"

"May have."

"And you also told the police that you were quite sure you cut your finger before you went to Chicago, true or false?"

"Probably."

"Probably?" More quibbling, but that's what he had said in his deposition. "They asked you if you had been bleeding at Nicole's, or cut it at Nicole's, in the past couple of weeks, and you said no, you're quite sure you cut it last night." I was taking those statements right out of his June 13 police statement, I wasn't characterizing or tinkering with them. "Do you remember that?" I began to read from that statement. "Page 22, line 27:

"'Q. Do you recall having that cut on your finger the last time you were at Nicole's house?'

"'A. Oh, a week ago?'

"'Q. Yeah.'

"'A. No.'

"'Q. Oh, so it's since then?'

"'A. Oh, I'm pretty sure, yeah. Yeah, just last night.'

"'Q. Okay. Somewhere last night you cut it?'

"'A. Yeah, yeah.'

"'Q. Somewhere after the recital?'

"'A. Somewhere when I was rushing to get out of my house.'

"'Q. Okay. After the recital?'

"'A. Yeah.'

"'Q. What do you think happened? Do you have any idea?'

"'A. I have no idea, man.'"

I looked up and turned to him. "There's no doubt that you told the police you cut your hand the night before, when you were leaving for the airport, true?"

What was he going to say? "True."

"And you told the police that you had no idea how you did it, right?"

"That's correct."

"And you told the police that you reopened that cut, or *may have* reopened that cut, in Chicago, right?"

"Yes."

He was set up perfectly. He cut himself at Rockingham after the recital. He reopened the cut in Chicago. He had tried earlier to deny that the cut he "reopened" in Chicago was on his middle finger, so now I put it to him, "Tell the jury, which cut did you reopen in Chicago, sir. Point to it."

Simpson would not be led. "The police—" he began.

"Just point to the cut on your finger!"

"Well, I don't know because—"

"—That you reopened!"

"You haven't talked about everything that's in there." He was doing his damnedest to introduce his unrequired details and his alternate takes and everything else to explain away his incriminating admissions. I cut him off.

"No, no, no!" I exclaimed. "We'll do this one step at a time!"

"I don't know. I never saw—"

"Excuse me, sir. I just want you to point—"

Baker broke in. "Your Honor!"

I protested. *"He's not answering my question!"*

"That's because you won't let him!" Baker said angrily. "You keep interrupting him. Let him answer the question."

Judge Fujisaki: "Overruled. Ask your question."

I modulated my tone and brought the level down. "Mr. Simpson . . ." Tensely contained, I sounded like I felt, walking a thin line between civility and anger. "Point to the cut on your finger that you sustained in Los Angeles between 10:00 and 11:00 P.M. on June 12 and that you reopened in Chicago the next morning." It was a very simple request, and I was speaking in little more than a whisper. *"Just point to it."*

The jury was mesmerized. I wasn't watching them, but I knew they were riveted. The examination was not simply a series of questions, it was a performance. Simpson and I had developed a dynamic: I was ridiculing, sneering, challenging, angry, bemused, incredulous; he was backtracking, filling, lying, caught in one trap after another and desperately trying to claw his way out. This was quite a show, and the jury was enjoying it.

Simpson would not explain the cut. "I can't," he said, "'cause I never saw a cut that night."

"Well, you know the finger that you cut in Chicago, right?" He had a scar on it!

"Yes."

"So point to that."

"The finger that I cut in Chicago is here." He must have thought he was making some fine distinction.

"Let the record reflect Mr. Simpson is pointing to the middle finger of his left hand, just above the knuckle."

Though he had every opportunity, Simpson refrained from flashing me the bird.

"Is that scar the cut that you incurred in Los Angeles between 10:00 and 11:00 P.M., that you recut in Chicago? Yes or no?"

"I would have to say no." It was an absurd answer, but now he owned it.

I wanted to be absolutely certain I had phrased the question correctly. I didn't want Simpson arguing legalisms later on. "Is that the cut you reopened in Chicago?" I asked. "Yes or no?"

"I would say no."

I was still not satisfied. Simpson was such a conniver that I would not put it past him to argue that his denial had not been definitive, so I asked him directly, "What do you mean, you 'would say'? What happened? *Can't you just answer the question?*"

This was for effect. I wanted the jury to understand how far and to what extremes Simpson would go not to be honest with them. Of course he could answer the question—if he confessed to the murders.

From across the room, Baker objected. "That's argumentative, Your Honor."

The judge overruled. "Answer it." What an abrupt directive. This was no Lance Ito. He was the Anti-Ito.

"You want me to explain?" Simpson asked hopefully.

I did not. "I'm not asking you what you 'would say.' When you told the police that you cut your finger in Los Angeles, and that you cut it again in Chicago, I would like you to tell us what cut you were referring to."

"I think earlier I told you I assumed, because I saw blood the night before, that I had cut my finger. I made it clear to the police that I never saw a cut"—that was a lie—"*on numerous occasions* that day. I made an assumption, which I realize I shouldn't have made, because I saw blood on my finger. I assumed I had cut my hand. Since I didn't see a cut, and since there was no other cut on my hand when I returned from Chicago, and I was with the police and I was with Nurse Peratis, there was no other cut on my hand . . ." He was getting all his well-rehearsed arguments in as best he could. "I made an assumption, and I was wrong making that assumption." (*E.g.: I take full responsibility but I did not hit her; same technique.*)

"You were wrong when you told the police that you reopened that cut or that you cut it in Chicago. Yes or no? You were wrong?"

"I was wrong."

"Wrong about crucial questions given to you hours after Nicole's murder, true?"

"At the time I didn't know what was crucial."

Give me a break! *We've found blood all over a crime scene; I see you've got a cut there, why don't you tell us about it and you're home free.* He didn't know it was crucial?!

Baker broke in again. "This is argumentative."

You're not supposed to direct comments to opposing counsel, but I couldn't resist. "It's not argumentative!"

"Again—"

"Absolutely not argumentative!"

The Court overruled his objection.

I set Simpson up some more. June 13 had been the first time he had been interviewed in connection with Nicole's murder, yet he was making assumptions instead of simply telling the truth. When the police told him there was blood dripped in his house, driveway, and car at Rockingham, and asked if that blood was his, Simpson had said, "If it's dripped, it's what I dripped running around trying to leave."

"An important question like that and you just made an assumption?" I asked him. "Is that what you're saying?"

"I saw one drop of blood and some blood on my pinkie, which I told them, and so I assumed—"

"So you told the police that, no question about that in your mind, there's blood coming from you someplace on the evening of June 12, correct?"

"Since I saw a drop of blood on my counter, and I saw a drop of blood on my pinkie, I assumed it came from me."

This was a preposterous story and demanded to be reduced to absurdity. "Now, tell the jury how you cut yourself such [as] to have blood that was on the counter and blood on the finger."

Even Simpson could not pony up the strength to give a convincing lie. "I don't know," he testified. "As I said, I didn't feel the cut, I didn't see any other blood anywhere. . . . I saw a drop of blood on my counter and I looked at my hand and saw a drop of blood on my pinkie, and that's all I saw."

"You have no idea how blood got on you that night. Is that what you're saying?"

"Yes."

In the gallery, people were shaking their heads in disbelief. Several people in the media later told me they wanted me to stop; it was too painful. "I couldn't take it," one said. "Enough is enough. You're piling on." Simpson was getting beaten up so badly, punished so mercilessly, there was some concern he would end up earning sympathy by looking like a victim.

Fred Goldman had none of those concerns. He felt vindicated. He wanted the examination to go on and on forever.

After a break, I took Simpson to his least favorite place, his hideaway hotel room in Chicago. I asked about the immaculate breaking of the hotel water glass. "At one point going back and forth, a glass broke," Simpson said. Not good enough.

"What do you mean, 'a glass broke'? *You* broke it, right?"

"Yes."

Hotel drinking glasses are thick and sturdy, made to withstand lots of uncaring travelers and careless wear. They are not fine crystal. I had planned to bring a water glass from the DoubleTree and slam it on the lectern, to show how hard it was to break and how difficult it would be to do so without remembering. But that morning I forgot the glass.

"Tell the jury exactly how you broke the glass," I said.

"I couldn't tell you," he answered. "I don't know."

"How did you break it? What did you do?"

"I don't know. I really couldn't tell you."

"You know when you break a glass. When did you break this glass?"

"I don't know." He could not tell the jury how he broke the glass that supposedly gave him the scar he was carrying to this day.

I pursued him. "At what point in time did you break this glass? Tell us exactly when it occurred."

"As I have told you *on numerous occasions,* Mr. Petrocelli, it was during the course of going back and forth trying to pack, trying to get my flight out of there, I was going back and forth, back and forth. In the midst of that, at one of the times I was in and out of that bathroom, the glass broke." It was at this point in the deposition that he himself had broken down and walked out. Now his voice, through tone and delivery, was designed to push me away. I did not know whether Simpson was better prepared to take on the subject this time, I did know I wasn't going anywhere; we would be with this topic for a while.

Did he throw the glass at the mirror? No. Did he throw it at the shower? In the toilet? On the floor? At anything? No. Did he step on it? Kick it? Did he do anything with the glass in an act of rage or violence? No. Did he slam it on the counter? "I may have."

Bam! I banged Yvette's plastic water bottle on the witness stand. "Is that what you're saying?"

"I may have."

"Is that the best you can do for this jury?"

"Yes."

How did he cut himself? He didn't know. We were looking at a picture of the pristine hotel bathroom, photographed exactly as Simpson had left it. "I was going back and forth on the phone and at one point I noticed blood. . . . I'm strictly taking a shot here. I, at some point when I was trying to get in the sink, I think I cut my hand, but I couldn't tell you when. I was back and forth to the phone so many times and I was also packing and at some point in there I cut my hand. . . . At some point I was packing my stuff. I made sure the glass was out of my way as I was putting my things back in my overnight kit. I was going back and forth to the telephone and somewhere in there my hand was cut."

This was a mantra, in the manner of his other mantras: *My hand was cut; I take full responsibility; my hand touched her face; a glass broke.*

Supposedly, he cut himself while sweeping the broken glass into the sink. Backhanded. Simpson is right-handed, but the scar is on the knuckle of the middle finger of his left hand. "I'm sure I used both hands," he said. "You know, I can use both of my hands!"

"Tell us how glass came into contact to that part of your finger, sir, while you were sweeping the glass or picking up the pieces." *How did she get the bruises on her face?* Same question.

"As I've told you on numerous occasions. . . . It was during the process of going back and forth to the telephone, trying to pack my clothes, moving the glass out of the way so I can put my toiletries away, that I cut my hand. I can't tell you any more than that."

"You're unable to give us anything more definitive than that, sir?"

"That's correct."

"You cannot tell the jury how the glass actually cut your finger?"

"No."

"That is correct?"

"That is correct."

Simpson also swore he had no injury to his fourth finger when he came back to Los Angeles. "I know it wasn't there when the police had my hand on the paper with Nurse Peratis and they were inspecting my hand. I know it wasn't there then. . . . I know when I was with Vannatter and Lange and Nurse Peratis, all three of them took my hand, they . . . looked at my hand and there was no other cut there. . . . They talked to me about the injury, and I'm sure that they would have noted it if there was another injury there, and it was not there." He was always prepared to dump his prepared speech into our text. There was also an element of glee to this prepared testimony that invited skepticism. I didn't mind his soliloquy; Skip Taft had seen things differently.

Plus, there was a flaw in his logic. These superbly skilled police officers who were examining him and supposedly cataloging every wound, were, according to Simpson, the same bumbling, stumbling cops who processed the crime scene wrong, missed important evidence and could not identify what evidence they did find, were corrupt, racist, morally bankrupt, and generally contaminated everything. These were the people whose honesty and powers of observation he was banking on. Which way did he want it?

Steve put a photo of Simpson's hands on the ELMO. The fingernail marks? Perhaps it was Justin. "You're saying it was Justin's? Your son's?"

"I think Justin is the only person that between the thirteenth and fifteenth that I was in any real heavy physical thing with." Simpson shamelessly blamed Nicole's death marks on their young child. I pursued him angrily.

"You're talking about a seven-year-old, eighty-pound boy. You're not saying to the jury that Justin gouged you with his fingernails and caused that injury."

"Not at all." Simpson saw this was a bad idea.

"You're not saying that?"

"Not at all. But he's the only person I was in any kind of physical wrestle with."

The curved marks on his hands on June 15, "How did you get that injury?"

"I don't know."

"Can't give a single explanation, true?"

"True."

"Did you have this injury on the top of your middle finger when you came back from Chicago?"

"I certainly did not see it. Neither did Vannatter or Lange, for that matter."

"Move to strike."

"Stricken."

From the cuts we went to Simpson's clothing. In his deposition he said he had changed clothes in his hotel room and put on the black pants and white shirt he was seen wearing when he arrived at Rockingham the next day. However, both Raymond Kilduff, the Hertz vice president who had accompanied Simpson back to O'Hare in Chicago, and Mark Partridge, the passenger who sat next to him on the flight to Los Angeles, had testified in deposition that they had seen him wearing a blue jean out-fit, the same one Allan Park had seen him wear to Chicago the previous night. What to do?

Simpson said he threw up on the pants. On the airplane back to Los Angeles. Or *maybe* he did. "I do remember throwing up on the airplane, and bleeding, where the girl brought me a napkin. And I don't remember if I changed pants on the airplane. I could have." Never mind that no one, not the passenger sitting next to him or the stewardess or anyone else, had any recollection of this.

This was new, I hadn't heard of this throwing up business before. Finally, despite the fact that witnesses had him leaving Chicago in blue jeans and arriving at Rockingham in black slacks, Simpson returned to his deposition story that he put on the black pants in his Chicago hotel room. Both Cathy Randa and Skip Taft, who picked him up at the airport, would swear they made no stops and that Simpson did not change clothes.

My own feeling is that he bled on the blue jeans on the way to Chicago, perhaps when he put his fingers in the pants pockets. He put the same jeans on when he left Chicago and wore them on the airplane, as two witnesses on the plane confirmed. When he got off the plane at LAX, he changed—sometime, somewhere—before arriving at Rockingham. He did not want to stroll into a murder investigation with blood stains on his jeans—imagine how that would look.

Simpson was met at Rockingham by noted criminal defense attorney Howard Weitzman. Why? Because, Simpson said, on the plane home he was chatted up by the guy sitting next to him, a lawyer, who told him to get one. "Is it your testimony that the only reason that Howard Weitzman was waiting for you when you got to Rockingham is because some guy you never met before on an airplane told you so? . . . That's your testimony?"

"That's absolutely correct."

We moved along. Simpson said, the next day, he had called the Hertz employee in Chicago, Jim Merrill, not to check on the whereabouts of his golf clubs and golf bag, but to apologize for his rude behavior the day before. *Look, I was having a bad day, my wife got murdered. Sorry I was so rude. Oh, by the way, seen my clubs?*

After he'd hung up with Merrill, Simpson had headed out to LAX with Robert Kardashian. "Isn't it true," I asked, "that you specifically asked Mr. Kardashian at the office, in the presence of Skip Taft, to take you to the airport and get your golf clubs?"

"That's not correct," he answered. ". . . We were driving around after going by Nicole's house and we were waiting for my children and we were on the Santa Monica freeway . . . and he said, 'What do you want to do?' I said, 'Just drive around,' and then at one point we were near the airport, I said we can get my clubs at the airport. . . . I was trying to kill fifty minutes waiting for my kids." Taft and Kardashian would do him in on this lie.

At the break, Tom suggested we go back in and get more blood, or rather, more admissions that Simpson had no explanations for the presence of his blood in incriminating sites. We pulled out a big board exhibit detailing the places at Bundy where his blood had been found. I wanted to prevent the defense from arguing that he had bled there on some prior occasion.

"Sir," I asked, "do you have any explanation whatsoever why there was blood found matching your blood at Bundy?"

"*Represented* to be my blood," Simpson insisted. It was really the only defense left to him.

"You have no explanation whatsoever for why each of those blood drops that was found had DNA matching your DNA, correct?"

"Correct."

"Same questions for the rear gate?"

"No explanation."

I showed him the board with the Rockingham blood drops and had him repeat that he did not remember bleeding in those locations on that evening. My question was "Do you have any explanation . . . ?" and I suppose he could have said, "I think the cops planted my blood." Had he done so, I would have changed my question to "You don't know that for a fact, do you? You didn't see that happen? You have no personal knowledge?" No, no, no. I would have followed with a string of questions, beginning with, "To your own personal knowledge, do you know how that blood got there?" No.

They'd had their chance. If there had been any real evidence of planting, for instance witnesses who saw cops sprinkling blood, dropping a glove, breaking into the LAPD lab or Simpson's Bronco, we would have heard about it a long time ago. But there was nothing.

I showed Simpson a picture of the socks. "Do you have any explanation, sir, for how blood matching your blood got on those socks?"

"No."

"Do you have any explanation for how blood matching Nicole's got on those socks?"

"No."

Tom said I hadn't covered all the blood spots in the Bronco, so I went back and established he had no explanation for them, either. We had covered all the blood evidence in the case and he had no explanation for any of it.

I moved to the murder clothes. This was going to be fun, because we could dress him from head to foot; we had pictures of Simpson wearing almost every piece of the murder ensemble.

We had enough sense not to put the gloves on Simpson. I was tempted, because Baker still had the opportunity to do so in his cross-examination as well as the defense case, and Richard Rubin had worked them in rather well. But the one element in a demonstration I could not control was Simpson, who obviously would make a great scene of struggling to put them on one more time. So I decided against it. Why take chances?

Simpson denied Nicole had bought the gloves for him, even though we had her sales receipt. As for the photographs of him wearing the gloves at football games, he conceded he was wearing gloves, which was big of him, but he did not know if they were Aris Leather Lights. He admitted he no longer had the gloves he was pictured wearing. If they weren't the murder gloves, where were they? He didn't have a clue.

We had found knit caps in his house. "You owned caps like that as of June 12, 1994, correct?"

"I could have, but I don't know." He was destroyed as a witness, by this time, his answers were just words. All he knew was, "I can't admit things. I have to say something, but I can't admit. If I admit, I lose the case." Nevertheless, he could not dispute the fact that he had owned a similar knit cap found by the police when they had searched his house. So we had him in the hat.

Sweatsuit. "I asked you at your deposition whether you owned any dark sweatsuit in June 1994, and you said you did not. Do you remember that?"

"Yes."

"You have the photo, Steve?" Onto the ELMO came a photograph from a magazine that had been sent to us by one of the many civilians who inundated us with what they hoped would be helpful material. This was gold: a color photo layout, over several pages, of Simpson wearing a dark sweatsuit weeks before the murder.

"You remember shooting an exercise video put out by *Playboy* in late May 1994?"

"Yes."

"And that's you wearing the dark sweatsuit, right?"

"If it is, it's their clothes." I showed him another picture, this time a close-up of him in the dark sweatpants.

"And that was one of the items that you wore in the shooting of that video."

"Possibly."

"You're wearing it, aren't you!" I was incredulous, mocking, derisive, but without too harsh an edge. I didn't want to offend the jury by being a jerk. As his answers became more off-the-wall I would not laugh, just snicker in utter disbelief.

"Yes."

The first photograph showed him in clothes that completely fit Kato's description: sharp dark sweatsuit with a white or silver zipper. Simpson said, "Can I see that other picture again?" Steve put it back up.

It was a strange moment. Simpson stared at the screen.

So where's the sweatsuit? He said he had returned the suit to the crew immediately after the shoot. We'd see about that.

We were down to the shoes, the best part of all. At his deposition, Simpson had been cocky. The footprints of the murderer, despite being pigeon-toed like his, could not be laid directly at his feet. We had gone to great lengths to identify the shoes as Bruno Maglis, but at the time we'd possessed no proof Simpson had ever owned a pair. He could deny ever wearing them, and there was nothing anyone could do to prove otherwise. From such a comfortable legal position—and faced with a lot of other work to be done—neither the criminal defense team nor Simpson and his present advisers had addressed the need to create a cover story.

Johnnie Cochran triumphantly told the jury, "There is no evidence that O.J. Simpson had any Bruno Magli shoes, ever."

All that changed when the Harry Scull, Jr. photo hit the newsstands.

I had three objectives: One, to show the jury that Simpson did, in fact, own the shoes; two, that he lied about owning them; and three, to make him go on record swearing that the Scull photograph was a fraud. I especially wanted the jury to see how he lied, got caught, and was now lying again in response to getting caught.

I pointed out that his deposition took place before the Scull photo was published, then read some of his depo testimony: "I would never have owned those ugly-ass shoes." Up on the large TV monitor flashed the perfect photograph of Simpson exactly as Scull had captured him, striding across the end zone.

"That is you, Mr. Simpson, is it not?"

I could not wait to get to this. After two days full of lying and getting hammered, the guy had no way out. We were going to close by burying him. It was going to be humiliating.

"It looks like me." Simpson braced for the assault.

"And you did attend a football game at Rich Stadium in Orchard Park, New York, on September 26, 1993, correct?"

"I could have, yes." The constant qualifier.

"What do you mean, 'could have'? Did you or did you not?"

"I don't know."

"Do you remember being there?"

"I don't know the dates, but I certainly attended a lot of games in Buffalo."

"Well, how is this for refreshing your recollection. The last time you saw the Bills play the Dolphins at Rich Stadium?"

"I don't recall when that was."

"That would have been that game, correct?"

More argument. This kind of obtuseness might have seemed effective to Simpson in the closed atmosphere of a deposition room, but in court it was strikingly counterproductive. I purposely let him slip and slide and waffle in front of the jury. I wanted them to hear him deny the undeniable.

I put up a large exhibit board including a blow-up of the Scull photo. "Now, Mr. Simpson, you are wearing Bruno Magli, size 12, in that photograph?"

"That photograph depicts that, but I wasn't wearing Bruno Magli shoes."

"Are you saying those are not Bruno Magli shoes?"

"They look like Bruno Magli shoes, yes."

"But you're not wearing them. Is that what you are saying?"

"That's what I'm saying."

"How can that be, sir?" I was standing right next to him, facing the jury.

"I don't know. I saw a picture of Mark Fuhrman and I playing golf together, and I never, ever played golf with him, either." Even now, a pathetic attempt to inject Fuhrman into his case. He would not do so unchallenged.

"What does this have to do with Mark Fuhrman?"

"I don't know. You asked me how that can be. I'm no expert on pictures, but I saw a picture of Mark Fuhrman and me playing golf, together in a golf cart."

"What you're saying to the jury is, that picture is a fraud?"

"I believe so, yes."

"What do you mean, you 'believe so'? Is it or is it not?"

"I would say it is." Baker objected; his client was no photo expert. The judge overruled.

"State your opinion," I countered. "Is it or is it not a fraud?"

"My opinion is that it is a fraud."

"Okay. What part of the picture is fraudulent?"

"I couldn't tell you exactly. . . . I had a tie sort of like that tie, I know. As I've told you in a deposition, the coat, I can't really tell; I've worn all kinds of sports coats. It looks like a nice sports coat. The collar on the shirt is definitely a collar that I've had shirts that look like that. The belt, I can't really tell. The pants look a little big on me. And the shoes, I don't know, weren't my shoes."

"You're absolutely positive about the shoes?"

"I'm pretty sure."

That was a surprise. "Pretty sure?"

On further reflection: "Well, I am sure."

"There is no doubt in your mind, is there, sir?"

"No, there's not."

There's no doubt?"

"I said no."

"None, right?"

"For the third time, no!"

Good. He had dug a hole he could never get out of. The photo was completely legitimate, we had proof, and his denials would be all the more damning for their ferocity. But I wasn't finished with him. I wanted to draw out this perjury in agonizing detail.

"Give us your definitive opinion: Are those pants yours or not? Yes or no?"

"I couldn't tell you. They're gray pants. They look big on whoever that might be."

"You have any reason to believe those pants are not yours?"

"Only the shoes lead me to believe those were not my pants."

"Forget the shoes. Focusing on the pants, are the pants yours?"

"I don't know."

"You don't know?"

"They look a little big in the legs."

"Let's go to the belt. Is the belt yours?"

"I can't tell."

"You don't know?"

"I can't tell."

"Is the jacket yours?"

"I don't know."

"You don't know?"

"It looks like it could be my jacket."

"You're saying you can't tell if that is your jacket or not?"

"It looks like my jacket, yes."

"Is that your opinion, that it is your jacket?"

"That would be my opinion, yes."

Okay, we got him in the jacket.

"And the tie?"

"I had a tie like that, so I would say yes."

"And the white shirt, is that your white shirt?"

"By the collar of the shirt, I knew I had shirts that looked like that, yes."

"And the hands and the upper torso, that's all you, right?"

"Yeah. Yes, I would say so."

"So it's basically the shoes that you question, right?"

"Yes. The pants somewhat, too."

I turned to Steve. "Do we have the video?" As if there was some possibility that we didn't. "Put it on."

We had dug up sideline video of Simpson doing the same Bills-Dolphins game, and there he was, dressed exactly as in the Scull photo. Unfortunately, the video didn't shoot him all the way down to his shoes, but the jacket, shirt, tie, belt, and top of his pants were all clearly visible.

"You don't have any reason to think that those are not your items that you are wearing?"

"From what I could see."

"And that TV footage is from the same game, right?"

"I would assume so, yes." At least now he had given up that pretense.

I put up the Scull photo and compared the two. "Same tie, same shirt, right?"

"That's right."

"So basically everything is there. You can see it there, right?"

"Yes."

"So did that change your mind a little bit on the pants? Make you sure that those pants were genuine?"

"No."

"That the pants you're wearing here," I pointed to the Scull photo, "are the same pants depicted here?" I pointed to the video.

"No, that didn't change my mind."

"Do you think the video is a fraud, too?"

"Not at all."

Scull had taken another photo of Simpson at the game, in the same clothes, but not showing his shoes. "Is it your opinion that that photograph is a fraud?"

"No."

The video wasn't a fraud, Scull's two other photos weren't frauds, he was in the same clothes; according to Simpson, the only fraud was the depiction of the shoes.

"You cannot bring to this courtroom the shoes depicted in that photograph?" I challenged him.

"The shoes depicted in that photograph?" Simpson reiterated. "No."

"By the way, you still think those shoes are ugly-ass shoes?"

"I don't think those are attractive shoes."

Two days of solid lying. It was time to wrap this up. Simpson said his passport was in his bag. (Paula said it was on the bedside table.) The judge asked him to pull the microphone closer to him; Simpson was so drained the judge was having trouble hearing him. He denied having the key to Nicole's condo. (The police had found it, on its Smokey the Bear key ring, in his bag.) He said the fake goatee had been put in his grip when it first arrived at Rockingham well before the murders. (His housekeeper said it was on his desk as late as June 9.) I introduced his deposition testimony in which he said seven thousand dollars had not been taken from his closet by the police at Rockingham. Apparently the cops were willing to frame him for murder but wouldn't steal seven grand from his closet.

"After you were informed that the police were coming to arrest you on the seventeenth, you decided to take off. True?"

"At one point, yes."

I thought the jury could draw its own conclusion. If he was fleeing, that was extremely incriminating. If he was running off to commit suicide, it was also incriminating, for the reasons I have mentioned: why would O.J. Simpson, with all his wealth, orphan his children and kill himself in grief over a woman he said he had stepped beyond?

I think he didn't know what he was going to do when he and Cowlings left Kardashian's house. He took his black grip; you don't need your black grip to kill yourself. He had his credit cards, his passport, a disguise, and a gun; he had his options open. If he was, as he said, going to visit Nicole's grave, it wasn't his final destination. He was going to run till he ran out of room.

I began to read a transcript of his rambling cell phone conversation with Detective Tom Lange, spoken as he was slowly cruising the freeway with a sizable police escort. ". . . Remember, you're saying the following: 'Just tell them all I'm sorry. You can tell them later on today and tomorrow that I was sorry and that I'm sorry that I did this to the police department.' Do you remember saying that? Yes or no?"

"And I also remember telling them I didn't do it."

"Do you remember saying that?"

"No, I don't remember that, no. But I probably did."

"Excuse me. Just answer the questions; we'll get through this. . . . Do you remember saying the following to Tom Lange: 'Hey, you've been a good guy, too, man. . . . You let me tell you, I know you're doing your job. You've been honest with me right from the beginning. . . . You're doing your job. I know you're doing a good job. . . . I'm the only one that deserves it.' Do you recall saying that?"

"I don't recall saying that at all."

"If it is on tape, you wouldn't dispute it, would you?"

"Let me hear the tape."

Even at the end, Simpson was cagey, always looking for an edge. On that tape, Simpson moans and groans in anguish—he surely was in pain; his life as "O.J." was over—and I did not want to create any sympathy for him. I ignored the request.

"You recall telling Mr. Lange near the end, 'You're a good guy. You did your job well.'"

"I don't recall saying it, but I think that is the way I was feeling towards the police at the time, yes."

I put down the transcript and paused to let everything sink in. Then I walked up close to him.

"Now, Mr. Simpson," I said quietly, "at no time did you tell Detective Lange on the phone, 'Why are you framing me?' You never said that, did you?"

"I didn't know what they were doing. I know I told them I didn't do it on numerous occasions on that ride."

I started raising my voice. "At no time did you say, 'Why have you planted all this evidence against me'?"

"I had no idea what the evidence was."

"You knew well there was blood. You knew there were gloves. . . . You knew there was blood found on your property and you knew there was blood found in your car, and you knew there was blood found on Bundy as of June 17, when they were going to arrest you, right?"

"I knew there was blood, yes."

"You never accused whoever you spoke to on the phone of framing you. True or untrue?"

"All I can do is say I told him time and time again, 'I didn't do this.'"

"Move to strike as nonresponsive."

"Stricken as nonresponsive."

"You never accused the person on the telephone from the police department when you were talking of planting evidence against you, correct?"

"Correct."

"Or framing you for a murder that you did not commit. Correct?"

"That's correct."

"And the reason you didn't do so, Mr. Simpson," I was in a crescendo, "is because you knew you committed those murders. Correct?!"

"That's incorrect." Simpson began huffing again.

"And that is why you were going to kill yourself, because you knew you were going to spend the rest of your life in jail. Correct?"

"That's incorrect!"

"And you knew that you dropped the blood at Bundy, correct?"

"That's incorrect!"

"And knew, sir, that you went there that night *and you confronted Nicole! And you killed her!*" I was yelling at Simpson now.

Baker was screaming: "YOUR HONOR, I AM GOING TO OBJECT!" He was overruled. Simpson had to answer.

"No, Mr. Petrocelli. That's totally, absolutely incorrect."

I quieted my voice. "And Ronald Goldman came upon you when you were there with Nicole," I said, the courthouse silent as if a storm had just passed, "and you did not expect him that night. Correct?"

"I don't know Ron Goldman."

"And Ronald Goldman got into a fight with you as he tried to stop you, and you cut him and you slashed him until he died, collapsed in your arms. True or untrue?"

"Untrue." Again, the exploding breaths.

"And you left him there to die, Mr. Simpson, with his eyes open, looking right at you. True or untrue?"

"That's untrue."

I closed my notebook and turned my back on him. "We have no further questions."

THIRTY-ONE

"The Real O.J."

I didn't even have a seat to go to. All the chairs were filled. The faces at our table, and in the rows right behind, shone as they looked at me. My blood was racing.

One year of anticipation, of preparation, one year of complete consumption by the case, culminating in two days of confrontation. And I had taken him apart. I had exposed Simpson as a liar, a deeply flawed liar, a man with no conscience. Yes, he had succeeded in maintaining himself, he had not burst into a rage in the courtroom. But that was a false goal. It was about the only thing he had actually achieved, and in the end I think it helped destroy him. He seethed where he should have been calm; he was disturbingly calm in exactly those places where he should have raged. Simpson sat on the stand revealed as a guilty man.

It was four P.M. I assumed court was done for the day and I could go back to the DoubleTree and breathe deeply.

"You may begin."

Baker bounced up, ready to counterattack. The judge was so eager to keep the trial going, he intended to use every half hour available.

Kelly and Brewer jumped up, too. "Your Honor," Brewer said, "we have some questions." Each had individual clients and wanted their own time to interrogate Simpson, but Fujisaki did not want them going over the same ground I had covered. He had to be convinced at sidebar that they should be given the opportunity to examine the defendant.

Brewer got to ask his first question, and Simpson did not even get the chance to answer before the judge interrupted. He sent the jury home for the day and told us to meet him in chambers.

"We've got a problem with a juror."

Juror number seventy-eight, an attractive young woman, had asked a deputy sheriff to relay a message to Steve Foster: she liked his tie. The deputy had told Steve, "Your tie was a topic of discussion at lunch today. Some of the jurors liked it."

Steve said, "Thanks. It's my favorite."

Later, the juror had asked the deputy, "Did you pass the message?" She was overheard telling the story, and someone ratted her out.

Now, I know Steve to be among the world's most honest and honorable people, with great respect for both the law and the workings of the court. He is in his early twenties and very exuberant, however, and I didn't know whether he fully appreciated that it is totally impermissible for anyone on either side of a case to have even the most idle banter with a juror. Steve was not yet enrolled in law school, and I was not completely confident that I had gone over all the rules with him. Within minutes he was brought into the judge's chambers, seated in the middle of the room, and questioned under oath. "Raise your right hand." His face, usually animated, was ashen. He was petrified.

I thought this was completely unfair; Steve should have been given access to counsel to advise him. Instead he was left to fend for himself. Things were happening too quickly.

I sat there hoping he said the right thing. A misstep in court could cost him severely in his fledgling career, and a mistrial here would be a disaster for us all.

Trying not to hyperventilate, Steve was asked one question. He told the truth and was excused. The deputy who had passed him the message was sworn in, then confirmed his account: Steve had not initiated the contact, had not reciprocated, had not made any effort whatsoever to contact the juror, had not actually spoken to the juror. All he had done was reflexively say, "Thanks," to the deputy. He had done nothing wrong. The judge accepted the facts. Steve was safe.

The juror, Ann Marie Jamison, was a fun-loving woman. She had earlier in the trial been reprimanded by Fujisaki because she brought in Halloween candy to give to all the lawyers. She had also worn a Halloween T-shirt to court that read "Let's Go Bump in the Night"—not the most appropriate attire for court. She didn't think she had done anything wrong, but Judge Fujisaki did not want even the first hint of the appearance of impropriety on the jury's part. He discharged her. Naturally, when she walked out of the courthouse, she was swarmed by the media.

We were vitally interested in Ms. Jamison's comments. She presented the first indication of what was going on in the jurors' minds. Interviewed on television, she said she did not believe Simpson was telling the truth. She would not reveal how she would have voted, but she felt Simpson was not being honest and that we were doing a good job. A great sign.

(After the trial was over, Steve got a call on his machine. "Hi, this is Ann Marie. I want your tie for my scrapbook. Call me." Steve, however, was engaged.)

This trial was an emotional roller-coaster. I had just finished one of the most anticipated examinations in legal history, but the lead story on the news that night was that a juror had been excused. Of course, the press, the pundits, the people on TV, and the viewing public, were not voting on the case, but I wanted the satisfaction of hearing how I'd destroyed Simpson, how he had been cut up and left for dead on the witness stand. I was frustrated that I didn't have the opportunity to revel in the moment. But Fred Goldman was ecstatic, the MSK team patted me on the back, and the trial went on.

In addition to my bruised ego, I was professionally frustrated. We had lost a good juror. Who would replace her?

As the trial wore on, we started to get into amiable banter with the defense lawyers about which jurors were ours or theirs. "Oh, we've got that juror." "Are you kidding? *You* got her?" "Yeah, she loves Baker." There was one woman in the front row who smiled at me all the time. I thought we had her until I noticed her smiling at the defense lawyers. She smiled at everybody! We were all trying in vain to translate facial expressions and body language; nobody had a clue.

The process to select the replacement juror was pretty elemental; all the alternates' numbers were placed in a hat. The juror we truly did not want was number 295. Her responses to the questionnaire and our verbal examination had left us feeling she would not be sympathetic to us. The defense, of course, wanted her on. She was African American. There was tension on both sides when Erin Kenney, Judge Fujisaki's clerk, reached into the hat and came up with a number.

"Two ninety-f . . . *four.*"

I may not have gotten my moment of triumph and relaxation, but at least we were back in business.

I would have preferred that Brewer and Kelly not examine Simpson at all. But they wanted a piece of him, which I understood. I would have, too, if I'd been in their position. But I had worked hard to decimate the guy, and I didn't want to give him a chance to get off the canvas. Brewer and Kelly understood that; they promised to be brief.

Near the end of Brewer's exam, he asked, "Who is the real O.J.?" I'm sure he was trying to encourage Simpson to brag about himself and thereby offend the jury.

But it was an open invitation to trouble. Simpson's entire defense— his *only* defense—was structured around "the real O.J.," the Heisman Trophy winner, the eternal superstar; we had just given him a ball he could run with.

And run he did, launching into a self-serving good-guy routine that was hard to shut down. "I always had time for people. I was involved in charities. Nicole's family and friends, when they had problems, they came to me. And I'd like to think I was a good friend to all of them." It made me very anxious. I snuck a peek at the defense table, and they were smiling, looking our way with "How does it feel?" grins.

Kelly compared Simpson's fleeing Bundy and skulking back in the dark to Rockingham after the murders with his 1989 beating of Nicole, when he fled from the police. Both lawyers were on and off in a short time. We then took a ten-minute break before Baker's cross-examination was to begin.

We had all been very concerned, from the time we first considered putting Simpson on the stand, that he would be cross-examined by Baker at great length in our case, then perhaps given a second chance to tell his story when called to testify in the defense case. We spent a good part of the summer arguing whether taking a shot at him was worth the risk of his getting two shots at us. But in the hallway, Baker pulled me aside.

"In light of Brewer's examination," he told me, "I don't have any questions to ask him." I thought he was joking.

Back in the courtroom, Baker addressed the court. "Your Honor, I apologize. I changed my mind." He would not cross-examine Simpson; he was going to wait until his case to put him on.

A few minutes of self-serving palaver about the "real O.J." was supposed to nullify two full days of scorched-earth devastation? In Baker's dreams. By now he knew this judge would never allow him to repeat areas of testimony wholesale, although I suspect Fujisaki would have given Simpson some latitude because he was the key witness and a party to the case. Of course, Baker knew I would have been able to come right back and attack his client some more on redirect.

More than that, though, Simpson had performed miserably, and the defense needed time to regroup. They probably surmised that six weeks down the road the jury might forget Simpson's debacle and they could start fresh. It probably wasn't a bad strategy. They *needed* to start fresh.

Right around the holiday we lost an alternate juror, a big Hispanic man who sat in the seat directly next to Simpson and smiled at him a couple of times as he got off the witness stand. He was bounced because he sent a greeting card to a friend saying he was on the Simpson jury. I had worried about this man, but when he was interviewed on television after his dismissal, he said he didn't believe Simpson. On the one hand, this was an excellent sign; two jurors had independently said Simpson was a liar. It was a very good barometer of the larger jury's leanings. On the other, neither of those jurors was on the panel anymore.

The court took six and a half days off over the Thanksgiving holiday, which was torture for me. I thought this was hurting our momentum. All I wanted to do was wolf down some turkey and stuffing and get back to work at the DoubleTree. I had my holiday dinner at my brother Gabriel's house, with my wife and family. I watched the football games, I made some small talk—but my mind was a million miles away. It was focused entirely on an ex–football player turned murderer. I was obsessed to the point of excluding almost everything and everybody around me who wasn't connected to the case. Marian, my wife, didn't know what to do with me—especially when, one day, I called home only to get a recording saying my phone service had been disconnected. Sure enough, I hadn't bothered to pay my bills in months—they were all bundled up, kept and ignored at the DoubleTree. It turned out, I was so delinquent on my mortgage payment, foreclosure proceedings had started on our house. My secretary, Maria, came to the rescue, taking over my financial affairs until the trial ended. My entire family was quite relieved to have a phone again, not to mention a roof over our heads.

It was now time to put on our impeachment case. I wanted only witnesses who would have the most impact, so I went about reducing our line up.

Linda Schulman, a close friend of Nicole's in the 1980s, was prepared to testify that Nicole had both shown her bruises and told her Simpson hit her with a wine bottle. I was going to have big hearsay problems, and Simpson had pretty well battered his own credibility on the issue already, so we eliminated Schulman as a witness.

Wayne Hughes was going to tell the jury of the time Nicole showed him a large bruise under her breast where Simpson had hit her. He also could testify that Simpson told him, in 1989, that he had caught Nicole with "too much backhand," a contradiction to Simpson's defensive depiction of his role in the incident. Unfortunately the judge said the first incident was too far removed from the date of the crime—it happened in the early eighties—so I scrapped Hughes, too.

I planned to call Ron Shipp, an experienced former LAPD officer and onetime Simpson friend, to discuss a conversation on the night of June 13 in Simpson's bedroom, in which Simpson said he'd been having dreams about killing Nicole and asked whether such thoughts would register on a polygraph test. This showed extreme consciousness of guilt; Simpson was trying to figure out how he might explain failing a lie detector test, which the police wanted him to take.

Shipp's recollection of the conversation was borne out by Simpson's own statement to the police earlier that day, in which he said he had been having "weird thoughts" about Nicole. In his deposition Simpson had admitted those "weird thoughts" had to do with violence, then gave an absurd explanation that it was not his own violence against Nicole he had been thinking of, but the fact that he wished his maid, Michelle, would have retaliated after Nicole slapped her in March 1994. His wife had just been killed, and he was wishing his maid had given her a good smack three months earlier.

Aware that Shipp had knowledge of police technology, Simpson had also asked in that conversation how long DNA test results took to come back from the lab. What would his interest in DNA stem from, except his own fear of being identified as the killer?

I had set up Shipp's testimony in my opening statement and in my questions to Simpson, but I made a difficult, last-minute decision not to call him. I believed him, but the defense would have called Arnelle Simpson and other relatives to swear that Shipp had never been alone in a room with Simpson and that he had been drinking. I also knew that Shipp was vilified in some segments of the black community as a traitor for testifying against Simpson in the criminal trial, and that concerned me. We had kept race out of the case so far, and I was determined to keep it out.

Despite the power of her testimony, I also decided not to call Faye Resnick because of the ruckus it would cause. Simpson was dying to delve into "Faye's world," even though he had nothing on her. I didn't want to give him the chance to veer our trial away from him.

Beverly De Teresa was the first-class flight attendant on Simpson's red-eye flight from Los Angeles to Chicago the night of the murders. The galley, her base of operations, was right next to the lavatory, which she remembered Simpson going in and out about ten times, once every fifteen minutes. Each time he stayed inside one or two minutes, she said, and although she was often standing right next to the door, she never heard the toilet flush. Noting that Simpson did not drink enough water to justify the number of trips to the bathroom, she told the captain and first officer she thought he must have a urinary tract infection.

My interpretation is that Simpson's finger was bleeding and he was continually cleaning the cut with water, stopping the flow with pieces of paper towel or toilet paper. Rather than throw the bloody paper in the trash or flush it down the toilet, where it might possibly be found— the movies offer ample examples of this kind of thorough detective work—Simpson may well have been drying his finger on the inside of his blue jeans pocket or stuffing the bits of paper in his pockets, which would account for the change of clothes before arriving at Rockingham the next day.

Ms. De Teresa also remembered Simpson coming out of the bathroom and staring right through her—*at least four times.* She tried to make conversation with him, but he again stared right through her. It frightened her. She thought, What is wrong with this man?

However, she did not make these experiences known until quite some time later. She had made notes but couldn't find them. Her police statement, like so many others, was nowhere near as detailed and revealing as later interviews with investigators; some of her most powerful observations—for instance, the vacant staring—were not elicited by or told to the police and did not appear on their report. When she heard news of the murders the next day, she didn't immediately pick up the phone to give these details to the police, as one would have hoped. She had great testimony, but I did not want to give the defense the opportunity to say her actions were not consistent with her observations.

I figured I would lie in the weeds and bait the defense into calling Cora Fischman to corroborate Simpson's side of his relationship with Nicole, after which a relentless cross-examination would bring out all the damaging admissions she had made in her deposition. They got smart, however, and never called her.

We called over twenty witnesses in rapid-fire succession over four days. India Allen: Saw Simpson slap Nicole in a parking lot in the early eighties. Baker tried to impeach her by noting that she was a former *Playboy* model. Doesn't make her a liar. Now married with kids.

Albert Aguilera: Saw Simpson hit Nicole while he was walking on Victoria Beach near Laguna Niguel, Fourth of July weekend; he thought it was 1986. Baker tried to impeach him on the year.

Charles Cale: Lived near Simpson on Rockingham. Was walking his dog on Rockingham between 9:30 and 9:45 P.M. and did not see the Bronco. At 9:45 P.M. observed the spot where Simpson said he parked and testified that the Bronco was not there. Saw the Bronco parked on Rockingham at 7:00 A.M. when he walked his dog the next morning.

Al Cowlings: Stuck with his story that Simpson sent him to retrieve a jewelry pouch from the trash. Recanted his deposition testimony that he alone went to check on Nicole in 1989; now O.J. went, too. Cowlings had made his living as a defensive lineman; now he was a blocking back.

Jackie Cooper: Confirmed Simpson had told him over the 1994 Memorial Day weekend that Nicole had broken up with him, that he was unhappy about it, that this time it was final. Simpson testified he was over Nicole; Cooper testified that he was still anguished. Baker cross-examined by pointing out Cooper had not told this to the police. Indeed he hadn't; they'd never asked.

Donna Estes: Corroborated Cooper. Simpson had told her about the argument with Paula in which he admitted he still loved Nicole. All he could talk about was Nicole.

Craig Baumgarten: Simpson friend and golf partner; testified they talked on the morning of the murders about the fact that Paula was upset over not being invited to the recital; admitted confrontation with Simpson playing golf; said he'd never seen Simpson get so angry at him before.

Frank Olson: We presented videotaped testimony in which the Hertz executive explained how Simpson minimized the 1989 incident, how he described his unhappiness over his breakup with Nicole, and how image was everything to O.J.

Nancy Ney: There was a lot of legal skirmishing around Ms. Ney's testimony. She was a member of the board of directors of the Sojourn House, a domestic violence shelter and temporary home for battered women. On Tuesday, June 7, Ms. Ney had fielded a call on their hot line from a "Nicole," a Caucasian woman in her mid-thirties who had been married for eight years to a very high-profile person, was now divorced, had two small kids, lived in West Los Angeles, and was very frightened. The ex-husband, said "Nicole," had been calling her on the phone and begging her to come back. He had been stalking her in restaurants, in the market, on the street. Ms. Ney testified, "She said that he told her a few different times, if he ever caught her with another man, he would kill her."

This didn't see the light of day in the criminal trial; Judge Ito would not let it in on hearsay grounds. We took the same position we used to get Nicole's diary into evidence, saying Ms. Ney's testimony went to Nicole's state of mind: fear. This, in turn, was relevant to explain her conduct toward Simpson on the night of the recital. In his opening statement, Bob Baker had portrayed Simpson as Nicole's confidant and suggested there was no hostility between them. His arguments helped us to convince the judge that Nicole's state of mind was relevant.

Dr. Ron Fischman: This time the good doctor showed up without being served with a bench warrant. Dr. Ron, still a friend to Simpson, was forced to admit that Simpson had been having great difficulty with Nicole at the end, and felt rejected. Six days before the murders, Fischman testified, Nicole came into his kitchen, showed him the IRS letter, and was "extraordinarily angry."

We edited the Paula Barbieri deposition video to include her admission that she left a message breaking up with Simpson on the morning of the murders and that when she heard his return messages later that day, she understood that he had picked it up.

Leslie Gardner was the wardrobe stylist on the *Playboy* exercise video shoot who had given Simpson the dark sweatsuit in which he had been photographed, three weeks before the murders. Yvette Molinaro had done such a good job of pulling together this area of investigation that, as a reward, she put on this testimony. Gardner was an important witness; she placed Simpson directly in the murder clothes. Our theory was the blue/black fiber found on Ron's shirt came from this sweatsuit.

Gardner severely impeached Simpson. He had received various sweatsuits, Gardner said, some of which were cashmere but didn't fit and were returned. The rest were cotton blend, which Simpson kept, including the black sweatsuit he had been photographed in. He swore he had returned everything. But Gardner said neither she nor any crew member received the sweatsuit back. It was powerful testimony: Simpson denying possession of the killer's clothes.

Gigi Guarin: Simpson's housekeeper admitted that she saw the fake goatee and mustache on Simpson's office desk at Rockingham; Simpson claimed he had put it directly in his bag long before the murders. Clearly he had stuffed it in his bag while preparing to flee. She also testified that Chachi, Simpson's dog, was trained and was never a threat to run outside.

Dale St. John: Simpson's limousine driver for three and a half years had picked him up approximately one hundred times, and Simpson had always been there, had always buzzed him in immediately upon his arrival. He never once saw Chachi run out the gate and was never given instructions to be careful that Chachi stayed inside.

Randall Petee: A private investigator who test-drove from Bundy to Rockingham, taking several routes at several speeds. He established that the drive time between Nicole's condo and Simpson's estate was anywhere from four minutes three seconds to five minutes thirty-five seconds. There was sufficient time to commit the murders at 10:40, hastily leave the scene, drive to Rockingham, and bump into Kato's wall at 10:50, 10:51.

The testimony of the Chicago witnesses James Merrill, Raymond Kilduff, and Mark Partridge were introduced in the same manner. Merrill, the Hertz sales representative who picked Simpson up at O'Hare airport on the night of the murders, testified that in retrieving his luggage, Simpson got up from where they were sitting, walked over, and personally retrieved his golf bag, which was covered by a travel bag, from the luggage carousel. (Celebrity that he is, this was a rare action for Simpson.) The next morning, Simpson called him several times, frantically asking Merrill, who lived over a half hour away, to get him to the airport. Ultimately, Simpson left before Merrill arrived—with Simpson's golf clubs. Merrill also testified about the call he received from Simpson the following day, ostensibly to apologize for his rudeness but during which the conversation soon turned to Simpson's clubs, what flight they left on, and their baggage ticket number.

Kilduff, a Hertz vice president of sales, drove Simpson from his Chicago hotel to the airport and recalled that Simpson "wanted to make sure his golf clubs got back." Simpson's duffel bag, which according to Merrill had appeared full the night before, was "virtually empty." Simpson was wearing the blue jean outfit on the way to the Chicago airport. (Simpson swore he had changed into his black pants and white shirt before he left the hotel.)

Partridge was particularly damaging. A balding copyright lawyer, he had been sitting next to Simpson on the flight back to Los Angeles and had taken notes of their conversation. He went so far as to put a "c" with a little circle around it at the bottom of the page. He said Simpson was wearing the blue jean outfit and no socks the entire trip. Simpson told him Nicole and a man had been killed, and that they had been found in the garden by the street where Nicole lived.

The problem this testimony presented for Simpson was monumental: he had not been told all this information as of the time he was revealing it to Partridge. It's not information the police released so early in an investigation, particularly to a potential suspect. Detective Phillips told Simpson only that Nicole had been killed; he never mentioned a second victim, and he never told him it happened in the garden. Phillips also noted that Simpson didn't ask the questions people usually ask: How? Where? Are you sure? Arnelle Simpson, who had spoken to her father by telephone, didn't know all of this information, either. There was no way Simpson could have had this information except from firsthand knowledge.

I expected Skip Taft's testimony to last about five minutes. His deposition had been clear: Did he see two to three cuts on Simpson's fingers on June 13 at Parker Center? Yes. It was devastating testimony, directly impeaching Simpson, who swore for two days he had only one cut. If the jury were to believe Simpson returned from Chicago with two to three cuts, not even Simpson himself could try to explain that. That was the end of the road for him.

About a minute into Taft's examination I got right to the point. "You saw some cuts on Mr. Simpson's left hand, correct?" I expected the right answer. To my horror, Taft sandbagged me.

"As I sit here today, I recall one cut."

I was caught up short. "In fact," I reminded him, "you saw more than one cut, correct?"

"No. I say, as I sit here today, I recall seeing one cut—and early in my deposition, that's what I said." Not only was he denying his prior testimony, I could see in an instant that he had dissected his deposition every which way to find some way out of burying his murdering friend of nearly thirty years.

This was such a surprise, I didn't even have my materials ready. Steve quickly put the photo of Simpson's hand up on the ELMO. "Do you see that cut on that finger, sir?"

"Yes."

"And you saw that cut at one on June 13, 1994, true?"

"No, not true."

"Now, you understood you were under oath and had to tell the truth?"

"Right. Absolutely."

I was getting hot. "You're a lawyer and you understand the obligation to tell the truth?"

"Absolutely."

Steve put the transcript of his deposition testimony up on the ELMO, and I began reading aloud from it. The testimony was clear; he saw two cuts. "Do you recall giving that testimony?"

"Yes, I do."

"So at your deposition, you said to me under oath that you saw at least two cuts, correct?" Was he really going to deny it?

"I said in one part of my deposition, that's correct. But . . . I think on page 118 and 119."

"You've really read this, haven't you."

"Of course."

Twenty pages later, however, he had admitted to seeing two. I read from his testimony:

"'Q. So you saw a total of three cuts at Parker Center on June 13, on Mr. Simpson, on the fingers of his left hand, right?'

"'A. I saw for sure two. I'm not sure of that third cut that you pointed out in that picture.'

"How about *that*, Mr. Taft!"

Baker flew out of his seat. "Wait a minute!"

"Put that on the ELMO!" I had no patience with this guy. If I'd been bamboozled at the beginning, I was recovered and focused now, storming around the courtroom.

"Your Honor," Baker complained, "what is this 'How about that?' That's not a question. If he wants to argue the case, he ought to wait until the end of the case to argue."

I calmed down enough to read more of Taft's previous testimony, in which he admitted to seeing two cuts. "Did you give that testimony under oath?" I asked Taft.

"Yes, I did."

"Are you now telling the jury that that was wrong? You saw one cut; is that your testimony today?"

"No," Taft answered. "My testimony today is that I'm sure I saw one cut." Taft was a lawyer. He turned to the jury and addressed them directly with a canned mea culpa. "I lost my time reference with respect to Mr.

Petrocelli showing me pictures and asking me if I saw them. I saw those pictures, ladies and gentlemen, many times afterwards, in meetings with attorneys. And you have to realize that on the thirteenth, we were all in a major state of shock."

"Have you finished?" I snapped.

"That's my answer," he insisted.

"Okay." Now I was really steamed. It was one thing for family to blindly lie for Simpson. But I naively expected more from Taft, a well-respected lawyer. Now I had no respect for him, and I lit him up. "You didn't tell me any of that, did you, sir, when you gave me that answer: 'I saw for sure two.' Correct? You didn't tell me?"

"Correct."

"You had every word in the universe to choose from when you answered my question, sir, and you said, 'I saw for sure two.' Correct?"

"Correct."

Tom and the team were furiously scribbling behind me, and when I'd picked up their notes as I passed the table, there were some good questions for me.

"Let me ask you this: Were you in a state of shock at your deposition?"

"No."

"Clear-headed when you gave that testimony?"

"I believe so."

This was the Simpson cabal in action. This was rooted in the Cowlings roundup and the Shapiro roundtable. "Before coming here and taking that witness stand and telling this jury that you saw one cut and not two, you understood the importance of saying that Mr. Simpson only had one cut on his finger at that time. True or untrue?"

"I understood the importance of telling the truth here today."

"Excuse me, Mr. Taft. Your Honor, could you direct him to answer my question!"

Judge Fujisaki scowled down at him. "Answer the question, Counsel." He called him *Counsel!* A not very subtle reminder to Taft that he better behave like an honorable lawyer. This was one of the few times I had seen the judge angry at a witness.

What did Skip Taft say? "I understood it was correct to tell the truth today."

I yelled at him. "You want to answer my question? Let's try it a third time."

He asked me to repeat it. "Okay. You understood the importance to Mr. Simpson's side of the case in saying that there was only one cut, not two, on his finger. Correct? You understood that?"

"I understood that I was here to tell my best recollection of the situation."

The judge had to have been deeply offended. "Excuse me, Mr. Taft," Judge Fujisaki interrupted. "I'm going to direct you just one more time to answer the question." The next time would bring out the handcuffs; he was threatening to lock Taft up for contempt.

"I can't answer the question the way you've put the question."

He still hadn't answered, but I didn't want to put Fujisaki on the spot. "You understood before you took the witness stand, and turned to the jury, and told them that you only saw one cut instead of two, *as you said at the deposition,* that Mr. Simpson had testified before this same jury that there was only the one cut on his finger." I wanted the jury to understand that he was trying to deceive *them.* Not me, *them. They* were Taft's victims, and they were the ones making the decisions. "You knew that, didn't you?"

"Yes, I did."

I sneered at him. "Of course you did. And you knew that Mr. Simpson, on that same witness stand where you are sitting, denied having that cut on his fourth finger, that you said he had in August. True?"

"True."

"I've got nothing further."

This guy disgusted me. After a year of hearing so many people tell so many unbelievable stories, and working my tail off to get three usable sentences out of a three-hundred-page deposition, to have this guy pull that stunt in open court was contemptible. It was a stupid thing for him to do; as bad as his depo testimony might have been for the defense, it was made wildly worse when it blew up in their face.

Baker compounded the mistake by invoking the LAPD's inattentive inspection of Simpson's hands and Taft's supposed early deposition testimony in an attempt to rehabilitate the witness. As he asked his questions, our entire table was busy finding more ammunition with which to destroy Taft. On redirect, I went right at him again.

Where in the deposition had he said he'd seen only one cut? "I want you to point to all the words that you are relying on." He indicated page 119. I started reading a page earlier.

"'Q. Now, when you were picking him up at the airport and going to Rockingham, did you know that he had a cut on his finger?'

"'A. I consciously, at this point, don't know that I knew.'"

In the car, Simpson had been wearing a Band-Aid on his hand. He had not yet arrived at Parker Center; Taft was now trying to rely on his uncertain observations in the car ride; but the damning observations elicited in deposition had occurred later, after they arrived at Parker Center.

"In fact, you were testifying under oath that when you did learn about the cut was later on, when you were at Parker Center with Howard Weitzman and Mr. Simpson and you, correct?"

"That's correct."

"Isn't it the truth, sir, that the first time that you really learned about a cut or cuts on Mr. Simpson's finger, and could see cuts or a cut, was at the room in Parker Center with Mr. Weitzman, yourself, and Mr. Simpson? Correct?"

"Correct."

"And what you were saying under oath in your deposition was that, in the car ride, because Mr. Simpson had a Band-Aid, you did not consciously see any cuts at that time. Correct?"

"Correct."

"So the only place where you actually observed a cut or cuts on Mr. Simpson's hand is at Parker Center, one P.M., on June 13. Correct?"

Taft was a defeated man. He was submitting now. "Correct."

"And this is where we started our examination some time ago, correct?"

"Correct."

I asked another of Lambert's questions: "You also knew, Mr. Taft, when you completed this deposition, that you had the right to review it. Correct?"

"Correct."

"You also knew, Mr. Taft, when you received this deposition, that you had the right, the absolute right, to make any changes at the time that you reviewed it. Correct?"

"Correct."

"And you did not do so, correct?"

"Correct."

"And the truth of the matter is, Mr. Taft, that you saw a cut on Mr. Simpson's middle finger in the room at Parker Center with Mr. Weitzman and yourself and Mr. Simpson. Correct?"

"I saw a cut on his middle finger."

"And you also saw the cut on his fourth finger, did you not?"

"No, that's not correct."

"You deny that under oath?"

"Yes, I do."

After all this time he was going to continue this charade. Okay. He'd gotten caught. Now he was going to get punished. "Let's take one more look."

Taft's face said, *Oh, no.* Baker objected, but Judge Fujisaki wasn't going to spare Taft now. I put up the same pictures I had used at the deposition and dragged him through it again, reading the testimony at which he definitively identified two cuts. "Do you recall giving that testimony?" I asked when I had finished reading.

"Yeah. . . . Whatever the deposition says."

"So you lied to me in your deposition?"

"No, I didn't lie to you." He was done.

At the break the Goldmans, Peter Gelblum, Tom Lambert, and members of the media were outraged. Several people told me, "You should report him to the bar. You should report him to the DA's office!" Fred wanted the transcripts sent over there right away. I wasn't concerned about the DA's office, I was focused on the rest of the trial.

Dan Leonard shrugged and gave me the Simpson defense in a nutshell: "Well, you've got to say one thing: He's a stand-up guy."

Robert Kardashian had flown off to New York when we tried to serve him with a trial subpoena. He did us a favor. We read his deposition testimony instead—in which he impeached Simpson by making it clear the bereaved widower had specifically asked the lawyer to drive him to LAX to retrieve his golf clubs. That ended our impeachment parade.

All that remained was to hear from the victims' families. In a taped depo, Sharon Rufo talked about her son. The tape was brief; so were her experiences.

Then John Kelly put Nicole's mother, Juditha Brown, on the stand. She talked lovingly about Nicole, and recounted the last hours they spent together. She also told of her conversation with Simpson on May 19, 1994, Nicole's birthday. "He said, 'She may not love me anymore.' And I said, 'Well, then, go on with your life.' And he said, 'I tell you, the first time when she left me, I take the blame; it was my fault. But the second time, it's gonna hurt.'"

Testifying was wrenching for her; she broke down on the witness stand and cried several times. Judge Fujisaki gave Kelly several harsh looks—*Get this over with!* I thought he was being unfair; this was the first and only time that Nicole's family members would testify. But the judge was a tough guy. I thought, Jeez, wait till he sees Fred.

At the end of her examination, Judy recalled her final moments at her daughter's coffin. "Mr. Simpson came in and he said, 'Could you move? Could you move? I have to be alone.' And I heard him say, 'I'm so sorry, Nic, I'm so sorry.' And he kissed her on the lips."

"And did you do anything then?" Kelly asked.

". . . I followed him and confronted him, very close, and I said, 'Did you have anything to do with this?' And he said, 'I loved your daughter.' And that was the end."

"Did he ever answer your question, though, Mrs. Brown?"

"No."

Kelly had no further questions. Baker sprang up. "Play the tape," he said.

On her first television interview after Nicole's death, Juditha and her husband, Lou, had sat with ABC's Diane Sawyer. She had told the same story: Simpson came in, she asked him if he had anything to do with the murders.

"And he said . . . ," Ms. Sawyer prompted.

"And he said, '*No,* I loved your daughter.'" According to this version, Simpson *had* answered, and he'd answered, "No." Baker's instant impeachment stung.

Baker then alluded to Judy's participation in the child custody suit taking place at the same time, to suggest that she would slant or bias her testimony in this case in order to win that one; if she could show that Simpson was a killer, maybe she could keep the kids.

At the break I asked Baker, "How did you have that tape ready to go?" I thought perhaps they had seen Kelly's notes. He was strutting around the room, grinning for the first time in quite a while, but he wouldn't tell me.

We had all but wrapped it up. The physical evidence was overwhelming, the domestic violence had been established, Simpson's motive and character were now well-known to the jury, the judge, the media, and everyone else in the courtroom. Judy Brown had had spoken for her daughter. Sharon Rufo said her piece. All that was left was Fred Goldman. He was our next and final witness.

Friday, December 6, 1996, was Fred's fifty-sixth birthday, and he wanted to testify on this special occasion. He thought the day he was born would be a fitting day to testify about the life and death of his only son. Rather than an annual celebration, the day would then mark a moment in time he would always remember.

Unfortunately, there were only forty-five minutes left until the end of the Friday session, so the judge decided to hold the entire exam over until the next Monday. Fred was very disappointed.

That Sunday I invited Fred to my home. It was one of the few days I didn't go in to the DoubleTree. I wanted to prepare him for Baker's cross-examination.

Bob Baker didn't like Fred Goldman. He thought Fred was a publicity hound, that he was selling his son's memory for a moment in the sun. The cross-examination promised to be intense, even ugly. "He will try to upset you," I advised, "to make you blow a fuse and turn into a raging maniac. I'm the last person in the world who is going to tell you, if Baker pisses you off, not to display your natural feelings; unlike the killer, who won't show anything because he has so much to hide, you have nothing to hide. Just be yourself; say and do whatever feels right.

"Just don't say anything nasty back to him. If he hurts you, show your hurt, but don't attack him; it is not becoming. Let Baker be the bad guy.

"Oh, and one more thing. Wear a tie."

"I don't want to wear a tie," he said. Fred, apparently, was not worried about showing the court a lack of respect. "Don't ask me again."

We held a mock session, as I do with all my witnesses. I played Baker, and I didn't hold back.

"You are better off now, Mr. Goldman, aren't you? You've made a lot of money off your son's death, haven't you? You were a salesman, now you are a spokesman for a national victims' rights organization. You speak out, you get on television, you've even got a book coming out soon. You are a household name. You *like* that, don't you, Mr. Goldman?"

Fred looked me straight in the eye and answered, "Mr. Baker, would you like to trade places?" I was not worried about Fred Goldman handling Bob Baker.

Fred refused to talk about my examination of him. "This is not something I need to prepare to do," he said firmly. "Don't even tell me what you're going to ask me, I don't want to know. I want it to be natural." Instead I invited him to help select the photographs we would use to show Ron during the important times of his life. We chose six or seven shots—Ron alone, Ron with Fred, Ron and Kim, Ron as a youngster and a grown man. We sat there and looked at Fred's boy. It was very difficult.

The Goldman family had a videotape of the bat mitzvah of Lauren—Patti's daughter, Ron's stepsister—and over the past week I had asked Steve Foster to prepare an edited version of the Goldmans' last major family event.

Sunday night I called the Goldmans' home. Fred and Patti weren't there. I left a message: "Fred, I'm asking you please to wear a tie." He walked into the DoubleTree at eight Monday morning with his collar buttoned, fingering his tie. "Here. Are you satisfied?"

I hadn't really gotten close to Fred Goldman until the trial. Yes, I had talked to him daily from the time we took the case, to keep him abreast of what was going on. But the early frustration around money raising had taken some time to get over, and then I'd been so involved in the witnesses and depositions and evidence that I had lost track of Fred's personal issues.

People thought Fred was a wealthy man, but he was a middle-class man who had had to work full-time as a salesman before running off to attend the tail end of each day's criminal trial sessions. He was finally able to give up that difficult juggling when he became an advocate and victims' rights spokesperson. He developed a burning passion for that kind of work, and his new job allowed him to attend the civil trial full-time. It wasn't until he showed up for trial every day that I understood his feelings, his convictions, his hopes, and we became close friends. Now, for the first time, he would get on the witness stand and talk about the loss of his son.

From the moment Fred rose, walked from the gallery, and took the stand, I knew this would not be easy. I stood in front of the counsel table and said, "Good morning, Mr. Goldman. I'd like to talk to you about your relationship with your son, Ron. We're going to have a conversation about Ron, just you and me."

Fred explained that he and Ron's mother, Sharon Rufo, had split up early in Ron's life, that he had raised both Ron and Kim in Illinois. We put up a picture of Fred's two children when they were small, and he talked about them. I asked him to tell us about Ron as a boy, and he described him in simple terms. The pictures came on and off the ELMO as Ron the boy became Ron the young man. "There was something special about our relationship," Fred said. "No matter what, nothing ever seemed to get in the way."

When Fred married Patti in 1987 the family moved to Southern California. "Ron absolutely loved California," he said. "He loved the mountains, loved the ocean." Fred's son went through a transformation. "He came here as a skinny kid, and Ron started to eat healthy, more healthy than ever before; he started to work out; stopped completely any drinking of beer; never smoked—stopped completely. His big push was to get as healthy as possible, and he did."

I had come to know Ron through Fred. I knew what kind of a man he had become. Ron was innocent, friendly, just one of those truly good kids. A little irresponsible, a late bloomer, but the kind of rare young man who volunteered at a cerebral palsy hospital, helping patients dress, taking them on outings. He wasn't trying to become a doctor, he wasn't doing it for professional reasons or out of ambition; he just liked to help people.

Fred explained how Ron didn't take well to school and went through a series of jobs, working enthusiastically as a camp counselor with inner-city kids.

In his twenties, Ron worked as a waiter, but his finances were not good. He got himself into $12,000 worth of debt, and after he and Fred visited a financial counselor and Ron tried to work it out, he filed for bankruptcy. Fred did not offer to give him the money. "Ron understood. . . . He wanted to handle it on his own." He moved back into Fred's house, got his feet back on the ground, and moved out again. He seemed to have grown up. "He made just enormous changes."

About six months before he was murdered, Ron came to his father with a business proposal. "He had an idea about a restaurant that he wanted to do, and wanted to know if I would invest in it. I told him that the answer was yes." After his son's death, he found a file among the papers in Ron's apartment. In it was a menu and a floor plan. We put the diagram on the TV monitor. "I never realized how far Ron had gotten with his plans and his dreams."

"Mr. Goldman," I asked softly, "what is the shape of that diagram? Does it have any significance?"

Fred broke down sobbing. The judge gave me the same look he'd given Kelly when Judy Brown was on the stand, but I shut him out; I wasn't going to rush this. It was Fred's time, and I was not about to let the judge take it away from him and the jury.

When Fred could pull himself back together, he answered. "It's the Egyptian symbol that Ron wore around his neck. It was the Egyptian symbol of an ankh."

"What does an ankh stand for?"

Fred broke down again, just sobbing and sobbing.

"It meant 'eternal life.'"

"And Ron wore it around his neck?"

"Yes."

I was concerned for Fred. He was lost in his emotion. "Are you able to finish this up?" I asked.

"Yeah," he said.

"Okay."

"Doesn't wear it anymore." He sighed. "Kim wears it now."

This is what Simpson did. When you kill someone you not only take his life, you take a big part of the lives of those around him.

I put up the last picture taken of Ron alive. He was holding a baseball bat, full of life. Fred could hardly look. "My favorite picture of him," he said.

He had been on the stand only twenty minutes, but I decided it was now time to finish. We played the video.

This was most difficult. Up on the big screen there was Ron, a good-looking kid, healthy, alive, dancing at his kid sister's bat mitzvah. He was the big brother, clearly the family star. Fred was there, and Patti and Kim and Lauren and a whirl of friends. Behind the music, you could hear Ron say, "I don't know where I'm going to be one year from now." I paused the video at a spot where Ron and Fred were singing together to the music of Bob Seeger's "Old Time Rock and Roll." I let the frozen image of the two of them looking each other in the eye, laughing, hang in the air.

The only sound in the courtroom was the sound of crying, including, for the first time, the jury.

"Mr. Goldman," I asked very quietly, "did you love your son?"

Fred was sobbing, almost doubled over. "Oh, God, yes." I could hardly hear him.

"Do you miss him?"

"More than you can imagine."

"Do you think about him every day?"

"There isn't a day that goes by that I don't think of Ron."

"Will your life ever be the same again?"

"Never ever be the same." I had tears streaming down my face as I stood before him. "A hole missing."

THIRTY-TWO

Breaking Down the Defense

Judge Fujisaki, barely able to restrain his own tears, said, "Take a brief, ten-minute recess, ladies and gentlemen," and hurried off the stand. The jury filed out somberly. Fred stood up in tears. We embraced in front of the witness stand. Kim and Patti were crying, as were all the members of our team. It was a release for all of us. Even the hardened reporters couldn't hide their emotions. Simpson was gazing up at the ceiling as his lawyers huddled.

Baker got lucky; the ten-minute break turned into a half hour. When court finally came back in session, the emotion had calmed. I waited to see if Baker would go after Fred as he'd been threatening, but he was smart enough not to grill him. His examination was perfunctory. Baker tried to imply that Fred was friendly with cops, and he put into evidence the amount of money Fred received for writing a book. When he asked how many press conferences Fred had held since the trial began, I objected and the court sustained. Baker had nothing else. We rested our case.

The defense case began immediately with Phil Vannatter. This was supposed to be a bloodbath. Baker tried to use the detective to lay out the familiar, by now worn-out story of the LAPD's rush to judgment: The police go to Bundy, they don't process the crime scene quickly, they don't call the coroner for hours; instead, four officers go running off to Simpson's property because they think he's a suspect, they climb the wall to get into

Rockingham but don't draw their weapons or act like people looking for a killer; they wake up Kato and Arnelle; Fuhrman finds the bloody glove, Fuhrman shows it to Vannatter, there is no blood or insect activity around the glove, *Fuhrman, Fuhrman, Fuhrman;* later in the day they go to Parker Center and interview Simpson, they photograph and look at his hands but see no other cuts, they take his blood, Vannatter carries it across town instead of booking it. The familiar litany, most of which we had thoroughly blunted by now.

If evidence was planted, how was it planted? Who planted it? When was it planted? Under what circumstances? Where are the witnesses? Perhaps in the criminal trial, simply raising such questions was sufficient to get Simpson off. Not here. Their story went nowhere. What did it prove? Nothing. They had no answers, because there were none.

Vannatter kept his cool. He had served the Los Angeles community for nearly three decades, only to be branded a perjurer by Simpson and his lawyers. He had been accused of framing an innocent man for double murder, but he answered Baker's disgraceful questions calmly, never got upset, and told the truth. Baker never touched him. Phil Vannatter walked off the stand and returned to his farm in Indiana.

Andrea Mazzola was a technician trainee at the Bundy crime scene who had been vilified at the criminal trial for poor evidence handling. Bob Blasier pointed out all the mistakes: "You did not examine your hands between collecting material that may have gotten on your hands from the knit cap, correct?" "You didn't examine your gloves for any possible trace evidence that might have come off the knit cap onto your gloves before you picked up the glove, correct?" She didn't do this, she didn't do that.

But so what? If she was not the ideal evidence collector, if she touched her nose after she touched Ron's glasses—if she was not up to the standards of Dr. Henry Lee—how did that make the evidence turn into O.J. Simpson's blood? Again, the defense provided no answers.

Nurse Thano Peratis testified at the criminal trial that he had taken 8 cc of blood from Simpson's arm. When only 6½ cc could be accounted for, the defense made the great leap and placed the remaining 1½ cc in Phil Vannatter's meat hooks, and from there sprinkled it all over the case. This was a major element in their O.J. conspiracy theory. Blasier put Peratis on the stand to testify about drawing Simpson's blood and to lay the groundwork for a replay of the missing blood argument.

As it turned out, Peratis, a frail, elderly man, was mistaken. Medvene had talked to him at length and found that, in drawing Simpson's blood, Peratis had not filled the 8 cc test tube to the top. In fact, because of Simpson's muscular arm, Peratis had to use a different syringe device that routinely draws out a bit less blood. "Good luck if you can fill the vial up all the time," Peratis said. "It looked like it was enough blood to test. I said, 'Officers, is this enough?' I heard a 'Yes.' I withdrew the needle." Nurse Peratis had innocently underestimated. *There was no missing blood!*

Simpson never missed an opportunity to invoke Peratis as the police representative who had examined his hand and would vouch for his statement that he had only one cut. Blasier tried to get him to admit this now. But here he was saying he treated only the finger. "That's the only place I looked, 'cause it was specifically mentioned to me. . . . I didn't do any full examination. . . . I didn't look to see if there was anything else."

They called a witness who sat across the plane from Simpson on the flight to Chicago. He swore he had put his feet up on the footrest, reclined, and specifically looked at Simpson's hands for a Super Bowl ring, but saw no cuts. Putting aside the fact that Simpson never played in a Super Bowl, the guy blew up in their face when first we showed there were no footrests on that plane, then produced a seating chart of the flight proving he couldn't see Simpson's hands from his seat.

You should always win each day during your case-in-chief, that's the time your strongest evidence is being disclosed, presented by you to your own advantage. We had won most, if not all, of our days, but now we were winning theirs. The defense was rolling out the same game plan used in the criminal trial, but it was out of steam and going nowhere. There was nothing to replace it, either. No new evidence, no new explanations, no other killer. There was nothing left in their bag of tricks.

Their most important witness the first week would be molecular biologist and laboratory director Dr. John Gerdes. He was the man who examined the LAPD crime lab for the criminal defense team and called it a "cesspool of contamination." He had been the centerpiece of their contamination defense. Our presentation of Fung and Yamauchi had gutted their contamination argument, and Dr. Gerdes was their last chance to resurrect it. Tom Lambert was ready for him.

After establishing his credentials, Dr. Gerdes testified on direct that in his professional opinion, the LAPD lab's "sample collection, manipulation, and PCR setup protocols are such that there's an unacceptable risk of cross-contamination" in this case. He covered outside lab results by saying, "If there were any errors made in terms of cross-contamination at the LAPD, the Department of Justice would simply repeat those errors." It was the "garbage in, garbage out" argument.

Bob Blasier played a videotape on which Andrea Mazzola could be seen demonstrating the gathering of evidence. Gerdes said, "You see her right hand? . . . [It] is resting on the pavement there, so even though it's gloved, she has now transferred anything that was on the pavement at that exact spot onto her glove."

Blasier exhorted him to continue rolling the videotape. "Let's go."

"She just picked up the tweezers in that right hand, so now she transferred anything that was on the pavement onto the tweezers . . . so now the tweezers are contaminated." On and on, minute observations, as if to say, "It's all wrong! Nothing can be relied on!" And to an untrained eye, that might seem true.

But Dr. Gerdes's testimony itself was all "garbage in."

Mistakes in procedure could not possibly explain the fact that all the test results pointed to Simpson. An expert of such renown would clearly know that if someone else's DNA had been picked up through an extraordinarily negligent method of collection, such DNA would have shown up not only on the swatches of blood taken by the criminalist, but also on the control swatches. *And every single control swatch in this case showed no evidence of anyone's DNA; they were all clean.* There had been no contamination.

Several days earlier Tom had filed a motion seeking to prevent Gerdes from testifying for the defense about certain validation studies run by the LAPD. It was these studies, test runs during which the lab was learning how to run their DNA test, on which Gerdes had based his severely critical opinions of the LAPD lab. But that's like basing a Major League scouting report on Little League batting practice. A year had gone by between those studies and their handling of the Simpson evidence, during which time the lab had become professionally proficient. None of those practice runs or validation studies involved the actual evidence in our case, much less Simpson's blood. Dr. Gerdes irresponsibly called the lab a "cesspool," even though he did not and could not base his conclusion on the actual bloodwork done in this case. The judge ruled Gerdes could testify, but accepted Tom's motion and barred Gerdes from talking about or basing his opinions on the validation studies.

Tom Lambert was pumped up for his cross-examination. There are some things you don't do, and misusing important scientific knowledge in the service of a double murderer was over Tom's line in the sand.

"Dr. Gerdes, would you please tell the jury how many times you have collected evidence at a crime scene?"

"I have never collected crime scene evidence."

Not only had he never tested crime scene evidence, his lab had never tested crime scene evidence, either. He had never given classes in forensic science. Conducted validation studies on forensic evidence samples? "No." Conducted experiments in the area of forensic evidence? "No." He had used the DQ Alpha test kit once in his life. The LAPD forensic scientist had run it "what, a thousand times?" Tom asked. "Two thousand?"

"I'm sure he has," said Gerdes, "yes." Gerdes also confessed that he never had run the D1S80 test, another type of DNA test.

"So you yourself have never done any forensic evidence testing, you don't run the test that we're discussing here, but you have testified frequently in court as an expert, isn't that right, sir?"

"That's right."

"Thirty-five times?"

"Correct."

"Every time on behalf of a person charged with rape, murder, or both?"

"Correct."

". . . Your testimony was always that the evidence was unreliable, is that right?"

"It's been critical of that specific type of DNA testing, yes."

"And that specific type of DNA testing is . . . now a well-established part of forensic science, isn't it, Doctor?"

"I think you can say that, yes."

When we broke for lunch I went right over and slapped Tom on the back, while Dr. Gerdes was still sitting in the witness chair, looking shell-shocked. When court resumed, Tom put the finishing touches on him. "I'd like to make sure that the jury is clear on what you are saying and what you are not saying here today. First, you're not opining that [the

RFLP DNA test results in the Simpson case] were in any way the result of contamination, are you, Doctor?"

He suspected one item, one drop of blood found at Bundy. "All the rest are valid results," he admitted.

"So all those test results are good test results"—Tom rubbed his nose in it—"that the jury can rely on?"

"In my opinion, that's true."

Tom proceeded to extract admission after admission from Gerdes. So much for the cesspool of contamination. He had testified at length at the criminal trial, and it was based upon his testimony that Scheck was able to argue that the LAPD lab was a "black hole." Not only had we neutralized this once damaging defense witness, we had turned him into an advocate for our side. The DNA tests were now validated by the defense's own expert.

Another day won.

Ed was up next. It was his job to cross Dr. Michael Baden, the defense's Werner Spitz. Baden was extremely important; he was the one person who could destroy the weak link in our chain. If he could convincingly argue that the struggle to kill Ron and Nicole took from ten to fifteen minutes, we could not convincingly argue that Simpson was that killer. There was a very small window of opportunity between 10:32 when Heidstra heard "Hey, hey, hey!" and 10:50, 10:51 when Kato heard three thumps on his wall, and if the killer spent fifteen minutes at his killings, he wasn't Simpson.

Dr. Baden was a well-known forensic pathologist, the former medical examiner for the city of New York, who had served with Spitz on the committees and panels investigating the assassinations of President Kennedy and Dr. Martin Luther King Jr. His credentials were extensive; he had performed more than twenty thousand autopsies and had testified at many trials, usually for the prosecution. He and Spitz were good friends.

The essence of Dr. Baden's testimony was that because of the blood spewed so widely on the ground and the blood staining downward on Ron Goldman's pants, shirt, and shoe, he believed that Ron had died after a long struggle, from the severing of his internal left jugular vein. He did not dispute that Nicole died quickly.

In the criminal trial, Dr. Baden posited that Ron oozed blood for ten, fifteen, perhaps twenty minutes before he died. The purpose of this testimony was to enable the defense to argue that Ron, unarmed, battled an infinitely more powerful, knife-wielding professional athlete in a tiny, caged area for more than a quarter of an hour. The sole purpose of this argument was to devise a murder scenario lasting long enough to disqualify Simpson as the perpetrator. For his services, Dr. Baden was being paid more than $100,000. Plus he got to be on television.

Baden began his examination by opining on the cause of the cut on the middle finger of Simpson's left hand. "My opinion, after going over this and consulting with Dr. Lee, was that it was most likely broken glass." He also opined that there was more than one killer. "It would not be, in my experience, possible to reliably prevent people from yelling, screaming, asking for help, from escaping, from taking many evasive actions, that were not done here in a public place with people walking around outside. So it's my opinion, it's more than likely there's more than one perpetrator." Coming from the distinguished doctor, it sounded like good, solid medical opinion.

Baden was familiar with Spitz's testimony, and so we had dueling experts. As to time of struggle, Baden said, "My opinion would be that once the neck wound was incurred and he started bleeding, he would be able to stand up for a few minutes, plus or minus five minutes, maybe three minutes or four minutes or five minutes, and then he would collapse. And he would stay that way for five or ten minutes longer, until the heart would stop beating completely."

Baden had already backed off. Now he had Ron Goldman on the ground after perhaps only three minutes. And this was on *direct* examination! I sat at the counsel's table next to Medvene and thought, Should we even cross-examine him?

But Baden continued. "Somehow, there had to be a delay between the jugular vein cut and the stab wound to the flank of at least five or ten minutes." So now, the defense was floating this theory: Presumably the killer wouldn't leave the scene until he knew everyone was dead, so he stuck around for the extra ten minutes while Ron Goldman slipped away, then stabbed him at least one more time before departing.

Baden testified that Ron bled outwardly from the wound to his jugular vein, but he had no creditable explanation, considering the lack of blood on the ground around the body, for where that blood would be.

When the time came, Ed went right after him. Baden was part of the Simpson team, Ed made clear; he held a press conference and appeared on TV several times in support of Simpson. "You appeared on television as recently as a month ago, after Dr. Spitz testified, to give some contrary version on the Rivera show? Could you answer that question, yes or no, sir?"

Dr. Baden did a remarkable thing. He slapped his forehead with the heel of his hand. We had no idea he would be so sensitive. "No! No, as you asked the question, that's not true!" Geraldo Rivera had two TV shows at the time: a daytime tabloid affair and the more dignified nighttime program regularly devoted to the Simpson case. Apparently Dr. Baden did not want to create any confusion. Once Ed established he was talking about the time "you got on that show with Mr. Dershowitz and talked about this case," he assented.

"That wasn't the purpose of my appearance. . . . It was one day to publicize an HBO special, that's what I was on for."

This $100,000 expert who was not shy about publicity was coming unglued.

Ed continued his attack. "Is it true there's certain magic words that people that testify a lot use, and one of them is 'consistent with.' Is that true?"

"I try, in all my testimony, to be beyond a reasonable [degree of] medical certainty."

"You said in the past that's up to ninety-five percent category, didn't you?"

"Or more."

"Are you telling this jury, with a reasonable degree of medical certainty—more than ninety-five percent—that it's your opinion there were two assailants that slaughtered Ms. Brown and Ron Goldman?"

"That opinion was not to a reasonable degree of medical certainty; it was more likely than not."

Baden had conveyed a misleading impression to the jury on direct, and he had been caught at it. He was an experienced testifier. Without making clear the subtle but crucial distinction to the jury, a 51 to 49 opinion appeared to be 95 to 5.

Baden explained that he hadn't asked Simpson about the superficial scratches to his hands but had inquired about the major ones. "He indicated to me that he didn't know where he'd gotten them, but he had gotten blood on his hand after rummaging through his car, looking for the *cell phone,* and while at his house."

An extraordinary admission. Simpson swore up and down that he was getting not his cell phone, but his cell phone *accessories,* yet here's Baden saying that on June 17 Simpson told him he was looking for his cell phone. The cell phone was in the Bronco at eleven. Another nail in the coffin.

Baden continued, "He often cut himself and he does have a lot of scars on him and—"

"You're not an advocate," Ed admonished him. Baden smacked himself on the forehead again.

Ed toyed with Baden, who didn't appear to understand the importance of the phone issue, and got him to repeat Simpson "had rummaged for the car *phone*" and "was looking for his car *phone*" before moving on. He returned to the length of struggle. "I said he stayed up for two or three minutes," Baden said under prodding.

"Now"—Ed was closing in—"you've told us under oath he's standing maybe two or three minutes before he's on the ground. Did you tell, in this TV program you went on a month ago, Mr. Rivera and the national TV audience, at that time we had him up at least five or ten minutes? . . . Just yes or no, sir, did you say that on TV?"

In fact, Baden, speaking *while Werner Spitz was still on the witness stand,* had said, "He's standing five to ten minutes." We played the video for him. It was devastating impeachment.

Blasier and Medvene went back and forth, redirect, recross. Ron was up for two or three minutes, down for five or ten. "I've given various numbers," Baden admitted. "I don't know how long he stood up. Two to five minutes, he'd be down on the ground."

Ed said very quietly, very slowly, "So many numbers you've given us."

He brought his cross to a close. "Are you suggesting to this jury, as you did on the Rivera show, that maybe the assailant didn't immediately, after two minutes, inflict the remaining blows, but he stopped and talked?"

"That he stopped, did something else."

"Sir, you said stopped and talked."

"That was an example."

"Sir, are you suggesting to the jury, as you did on the show, maybe there was another perpetrator with a gun? Are you telling the jury that's what you believe happened?"

"No."

By the end he was rendered silly. Ed had dismantled him.

The vaunted expert who would convince the jury that the Scull photo was a guy who ran a motorcade route through Dallas, narrating the assassination of President John F. Kennedy to his customers from a replica of the presidential limousine. As they pass through Dealey Plaza, shots ring out of the limousine's speakers.

When their initial photo expert went south on them after examining the photo in Buffalo, the defense had to find *someone* who would call it a fake. They found Robert Groden, a fifty-one-year-old JFK conspiracy buff with no formal training in photography, no college education, no certification by any professional organization; a man whose claim to fame was that he released the Zapruder film, showing the president being shot, to television in 1975. He claimed to be "the consultant" for the House Select Committee on Assassinations, formed to investigate the work of the Warren Commission. However, a bit of prodding revealed that he was a consultant who spent a great deal of his time analyzing one photo of Lee Harvey Oswald holding a gun, and this was eighteen years ago. Fourteen years prior to our trial, he said, the *National Enquirer* had asked him to authenticate a photograph. They called back once and never again. He wrote books, produced videos, and consulted on films that included footage of the Kennedy assassination. His day job was as a photo-processing machine repairman. The defense was paying him $2,000 a day to testify, and he was perfect for them: he was a man who never met a conspiracy he didn't like.

Outside the presence of the jury, a hearing was held to determine Groden's fitness as an expert. Peter Gelblum argued, "He's never qualified as an expert because he's *not* an expert." Nevertheless, Judge Fujisaki conceded that Groden was "something more than a lay witness" and allowed him to testify. But for the fact that Simpson and Baker rested their entire case on this character, I believe the judge would not have let him on the stand. However, the consequences of disallowing the defense's only expert witness willing to swear that the Scull photo was fraudulent would have been severe. They would have been left with nothing but Simpson's denials. The judge threw them a bone.

Peter Gelblum was preparing to do the cross-exam, and I'd been pumping him up for days. "Go get him, Pedro. Groden's your guy, you're going to eat him alive! You're the Grodenator!"

After all that, Groden turned out to be pretty slick on direct. The jury paid respectful attention as he handed out material and said, "My conclusion is that there is a high likelihood of forgery." He said he noticed a discrepancy between what appears on the negative itself and on the surrounding area. He compared the negative of Simpson in the end zone to the rest of the roll and saw problems in measurement, positioning, color, balance. He claimed he saw a difference in alignment between the photo of Simpson and the rest of the shots on the roll. He claimed he saw a "secondary edge." He held a pointer and walked up and down in front of the jury, tapping on the exhibit board. "You also notice that there is some kind of line running between the edge of the frame itself and the sprocket hole area. There is no natural phenomenon to allow for it." To an untrained eye, his positions appeared to have merit.

"Peter, is there anything to what this guy is saying?" I asked nervously.

"He's nuts!" Peter whispered.

Groden examined the sole of Simpson's shoe in the picture. "Whoever did this had it reflect as red instead of white, and the angle seems wrong."

To Groden, Simpson's white shirt was pink. "Mr. Simpson's shirt is pink," was his expert opinion. "The balance is off, and the problem that I described before with trying to exactly match a color balance during a re-creation, would, in fact, be indicated possibly by this, as well as a slightly out-of-focus attitude of that particular frame."

It was perfectly in focus! This guy was seeing things that weren't there. His learned opinion: The Scull photo was a fraud.

On cross, Peter blasted Groden over exaggerations in his résumé. He wasn't *the* photographic consultant for the House Select Committee. He didn't testify before the Assassination Records Review Board to render professional opinions; he testified in connection with an investigation— of himself. Peter then made the jury aware that Groden had been paid $50,000 by the *Globe* tabloid for autopsy photos of JFK, which he had obtained under highly questionable circumstances while consulting for the House Select Committee. Groden insisted they had paid him fifty grand for his story *and* the right to use the photos, not just for the photos. This was the level of class and candor the jury was getting from the defense's lone photography expert.

Peter was getting so disgusted with Groden that he started screaming at him—and Fujisaki had to reprimand him. But Peter was getting his point across: Groden was an impostor. On top of that, Groden fooled with the ELMO. Judge Fujisaki, seeing a blurry photo, raised his voice and said, "Just a minute! Did you guys screw this thing up?!"

Phil Baker quickly said, "I didn't touch it!" Steve Foster was the acknowledged ELMO master; he didn't do it. "It was Groden," I accused. The repairman.

Dan Leonard, trying to be helpful to the judge, said, "He can correct it in a second. Do you want to have him come down?" Groden fiddled with it.

"It used to be a thousand percent better than that!" said the judge.

Peter took Groden through his attacks on the Scull photo, demonstrating to the jury how implausible and silly they were. Simpson's shirt is white, not pink. There's no blue line there. The frames are the same size. Correct? Peter brought out that Groden, in making the crucial precise measurements of the various frames, first enlarged the frames—on a Xerox machine—at Kinko's! Groden appeared unfazed by this assault.

Rather than attack further—Groden would never recant—we sat back and waited. We had a rebuttal witness in the wings who would finish Groden off.

We proceeded to dispense with the remaining brainchilds of the Simpson Dream Team. In the criminal trial they put on an expert named Herb MacDonell, a criminalist well-known for his work on blood patterns and stains. MacDonell testified that he analyzed the stains on Simpson's socks and saw tiny spheres, or red balls, of blood, indicative of someone having placed—that is, planted—blood on the outside surface of the socks rather than its having splashed onto them during the murders. Baker put MacDonell on in the civil trial to say the same thing.

Ed found a criminalist named Richard Fox and asked him to give us his opinion about MacDonell's conclusions. Fox told us MacDonell was wrong. He explained that MacDonell's little spheres could be there from perspiration. You can bet Simpson was perspiring in those socks while butchering two people. Fox also explained that the red spheres most likely resulted from the criminalist's cutting of the socks when performing tests on them, causing tiny dried blood particles to flake onto the fabric. In fact, Fox performed an experiment replicating the cutting process, and the results showed the same little spheres of blood.

Medvene cross-examined MacDonell and confronted him with Fox's analysis and conclusions. MacDonell, of course, was not impressed. However, he did concede that when he was examining the bloodstains on the socks, he failed to manipulate the little red spheres to determine if they had flaked onto the sock fiber as Fox discovered. MacDonell had the ability to determine this for himself, but he did not.

Baker's last line of defense was a much ballyhooed part of Simpson's criminal defense effort to prove that his blood was planted on the back gate at the Bundy crime scene and on his socks. EDTA is a chemical preservative contained in purple-top blood vials to prevent blood from coagulating or clotting. When Simpson's blood was drawn by Nurse Peratis on June 13, it went into a purple-top vial containing EDTA. In the criminal case the prosecution came up with a way to disprove the idea of planting. If the blood had been planted, the theory was that it came from Simpson's reference vial, then was splattered on the back gate and placed on the socks. If it came from Simpson's reference sample, the blood would have EDTA in it; if the blood had no EDTA, it could not have been planted. So the prosecutors decided to have the blood tested for EDTA. In theory the idea was a good one. In practice it was not, because they had never had this kind of test done before.

The prosecutors sent samples of Simpson's bloodstains from the back gate and his socks to Washington, D.C., to be tested by an FBI chemist named Roger Martz. First, Martz tested a sample of blood from a purple-top container and found a high level of EDTA. Then Martz tested a blood sample from the sock and a sample from the back gate. Instead of finding no EDTA, Martz found very small traces of it. Puzzled by these results, he then took some blood from his own arm and tested it and also saw the same small signal of EDTA. He concluded that the small trace amounts showing in the evidence stains must have come from the infinitesimal levels of EDTA that can be found in everyone's blood. EDTA is used in numerous food substances and household products.

The defense, on learning these findings, celebrated wildly. Now they could argue from the prosecution's own proof that Simpson's blood had been planted. It had EDTA in it. Never mind that they were tiny amounts of EDTA. (Never mind that if Simpson's team really believed this, they would have tested every bloodstain for EDTA. To no one's surprise, they never tested one sample; if they did, they didn't tell anyone the results.)

We fully expected to be hit very hard with the EDTA defense in our case, so Tom went to work on it right away. He contacted a number of experts around the country to discuss Martz's test results. Meanwhile Martz himself figured out what had gone wrong. The equipment used to test the EDTA is extremely sensitive. When Martz ran the first test with EDTA-laced blood, a small amount of the EDTA stayed in the machine. The machine was not fully cleaned before the tests were run on Simpson's bloodstains, so when those tests were run, the machine picked up residue of EDTA from the first test.

We intended to call Roger Martz at our trial to explain all this, but shortly before the trial, the FBI refused to make him available. Apparently Martz and members of his lab were being questioned and criticized for improper lab practices—having nothing to do with the work done in Simpson's case. At the last minute, Tom was able to find a highly qualified expert as a replacement.

By the time the civil trial rolled around, the defense team knew all of this. Nonetheless, Bob Blasier put on Fredric Rieders, the same gruff Austrian-born chemist used by the criminal defense, to give his opinion that the trace amounts of EDTA found by Martz indicated the blood came from a purple-top container—in other words, it had EDTA in it; in other words, it was planted.

Tom Lambert cross-examined Rieders and forced him to admit that Martz's test results for the known blood sample spiked with EDTA showed a mountain of a signal, while the trace amounts from Simpson's blood showed a molehill. Clearly Simpson's blood did not have EDTA from a purple-top container. But Rieders stubbornly clung to his opinion, and we would have to call our own expert to bury the EDTA myth forever.

The same day Rieders was on the stand, Judge Nancy Wieben Stock announced her decision in the suit Lou and Judy Brown had brought against Simpson for custody of Justin and Sydney: Simpson got the kids.

This was awful. Not only were two little children being delivered into the hands of their mother's killer, but I was terrified that the jury would hear the news and react badly to it. They could easily come to the conclusion that if Simpson was awarded the children, the judge must have investigated and found Simpson innocent. Of course, the judge hadn't investigated the murders and had no real choice in the matter; Simpson had been acquitted, he was their father, he got control. But the jury might see things differently.

Juror #333, an older black woman, had expressed concern for the children during jury selection, and I hoped she and the rest of the jurors would not feel compelled now to find him not guilty for their sake. We had all worked hard to convince this jury that Simpson was a murderer, but if they thought it would not be in the children's best interest to learn that their father killed their mother, we were doomed.

So far, Simpson's record in trials was 2–0. Where was the justice?

THIRTY-THREE

More Ugly-Ass Shoes

We had a two-week break over Christmas, and I found it difficult to stay focused. The DoubleTree suite was desolate and empty—no bustle, no buzz—but I could not stay away from it for a week or even three days at a time. I needed my fix.

Even when I wasn't at work, the case haunted me. I was with my son and daughter, shopping for a present for my wife at the Northridge Mall, when who appeared at the same jewelry counter but one of the jurors. I quickly gave my kids my credit card and told them, "Don't say anything to him. I'm going outside." I thought I was safe, standing behind a post, but when Rachel and Adam returned, who was heading in my direction but juror #326. I was petrified. This was a mistrial in the making.

He saw me. I put up my hands as if to say, "Don't come near. Don't say anything." He kept on going.

I told my partners. Of course, I'd have to tell the judge. (Ultimately I finessed it, mentioning the incident in an "Oh, by the way" during a sidebar. Neither Baker nor the judge made an issue of it, but the episode didn't do my "vacation" any good.)

I spent Christmas Day with my family, but the rest of the time I was huddled in the suite, working on the outline for my cross-examination of Simpson. Baker was planning to call him to the stand right after the break.

Yvette helped me pull out everything he might testify to and plan our counterattack. Peter returned from a short vacation and began getting ready to complete Groden's examination and to put on Gerald Richards, our photo expert, in rebuttal. Tom and Ed were busy planning their rebuttal witnesses. We were all anxious to get back to court and bring the case to an end.

We also had pages and pages of objections to Dr. Lee's videotaped testimony, which the defense wanted to play for the jury. The judge said, "You guys work it out," so over the holiday I met with Bob and Phil Baker in their office to try to resolve the differences. We ended up talking quite pleasantly for a couple of hours.

"Boy," said Phil, "you really hammered our guy."

Bob said, "You weren't so effective the first day, but you were the second." I reciprocated by telling them again what a good job Phil had done with Bodziak. On the Dr. Lee matter, however, we couldn't agree on anything.

After Simpson's performance on the stand, I'd been flooded with photos and videos from people all over the country, all showing Simpson wearing shoes. In the hopes of finding another pair of Bruno Maglis, I had Yvette and Steve look at every one of them. Their search proved golden when a photo arrived from a Buffalo carpenter named Brian McCrone. His brother Tim, an attorney, had prevailed upon him to send it to us rather than sell it to the tabloids. "If your little girl was murdered and somebody out there had evidence to help you catch the man who did it, what would you hope that person did with that evidence, sell it to the *National Enquirer* or give it to the district attorney?" Brian McCrone had done the right thing.

The beauty of his photos was their happenstance. A carpenter takes his son to a football game, sees O.J. Simpson, snaps off two or three shots in the middle of all the other snapshots he's taking of the players at the game that day, and goes home. He had never sold them, he had never given an interview, he was just a guy who took his son to a game and came back with murder evidence. The pictures were pure.

Unfortunately McCrone was a better carpenter than he was a photographer; the shoes were there all right, but the shots were not high quality. They were a bit blurry, and we would have to blow them up in order to present them properly. The defense would surely attack the quality, and in the process we might end up diluting the importance of the picture-perfect Scull photo. Nevertheless, we had the McCrone photos if we needed them.

So I was sitting in the DoubleTree on Friday, December 27, when John Kelly called.

"Dan, you're not going to believe it!" He sounded more excited than usual. "I'm looking at a picture of Simpson in the shoes on the same day as Scull's photo, taken by another photographer!"

On a tip from Scull's lawyer, Michael O'Connor, Kelly had flown from New York to Buffalo and seen the Buffalo Bills' sports information director, Denny Lynch, who had put him in touch with a photographer named E. J. Flammer, who had put him in touch with his son, E. J. Flammer Jr., who had shown him the pictures.

"Is the picture clear?" I asked immediately.

"Dan, *it's absolutely clear!*"

"Is it the shoes?"

"*It's the Brunos!*" Kelly was almost sputtering. "And get this, there are *thirty* of them!"

Thirty photographs of Simpson in the Bruno Maglis? This doesn't happen.

"John, please don't say a word to anybody. Don't tell a soul." I didn't want the defense getting wind of this. Plus, I had to see for myself. "FedEx me the pictures and keep those guys quiet!"

"Absolutely."

But it wasn't kept too quiet—that evening it was on the news.

"Dan," Kelly said, "it wasn't me. An ABC cameraman was hanging around when I got to the airport and recognized me." He had some more bad news. "You're not going to believe this: McCelroy's involved." Rob McCelroy was the man who sold the Scull photo to the *National Enquirer.*

"Tell them they can't sell it!" I didn't want the defense claiming the photos were doctored for money.

"There are thirty pictures," said Kelly, "you can't doctor them all."

"Try to get a lid on the situation."

I was at the DoubleTree when Peter Gelblum called from the office the next morning, shouting.

"They're unbelievable! They're perfect! You're not going to believe them! *It's the shoes!*" He broke land speed records getting over.

Flammer hadn't sent all thirty, but he had printed up a representative sample, and Peter was right. There, standing on the field at Rich Stadium on September 26, 1993, in the midst of a group of middle-aged guys, was Simpson wearing the O.J. smile and the identical clothes Scull had photographed him in: the jacket, the tie, the white shirt, the slacks— the whole outfit—*the shoes!* Flammer had even kept his press pass from the game. On top of that, it turned out that one of the pictures had been printed in the Buffalo Bills newsletter. *Here's a picture of O.J. Simpson wearing the Bruno Magli shoes, printed in the newspaper seven months before the murders!*

I got on the phone with Kelly. "Who's Flammer? What kind of guy is he?"

Kelly told me, "His father is a Buffalo Bills booster who's in these pictures with O.J. The kid's a regular guy. He works in a photo shop. He just had the pictures and didn't realize they were important. The problem is, he's hired McCelroy to represent him, and he has a lawyer."

I immediately got on the phone and started negotiating with McCelroy. "Rob, you've got to work with us on this."

"In fairness to Flammer," he said, "he should earn some money. We're going to have an auction and bid these out to the media, and see how much they'll pay for them."

"I will do whatever I can to prevent the pictures from being copied so you can do what you want with them," I said. "But I want to have them for use in court before they're sold. You've got to do that for me. Too much is riding on this."

McCelroy turned out to be a decent guy and ended up cooperating. He gave us a complete set of the prints with a copyright notice on the back of each, reading "Do not reproduce." He said he would not put them up for sale until we used them in court and wanted to know when that would be.

Good question. If we didn't use them soon, if we held on to them for a week or two and didn't make them available to the defense, the judge might not allow us to use them at all. Peter wanted to enter them through Groden and just Grodenate him, but if we tried to use the photos with either Groden or Simpson on the stand, we had no way of authenticating them; Groden would say they were phonies, and I wouldn't put it past Simpson to deny he was even *in* Buffalo. We figured the defense wouldn't go anywhere near the issue of shoes in their examination of Simpson, so we might have no grounds for exploring the issue with him. We would have to wait until our rebuttal case, when we could put Flammer on to authenticate them.

We got in touch with Flammer and sent him a declaration, signed under penalty of perjury, authenticating the pictures and securing his agreement to come to the trial to testify about them. Such a declaration is hearsay and not admissible in court, but I thought Fujisaki would permit us to introduce the photos by assuring him we could bring in the proof later. TV news had eliminated the possibility of our presenting the photos as a surprise, but Peter and I decided that if he could set Groden up to say his opinion of the Scull photo might be different if other pictures taken the same day were introduced, we would spring it on him then.

We got to court Monday morning, January 6, the first day following our Christmas break. The defense was ready to fight for their lives to keep these new smoking guns out of the case. Dan Leonard argued to the judge that the appearance of these photos at this time was "highly suspicious." They wanted a two-week recess to investigate them. I said, "Your Honor, there's absolutely no basis for this position at all. Mr. Simpson took that stand under oath and said he was not wearing the shoes in [the Scull] photograph. He said the photograph was a fake. Mr. Baker told the jury the same thing. They put this would-be expert on the stand to say that this photo is a fake. . . . This is classical impeachment material, Your Honor, and they don't have any right to advance disclosure of it, even if we had obtained it in advance, which we did not."

When the judge so ordered, we produced copies of the photos for everyone involved; we produced Flammer's sworn affidavit of authentication. We were totally prepared. Leonard shouted to the courtroom, "This is a total sandbag!"

Judge Fujisaki looked at him and shook his head. "That's usually what impeachment amounts to, Counsel."

When the Flammer photos were brought back to the defense counsel's table, Bob Baker wouldn't even look at them. As they opened the envelope and huddled around the prints, staring at them one by one, Simpson pointed lamely. In his opening argument, Baker had said assertively and unequivocally that the Scull photo was "a phony. It isn't real. It was doctored!" Now he had no answer. Seated, he backed himself away from the crowd, his arms folded, eyes down, signaling to anyone who might be watching that he had been betrayed.

But betrayal implies trust and belief, and Baker had no right trusting or believing Simpson in the first place.

Groden resumed the stand. How sure was he that the Scull photo was a fraud? Beginning at 1 percent, moving to 50, 60, 65—"You're playing games," said Groden, "aren't you"—Peter was letting Groden hang himself, pushing him, and got him to say there was "greater than a ninety percent probability either the pants and/or the shoes, or the shoes alone, were changed, if indeed that was a legitimate picture of Mr. Simpson in the first place."

"If there were other photographs of Mr. Simpson taken on the same day, at the same game, in the same stadium, and he's wearing the same outfit and they're taken by a different photographer with a different camera, and he's wearing the same pants and same shoes, that would affect your opinion, wouldn't it, sir?"

Leonard objected. Judge Fujisaki said, "Based on the affidavit filed in support of plaintiff's position, motion overruled."

"No."

Peter looked at me. Though Groden hadn't answered as we hoped, I nodded. *Go for it!* I was afraid the defense might ask again for a postponement, anything could happen. We had our green light. It might yet turn. *Go!*

Peter pulled out the Flammer pictures. "You see the shoes Mr. Simpson is wearing?"

"Yes."

"I'll show you some more." He passed them around to the jurors. They didn't show any change in emotion, but I was preening. *This was so much fun!* My swivel chair was rocking. "I ask you if that changes your opinion?"

"It does not."

Peter showed him another photograph. "And I ask you if *that* changes your opinion?"

"Does not."

Peter showed him another. "I ask you if that changes your opinion?"
"Nope."

All the Flammer photos, including negatives, arrived in the courtroom the next week. Groden had plenty of time to examine them and
return to the stand to say they were not authentic. Instead he returned to
Dealey Plaza. The defense did not call anyone else to challenge the photos.
They wouldn't go near them. The photos just sat there in the courtroom.

The defense went through the motions all the rest of that week, but
Baker's fire was out. As his case was crumbling, Simpson was nevertheless
a presence. Fred Goldman, of course, refused to remain in the same room
with him anywhere but the courtroom. Once, when he walked into the
men's room and found Simpson there, he turned around and walked out.
"I guess Fred doesn't want to be my pissing partner," Simpson said. The
man was pathetic.

Kim Goldman gave Simpson the hate stare constantly, and he didn't
like it. It was all she could do to him for killing her brother. One day, as
the courtroom was emptying, he mimicked her back. Just at that moment,
Fred turned and thought Simpson was making fun of him.

"Don't you do that, you son of a bitch!" From across the room, Fred
was ready to charge him.

"Your daughter was staring at me!" yelled Simpson. The deputies
scurried to keep them apart.

Finally it was time for Simpson to tell his tale. Sure enough, right
out of the opening statement, it's the Heisman Trophy gambit. It was
pretty clear who was calling the shots. Baker appeared to be doing his
duty, finishing off the case for his client and getting the hell out of Dodge.
Did Simpson think that because he had been a great football player, the
jury would believe him incapable of committing this crime? Did he really
think he could con the jury with this monument to O.J.? What about
addressing the merits of the case?

When it came time to rebut the damaging quotes from his rookie
book, Simpson droned on about hazing rookies in the NFL and his playing jokes on the veterans and how this business about being an "effective
liar" was all a big joke. Baker, however, went too far.

"You have never *attempted* to lie, have you, on *anything* that's important relative to your life."

"No."

"Did you ever tell a fan during the years that you were in the NFL that you didn't have time for an autograph?"

"No."

"Did you ever spit on a referee?"

"No."

He'd been on the stand for fifteen minutes and we were still talking about football. This could be ESPN SportsCenter. Months ago I might have been concerned about a jury being swayed by a hero, but no longer. It was too late for that.

Finally he started dealing with specifics. India Allen said Nicole had been wearing a headband when Simpson hit her; Simpson said Nicole didn't wear headbands. The incident at Victoria Beach? "There's no way the guy could have seen me. It's always crowded. And I wasn't there at that time, anyway." He gave a litany of unrequired details.

Simpson dropped the names of his celebrity friends and talked about playing golf. The New Year's Eve incident? Nicole's fault. "I didn't slap her! I didn't hit her! My purpose was not to injure her in any way, shape, or form, but I was very physical with her. Once we got physical with each other, and my attempts to get her out of my bedroom, but I had no purpose to injure her at all!" *My* bedroom, not theirs! He was his own worst enemy.

"You ever take your hand back, close your fist, and intentionally hit Nicole?"

"Of course not," he said. "She would have looked a little different than she looked if I hit anybody, for that matter."

Simpson went on in excruciating detail about how the police were rude to him and that was why he ran to Allen Schwartz's house. He was "totally, one hundred percent responsible for whatever I did that night," but "whatever I did" didn't include slapping, kicking, or hitting Nicole.

He talked about his life with Paula, and his favorite subject, how Nicole begged him to come back. He went on in detail about all the ground rules *he* had laid down for their reconciliation. Baker tossed out quick questions, and Simpson delivered monologues: "My Story" by O.J. Simpson, always rich in detail, with the emphasis on how he was always trying to do the right thing, and be a good guy, and help everyone with problems, especially Nicole, who had so many.

He just trashed her. "When I would call her, I literally didn't know who I was talking to from day to day. One day she was upset about something and wouldn't tell me, the next day she would apologize and said she loved me. The next day I couldn't even get a word out of her. I was real concerned about what was going on." The implication was that she was bottoming out in Faye's world.

It was all so familiar, but the pundits ran with it. "O.J. was convincing." "The jury saw a powerful, charismatic man." He was none of that; he simply had his story down. You either accepted it without question or you were deeply offended. I was screaming at the TV screen, "What about the gloves? What about the knife? What about the cuts? What about the fact that he all but called her a tramp, a whore, a drug addict crashing up cars and having abortions? Where were you?!"

I kept track of Simpson's new stories. To cover some of his lies the first time on the stand, he now said he had *mistakenly* told the police he'd gone to Paula's after the recital. "I have a way of talking when someone will call and will say, 'What are you doing?' I'll say I'm going to somebody's place when, in fact, I was home. But I was sort of running both nights and things together because I didn't really have a Sunday night. . . ."

He "didn't really have a Sunday night" because he was murdering two people.

". . . Because I hadn't slept, and at the exact same time on Saturday night I was on my way to Paula's."

Closer inspection destroys that statement, however; Paula was home on Saturday night, but Simpson had told the police she was not home when he called her. It was not the same night; he was lying desperately, wildly. No more pretense of careful reconstruction. No time for that anymore. Just lie, lie, lie.

Suicide? He had no counter to our argument, so he simply denied it. "Did you ever tell anyone at the time that you had contemplated ending your life or thereafter, that you were in any way responsible for Nicole Brown Simpson's death?"

"Never," Simpson said, "never at any time, and never would I, 'cause I wasn't."

Baker's final question revealed what I guess it was all about to O.J. "Have you just about lost every *material possession* that you've had as a result of this incident?"

I objected because finances was an area that we were not allowed to get into, and the court sustained me. Baker had nothing further. I should have let Simpson answer that question and talk about all the material things he'd lost. The one loss he would not have mentioned was Nicole.

The defense case was notable for what it did not produce. They never called a DNA expert to challenge any of the blood tests that implicated Simpson, nor did they produce a witness to testify that any of the hair and fiber matches that we established belonged to Simpson were erroneous. They couldn't find a DNA or a hair-and-fiber Robert Groden. Simpson, of course, said nothing about this evidence.

I had spent much of the past two weeks fretting about facing Simpson a second time. I just couldn't concentrate, couldn't get revved up. I had done it, and I didn't know if, given another shot, I could do it any better. I was spent on the issue. Nevertheless, the jury would remember best the examination they had seen most recently, so it was important that I not let down now. I stood up and went right at him.

"You told this jury on Friday, Mr. Simpson, that you never, ever attempted to lie about anything in your life. Do you remember that?"

"Not anything that was germane to anything."

"Excuse me." I had to reestablish the ground rules. "Do you remember that testimony? Please answer yes or no."

"Yes."

"And when you told this jury on Friday that you never, ever attempted to lie about anything important, you understood that your credibility is a crucial issue in this case, right?"

It was clear throughout the first round of our examination that the jury hadn't believed him, so now he was going to do whatever he could to convince them he was a man of flawless character, one who would never lie and, indeed, testified that he never even attempted to lie. Baker objected: "Argumentative, Your Honor." The court: "Sustained."

This was a surprise. My question was well within the bounds of acceptability; the judge should not have sustained that objection. Apparently I was going to be in for some tough sledding.

"You understand that it's important that you are believed by this jury, correct?"

"Same thing, Your Honor." Baker had adapted to our offense and obviously developed a new game plan. He was going to object more often. The judge overruled this one.

"I believe it's important for me to be honest to the jury," Simpson intoned.

"Can you answer my question, sir?"

"I can't answer your question the way it's worded. I believe it's important for me to be honest to the jury." Another element in their new plan of attack was clearly that Simpson himself was going to argue with me more. We went back and forth for several minutes, and when it was clear that Simpson wasn't going to move off this particular dime, the judge said, "Move on to the next question. You got your answer."

"You have lied repeatedly to this jury, haven't you, sir?"

Simpson looked at me. "No."

"And you have lied repeatedly throughout your life, haven't you?"

"No."

Baker, by this time, was yelling. "Your Honor, this is argument!" Overruled. "When you were married to Nicole, you were repeatedly unfaithful to her, were you not?"

"There were times," he admitted.

He said he never even attempted to lie about anything important, yet he had repeatedly cheated on his wife. That's not a lie? Apparently Simpson didn't think so. We had a big argument at sidebar on the issue, and finally the judge ruled in my favor. Finally I was able to ask him, "Are you saying that you don't consider it a lie to your wife to cheat on her?" I had him in a no-win situation. Either he said that cheating was a lie, in which case not only had he admitted to lying, but he had also committed perjury by having said he never even attempted to tell a lie. Or else he said cheating was not a lie, in which case he presented himself as a completely amoral, remorseless, deceitful womanizer. Which one would it be?

"It's not the word I would use for it, no." He decided it was worse to be a perjurer than a philanderer. "I would say morally, it was wrong."

After a long argument at sidebar with the jury out of the courtroom, during which the judge had to read cases and research the point, I was able to introduce Nicole's diary into evidence. The jury would be allowed to read things like "He beat the holy shit out of me," not as fact, but as "admissible hearsay," to show Nicole's state of mind and feelings regarding the relationship. It was relevant to show the progression of that relationship up to and including the night of June 12.

But their strategy was working. I was making my points, but having to fight through many more objections than before. The examination wasn't smooth, it didn't flow, and it wasn't as effective as I'd hoped.

"Did Nicole lie to you frequently in the course of your marriage?"

"Lie to me?"

"Was she a liar?"

"She's lied. But I can't say frequently." So now Nicole was a liar, but Simpson wasn't.

I tried to rebut the rendition of the New Year's Eve incident Simpson presented on direct examination, but Baker objected and the judge sustained, saying I already had my information. "Let's not waste our time." He'd had enough of Simpson. He wanted to get this case to the jury.

I was very frustrated. Baker kept objecting, the judge kept sustaining, and the entire defense team seemed to be feeling more confident as a result. I had wanted to remind the jury of all the evidence they had heard earlier in the case, but I had closing argument to do that. So I decided to scrap the rest of my examination. It was time to bring this thing to a close. And I had saved the best for last.

"You testified that the shoes you were wearing on September 26, 1993, that were depicted in the photo, were not shoes that you were actually wearing. Do you remember that?"

"I testified that I didn't recognize those shoes, no." This was not responsive, nor was it what he'd said previously. Simpson was arguing with me on all the answers now.

"And you said that you thought the picture was fraudulent, right?"

"I think you said something about if these are Bruno Magli shoes, and I testified I didn't believe so, yes." That wasn't responsive, either.

"You said you weren't wearing Bruno Magli shoes of the type depicted in that photograph. . . . Do you remember all of that?" I wanted to set this up with the jury, to feed their own recollection and show the progression of lies.

"Yes, I said those shoes are not shoes that I recognized that I ever owned."

"And you said there was no doubt in your mind that those were not shoes that you were wearing, do you remember that?"

"I never buy any shoes that I never owned." This garbled sentence must have been an attempt to create a distinction between wearing shoes and owning them.

"There wasn't any doubt in your mind, correct?"

"I don't believe I've ever owned those shoes, no."

"Sir, since you gave testimony, you have learned that there are thirty new photographs of you wearing shoes."

"Other photos, yes."

"Let me show you." There were eight prints and two contact sheets. "These photos are true and correct depictions of you, correct?"

"To an extent, yes, that looks like me." Only O.J. Simpson could give that answer.

"Do you have any reason to believe that there's anything wrong with you in this photo?" I held one up.

"Yes, I have an opinion. My only opinion is I do not recognize ever owning these shoes."

"So you don't believe that you were wearing shoes like this in this photo? Is that what you're saying?"

"I don't believe I ever *owned* shoes like that." Did Simpson actually think that at the end of this trial, he was going to be able to weasel out of these photographs by saying they weren't his? Maybe he borrowed them. Maybe the cameraman gave them to him. Maybe they were on extended loan from Bruno Magli himself.

"Were you *wearing* them?"

"I don't believe so, no."

Steve Foster put up the Scull photo. "I never recall owning shoes like that, ever," Simpson swore. I made him admit he didn't recall wearing any of the shoes in any of the photos. Back to the Flammer photos, he once again quarreled with the pants. "I'm normally a pretty sharp dresser, and that is very not like me. They don't look like they fit."

"So your opinion, sir, is that all of these pictures are once again doctored; is that right?"

"I don't know." He was starting to wriggle. "I just know that the pants don't look right to me. I don't ever recall owning shoes like these."

"You're saying you don't recall the shoes? Or are you saying, sir, you did not wear those shoes in those photographs?"

"I would say no."

I made him repeat it. "What is it?"

"I would say no, I didn't wear those shoes."

Again. "You did not wear those shoes, right?"

"No."

"Do you have any explanation for why all these photographs show you wearing those shoes?"

"No."

It took a little more work, but I had him. I dropped them one by one. "Do you have any explanation, sir?"

"No."

Now he was back to where I wanted him: somber. No more lilt now, he was out of O.J. world and into mine. He looked as though he'd given up again.

I showed him the November 1993 Buffalo Bills newsletter which, in a twist of irony, commemorated Simpson's record-breaking year twenty years earlier and featured an action picture of him on the cover. Inside was Flammer's photo of Simpson wearing the murder shoes. "Well, I can't tell the shoes in this photograph," he said. It didn't make a difference what his answers were, at this point. I put the printed photograph up on the ELMO.

"You don't have any reason to doubt that you're wearing the shoes in that picture in the newspaper, many months before Nicole's murder?"

"I can't tell those shoes from these shoes."

"Remember testifying in your deposition that the shoes of the type depicted in the Scull photo were ugly aesthetically and stylewise?"

"No."

"You don't remember that?"

"No, I remember saying that about the shoes that were shown to me in court." It was a distinction Medvene had made at the mock trial, but it was way too late for that argument.

"And you testified that you believed that the shoes that I showed you in the Scull photo the last time that you testified were also ugly, correct?"

"No. I'm sure I said that they looked better than what they showed me in court, but they still didn't look like shoes I would wear." The jury had heard his original testimony, and I knew they were aware of the differences.

"They were not attractive, correct?"

"I think I told you that they weren't as bad-looking as the ones that were shown me in court, but I still didn't think they were shoes that I would wear."

I repeated: "And you also said they were not attractive, correct?"

Finally. "I don't think they are attractive, even looking at them now."

"And you're *positive* you're not wearing those shoes?"

"Yes."

"Mr. Simpson, when you testified last time on this witness stand, in November, you did not know about the existence of these thirty photographs, correct?"

"No."

"And you told this jury that you were not wearing those shoes depicted in the Scull photograph. Correct?"

"Correct."

"And now there are thirty pictures that have come forward showing that you are wearing the same shoes. Correct?"

At this point I felt I had assumed the role of, in effect, the jury's lawyer. He had lied repeatedly to them, and they knew he had lied. I looked him right in the eye and pointed to the jury box. I was close enough to touch them.

"You lied to this jury!" It was me and them now.

"No."

"You lied to this jury, didn't you?"

"No."

"It's still your testimony, sir, that you would never attempt to tell a lie, correct?"

"Not in a court of law, no," he maintained.

"Or in anything important in your life." Baker had given me the perfect opening. "Correct?"

"Certainly not nothing close to this important."

I was finished with Simpson for good.

Baker didn't have much to add. He closed by asking the single question I hoped he would ask. "O.J.," he began. He was still invoking "O.J."

"On June 12, 1994, did you, with your children in the house, upstairs in their bedroom, asleep, murder your wife—your ex-wife—and leave her body where the kids would find it?"

Simpson again turned to the jury as if stage-managed. This time they wouldn't look at him. Half had their eyes downward, refusing to meet his gaze; the rest stared anywhere but at the defendant. These were monumental lies he was telling, not only hollow but offensive.

"No," he swore. "*Absolutely* not!"

THIRTY-FOUR

Close Strong

S impson put his daughter on the stand to do his final dirty work. The first thing she did was tell the jury she was born on the day her father got the Heisman Trophy. After that, she turned her attention to the night of the murders, claiming she went to the *front* of the house to let the cops in. She said, "There's no time for me to run to turn the alarm off. I—I—I have to do it immediately." She went on to say that Chachi was a threat to run out and that she told her father, "Nicole is dead and there was somebody else with her." She did *not* say she told him they were at Bundy or in the garden.

I thought it was terrible that they sent this young woman up there to do this, and while I was careful to be respectful, I had to make the jury aware of the gaping holes in her story. Her testimony concerning the house alarm system contradicted her testimony at the criminal trial; there she said the alarm sensor had a forty-second delay during which it could be disarmed. Clearly she had not disarmed anything when she was with the police; there had been no warning beeps because the system was not on. I made my points, the defense tried to rehabilitate her, then they rested.

It was time to put on our rebuttal case. The rebuttal phase is the plaintiff's opportunity to put on witnesses to respond to new points raised by the defense, and the defense's chance to put on witnesses to respond to the plaintiff's rebuttal witnesses. This funneling process continues until neither side has anything left to rebut or the judge blows the whistle. Usually, the latter.

After the defense rested, we all felt we had put on a near perfect case. In contrast, we believed they'd had an aimless, sputtering defense case. "Less is more" had not failed us yet, so the temptation was enormous to put on no rebuttal case at all. That would have closed the evidence phase, leaving only final summation to the jury. If we elected to put on any rebuttal witnesses, we risked opening new doors, creating new opportunities for the defense to snatch victory from the jaws of defeat. This was the last thing we wanted to do.

But our hand was forced, because we had to put on E. J. Flammer to authenticate the thirty new photos. Plus, we needed Jerry Richards to lay to rest any doubt about the authenticity of the thirty-one pictures of Simpson wearing the murder shoes.

As long as we were going to have a rebuttal case, we decided to address a few additional points the defense made and put in the record all the ammunition needed to destroy the last vestiges of the defense case. In closing argument, we would arm the jury with this ammunition. The whole thing would be short and sweet. But extremely potent.

Our rebuttal case took two and a half days. After E. J. Flammer Jr. authenticated his photos, Jerry Richards was brought to the stand to substantiate them. Richards had spent twenty-three years in the FBI, rising to become chief of the FBI's questioned documents examination unit. He was an expert in forensic photography, which he taught at George Washington University. Peter Gelblum presented his extensive credentials in all their glory: twice past president of the Mid-Atlantic Association of Forensic Scientists, member of the Evidence Photography International Council, member of the Photographic Historic Society; writer of numerous published articles, including "Applications of Electronic Video Techniques to Infrared and Ultraviolet Examinations." He did not give tours of Dealey Plaza complete with simulated gunfire. Richards was the anti-Groden.

I gave him the nickname "Mr. Wizard." Richards pulled out his state-of-the-art instruments and measuring equipment, one piece of which fit over his head like a space helmet. He was operating the ELMO, and everything worked perfectly. Not only did Richards produce precise measurements proving the reliability of the negative, he explained that copy machine enlargements such as the ones Groden had made at Kinko's, create distortions that render useless all measurements taken from them. Richards gave simple, obvious explanations to all the other fictional abnormalities listed by Groden.

Richards examined the Scull photo for retouching marks, signs of digital alteration, physical defects, scratches, anomalies. He looked at the grain structure under a variety of magnifications; he scanned the entire negative millimeter by millimeter; he viewed all the negatives on Scull's roll for perspective, dimensional sizes, cut lines. His expert opinion: "There's no doubt in my mind regarding the shoes in this particular photograph, that these have not been altered or changed in any way."

Dan Leonard had to cross-examine him. He told me, "I get all the hard ones, don't I? Gee, you think you could have found someone a little tougher for me?" Leonard was right. He didn't touch Richards—mostly because Richards was untouchable. Groden's opinions were shown to be absolutely worthless. And, of course, wrong.

We then concluded the rest of the rebuttal case. Richard Fox ("Fox on Socks") explained the mystery of the little round balls of blood on Simpson's socks. Dr. Terry Lee delivered the last rites to the EDTA myth, explaining the mishap with the testing equipment. Tom called Dr. Bradley Popovich, a renowned DNA expert, to testify that he reviewed all the DNA test work done in the case and found no evidence whatsoever of contamination. Ed called shoe expert Bill Bodziak back to the stand to tell the jury what they already knew: the new Flammer photos showed Simpson wearing the murder shoes.

I rose and rested our case. Baker rested. It was over. Only closing arguments remained.

I picked up my briefcase and put my arm around Fred as we left the courtroom. I said to him, "Whatever happens, we proved he killed your son. We proved that to this jury. We proved that to the world. *Everybody* knows."

Back at the DoubleTree we all felt like celebrating. But there was still work to do. This was a Thursday. With the court on holiday the next Monday to celebrate Dr. Martin Luther King Jr.'s birthday, the close wouldn't start until Tuesday; we had time to do some crafting.

Fred said he wanted to meet with us privately, so Tom, Ed, Peter, Yvette, Steve, and I sat with him in the back room. "I just want you all to know," he began, "how proud I am of all of you, and the work you all did, and how you did it with dignity. You showed yourselves to be true professionals, and I truly want to thank you. My family thanks you. The country thanks you. We will be proud of you forever."

Lawyers are in a tough business, dealing with financial issues that are very important to the people whose nickel it is, but we don't have many moments like that. We have grateful clients, sure, but this was a man who had lost his son forever and was pouring out his heart, thanking us for *our* dignity, when he had shown so much of his own.

I thanked him, told him how proud and privileged we were, all of us, to have had the opportunity to represent him. It was an honor that he had placed his trust and confidence in us; we deeply cared about him and his family and always would. We embraced, Fred left, and we got back to work.

For the last several weeks I had been thinking about how we should handle closing argument. My strong preference was to do it myself. I'd been the lead plaintiffs' attorney, I represented continuity, I had been the man who confronted Simpson, and I felt I was the one the jury expected to hear from.

But it wasn't as simple as that. John Kelly and Mike Brewer had their own clients, so I broke off chunks that would not disrupt the flow of my principal argument and gave those pieces to them. Kelly would talk about Nicole, and Simpson's abuse of her. Brewer would talk about his client and could explain the special verdict form the jury would have to fill out.

The situation with my partners was another matter. A closing argument is a piecing together of all the individual tiles of a case into a revealing mosaic. A trial is an awkward process, with bits and pieces of evidence coming together, then being put aside as others are introduced. Although we had presented our case in a logical, coherent order, it doesn't always happen that a jury understands why the pieces are there. It is our job to put those pieces in place and complete the picture. I wanted to do it, felt strongly that I should. However, Tom knew the science better than I and had been a commanding figure when presenting it during the trial. I asked him to handle that part in the rebuttal closing. Asking everyone else for their help and input, I then set about the task of constructing the close.

How to open? I wanted to attack. An all-out assault on his celebrity, his image, his credibility. Everyone agreed. We certainly had done this during the course of the trial; now we had to bring the point forcefully home. After that, all we had to do was review the facts. I asked everyone for memos on the areas they covered.

Peter Gelblum and I worked out the structure for the argument much as we had worked out the Simpson examination. We also designed several additional exhibit boards. A closing argument is a dog-and-pony show, and you want to use as many exhibits as possible to break up the monotony.

The DoubleTree was overflowing with media. If we lost, the gag rule would die with the verdict; if we won, it would be extinguished with the end of the trial's second stage, for the punitive damages. All the top interviewers sent their producers to get an exclusive, and these producers were very good at their job. Friendly, ingratiating without being too sickening or sycophantic, they shot the breeze around the Gag-Free Zone at Happy Hour and were fun to be with. Who wouldn't like to hear, "You guys have done a fabulous job," "You should have handled the criminal case," and "O.J. is so guilty, it's unbelievable"? It was pretty heady stuff.

Dateline producer Libby Rager tried to convince me to do my first posttrial interview with Stone Phillips, and I sat there saying, "I don't know if we're going to win this case."

"Win or lose, you're going to have to talk about it."

I hadn't thought of it that way. If I lost, I figured I would simply hibernate for the rest of my life.

At that moment, however, hibernation was not a possibility. The phones never stopped ringing.

I dictated the first fifteen minutes of my closing argument into a tape machine, then reworked and reworked and reworked it until it was more than memorized, it was ingrained. Beyond that, I had talking points. Like Fred Goldman before his appearance on the witness stand, I didn't want to sound rehearsed, so I *didn't* rehearse. I didn't have to. By this time I was oozing this case out of every pore.

People were contributing phrases. Arthur Groman wanted to know, "What kind of man would say cheating on his wife is not a lie?" Tom told me, "You should say, 'There's a killer in the courtroom. There is a murderer amongst us.'" I wasn't so sure about the last sentence, but the first stuck with me.

I worked four straight days organizing. Which points were worth making, which were not? What should go first, what should follow? Words seemed inadequate to describe how I felt. All the anger, the frustration, the hurt, pain, and anguish I felt for my client and his family; all the roadblocks, the deceit, the lies; the memory of Simpson leaving the courtroom to a hero's welcome, laughing at America, having beaten the system in front of their eyes—all of that welled up inside, and I felt a rage of my own. I had to find an acceptable way, short of using a knife, to get it out.

I felt responsible. The truth was that O.J. Simpson was a killer, and it was my personal responsibility to make the jury see that truth and act on it. I knew our case, and I knew we were right. In any moment of anxiety or upset or weakness, I could always lean on the trunk of that certainty. It was my job to gather the jury under its shade as well.

Peter Gelblum and I constructed the final master closing argument outline. The whole case lay in our computer and between the covers of my notebook, which I carried with me everywhere as if it were an illuminated manuscript.

Tuesday morning I ate breakfast at the DoubleTree, got my mints, gathered the troops, and headed over. "Let's rock and roll!"

The walk to the courthouse was an even more tumultuous mob scene than the one before I examined Simpson. I thought I had seen the top of the meter, but this busted the needle. I was happy to get inside.

"Judge, I want to take up some matters, if it please the court."

"It doesn't, but go ahead." A rare joke from Fujisaki.

Before I could address the jury, we made the trial all or nothing by dropping our claim of negligence. The jury now had to find that Simpson had acted intentionally or had not acted at all. (In that way the judgment would be bankruptcy-proof; a verdict of negligence was dischargeable, a verdict of intentional misconduct requires that the judgment be paid.)

The jury filed in, serious, dignified as usual. I looked at them, one by one. They had given up a substantial portion of their lives to this case, and I thanked them for their sacrifice and commitment. I wanted them to know that we appreciated them. Then, I began.

"We are here to determine responsibility for the deaths of Ronald Goldman and Nicole Brown Simpson." Immediately: responsibility. "Two vital people who had most of their lives ahead of them. Here they are in life." This was not some intellectual pursuit, this was not a national referendum on race or an examination of the judicial system; this was a trial to determine who was responsible for killing Ron and Nicole. I put up Ron's picture, holding a baseball bat, Fred's favorite. He looked as though he were having fun, he looked so alive.

"Today, Ron Goldman would have been twenty-nine years old, and I think he would have had that restaurant that he wanted to open, shaped in the design of the ankh, the Egyptian symbol for eternal life, which Ron always wore around his neck and even had tattooed on his shoulder."

I put Nicole's picture on the ELMO. It was taken June 7. On the witness stand, her mother had remarked how beautiful she looked in that picture. "On a day not unlike today, I think she would have, like she did every day, gotten up and taken care of her children, fed them, taken them to school, karate lessons, dance lessons, brought them home, fed them dinner, played with them, put them to bed."

I chose something important to each: Ron's restaurant, Nicole's kids. "Ron Goldman will never get to open his restaurant, ladies and gentlemen, and Nicole Brown Simpson will never see her children grow up because on a Sunday evening in 1994 these two vital people, their lives came to a sudden end in a few moments of uncontrollable rage."

I had constructed the opening phrases very carefully. For instance, "a few moments," not a long struggle.

"Here they are in death." The contrast between the two attractive young people and the bloody, crumpled bodies was stark. "I apologize for the photograph.

"Nicole, as you can imagine, was helpless at the hands of this enraged man, and she died within moments of the gaping cut to her throat. Ron Goldman, instead of running from danger, tried to help a friend. But he, too, was defenseless against this powerful man with a six-inch knife, stabbing over and over and over again until Ron collapsed to the ground and died with his eyes still open."

It was important to me, because I knew it was so important to Fred, to emphasize that Ron could have run but didn't; he died helping someone.

"Now, had Ron lived, ladies and gentlemen, he'd have been on *this* witness stand"—I smacked the railing—"and he would have relived what happened that night, and he would have told us what he saw.

"But that is why Ron Goldman was killed. So he could not tell you what he saw that evening." The contrast between what he would have seen and his open eyes at death could not have been lost on the jury.

"But even though Ron's and Nicole's voices will not be heard in this courtroom—they will not be on that stand—their last struggling moments to stay alive, ladies and gentlemen, provided us the key evidence to identify their killer. They managed to get a glove pulled off, a hat to drop off, they managed to dig nails into the left hand of this man, cause other injuries to his hand, forcing him to drop his blood next to their bodies as he tried to get away."

I was careful throughout the argument never to commit to any specific, precise version of how this happened. I didn't say who pulled off the glove or how the hat dropped. I didn't have to.

"And by their blood, they forced him to step, step, step"—I just began stepping: I hadn't planned to, but I picked up my feet gingerly; you could almost hear the wet blood sticking to my soles—"as he walked to the back, leaving shoe prints that are just like fingerprints in this case, that tell us who did this, who did this unspeakable tragedy.

"So these crucial pieces of evidence, after all, are the voices of Ron and Nicole speaking to us from their graves"—I was speaking loudly and forcefully, not from memory, but from conviction—"telling us, telling *all of you*"—I made a circle around the jury with my finger and then pointed directly at Simpson—"that there is a *killer in the courtroom!*" I was shouting.

Simpson hadn't been watching. To deal with his anxiety, he appeared to be scribbling furiously on a notepad. The courtroom was deathly silent. When I raised my voice and then paused, he looked up startled, a "Who, me?" expression crossing his face. He realized everyone was looking at him, and he puffed up his cheeks, as he had done in so many other embarrassing moments when he had no answers on the witness stand. I was still pointing at him.

"*That* is the man who attacked them"—I stared at him eye to eye; this time he could not avoid me—"who confronted them, and who *killed* them on that Sunday evening in June. The defendant, Orenthal Simpson." The "James" didn't slip out this time.

I had made my segue from the victims to the killer. "You heard his voice on the witness stand." Contrasted with their voices, which we would not hear.

"We did not merely prove that he did these things by a preponderance of the evidence, which . . . is the burden of proof that we have to meet in this case. We didn't prove it merely by clear and convincing evidence, which is yet another burden of proof. We didn't prove it merely by proof beyond a reasonable doubt, which is the standard of proof that applies in criminal cases.

"We proved it to a certainty."

Why was I creating such elevated standards? Why make things difficult?

First of all, I was careful; I told the jury that we had proved the case beyond the standards of this court. But more than that, I didn't want them to think we thought there was any question at all. Chris Darden, in his apologetic closing argument, had said, "We hope we presented the best evidence we could. And if we didn't present the best evidence we could, don't hold that against us." No wonder he lost. I wanted the jury to know we were working from *absolute* certainty and that we intended to win.

I moved to a series of rhetorical questions. "What did his fine lawyer, Mr. Baker, ask him about? Did Mr. Simpson explain why his blood and his DNA were found dripped on the ground near the two victims? Did he talk about that? Did he explain why his glove was found next to these two murdered people? Did he explain that? Did he explain why his other glove was found back at his house? Did he explain that?!" The approach worked two ways: I was reviewing key evidence and at the same time pointing out that he hadn't spoken when he'd had the opportunity.

"*Did he explain why his hat, his knit cap, was at the murder scene? Why it had his head hairs in it? Why it had his clothing fibers? Did he explain it? Did he explain any of that?*" It's fair to say I was yelling these things. "*Not one word!*

". . . Did he say anything about the thirty photographs, *over* thirty photographs, in fact, of him wearing those 'ugly-ass' Bruno Magli shoes that he swore to you, under oath on that witness stand"—I was pounding on the stand by now—"that he never owned and never wore? Did he talk abut those photos?

"No, he didn't!"

I was transported. Everything I hated about the man fueled me. Still, I was working toward a goal.

"Did he explain to you how he could cut himself the night of the murders *between ten and eleven times*," I said incredulously, "at the time these murders occurred, on his left finger, and yet not know how? 'I don't know how I cut myself.'" I mocked him. "Did he even talk about that? Did he explain to you how he could cut himself so badly in Chicago—he claims so bad as to leave a permanent scar on that finger—and yet not know how he did it? Did he talk about that?"

The jury's eyes followed me as I walked, but they themselves were taut. To involve them, I asked them a question.

"What did he choose to say?" I paused, then wagged my head like Simpson and spoke like Ronald Reagan: "'Well . . .'

"He talked about his accomplishments as a football player. How he won the Heisman Trophy." If that was part of their closing, I figured I would trump it immediately. "He talked and talked and talked about golf. A lot about golf. And he went to great lengths, ladies and gentlemen, to talk about his character. . . . We heard about how he always tries to help others. We heard that he still goes to his mother for advice. And then he talked of his honesty, and he told us, looking you straight in the eye, right here"—I brought his duplicity to within three feet of them—"and said, 'I have never, ever *attempted* to tell a lie about anything important in my life.'

". . . These are the things Mr. Baker asked him about, and these are the things he spoke about." I wanted to bring Baker into the condemnation as well. If the jury liked Baker, they might vote for Simpson, so Baker was in on this, too.

"The bottom line here, ladies and gentlemen, is that they would like you to believe that that handsome man with the charming smile, the expensive suit, who's lived the life of fame, celebrity, and fortune, and who claims to be dedicated to his family, flawless in character, incapable of telling a lie—that that man could not possibly be responsible for the deaths of Nicole Brown Simpson and Ronald Goldman." That was the thrust of his case: *It can't be me, I'm O.J.*

"He'll talk about responsibility. . . ."

On the large television screen appeared the picture of a beaten Nicole. "What kind of man, ladies and gentlemen, confronted with this bruised and battered picture of Nicole, says, 'I take full responsibility for causing all those injuries, but I didn't hit her, I didn't strike her, I didn't slap her, I didn't do anything wrong'?" I started strong.

"What kind of man, who has shared a bedroom with his wife for ten years, calls it *my* bedroom, *my* house, *my* property, *me?*

"What kind of man takes a baseball bat to his wife's car, right in front of her, and then says . . . he was not in a state of rage and she wasn't upset at all, not the slightest, even though she went to call the police for help?

"What kind of man"—Arthur Groman's phrase was in his face like a jab—"kicks open a door so hard as to break it in pieces and then . . . actually went on to blame it on his kids?

"What kind of man says his deceased wife's voice on a 911 tape . . . is lying when she says she's afraid and when she says that he's going to 'beat the shit out of me,' to use her words. What kind of man says his deceased wife is *lying,* when you heard her voice trembling on that tape?"

I was bellowing.

"What kind of man says *cheating on your wife isn't a lie,* which is what he said!

"What kind of man says that his wife's most private writings about her feelings . . . in fact, her last written words . . . are a, quote, *pack of lies?*"

I paused to let the words sink in.

"What kind of man comes into court and looks you straight in the eye and says, 'I never lied about anything important in my life,' and then lied about everything important in this case?

"Well, let me tell you what kind of man says those things." I looked straight at him. "A guilty man. A *guilty* man! A man with no remorse. A man with no conscience." No one in the room was moving except Simpson. He was scribbling on his notepad while Baker sat, arms crossed, head tilted to one side as if just biding his time. I felt as if I were swinging a club.

"This man is so obsessed with trying to salvage his image and protect himself that he'll come into the courtroom, knowing the whole world is watching, and he will smear the name and reputation of the mother of his children while she rests in her grave. This is a man, ladies and gentlemen, who I submit to you has lied and lied and lied to you about every important fact in this case." I stopped.

"Every one."

I felt in total command of the courtroom. I felt in total command of what I was saying, and what I was saying was true; there was no greater feeling. I kept pounding him.

"O.J. Simpson has been marketing, manufacturing, packaging, and selling his image to the American public for over thirty years. And you know what they tried to do in this courtroom, he and his defense team? To sell you an image: 'O.J.,' 'Juice,' an image, a personality. I even asked him, 'Are you an actor?' He says, no, 'I'm a personality.'

"We are not here, though, in this important trial, to be sold anything. And we're not here to talk about 'O.J.' and 'Juice' and talk about images. We're here to talk about a man named Simpson. A deeply flawed man named Simpson, and what he did on June 12, 1994."

I began to review the evidence. No burglary, no vandalism, no sexual assault; there was a Ferrari in the garage and jewelry in the house, none of which was touched. The children were upstairs; no one had tried to harm them. We brought out our visual aids and reviewed Bundy. I presented Tom's overview of the blood evidence. "Do you remember when Mr. Lambert read to you something called Defendant's Responses to Request for Admissions? . . . They establish that those blood drops are Mr. Simpson's blood. And you have to accept that. They don't contest it. . . . Mr. Simpson, of course, gave you no explanation how his blood could have gotten there innocently. He had no explanation for why his blood was at Bundy. In fact, he had no explanation for any of this evidence. Nothing." The DNA test range was from 1 in every 170 million people to 1 in every 2.2 billion. The killer was Simpson; the next guy in line was number 2,000,000,001.

On the issue of the Brunos, I would not let Simpson off the hook. They had framed the issue at the beginning of the case; they agreed that the killer wore the shoes. They didn't challenge Bodziak when he stated that the shoes were Bruno Magli Silga sole size twelve; they simply stated that Simpson wasn't wearing them. They had based their defense on decrying the Scull photo as a doctored phony. Baker had said so himself. "So, by his own reasoning," I told the jury, "if that photo is real, O.J.

Simpson is the killer. The shoes are on his feet. That's it. It's the end of the ball game. There's nothing more to talk about.

"Not only that photo. The thirty new photographs of him at that same game; if those photos are real, O.J. Simpson's the killer."

And, of course, they had never addressed the Flammer photos at all. How could they, when one was published in the newspaper seven months before the killings? "It didn't happen. There is no such testimony.

"They can talk all they want about police conspiracies, LAPD frame-ups, all these wild ideas. . . . What are they going to do about this evidence? This doesn't involve the Los Angeles Police Department. What are they going to say? Oh, because they were selling pictures. . . . Everybody in this case has sold something."

Chachi, I could never resist Chachi. "How many witnesses did I have to call to the stand to show that the dog never runs out, this old, lame, arthritic dog. . . . The dog's not going anywhere, the dog's sitting there, and he ain't moving."

Simpson's blood inside the Bronco? How did he get it on the inside notch of the driver's side door handle, when he said he reached in with his right hand to get his cell phone? I'll tell you how: while he was pulling the door shut with his left hand, having climbed in after killing two people. "Why is there *any* blood?" I asked. "Is there any blood in your car that night? My car?

"Now, how does Ron Goldman's blood get in O.J. Simpson's car? Do you really need to ask it over and over again?"

The blood at Rockingham: "They had no blood to plant! So what is his blood doing dripped all over the driveway?"

The bloody glove found at Rockingham, the one that Fuhrman was accused of planting, was one of the most important pieces of evidence in the case because it was filled with so many other pieces of evidence. It had been one of the greatest downfalls of the criminal trial, and I strongly felt the need to drill home the fact that this glove was untainted.

"It's got everything on it, ladies and gentlemen": the victims' hair, Simpson's blood, fibers from his clothing, fibers from his car. "It's a glove that he used to hold the knife in his right hand. . . . And *there's no evidence that that glove was anywhere else, other than the back of Rockingham,* where it was found." It had been tested and found to have Simpson's blood on it in various locations. "Now, that is further absolute proof that this glove could not have been planted, 'cause if this glove was at Bundy, left by another killer, how would it have O.J. Simpson's blood on it?"

When the court took an hour-and-a-half lunch break, the media stampeded to file their stories. I was getting pats on the back from the team, but like the dugout while a pitcher is throwing a no-hitter, the DoubleTree room was crazy-calm; they didn't want to get in my way.

Simpson hated the cuts. He had broken down or gotten extremely agitated every time I had grilled him on them, so after the break I concentrated hard on what I knew was a sensitive area. "They found blood dripped all over his house," I told the jury, "so he had to admit he cut himself." I wanted them to understand why he had told the police it had happened in Los Angeles, before he went to Chicago. Simpson hadn't met Barry Scheck or the distinguished Dr. Henry Lee yet, so when it came time for a cover story he had come up with the obvious answer that would come to a layperson who had never heard of contamination: "Hey, I cut myself." How had he cut himself? "I have no idea, man."

"He was able to hide some of them, by the way," I explained, "between his fingers, which he never showed to anybody. You'll see when he takes the photograph, he keeps his fingers together, and he hid the one inside the fourth finger." Yet in deposition, his good friend and attorney Skip Taft, "testified in crystal-clear terms that he saw the cut on Mr. Simpson's fourth finger that day while he was being interviewed by police.

"By the time he came into court to testify, he knew Mr. Simpson had said he only had one cut, and he knew he had a big problem, so he went to bat for his buddy and lied under oath. That's Skip Taft."

Steve put a picture of Simpson's cut hand on the ELMO and blew it up to life-size. I walked to the monitor. "Even though Mr. Simpson only talks about one cut, there's the second cut there"—I pointed to it—"right there, maybe even a third." I looked at the killer's hand. "Dr. Spitz says these really aren't cuts," I said, turning to the jury, "these are fingernail gouges." I turned back and put my fingers on the screen, the tips right on the marks on Simpson's hand. They fit perfectly. *The last person to put his fingers there was either Ron or Nicole, as they struggled, as they were dying.*

"These are victims trying to unclaw his fingers."

I took the jury through all the physical evidence, I reviewed the chronology of his desperate attempts to win Nicole back, his relationship with Paula, the reconciliation, and the downward spiral when she dumped him. We had made all the arguments during the trial, so mostly I hit the hot spots. I talked for about five hours but had not finished by the close of court that afternoon.

When the team and I exited the side door and began the walk back to the DoubleTree, people were screaming! The phrase "killer in the court-room" had been played on radio and television all day and had immediately entered the Simpson saga lexicon. The media carnival followed us back to the hotel, calling questions I was not permitted to answer.

Back in the room I got nothing but warm hugs from Fred, Patti, and Kim. I wasn't done, so no one wanted to jinx me, but everyone in the room was ecstatic. The Browns came up and said to me, "You really understand." I had spent so much time dealing with their daughter's life, but I had met them only once or twice before. I felt so gratified that they were pleased.

When we turned on the television, the reviews were positive. I was sky-high, so I went to the Gag-Free Zone. In the trial's waning days, I had taken to having an early-evening drink there and smoking a cigar. During the trial, the crowd had consisted of maybe twenty regulars, but now there had to be close to a hundred people bellying up to the bar and sprawling into the corner tables. Everyone was bad-mouthing the competition and hitting me up for the first interview. It was overwhelming. Thrilling and ego gratifying, but also a little scary.

It was all I could do to get to sleep that night.

The next morning, when court opened, the place was so full that other judges and their wives were standing against the wall in back of the gallery. I said, "Thank you, Your Honor. I will be concluding this morning in about an hour or so."

"You said an hour at four yesterday." Fujisaki never let up.

I continued reminding the jury of the devastating witnesses we had presented. "Now comes another big lie: Mr. Simpson tells us with a straight face he never picked up that message from Paula. . . . But we *know* he picked it up. We know from at least three places." I moved on to the recital, the conversation with Ron Fischman, the conversation in which he told Kato that Nicole was playing hardball, his phone call to Nicole at nine that night.

"He said, 'Can I speak to Sydney, is she asleep?' or words to that effect. Sydney takes the phone. He hangs up after he speaks to his daughter, and that's the end of the call. That's what he says. There's nobody here to contradict that.

"But . . . that doesn't sound like things are all too well. How about, 'How was your dinner?' . . . 'How was the family?' . . . 'Wasn't that recital wonderful?' . . . Wouldn't that be normal conversation? Mr. Simpson will probably never tell us what happened in that conversation, nor will he ever tell us what happened in the next hour and a half. But I tell you, ladies and gentlemen, and there's absolutely no question about this: The next time he saw Nicole Brown Simpson after he hung up that phone, he had a knife to her throat. . . .

"Who can imagine the words of hatred, revenge, that he last spoke to her? Who can imagine? Rage. Words of rage.

"In the end, it all comes down to this: There's blood, there's hair, there's fiber, there's cuts, there's sweatsuits, there's hats, there's no alibi, there's plenty of time, and there's motive. And that's on our side. What's on his side?"

I took a long time before answering.

"His word that he didn't do it." I sneered. "His credibility. His truth. That's what's on his side." I looked directly at the jury. "Did he tell the truth to you? He's lied to you about everything important in this case."

We brought out an exhibit board created especially for this moment. "Apart from the physical evidence that tells us he is lying, for him to be innocent and for him to be believed, you have to disbelieve *all* of them." I pointed to the sixty-odd people and documents listed. We had nicknamed this exhibit the "Liars Board."

"Either Simpson is lying or all of these witnesses and documents are either lying or mistaken or faked."

It was an impressive list of witnesses, photographs, and documents that put the lie to O.J. Simpson.

The four-foot-high board was standing to the jury's right. "All these people, all these writings, all these photographs, they either have to be fraudulent, lying, altered, mistaken. Bottom line, they all have to be wrong, and only he is right.

"And here's the man who told you that he never, ever even *attempted* to tell a lie about anything important. A man who wrote in his autobiography, 'I am a pretty effective liar,' and then tried to disavow it.

"His own counselor, Lenore Walker, she's wrong; all those things in her notes, they're wrong.

"Medical records of Nicole's '89 beating: Wrong.

"People who witnessed domestic violence incidents: Wrong.

"GTE telephone records showing he picked up the message: Wrong.

"His good friend, Jackie Cooper, about obsessing about Nicole: Wrong.

"His lawyer, Skip Taft, who saw the cut on his fourth finger the day when he came back from Chicago: Wrong." Taft continued to bother me, so I added, "And then he agreed to lie for Mr. Simpson.

"His lawyer friend of, what, twenty, thirty years, Robert Kardashian: Wrong. Lied. He lied! He lied when he said Simpson asked him to go get the golf clubs. That was a lie."

I had to laugh. "And Orenthal James Simpson, I guess he's got to be a liar, too, because he told us how mistaken he was when he told the police all those things that he now wants to recant. . . . 'I was wrong.' 'I was assuming. . . .'

"This is just a good illustration of how a liar gets trapped in his lies." We then brought out the Bruno board—an impressive display of the thirty Flammer photos, plus the Scull photo, showing Simpson in the Bruno Magli shoes. In the center of the board, in a plastic sleeve, was the Buffalo Bills November 1993 newsletter—with the photo of Simpson in the killer's shoes. I then role-played Simpson. "'Hmmm . . . That's a Bruno Magli. That sure looks like me. I was at that game. Those are my clothes. I got it: The picture's a fake, it's a fraud.'" And to authenticate it? "He has the best lawyers in this courtroom. He could have hired the best experts. He brought in a guy named Groden."

Finally it was time to come full circle. I brought my voice down and walked to the end of the counsel's table where Fred was sitting, just a few feet from the jury.

"We're going to talk very, very briefly about my client, Fred Goldman, my client's loss, the loss of his son." I spoke slowly. "I don't need to tell you that there is no amount of money that could ever compensate Fred Goldman for the loss of his son. We cannot put a value on human life. . . . There can never be true justice for Fred Goldman. . . . True justice would be to see Ron Goldman walk through those doors right now"—I pointed to the large wooden doors at the back of the courtroom and looked out there; I could feel in the crowd a strong temptation to follow my lead, but no one actually turned—"or Nicole Brown Simpson, playing with her children. That's true justice.

"That will never happen. They're gone forever. There's nothing I can do, there's nothing you can do, there's nothing this good judge can do, and there's nothing that man can do"—I pointed to Simpson—"to bring these people back.

"All you have in your power to do is bring about some small measure of justice by recognizing the incalculable loss my client has suffered, and to require the man who is *responsible* for this to pay for the loss he caused this man.

"I would like to say a few words about that loss."

I had been pacing. But now I was still. "I think we would agree, whatever your ethnic, racial, cultural background is, there isn't any loss greater than a parent losing a child." I had found a universal bond. "That loss is no less if a child grows into a young man. We don't have to look beyond this courtroom." I turned and looked at Bob Baker and his son, Phil. "In fact, we don't have to look beyond the counsel's table to see the love and the pride that a father has for his grown son. You've seen that right here in this courtroom."

I had been waiting for a year and a half to make that comment. Baker was up front, his son at the kid's table, and neither of them registered an emotion. For one of the few times in the trial, they were hard to read.

"That is the love and pride that Fred Goldman will have only in memory. In memory," I repeated, "in his heart and his soul.

"Ron will never see the beaming look of satisfaction on Fred's face as he might have ushered him through his restaurant. Fred will never sit down with Ron at a Fourth of July picnic or Passover seder, or a birthday party. He will never share the joy of running off to the hospital to see his grandchild. . . . He will never see again the smile on his son's face. He will never see any tears in his eyes."

Fred was having a tough time. I was standing next to him as I faced the jury, my right hand on his shoulder, and he was starting to weep.

"Fred has lost all of that and infinitely more, and his life will never be the same. You can't give him back his son. All you can do is make Mr. Simpson pay for what he did."

We left the amount of compensation to the jury's discretion. It would have been pointless—in fact, offensive—to mention a number; a son is priceless.

We played the bat mitzvah video, this heartbreaking video, and froze the final frame showing Ron and Fred on stage, arms around each other, in celebration. Then we faded to black.

All I could hear in the courtroom were people sobbing.

I had wanted to end with a poem, and Arthur Groman had brought me one. I shared it with the jury.

"There was a sixteenth-century poet named Guillaume du Bartas, who best expressed a relationship between a father and son in a few simple words. Let me read them to you:

> 'My lovely living boy,
> My hope, my happiness,
> My love, my life, my joy.'"

I turned from the jury and looked into my client's eyes.

"Fred Goldman's lovely, living boy is no more."

I walked to my notebook, which was sitting on the lectern, and closed it.

THIRTY-FIVE

Duty Performed or
Duty Violated

In John Kelly's closing, he defended Nicole against the scurrilous attacks made on her by Simpson and his entourage, read important selections from Nicole's diary, and created a dramatic call and response between Simpson's accusations and audiotapes of Nicole herself—the 911 tape, the surreptitious tape—talking about her belief that he would kill her. Kelly's argument picked up the theme of responsibility and was both powerful and effective.

Brewer explained the law concerning battery and wrongful death, talked about the burden of proof, and closed by talking about Ron's mother and the "unbreakable bond" between a mother and son. He closed by reading a poem written for the occasion by Sharon Rufo.

After the lunch break, Baker was the next scheduled speaker, and he was still trying to sneak the specter of Mark Fuhrman into this trial. Before he began his close, I asked to see the exhibits he was going to use. One was called "Missing Witnesses," and among the four names was Fuhrman. I objected. Mark Fuhrman had taken the Fifth; it was improper for Baker to argue that he was missing when he had absented himself. Judge Fujisaki agreed and ordered Fuhrman's name to be removed. It was taped over.

The day before, I had seen Simpson at the counsel table, toying with the murder gloves. The thought occurred to me that Baker, in closing argument, might have him put them on. When we got back from lunch I noticed the gloves in an envelope near the witness stand. I figured Baker was going to try something. Now, there is nothing wrong with using and discussing the gloves in closing argument, but he was not allowed to put them on Simpson. He had not put them on Simpson during the trial, and the time for evidence was over. I didn't want to object in front of the jury and appear to be concerned that they would not fit—I didn't want to hear the "fit/acquit" rhyme in this courtroom—so I asked for a ruling before they were led in. Baker, insistent as always, said, "I will put them on Mr. Simpson during my final argument." Whether he actually intended to do so or was simply pulling my chain, I don't know. In any case, Judge Fujisaki didn't let him.

"It's demonstrative!" cried Baker.

"That's called demonstrative *evidence*," said the judge. "Sustained."

Baker was battling the flu but couldn't fight through it. That told me a lot about his convictions for his client and his case. He didn't appear to have the spirit or passion to fight through it.

"Now, any one of us, all the people in the gallery," Baker said in his closing statement, "can go down to the first floor of this building, and for about two hundred dollars, file a lawsuit. And they can charge somebody else, another human being, or a corporation, with malfeasance, doing something wrong, and seek to collect hundreds of thousands of dollars, or millions of dollars. That's an enormous privilege we have as citizens and noncitizens in this country."

I thought that was an outrageous statement. Maybe that works against ambulance chasers trying to collect on a sprained neck, but it had nothing to do with us. The idea that he would reduce our case to $200 was offensive.

Baker appeared scattered. He launched into a rambling argument about how we put on our witnesses for very limited purposes and, therefore, were trying to hide the truth. He didn't seem to have a cohesive game plan at all. This was not the confident, assertive, persuasive lawyer who had powered through jury selection and opening arguments four months before.

He tried to convince the jury we had not met our burden of proof. I expected Simpson's advocate to get up and say, "He is absolutely innocent, and he didn't do this, and I don't care what the burden of proof is!" Maybe he couldn't make that argument with a straight face. No matter, he was not advancing the ball.

He argued for nullification. "There are, ladies and gentlemen, an immense amount of people who want to see my client found responsible. They want to see you render a verdict that Mr. Simpson killed Nicole Brown Simpson and Ron Goldman. And I'm not just including the plaintiffs, I'm including those people on either side. I'm including the media. Because, ladies and gentlemen, if in fact you find him not responsible, the gravy train is over."

Then, almost out of nowhere, Baker said, "You have just been subjected to a ploy for your sympathy. You know, I was kind of amazed that Mr. Petrocelli had to bring up myself and my son." Clearly the scene had bothered him, but what was he amazed about? My point was that a father loves his son, very much a core issue in this trial. Baker was angry, but I didn't know what he would do with it.

"I can tell you this," he said, "I would have a terrible time if I lost him. But I wouldn't ever take four hundred and fifty thousand dollars for a book. I wouldn't ever prosecute an innocent man."

Here we go. Goldman: greedy, money-hungry man of gold. This was two references to money in the span of ten minutes.

"I think that you have gotten the flavor of this case over the four months. It's law enforcement versus O.J. Simpson. There's no doubt about it, they're linked at the hip, or any other place you want to join them." He accused the FBI and LAPD of giving away "thousands upon thousands of dollars of their services. For what? To assist a private litigant. To assist Mr. Goldman in getting a judgment against my client." There were many parties, not simply Fred Goldman. "This isn't a fight for justice," he said, "it's a fight for money."

Baker went on to make a massive attack asserting that the FBI and the police were all biased because they were assisting in presenting our case, again trying to appeal to the jury on some emotional ground that there is a grand conspiracy to "do in" O.J. He still had not explained one single piece of damning evidence.

Baker attacked the motive case. Rage? What rage? It was the area in which Simpson could lie with the most impunity. "Did he hit her? No!"

When he reached Paula's "Dear John" message Baker said, "Did he pick up the message that she had broken up with him? . . . *I don't know. It's not a significant thing.*"

He did not know? His client had said *adamantly* that he did not pick up the message. Not even Baker believed him! He was telling the jury, "I don't believe Simpson"! What do you mean, you don't know? You *can't* say you don't know! Tell the jury what you really mean: *Even though my client has told you, under oath, over and over and over again that he didn't pick it up, I don't know, maybe he did!*

I don't like sitting and listening to other lawyers making their arguments against me. I can't stand it, and going into the day's session, I'd thought I would have to be sedated just to listen to Baker. But as he moved along, I told my partners, "So far, I'm not seeing anything." I never did.

Bob Blasier performed his part of the closing from a wheelchair because he had had serious back surgery in December. He handled the science arguments, the contamination theorizing, the length of struggle, in almost identical manner as the criminal defense and was on the wrong side of the Baden/Spitz mismatch. He talked in a monotone, and I felt we had clearly overcome the force of his arguments, but the jury was taking notes. Lots of notes! Why were they doing that? Tom told me uneasily, "They didn't take this many notes during your argument."

We began to fret that the jury was taking his points to heart, so we concentrated on preparing rebuttals for all the moments in his closing during which notes were taken. Tom was ready to pounce on him.

Dan Leonard rose for the defense. "If it please the court, brother Counsel, ladies and gentlemen of the jury: Good afternoon." I kind of liked that "brother" business, which he brought with him from Boston. He was there, lacking decent expert testimony, to undermine the photographic testimony. "Common sense," he said, "will tell you that these are photographs that come too late and cost too much." But rather than examine the photographs, he questioned the fact that no one had located the salesperson who sold the Bruno Magli shoes to Simpson. From lack of a salesperson he leapt to the conclusion that Simpson never owned the shoes.

Money was another of his recurring themes. "Money makes the world go around. Money spins the globe. People kill each other over money. . . . Money makes people do a lot of things. . . . Money. Is that what this is all about? Is that what this evidence is all about, store-bought evidence, evidence with a price list?" He professed taking offense that

Flammer's pictures were being sold, but he could not dispute their authenticity. He never tried.

After court I told him, "Well, Dan, you took a hit for the team." He just shrugged, as usual.

After a three-day weekend off, Baker came back to finish the defense's closing. He was still fighting the flu but appeared stronger. He tried one last time to play the "Fuhrman" card. "There's one man that wants to be, more than anybody, the linchpin of that case, and that's somebody who you've, I'm sure, now felt there has been an effort to keep out of this trial: Mark Fuhrman."

"Objection!"

"Sustained." The court had given a direct order that this was impermissible because Fuhrman had taken the Fifth. "Jury to disregard that comment."

"In bad faith," I added. "And he knows better."

"I know the truth," Baker grandstanded.

"You know better," I told him.

Nonetheless, Baker would not stop. "The rogue Fuhrman . . ." "Fuhrman climbs the wall . . ." "And we didn't have the benefit of Fuhrman's testimony here." Objection. Sustained. He kept going.

Baker was desperate. He stated in open court that there was an answering machine tape of Simpson's 10:03 call to Paula. There was absolutely no evidence of such a tape, and he knew it. "Your Honor"—I was furious and barked out loudly—"make him point to the evidence where there's such a tape!" The judge called us to the bench, but Baker spoke plenty loud enough to be heard by the jury.

"There was a tape made by Paula Barbieri's answering machine. It was analyzed by the LAPD . . ." The judge asked the jury to step into the hallway.

"They are trying to imply to the jury that there was a tape," I complained, "that the police looked at it, they analyzed it, and they determined that the call didn't come from the cell phone. That's exactly what he's arguing. I want this jury admonished!"

Baker: "Oh, be quiet."

"If there was such a tape, I'd be all over that tape and I'd bring it into court, Your Honor. . . . I want this jury admonished!"

These were the types of battles Judge Fujisaki had been successful in avoiding throughout the trial. But Baker was pulling out all the stops now. Fujisaki agreed with me and told the jury there was no such tape in evidence.

"There's no evidence," Baker continued to the jury, "but the imagination of Mr. Petrocelli that O.J. Simpson was in his Bronco at 10:03, driving the vehicle."

They were so desperate, they were making up evidence. They were cheating. And it got worse.

"Mr. Petrocelli got up here and told you in a very emotional appeal that Ron Goldman would probably be opening his restaurant now, and he would be going into that restaurant. Let's examine reality.

"Fred Goldman, for reasons that he called 'tough love,' didn't help his son, and he had to go through bankruptcy. Ron Goldman wouldn't have a restaurant now. He'd be lucky to have a credit card."

I was stunned. It was a shameful thing to say, particularly with the young man's father in the room. It was unnecessary, pointless, ugly. I stewed but said nothing for the moment. Baker closed not long thereafter.

"You can't give Ron Goldman's life back, but you can give back Mr. Simpson *his* life," he said, "and give Justin and Sydney their dad back. Thank you very much."

The plaintiff has a tremendous advantage in getting the last word. Their entire case? "Ladies and gentlemen," I told the jury, "it's a fraud. It's a fraud on you. It's a big lie." I laid out the evidence one more time, this time even more heatedly than before. There was no doubt. Baker had pulled out Johnnie Cochran's old saw, "If you can't trust the messenger, you can't trust the message." I said, "If there is a messenger in this case you cannot trust, it is O.J. Simpson."

I turned the podium over to Tom Lambert, who went into a point-by-point refutation of everything Bob Blasier had presented, particularly the material on which the jury had taken copious notes: the blood evidence, hair-and-fiber evidence, the sock, the Bronco blood collection. Having shown how none of the evidence could have been planted, he then destroyed the contamination argument. In the end, there was nothing left.

Finally, I had the last word. I picked off their arguments one by one—among them, that professional hit men killed Ron and Nicole. "Is a professional assassin going to leave all that evidence behind? Is a guy who's in the business of killing people, does he leave all of his blood? Does he leave his hat? Does he leave his glove? Does he leave all the evidence *on* the glove?"

Baden's theory of two killers? There was no blood, hair, clothing, or other evidence of a second killer. There was only O.J. Simpson's evidence.

Frame-up by the LAPD? He was their darling. I played the 1993 tape of the cops responding at Gretna Green: "Because of your celebrity status, we are going to keep this as small as possible." "That describes the relationship of the Los Angeles Police Department towards O.J. Simpson," I told the jury. "They treated him like gold."

Finally, I came to Simpson himself. "It doesn't make a difference to him how many witnesses we bring in here," I said. "And it doesn't make a difference to him how many of his lies we expose. None of this matters to him because this man has no sense of responsibility. . . .

"Mr. Baker says, 'We're not here to talk about responsibility, we're here to talk about money.'" I was ready to go after him now. "I was amazed yesterday to hear him say"—and I mocked his angry tone—"'Ron Goldman, he wouldn't have a restaurant now. *He'd be lucky to have a credit card.*' Let me explain something, just in case you're confused.

"We're not seeking any damages for Ron Goldman's earnings. We're not seeking any damages for how successful his restaurant would have been. . . . Whether Ron Goldman had a successful restaurant or not has nothing to do with this case. *We ask that you determine who his killer is,* and we ask that you award damages for this man's loss." I pointed to Fred, sitting nearby. "His life will never be the same."

I looked across at the defense table. "Mr. Baker got up here—in one of the lowest moments of this trial—and he *mocked* this young man who lies in his grave." Baker looked at me, showing nothing.

"Now, I want you to think about this." I paused. "If O.J. Simpson were innocent—*truly* innocent—would he let his lawyer mock this young man? This young man tried to save the life of the mother of his children. He is a *hero* to O.J. Simpson." Who knows, if Ron had not come by, maybe the "real killer" would have murdered his children as well. "Only a *guilty* man has his lawyers stand up there and disparage this person, and disparage his loss, and cheapen his loss. And Mr. Baker has the *nerve* to tell you it only costs two hundred dollars to file a lawsuit. Can you imagine that?"

I turned toward Baker and then the jury. "He is right." Was I actually conceding a point? No. "It costs two hundred dollars to file a lawsuit. Is that what he thinks this is about?" I glared at him. "It's not about Mr. Simpson's blood or his gloves or hat and shoes and all the other evidence? It's not about any of that? It's about the fact that Mr. Goldman has two hundred dollars to file a lawsuit?" I was pouring out my outrage.

"And in their zeal to get your verdict, have they become so insensitive to the greatest of human tragedies, the loss of life, that they want to speak about these two dead people in terms of two hundred dollars? *My stomach turned when I heard that!*" I wheeled toward Simpson, put my left hand in my pants pocket, and pulled out all the bills I had.

"You know, Mr. Simpson"—and I yelled as loudly as I could—"*here's two hundred dollars!* You want it?" Simpson looked up, bug-eyed and startled. I shifted the cash to my right hand and pointed it in the direction of his face. *"Give me back my client's son!"*

"Give it up!" screamed Baker.

"They want this verdict that bad, take it! Give my client back his son and we will march out of here in a heartbeat!" I turned back to the jury.

"Enough is enough!" It was me and them again. "The time has come to put this to rest. Two people lost their lives. They deserve their due. They deserve their final peace. *Their lives matter; their lives counted!* And *that* man"—I pointed—"who *took* their lives, should be held accountable!"

"That's not the law, Your Honor," shouted Baker, all of a sudden a purist. "That's not why we're here."

"Overruled."

I had been looking for a quotation that spoke to a jury's responsibility, and Arthur Groman had again proved eloquently indispensable. "The great American lawyer Daniel Webster," I told the jury, "over one hundred and fifty years ago, addressed a jury just like this one in a case involving murder. Just like this one," I repeated. "And he spoke of your duty, and he said: 'Absence of duty pursues us forever. If we take to ourselves the wings of the morning, and dwell in the uttermost parts of the sea, duty performed or duty violated is still with us, for our happiness, for our misery.'

"Ladies and gentlemen, your sense of duty performed or duty violated will be with you forever. And I have no doubt you will perform your duty. I have no doubt that you will do justice.

"Thank you."

I closed my notebook for good.

THIRTY-SIX

Responsibility

In charging the jury, Judge Fujisaki instructed them they were not bound by the criminal jury's verdict and explained that the double jeopardy clause of the Constitution does not prohibit a civil case being brought by the victims' families. Similarly, he said the verdict in the custody case had nothing to do with ours. Then the jury went to deliberate, the judge retired to his chambers, Simpson and the defense packed up and left, most of the media buzzed off, Fred went home. I stuck around.

I could not leave the courtroom. I sat there trying to figure out what to do. There was nothing more to read, no one else to talk to, no alternate avenues of attack to explore. It was excruciating; I did not realize how painful the waiting would be.

I came back the next day, Wednesday, with Kelly and a couple of others, and we just hung out. We saw the jurors going to and from the jury room on breaks. They saw us, but they didn't see the defense lawyers, because the defense didn't show up. When one of their lawyers called and found we were there, they passed a message to the clerk, who passed it to the judge, who threw us out of the courtroom and locked the door.

I went back to the DoubleTree and collapsed. I'd had a 101-degree temperature for the past three days but hadn't known it. The flu was spreading all over the city, and now I was worried that the jurors would come down with it and be forced to drop out during deliberations. Ed had stayed in his office, Peter had gone back to prepare for the punitive damage phase, but Tom, the ultimate team player, stayed and pumped me full of orange juice and companionship.

By midday Wednesday, I was nuts. "What the hell is taking them so long? Why haven't they just decided?" I wasn't rational. The criminal jury had been scorned for deciding a nine-month trial in no time at all. It was good that this jury was being deliberate.

They wanted a read-back of testimony regarding cross-hybridization or contamination of DNA. We piled back into the courtroom. At this point we found out that Juror #12 was the foreman. (Arthur Groman and Tom won the betting pool. He'd been my second choice.) We started reading tea leaves. "Why do they want such arcane technical matter? Does that help us? Is that a good sign? A bad sign? Tom, what are they doing?" He told me they were just trying to be careful and thorough. That didn't pacify me very much. I was just torturing myself. The media, of course, were doing this in spades.

Another read-back, this time for a whole stack of material. In my flu-ridden stupor, this was the worst thing I had ever experienced. Everything was getting away from me. During the trial, I was in control; there was another question to ask, another witness to put on, another argument to make. But now it was over, there was nothing I could do. I was utterly helpless and hopeless.

The Goldmans, to their credit, went on with their other responsibilities. Kim went back to work, Fred and Patti had things to do; they left numbers for us to call them whenever there was a development.

I was achy, chilled, sore, feverish. Finally Tom said, "You should go home. We'll call you."

"I'm not going home, I can't go home, I'll be wasted at home." Friends were knocking on the DoubleTree door, and I finally had the chance to talk to them; media folks, who had become part of the family, were coming in and asking questions.

At night, feverish, propped up on a pillow, I would watch the pundits speculating on TV and scream at them. By the end of Thursday I was really struggling.

We came in Friday, and Erin Kenney, the judge's efficient clerk, called. "Mr. P., the judge needs to see everyone."

Oh, no. "Don't tell me it's a juror problem." I could tell by the tone in her voice.

The judge had gotten a letter from the district attorney's office. Juror #7's daughter worked for the DA's office and knew Christopher Darden, and Juror #7 had not disclosed this. Clearly, it was an oversight. Judge Fujisaki said, "We have a problem now." Baker wanted a mistrial. The judge decided to dismiss the juror, replace her with an alternate. After already having deliberated for two and a half days, a replacement juror was selected and the jury was instructed to begin all over again. Juror #7 had been the only black woman on the panel; her replacement was a young Asian man.

Juror #7's name turned out to be Rosemary Caraway. *Hard Copy* called to say she was going on their show that night. That was the last thing I needed, a juror going on the air to discuss deliberations that were still in progress. The media was descending on her. I heard they were following her home in helicopters, trying to get interviews. The whole thing was unraveling. I got her number from the court and called her myself; she had been discharged, this was legal. Her daughter answered. I pleaded that her mother *not* go on the air, that the entire case was in her hands. The daughter said, "My mother's not going on television! I'm tired of all these media around my house. Why don't they leave us alone? We want our privacy!" *Boom,* she hung up the phone. Ms. Caraway did not appear on TV.

Meanwhile the judge informed us that two criminal trial jurors, Brenda Moran and Gina Rossborough, had tried to contact two jurors on our case—one by letter, the other by phone—advising them to contact their agent for posttrial representation. I do not know how the addresses and phone numbers of our jurors got out—it was extremely private information, sealed by the court and illegal for attorneys to be involved in their dissemination—but again the process was threatened.

Again the defense called for an investigation and a mistrial. "This is an absolute outrage!" I told the judge. "O.J. Simpson's criminal jurors, who went and attended a victory party after the criminal trial, they're contacting our jurors *and the defense lawyers are trying to get a mistrial!* What's going on here?"

On his own, without telling us, Judge Fujisaki brought in the sheriff's department. I was watching on TV as the sheriffs, late at night, were hauling computer equipment out of Brenda Moran's house. Fujisaki was something else.

The judge interviewed all the jurors individually, then kept the two jurors on the panel and ordered the entire jury to turn off everything: TV, answering machine; don't look at your mail. He wanted them self-sequestered.

It didn't stop. Very early in the trial, the judge received a complaint from the sister of Juror #6, stating that the juror had used the word "nigger," didn't like blacks, and shouldn't be on the jury. When he brought in the juror, she had begun to cry. A Hispanic woman, she said her sister hated her because of a dispute over family property, that she herself worked at the post office with many blacks, had nothing against blacks, was not a bigot, and didn't even want to be on this jury. The judge believed her and kept her on. These proceedings had been held in the judge's chambers and the record sealed. Now, four months later with a verdict in reach, this incident got leaked.

I was trying desperately to hold this jury together. I do not know whether the same can be said for the defense.

By Tuesday afternoon, February 5, after deliberating for five days, they asked for a read-back about Al Cowlings jumping the fence in 1989. "I'm outta here," I told Tom. "Who the hell knows what they're thinking? That's got to be the most unimportant fact in the whole case. The State of the Union address is tonight, there's probably going to be a lot of traffic, there's no point in my waiting around, I'm going home."

The phone rang. It was Erin.

"They're back!"

It was about a quarter to four in the afternoon. I figured the judge would review the verdict and read it in the morning. "No," she told me, "he wants it tonight." He didn't want it to leak.

Our place exploded into motion, calls to everyone, "Get here!" I started slapping Tom on the back. "This is it! This is it!" He looked worried. "What?"

"They were just dealing with an issue about this Cowlings thing," he said, "which is a liability issue, just a half hour ago. There's no way they could have decided liability and then done damages." If they were going to vote in our favor, damages should have taken hours to resolve; if they were voting for Simpson, there were no damages and it took no time. It made perfect sense. We'd lost.

"It can't be. It can't be!" I was trying to convince myself. But I refused to believe we had lost.

We needed a sheriff's department escort to get out of our room and down the elevator at the DoubleTree. They cleared the way from the hotel to the courthouse with sheriffs on horseback. The feeling was electric! People were cheering and yelling and screaming louder than ever before. It was getting dark, and the camera lights blazed a trail for us. Walking over, I was trying to take it all in. I kept thinking, I will never experience this again.

In the hall outside the courtroom, I turned and looked out on the grounds. They roiled, like the ocean in a bad storm.

Simpson marched in, and Baker patted him on the back. I had heard that they'd split; they weren't getting along. I saw no evidence of it. When Simpson moved on, I went to Baker. "It's over," I said, extending my hand. "Whatever it is, it is. I've enjoyed working with you, and it's been a real learning experience for me."

Baker raised his chin. "Ah, you guys won hands down. I've been through too many of these, I know when a jury's coming in against me." He looked at me. "They're coming in big, too."

I felt a little better after talking to him. I did not share Tom's analysis with Baker.

During the day, the court bustles with people suing and being sued. Lawyers and judges and court personnel move through the hallways in the rhythms of their own world. But it was after business hours, and no one else was in the building except the Simpson trial players and maintenance personnel. The courthouse air-conditioning system had been turned off, and the place was getting hot.

The Browns were out of town, but Kelly was ducking the clerk's calls: he refused to hear the verdict without his clients being in the courtroom. Good for him. Finally, around seven P.M., they showed up.

Judge Fujisaki entered, sat down, and said, "Bring in the jury."

No smiles, no eye contact, no clues.

The jury had reached a verdict at 3:45 that afternoon. The bailiff, Vicky McKown, handed the sealed envelope to the foreman, Juror #12, who opened it and reviewed the verdict form to make certain it presented the verdict as rendered. Peter Gelblum had typed the three-page form; he knew exactly which and how many boxes had to be checked for us to win, and he watched the juror's eyes. Were they hitting the check marks? If there was a number at the bottom, there were damages and we'd won. If not, we were a loser. Was there a number? The foreman read the form slowly, carefully. His silent reading took several minutes, but Peter couldn't tell.

I couldn't look at all. I was so afraid I would be able to tell the verdict if I saw the foreman's eyes, and I didn't want to know that way. My heartbeat is not something I normally notice, but there it was. And beating hard. Tom, sitting right next to me, drummed his sweaty hands on the table, as he always does when he's anxious. I whispered, "We're going to win because it's the right thing."

The foreman handed the form back to the bailiff, who gave it to the clerk, who gave it to Judge Fujisaki. He looked at every page. No expression. Not a sign.

"Clerk will read the verdict."

With two hands on the form, clerk Erin Kenney read:

"We, the jury . . . find the following special verdict on the question submitted to us:

"Question number one, do you find by a preponderance of the evidence that defendant Simpson willfully and wrongfully caused the death of Ronald Goldman? Write the answer yes or no below.

"Answer: Yes."

I heard a scream. I turned and put my hand on Fred's knee. Fred's face showed pained release. Maybe now he could breathe a little easier.

"Excuse me," said Judge Fujisaki. "*Hold it!* If there's any display, I am going to clear the courtroom."

I looked at Simpson. He wasn't looking at anybody, just studying the ceiling tiles. I looked at the jury and began shaking my head, *Yes!* They acknowledged me, shaking their heads in agreement. They had performed their duty.

Erin proceeded to read the operative question about Nicole: Did O.J. Simpson maliciously assault and attack her?

Answer: Yes.

The judgment was as clear and definite as it could be: He killed her.

Erin read the rest of the verdict. At some point I heard the number $8.5 million. Baker had called it: big.

When the judge polled the jury, we learned the verdict had been unanimous: twelve–zip. That gave us ultimate satisfaction. Unanimous. On all counts. No doubt. Then the tears started.

Back at the DoubleTree there must have been near a hundred people crammed into our small suite. Someone had sent champagne, and we were popping corks and giving toasts to all of us, to Ron and Nicole, to justice. I charged around saying, "We kicked their ass. *We kicked their ass!*"

"Tom, what the hell happened? How did they decide damages so fast?" We never found out.

At about ten that night I drove home to the Valley. By myself. (My wife and son had come in her car.) I noticed when the digital clock said "10:03." I drove slowly. No pressure, no anxiety, completely free for the first time in over a year. Finally a jury had declared the truth of what happened on June 12, and I felt totally vindicated. As a lawyer, you live to deliver results for your client, and there could be no result—or feeling—better than this.

Although this was not a happy occasion for Fred, Kim, and Patti, it was vindication for them, too.

O.J. Simpson is still a free man. He killed two people, yet he will get to enjoy the rest of his life while Ron and Nicole lie in their graves and their families continue to suffer. He will never accept responsibility for having killed them; he has never accepted responsibility for anything in his life. But he will bear it. He can lie all he likes; the truth is, he's a murderer.

THIRTY-SEVEN

The Pursuit of Justice

W e had one final task. We were required by law to prove Simpson's financial condition, to enable the jury to decide how much punitive damages to assess against him.

Although the issue was important, I had great difficulty motivating myself to complete this last phase of the trial. It was anticlimactic. The jury had rendered their verdict: Simpson was a killer. That was what the trial was about, that was what mattered. But as I thought about it more, the other half of the equation also mattered. Simpson deserved to be punished for what he did, society demanded he be punished, and the victims and their families were owed it.

Peter Gelblum presented our evidence of Simpson's financial condition through our expert forensic accountant, Neill Freeman. Freeman combed through Simpson's financial records and concluded he was worth nearly $30 million (pretax). Freeman also quantified how much money Simpson had earned so far as a result of killing two people:

Book (*I Want to Tell You*)	$991,743
Video	303,500
Star Photos	433,693
Interviews	75,300
Autographs/Memorabilia	1,013,900
TOTAL	$2,818,136

Freeman was followed to the stand by Mark Roesler, an expert in the business of celebrity names and likenesses. Roesler estimated Simpson's celebrity value at $25 million, explaining he was worth substantially more because of his notoriety as a famous killer.

Not surprisingly, Simpson did not testify in his own behalf. He didn't even show up. He sent Skip Taft and others to swear to the jury that he was broke. With Taft on the stand, Peter elicited the disturbing fact that one month after the murders Simpson trademarked his name on over five hundred different goods and products, *including cutlery.* O.J. Knives. The man had no shame.

I gave the final argument to the jury. Pointing to Simpson's empty seat in the courtroom, I asked the jury, "Is he here, ladies and gentlemen? You see, he still refuses to accept responsibility. He can't come here and face you, because you are the truth; you have declared that he is a killer, and he can't face you, you, and you," as I pointed to various members of the jurors. "That's why he sent his messenger to tell you that he's broke and he'll never earn a dime again for the rest of his life. I guess he'd like you to believe that he'd be lucky to own a credit card."

I cataloged the evidence of Simpson's wealth and concluded my argument.

"Even though he will not come here and listen to you, you must send him a message. You must send him a message as loud as humanly possible, so that he can hear it on whatever golf course he is hiding out on right now.

"You send him a message with your verdict: You cannot kill two people and get away with it, no matter how much money you have, no matter how many lies you tell."

After deliberating one day, the jury returned a verdict of $25 million in punitive damages against Simpson. As far as I was concerned, he was lucky it wasn't more. The total award was $33.5 million. Small price for killing two people.

When I was a brand-new lawyer starting my practice, I met a big, heavy-set guy with a thick New York accent, named Harold Young. Harold had been one of the New York court system's finest court reporters before moving to Los Angeles, and he brought with him a world of wonderful stories about the uniquely New York trials and cases he had handled. He was many years older than I and was the reporter at one of my first depositions. These are nervous moments for a young attorney, and during a break Harold had pulled me aside and said, "You know, you're going to be a good lawyer. You're really quite good." That a man of his stature and experience had such kind words for me was very important at that time of my life.

As I grew older, I involved Harold in my cases whenever I could. I had used him in the Armand Hammer estate case, my most important one to date, but he had retired by the time I started working on Simpson.

Several years earlier, Harold's family had gone through a terrible tragedy: his son had been murdered. Harold and his wife had been devastated and in their grief had become active in an organization called Parents for Murdered Children.

After the Simpson trial, I got a call from Harold's wife. Harold had died just before our trial. She asked if I would speak at a memorial service being held by the organization. I told her how much Harold had meant to me and said I would be honored.

The service was held on a Sunday, at a hillside chapel in Whittier, California. I was introduced to the large gathering as a man who fought for victims, a "champion of justice." I did not feel worthy of the words.

Ringing the walls were poster-size photographs of children who had been murdered, all different ages, who were being mourned. Murdered children. I knew something about that.

I looked around. It was a mournful sight, all these young lives lost. I talked about Fred Goldman and his courageous fight for justice.

"Justice not so much for him or his family, but for the life of his son. Justice for the lives of all your loved ones. They did not live to die in vain.

"What is important is the pursuit of justice. The pursuit of justice."

ACKNOWLEDGMENTS

I am forever indebted to Mitchell, Silberberg & Knupp for what the law firm has enabled and encouraged me to do throughout my professional career. Their decision to accept and prosecute *Goldman* v. *Simpson* to the highest standards of the profession makes me proud and privileged to practice law with the firm. There are so many people at MSK who contributed to the success of our case. Not just those who worked on the case but all the lawyers and staff who worked hard to take up the slack to give our case the help and resources needed to bring it to fruition. To all of you I owe you a debt of gratitude.

The behind-the-scenes people at MSK were as important as those in the courtroom. Jerry Kaufman, Francine Peterman, and Linda Schwartz-Wright gave us a fully equipped war room at MSK, and a second one for the trial, and in between provided all the administrative and technical support and resources that we could ask for. Many thanks to Joycelyn Furginson and Nadine Wolf for their work in transcribing many of the tapes and documents generated by the lawyers on the team and for their hard work after the trial in helping me with this book. Thanks also to Dante Tibay and his colleagues in the duplicating department that helped us into the wee hours of many mornings.

My dear friend and secretary, Maria Johnson, bore the brunt of the madness and hysteria of the Simpson case, fielding the calls, clues, tips, letters, donations, and the incessant demands of the media and the public, and she handled it with consummate professionalism. Without her, I never could have done my job. After the trial she helped me with the research and preparation for this book. I am deeply indebted to her.

Carolyn Walker was superhuman. She was the commander-in-chief of our trial war room. She took care of everything and everyone, working day and night, seven days a week, always cheerful, always helpful, at great personal sacrifice. She was the glue that held us together, and we never could have made it without her.

Steve Foster was a gift that was too good to be true. He singlehandedly did the work of many people, did it with infectious enthusiasm, and did it better than anyone could have imagined. He was our secret weapon. Steve, hurry up and finish law school and come back to work. A special thanks to Steve's assistant, Joe Lester, for helping out when we needed him.

Yvette Molinaro worked endlessly helping other members of the trial team and took responsibility for important areas of her own. Her energy and enthusiasm kept us going at all times. We would not have gotten very far without the work of Jeff Goldman, Matt Railo, and Michael Tsao. These lawyers worked long days and nights back at the office and their excellent work product made possible the results achieved in the courtroom. Special thanks to Ron DiNicola for his guidance and assistance in raising funds.

Since I started at MSK, I always wanted to try a case with Ed Medvene. Although it took seventeen years, it was worth the wait. His advice, experience, and work were a large part of our success. I will never forget the lessons he has taught me.

Peter Gelblum was like a brother to me. His superb work, his close collaboration with me every step of the way, and his friendship and companionship have given me memories I will treasure forever. Peter, thank you for being there with me.

There is no finer lawyer than Tom Lambert. He has been a role model for me, and I would not be where I am without him. He helped me steer the course and gave me a chance to flourish. His brilliant work was second only to his team spirit.

Arthur Groman has meant more to me than anyone in my professional career. He taught me what it means to be a lawyer. He set the standards and challenged us to exceed them. I will never be able to thank him enough.

I wish to thank Paul Marciano and his brothers, Maurice and Armand, for their loyal support, encouragement, and confidence. Without their help, we would not have been able to get our case off the ground. Special thanks to Susan Tenney, Susan Mock, Sherry Koopman, and all the other people at Guess?, Inc. who put in their own time to help make our case a reality.

Phyllis and Brian Harvey, thank you for having the vision and the desire to do something for someone else. Your generosity and spirit set the example for others.

Bill Hodgman and the Los Angeles District Attorney's Office helped us complete what they started. I am also grateful to the Los Angeles

County Sheriff's Department and Santa Monica City Police Department for their professional and expert assistance in providing security and good cheer for all the trial participants and their friends and family.

MSK enjoyed working with a number of co-counsel on the case: Michael Brewer, Chris Olsen, Nick Hornberger, and Bill Driscoll represented Sharon Rufo. John Kelly, Paul Callan, Natasha Roit, and Ed Horowitz represented the Estate of Nicole Brown Simpson. All the lawyers checked their egos at the door and worked together as a unified team.

I wish to thank Steve Ross, who believed that this story should be told and whose constant enthusiasm and support were vital. Peter Gethers provided superb editorial guidance and was a constant source of calm. I am thankful to all the people at Crown Publishers who had so much confidence in this book and worked so hard to bring it to the public, including Alberto Vitale, Chip Gibson, Andrew Martin, Joan De Mayo, Tina Constable, and Brian Belfiglio. Amy Boorstein, June Bennett-Tantillo, Jane Searle, and Sona Vogel did yeomen's work to bring the manuscript to print under great pressure. Special thanks to Greg Mitchell for his invaluable indexing of my transcriptions.

My deepest appreciation to Len Riggio for giving me the inspiration and courage to write this book. And thanks to Rafe Sagalyn, Rob Lee, Esther Newberg, and Phil Davis for helping to make it happen.

We are grateful to all the people at DecisionQuest for their research, analysis, and graphics work. Don Vinson, Phil Anthony, Steve Patterson, Norma Silverstein, Donna Edmonds, Jane Darcy, and their entire team deserve recognition. Special thanks to Paul Mones for sharing his special skills and talents in helping us to understand domestic violence.

I wish to specially thank Michelle Caruso for her friendship, guidance, and help. She was a constant source of encouragement and confidence.

My deepest gratitude goes out to the family of Nicole Brown Simpson. You have endured with grace and dignity. Thank you for trusting us to tell Nicole's story.

To the millions of people who encouraged and empowered us to pursue justice, thank you for putting your faith in us. Our verdict is a triumph of justice for all of you.

To my friend and collaborator, Peter Knobler, what can I say? You immersed yourself in this book with passion and zeal and brilliance. You made great personal sacrifices to make this book special, and I will always be grateful. You are the best. Go Yanks!

To my brothers, Gabriel, John, and Dennis, and all their families, thank you for being loving brothers and guiding me through life. You have always been there for me.

To my loving parents, Anna and Ralph Petrocelli, I am blessed to have been raised by you. What you have taught and given me is priceless.

To my own family, Marian, Rachel, and Adam, thank you for putting up with me and without me and for giving me a chance to pursue my dreams. I love you all.

To the Goldman family, Fred, Patti, Kim, Michael, and Lauren, you have become like family to me. You have carried yourselves with courage and dignity and it has been an honor to be your lawyer.

INDEX